www.wadsworth.com

www.wadsworth.com is the World Wide Web site for Wadsworth and is your direct source to dozens of online resources.

At *www.wadsworth.com* you can find out about supplements, demonstration software, and student resources. You can also send email to many of our authors and preview new publications and exciting new technologies.

www.wadsworth.com
Changing the way the world learns®

The Color of Justice

Race, Ethnicity, and Crime in America

Third Edition

SAMUEL WALKER
University of Nebraska at Omaha

CASSIA SPOHN
University of Nebraska at Omaha

MIRIAM DELONE
University of Nebraska at Omaha

THOMSON

WADSWORTH

Australia • Canada • Mexico • Singapore • Spain
United Kingdom • United States

Senior Acquisitions Editor, Criminal Justice:
  Sabra Horne

Assistant Editor: Dawn Mesa

Editorial Assistant: Paul Massicotte

Technology Project Manager: Susan DeVanna

Marketing Manager: Dory Schaeffer

Marketing Assistant: Neena Chandra

Advertising Project Manager: Stacey Purviance

Project Manager, Editorial Production: Katy
  German/Jennie Redwitz

Print/Media Buyer: Kris Waller

Permissions Editor: Sarah Harkrader

Production Service: G&S Typesetters, Inc.

Copy Editor: Cynthia Lindlof

Cover Designer: Bill Stanton

Cover Image: Garry Gay/Getty Images

Compositor: G&S Typesetters, Inc.

Text and Cover Printer: Transcontinental
  Printing/Louiseville

For more information
about our products, contact us at:
**Thomson Learning Academic
Resource Center
1-800-423-0563**

For permission to use material from this text,
contact us by: **Phone:** 1-800-730-2214
Fax: 1-800-730-2215
Web: http://www.thomsonrights.com

Library of Congress Control Number:
2002116013

ISBN 0-534-59499-9

**Wadsworth/Thomson Learning
10 Davis Drive
Belmont, CA 94002-3098
USA**

Asia
Thomson Learning
5 Shenton Way #01-01
UIC Building
Singapore 068808

Australia/New Zealand
Thomson Learning
102 Dodds Street
Southbank, Victoria 3006
Australia

Canada
Nelson
1120 Birchmount Road
Toronto, Ontario M1K 5G4
Canada

Europe/Middle East/Africa
Thomson Learning
High Holborn House
50/51 Bedford Row
London WC1R 4LR
United Kingdom

Latin America
Thomson Learning
Seneca, 53
Colonia Polanco
11560 Mexico D.F.
Mexico

Spain/Portugal
Paraninfo
Calle/Magallanes, 25
28015 Madrid, Spain

Contents

Foreword

Today there are more African American men in prison and jail than in college.

This statistic, recently reported by The Sentencing Project, a Washington, DC, policy research group, is alarming for what it says about national priorities and the collateral consequences of criminal justice policy. We know, for example, that going to college improves one's life chances in several respects, including lifelong earnings and other measures of well being. We also know that being incarcerated affects most of those same prospects negatively. Putting these facts together, we can say that as a result of today's incarceration policies, more African American men will experience the lifelong debilitating effects of incarceration than the lifelong beneficial effects of college.

The odds of going to prison for an African American male born today are nearly one in three, and this rate is several times higher than the rate for white males and more than ten times higher than that for white females. The concentration of prison and jail activity among people of color living in impoverished urban neighborhoods is at least 10 and sometimes as much as 50 times higher than other neighborhoods.

There can be no denying that criminal justice policy and practice operate under the cloud of a racial dynamic. People may dispute what causes that dynamic, and they may disagree about its consequences. But there is no disputing the fact that criminal justice means something different for people of color than it does for others in the United States. This difference in personal experience of justice translates into significant impediments to a larger sense of justice and fairness among those of minority racial and ethnic backgrounds.

As editor of the Wadsworth Contemporary Issues in Crime and Justice Series, I am pleased to introduce the third edition of *The Color of Justice: Race, Ethnicity, and Crime in America*. The series is devoted to providing an in-depth investigation of current issues in crime and justice that cannot receive adequate treatment in standard introductory textbooks. Surely there can be no topic of more burning importance than that of racial and ethnic fairness in the criminal justice system.

This edition of *The Color of Justice* provides the best, most comprehensive exploration available today of the problem of race and ethnic variability in criminal justice practices. Professors Walker, Spohn, and DeLone have assembled the most up-to-date statistics and have supplied the most insightful and incisive analysis of any book on this topic now available. In the new edition the authors not only cover the topics that made previous editions bestsellers in this series, but they also have updated the review of research to incorporate new and provocative studies, and they have added material that reflects new insights regarding the implications for race and ethnicity of the attacks on the World Trade Center of September 11, 2001.

This book has become a standard text in its area. The reasons are several. First, the presentation of data and interpretation of studies is comprehensive, covering a wide range of material within a broad understanding of criminal justice, from the passage of laws to their enforcement and the resulting sanction imposed. Second, the book goes beyond the usual division of black and white. America today is multiracial and multiethnic, and one cannot study these topics without recognizing the substantial diversity that is the U.S. population. This book makes a conscious effort to go beyond the usual distinctions and to investigate racial and ethnic questions of a much wider variety. Third, this book does not hawk a particular point of view. When dealing with a topic in which emotions often run stronger than reason, this book offers a careful analysis and an impartial interpretation of what is known about the subject. The evidence is provided to the reader as a guidepost to an informed perspective, but the perspective itself is left to the reader to develop as the evidence is pondered and digested.

To these three strengths must be added an observation: No aspect of criminal justice is left out. The book addresses the broad questions of social structure and social values, just as it confronts the much narrower questions of law enforcement decisions and criminal justice system classification. In this sense, the book will address a topic that will be of direct importance to almost any reader who picks it up.

What this book represents then is a rare gem of a contribution. Comprehensive, critical, and authoritative, but not at all pedantic, the authors provide a book that will inform the reader, stimulate class discussion, and take the intellectual understanding of those who read it to a higher level. I commend it to you with enthusiasm.

Todd R. Clear

Preface

Since the second edition of *The Color of Justice* was published, issues of race and ethnicity in relation to crime have, if anything, become even more prominent in American political life. Racial profiling—that is, the practice of police officers' making traffic stops solely on the basis of the drivers' race—continues to be a source of national controversy. The debate over the death penalty has also entered a new phase in just the last few years, with new and disturbing evidence of miscarriages of justice in which innocent people have been sentenced to death.

We decided to write this book together because all three of us have addressed questions of race, ethnicity, and crime for many years in our research and teaching. It seemed natural to combine our experience, insights, and ideas into one book.

We would like to thank the following reviewers for their suggestions on how we might improve this edition:

Mary Atwell, Radford University

Stephanie Bush-Baskette, Florida State University

Charles Crawford, Western Michigan State University

Tara Gray, New Mexico State University—Las Cruces

Becky L. Tatum, Georgia State University

We remain grateful as well for helpful comments from the reviewers of the previous edition: Orie A. Brown, California State University, Fresno; James G.

Fox, Buffalo State College; Marianne O. Nielson, Northern Arizona University; Katheryn Russell, University of Maryland; Jill Shelley, Northern Kentucky University; and Marjorie Zatz, Arizona State University.

We would also like to thank Greg DeLone for suggesting the title of this book.

Samuel Walker
Cassia Spohn
Miriam DeLone

1

Race, Ethnicity, and Crime

The Present Crisis

More than 100 years ago, the great African American scholar W. E. B. Du Bois declared, "The problem of the twentieth century is the problem of the color line."[1] By that he meant that racism and racial discrimination were the central problems facing modern society.

Much the same can be said about crime and justice in American society today. Nearly every problem related to criminal justice issues involves matters of race and ethnicity:

- In 2001, the incarceration rate for African Americans in state prisons and local jails was 6 times the rate for whites (2,209 vs. 366, respectively, per 100,000). The incarceration rate for Hispanic Americans was twice that for whites overall (759 per 100,000).[2]

- Hispanics and Latinos are the fastest-growing group in the U.S. population, rising from 9 percent of the population in 1990 to 12 percent in 2000—and projected to be 18.2 percent by the year 2025. At the same time, Asian Americans and Pacific Islanders now constitute 4 percent of the population.[3] The arrival of many immigrants who do not speak English and who often have cultural patterns different from those of the majority American society, creates problems throughout the entire criminal justice system:

    Cultural practices that are misunderstood and sometimes regarded as criminal in this country

Inability to communicate effectively with police officers

Inability to communicate effectively with attorneys and judges in court

Cultural and language barriers in the delivery of correctional treatment programs

- In Cincinnati, the fatal shooting of a young African American man in April 2001, the 15th such shooting in 6 years, sparked a riot with significant property destruction and the imposition of a citywide curfew. This riot was only the latest in a long series of urban disorders that have punctuated the last 100 years.[4]

- A series of Justice Department reports has found very high crime rates and inadequate law enforcement protection on Native American reservations.[5]

- Across the country, there have been allegations of "racial profiling": the charge that police officers stop African American drivers because of the color of their skin and not because of actual violations of traffic laws.[6]

- Since the mid-1960s, crime has been a central issue in American politics. For many white Americans, the crime issue is an expression of racial fears: fear of victimization by African American offenders and fear of racial integration of neighborhoods.

- For its annual report on *The State of Black America,* The National Urban League surveyed 800 African Americans. One question asked, "In general, do you think the criminal justice system in the United States is biased in favor of blacks, is it biased against blacks, or does it generally give blacks fair treatment?" Seventy-four percent of the respondents thought that it is biased against African Americans, whereas only 15 percent thought that the system is fair.[7]

In short, on both sides of the color line, there are suspicion and fear: a sense of injustice on the part of racial minorities and fear of black crime on the part of whites. American society is deeply polarized over the issues of crime, justice, and race.

This polarization of attitudes toward crime is especially strong with respect to the death penalty. In 2001, 43 percent of African Americans opposed the death penalty, compared with only 22 percent of whites. Hispanic Americans fell squarely in between, with 33 percent opposing the death penalty.[8]

Even though African Americans are more likely to be the victims of crime, whites also express high levels of fear of crime. For many whites, *crime* is a code word for fears of social change. A study of community crime control efforts in Chicago, for example, found that neighborhood organizations usually were formed in response to perceived changes in the racial composition of their neighborhoods.[9]

THE SCOPE OF THIS BOOK

This book offers a comprehensive, critical, and balanced examination of the issues of crime and justice with respect to race and ethnicity. We believe that none of the existing books on the subject is completely adequate.[10]

First, none of the previous books or articles offers a comprehensive treatment of all criminal justice issues. There are many excellent articles on particular topics, such as the death penalty or police use of deadly force, but none covers the full range of topics in a complete and critical fashion. As a result, there are often no discussions of whether relatively more discrimination exists at one point in the justice system than at others. For example, is there more discrimination by the police in making arrest decisions than, say, by prosecutors in charging? Christopher Stone, director of the Vera Institute of Justice, points out that our knowledge about most criminal justice issues is "uneven."[11] There are many important questions about which we just do not have good information.

Second, the treatment of race and ethnicity in introductory criminal justice textbooks is very weak. The textbooks do not identify race and ethnicity as a major issue and fail to incorporate important literature on police misconduct, felony sentencing, the employment of racial minorities, and other important topics.[12]

Third, few books or articles discuss all racial and ethnic groups. Most focus entirely on African Americans. Coramae Richey Mann points out that "the available studies focus primarily on African Americans and neglect other racial minorities."[13] There is relatively little research on Hispanic Americans and almost nothing on Native Americans or Asian Americans.[14] This edition of *The Color of Justice* adds new material on Americans of Middle Eastern origin, who, in the wake of the terrorist attacks on September 11, 2001, allege that they have been the victims of racial profiling and other forms of discrimination.[15]

Increasing evidence indicates that there are important differences between the experiences of various racial and ethnic groups with respect to crime and justice. The *contextual approach* in this book emphasizes the unique historical, political, and economic circumstances of each group. Alfredo Mirandé, author of *Gringo Justice,* argues that historically "a double standard of justice" has existed, one for Anglo-Americans and one for Chicanos.[16] Marianne O. Nielsen, meanwhile, argues that the subject of Native Americans and criminal justice "cannot be understood without recognizing that it is just one of many interrelated issues that face native peoples today," including "political power, land, economic development, [and] individual despair."[17]

Consequently, there are no useful comparisons of the experiences of different groups. We do not know, for example, whether Hispanic Americans are treated worse, better, or about the same as African Americans. We have chosen to title this book *The Color of Justice* because it covers *all* people of color.

Fourth, many of the books on the subject do not offer a sufficiently critical perspective. The handling of the evidence is often superficial, ignoring many of the complexities related to specific issues. Too often authors rely only on evidence that supports their preconceptions. We disagree with William Wilbanks's argument that racism in the criminal justice system is a "myth."[18] We also reject Christopher Stone's conclusion, in his report to the President's Initiative on Race, that there is "strong reason for optimism" in the data on race and criminal justice.[19] The authors of this book are not quite so optimistic: there are some areas of progress in the direction of greater equality and fairness in the criminal justice system, but serious problems remain.

Finally, as Hawkins points out, American sociologists and criminologists have done a very poor job of studying the relationship of race, ethnicity, and crime. In particular, there is an absence of solid theoretical work that would provide a comprehensive explanation for this extremely important phenomenon. The main reason for this, according to Hawkins, is that "public discourse about both crime and race in the United States has always been an ideological and political mine field."[20] On the one side have been racist theories of biological determinism that attribute high rates of crime among racial and ethnic minorities to genetic inferiority. On the other side, the mainstream of American criminology has reacted by downplaying racial differences in criminal behavior and emphasizing the inadequacy of official crime data. The extreme sensitivity of the subject has tended to discourage rather than stimulate the development of theoretical studies of race, ethnicity, and crime.

The Color of Justice has several objectives. First, it seeks to synthesize the best and most recent research on the relevant topics: the patterns of criminal behavior and victimization, police practices, court processing and sentencing, the death penalty, and prisons and other correctional programs.

Second, it offers an interpretation of what the existing research means. Is there systematic discrimination in the criminal justice system? If so, where does it exist? How serious is it? What are the causes? Have any reforms succeeded in reducing it?

Third, *The Color of Justice* offers a multiracial and multiethnic view of crime and justice issues. The United States is a multicultural society, with many different races, ethnic groups, and cultural lifestyles. Unfortunately, most of the research has ignored the rich diversity of contemporary society. There is a great deal of research on African Americans and criminal justice but relatively little on Hispanics, Native Americans, and Asian Americans. In addition, much of the criminal justice research confuses race and ethnicity.

Finally, *The Color of Justice* does not attempt to offer a comprehensive theory of the relationship of race, ethnicity, and crime. Although Hawkins makes a persuasive case for the need for such a theory, this book has a more limited objective. It seeks to lay the groundwork for a comprehensive theory by emphasizing the general patterns in the administration of justice with respect to race and ethnicity. We feel that the available evidence permits us to draw some conclusions about that subject. The development of a comprehensive theory will have to be the subject of a future book.

GOALS OF THE CHAPTER

As an introduction to the book, Chapter 1 provides a foundation for a discussion of race, ethnicity, and crime involving several basic issues. The first issue involves *race* and *ethnicity*. When we speak of race and ethnicity, what are we talking about? The second issue is the question of *disparities* and *discrimination*. What exactly do these two terms mean? What kind of evidence is necessary to establish that discrimination exists? This chapter is designed to provide clarification of these issues.

The first section of this chapter describes the racial and ethnic categories used in the United States. It also discusses the quality of data on race and ethnicity reported by the different criminal justice agencies.

The second section examines the distribution of racial and ethnic groups in the United States. The uneven distribution of racial and ethnic minority groups means that race and ethnicity have a very different impact on the criminal justice systems in various parts of the country.

The third section addresses the distinction between disparity and discrimination. One of the central controversies in criminal justice is whether the overrepresentation of racial minorities in the justice system is the result of discrimination or whether it represents disparities that can be explained by other factors.

THE COLORS OF AMERICA:
RACIAL AND ETHNIC CATEGORIES

The 2000 census revealed that the United States is increasingly a multiracial, multiethnic society. The population was 82.2 percent white, 12.8 percent African American, 0.9 percent Native American, 11.8 percent Hispanic, and 4.1 percent Asian/Pacific Islander. (The difference between race and ethnicity is explained in detail in the next section.) These figures represent significant changes from just 20 years ago, and demographers are predicting steady changes in the immediate future. As Figure 1.1 indicates, Hispanics are the fastest-growing racial or ethnic group in the United States, increasing from 6.4 percent of the population in 1980 to an estimated 24.3 percent by the year 2050.[21]

Racial and Ethnic Categories

Race and ethnicity are extremely complex and controversial subjects. The categories we use are problematic and do not necessarily reflect the reality of American life.

Race Traditionally, race has referred to the "major biological divisions of mankind," which are distinguished by color of skin, color and texture of hair, bod-

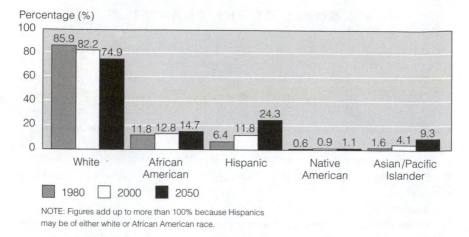

NOTE: Figures add up to more than 100% because Hispanics may be of either white or African American race.

FIGURE 1.1 Changing Population of the United States, 1980, 2000, 2050 (estimated)

SOURCE: Bureau of the Census, *Statistical Abstract of the United States, 2001,* Table 10.

ily proportions, and other physical features.[22] The traditional approach identifies three major racial groups: Caucasian, Negroid, and Mongoloid.

Experts on the subject today do not accept the strict biological definition of race. Because of intermarriage and evolution over time, it is virtually impossible to identify exclusive racial categories. Scientists have not been able to determine meaningful differences between people who are referred to as white, black, and Asian. Yinger maintains that "we cannot accept the widespread belief that there are a few clearly distinct and nearly immutable races. Change and intermixture are continuous."[23]

Anthropologists and sociologists regard the concept of race as "primarily a social construct."[24] That is to say, groups define themselves and have labels applied to them by other groups. Usually, the politically and culturally dominant group in any society defines the labels that are applied to other groups. At times, however, subordinate groups assert themselves by developing their own labels. Racial designations have changed over the centuries as a result of changes in both political power and racial attitudes. Yinger argues that the critical categories for social analysis are the "socially visible 'racial' lines, based on beliefs about race and on administrative and political classifications, rather than genetic differences."[25]

A good example of the politics of racial categories is the history of the classification and labeling of African American people in the United States. Historically, the attitudes of whites—and official policy—embodied the racist "drop of blood" theory: anyone with the slightest African ancestry was defined as "black," even when a majority of that person's ancestors were white or Caucasian.[26] Following this approach, many data sets in the past used the categories of "white" and "nonwhite." The federal government today prohibits the use of the "nonwhite" label.[27]

**BOX 1.1   American Anthropological Association,
Statement on "Race," 1998 (excerpt)**

In the United States both scholars and the general public have been conditioned to viewing human races as natural and separate divisions within the human species based on visible physical differences. With the vast expansion of scientific knowledge in this century, however, it has become clear that human populations are not unambiguous, clearly demarcated, biologically distinct groups. Evidence from the analysis of genetics (e.g., DNA) indicates that most physical variation, about 94%, lies *within* so-called racial groups. Conventional geographic "racial" groupings differ from one another only in about 6% of their genes. This means that there is greater variation within "racial" groups than between them. In neighboring populations there is much overlapping of genes and their phenotypic (physical) expressions. Throughout history whenever different groups have come into contact, they have interbred. The continued sharing of genetic materials has maintained all of humankind as a single species.

SOURCE: The full statement, along with other materials, can be found on the Web site of the American Anthropological Association (www .aaanet.org).

The problem with traditional racial categories is obvious when we look at American society. Many people have mixed ancestry. What, for example, is the "race" of the child whose father is African American and mother is white? Or the child whose mother is Japanese American and whose father is white? Or the child whose mother is Native American and whose father is Hispanic? Many "white" Americans have some ancestors who were African American or Native American. Few African Americans have ancestries that are purely African.

Issues related to classifying multiracial and multiethnic people are not abstract ideas; they have very real, and often cruel, human meaning. An article in the *New Yorker* magazine highlighted the case of Susan Graham of Roswell, Georgia, who complained, "When I received my 1990 census form, I realized that there was no race category for my children." She is white, and her husband is African American. She called the Census Bureau and was finally told that children should take the race of their mother. No rational reason was given about why the race of her husband, the children's father, should be arbitrarily ignored. Then, when she enrolled the children in kindergarten, the school classified them as "black." Thus, she pointed out, "My child has been white on the United States census, black at school, and multiracial at home—all at the same time."[28]

The bureaucratic problems related to classification of people have important human implications. Classification systems label people and inevitably tend to imply that some groups are inferior to others. The Association of Multi-Ethnic Americans and related groups are particularly concerned about the impact of classifications and labels on children.[29]

Focus on an Issue
The Bell Curve Controversy: Race and IQ

A national storm of controversy erupted in the fall of 1994 over a book titled *The Bell Curve* (Herrnstein & Murray, 1994). The authors argue that success in life is determined largely by IQ: the smarter people succeed, whereas those with lower intelligence, as measured by standard IQ tests, fail and end up at the bottom of the social scale. The authors contend that those at the low end of the IQ scale do poorly in school and are more likely to be unemployed, receive welfare, and commit crime.

The most provocative and controversial parts of their thesis are the points that intelligence is inherited and that there are significant differences in intelligence between races. The authors cite data indicating that Asian Americans consistently score higher on IQ tests than white European Americans, who, in turn, score higher than African Americans. Herrnstein and Murray are very clear about the policy implications of their argument: Because intelligence is mainly inherited, social programs designed to improve the performance of poor children, such as Head Start, are doomed to failure and should be abandoned.

The Bell Curve was attacked by psychologists, anthropologists, and sociologists, among others (Fraser, 1995). Critics disputed the authors' assumptions that there is some entity called "intelligence" that is inherited and that IQ tests are a valid measure of intellectual capacity. They also disputed their handling of the evidence regarding intelligence tests, the impact of environmental factors as opposed to inherited factors, and the effect of programs such as Head Start. There is evidence, for example, that Head Start does improve IQ test scores, as well as children's later success in life.

This book is not the place for a full-scale critique of *The Bell Curve,* although we do reject its basic argument. One point is relevant to the discussion in this chapter, however. Herrnstein and Murray argue that there are basic, inherited differences in intelligence between races. We reject that argument on the grounds that the vast majority of anthropologists and sociologists do not accept the idea of separate races as distinct biological entities. If there are no scientifically valid racial differences, the basic argument of *The Bell Curve* falls apart.

In response to the long controversy, the American Anthropological Association (AAA) in 1994 issued an official "Statement on 'Race' and Intelligence." (Note in this statement and the one cited in Box 1.1 that the AAA places the word *race* in quotation marks as a way of indicating that the concept does not have any scientific validity.) The AAA makes the following statement:

The American Anthropological Association (AAA) is deeply concerned by recent public discussions which imply that intelligence is biologically determined by race. Repeatedly challenged by scientists, nevertheless these ideas continue to be advanced. Such discussions distract public and scholarly attention from and diminish support for the collective challenge to ensure equal opportunities for all people, regardless of ethnicity or phenotypic variation.

Earlier AAA resolutions against racism (1961, 1969, 1971, 1972) have spoken to this concern. The AAA further resolves:

WHEREAS all human beings

are members of one species, *Homo sapiens,* and

WHEREAS, differentiating species into biologically defined "races" has proven meaningless and unscientific as a way of explaining variation (whether in intelligence or other traits),

THEREFORE, the American Anthropological Association urges

the academy, our political leaders and our communities to affirm, without distraction by mistaken claims of racially determined intelligence, the common stake in assuring equal opportunity, in respecting diversity and in securing a harmonious quality of life for all people.

SOURCE: The full AAA statement is available on the organization's Web site (www.aaanet.org).

The problem of classifying multiethnic and multiracial people has important implications for criminal justice data. What if the National Crime Victimization Survey (NCVS) calls the Graham household? Would their household be classified as "white" or "black"? What if one of their children were the victim of a robbery? Would the victimization survey record that as a "white" or "black" victimization?

The National Urban League surveyed 800 African American adults, asking them which term they preferred. About half (51 percent) preferred *black,* and 43 percent preferred *African American.*[30]

As these examples suggest, the complex multicultural reality of American society means that the categories used by government agencies such as the Census Bureau are, as one person put it, "illogical."[31]

Many people have protested the requirement of having to choose one or another racial category. The Association of MultiEthnic Americans (AMEA) was established to fight for the right of people with mixed heritage to acknowledge their full identity. AMEA proclaimed "victory" in October 1997 when the Office of Management and Budget (OMB) adopted new federal guidelines allowing people to identify themselves in terms of more than just one race.[32] (The U.S. census classifies people on the basis of self-identification.)

In this historic change, the OMB replaced guidelines that had been in effect since 1977. Most of the data in this book use the racial categories established by the OMB, which are required for use by all federal agencies, including the Census Bureau.

In addition, the OMB revised the names used for some racial groups.[33] The new categories are (1) American Indian or Alaska Native; (2) Asian; (3) Black or African American; (4) Hispanic or Latino; (5) Native Hawaiian or Other Pacific Islander; and (6) white. Previously, OMB used only the term *black;* the new category is *Black or African American.* Persons may also identify themselves as Haitian or Negro. Previously, only the term *Hispanic* was used. The new guidelines use *Hispanic or Latino.* The OMB considered, but rejected, a proposal to use *Native American* and retained the old term *American Indian.*

OMB Racial and Ethnic Group Definitions The OMB defines a black or African American person as anyone "having origins in any of the black racial groups of Africa." It defines a white person as anyone "having origins in any of the original peoples of Europe, the Middle East, or North Africa." Accordingly, a person who is from Morocco or Iran is classified as "white," and someone from Nigeria or Tanzania is classified as "black."

The category of American Indians includes Alaska Natives and "original peoples of North and South America (including Central America)." Asian includes people from the Far East, Southeast Asia, or the Indian subcontinent. Pacific Islanders are no longer in the same category with Asians and are now included with Native Hawaiians in a separate category.

The OMB concedes that the racial and ethnic categories it created "are not anthropologically or scientifically based." Instead, they represent "a social-political construct." Most important, OMB warns that the categories "should not be interpreted as being primarily biological or genetic in reference."[34]

Ethnicity Ethnicity is not the same thing as race. *Ethnicity* refers to differences between groups of people based on cultural customs, such as language, religion, foodways, family patterns, and other characteristics. Among white Americans, for example, there are distinct ethnic groups based primarily on country of origin: Irish Americans, Italian Americans, Polish Americans, and so on.[35] Yinger uses a three-part definition of ethnicity: (1) The group is perceived by others to be different with respect to such factors as language, religion, race, ancestral homeland, and other cultural elements; (2) the group perceives itself to be different with respect to these factors; and (3) members of the group "participate in shared activities built around their (real or mythical) common origin and culture."[36]

The Hispanic or Latino category is extremely complex. First, Hispanic is an ethnic designation, and individuals may belong to any racial category. Thus, some Hispanics identify themselves as white, others consider themselves African American, and some identify as Native Americans. In the past, criminal justice agencies, following the federal guidelines, have classified Hispanics as white but have not also collected data on ethnic identity. As a result, most criminal justice data sets do not provide good longitudinal data on Hispanics.

Second, the Hispanic American population is extremely diverse with respect to place of origin, which includes Mexico, Puerto Rico, Cuba, Central America, South America, and others. The traditional distinctions are not entirely logical. Mexico and Cuba are countries, whereas Central America and South America are regions consisting of several nations. Mexican Americans are the largest single group within the Hispanic community, making up 58.4 percent of the total in the 2000 census. Puerto Ricans are the second largest (9.6 percent), and Cubans are third (3.2 percent).

"Minority" Groups The term *minorities* is widely used as a label for people of color. The United Nations defines minority groups as "those nondominant groups in a population which possess and wish to preserve stable ethnic, religious or linguistic traditions or characteristics markedly different from those of the rest of the population."[37] The noted sociologist Louis Wirth adds the element of discrimination to this definition: Minorities are those who "are singled out from the others in the society in which they live for differential and unequal treatment, and who therefore regard themselves as objects of collective discrimination."[38]

Use of the term *minority* is increasingly criticized. Among other things, it has a pejorative connotation, suggesting "less than" something else, which in this context means less than some other groups. The new OMB guidelines for the Census Bureau and other federal agencies specifically "do *not* identify or designate certain population groups as 'minority groups.'"[39] Many people today prefer to use the term *people of color.*

The Politics of Racial and Ethnic Labels

There has always been great controversy over what term should be used to designate different racial and ethnic groups. The term *African American,* for example, is relatively new and became widely used only in the 1980s. It has begun to replace *black* as the preferred designation, which replaced *Negro* in the 1960s. *Negro,* in turn, replaced *colored* about 25 years earlier. The leading African American civil rights organization is the National Association for the Advancement of Colored People (NAACP), founded in 1909. Ironically, *colored* replaced *African* much earlier. In some respects, then, we have come full circle in the past 150 years. As John Hope Franklin, the distinguished African American historian and chair of the President's Initiative on Race, points out in the seventh edition of his classic history of African Americans, *From Slavery to Freedom,* the subjects of his book have been referred to by "three distinct names . . . even during the lifetime of this book."[40]

Preferred labels can change quickly in a short period of time. The term *African American,* for example, replaced *black* as the preferred label among African Americans in just 5 years (although a majority say that it does not matter).[41]

The controversy over the proper label is *political* in the sense that it often involves a power struggle between different racial and ethnic groups. It is not just a matter of which label but who chooses that label. Wolf argues that "the function of racial categories within industrial capitalism is exclusionary."[42] The power to control one's own label represents an important element of police power and autonomy. Having to accept a label placed on you by another group is an indication of powerlessness.

The term *black* emerged as the preferred designation in the late 1960s as part of an assertion of pride in blackness and quest for power by African Americans themselves. The African American community was making a political statement to the majority white community: "This is how we choose to describe ourselves." In a similar fashion, the term *African American* emerged in the 1980s through a process of self-designation on the part of the African American community.

In this book, we use the term *African American.* It emerged as the preferred term by spokespersons for the African American community and has been adopted by the OMB for the 2000 census (and can be used along with *black, Negro,* and *Haitian*). It is also consistent with terms commonly used for other

---

BOX 1.2   Donde está la justicia?

The U.S. government uses the term *Hispanic* to recognize individuals' common Spanish descent. The term refers, in part, to people with ties to nations where Spanish is the official language. The U.S. government and legal system historically have insisted on categorizing all Spanish-speaking people as Hispanic and treating them as a monolithic group, regardless of cultural differences.

The term *Latino*, on the other hand, generally refers to people with ties to the nations of Latin America and the Caribbean, including some nations where Spanish is not spoken such as Brazil. It also encompasses per-sons born in the United States whose families immigrated to this country from Latin America in the recent past, as well as those whose ancestors immigrated generations ago. Like the term *Hispanic,* the categorization *Latino* is a general one that does not recognize the diversity of ethnic subgroups (for example, Puerto Rican, Dominican, Guatemalan, Peruvian, and Mexican).

SOURCE: Francisco A. Villarruel and Nancy E. Walker, *Donde está la justicia? A Call to Action on Behalf of Latino and Latina Youth in the U.S. Justice System* (East Lansing, MI: Institute for Youth, Children, and Families, 2002).

---

groups. We routinely refer to Irish Americans, Polish Americans, and Chinese Americans, for instance, using the country of origin as the primary descriptor. It makes sense, therefore, to designate people whose country of origin is Africa as African Americans. The term *black* refers to a color, which is an imprecise descriptor for a group of people whose members range in skin color from a very light yellow to a very dark black.

There is a similar controversy over the proper term for Hispanic Americans (see Box 1.2). Not everyone, including some leaders of the community itself, prefers this term. Some prefer *Latino,* and others use *Chicano.* A 1994 Gallup Poll found that 62 percent of Hispanics preferred that term; only 10 percent preferred *Latino,* and 24 percent said that it did not matter.[43] Some white Americans incorrectly refer to Hispanics as Mexican Americans, ignoring the many people who have a different country of origin. The OMB has accepted the term *Latino,* and the 2000 census uses the category of Hispanic or Latino.

In this book we use the term *Hispanic.* It is more comprehensive than other terms and includes all of the different countries of origin.

We use the term *Native Americans* to designate those people who have historically been referred to as American Indians. The term *Indians,* after all, originated through a misunderstanding, as the first European explorers of the Americas mistakenly thought they had landed in Asia.

The term *Anglo* is widely used as a term for whites, but it is not an accurate descriptor. Only a minority of white Americans trace their ancestry back to the British Isles. The pejorative term *WASP* (white, Anglo–Saxon, Protestant) is also inaccurate because many white Americans are Catholic, Jewish, or members of some other religious group. Therefore, in this book we use the term *white.*

Actually, however, the term *white* is as inaccurate as *black*. People who are commonly referred to as white include a wide range of skin colors, from very pale white to a dark olive or brown. The term *Caucasian* may actually be more accurate.

The Quality of Criminal
Justice Data on Race and Ethnicity

Serious analysis of the racial and ethnic dimensions of crime and justice requires good data. Unfortunately, the official data reported by criminal justice agencies are not always reliable.

The first problem is that, overall, the body of literature is very small, and many important subjects have not been researched at all. The majority of the published research to date involves African Americans. Although there are important gaps and much remains to be done, we do have a reasonably good sense of how African Americans fare at the hands of the police, prosecutors, judges, and correctional officials. Hispanic Americans, however, have been neglected.[44] Even less research is available on Native Americans[45] and Asian Americans. Consequently, we will not be able to discuss many important subjects in detail in this book (for example, the patterns of police arrest of Hispanics compared with those of whites and African Americans).

A second problem involves the quality of the data. Criminal justice agencies do not always use the same racial and ethnic categories. The problem is particularly acute with respect to Hispanic Americans. Many criminal justice agencies collect data only on race and use the census categories of white and black, counting Hispanics as whites. This approach, however, masks potentially significant differences between Hispanics and non–Hispanic whites. This has important implications for analyzing the nature and extent of disparities in the criminal justice system. If we assume that Hispanics are arrested at a higher rate than non–Hispanic whites (a recent report finds that they are stopped by the police at a much lower rate than the other two groups),[46] the available data not only eliminate Hispanics as a separate group but also raise the overall non–Hispanic arrest rate. This result would narrow the gap in arrest rates between whites and African Americans and understate the real extent of racial disparities in arrest.

Some data systems use the categories of white and nonwhite. This approach incorrectly treats all people of color as members of the same race. As noted earlier, the OMB prohibits government agencies from using the term *nonwhite*.

The Uniform Crime Reports (UCR) data from the Federal Bureau of Investigation (FBI) are useless with respect to many important issues related to race, ethnicity, and crime. First, the data used to create the Crime Index, "crimes known to police," do not include data on race and therefore do not tell us anything about rates of offending. Second, the data on arrests utilize the categories of white, black, American Indian or Alaska Native, and Asian or Pacific Islander. There is no separate category for Hispanics.

With respect to Native Americans, LaFree points out that they "fall under the jurisdiction of a complex combination of native and nonnative legal entities" that render the arrest data "problematic."[47] Snyder-Joy characterizes the Native American justice system as "a jurisdictional maze" in which jurisdiction over various criminal acts is divided among federal, state, and tribal governments.[48] It is not clear, for example, that all tribal police agencies report arrest data to the FBI's UCR system. Thus, Native American arrests are probably significantly undercounted.

A third problem is that the FBI has changed the categories for Asian Americans over the years, making longitudinal analysis impossible.

The appendices in the *Sourcebook of Criminal Justice Statistics* reveal a serious lack of consistency in the use of the Hispanic designation among criminal justice agencies.[49] In the National Corrections Reporting Program, for example, Colorado, Illinois, Minnesota, New York, Oklahoma, and Texas record Hispanic prison inmates as "unknown" race. Ohio records Native Americans and Asian Americans as "unknown" race. California, Michigan, and Oklahoma classify only Mexican Americans as Hispanic, apparently classifying people from Puerto Rico, Cuba, and South America as non-Hispanic.

In addition, the criminal justice officials responsible for classifying persons may be poorly trained and may rely on their own stereotypes about race and ethnicity. The race of a person arrested is determined by the arresting officer and indicated on the original arrest report. In the Justice Department's Juvenile Court Statistics, race is "determined by the youth or by court personnel."[50] We are not entirely sure that all of these personnel designate people accurately.

In short, the official data reported by criminal justice agencies are very problematic, which creates tremendous difficulties when we try to assess the fate of different groups at the hands of the criminal justice system. The disparities that we know to exist today could be greater or smaller, depending on how people have been classified. We will need to be sensitive to these data problems as we discuss the various aspects of the criminal justice system in the chapters ahead.

THE GEOGRAPHY OF
RACIAL AND ETHNIC JUSTICE

Because of two factors, the "geography of justice" in the United States varies across the country. First, the primary responsibility for criminal justice lies with city, county, and state governments. The federal government plays a very small role in the total picture of criminal justice. Second, the major racial and ethnic groups are not evenly distributed across the country. California and Texas alone have a disproportionate share of the Hispanic population, for example. As a result, the salience of race and ethnicity varies widely from jurisdiction to jurisdiction.

Although the United States as a whole is becoming more diverse, most of this diversity is concentrated in a few regions and metropolitan areas. One study concluded that "most communities lack true racial and ethnic diversity."[51] In 1996 only 745 of the 3,142 counties had a white population that was below the national average. Only 21 metropolitan areas qualified as true "melting pots" (with the percentage of the white population below the national average, and at least two minority groups with a greater percentage than their national average).[52]

More than half of all racial and ethnic minorities live in just five states (California, Texas, New York, Florida, and Illinois), with 20 percent in California alone. More than half (52.3 percent) of the African American population is located in the seventeen states in the Southeast. The other major concentration is in the big cities of the North and the Midwest. For example, African Americans represent 82 percent of the population in Detroit, 67 percent in Atlanta, and 46 percent in Cleveland.[53]

The distribution of the Hispanic population is even more complex. More than half (51 percent) live in just two states, Texas and California. About 83 percent of these people are Mexican Americans. Puerto Rican Americans are concentrated on the East Coast, with almost 41 percent living in New York and New Jersey. About 67 percent of all Cuban Americans live in Florida.[54] Native Americans are also heavily concentrated. Just under half (45 percent) live in four states: Oklahoma, Arizona, New Mexico, and California.[55]

The uneven distribution of the major racial and ethnic groups is extremely important for criminal justice. Crime is primarily the responsibility of state and local governments. Thus, racial and ethnic issues are especially salient in those cities where racial minorities are heavily concentrated. For example, the context of policing is very different in Detroit, which is 82 percent African American, than in Minneapolis, where African Americans are only 18 percent of the population. Similarly, Hispanic issues are far more significant in San Antonio, which is 59 percent Hispanic, than in many other cities where few Hispanics live.[56]

The concentration of racial and ethnic minority groups in certain cities and counties has important implications for political power and the control of criminal justice agencies. Mayors, for example, appoint police chiefs. In recent years, African Americans have served as mayors of most of the major cities: New York, Los Angeles, Chicago, Philadelphia, Detroit, Atlanta, Washington, DC, and others. There have also been African American police chiefs or commissioners in each of these cities.

The concentration of African Americans in the Southeast has at least two important effects. This concentration gives this group a certain degree of political power that translates into elected African American sheriffs and mayors. These officials, in turn, may appoint African American police chiefs. For instance, by 1999 the State of Mississippi had 850 elected African American officials, more than any other state, including several elected sheriffs.[57]

DISPARITY VERSUS DISCRIMINATION

Perhaps the most important question with respect to race and ethnicity is whether there is discrimination in the criminal justice system. Many people argue that it is pervasive, whereas others believe that intentional discrimination does not exist. Mann presents "a minority perspective" on the administration of justice, emphasizing discrimination against people of color.[58] Wilbanks, on the other hand, argues that the idea of systematic racism in the criminal justice system is a "myth."[59]

Debates over the existence of racial discrimination in the criminal justice system are often muddled and unproductive because of confusion over the meaning of "discrimination." It is, therefore, important to make two important distinctions. First, there is a significant difference between disparity and discrimination. Second, discrimination can take different forms and involve different degrees of seriousness. Box 1.3 offers a schematic diagram of the various forms of discrimination, ranging from total, systematic discrimination to pure justice.

Disparity refers to a difference, but one that does not necessarily involve discrimination. Look around your classroom. If you are in a conventional college program, almost all of the students will be relatively young (between the ages of 18 and 25). This represents a disparity in age compared with the general population. There are no children, few middle-aged people, and probably no elderly students. This is not a result of discrimination, however. These older groups are not enrolled in the class mainly because the typical life course is to attend college immediately after high school. The age disparity, therefore, is the result of factors other than discrimination.

The example of education illustrates the point that a disparity is a difference that can be explained by legitimate factors. In criminal justice, the crucial distinction is between legal and extralegal factors. *Legal factors* include the seriousness of the offense and an offender's prior criminal record. These are considered legitimate bases for decisions by most criminal justice officials because they relate to an individual's criminal behavior. *Extralegal factors* include race, ethnicity, gender, social class, and lifestyle. They are not legitimate bases for decisions by criminal justice officials because they involve group membership and are unrelated to a person's criminal behavior. It would be illegitimate, for example, for a judge to sentence all male burglars to prison but place all female burglars on probation, despite the fact that women had committed the same kind of burglary and had prior records similar to those of many of the men. Similarly, it would be illegitimate for a judge to sentence all unemployed persons to prison but grant probation to all employed persons.

Discrimination, on the other hand, is a difference based on *differential treatment* of groups without reference to an individual's behavior or qualifications. A few examples of employment discrimination will illustrate the point.

Until the 1960s, most Southern police departments did not hire African American officers. The few that did, moreover, did not allow them to arrest whites. Many Northern police departments, meanwhile, did not assign African American officers to white neighborhoods.[60] These practices represented differential treatment based on race—in short, discrimination. Also during that time period, airlines hired only young women as flight attendants. This approach represented a difference in treatment based on gender rather than individual qualifications. (The flight attendants were also automatically terminated if they

---

BOX 1.3 Discrimination–Disparity Continuum

Systematic Discrimination	Institutionalized Discrimination	Contextual Discrimination	Individual Acts of Discrimination	Pure Justice

Definitions

Systematic discrimination—Discrimination at all stages of the criminal justice system, at all times, and all places.

Institutionalized discrimination—Racial and ethnic disparities in outcomes that are the result of the application of racially neutral factors, such as prior criminal record, employment status, and demeanor.

Contextual discrimination—Discrimination found in particular contexts or circumstances (for example, certain regions, particular crimes, or special victim–offender relationships).

Individual acts of discrimination—Discrimination that results from the acts of particular individuals but is not characteristic of entire agencies or the criminal justice system as a whole.

Pure justice—No racial or ethnic discrimination at all.

---

married; because no male employees were fired for being married, this practice represented a form of sexual discrimination.)

African Americans were excluded from serving on juries because they were illegally disenfranchised as voters and, therefore, were not on jury lists. This practice represented racial discrimination in jury selection. But let's imagine a rural county in the northwestern United States where there are no African American residents. The absence of African Americans from juries would represent a racial disparity but not discrimination. Consider another hypothetical case. Imagine that a police department arrested only African Americans for suspected felonies and never arrested a white person. That situation would represent racial discrimination in arrest.

The questions we deal with in the real world, of course, are not quite so simple. There are, in fact, racial disparities in jury selection and arrest: African Americans are less likely to serve on juries, and more African Americans are arrested than whites. The question is whether these disparities reflect discrimination.

It is also important to remember that the word *discrimination* has at least two different meanings. One has a positive connotation. When we describe someone as a "discriminating gourmet" or a "discriminating music lover," we mean that he or she has good taste and chooses only the best. The person discriminates against bad food and bad music. The other meaning of *discrimination* has a negative connotation. We say that someone "discriminates against racial minorities." This statement means that the person makes invidious distinctions, based on negative judgments about an entire group of people. That is, the person discriminates against all African Americans without reference to a particular person's qualities (for example, ability, education, or experience).

The Discrimination–Disparity Continuum

To help clarify the debate over this issue, let's review Box 1.3. *Systematic discrimination* means that discrimination occurs at all stages of the criminal justice system, in all places, and at all times. That is to say, there is discrimination in arrest, prosecution, and sentencing (stages); in all parts of the country (places); and without any significant variation over time.

Institutionalized discrimination involves disparities in outcomes (for example, more African Americans than whites are sentenced to prison) that result from established (institutionalized) policies. Such policies do not directly involve race. As Georges-Abeyie explains, "The key issue is result, not intent. Institutionalized racism is often the legacy of overt racism, of de facto practices that often get codified, and thus sanctioned by de jure mechanisms."[61]

A local criminal court, for example, has a bail policy granting pretrial release to defendants who are currently employed. This policy is based on the reasonable assumption that an employed person has a greater stake in the community and is less likely to flee than an unemployed person. The policy discriminates against the unemployed, and, because racial minorities are disproportionately represented among the unemployed, they are more likely to be denied bail. Thus, the bail policy has a race effect: a racial disparity in the outcomes that is the result of a criterion other than race. The racial disparity exists not because any judge is racially prejudiced, but because judges apply the rules consistently.

Employment discrimination law recognizes the phenomenon of institutionalized discrimination with reference to "disparate impact." A particular hiring policy may be illegal if it has an especially heavy impact on a certain group and is not demonstrably job related. In policing, for example, police departments formerly did not hire people who were shorter than 5'6". This standard had a disparate impact on women, Hispanics, and Asian Americans and is now no longer used.

Contextual discrimination involves discrimination in certain situations or contexts. One example is the victim–offender relationship. As we will see in Chapter 8, the odds that the death penalty will be given are greatest when an African American murders a white person, whereas there is almost no chance of a death sentence when a white person murders an African American.[62] This factor has been found in the context of other felony sentencing as well. It also appears that drug enforcement has a much heavier impact on African Americans and Hispanics than routine police work does.[63]

Organizational factors represent another contextual variable. Some police departments encourage aggressive patrol activities (for example, frequent stops and frisks). The Kerner Commission found that "aggressive preventive patrol" aggravated tensions between the police and racial minority communities.[64] Thus, departments with different patrol policies may have less conflict with minority communities. Some police departments have very bad records in terms of use of physical force, but others have taken steps to curb misconduct.

Individual acts of discrimination involve those carried out by particular justice officials: one police officer is biased in making arrests, whereas others in the department are not; one judge sentences minorities very harshly, whereas other judges in the same court do not. These are discriminatory acts, but they do not represent general patterns of how the criminal justice system operates.

Finally, at the far end of the spectrum in Box 1.3 is the condition we label *pure justice*. This means that there is no discrimination at any time or place in the criminal justice system.

In a controversial analysis of the administration of justice, Wilbanks argues that the idea of a racist criminal justice system is a "myth." He claims that "there is racial prejudice and discrimination within the criminal justice system" but denies that "*the system* is characterized by racial prejudice and discrimination."[65] Using our discrimination–disparity continuum, Wilbanks falls somewhere in the area of contextual discrimination and individual discrimination. Mann, on the other hand, argues that there is systematic discrimination: "The law and the legal system [have] perpetuated and [continue] to maintain an ingrained system of injustice for people of color."[66]

Throughout the chapters that follow, we will encounter the question of whether disparities represent discrimination. For example, there are racial and ethnic disparities in arrests by the police. In Chapter 4, we examine the evidence on whether these data indicate a clear pattern of discrimination—and if so, what kind of discrimination (contextual, individual, or systematic). Chapter 4 also examines the difficulties in interpreting traffic stop data to determine whether there is a pattern of illegal racial profiling. There is also evidence of disparities in plea bargaining and sentencing. Chapters 5, 6, and 7 wrestle with the problem of interpreting the data to determine whether there are patterns of discrimination. Chapter 8 examines the data on the death penalty and the race of persons executed.

A THEORETICAL PERSPECTIVE
ON RACE, ETHNICITY, AND CRIME

There are many different theories of crime and criminal justice. We believe that the available evidence on race, ethnicity, and crime is best explained by a theoretical perspective known as *conflict theory*.

The basic premise of conflict theory is that the law is used to maintain the power of the dominant group in society and to control the behavior of individuals who threaten that power.[67] A classic illustration of conflict theory involves the law of vagrancy. Vagrancy involves merely being out in public with little or no money and no clear "purpose" for being there. Vagrancy is something engaged in only by the poor. To make vagrancy a criminal act and to enforce vagrancy laws are means by which the powerful attempt to control the poor.

Conflict theory explains racial disparities in the administration of justice as products of broader patterns of social, economic, and political inequality in U.S. society. These inequalities are the result of prejudicial attitudes on the part of the white majority and discrimination against minorities in employment, education, housing, and other aspects of society. Chapter 3 explores these inequalities in detail. Conflict theory explains the overrepresentation of racial and ethnic minorities in arrest, prosecution, imprisonment, and capital punishment as both the product of these inequalities and an expression of prejudice against minorities.

Conflict theory has often been oversimplified by both advocates and opponents. Criminal justice research has found certain "anomalies" in which racial minorities are not always treated more harshly than whites. For example, there are certain situations in which African American suspects are less likely to be arrested than white suspects. Hawkins argues that these anomalies can be explained through a revised and more sophisticated conflict theory that takes into account relevant contingencies.[68]

One contingency is crime type. Hawkins claims that African Americans may be treated more leniently for some crimes because officials believe that these crimes are "more normal or appropriate for some racial and social class groups than for others."[69] In the South during the Segregation Era, for example, African Americans often were not arrested for certain crimes, particularly crimes against other African Americans. The dominant white power structure viewed this behavior as "appropriate" for African Americans. The fact that minority offenders were being treated leniently in these situations is consistent with conflict theory because the outcomes represent a racist view of racial minorities as essentially "childlike" people who cannot control their behavior.

A second contingency identified by Hawkins involves the race of the offender relative to the race of the victim. Much research has found that the criminal justice system responds more harshly when the offender is a minority and the victim is white, particularly in rape and potential death penalty murder cases. According to conflict theory, such crimes are viewed as challenges to the pattern of racial dominance in society. The same crime is not perceived as a threat when it is intraracial (for example, white offender/white victim, African American offender/African American victim). A relatively lenient response to crimes by minorities against minorities or crimes in which a racial or ethnic minority is the victim is explained by conflict theory in terms of a devaluing of the lives of minority victims.

There may also be important contingencies based on population variables. It may be that crimes by racial minorities are treated more harshly when minorities represent a relatively large percentage of the population and therefore are perceived as a social and political threat. At the same time, some research on imprisonment has found that the disparity between white and African American incarceration rates is greatest in states with small minority populations.[70] In this context, minorities have little political power.

Alternative Theories

Conflict theory is a sociological explanation of criminal behavior and the administration of justice in that it holds that social factors explain which kinds of behavior are defined as criminal; which people commit crime; and how crimes are investigated, prosecuted, and punished. Sociological explanations of crime are alternatives to biological, psychological, and economic explanations. These other factors may contribute in some way to explaining crime but, according to the sociological perspective, do not provide an adequate general theory of crime.[71]

Conflict theory also differs from other sociological theories of crime. Consensus theory holds that all groups in society share the same values and that criminal behavior can be explained by individual acts of deviance. Conflict theory does not see consensus in society regarding the goals or operation of the criminal justice system. Conflict theory also differs from Marxist theory, even though there are some areas of agreement. Conflict theory and Marxist theory both emphasize differences in power between groups. Conflict theory, however, does not hold that there is a rigid class structure with a ruling class. Instead, it is consistent with a pluralistic view of society in which there are different centers of power—business and labor, farmers and consumers, government officials and the news media, religious organizations, public interest groups, and so forth—although they are not necessarily equal. The pluralistic view also allows for changes in the relative power of different groups.

CONCLUSION

The question of race and ethnicity is a central issue in American criminal justice—perhaps the central issue. The starting point for this book is the overrepresentation of racial and ethnic minorities in the criminal justice system.

This chapter sets the framework for a critical analysis of this fact about contemporary American society. We have learned that the subject is extremely complex. First, the categories of race and ethnicity are extremely problematic. Much of the data we use are not as refined as we would like. Second, we have learned that there is much controversy over the issue of discrimination. An important distinction exists between disparity and discrimination. Also, there are different kinds of discrimination. Finally, we have indicated the theoretical perspective about crime and criminal justice that guides the chapters that follow.

DISCUSSION QUESTIONS

1. What is the difference between *race* and *ethnicity*? Give some examples that illustrate the differences.

2. When social scientists say that the concept of race is a "social construct," what exactly do they mean?

3. Do you think the U.S. census should have a category of "multicultural" for race and ethnicity? Explain why or why not. Would it make a difference in the accuracy of the census? Would it make a difference to you?

4. Explain the difference between *discrimination* and *disparity*. Give one example from some other area of life.

NOTES

1. W. E. B. Du Bois, *The Souls of Black Folk* (Chicago: McClurg, 1903), p. 13.

2. Bureau of Justice Statistics, *Prison and Jail Inmates at Midyear 2001,* NCJ 191702 (Washington, DC: U.S. Government Printing Office, 2002). Available at www.ncjrs.org.

3. U.S. Census Bureau, *Statistical Abstract of the United States, 2001* (Washington, DC: U.S. Government Printing Office, 2002), table 10.

4. The Cincinnati consent decree is available on several Web sites: www.usdoj.gov/crtsplit; www.policeaccountability.org; and the City of Cincinnati Web site.

5. Stewart Wakeling, Miriam Jorgensen, Susan Michaelson, and Manley Begay, *Policing on American Indian Reservations: A Report to the National Institute of Justice,* NCJ 188095 (Washington, DC: U.S. Government Printing Office, 2001). Available at www.ncjrs.org.

6. David Harris, *Profiles in Injustice: Why Racial Profiling Doesn't Work* (New York: New Press, 2002); ACLU, *Driving While Black* (New York: Author, 1999). See www.profilesininjustice.com.

7. National Urban League, *State of Black America, 2001.* (New York: Author, 2001). Available at www.nul.org/soba.

8. Bureau of Justice Statistics, *Sourcebook of Criminal Justice Statistics, 2000,* online edition, p. 143. Available at www.albany.edu/sourcebook.

9. Dennis Rosenbaum, D. A. Lewis, and J. Grant, "Neighborhood-Based Crime Prevention: Assessing the Efficacy of Community Organizing in Chicago," in *Community Crime Prevention: Does It Work?* ed. Dennis Rosenbaum (Newbury Park, CA: Sage, 1986), pp. 109–136.

10. See, for example, Gregg Barak, Jeanne M. Flavin, Paul S. Leighton, *Class, Race, Gender, and Crime* (Los Angeles: Roxbury, 2001); Michael Tonry, *Malign Neglect* (New York: Oxford University Press, 1994); Coramae Richey Mann, *Unequal Justice* (Bloomington: Indiana University Press, 1988); Ronald Barri Flowers, *Minorities and Criminality* (Westport, CT:

Greenwood, 1988); William Wilbanks, *The Myth of a Racist Criminal Justice System* (Monterey, CA: Brooks/Cole, 1987); Joan Petersilia, *Racial Disparities in the Criminal Justice System* (Santa Monica, CA: Rand, 1983); National Minority Advisory Council on Criminal Justice, *The Inequality of Justice: A Report on Crime and the Administration of Justice in the Minority Community* (Washington, DC: U.S. Government Printing Office, 1982); Elton Long, James Long, Wilmer Leon, and Paul B. Weston, *American Minorities: The Justice Issue* (Englewood Cliffs, NJ: Prentice-Hall, 1975).

11. Christopher Stone, "Race, Crime, and the Administration of Justice: A Summary of the Available Facts," paper presented to the Advisory Board of the President's Initiative on Race, May 19, 1998.

12. Samuel Walker and Molly Brown, "A Pale Reflection of Reality: The Neglect of Racial and Ethnic Minorities in Introductory Criminal Justice Textbooks," *Journal of Criminal Justice Education* 6 (spring 1995): 61–83.

13. Mann, *Unequal Justice,* p. viii.

14. National Minority Advisory Council on Criminal Justice, *The Inequality of Justice,* chap. 2, "Impact of Criminal Justice on Hispanic-Americans"; chap. 3, "Impact of Crime and Criminal Justice on American Indians"; chap. 4, "Impact of Crime and Criminal Justice on Asian-Americans."

15. See the Web site of the American-Arab Anti-Discrimination Committee at www.adc.org.

16. Alfredo Mirandé, *Gringo Justice* (Notre Dame, IN: University of Notre Dame Press, 1987), p. ix.

17. Marianne O. Nielsen, "Contextualization for Native American Crime and Criminal Justice Involvement," in *Native Americans, Crime, and Justice,* ed. Marianne O. Nielsen and Robert A. Silverman (Boulder, CO: Westview, 1996), p. 10.

18. Wilbanks, *The Myth of a Racist Criminal Justice System.*

19. Stone, "Race, Crime, and the Administration of Justice," p. 1.

20. Darnell F. Hawkins, "Ethnicity, Race, and Crime: A Review of Selected Studies," in *Ethnicity, Race, and Crime,* ed. D. F. Hawkins (Albany: State University of New York Press, 1995), p. 40.

21. Bureau of the Census, *Statistical Abstract, 2001,* table 10.

22. The concept of race is both problematic and controversial. For a starting point, see Ashley Montagu, *Statement on Race,* 3d ed. (New York: Oxford University Press, 1972), which includes the text of and commentary on four United Nations statements on race.

23. J. Milton Yinger, *Ethnicity: Source of Strength? Source of Conflict?* (Albany: State University of New York Press, 1994), p. 19.

24. Paul R. Spickard, "The Illogic of American Racial Categories," in *Racially Mixed People in America,* ed. Marla P. Root (Newbury Park, CA: Sage, 1992), p. 18.

25. Yinger, *Ethnicity,* p. 19.

26. Christine B. Hickman, "The Devil and the One Drop Rule: Racial Categories, African Americans, and the U.S. Census," *Michigan Law Review* 95 (March 1997): 1161–1265.

27. U.S. Office of Management and Budget, Directive 15, *Race and Ethnic Standards for Federal Statistics and Administrative Reporting,* OMB Circular No. A-46 (1974), rev. 1977 (Washington, DC: U.S. Government Printing Office, 1977).

28. Lawrence Wright, "One Drop of Blood," *The New Yorker* (July 25, 1994), p. 47.

29. See the Association of MultiEthnic Americans Web site at www.ameasite.org.

30. National Urban League, *State of Black America, 2001.* Available at www.nul.org/soba.

31. Ibid.

32. AMEA Web site: www.ameasite.org.

33. Office of Management and Budget, "Revisions to the Standards for the Classification of Federal Data on Race and Ethnicity" (October 30, 1997). Available at www.whitehouse.gov/omb/fedreg/ombdir15.html.

34. Ibid.

35. James Paul Allen and Eugene James Turner, *We the People: An Atlas of America's Ethnic Diversity* (New York: Macmillan, 1988).

36. Yinger, *Ethnicity,* pp. 3–4.

37. Quoted in Yinger, *Ethnicity,* p. 21.

38. Louis Wirth, "The Problem of Minority Groups," in *The Science of Man in the World Crisis,* ed. Ralph Linton (New York: Columbia University Press, 1945), p. 123.

39. Office of Management and Budget, "Revisions to the Standards."

40. John Hope Franklin and Alfred A. Moss Jr., *From Slavery to Freedom: A History of African Americans,* 7th ed. (New York: Knopf, 1994), p. xix.

41. George Gallup Jr., *The Gallup Poll Monthly* (August 1994), p. 30.

42. Eric R. Wolf, *Europe and the People without History* (Berkeley: University of California Press, 1982), pp. 380–381.

43. Gallup, *The Gallup Poll Monthly,* p. 34.

44. Mirandé, *Gringo Justice.*

45. Nielsen and Silverman, eds., *Native Americans, Crime, and Justice.*

46. Bureau of Justice Statistics, *Contacts Between the Police and the Public* (Washington, DC: U.S. Government Printing Office, 2001).

47. Gary LaFree, "Race and Crime Trends in the United States, 1946–1990," in *Ethnicity, Race, and Crime,* pp. 173–174.

48. Zoann K. Snyder-Joy, "Self-Determination and American Indian Justice: Tribal versus Federal Jurisdiction on Indian Lands," in *Ethnicity, Race, and Crime,* p. 310.

49. Bureau of Justice Statistics, *Sourcebook of Criminal Justice Statistics, 1998* (Washington, DC: U.S. Government Printing Office, 1999), app. 4.

50. Ibid., app. 13.

51. William H. Frey, "The Diversity Myth," *American Demographics* 20 (June 1998): 41.

52. Ibid.

53. U.S. Census Bureau, *Statistical Abstract, 2001,* table 35, p. 38.

54. Ibid., table 23, p. 25.

55. Ibid., table 24, p. 27.

56. Ibid., table 36, p. 39.

57. Ibid., table 400, p. 250.

58. Mann, *Unequal Justice,* pp. vii–xiv.

59. Wilbanks, *The Myth of a Racist Criminal Justice System.*

60. W. Marvin Dulaney, *Black Police in America* (Bloomington: Indiana University Press, 1996).

61. D. E. Georges-Abeyie, "Criminal Justice Processing of Non-White Minorities," in *Racism, Empiricism, and Criminal Justice,* ed. B. D. MacLean and D. Milovanovic (Vancouver: Collective, 1990), p. 28.

62. David C. Baldus, George G. Woodworth, and Charles A. Pulaski, *Equal Justice and the Death Penalty: A Legal and Empirical Analysis* (Boston: Northeastern University Press, 1990).

63. Jerome G. Miller, *Search and Destroy* (New York: Cambridge University Press, 1996).

64. Kerner Commission, *Report of the National Advisory Commission on Civil Disorders* (New York: Bantam Books, 1968), p. 304.

65. Wilbanks, *The Myth of a Racist Criminal Justice System,* p. 5.

66. Mann, *Unequal Justice,* p. 160.

67. Richard Quinney, *The Social Reality of Crime* (Boston: Little, Brown, 1970).

68. Darnell Hawkins, "Beyond Anomalies: Rethinking the Conflict Perspective on Race and Criminal Punishment," *Social Forces* 65 (March 1987): 719–745.

69. Ibid.

70. Alfred Blumstein, "Prison Populations: A System out of Control," in *Crime and Justice: A Review of Research,* ed. Michael Tonry and Norval Morris, vol. 10 (Chicago: University of Chicago Press, 1988), p. 253.

71. Freda Adler, Gerhard O. W. Mueller, and William S. Laufer, *Criminology,* 2d ed. (New York: McGraw-Hill, 1995).

2

Victims and Offenders

Myths and Realities
about Crime

O n Wednesday, April 19, 1989, at 10:05 P.M., "a 28-year-old investment
banker, jogging through Central Park, was attacked by a group of teenagers. They kicked and beat her, smashed in her head with a pipe and
raped her."[1] The offenders were later identified as minority youth from East
Harlem. The *New York Times* reported that "the attack sparked angry cries for
vengeance and increased police patrol, partly, some have argued, because those
charged in the attack were minority group teenagers and the victim was an affluent white woman."[2]

Does this incident reflect a "typical" criminal event? Many people believe
that it does: a white victim falling prey to the violence of minority gang activity. But the evidence suggests that it is *not* the typical criminal event. First, over
80 percent of crime reported to the police is property crime.[3] Second, a disproportionate number of crime victims are minorities. Third, interracial (between-
race) crimes are the exception, not the rule. Finally, not all group activity is gang
activity, not all gang actions are criminal, and not all gang members are racial
or ethnic minorities.

An article in the *New York Times* several weeks after the well-publicized
event described here helps put this victimization in perspective. Twenty-nine
rapes were reported in the city that week (April 16–22, 1989), with 17 African American female victims, 7 Hispanics, 3 whites, and 2 Asians.[4] Thus, the
typical rape victim was in fact a *minority* female. Although the 29 reports from
the New York Police Department did not indicate the race of the offender, other

sources, including the national victimization data discussed later in this chapter, demonstrate that rape is predominantly an intrarracial (within-race) crime.[5]

GOALS OF THE CHAPTER

In this chapter, we describe the context of crime in the United States. We use several different sources of data to paint a picture of the crime victim and the offender. We compare victimization rates for racial and ethnic minorities to the rates for whites, focusing on both household victimization and personal victimization. We also compare offending rates for racial minorities and whites. We then present statistics to document the fact that crime is predominantly an intraracial, rather than an interracial event. We also focus on the most noted exception to the intraracial crime pattern: hate crime. We end the chapter with a discussion of ethnic youth gangs and their role in the United States.

A BROADER PICTURE
OF THE CRIME VICTIM

Our perceptions of crime are shaped to a large extent by the highly publicized crimes featured on the nightly news and sensationalized in newspapers. We read about young African American or Hispanic males who sexually assault, rob, and murder whites, and we assume that these crimes are typical. We assume that the typical crime is a violent crime, that the typical victim is white, and that the typical offender is African American or Hispanic. As Silberman observed, this topic is difficult to address:

> In the end, there is no escaping the question of race and crime. To say this is to risk, almost guarantee, giving offense; it is impossible to talk honestly about the role of race in American life without offending and angering both whites and blacks—and Hispanic browns and Native American reds as well. The truth is terrible, on all sides; and we are all too accustomed to the soothing euphemisms and inflammatory rhetoric with which the subject is cloaked.[6]

In short, compelling evidence suggests that the arguably prominent picture of crime, criminal, and victim just described is at best incomplete and at worst inaccurate, particularly as it concerns race and ethnicity of crime victims. Recent victimization data, in fact, reveal that racial minorities are more likely than whites in most circumstances to be victimized by crime.

In the sections that follow, we use victimization data to paint a broad picture of the crime victim, allowing for a view of which racial and ethnic groups are disproportionately the victims of crime. We begin by discussing the National Crime Victimization Survey, the source of most data on criminal victimization in the United States. We then compare the household victimization rates of African Americans and whites, as well as Hispanics and non-Hispanics. Personal victimization rates (property and violent offense) are then compared for African Americans, Hispanics, and whites. We conclude with a discussion of homicide victimization events.

The National Crime Victimization Survey

The most systematic source of victimization information is the National Crime Victimization Survey (NCVS).[7] The survey, which began in 1973, is conducted by the Bureau of the Census for the Bureau of Justice Statistics (BJS).[8] Survey data are used to produce annual estimates of the number and rate of personal and household victimizations for the nation as a whole and for various subgroups of the population.

Interviews are conducted at a 6-month interval to ask whether household members have been the victims of selected major crimes during the last 6 months.[9] Information is collected from persons aged 12 and older who are members of the household selected in the sample. The sample is chosen on the basis of the most recent census data to be representative of the nation as a whole. The NCVS data presented here are estimates based on the interviews of 86,600 households and 159,420 people aged 12 and older.[10] The response rates for the 2000 survey were very high: 93.4 percent of eligible households and 89.6 percent of eligible individuals responded.[11]

Members of selected households are contacted either in person or by phone every 6 months for 3 years. They complete household questionnaires to describe the demographic characteristics of the household (income, number of members, and so on). The race and ethnicity of the adult completing the household questionnaire is recorded from self-report information as the race and ethnicity of the household. Incident questionnaires are completed for both household offenses and personal victimizations. The designated head of the household is questioned about the incidence of household burglary, household larceny, and motor vehicle theft. Personal victimization incident questionnaires are administered to household members aged 12 and older, probing them to relay any victimizations of rape, robbery, assault, and personal larceny. Those who report victimizations to interviewers are asked a series of follow-up questions about the nature of the crime and the response to the crime. Those who report personal victimizations are also asked to describe the offender and their relationship (if any) with the offender. Some sample personal victimization questions follow:

During the last six months . . .

Did anyone beat you up, attack you, or hit you with something such as a rock or a bottle?

Did anyone take something directly from you by using force, such as by a stickup, mugging, or threat?

Was anything stolen from you while you were away from home, for instance at work, in a theater or restaurant, or while traveling?

In many ways, the NCVS produces a more complete picture of crime and the characteristics of those who are victimized by crime than official police records. For one thing, respondents are asked about victimizations not reported to the police. In addition, the survey includes questions designed to elicit detailed information concerning the victim, the characteristics of the offender(s), and the context of the victimization. This information is used to calculate age-, sex-, and race-specific estimates of victimization. In addition, estimates of interracial and intraracial crime can be calculated.

The NCVS also has several limitations. For example, it does not cover commercial crime, kidnapping, or homicide; the estimates produced are for the nation as a whole, central city compared to suburban areas, but not for states or local jurisdictions; homeless people are not interviewed; and responses are susceptible to memory loss and interviewer bias. In addition, the information on race is often limited to white, African American, and other, whereas ethnicity is limited to Hispanic and non-Hispanic, with the latter being available for selected issues only. It is important to remember that Hispanics may be of any race (see Chapter 1). NCVS designations are determined by census categories, so the Hispanic category includes all individuals of Spanish origin (Mexican American, Chicano, Mexican, Puerto Rican, Cuban, Central or South American) regardless of racial identity.

Household Victimization

As noted, the NCVS questions the designated head of household about crimes against the household—burglary, household larceny, and motor vehicle theft. It is clear that household victimization rates vary by race and ethnicity, indicating that African American households are more vulnerable than white households, and Hispanic households are more vulnerable than non-Hispanic ones.[12]

In 2000, households headed by African Americans had a higher victimization rate than white households (see Figure 2.1) for all designated household offenses (212.2 per 1,000 households compared to 173.3 per 1,000 households). This general pattern also characterized each of the three household crimes. That is, the rate for African American households exceeded the rate for white households for burglary (47.6 compared to 29.4) and household larceny (151.4 compared to 136.0). The greatest disparity was in motor vehicle theft rates, with African American households victimized at a rate nearly twice that of white households (13.2 compared to 7.9).

The BJS also estimates that victimization rates for Hispanic households are markedly higher than the victimization rates for non-Hispanic households.[13] Figure 2.2 shows higher rates for Hispanics than non-Hispanics for all household crimes combined (227.0 per 1,000 households compared to 173.4 per 1,000 households). Burglary and household larceny rates indicate that households headed by Hispanics have higher victimization rates than non-Hispanic ones (41.7 compared to 31.0; 165.6 compared to 134.7). Motor vehicle theft reflects

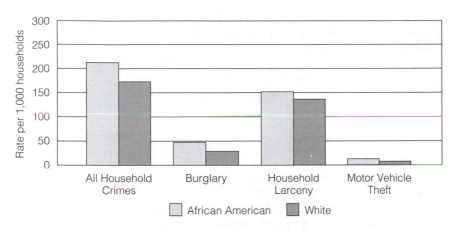

FIGURE 2.1 Household Victimization Rates, by Race of Head of Household, 2000

SOURCE: Callie Marie Rennison, *Criminal Victimization 2000: Changes 1990–2000 with Trends 1993–2000* (Washington, DC: Bureau of Justice Statistics, 2001). Available at www.ojp.usdoj.gov/bjs.

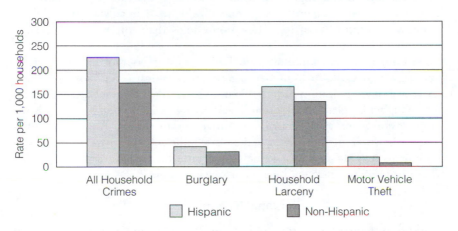

FIGURE 2.2 Household Victimization Rates, by Ethnicity of Head of Household, 2000

SOURCE: Callie Marie Rennison, *Criminal Victimization 2000: Changes 1990–2000 with Trends 1993–2000* (Washington, DC: Bureau of Justice Statistics, 2001). Available at www.ojp.usdoj.gov/bjs.

the greatest disparity, with rates twice as high for Hispanic households as for non-Hispanic households (19.7 compared to 7.6).

The Effect of Urbanization The racial differences in household victimization rates discussed thus far are differences for the United States as a whole. These patterns vary, however, depending on the degree of urbanization (see Table 2.1).[14] Household victimization rates are highest for African Americans in urban areas, for white households in suburban areas, and for the combined "other" racial group (Native American/Alaska Native and Asian/Pacific Islander) in the rural areas. The pattern shown in Figure 2.1 of African Ameri-

Table 2.1 Racial and Ethnicity Property Crime Victimization Rate by Urban, Suburban, and Rural Setting, 1993–1998

	CRIME RATE PER 1,000 HOUSEHOLDS		
	Urban	Suburban	Rural
Race			
African American	348.6	295.5	200.0
White	341.7	252.4	210.6
Other	295.4	253.9	342.8
Ethnicity			
Hispanic	386.4	337.8	271.6
Non-Hispanic	335.2	249.9	209.6

SOURCE: Detis T. Duhart, *Urban, Suburban and Rural Victimization, 1993–1998* (Washington, DC: Bureau of Justice Statistics, 2000). Available at www.ojp.usdoj .gov/bjs/.

can households having higher victimization rates than white households does reverse under some circumstances.[15] Specifically, rural area data reflect slightly higher victimization rates for white households than for African American households.

Although the analysis presented in Table 2.1 offers no information by crime type, analysis of earlier years of victimization data indicate even more variations in the typical victimization pattern. Crime-specific data from suburban areas reflected higher burglary and household larceny figures for white households and a higher combined victimization rate for suburban African American households.[16] In rural areas, crime-specific data indicated that African American households had higher motor vehicle theft rates than white rural households, which had the highest combined victimization rates.[17]

Personal Victimization

In addition to questioning the head of the household about crimes against the household, the NCVS interviewers ask all household members over the age of 12 whether they themselves have been the victim of an act of rape (worded as sexual assault), robbery, assault, or theft within the past 6 months. This information is then used to estimate victimization rates for the nation as a whole and for the various subgroups in the population.

Consistent with the pattern of racial disparity found in household victimizations, these estimates reveal that African Americans are more likely than either whites or members of "other" racial groups to be the victims of personal crimes. Table 2.2 shows that the overall victimization rate (which combines crimes of violence and personal theft) for African Americans is 37.2 per 1,000 persons in the population over age 12; 28.2 per 1,000 for whites; and 22.5 per 1,000 for other races (combined group of Native American/Alaska Native and Asian/Pacific Islanders). To estimate victimization rates for Native Americans and Asian Americans, the Bureau of Justice Statistics combined six years of data (1993–1998). These data are discussed in Boxes 2.1 and 2.2.

Table 2.2 Personal Victimization Rates by Type of Crime and by Race and Ethnicity of Victims, 2000

| | VICTIMIZATION RATES[a] | | | | |
| | RACE | | | ETHNICITY | |
	White	African American	Other	Hispanic	Non-Hispanic
Crimes of violence	27.1	35.3	20.7	28.4	27.7
Rape	1.1	1.2	1.1	0.5	1.2
Robbery	2.7	7.2	2.8	5.0	3.0
Assault	23.3	26.9	16.7	23.0	23.5
Aggravated	5.4	7.7	5.2	5.6	5.7
Simple	17.9	19.2	11.5	17.4	17.8
Crimes of theft	1.1	1.9	1.8	2.4	1.1
Total	28.2	37.2	22.5	30.8	28.8

SOURCE: Callie Marie Rennison, *Criminal Victimization 2000: Changes 1990–2000 with Trends 1993–2000* (Washington, DC: Bureau of Justice Statistics, 2001). Available at www.ojp.usdoj .gov/bjs.

[a]Victimization rates per 1,000 persons aged 12 and older.

The racial differences are much greater for crimes of violence than for crimes of theft. In particular, African Americans are nearly 3 times as likely as whites to be the victims of robbery and are clearly more likely to be the victims of aggravated assault than whites or other races. On the other hand, the victimization rates by race are far more similar for simple assaults and crimes of theft. Few differences emerge in the reported rape victimization rates.

Table 2.2 also displays personal victimization rates by ethnicity. Overall, Hispanics have slightly higher victimization rates than non–Hispanics (30.8 per 1,000 persons over age 12 compared to 28.8 per 1,000). The largest victimization differences appear in the cases of robbery and personal theft. Although Hispanics are almost twice as likely to be victims of robbery than non-Hispanics, aggravated and simple assault rates are similar between the groups.

The Effects of Urbanization A recent analysis of victimization trends by the BJS using NCVS data from 1993 to 1998 indicates that urbanization is a key aspect of understanding victimization. As the data in Table 2.3 reveal, victimization rates are highest for most groups in urban areas. Overall, urban residents report 38 percent of all victimizations, while making up only 29 percent of the U.S. population.[18] Suburban residents make up 50 percent of the population and experience 47 percent of the victimizations. Rural residents are least likely to experience criminal victimization, as they make up 20 percent of the population and experience 20 percent of the criminal victimization.

The national figures for violent victimization shown in Table 2.2 indicate that African Americans have higher overall victimization rates than whites. As we see from Table 2.3, this difference is fueled mostly by the extreme differences in urban victimization rates. African Americans report higher violent

Table 2.3 Violent Crime Rates by Race and Ethnicity for Urban, Suburban, and Rural Areas, 1993–1998

	RATE PER 1,000 PERSONS OVER AGE 12		
	Urban	Suburban	Rural
Race			
African American	68.0	48.5	31.1
White	59.1	43.8	34.0
Other	35.7	34.8	68.3
Ethnicity			
Hispanic	51.7	49.7	46.5
Non-Hispanic	60.9	43.1	33.7

SOURCE: Detis T. Duhart, *Urban, Suburban and Rural Victimization, 1993–1998* (Washington, DC: Bureau of Justice Statistics, 2000). Available at www.ojp.usdoj.gov/bjs/.

victimization rates than whites (68 per 1,000 persons aged 12 and older compared to 59.1 per 1,000), and both groups have much higher rates than those for the "other" racial group, which includes Native Americans/Alaska Natives and Asian/Pacific Islanders (35.7 per 1,000). In suburban areas, violent crime victimization rates are more similar for African Americans and whites (48.5 per 1,000 compared to 43.8 per 1,000), and again are higher than rates for the "other" racial grouping (34.8 per 1,000). Although violent victimization rates remain at somewhat similar levels in rural areas, these areas are the only places where white rates are slightly higher than the African American rates (34.0 per 1,000 compared to 31.1 per 1,000). However, the highest victimization rate for any racial group is that of the combined "other" group in the rural setting (68.3 per 1,000).

A number of comparisons can also be drawn from the ethnicity data reported in Table 2.3. Hispanics have a higher victimization rate than non-Hispanics in nationwide victimization data (see Table 2.2), but this difference seems to be fueled primarily by higher rates in suburban and rural victimization rates. Hispanic violent victimization rates compared to those of non-Hispanics are somewhat higher in suburban areas (49.7 per 1,000 compared to 43.1 per 1,000), but substantially higher for Hispanics in rural areas (46.5 per 1,000 compared to 33.7 per 1,000). Conversely, the violent victimization rates for Hispanics in urban areas are markedly lower than for non-Hispanics (51.7 per 1,000 compared to 60.9 per 1,000).

The Effects of Gender and Urbanization The intersection of race/ethnicity, urbanization, and gender is not always a focus of the BJS analyses of NCVS data. However, a recent analysis of these data reveals that victimization rates vary for African American men and women in urban and nonurban settings. African American males have a higher violent crime victimization rate than white males; however, this picture of victimization rates arises from higher African American male victimization rates only in urban areas.[19] In suburban and rural areas, white males have higher violent victimization rates.[20] Robbery rates stay higher for African American males regardless of urbanization, but white male victimization rates are close to or even exceed those of African American males for aggravated assault in suburban and rural areas.[21]

Although female victimization rates are often expected to be lower than those of males, in many cases, African American female violent victimization rates are closer to the rates of African American males than of white females.[22] That is, African American female violent victimization rates often match or even exceed the rates recorded for white males. This situation is more likely in robbery offenses and less likely in rural areas.[23] African American female violent victimization rates are consistently higher than those of white females in urban and suburban areas, but not in rural areas.[24] The personal violence victimization rate for rural white females seems to arise from high simple assault rates, as robbery rates and aggravated assault rates remain higher for African American females than for white females.[25]

Trends in Household and Personal Victimization

A review of NCVS data from 1973 to 2000 indicates that most of the general patterns of victimization noted previously have not changed over time.[26] The household victimization data for these years illustrate that property victimization rates for African American households consistently exceed the rates for white households, and Hispanic victimization rates exceed those for non-Hispanic households; however, some variations occur when considering urbanization and crime type. Moreover, rates of robbery and aggravated assault victimization for African Americans are repeatedly higher, but simple assault rates remain similar to white victimization rates. Violent victimization rates are higher for Hispanics than non-Hispanics, driven mostly by higher robbery rates. Personal theft rates are characterized by a convergence of rates for these two groups over time; however, African American rates remain somewhat higher than rates for whites, and Hispanic rates remain somewhat higher than non-Hispanics rates.

The addition of urbanization to the discussion of race, ethnicity, and victimization offers an interesting, although divergent, pattern for different race and ethnicity groups. Urban areas consistently have the highest household and personal victimization rates. African Americans consistently have the most disproportionately high violent and household victimization rates, but only in urban areas. Suburban victimization rates are more similar across racial groups. However, rural victimization rates often show the lowest victimization rates for African Americans; the "other" combined racial group has disproportionately high victimization rates in rural areas. Similarly, the highest victimization rates for African Americans are in urban areas, and the victimization rates for the "other" racial group are highest in the rural areas.

Hispanic victimization rates reflect a combination of these patterns: Hispanic household victimization rates are similar to those of African Americans in that the highest victimization rates are in urban areas; however, Hispanics retain a disproportionately higher victimization rate than non-Hispanics in urban, suburban, and rural areas. Personal victimization rates for Hispanics are

---

BOX 2.1   Native Americans and Violent Crimes

Information on the victimization rates of Native Americans is difficult to compile. This group represents approximately 1 percent of the population. Given that the incidence of victimization in the general population is a rare event, documenting a rare event in a small population is challenging. The BJS has pooled data from a number of years (1993–1998) to reveal a picture of Native American (nonfatal) violent victimization: 118.8 violent victimizations occurred per 1,000 population of Native Ameri- cans aged 12 and older. Ths average violent victimization for Native Americans was 2.5 times the rate for whites (45.4 per 1,000), 2 times the rate for African Americans (56.5 per 1,000), and 4.5 times the rate for Asians (25.5). In contrast to the general intraracial victimization patterns of white and African American crime, Native Americans report that 7 of 10 violent offenses are of someone they perceived to be of a race other than Native American (Rennison, 2001; Greenfeld & Smith, 1999).

---

similar to those of the "other" combined racial group, with disproportionately high rates for Hispanics in suburban and rural areas only.

Perhaps the pattern of higher victimization for African Americans in urban areas and higher victimization for other minority groups in rural areas has to do with issues of racial composition. Urban populations are disproportionately African American, and rural areas are disproportionately white.[27] The movement of Hispanic populations to fill labor needs in rural areas that have traditionally been predominantly (90 percent or more) white has left such groups open to higher risks of victimization.

Lifetime Likelihood of Victimization

Although annual victimization rates are important indicators of the likelihood of victimization, they "do not convey the full impact of crime as it affects people."[28] To gauge the impact of crime, we must consider not just the odds of being victimized within the next few weeks or months, but the possibility of being robbed, raped, assaulted, or burglarized at some time in our lives. Even though the odds of being victimized during any 12-month period are low, the odds of ever being victimized may be high. Only 16 out of 10,000 women are rape victims annually, for example, but the lifetime likelihood of being raped is much greater: nearly 1 out of every 12 females (and 1 out of every 9 African American females) will be the victim of a rape at some time during her life.[29]

The BJS used annual victimization rates for a 10-year period to calculate lifetime victimization rates. Table 2.4 presents these rates, which indicate that about five out of six people will be victims of a violent crime at least once during their lives and that nearly everyone will be the victim of a personal theft at least once. There is no difference in the African American and white rates for personal theft and only a slight difference in the rates for violent crimes.

For the individual crimes of violence, the lifetime likelihood of being assaulted is nearly identical for African Americans and whites: about three of every

Table 2.4 Lifetime Likelihood of Victimization

	PERCENTAGE WHO WILL BE VICTIMIZED [a]	
	African Americans	Whites
Violent crimes	87	82
Robbery	51	27
Assault	73	74
Rape (females only)	11	8
Personal theft	99	99

SOURCE: Bureau of Justice Statistics, U.S. Department of Justice, *Lifetime Likelihood of Victimization* (Washington, DC: U.S. Government Printing Office, 1987).

[a]Percentage of persons who will experience one or more victimizations starting at 12 years of age.

BOX 2.2 Asian Americans and Violent Crime

Asian Americans make up less than 4 percent of the population. To estimate their victimization rates, the BJS pooled several years of NCVS data (1993–1998) (Rennison, 2001). These data indicate that Asian Americans have the lowest overall victimization rates (25.5 per 1,000 population aged 12 and older) compared to whites (45.5 per 1,000), African Americans (56.5 per 1,000), and Native Americans (188.8 per 1,000). Rates for individual violent victimizations indicated that only for robbery are Asian American victimization rates higher than those of the next lowest group (whites). The persistent pattern of intraracial crime events does not hold true for Asian American victimizations. When Asian American respondents were asked to report the perceived race of the offender, less than 30 percent of offenders were identified as Asian Americans, 35 percent as white, and 26 percent as African American.

---

four persons, regardless of race, will be assaulted at some time during their lives. There are, on the other hand, large racial differences for robbery, with African Americans almost twice as likely as whites to be robbed. The lifetime likelihood of rape is also somewhat higher for African American females than for white females. Thus, for the two most serious (nonmurder) violent crimes, the likelihood of victimization is much higher for African Americans than for whites.

Homicide Victimization Rates

The largest and most striking racial differences in victimization are for the crime of homicide. In fact, all of the data on homicide point to the same conclusion: African Americans, and particularly African American males, face a much greater risk of death by homicide than do whites.

Although the NCVS does not produce estimates of homicide victimization rates, there are a number of other sources of data. A partial picture is available

Focus on an Issue

Victim Assistance: Should Race Matter?

Most observers agree that the American criminal justice system should treat suspects and offenders in a color-blind fashion, but how should we treat victims? Barak, Flavin, and Leighton (2001) argue that victim assistance should take the race, ethnicity, gender, and even class of the victim into consideration. They state, "Victim counseling needs to be sensitive to cultural values through which the victimization experience is interpreted. Rehabilitation and intervention programs likewise need to build on cultural values for maximum

effectiveness" (p. 102). For example, a victim of domestic violence may need different services depending on her social realities: a Hispanic woman with children, no employment history, and a limited working knowledge of English compared to a white woman with children, a professional employment history, and a command of English.

Do you agree? Should the criminal justice system be entirely color-blind? Or does justice actually require the system to be color-conscious in some situations?

from the Supplemental Homicide Reports (SHR) submitted by law enforcement agencies to the FBI as part of the Uniform Crime Reports (UCR) Program. This information is collected, when available, for single-victim–single-offender homicides. These data reveal that a disproportionate number of homicide victims are African American. From 1976 to 1999, African Americans constituted no more than 15 percent of the population but over 46 percent of all homicide victims.[30]

The race and sex differences in the likelihood of death by homicide are revealed more clearly by comparing the *rates* of death by homicide (per 100,000 population) for various subgroups of the population.[31] These data reveal that homicide is a more significant risk factor for African Americans than for whites. Although homicide rates have decreased among all groups since the early 1990s, the homicide rate in 1999 for African Americans (20.6 per 100,000 specified population) remained nearly 6 times the rate for whites (3.5 per 100,000). Even more striking, the rate for African American males was nearly 8 times the rate for white males and was 24 times the rate for white females. The rate for African American females exceeded the rate for white females, appearing closer to that of white males.

Summary: A More Comprehensive
Picture of the Crime Victim

The victimization data presented in the preceding sections offers a more comprehensive picture of the crime victim than that found in common perceptions and media presentations. These data reveal that African Americans, Asian/Pacific Islanders, Native Americans, and Hispanics are often more likely than whites and non-Hispanics to be victims of household and personal crimes. These racial and ethnic differences are particularly striking for violent crimes, especially robbery. African Americans—especially African American males—also face a much greater risk of death by homicide than whites. It thus seems fair to conclude that in the United States, the groups at greatest risk of becoming crime victims are those that belong to racial and ethnic minorities.

PICTURE OF THE TYPICAL OFFENDER

For many people, the term *crime* evokes an image of a young African American male who is armed with a handgun and who commits a robbery, a rape, or a murder. In the minds of many Americans, *crime* is synonymous with *black crime*.

It is easy to see why the average American believes that the typical offender is African American. The crimes that receive the most attention—from the media, politicians, and criminal justice policymakers—are "street crimes" such as murder, robbery, and rape. These are precisely the crimes for which African Americans are arrested at a disproportionately high rate. In 2000, for example, 48.8 percent of those arrested for murder, 53.9 percent of those arrested for robbery, and 34.1 percent of those arrested for rape were African American.[32]

Arrest rates for serious violent crimes, of course, do not tell the whole story. Although violent crimes may be the crimes we fear most, they are not the crimes that occur most frequently. Moreover, arrest rates do not necessarily present an accurate picture of offending. Many crimes are not reported to the police, and many of those reported do not result in an arrest.

In this section, we use a number of criminal justice data sources to paint a picture of the typical criminal offender. We summarize the offender data presented in official police records, victimization reports, and self-report surveys. Because each of these data sources varies both in terms of the offender information captured and the "point of contact" with the offender, the picture of the typical offender that each produces also differs somewhat. We note these discrepancies and summarize the results of research designed to reconcile them.

Official Arrest Statistics

The UCR system, which has been administered by the FBI since 1930, presents annual data on arrests. Today, the program compiles reports from over 17,000 law enforcement agencies across the country representing 95 percent of the total U.S. population. The annual report *Crime in the United States* offers detailed information from local, state, and federal law enforcement agencies on crime counts and rates, as well as arrest information.

Problems with UCR Data The information on offenders gleaned from the UCR is incomplete and potentially misleading because it includes only offenders whose crimes result in arrest. The UCR data exclude offenders whose crimes are not reported to the police, as well as offenders whose crimes do not lead to arrest. A second limitation is that the UCR data include arrest statistics for four

Focus on an Issue:
The Creation of Victims and Offenders of Color

Silberman (1978) makes the following observation on the common misconceptions of race and crime:

> For most of their history in this country . . . blacks were victims, not initiators, of violence. In the Old South, violence against blacks was omnipresent—sanctioned both by customs and by law. Whites were free to use any methods, up to and including murder, to control "their Negros." . . . There was little blacks could do to protect themselves. To strike back at whites, or merely to display anger or insufficient deference, was not just to risk one's own neck, but to place the whole community in danger. It was equally dangerous, or at best pointless, to appeal to the law. (p. 124)

Indeed, the purpose of the Fourteenth Amendment to the U.S. Constitution following the Civil War was to create a situation of full citizenship for former slaves. One of the implications of this newfound status of citizenship was that African Americans were formally conferred the status of victim and offender in the eyes of the law. Prior to this time, actions of assault, rape, and theft against slaves and by slaves were handled informally, or even as civil matters. Even African American offenders were not necessarily viewed as subject to formal criminal trial and adjudication, especially if the "victims" were slaves, too.

One frequently retold example of a slave's lack of status as a citizen is the case of Margaret Garner. This female slave escaped with her children to Ohio from a Kentucky plantation in 1855. Once discovered by her master, who was given the right of retrieval under federal law, she responded to the threat of capture by murdering one of her children and attempting to murder her other children. Outrage at her actions led to the unprecedented call for the intervention of the formal justice of the American judicial system. This situation was complicated by the legal issue of citizenship. In short, the slave could not be tried as a citizen nor was the victim of the murder a citizen. The issues were merely of a civil nature. Although most would agree the child was a victim, she was not so in the eyes of the law. Garner was, in fact, tried for her destructive actions to the master's property. This case became the foundation for Toni Morrison's *Beloved: A Novel* (1988) and was later adapted as the movie *Beloved* (1998) (Weisenburger, 1988).

---

racial groups (white, African American, Native American, and Asian) but do not present any information by ethnicity (Hispanic versus non-Hispanic).

A substantial proportion of crime is not reported to the police. In fact, the NCVS reveals that fewer than half of all violent victimizations and only one-third of all property victimizations are reported to the police.[33] Factors that influence the decision to report a crime include the seriousness of the crime and the relationship between the victim and the offender. Violent crimes are more likely than property crimes to be reported, as are crimes committed by friends or relatives rather than strangers.[34]

Victimization surveys reveal that victims often fail to report crimes to the police because they believe that nothing can be done, the event is not impor-

Focus on an Issue

A Proposal to Eliminate Race from the Uniform Crime Report

In October 1993, a group of mayors, led by Minneapolis mayor Donald Fraser, sent a letter to the U.S. Attorney General's Office asking that the design of the UCR be changed to eliminate race from the reporting of arrest data. The mayors were concerned about the misuse of racial data from crime statistics. They charged that the current reporting policies "perpetuate racism in American society" and contribute to the general perception "that there is a causal relationship between race and criminality." Critics of the proposal argued that race data are essential to battling street crime because they reveal who the perpetrators are.

Although the federal policy of reporting race in arrest statistics has not changed, Fraser was instrumental in pushing a similar request through the Minnesota Bureau of Investigation. The final result in Minnesota was the following disclaimer in state crime publications: "Racial and ethnic data must be treated with caution. . . . [E]xisting research on crime has generally shown that racial or ethnic identity is not predictive of criminal behavior within data which has been controlled for social and economic factors." This statement warns that descriptive data are not sufficient for causal analysis and should not be used as the sole indication of the role of race and criminality for the formation of public policy.

Using inductive reasoning, we can conclude that the overrepresentation of minority race groups in arrest data can be suggestive of at least two causal inferences: (1) certain racial groups are characterized by differential offending rates, and (2) arrest data are reflective of differential arrest patterns targeted at minorities. What steps must a researcher take to move beyond descriptions of racial disparity in arrest data to an exploration of causal explanations for racial patterns evident in arrest data?

---

tant enough, the police do not want to be bothered, or it is a private matter.[35] Failure to report might also be based on the victim's fear of self-incrimination or embarrassment due to criminal justice proceedings that result in publicity or cross-examination.[36]

The NCVS indicates that the likelihood of reporting a crime to the police also varies by race. African Americans are slightly more likely than whites to report crimes of theft and violence to the police, whereas Hispanics are substantially less likely than non-Hispanics to report victimizations to the police.[37] Hindelang found that victims of rape and robbery were more likely to report the victimization to the police if the offender was African American.[38]

Even if the victim does decide to report the crime to the police, there is no guarantee that the report will result in an arrest. The police may decide that the report is unfounded; in this case, an official report is not filed, and the incident is not counted as an offense known to the police. Furthermore, even if the police do file an official report, they may be unwilling or unable to make an arrest. In 2000, only about 20 percent of all Index crimes were cleared by the police; the clearance rate for serious crimes ranged from 13.4 percent for burglary to 63.1 percent for murder.[39]

Police officer and offender interactions may also influence the inclination for the police to make an arrest, and cultural traditions may influence police–citizen interactions. For instance, Asian communities often handle delinquent acts informally, whereas other communities would report them to the police.[40] Hispanic cultural traditions may increase the likelihood of arrest if the Hispanic tradition of showing respect for an officer by avoiding direct eye contact is interpreted as insincerity.[41] African Americans who appear hostile or aggressive may also face a greater likelihood of arrest.[42]

The fact that many reported crimes do not lead to an arrest, coupled with the fact that police decision making is highly discretionary, suggests that we should exercise caution in drawing conclusions about the characteristics of those who commit crime based on the characteristics of those who are arrested. To the extent that police decision making reflects stereotypes about crime or racially prejudiced attitudes, the picture of the typical offender that emerges from official arrest statistics may be racially distorted. If police target enforcement efforts in minority communities or concentrate on crimes committed by racial minorities, then obviously racial minorities will be overrepresented in arrest statistics.

A final limitation of UCR offender information centers around the information not included in these arrest reports. The UCR arrest information fails to offer a complete picture of the white offender entering the criminal justice system. Specifically, additional sources of criminal justice data present the white offender as the typical criminal offender in the case of many economic, political, and organized-crime offenses. Russell, in detailing the results of her "search for white crime" in media and academic sources, supports the view that the occupational (white-collar) crimes for which whites are consistently overrepresented may not elicit the same level of fear as the street crimes highlighted in the UCR, but nonetheless these crimes have a high monetary and moral cost.[43]

Arrest Data The arrest data presented in Table 2.5 reveal that the public perception of the typical criminal offender as an African American is generally inaccurate. Examination of the arrest statistics for all offenses, for instance, reveals that the typical offender is white; over two-thirds (69.7 percent) of those arrested in 2000 were white, less than one-third (27.9 percent) were African American, and less than 3 percent were Native American or Asian. Similarly, over half of those arrested for violent crimes and nearly two-thirds of those arrested for property crimes were white. In fact, the only crimes for which the typical offender was African American were robbery and gambling.[44]

Examination of the percentage of all arrests involving members of each racial group must be done in the context of the distribution of each group in the population. In 2000, whites made up approximately 83 percent of the U.S. population; African Americans, 13 percent; Asians, 3 percent; and Native Americans, less than 1 percent. A more appropriate comparison, then, is the percentage in each racial group arrested *in relation to* that group's representation in the

---

**BOX 2.3   The Operationalization of Race
                       in Criminal Justice Data**

The concept of race is measured—operationalized—in a number of ways, depending on the discipline and the research question. Most biologists and anthropologists recognize the difficulties with using traditional race categories (white, black, red, yellow) as an effective means of classifying populations, and most social scientists rely on administrative definitions for record keeping, empirical analysis, and theory testing. Given these conditions, however, the term *race* still carries the connotation of an objective measurement with a biological or genetic basis.

As Knepper (1996) notes, the recording of race in the UCR can be traced to a practice that has no formal theoretical or policy relevance. From available accounts, this information was recorded because it was "available" and may be a side effect of efforts to legitimize fingerprint identification. Currently, the UCR manual gives detailed information on the definitions for Index offenses and Part 2 offenses, as well as specific instructions about the founding of crimes and the counting rules for multiple offenses. What is lacking, however, are specific instructions on the recording of race information. Administrative or census definitions provided by local law enforcement agencies on agency arrest forms are calculated and reported, but no criteria for the source of the information are given. Thus, some records will reflect self-

reporting by the offender, and others will reflect observations of police personnel. Some police arrest reports use the categories of black, white, Native American, and Asian, whereas many use the category of "other." Still others use Hispanic in the race category, rather than as a separate ethnicity. Given that the FBI does not currently request or report ethnicity in the UCR, much information is lost.

The NCVS attempts to collect race and ethnicity information consistent with census definitions. Given their sampling procedures, information is often collapsed into merely black, white, and other (as the combined category for Asian/Pacific Islander and Native American/Alaska Native). An attempt is made to acknowledge one ethnicity, Hispanic. Household information reflects the self-reported race of the individual with sufficient knowledge (and interest) in answering demographic questions about the family and the household incident questions. However, although the 2000 census format allows respondents to pick more than one racial identification, no multiracial household category is available for NCVS respondents. For personal offenses, the race and ethnicity information is available as self-report information from the respondent reporting a victimization. However, the offender race information is based on victim perception of the offender.

---

general population, rather than simply describing the typical offender by the largest proportion of offenders by racial group.

Thus, although whites are the persons most often arrested in crime categories reported in the UCR, it appears that African Americans are arrested at a disproportionately high rate for *nearly* all offenses. The total combined rate for all offenses (see Table 2.5) indicates that the arrest rate for African Americans is 2 times higher than would be predicted by their representation in the population. The disproportion is even larger for the most serious Part 1/Index

Table 2.5 Percentage Distribution of Arrests by Race, 2000

	% White	% African American	% Native American	% Asian American
Total	69.7	27.9	1.2	1.2
Part 1/Index crimes	64.5	32.9	1.2	1.5
Murder and nonnegligent manslaughter	48.7	48.8	1.0	1.5
Forcible rape	63.7	34.1	1.1	1.1
Robbery	44.2	53.9	0.6	1.2
Aggravated assault	63.5	34.0	1.1	1.3
Burglary	69.4	28.4	0.9	1.2
Larceny-theft	66.7	30.4	1.3	1.6
Motor vehicle theft	55.4	41.6	1.1	1.9
Arson	76.4	21.7	0.9	1.0
Violent crime	59.9	37.8	1.0	1.3
Property crime	66.2	31.0	1.2	1.6
Part 2				
Other assaults	66.0	31.5	1.4	1.1
Forgery and counterfeiting	68.0	30.0	0.6	1.4
Fraud	67.3	31.5	0.6	0.7
Embezzlement	63.6	34.1	0.4	1.9
Stolen property: buying, receiving, possessing	58.9	39.1	0.7	1.2
Vandalism	75.9	21.6	1.4	1.1
Weapons: carrying, possessing, etc.	61.3	36.8	0.7	1.2
Prostitution and commercialized vice	58.0	39.5	0.8	1.7
Sex offenses (except forcible rape and prostitution)	74.4	23.2	1.1	1.3
Drug abuse violations	64.2	34.5	0.5	0.7
Gambling	30.7	64.4	0.4	4.4
Offenses against family and children	67.6	29.6	1.0	1.7
DUI	88.2	9.6	1.3	0.9
Liquor law violations	85.6	10.6	3.0	0.8
Drunkenness	84.7	13.7	1.1	0.5
Disorderly conduct	65.3	32.6	1.4	0.7
Vagrancy	53.6	43.4	2.6	0.5
All other offenses (except traffic)	65.8	31.6	1.3	1.3
Suspicion	69.0	29.6	0.3	1.2
Curfew and loitering law violations	72.2	24.7	1.1	2.0

SOURCE: *Crime in the United States, 2000* (Washington, DC: U.S. Department of Justice, 2001). Available at www.fbi.gov/ucr/ucr.htm.

offenses reported in the UCR. The arrest rate is 2.5 times higher for African Americans than would be predicted by their representation in the population.

Among the individual offenses, however, the degree of African American overrepresentation varies. The largest disparities are found for robbery and murder. The arrest rate for African Americans is nearly 4 times what we would expect for murder and robbery. The differences are also pronounced for rape, motor vehicle theft, gambling, vagrancy, stolen property offenses, and weapons offenses.

Table 2.5 also presents arrest statistics for whites, Native Americans, and Asian Americans. Whites are overrepresented for some UCR offenses. Specifically, whites are overrepresented in DUI and liquor law violations compared to their representation in the general population, but the number of arrests for drunkenness is consistent with whites' representation in the population.

The overall pattern for Native American arrest figures is a slight overrepresentation compared to their representation in the population (1.2 percent arrested versus 0.8 percent in the population); however, the pattern across crimes is more erratic. For Part 1/Index crimes, Native Americans are slightly more likely to be arrested for property crimes (particularly larceny-theft) than their representation in the population suggests. Native Americans are overrepresented in several Part 2 offenses, including other assaults, vandalism, liquor law violations, disorderly conduct, and vagrancy. The proportion of Native American offenders arrested for a number of offenses is consistent with their proportion in the population: murder, robbery, fraud, embezzlement, receiving stolen property, prostitution/commercialized vice, gambling, and drug abuse violations. Additionally, the arrest figures for a number of other offenses are lower than what is expected given the proportion of Native Americans in the population: robbery, embezzlement, gambling, and suspicion.

Caution is required when interpreting Native American arrest figures, as arrests made by tribal police and federal agencies are not recorded in UCR data. Using information from the Bureau of Indian Affairs, Peak and Spencer found that although UCR statistics revealed lower than expected homicide arrest rates for Native Americans, homicide rates were 9 times higher than expected across the 207 reservations reporting.[45]

For overall figures and each Index offense, Asian Americans are underrepresented in UCR arrest data (1.2 percent of arrestees in 2000). The notable exception to the pattern of underrepresentation is the Part 2 offense of gambling. Although 2000 data reveal that Asian Americans make up 4.4 percent of arrests for gambling, UCR arrest figures have been as high as 6.7 percent. The arrest rate for this offense can reach twice what is expected given the representation of Asian Americans in the population.

Perceptions of Offenders by Victims

Clearly, African Americans are arrested at a disproportionately high rate. The problem, of course, is that we do not know the degree to which arrest statistics accurately reflect offending. As noted previously, not all crimes are reported to the police, and not all of those that are reported lead to an arrest.

Focus on an Issue
Racial and Ethnic Identification of Terrorists

Determining a profile of terrorists through the traditional format of the UCR system is difficult. First, terrorist acts, even those resulting in deaths, are not always reported in the UCR. For example, the deaths that occurred as a result of the domestic terrorist bombing in Oklahoma City on April 19, 1995, were recorded in the Oklahoma UCR figures; however, the deaths that occurred in various locations on September 11, 2001, as a result of international terrorist actions will not be recorded in the UCR. Second, if there is not a recorded event, there will be no recorded arrest and no subsequent offender information by race, age, or gender. For example, Tim McVeigh's arrest for the Oklahoma City bombing appeared in the arrest figures in Oklahoma, including his race, gender, and age; however,

the suspected terrorists from September 11—even if they were alive—would not be included in arrest figures.

An argument can be made that terrorist acts are also hate crimes; however, additional concerns arise with the recording of hate crime incidents that offer challenges for identifying victims and offenders. The FBI reports ask for victim and offender to be identified by racial categories used in the U.S. census: white, African American, Native American/Alaska Native, and Asian/Pacific Islander. These categories are very broad; for example, victims from Saudi Arabia and Iraq are identified as white, whereas victims from Pakistan and India are identified as Asian. Moreover, ethnicity is recorded only for victims, not for offenders, and is defined only as Hispanic or non-Hispanic.

One way to check the accuracy of arrest statistics is to examine data on offenders produced by the NCVS. Respondents who report a face-to-face encounter with an offender are asked to indicate the race of the offender. If the percentage of victims who report being robbed by an African American matches the percentage of African Americans who are arrested for robbery, we can have greater confidence in the validity of the arrest statistics. We can be more confident that differences in the likelihood of arrest reflect differences in offending.

If, on the other hand, the percentage of victims who report being robbed by an African American is substantially smaller than the percentage of African Americans who are arrested for robbery, we can conclude that at least some of the disproportion in the arrest rate reflects what Hindelang refers to as "selection bias" in the criminal justice system. As Hindelang noted, "If there are substantial biases in the UCR data for *any* reason, we would expect, to the extent that victimization survey reports are unbiased, to find large discrepancies between UCR arrest data and victimization survey reports on racial characteristics of offenders."[46]

Problems with NCVS Offender Data   There are obvious problems in relying on victims' "perceptions" of the race of the offender. Respondents who report a victimization are asked if the offender was white, black, or some other

**Table 2.6 Perceived Race of Offender
for Single-Offender Crimes of Violence**

Type of Crime	PERCEIVED RACE OF THE OFFENDER		
	White	African American	Other
All crimes of violence	63.1%	27.3%	8.0%
Rape/sexual assault	68.8	24.6	6.6
Robbery	33.9	53.3	10.9
Assault	65.6	24.9	7.8
Aggravated	59.6	27.7	11.2
Simple	67.3	24.1	6.9

SOURCE: Bureau of Justice Statistics, *Criminal Victimization in the United States, 1996* (Washington, DC: U.S. Department of Justice, 2000).

race. These perceptions are of questionable validity because victimizations often occur quickly and involve the element of shock. In addition, victim memory is subject to decay over time and to "retroactive reconstruction" to fit the popular conception of a criminal offender. If a victim believes that the typical criminal is African American, this may influence his or her perception of the race of the offender.

There is another problem in relying on victims' perceptions of offender race. To the extent that these perceptions are based on skin color, they may be unreliable indicators of the race of offenders whose self-identification reflects their lineage or heritage rather than the color of their skin. Thus, individuals may appear in different racial groupings in victimization reports than they do on a police arrest report. A light-skinned offender who identifies himself as Hispanic and whose race is thus recorded as "other" in arrest data might show up in victimization data as white. If this occurs with any frequency, it obviously will affect the picture of the offender that emerges from victimization data.

Perceptions of Offenders With these caveats in mind, we present the NCVS data on the perceived race of the offender for single–offender violent victimizations. As Table 2.6 shows, although the typical offender for all of the crimes except robbery is white (or is perceived to be white), African Americans are overrepresented as offenders for all of the offenses listed. The most notable disproportion revealed by Table 2.6 is for robbery, with over half (53.3 percent) of the offenders in single-offender robberies identified as African American. Also, African Americans are overrepresented as offenders for rape/sexual assault, aggravated assault, and simple assault, but not as severely as for robbery.

We argued earlier that one way to check the accuracy of arrest statistics is to *compare* the race of offenders arrested for various crimes with victims' perceptions of the race of the offender. Table 2.7 presents these comparisons. There is a relatively close match in the figures for white offenders for aggravated as-

Table 2.7 A Comparison of UCR and NCVS Data on Offender Race

	WHITES		AFRICAN AMERICANS		OTHER	
	Arrested	Perceived	Arrested	Perceived	Arrested	Perceived
Rape	56.1	68.8	41.6	24.6	3.2	6.6
Robbery	39.8	33.9	58.2	53.3	2.0	10.9
Aggravated assault	59.6	59.6	38.1	27.7	2.3	11.2
Simple assault	62.4	67.3	35.1	24.1	2.5	6.9

SOURCES: Federal Bureau of Investigation, *Crime in the United States, 1996* (Washington, DC: U.S. Government Printing Office, 1997); Bureau of Justice Statistics, *Criminal Victimization in the United States, 1995* (Washington, DC: U.S. Government Printing Office, 2000).

NOTE: This table reports the percentage of whites and African Americans arrested in 1996 compared to percentage of those who reported being victimized in 1995 and who perceived the offender (in single-offender victimizations) to be white or African American.

sault. However, noticeable gaps in the rape and simple assault comparisons suggest whites may be underrepresented in arrest data. Moreover, whites appear to be overrepresented for only one offense: robbery arrests. For African Americans, on the other hand, the pattern is more consistent. That is, African Americans are represented in arrest figures in much higher proportions than the perception of offenders from victim interviews suggests.[47] These comparisons indicate that the racial disproportion found in arrest rates for these offenses cannot be used to resolve the dilemma of differential arrest rates by race versus a higher rate of offending among African Americans. It may be reasonably argued that such evidence actually suggests the presence of both differentially high offending rates by African Americans for serious violent offenses *and* the presence of differentially high arrest rates for African Americans, particularly for rape offenses.

The comparison of other race figures offers a consistent pattern of underrepresentation of "other" race in arrest figures. This observation could mean that Asians/Pacific Islanders and Native Americans/Alaska Natives are committing crimes at a higher rate than the rate at which they are being arrested. However, these figures also suggest that NCVS respondents may be classifying offenders they perceive as Hispanic/Latino/Mexican in appearance to be of "other" race. Citizens commonly assume that Hispanic is a racial category, not an ethnic category. Therefore, dark-skinned offenders who do not appear African American may be classified as "other," as Hispanic is not an option to the race-identification question. Additionally, NCVS respondents are not asked to identify the perceived ethnicity of the offender.

Hindelang used early victimization data to determine which of these explanations was more likely. His initial comparison of 1974 arrest statistics with victimization data for rape, robbery, aggravated assault, and simple assault revealed some evidence of "differential selection for criminal justice processing" for two of the offenses examined.[48] For rape and aggravated assault, the percentage of African American offenders in the victimization data was smaller

(9 percentage points for rape, 11 percentage points for aggravated assault) than the proportion found in UCR arrest statistics.

However, once Hindelang controlled for victimizations that were reported to the police, the discrepancies disappeared and the proportions of offenders identified as African American and white were strikingly similar. Hindelang concluded that "it is difficult to argue [from these data] that blacks are no more likely than whites to be involved in the common law crimes of robbery, forcible rape, assault."[49]

Hindelang's analysis of victimizations reported to the police also revealed a pattern of differential reporting by victims. Specifically, Hindelang found that for rape and robbery, those victimized by African Americans were more likely than those victimized by whites to report the crime to the police. Hindelang suggested that this is a form of selection bias—victim-based selection bias.

Hindelang concluded his comparison of UCR arrest rates and victimization survey data by separating the elements of criminal justice system selection bias, victim-based selection bias, and differential offending rates. He argued that both forms of selection bias were present, but that each was outweighed by the overwhelming evidence of differential involvement of African Americans in offending.

Self-Report Surveys

Self-report surveys are another way to paint a picture of the criminal offender. These surveys question respondents about their participation in criminal or delinquent behavior. Emerging in the 1950s, the self-report format remains a popular source of data for those searching for descriptions and causes of criminal behavior. One of the advantages of asking people about their behavior is that it gives a less distorted picture of the offender than an official record because it is free of the alleged biases of the criminal justice system. However, it is not at all clear that self-report survey results provide a more *accurate* description of the criminal offender.[50]

Problems with Self-Report Surveys One of the major weaknesses of the self-report format is that there is no single design used. Moreover, different surveys focus on different aspects of criminal behavior. Not all self-report surveys ask the same questions or use the same or similar populations, and very few follow the same group over time. Typically, the sample population is youth from school settings or institutionalized groups.

In addition to the problems of inconsistent format and noncomparable samples, self-report surveys suffer from a variety of other limitations. The accuracy of self-report data is influenced by the respondent's honesty and memory and by interviewer bias.

One of the most confounding limitations in criminal justice data sets is present with self-report surveys: the comparisons are overwhelmingly comparisons of African Americans and whites. Little can be said about Native Americans, Asian Americans, or Hispanic Americans. Some studies suffer from the additional limitation of homogeneous samples with insufficient racial representation. These limitations make it difficult to draw conclusions about how many members of a racial group commit delinquent activity (prevalence) and how frequently racial minorities commit crime (incidence).

Although self-report surveys generally are assumed to be reliable and valid, this assumption has been shown to be less tenable for certain subgroups of offenders.[51] Specifically, it has been shown that there is differential validity for white and African American respondents. *Validity* is the idea that, as a researcher, you are measuring what you think you are measuring. Reverse record checks (matching self-report answers with police records) have shown that there is greater concurrence between respondent answers and official police arrest records for white respondents than for African American respondents.[52] This indicates that African American respondents tend to underreport some offending behavior.

Elliot, Huizinga, Knowles, and Canter caution against a simplistic interpretation of these findings.[53] They find that African American respondents are more likely to underreport Index-type offenses than less serious offenses. Therefore, they suggest that this finding may indicate the differential validity of official police records rather than differential validity of the self-report measures by race. An example of differential validity of police records would occur if police report the clearly serious offenses for whites and African Americans but report the less serious offenses for African Americans only. In short, most self-report researchers conclude that racial comparisons must be made with caution.

Characteristics of Offenders Typically, juvenile self-report surveys record demographic data and ask questions about the frequency of certain delinquent activities in the last year. The delinquent activities included range in seriousness from skipping class to drinking liquor, stealing something worth more than $50, stealing a car, or assaulting another person.[54]

Early self-report studies, those conducted before 1980, found little difference in delinquency rates across race (African American and white only). Later, more-refined self-report designs have produced results that challenge the initial assumption of similar patterns of delinquency.[55] Some research findings indicate that African American males are more likely than white males to report serious criminal behavior (prevalence). Moreover, a larger portion of African Americans than whites report a high frequency of serious delinquency (incidence).[56]

Perhaps the most recent and comprehensive analysis of the race and prevalence and race and incidence issues was done by Huizinga and Elliot with six waves of the National Youth Survey (NYS) data.[57] This self-report survey is a longitudinal study that began in 1976 using a national panel design. This study offers the only national assessment of individual offending rates based on self-report studies for a 6-year period.

Huizinga and Elliot explored whether African American youth have a higher prevalence of offending than whites and whether a higher incidence of offending by African Americans can explain differential arrest rates. Their analysis revealed few consistent racial differences across the years studied, either in the

> ### BOX 2.4   Monitoring the Future
>
> The only student-based self-report survey done on a yearly basis with a nationwide sample is Monitoring the Future. Responses to their delinquency questions reveal few differences between white and African American youth in self-reported delinquent behavior. White youth were slightly more likely to report having been in a serious fight in the last year, having used a weapon to get something from a person, having taken something from a store, and having taken a car that did not belong to someone in the family. African American youth were slightly more likely to report having taken something from a store without paying for it, having taken something not belonging to them worth under $50, and having gone into some house or building without permission.
>
> SOURCE: Principal investigators of the Monitoring the Future project are Lloyd D. Johnston, Jerald G. Bachman, and Patrick M. O'Malley. Data available in the *Sourcebook of Criminal Justice Statistics, 2000*. Available at www.albany.edu/sourcebook/.

proportion of African American and white youth engaging in delinquent behavior or in the frequency with which African American and white offenders commit delinquent acts. Contrary to Hindelang, they suggest that the differential selection bias hypothesis cannot be readily dismissed, as the differential presence of youth in the criminal justice system cannot be explained entirely by differential offending rates.

Drug Offenders A prevalent image in the news and entertainment media is that of the drug user as a person of color. In particular, arrest data reflect an overrepresentation of African Americans for nonalcoholic drug abuse violations and an overrepresentation of Native Americans for alcohol-related offenses. A more comprehensive picture of the drug user emerges from self-report data that ask respondents to indicate their use of and prevalence of use behavior for particular drugs. In a recent report on the use of drugs among people of color, the National Institutes of Health (NIH) summarizes the current body of research as indicating the following:[58]

- African American youth report less alcohol use than white youth and report similar prevalence levels for use of illicit drugs compared to other racial and ethnic groups. (NIH does note research suggesting that African Americans experience higher rates of drug-related health problems than users from other race/ethnicity groups).

- Asian/Pacific Islander youth responding to sporadic state-level surveys and several years of pooled national data consistently report less drug use than other non-Asian populations.

- Native American youth begin using a variety of drugs (not limited to alcohol) at an earlier age than white youth. Inhalant use is twice as high among Native American youth.

- Hispanics are found to have a higher reported use of illicit drug use than non-Hispanic whites.

In short, there is no clear picture of the typical drug user or abuser. Additional race differences are evident in results from a recent school-based survey by the Centers for Disease Control and Prevention that indicate that self-reported lifetime crack use is highest among Hispanic students, followed by lower percentages for whites and even lower percentages for African Americans. However, the National Household Survey on Drug Abuse data reveal the disturbing observation that a far greater number of African American and Hispanic youth (approximately one-third) reported seeing people sell drugs in the neighborhood occasionally or more often than did whites (less than 10 percent).

Summary: A Picture of the Typical Criminal Offender

The image of the typical offender that emerges from the data examined here conflicts somewhat with the image in the minds of most Americans. If by the phrase *typical offender* we mean the offender who shows up most frequently in arrest statistics, then for all crimes except murder and robbery, the typical offender is white, not African American.

As we have shown, focusing on the *number* of persons arrested is somewhat misleading. It is clear from the data discussed thus far that African Americans are arrested at a disproportionately high *rate*. This conclusion applies to property crime as well as violent crime. Moreover, victimization data suggest that African Americans may have higher offending rates for serious violent crime, but examinations of victim perception of offender with official arrest data reveal that some of the overrepresentation of African American offenders may well be selection bias on the part of criminal justice officials, but this dilemma remains unresolved.

If one aspect of the view of the typical criminal offender is that the typical drug offender is a minority, we have shown that self-report data from youth populations in the United States reveal that people of color do not have consistently higher drug use rates than whites. This picture varies slightly by type of drug, with Hispanic youth showing higher rates of use with some drugs and Native American youth with other drugs. However, there is little evidence of differential patterns of higher use rates by African Americans than by other racial groups.

CRIME AS AN INTRARACIAL EVENT

In the minds of many Americans, the term *crime* conjures up an image of an act of violence against a white victim by an African American offender.[59] In the preceding sections, we demonstrated the inaccuracy of these perceptions of victims and offenders; we illustrated that the typical victim is a racial minority and that the typical offender, for all but a few crimes, is white. We now turn to a discussion of crime as an *intraracial* event.

Focus on an Issue
The Politicization of Interracial Crime

Willie Horton played an important role in the 1988 presidential campaign. He was featured in campaign ads and was frequently mentioned in speeches given by the Republican candidate and his supporters. By the end of the campaign, Willie Horton was a household name. Willie Horton was a convicted murderer from Massachusetts. While serving a lengthy prison term, he became eligible for a furlough program and occasionally was allowed to leave the prison for short periods of time. On one such trip, he fled to Maryland, where he committed a brutal rape. Willie Horton was African American; his victim was white. George Bush, the Republican candidate, used Willie Horton to portray Michael Dukakis, the Democratic

nominee for president, as "soft on crime." Although Dukakis played no part in the decision to allow Willie Horton out on furlough, he had been governor of Massachusetts at the time.

Critics of the Republicans' tactics disputed their claim that the "Willie Horton incident" was simply being used to illustrate what was wrong with the American criminal justice system. They charged that it was no coincidence that Horton was African American and his victim white. They charged that the campaign ads featuring Horton's picture had racist overtones and that use of the incident exemplified political pandering to public fears and stereotypes about crime.

The National Crime Victimization Survey

Few criminal justice data sources, including the NCVS, offer comprehensive information on the racial makeup of the victim–offender dyad. Recall that the NCVS asks victims about their perceptions of the offender's race in crimes of violence, and data presented distinguish among only African Americans, whites, and "others"(victims' perceptions of the offender as Hispanic are not available).

With these limitations in mind, we can examine NCVS data on the race of the victim and the perceived race of the offender in single-offender violent victimizations.[60] These data indicate that almost all violent crimes by white offenders were committed against white victims (73 percent). This pattern also characterizes the individual crimes of robbery and assault. The typical white offender, in other words, commits a crime against another white person.

This intraracial pattern of violent crime perceived to be committed by African Americans is also reported by African American victims. However, African American robbery offenders, depending on the type of robbery, are roughly as likely to have white victims as African American victims.

UCR Homicide Reports

A final source of data on the victim–offender pair is the Supplemental Homicide Reports. Contrary to popular belief, a 24-year review of UCR Supplemental Homicide Reports reveals that homicide is essentially an intraracial event.[61]

Focus on an Issue
Politicizing Black-on-Black Crime

Much attention has been devoted to "black-on-black" crime. . . . It is not unusual to see in the written press or to hear in the electronic media stories depicting the evils of living in the black community. [This] has occurred with such frequency that some individuals now associate black people with criminality. Simply put, it has become fash-ionable to discern between crime and black-on-black crime. Rarely does one read or hear about white crime or "white-on-white" crime. This is troubling when one considers that most crimes, including serious violent crimes, are committed by and against whites as well as blacks (Bing, 1994).

Specifically, 94 percent of African American murder victims were slain by other African Americans, and 86 percent of whites were victimized by whites.[62] The small percentage of interracial homicides are more likely to occur with young victims and young offenders, and they are slightly more likely to be black-on-white offenses than white-on-black offenses.[63]

Summary: Crime as an Intraracial Event

The general pattern revealed by the data discussed here is one in which white offenders consistently victimize whites, and African American offenders, particularly African American males, more frequently victimize both African Americans and whites. As noted, the politicizing of black criminality continues, while the emergence of and subsequent focus on racial hoaxes persist.[64]

Some researchers have challenged the assertion that crime is predominantly intraracial.[65] These critics point to the fact that a white person has a greater likelihood of being victimized by an African American offender than an African American has of being victimized by a white offender. Although this is true, it does not logically challenge the assertion that crime is predominantly an intraracial event. Remember that the NCVS reveals that the typical offender is white, not African American.

Using the percentages presented in Table 2.7 for all crimes of violence, we can determine that of the 7,051,940 victimizations, 4,349,712 victimizations involved white offenders and white victims, and 852,414 involved African American offenders and African American victims.[66] Interracial events are more rare, constituting less than 18 percent of these crimes of violence.[67]

The exception to the predominant intraracial pattern of crime noted previously, occurred in the Native American and Asian American victimization patterns. Native Americans report most victimizations occurring by whites, and Asian Americans report victimizations occurring almost equally by whites, African Americans, and other racial groups (with no group committing the majority of offenses).

CRIME AS AN
INTERRACIAL (HATE) EVENT

Not all interracial criminal events are considered hate crimes. The term *hate crime* (or *bias crime*) is most often defined as a common law offense that contains an element of prejudice based on the race, ethnicity, national origin, religion, sexual orientation, or disability status of the victim (some statutes add gender). Generally, hate crime legislation is enacted in the form of enhancement penalties for common law offenses (ranging from assault to vandalism) that have an element of prejudice. Justifications for the creation of such legislation include the symbolic message that certain actions are exceptionally damaging to an individual when they are "provoked" by the status of race and ethnicity and that such actions are damaging to the general community and should be condemned.

Congress has mandated the FBI to collect and disseminate information on hate crime in the United States.[68] In 2000, the FBI Hate Crime Data Collection Program received reports from 11,690 law enforcement agencies (in 48 states and the District of Columbia), representing nearly 85 percent of the U.S. population. The FBI offered this caution in its annual report: "The reports from these agencies are insufficient to allow a valid national or regional measure of the volume and types of crimes motivated by hate; they offer perspectives on the general nature of hate crime occurrence."[69]

The FBI received reports of 8,063 bias-motivated criminal incidents in 2000, consisting of 9,430 offenses and 9,924 victims.[70] Most offenses reported (65 percent) involved crimes against a person, with 34.4 percent of the offenses designated as property offenses.[71] A small number of offenses (0.6 percent) were designated as crimes against society.[72] The most common offense was the crime of intimidation (34.9 percent), followed by destruction/vandalism of property (29.3 percent), simple assault (17.1 percent), and aggravated assault (12.6 percent).[73]

Over half of the reported hate crime offenses involved race bias (54.9 percent), with another 12.4 percent reflecting bias based on ethnicity/national origin (see Figure 2.3). The victims of race bias crimes were reflective of all race categories, including a multiracial group category. The ethnicity/national origin information is available for Hispanic and Other ethnicity/national origin. African Americans and Hispanics are the most common hate crime victims in their respective categories, with Asian Americans and mixed-race victims being overrepresented as well. White victims are not overrepresented in relation to their presence in the population but are the second-largest group of hate crime victims.

Offender information is also available in reports from the FBI Hate Crime Data Collection Program. This information is that provided by victims reporting their perceptions to the police, rather than arrest information. In 57.6 percent of the hate crime offenses reported, the victim knew the offender and reported the perception of race.[74] In these cases, suspected offenders were most often identified as white (75.6 percent), but suspected offenders represented all four race categories and were occasionally identified as multiracial.[75] In short,

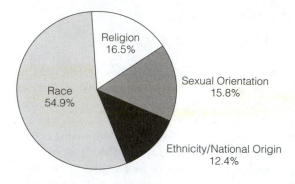

FIGURE 2.3 Hate Crime Offenses by Bias Type, 2000

SOURCE: FBI Hate Crime Report, 2000.

NOTE: Disability status (antiphysical and antimental) constitutes .003 percent of offenses in 2000 and is not included in this figure.

all race groups have individuals who have been victimized by bias crimes, and all race groups have individuals who are suspected offenders of bias crimes.

Information on the trends of victimization and offending in bias crime events is limited, but patterns for both whites and African Americans have emerged. Whites are most often victimized by African Americans, and African Americans are most often victimized by whites.[76] Native Americans are most often victimized by whites, and although they are rarely identified as offenders, Native Americans are more likely to victimize whites than other race groups.[77] Asian Americans most often identify their offenders as white, whereas the offender identified as Asian American is found to victimize whites and African Americans more than the other racial groups.[78]

Jacobs argued that hate crime statutes create a law unlikely to deter and its implementation will widen social division.[79] He also argued that hate crime legislation represents an ill-advised insertion of the civil rights paradigm into the criminal law. Specifically, he reasons that civil rights legislation is an attempt to extend "positive rights and opportunities to minorities and women . . . directed at the conduct of government officials and private persons who govern, regulate, or sell goods and services. By contrast, hate crime law deals with conduct that is already criminal and with wrongdoers who are already criminals."[80] He concluded that the "possibility that criminals can be threatened into not discriminating in their choice of crime victims is slight."[81]

ETHNIC YOUTH GANGS

In the minds of most Americans, the words *gang, race,* and *crime* are inextricably linked. Recall the incident described at the beginning of this chapter—a woman raped and attacked by a group of minority teenagers in Central Park. The media labeled these youth a "gang." This designation, however, was challenged by those who argued that the teenagers involved in the incident were not organized, had no gang identity, and behaved more like a mob than a gang.[82]

A comprehensive review of recent research on ethnic youth gangs is beyond the scope of this chapter. Instead, we discuss some of the prevailing myths about gangs and gang membership and summarize research on ethnic gang activities. Although there is no universally accepted definition of *gang,* the term is generally used to refer to a group of young people who recognize some sort of organized membership and leadership and who, in addition, are involved in criminal activity.[83]

Gang Myths and Realities

We have shown that popular perceptions of crime, crime victims, and criminal offenders often are inaccurate. Many of the prevailing beliefs about gangs are similarly mistaken. In the sections that follow, we discuss some of the myths surrounding gangs and gang activity. We show that even though there is an element of truth in each of these myths, there are also a number of inaccuracies.

Myth 1: Gangs are only found in large cities. It is important to understand that the gang phenomenon is not a homogeneous one. Although many gangs *are* located in urban areas, gangs are increasingly found in suburban[84] and rural communities,[85] as well as on Indian reservations.[86] The 1999 National Youth Gang Survey collected by the National Youth Gang Center from law enforcement agencies reported that gangs were present in 66 percent of large cities, 47 percent of suburban areas, 27 percent of small cities, and 8 percent of rural counties.[87]

Myth 2: All gang members are African American and belong either to the Bloods or Crips. The Bloods and the Crips *are* predominantly African American and are very widely known. These two gangs are heavily involved in illegal drug activities and are characterized by a confederation of local gangs that stretches across the country.[88] They are not, however, exclusively African American. Mydans provided examples of well-to-do white youth joining California Bloods and Crips.[89]

Although members of the racial minority groups we focus on in this book are overrepresented in gangs, they do not constitute the entire gang problem. (It is somewhat misleading to categorize gangs as *Hispanic* or *Asian*. These categories are very broad and mask the variety within each group. In reality, gangs are ethnically specific by nationality. There are Puerto Rican, Cuban, Mexican American, Vietnamese, Cambodian, Korean, Chinese, and Japanese gangs.)

The earliest gangs in the United States were predominantly white and first documented just after the Revolutionary War.[90] Moreover, the seminal studies of youth gangs conducted in the early 1900s documented predominantly white ethnic gangs composed of youth from Eastern European countries.[91] Currently, white ethnic gangs are not as prevalent. Covey, Menard, and Franzese[92] argue that "the relative absence of white ethnic gangs in official studies may be a product of a number of factors including the difficulty of identifying them[93] and biases in reporting and public perception."[94] Many of the white ethnic groups that do exist are characterized by white supremacist activities or satanism.

Myth 3: All gangs are involved in selling drugs and drug trafficking. Many, but not all, gangs are involved in illegal drug activities. However, at least some of these gangs existed before they began selling drugs. It is possible that gangs have been exploited because of their structure and organization to sell drugs and that this lucrative activity serves as a reason for recruitment and expansion.

Drug use is common in most gangs, but the emphasis placed on drug sales varies by the character and social organization of the gang.[95] Many researchers challenge the idea that selling drugs is usually an organized gang activity involving all gang members.[96] In their study of Denver youth, Esbensen and Huizinga distinguished between a gang involved in drug activity and individual gang members selling drugs. They found that 80 percent of youth respondents said that their gangs were involved in drug sales, but only 28 percent admitted to selling drugs themselves.[97] In short, although gang members were found to be more active in drug-related crimes (use and sales) than nongang youth, not all gang members sold drugs.

In a recent National Youth Gang Survey, law enforcement agencies reported that 51 percent of all gangs in rural counties were believed to be organized specifically for the purpose of drug trafficking, whereas 41 percent of those in large cities were identified as organized for drug trafficking.[98] Drug trafficking by gangs is perceived as being less common in suburban areas (39 percent of all gangs) and small cities (26 percent of all gangs).[99]

Related to the myth that all gang members sell drugs is the notion that drugs and violence are inextricably linked. In fact, there is a complex relationship between drugs and violence in gangs. Fagan found that regardless of the level of drug dealing within a gang, violent behaviors still occurred, with the majority of incidents unrelated to drug sales.[100] He concluded that "for gang members, violence is not an inevitable consequence of involvement in drug use and dealing."[101] Curry and Decker also noted the prevalence of violence in gang activity, pointing out that much of this violence is also intraracial.[102]

Myth 4: Gangs are the result of poverty and a growing underclass. It is overly simplistic to attribute the existence of gangs solely to poverty. A recent National Youth Gang Survey indicated that although the majority of gang members are identified as underclass, 35 percent are identified as working class, 12 percent as middle class, and 3 percent as upper middle class.[103] Gangs exist for a variety of reasons: the growth of the underclass,[104] the disintegration of the African American and Hispanic family,[105] poverty,[106] difficulty assimilating into American culture,[107] marginality,[108] political and religious reasons,[109] and general rebellion against adult and conventional society.[110] However, Curry and Decker did argue that gang formation and gang delinquency are more likely to be explained at a community level than at an individual level.[111]

Myth 5: All gang members are males. Although it is true that males are overrepresented in gang membership, there are female gang members and female gangs. The early sociological literature on gangs discussed only males; females who accompanied male gang members were often described in terms of an "auxiliary"—present, but not a formal part of the criminal activity.

More-recent studies have found both fully active female gang members and a few solely female gangs. Researchers estimate that females represent between 10 percent[112] and 25 percent[113] of all gang members. Campbell identified several all-female gangs in New York City. The Sandman Ladies, for example, were Puerto Rican females with a biker image. The Sex Girls were African American and Hispanic females who were involved in drug dealing.

The presence of female gang members differs by ethnicity as well. Females are found in Hispanic gangs, African American gangs, and white ethnic gangs but appear to be conspicuously absent in both journalistic and scholarly accounts of Asian American gangs.[114]

Varieties of Ethnic Gangs

We have noted that, contrary to popular wisdom, all gang members are not African Americans. There are Hispanic, Native American, Asian, and white gangs as well as African American gangs. The 1999 National Youth Gang Survey conducted by the National Youth Gang Center indicates that 47 percent of gang members are identified as Hispanic, 31 percent as African American, 13 percent as white, 7 percent as Asian, and 2 percent as other.[115]

Covey et al. stated that "[ethnicity] is not the only way to understand gangs, but gangs are organized along ethnic lines, and it would be a mistake to ignore ethnicity as a variable that may affect the nature of juvenile gangs."[116] Most ethnic gangs reflect a mixture of their members' culture of origin and the American "host" culture; indeed, many gangs form as the result of a clash between the two cultures.

African American The most widely known African American gangs are the Bloods and the Crips. Each gang has unique "colors" and sign language to reinforce gang identity. It is believed that these gangs are really "national confederations of local gangs" in American cities.[117] They are characteristically very territorial and often are linked to drug distribution.

Other African American gangs exist across the United States. Researchers have identified many big-city African American gangs that are oriented toward property crime rather than drug sales.[118] In addition, African American gangs have formed around the tenets of Islam, with corresponding political agendas.[119]

Native American Native American youth are becoming part of the gang culture in the United States as the presence of gangs emerges in the semisovereign tribal lands throughout the country. They are also becoming members of gangs located in urban and rural nonreservation areas. Specifically, the Navajo nation has documented the presence of youth gangs consisting of tribal members and recently reported the presence of more than 50 gangs with nearly 1,000 members on the tribal lands.[120] These gangs often take their names from more established urban gangs, such as Crips or Bloods, and are characterized by violence but appear to be less coordinated than the established gangs.[121]

Asian As previously stated, there are a variety of Asian ethnic gangs. Most Asian gang researchers attribute the formation of these gangs, at least in part, to feelings of alienation because of difficulty assimilating into American culture.[122] Similarities between Asian gangs include an emphasis on economic activity and a pattern of intraracial victimization. Asian gangs are found primarily in coastal cities such as New York City, San Francisco, Boston, and Portland, which have large Asian immigrant populations.[123]

The origins of Chinese American gangs can be traced to the early 1890s and the secret "Tong" societies.[124] Chinese American gang activity has increased since the relaxation of immigration laws in the mid-1960s.[125] The research on Chinese American gangs shows a commitment to violence for its own sake (gang warfare) and as a means for attaining income (robbery, burglary, extortion, protection).[126] Chin noted that, generally, the structure of Chinese American gangs is very hierarchical; he also explained that gang members may participate in legitimate business, establish drug distribution and sales networks, and form national and international networks.[127]

Vietnamese American gang activity is not as structured as that of Chinese American gangs. The rise in gang activity for this ethnic group can also be tied to an influx in immigration. Overall, Vietnamese American gang activity is less violent, typically economically oriented, and most likely to target other Vietnamese Americans.[128]

Hispanic   Hispanic gangs have identifiable core concerns: brotherhood/sisterhood, machismo, and loyalty to the barrio (neighborhood).[129] Many Hispanic gangs have adult as well as juvenile members,[130] and gang members may be involved in the use and sale of drugs. The importance of machismo may explain the emphasis of many Hispanic gangs on violence, even intragang violence.

White   The white ethnic gangs—composed of Irish, Polish, and Italian youth—identified by researchers earlier in this century are less evident in today's cities. Contemporary white ethnic gangs are most often associated with rebellion against adult society, with suburban settings, and with a focus on white supremacist or satanist ideals.

"Skinheads" may be the most well-known example of a white ethnic gang. Covey et al. describe them in this way: "Skinhead gangs usually consist of European American youths who are non-Hispanic, non-Jewish, Protestant, working class, low income, clean shaven and militantly racist and white supremacist."[131] Skinheads have been located in cities in every region of the country and have been linked to adult domestic terrorist organizations such as the White Aryan Resistance (WAR) and other neo-Nazi movements. Skinheads are unique in the sense that they use violence not to protect turf, protect a drug market, or commit robberies, but rather "for the explicit purpose of promoting political change by instilling fear in innocent people."[132]

"Stoner" gangs, another form of white ethnic gangs, are characterized by an emphasis on satanic rituals. This doctrine is supplemented by territoriality and the heavy use of drugs.[133]

In recognizing the racial nature of gangs, it is important to clarify the role of racism in the formation of gangs. Most gangs are racially and ethnically homogeneous. Some researchers argue that this situation is merely reflective of the racial and ethnic composition of neighborhoods and primary friendships. That is, "where schools and neighborhoods are racially and ethnically mixed, gangs tend to be racially and ethnically mixed."[134]

Although violent conflicts do occur between and within ethnic gangs, violence is seldom the reason for gang formation. Racism as a societal phenomenon that creates oppressive conditions can contribute to gang formation. However, individual racism explains very little in terms of the formation of gangs or the decision to join gangs. Skinhead membership is a notable exception, being almost exclusively a function of individual racism.[135]

CONCLUSION

We began this chapter with a description of the sexual assault of a white woman by a group of minority youth in New York City's Central Park. We argued that incidents like this shape perceptions of crime in the United States. In the minds of many Americans, the typical crime is an act of violence involving a white victim and a minority offender. We have used a variety of data sources to illustrate the inaccuracy of these perceptions and to offer a more comprehensive view of victimization and offending.

We have shown that people of color are overrepresented as victims of both household and personal crime and have demonstrated that this pattern is particularly striking for crimes of violence. We have demonstrated that although the typical offender for all crimes except robbery and gambling is white, African Americans are arrested at a disproportionately high rate. We have also shown that most crimes involve an offender and victim of the same race, which means that crime is predominantly an intraracial event.

The information provided in this chapter may raise as many questions as it answers. Although we have attempted to paint an accurate picture of crime and victimization in the United States, we are hampered by limitations inherent in existing data sources. Some victimization events are not defined as crimes by the victims, many of those that are defined as crimes are not reported to the police, and many of those reported to the police do not lead to an arrest. There is no data set, in other words, that provides information on all crimes that occur.

We have attempted to address this problem by using several different sources of data. We believe that we can have greater confidence in the conclusions we reach if two or more distinct types of data point in the same direction. The fact that both NCVS and SHR data consistently reveal that racial and ethnic minorities are more likely than whites to fall victim to crime, for example, lends credence to the need for a more comprehensive picture of victims and offenders. Similarly, the fact that a variety of data sources suggest that crime is predominantly an intraracial event enhances our confidence in this conclusion.

We have less confidence in our conclusions concerning the racial makeup of the offender population. Although it is obvious that African Americans are arrested at a disproportionately high rate, particularly for murder and robbery, it is not clear that this reflects differential offending rather than selective enforcement of the law. Arrest statistics and victimization data both indicate that African Americans have higher rates of offending than whites, but some self-report studies suggest that there are few, if any, racial differences in offending. We suggest that this discrepancy limits our ability to draw definitive conclusions about the meaning of the disproportionately high arrest rates for African Americans.

One final caveat seems appropriate. The conclusions we reach about victims and offenders are based primarily on descriptive data: percentages, rates,

and trends over time. These data are appropriate for describing a disproportionate representation of people of color as victims of crime and as criminal offenders, but these data are not sufficient for drawing conclusions concerning
causality. The data we have examined in this chapter can tell us that the African American arrest rate is higher than the white arrest rate for a particular
crime, but they cannot tell us why this is so. We address issues of causation in
subsequent chapters.

DISCUSSION QUESTIONS

1. Why is urbanization such a key issue in understanding victimization?
    Why is the impact of urbanization unique for separate racial and ethnic
    groups with regard to victimization rates? What kind of victimization
    prevention policies can you suggest, based on these observations?

2. The descriptive information in UCR arrest data depicts an overrepresen-
    tation of African American offenders for most violent and property
    crimes. What are the possible explanations for such disparity? Is this pic-
    ture of the offender the result of differential offending rates or differential
    enforcement practices? What must a researcher include in a study of
    "why people commit crime" to advance beyond a description of disparity
    to test for a causal explanation?

3. Should hate be a crime? What arguments can be made to support the use
    of sentencing-enhancement penalties for hate crimes? What arguments
    can be made to oppose such statutes? Are hate crime laws likely to deter
    offenders and reduce crime?

4. If most youth gangs are racially and ethnically homogeneous, should law
    enforcement use race- and ethnic-specific strategies to fight gang forma-
    tion and to control gang crime? Or, should law enforcement strategies be
    racially and ethnically neutral? What dilemmas are created for police de-
    partments who pursue each of these strategies? Is the likely result institu-
    tional or contextual discrimination?

NOTES

1. Don Terry, "In a Week of an Infamous
Rape, 28 Other Victims," *New York Times*
(May 29, 1989), p. 25.

2. Ibid.

3. According to UCR index crime totals
for 2000, roughly 90 percent of crimes
were property crimes. It is believed that
rapes are severely underreported, but similar arguments can be made for property
crimes, especially fraud. Even if the rape
numbers are low, the numbers of violent

criminal events do not overshadow property crime.

4. Terry, "In a Week of an Infamous
Rape," p. 25.

5. Robert M. O'Brien, "The Interracial
Nature of Violent Crimes: A Reexamination," *American Journal of Sociology* 92
(1987): 817–835.

6. Charles Silberman, *Criminal Violence,
Criminal Justice* (New York: Random
House, 1978), pp. 117–118.

7. The National Crime Survey (NCS) was recently renamed the National Crime Victimization Survey (NCVS) to clearly emphasize the focus of measuring victimizations.

8. The Bureau of Justice Statistics was formerly the National Criminal Justice and Information Service of the Law Enforcement Assistance Administration.

9. Bureau of Justice Statistics, *Criminal Victimizations in the United States: 1973–92 Trends* (Washington, DC: U.S. Government Printing Office, 1994).

10. Callie Marie Rennison, *Criminal Victimization 2000: Changes 1999–2000 with Trends 1993–2000* (Washington, DC: Bureau of Justice Statistics, 2001). Available at www.ojp.usdoj.gov/bjs/.

11. Ibid.

12. Ibid.

13. Ibid.

14. Detis T. Duhart, *Urban, Suburban and Rural Victimization, 1993–1998* (Washington, DC: Bureau of Justice Statistics, 2000). Available at www.ojp.usdoj/bjs/.

15. Ibid.

16. Bureau of Justice Statistics, *Criminal Victimization in the United States, 1994* (Washington, DC: U.S. Government Printing Office, 1996).

17. Ibid.

18. Duhart, *Urban, Suburban and Rural Victimization.*

19. Bureau of Justice Statistics, *Criminal Victimization, 1994.*

20. Ibid.

21. Ibid.

22. Ibid.

23. Ibid.

24. Ibid.

25. Ibid.

26. Lawrence Greenfeld and Steven K. Smith, *American Indians and Crime* (Washington, DC: Bureau of Justice Statistics, 1999); Rennison, *Criminal Victimization 2000.*

27. Duhart, *Urban, Suburban and Rural Victimization.*

28. Bureau of Justice Statistics, *Lifetime Likelihood of Victimization* (Washington, DC: U.S. Department of Justice, 1987), p. 1.

29. Ibid., p. 3.

30. James Alan Fox and Marianne W. Zawitz, *Homicide Trends in the United States* (Washington, DC: U.S. Government Printing Office, 2001). Available at www.ojp.usdoj.gov/bjs.

31. Ibid.

32. U.S. Department of Justice, *Crime in the United States, 2000* (Washington, DC: U.S. Government Printing Office, 2001). Available at www.fbi.gov/ucr/ucr.htm.

33. Rennison, *Criminal Victimization 2000.*

34. Ibid.

35. Ibid.

36. D. L. Decker, D. Shichor, and R. M. O'Brien, *Urban Structure and Victimization* (Lexington, MA: D. C. Heath, 1982), p. 27.

37. Rennison, *Criminal Victimization 2000.*

38. Michael J. Hindelang, "Race and Involvement in Common Law Personal Crimes," *American Sociological Review* 43 (1978): 93–109.

39. U.S. Department of Justice, *Crime in the United States, 2000.*

40. John Huey-Long Song, "Attitudes of Chinese Immigrants and Vietnamese Refugees toward Law Enforcement in the United States," *Justice Quarterly* 9 (1992): 703–719.

41. Margorie Zatz, "Pleas, Priors and Prison: Racial/Ethnic Differences in Sentencing," *Social Science Research* 14 (1985): 169–193.

42. Donald Black, "The Social Organization of Arrest," in *The Manners and Customs of the Police,* ed. Donald Black (New York: Academic Press, 1980), pp. 85–108.

43. Katheryn K. Russell, *The Color of Crime* (New York: New York University Press, 1998).

44. In some years, UCR arrest data indicate that African Americans make up half of the murder arrestees, but this pattern is not constant.

45. K. Peak and J. Spencer, "Crime in Indian Country: Another Trail of Tears," *Journal of Criminal Justice* 15 (1987): 485–494.

46. Hindelang, "Race and Involvement in Common Law Personal Crimes," p. 93.

47. Granted, the robbery arrest figures do include commercial offenses, but we are not looking at the volume of offenses, but rather the demographics of who is arrested.

48. Hindelang, "Race and Involvement in Common Law Personal Crimes," p. 99.

49. Ibid, pp. 100–101.

50. Gwynn Nettler, *Explaining Crime,* 3d ed. (New York: McGraw-Hill, 1984).

51. Patrick G. Jackson, "Sources of Data," in *Measurement Issues in Criminology,* ed. Kimberly Kempf (New York: Springer-Verlag, 1990).

52. Michael Hindelang, Travis Hirschi, and Joseph G. Weis, *Measuring Delinquency* (Beverly Hills, CA: Sage, 1981); Delbert Elliot, David Huizinga, Brian Knowles, and Rachel Canter, *The Prevalence and Incidence of Delinquent Behavior: 1976–1980: National Estimates of Delinquent Behavior by Sex, Race, Social Class and Other Selected Variables* (Boulder, CO: Behavioral Research Institute); Robert M. O'Brien, *Crime and Victimization Data* (Beverly Hills, CA: Sage, 1985).

53. Elliot et al., *Prevalence and Incidence of Delinquent Behavior.*

54. National Youth Survey questionnaire, in O'Brien, *Crime and Victimization Data.*

55. O'Brien, *Crime and Victimization Data.*

56. Delbert S. Elliot and S. S. Ageton, "Reconciling Race and Class Differences in Self-Reported and Official Measures of Delinquency," *American Sociological Review* 45 (1980): 95–110; Hindelang et al., *Measuring Delinquency.*

57. David Huizinga and Delbert S. Elliot, "Juvenile Offenders: Prevalence, Offender Incidence, and Arrest Rates by Race," *Crime and Delinquency* 33 (1987): 206–223.

58. National Institutes of Health, *Drug Use among Racial/Ethnic Minorities,* Report No. 95-3888 (Washington, DC: U.S. Government Printing Office, 1995).

59. Lori Dorfman and Vincent Scharaldi, "Off Balance: Youth, Race and Crime in the News" (Berkeley, CA: Berkeley Media Studies Group, 2001). Available at www.buildingblocksforyotuh.org/media.html.

60. NCVS, 1994.

61. Fox and Zawitz, *Homicide Trends in the United States.*

62. Ibid.

63. Ibid.

64. Bing, "Politicizing Black-on-Black Crime"; Russell, *The Color of Crime.* Russell defines a racial hoax as an event where "someone fabricates a crime and blames another person because of his race or when an actual crime has been committed and the perpetrator falsely blames someone because of their race" (p. 70).

65. William Wilbanks, "Is Violent Crime Intraracial?" *Crime and Delinquency* 31 (1985): 117–128.

66. Bureau of Justice Statistics, *Criminal Victimization, 1995.*

67. Ibid.

68. Hate Crimes Act of 1990; Violent Crime and Law Enforcement Act of 1994; Church Arson Prevention Act of 1996.

69. Federal Bureau of Investigation, *Hate Crime Statistics, 2000,* p. 2. Available at www.fbi.gov/ucr/ucr.htm.

70. Ibid.

71. Ibid.

72. Ibid.

73. Ibid.

74. Ibid.

75. Ibid.

76. Ibid.

77. Ibid.

78. Ibid.

79. James Jacobs, "Should Hate Be a Crime?" *Public Interest* (1993): 3–14.

80. Jacobs, "Should Hate Be a Crime?" p. 11.

81. Ibid., pp. 11–12.

82. A. K. Cohen, "Foreword and Overview," in *Gangs in America,* ed. C. Ronald Huff (Newbury Park, CA: Sage, 1990).

83. Herbert C. Covey, Scott Menard, and Robert J. Franzese, *Juvenile Gangs* (Springfield, IL: Charles C. Thomas, 1992).

84. J. W. C. Johnstone, "Youth Gangs and Black Suburbs," *Pacific Sociological Review* 24 (1991): 355–375; E. G. Dolan and S. Finney, *Youth Gangs* (New York: Simon & Schuster, 1984).

85. "Gangs Plague Reservations," *Omaha World Herald* (October 9, 1997).

86. Ibid.

87. *Highlights of the 1999 National Youth Gang Survey* (Washington, DC: Office of Juvenile Justice and Delinquency Prevention, 2000). Available at www.iir.com/nygc/.

88. Covey et al., *Juvenile Gangs.*

89. S. Mydans, "Not Just the Inner City: Well-To-Do Join Gangs," *New York Times* (April 10, 1991), p. A-7, national edition.

90. James Howell, *Youth Gangs: An Overview* (Washington, DC: Office of Juvenile Justice and Delinquency Prevention, 1998).

91. Frank Thrasher, *The Gang* (Chicago: University of Chicago Press, 1927).

92. Covey et al., *Juvenile Gangs, p. 64.*

93. C. J. Friedman, F. Mann, and H. Aldeman, "Juvenile Street Gangs: The Victimization of Youth," *Adolescence* 11 (1976): 527–533.

94. William J. Chambliss, "The Saints and the Roughnecks," *Society* 11 (1973): 341–355.

95. C. Ronald Huff ("Youth Gangs and Public Policy," *Crime and Delinquency* 35 [1989]: 528–537) identifies three gang types: hedonistic, instrumental and predatory. Jeffrey Fagan ("The Social Organization of Drug Use and Drug Dealing among Urban Gangs," *Criminology* 27 [1989]: 633–666) identifies four gang types: social gangs, party gangs, serious delinquents, and organized gangs.

96. Malcomb W. Klein, Cheryl Maxson and Lea C. Cunningham, "'Crack,' Street Gangs and Violence," *Criminology* 29 (1991): 623–650; Scott H. Decker and Barrick Van Winkle, "Slinging Dope: The Role of Gangs and Gang Members in Drug Sales," *Justice Quarterly* 11 (1994): 583–604.

97. Finn-Aage Esbensen and David Huizinga, "Gangs, Drugs and Delinquency," *Criminology* 31 (1993): 565–590.

98. *Highlights of the 1999 National Youth Gang Survey.*

99. Ibid.

100. Fagan, "The Social Organization of Drug Use."

101. Ibid.

102. David G. Curry and Scott H. Decker, *Confronting Gangs: Crime and Community* (Los Angeles: Roxbury, 1998).

103. *Highlights of the 1999 National Youth Gang Survey.*

104. J. M. Hagedorn, *People and Folks* (Chicago: Lake View Press, 1989); Huff, *Gangs in America.*

105. W. K. Brown, "Graffiti, Identity, and the Delinquent Gang," *International Journal of Offender Therapy and Comparative Criminology* 22 (1978): 39–45.

106. J. W. C. Johnstone, "Youth Gangs and Black Suburbs," *Pacific Sociological Review* 24 (1981): 355–375.

107. Thrasher, *The Gang;* J. D. Moore and Vigil R. Garcia, "Residence and Territoriality in Chicano Gangs," *Social Problems* 31 (1983): 182–194; Ko-Lin Chin, Jeffrey Fagan, and Robert J. Kelly, "Patterns of Chinese Gang Extortion," *Justice Quarterly* 9 (1992): 625–646; Calvin Toy, "A Short History of Asian Gangs in San Francisco," *Justice Quarterly* 9 (1992): 645–665.

108. M. G. Harris, *Cholas: Latino Girls in Gangs* (New York: AMS Press, 1988); J. D. Vigil, *Barrio Gangs* (Austin: University of Texas Press, 1988).

109. Anne Campbell, *Girls in the Gang: A Report from New York City* (Oxford: Basil Blackwell, 1984); Dolan and Finney, *Youth Gangs.*

110. James F. Short Jr. and Fred L. Strodbeck, *Group Process and Gang Delinquency* (Chicago: University of Chicago Press, 1965).

111. Curry and Decker, *Confronting Gangs.*

112. Mydans, "Not Just the Inner City."

113. Esbensen and Huizinga, "Gangs, Drugs and Delinquency"; Jeffrey Fagan, "Social Process of Delinquency and Drug Use among Urban Gangs," in *Gangs in America,* ed. C. Ronald Huff (Newbury Park, CA: Sage, 1990); Anne Campbell, *The Girls in the Gang,* 2d ed. (Cambridge, MA: Basil Blackwell, 1991).

114. Covey et al., *Juvenile Gangs.*

115. *Highlights of the 1999 National Youth Gang Survey.*

116. Covey et al., *Juvenile Gangs.*

117. Ibid.

118. C. Ronald Huff, "Youth Gangs and Public Policy," *Crime and Delinquency* 35 (1989): 524–537; Campbell, *Girls in the Gang.*

119. Campbell, *Girls in the Gang.*

120. "Gangs Plague Reservations," *Omaha World Herald* (October 9, 1997).

121. Ibid.

122. James D. Vigil and S. C. Yun, "Vietnamese Youth Gangs in Southern California," in *Gangs in America,* ed. C. Ronald Huff (Newbury Park, CA: Sage, 1990);

Chin et al., "Patterns of Chinese Gang Extortion"; Toy, "A Short History."

123. Covey et al., *Juvenile Gangs,* p. 67.

124. Ibid.

125. Chin et al., "Patterns of Chinese Gang Extortion"; Toy, "A Short History."

126. Chin et al., "Patterns of Chinese Gang Extortion."

127. K. Chin, "Chinese Gangs and Extortion," in *Gangs in America,* ed. C. Ronald Huff (Newbury Park, CA: Sage, 1990).

128. Vigil and Yun, "Vietnamese Youth Gangs."

129. Covey et al., *Juvenile Gangs.*

130. Ibid.

131. Ibid., p. 65.

132. Mark S. Hamm, *American Skinheads* (Westport, CT: Praeger, 1994), p. 62.

133. I. A. Spergel, "Youth Gangs: Continuity and Change," in *Crime and Delinquency: An Annual Review of Research,* Vol. 12, ed. Michael Tonry and Norval Morris (Chicago: University of Chicago Press, 1990).

134. Covey et al., *Juvenile Gangs.*

135. Hamm, *American Skinheads.*

3

Race, Ethnicity, Social Structure, and Crime

In 1968, the Kerner Commission warned that "our Nation is moving toward two societies, one black, one white—separate and unequal."[1] Twenty-four years later, political scientist Andrew Hacker published a book on American race relations titled *Two Nations: Black and White, Separate, Hostile, Unequal.*[2] Hacker's subtitle indicates that the Kerner Commission's dire warning has come true: instead of moving toward greater equality and opportunity, since the 1960s we have moved backward.

GOALS OF THE CHAPTER

Race discrimination and social and economic inequality have a direct impact on crime and criminal justice. They account for many of the racial disparities in the criminal justice system. The goals of this chapter are to examine the broader structure of American society with respect to race and ethnicity and to analyze the relationship between social structure and crime. As we learned in Chapter 2, racial and ethnic minorities are disproportionately involved in the criminal justice system, both as crime victims and as offenders. In very general terms, there are two possible explanations for this overrepresentation. The first is discrimination in the criminal justice system. We explore the data related to this issue in Chapters 4, 5, 6, and 7. The second explanation involves structural inequalities in American society. This chapter examines the relationships among race and ethnicity, the social structure, and crime.

We should first define what we mean by social structure. *Social structure* is "a general term for any collective social circumstance that is unalterable and given for the individual."[3] The analysis of social structure reveals *patterned relationships between groups of people* that form the basic contours of society. The patterned relationships are related to employment, income, residence, education, religion, gender, and race and ethnicity. In combination, these factors explain a person's circumstances in life, relationships with other groups, attitudes and behavior on most issues, and prospects for the future.

This chapter will explore three distinct issues related to the relationships among inequality, race and ethnicity, and crime:

1. *The extent of racial and ethnic inequality*. The first issue we examine is the nature and extent of inequality in American society with respect to the economic status of racial and ethnic minorities. What is the economic status of people of color compared with that of whites? Is the gap between whites and people of color narrowing or growing?

2. *Inequality and crime*. The second issue is the relationship between inequality and crime. In what ways is inequality associated with crime? To what extent do the leading theories of crime help explain the relationship between inequality and crime?

3. *The impact of the civil rights movement*. The third issue is the impact of efforts designed to reduce inequality. Have civil rights laws effectively eliminated discrimination in employment, housing, and other areas of American life? If Hacker is right that the United States is "two nations: separate, hostile, [and] unequal," how do we explain the failure of the national effort to eliminate discrimination? At the same time, have various economic programs designed to increase economic opportunity—from the liberal War on Poverty in the 1960s to conservative Reaganomics in the 1980s to the neoliberal policies of President Bill Clinton in the 1990s—achieved their goals and reduced poverty? If not, how do we explain the persistence of economic inequality?

ECONOMIC INEQUALITY

The first important issue is the nature and extent of inequality in the United States. The data indicate three important patterns: (1) a large gap between rich and poor, without regard to race or ethnicity; (2) a large economic gap between white Americans and racial minorities; and (3) the growth of the very poor—a group some analysts call an underclass—in the past 30 years. The standard measures of economic inequality are income, wealth, unemployment, and poverty status. All of these measures indicate deep and persistent inequality in society generally and with respect to race and ethnicity.

Income

Median family income is a standard measure of economic status. Data from the 2000 census reveal wide gaps between racial and ethnic groups. In 2000, the median income for all families in the United States was $50,890, but $56,442 for non-Hispanic white families, $34,192 for African American families, and $35,054 for Hispanic families (see Figure 3.1). Thus, the median family income for African Americans is 60.4 percent of that for white Americans (essentially unchanged from the 61 percent figure in 1990), whereas for Hispanics it is 62 percent of that for white families (up from 58 percent in 1990).[4] African Americans made significant progress relative to whites in the 1950s and 1960s but then stagnated in the 1970s. The National Research Council concluded, "Since the early 1970s, the economic status of blacks relative to whites has, on average, stagnated or deteriorated."[5]

The median family income figures mask significant differences *within* racial and ethnic groups. One of the most significant developments over the past 40 years has been the growth of an African American middle class.[6] This is the result of two factors. First, the civil rights movement opened the door to employment for racial and ethnic minorities in many job categories where they previously had been excluded: white-collar, service, and professional-level jobs. At the same time, the changing structure of the American economy has been characterized by tremendous growth in the white-collar sector. An increasing number of African Americans and Hispanics have been able to take advantage of these new opportunities; however, the percentage of African Americans among the very poor has also increased. Thus, among racial and ethnic minorities there is a greater gap between the middle class and the poorest than at any other time in our history.

Wealth

The data on family wealth reveal an even larger gap between whites and minorities. The distinction between income and wealth is important. *Income* measures how much a person or family earns in any given period. *Wealth,* on the other hand, measures all of their accumulated assets: home, cars, savings, stocks, and so forth. The family that owns a house, for example, has far more wealth than the family that rents. The 1995 median wealth of white families was $49,030, compared with only $7,073 for African Americans and $7,255 for Hispanics (see Figure 3.2).[7]

The reasons for the huge wealth gap are easy to understand. Middle-class people are able to save each month; the poor are not. These savings are used to buy a house, stocks, or other investments. The family's net wealth increases as the value of their home rises. Affluent whites, moreover, usually buy houses in neighborhoods where property values are rising rapidly. Lower-middle-class families, regardless of race, are often able to buy homes only in neighborhoods where property values are stagnant. As a result, their wealth does not increase very much. The poor, of course, are not able to save or invest anything, and they continually fall behind everyone else in terms of wealth.

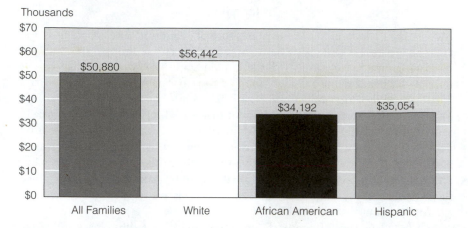

FIGURE 3.1 Median Family Income, 2000

SOURCE: U.S. Bureau of the Census, *Statistical Abstract of the United States, 2002* (Washington, DC: U.S. Government Printing Office, 2002), p. 436.

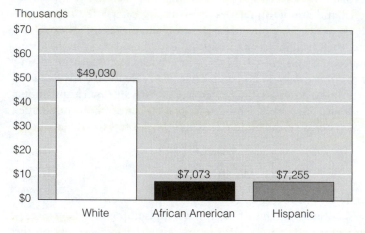

FIGURE 3.2 Median Family Net Worth, 1995

SOURCE: U.S. Bureau of the Census, *Household Net Worth and Asset Ownership* (Washington, DC: U.S. GPO, 2001), p. 5.

Wealth plays an important role in perpetuating inequality. It cushions a family against temporary hard times, such as loss of a job. The lower-middle-class person who is laid off, even temporarily, may lose his or her home; as a result, the family slides down the economic scale. Wealth is also transferred to the next generation. Families with savings can afford to send their children to private colleges and graduate or professional schools. They can also help their children buy their first home by giving or loaning them all or part of the down payment. Finally, when they die, their children inherit their estate in the form of cash, stock, or property. Poor and even many lower-middle-class families are not able to help their children in any of these ways. Wealth, in these respects, forms an important part of the social capital (see discussion later in the chapter) that shapes a person's advantages, or lack of advantages, in life.

Unemployment

In 2000, the official unemployment rate for the United States was 4.0 percent, a considerable improvement over the 5.6 percent rate for 1995. Because of the booming economy in the 1990s, this was the lowest the unemployment rate had been since the early 1970s. In 1985, it reached a high point of 7.2 percent. It is worth noting that the crime rate in the late 1990s was the lowest it had been since the 1960s. There have always been significant differences in the unemployment rates for different racial and ethnic groups. The unemployment rate for whites in 2000 was 3.5 percent, compared with 7.7 percent for African Americans and 5.7 percent for Hispanics. The African American unemployment rate has been consistently twice as high as or higher than the white rate. In 1985, for example, the African American unemployment rate was 15.1 percent, compared with 6.2 percent for whites and 10.5 percent for Hispanics.[8] Thus, even though African Americans benefit from economic good times, they have not been able to overcome their relative disadvantage with respect to the unemployment rate.

The official data on unemployment tell only part of the story, however. First, there are serious problems with the official unemployment rate, just as there are problems with the official crime rate. The official unemployment rate counts only those people who are actively seeking employment. It does not count three important groups: (1) discouraged workers who have given up and are not looking for work; (2) part-time employees who want full-time jobs but cannot find them; and (3) workers in the "underground economy," who are paid in cash to avoid paying taxes and Social Security withholding. Many economists believe that racial minorities are disproportionately represented among those not counted by the official unemployment rate.[9]

Equally important, the official unemployment rate is much higher for teenagers than for adults. The unemployment rate for African Americans between the ages of 16 and 19 was 24.7 percent in 2000, compared with 11.4 percent for white teenagers and 16.7 percent for Hispanic teenagers. The African American teenage unemployment rate had fallen dramatically since 1985, when it was a staggering 40.2 percent, but in 2000 it was still twice the white rate.[10]

The unemployment rate data reveal important differences within the Hispanic community related to national origins. In 2000, the unemployment rate for Hispanics of Mexican origin was 4.1 percent, compared with 4.0 percent for those of Puerto Rican origin and only 2.7 percent for those of Cuban origin.[11]

Later in this chapter, we discuss the major theories of crime as they relate to race and ethnicity. For virtually every theory, the teenage unemployment rate is particularly important in terms of the likelihood of participation in crime. The peak years of criminal activity for Index crimes are for persons between the ages of 14 and 24. Official arrest data indicate that involvement in crime peaks at age 18 for violent crimes and at age 16 for property crimes. The lack of meaningful job opportunities for teenagers is an important factor in the high rates of crime. The persistently higher rates of unemployment for African American and Hispanic teenagers help explain their higher rates of criminal activity compared with those of whites.

Poverty Status

Yet another measure of economic status is the percentage of families in poverty. The federal government first developed an official definition of poverty in 1964 designed to reflect the minimum amount of income needed for an adequate standard of living. In 2000, the official poverty line was $8,794 for a single person and $17,603 for a family of four.[12] In 2000, 11.3 percent of all Americans were below the poverty line. The percentage has fluctuated over time, from 22.2 percent in 1960 to 11.4 percent in 1978. In 2000, 7.7 percent of all non-Hispanic whites were below the poverty line, compared with 22.1 percent of African Americans and 21.2 percent of Hispanics.

The most disturbing aspect of the poverty figures is the percentage of children living below the poverty line. In 2000, 32.9 percent of all African American children under the age of 6 and 28.3 percent of all Hispanic children were living in poverty, compared with only 9.4 percent of non–Hispanic white children.[13] Because childhood poverty status is associated with so many other social problems—inadequate nutrition, single-parent households, low educational achievement, high risk of crime victimization, and high rate of involvement in crime—the data suggest a grim future for a very large percentage of racial and ethnic minority children.

Human Capital and Social Capital

Sociologists and economists have been concerned about the transmission of inequality from one generation to the next.[14] This problem can be understood not just in economic terms but also in reference to noneconomic resources, referred to as human capital and social capital.

Human capital includes values, habits, and outlook, which in turn shape behavior. Sociologists and psychologists generally agree that the family is the primary unit for transmitting values to children. These values include, for example, self-respect, self-reliance, hard work, and respect for other people. If a family is dysfunctional, these values are not effectively transmitted to the children. The condition of poverty is generally associated with single-parent families, which are less able to transmit positive values.

Social capital is defined by the World Bank as "the institutions, relationships, and norms that shape the quality on quantity of a society's social interactions."[15] The sources of social capital include families, communities, and organizations. With respect to employment, one important form of social capital is having family, friends, or neighbors who are able to offer jobs (for example, in a small family business) or personal referral to someone who is able to offer a job. This process is often referred to as *networking* and is generally recognized as extremely important in terms of finding jobs and advancing careers. In extremely poor neighborhoods, however, there are few people with jobs to offer or with family or friends who can make good job references. Criminologist Elliot Currie illustrated the point by citing a comparative study of juvenile delinquents who graduated from the Lyman School in Massachusetts and the Wiltwyck School in New York in the 1950s. The predominantly white Lyman graduates often had personal connections who helped them find good employment. One graduate explained: "I fooled around a lot when I was a kid. . . . But then I got an uncle on the [police] force. When I was twenty he got me my first job as a traffic man."[16] The predominantly African American and Hispanic graduates of Wiltwyck did not have similar kinds of personal resources. As a result, they recidivated into criminal activity at a much higher rate. In short, the conditions of extreme poverty diminish the human and social capital that young people possess, and as a consequence, contribute to higher rates of criminal activity.

The noted sociologist Alejandro Portes points out, however, that social capital can have a downside. Different communities in a large metropolitan area may each be well organized but still be in conflict and working at cross-purposes. For example, several may be demanding improvements in the streets and parks in *their* neighborhoods. All may be demanding more police protection at the same time, when police resources are already stretched thin. Finally, effective networks of groups in neighborhoods may direct their activity to criminal enterprises: drug trafficking, gambling, and so on. All of these aspects of social capital can hinder positive social and economic development.[17]

The World Bank argues that government institutions, "the public sector," are an important part of the network of social capital. Assume for the moment that a neighborhood has stable families and a strong sense of community. Responsive government institutions can help translate their aspirations and efforts into effective services: good schools, attractive parks for recreation, a public transportation system that allows people to find and hold jobs, and so on. Obviously, the police and the criminal justice system are an important element of this process. If the police effectively control crime and disorder, community members will feel better about their neighborhood and feel empowered to work for its improvement. The community policing movement of the past 20 years has been built on the idea that policing can be made more effective through partnerships with community organizations.

If, on the other hand, neighborhood residents do not trust the police, they are less likely to cooperate with them in solving crime and other problems. Residents will also feel worse about their neighborhood. For this reason, the quality of police–community relations is extremely important. Chapter 4 discusses in detail the state of police–community relations and the effectiveness of programs to improve them.

Progress, Stagnation, or Regression?
The Debate over the Status of African Americans

In a comprehensive survey of American race relations, the National Research Council concluded, "The status of black Americans today can be characterized as a glass that is half full." Despite considerable progress in race relations since the 1960s, there remain "persisting disparities between black and white Americans." Although civil rights laws and economic change have allowed "a substantial fraction of blacks to enter the mainstream of American life," the majority of African Americans have not achieved social or economic equality with whites.[18] Hispanics, Native Americans, and other racial and ethnic minorities experience similar inequalities in social and economic status.

Not everyone agrees with this pessimistic assessment, however. In *America in Black and White: One Nation, Indivisible,* Stephan and Abigail Thernstrom argue that African Americans have made remarkable progress since the 1940s, economically, socially, and politically. "The signs of progress are all around us," they observe, "although we now take that progress for granted."[19] Using Gunnar Myrdal's classic study of American race relations, *An American Dilemma* (1944), as their baseline, they find that the percentage of African American families in poverty fell from 87 percent in 1940 to 21.9 percent in 2000. The number of African Americans enrolled in college increased 30-fold in the same period, rising from 45,000 students in 1940 to 1.4 million in the late 1990s. Whereas 60 percent of employed African American women worked as domestics in 1940, today more than half are in white-collar jobs. The number of African American elected officials rose from a national total of only 103 in 1960 to 8,896 by 1999. African Americans serve as mayors and police chiefs in major cities all across the country. Contrary to Andrew Hacker's pessimistic assessment that we are "two nations," the Thernstroms argue that we are today less separate, less unequal, and, in their view, less hostile than was the case in 1940.[20]

Where does the truth lie? Is the United States progressing, stagnating, or regressing in terms of social and economic inequality? The answer is that there is a degree of truth in all three interpretations. It depends on which segment of the population we are talking about. We can make sense of this complex subject by taking the approach we suggested in Chapter 1: disaggregating it into distinct components and contexts.

First, different time frames lead to different interpretations. The Thernstroms' optimistic interpretation uses 1940 as a baseline. Few can question their data on racial progress since that time. After all, 1940 was still a time of institutionalized racial segregation in the South and blatant discrimination in other parts of the country. But even the Thernstroms concede that progress has stagnated in the past 20 years. Using 1973 as a baseline leads to a far more pessimistic interpretation.

Second, the aggregate status of African Americans encompasses two divergent trends: the generally rising status of a new middle class and the deteriorating status of the very poor.[21] The same is true for other people of color. Some Hispanics are also doing very well and are integrating into the mainstream of American life. Others are trapped at the bottom of society, and in many respects they are doing much worse than before. Asian Americans are also divided into those who are doing well and those who are not.

The 2000 census figures reveal that the gap between the richest and poorest Americans actually grew during the prosperous 1990s (the Clinton years), just as it did during the 1980s (the Reagan years). Table 3.1 indicates the share of all national income earned by the richest 5 percent of the population, the richest 20 percent, and the poorest 20 percent. The gap was narrowest in the 1970s but has steadily increased ever since. A disproportionate percentage of the very poor are African American and Hispanic. Their economic status has been getting worse over the last 25 years.[22]

Table 3.1 Percentage of Aggregate Wealth Held by the Richest and the Poorest Households

	Poorest 20%	Richest 20%	Richest 5%
1998	3.6	49.2	21.4
1988	3.8	46.3	18.3
1978	4.3	43.7	16.2
1968	4.2	42.8	16.6

SOURCE: U.S. Census Bureau, *Current Population Survey, March 1968–1999* (Washington, DC: U.S. Government Printing Office, 2000), table 2.

This book is concerned with crime. From that perspective, the persistence of a very poor group at the bottom of society assumes special importance. Predatory crime has always been concentrated among the very poor. In 2000, the violent crime rate was more than twice as high for the poorest Americans as for the wealthiest: 60.3 per 1,000 for people with incomes of $7,500 or less and 22.3 per 1,000 for those with incomes of $75,000 or more.[23] The reasons for this are explained later in this chapter in the discussion of the different theories of crime.

The real point of disagreement between those who take an optimistic view, such as the Thernstroms, and those who take a more pessimistic view is the *cause* of the stagnation over the past 20 years. Many observers blame the changes in the economy, including the disappearance of industrial-level jobs, particularly from the inner city. The Thernstroms blame affirmative action and racial preferences in particular. They argue that the greatest gains in racial equality were made during the years when the civil rights movement emphasized color-blind policies and that stagnation set in during the 1970s when civil rights leaders emphasized racial preferences.

We would reply by arguing that the civil rights movement eliminated the most blatant forms of discrimination (for example, disenfranchisement of African Americans in the South and law schools not admitting African Americans). It is not surprising that the elimination of these barriers would lead to some rapid progress, primarily by those who were equipped to take advantage of the new opportunities. The growth of political and civil rights, however, did not necessarily address *economic* inequality, particularly for those not yet equipped to take advantage of expanding opportunities. The Thernstroms have a point that affirmative action programs have not really helped those at the very bottom. But they are also wrong in arguing that affirmative action is the *cause* of the plight of the very poor.

The Debate over the Underclass

Those observers who take the most pessimistic view often use the term *underclass* to describe the very poor who are concentrated in the inner cities.[24] The question of the existence of an underclass is more than a matter of semantics.

It makes a great deal of difference whether the term is merely another euphemism for poor people (that is, "the poor," "the deprived," "the impoverished,"
"the disadvantaged," "the at-risk," and so on), which implies that the economic status of people at the bottom has not changed in any fundamental way,
or whether it describes the emergence of a new kind of poverty in America.[25]

From our perspective, the crucial point about the development of an underclass is that the conditions affecting the very poor have three important effects.
First, they tend to perpetuate poverty. Second, they create conditions, such as
family breakdown, that lead to higher involvement in crime. Third, members
of the underclass lack and are unable to develop the social capital—education,
skills, and networks—that are likely to help individuals rise out of severe poverty (see the discussion of social capital later).

Evidence suggests that the nature of urban poverty has changed in significant ways. First, the industrial sector of the economy has eroded, eliminating
the entry-level jobs that were historically available to the poor. Second, conditions in the underclass generate circumstances and behavior that perpetuate
poverty.[26]

Gary Orfield and Carole Ashkinaze's study of economic conditions in Atlanta during the 1980s found growing inequality amid overall growth and pros-
perity. The authors found that although most people in the Atlanta metropolitan area fared better economically, "the dream of equal opportunity is fading
fast for many young blacks in metropolitan Atlanta." For the African American poor in the inner city, "many of the basic elements of the American dream
—a good job, a decent income, a house, college education for the kids—are
less accessible . . . than was the case in the 1970s."[27] Most of the economic
growth occurred in the largely white suburbs, whereas opportunities declined
in the predominantly African American inner city. At the same time, most of
the expanding opportunities occurred in the service sector of the economy: either in white-collar professional-level jobs or in minimum-wage service jobs
(for example, fast-food). The poor cannot realistically compete for the professional-level jobs, and many of the service-sector jobs do not pay enough
to support a family. A minimum-wage job paying $5.15 per hour (the feder-
ally mandated level as of 1998) yields an annual income of $10,300 ($5.15 ×
40 hours/week × 50 weeks). This is substantially less than the official poverty
line of $17,603 for a family of four.

Patterns of residential segregation contribute to the development of the urban underclass. Job growth over the past 20 years has been strongest in suburban areas outside the central cities. Inner-city residents, regardless of color, find
it extremely difficult both to learn about job opportunities and to travel to and
from work. Public transportation systems are either weak or nonexistent in
most cities, particularly with respect to traveling to suburban areas. A private
car is almost a necessity for traveling to work. Yet, one of the basic facts of
poverty is the lack of sufficient money to buy a reliable car. Concentration of
the very poor and their isolation from the rest of society erode the social networks that are extremely important for finding employment. Studies of the
job-seeking process have found that whites are more likely to be referred to

jobs by friends or family who have some information about a job or connection with an employer. Racial and ethnic minorities are less likely to have these kinds of contacts, which are an important element of social capital. The problem is especially acute for members of the underclass, who are likely to have very few personal contacts that lead to good jobs.[28]

The pessimistic analysis of the changes in Atlanta in *The Closing Door* is still compatible with the more optimistic aspects of the Thernstroms' analysis. Atlanta has a large and growing African American professional and middle class. These individuals and families live in the suburbs, as do their white counterparts. Their very real progress, however, coexists in the Atlanta metropolitan area with the lack of progress by very poor African Americans trapped in the inner city.

Crutchfield explains the economic situation in the inner city in terms of a *dual labor market*. What economists call the *primary* market consists of good, well-paying jobs with fringe benefits (especially health-care coverage) and good prospects for the future. The *secondary* market consists of low-paying jobs with limited fringe benefits and uncertain prospects for the future. He argues that the secondary market "has an effect on individual propensity to engage in crime." Individuals are less "bonded" to their work (and, by extension, to society as a whole) and to the idea that hard work will lead to a brighter future. Additionally, the inner city involves concentrations of people in the secondary market, who then "spend time with each other, socialize with one another, and at times even victimize each other."[29]

The pattern of economic change that affected Atlanta, a growing city, had even more negative effects on declining industrial cities such as New York and Chicago. Economic expansion there was concentrated in the suburban areas, and the inner cities declined significantly. Such older industrial cities did not experience the same rate of growth in the suburbs, and the decline in industrial jobs was even more severe. The relationship of the underclass to crime becomes clearer when we look at it from the standpoint of neighborhood community social structure.

COMMUNITY SOCIAL STRUCTURE

The social structure of communities has an important impact on crime. *Community* in this respect refers to both large metropolitan communities and local neighborhoods. The social structure of a community involves the spacial distribution of the population, the composition of local neighborhoods, and patterns of interaction between and within neighborhoods.

Residential Segregation

American metropolitan communities are characterized by strong patterns of residential segregation. As already indicated, this has an impact on patterns of criminal activity.

Residential segregation itself is nothing new. Historically, American cities have always been segregated by race, ethnicity, and income. New arrivals to the city—either immigrants from other countries or migrants from rural areas—settled in the central city, with older immigrant groups and the middle class moving to neighborhoods farther out or to suburban communities. Racial and ethnic segregation in housing has been the result of several factors: the historic practice of de jure segregation, covert discrimination, and group choice. In the South and some Northern communities, local ordinances prohibited African Americans from living in white neighborhoods. Particularly in the North, many property owners adopted restrictive covenants that prohibited the sale of property to African Americans or Jews. Real estate agents maintained segregation by steering minority buyers away from white neighborhoods. Banks and savings and loan companies refused to offer mortgages in poor and minority neighborhoods—a practice known as "redlining." Finally, segregation has been maintained by personal choice. People often prefer to live among members of their own group. Thus, European immigrants tended to form distinct ethnic neighborhoods, many of which still exist (for example, Little Italy and Chinatown).

Despite federal and state laws outlawing housing discrimination, residential segregation persists today. Social scientists have devised an index of residential segregation that measures the proportion of neighborhoods in any city that are racially homogeneous. The data indicate that in the 1980s, from 70 to 90 percent of the people in the major cities lived in racially homogeneous neighborhoods. The residential segregation indices for both Detroit and Chicago in 1980 were 88, meaning that 88 percent of all people lived in either all-white or all–African American neighborhoods. In practical terms, this means that for a white person living in Detroit, an estimated 93 percent of the "potential" contacts with other people would involve other whites. For African Americans, 80 percent of the "potential" contacts would involve other African Americans. In New York City and Los Angeles, the residential segregation indices were 78 and 79, respectively.[30]

Residential Segregation and Crime Residential segregation has a direct impact on crime. Most important, it concentrates high-rate offenders in one area, which has two significant consequences. First, the law-abiding residents of those areas suffer high rates of robbery, burglary, and other predatory crimes. The NCVS consistently finds that both racial and ethnic minorities and poor people are victimized more than white and middle-class people. The violent crime rate for the very poor (60.3 per 1,000) is more than twice that of the richest Americans (22.3 per 1,000).[31]

Second, the concentration of high-rate offenders in one area has an important effect on the propensity of individuals to engage in criminal activity. Several of the theories of crime discussed later place this phenomenon in a broader framework. Teenagers in those areas are subject to disproportionate contact with persons who are already involved in criminal activity. These teenagers have comparatively less contact with law-abiding peers. As Crutchfield points

out, unemployed or marginally employed people in the secondary labor market "spend more time with each other," and as a result, they are more likely to
influence each other in the direction of a greater propensity to commit crime.[32]
Even in stable families, the sheer weight of this peer influence overwhelms positive parental influence. In the worst of situations, teenagers are coerced into
joining crime-involved gangs. Thus, many individuals are socialized into crime
when this would not be the case if they lived in a more diverse neighborhood
with lower crime.

In one of the great ironies of recent history, some of the great gains of the
civil rights movement have hurt the poorest racial minority communities. Since
the 1960s, the civil rights movement has opened up employment opportunities
in business and the professions, creating a greatly expanded African American
middle class. At the same time, the end of blatant residential segregation has
created housing opportunities for families in the new African American middle
class. Following the example of their white counterparts, these families move
out of low-income, inner-city neighborhoods and into the suburbs.

The result is that the old neighborhoods abandoned by the African American middle class are stripped of important stabilizing elements—what Wilson
refers to as a "social buffer."[33] The neighborhood loses its middle-class role
models, who help socialize other children into middle-class values, and an important part of its natural leadership: the people who are active in neighborhood associations and local school issues. Skogan reports that educated, middle-
class, home-owning residents are more likely to be involved in neighborhood
organizations than are less educated, poorer, renting residents.[34] And, as we have
already noted, the middle class is composed of the people who can provide the
social networks that lead to good jobs.

All of these factors contribute directly to neighborhood deterioration and
indirectly to crime. As more of the people with better incomes move out, the
overall economic level of the neighborhood declines. Houses often go from
owner-occupied to rental property. As the area loses purchasing power, neighborhood stores lose business and close. Wilson and Kelling, two of the early theorists of community policing, argue that the physical deterioration of a neighborhood (abandoned buildings and cars, unrepaired houses, and so forth) is a
sign that people do not care and, consequently, is an "invitation" to criminal
behavior.[35] As the composition of the neighborhood changes, meanwhile, an
increasing number of crime-involved people move in, changing the context of
peer pressure in the neighborhood.

Skogan describes the impact of fear of crime on neighborhood deterioration as a six-stage process. It begins with withdrawal. People choose to have less
contact with other neighborhood residents; the ultimate form of withdrawal is
to move away. This leads to a reduction in informal control over behavior by
residents: people no longer monitor and report on the behavior of, say, their
neighbors' children. Then, organizational life declines: fewer residents are active in community groups. These factors lead to an increase in delinquency and
disorder. As the neighborhood becomes poorer, commercial decline sets in.
Local shops close and buildings are abandoned. The final stage of the process is

collapse. At this point, according to Skogan, "there is virtually no 'community' remaining."[36]

Community policing, it should be noted, is designed to stop this process of deterioration. First, many community policing efforts address small signs of disorder that cause people to withdraw. Second, police-initiated partnerships and block meetings are designed to strengthen networks among residents and help to give them a feeling of empowerment or collective efficacy in dealing with neighborhood problems.[37]

The Impact of Crime and Drugs Crime has a devastating impact on neighborhoods—an impact that is intensified in very poor neighborhoods. First, it results in direct economic loss and physical harm to the crime victims. Second, the resulting high fear of crime damages the quality of life for everyone in the area. Third, persistent high rates of crime cause employed and law-abiding people to move out of the neighborhood, thereby intensifying the concentration of the unemployed and high-rate offenders. Fourth, crime damages local businesses, in the form of both direct losses and inability to obtain insurance. Eventually, many of these businesses move or close, with the result that the immediate neighborhood loses jobs. Those that stay frequently charge higher prices in order to make up for their losses.

The drug problem has hit poor neighborhoods with devastating effect, particularly with the advent of crack cocaine in the mid-1980s. Drug trafficking fostered the growth of gangs and led to an increase in gang-related violence, including drive-by shootings that sometimes kill innocent persons. Moreover, crack cocaine appears to be more damaging to family life than other drugs are. Mothers addicted to crack seem more likely to lose their sense of parental responsibility. The phenomenon of pregnant women becoming addicted to crack has resulted in a serious problem of crack-addicted babies.[38]

In some drug-ridden neighborhoods, the drug trade is the central feature of neighborhood life. Entire blocks have become "drug bazaars," with open drug sales. The drug trade is often a highly organized and complex activity, with people watching for the police, negotiating the sale, obtaining the drugs, and holding the main supply. The buyers are frequently outsiders, and the drug market represents what economists call *economic specialization,* with one part of society providing services to the rest of society.[39] Police departments have experimented with drug enforcement crackdowns (short-term periods of intensive arrest activity), but there is no evidence that this strategy has any long-term effect on reducing the drug trade.[40]

When drug and gang activity begins to dominate a neighborhood, it becomes virtually impossible for law-abiding residents to shield themselves and their children from illegal activity. The peer pressure on juveniles to join gangs becomes extremely intense. Often, kids join gangs for their own protection. Because of drive-by shootings and other gang-related violence, the streets are even less safe than before. This is the stage that Skogan describes as neighborhood "collapse."[41]

THEORETICAL PERSPECTIVES
ON INEQUALITY AND CRIME

The second important issue addressed in this chapter is the relationship between inequality and crime. We have established that significant economic inequality prevails between the white majority and racial and ethnic minorities. To what extent does this inequality contribute to the racial and ethnic disparities in crime and criminal justice? To help answer this question, we turn to the major theories of criminal behavior. In different ways, each one posits a relationship between inequality and crime that helps explain the disparities within crime and criminal justice.

Social Strain Theory

Robert Merton's social strain theory holds that each society has a dominant set of values and goals along with acceptable means of achieving them. Not everyone is able to realize these goals, however. The gap between approved goals and the means people have to achieve them creates what Merton terms *social strain*.[42]

As Steven F. Messner and Richard Rosenfeld argue in *Crime and the American Dream*, the dominant goals and values in American society emphasize success through individual achievement.[43] Success is primarily measured in terms of material goods, social status, and recognition for personal expression (for example, through art or athletics). The indicators of material success include a person's job, income, place of residence, clothing, cars, and other consumer goods. The accepted means of achieving these goals are also highly individualistic, emphasizing hard work, self-control, persistence, and education. The American work ethic holds that anyone can succeed if only he or she will work hard enough and keep trying long enough. Failure is regarded as a personal, not a social, failure. Yet, as we have seen, many people in America do not enjoy success in these terms: unemployment rates remain high, and millions of people are living in poverty; minorities are the victims of racial and ethnic discrimination.

Merton's theory of social strain holds that people respond to the gap between society's values and their own circumstances in several different ways: rebellion, retreatism, and innovation. Some of these involve criminal activity. *Rebellion* involves a rejection of both society's goals and the established means of achieving them, along with an attempt to create a new society based on different values and goals. This stage includes revolutionary political activity, which in some instances might be politically related criminal activity such as terrorism.

Retreatism entails a rejection of both the goals and the accepted means of achieving them. A person may retreat, for example, into drug abuse, alcoholism, vagrancy, or a countercultural lifestyle. Retreatism helps explain the high rates of drug and alcohol abuse in America. Many forms of drug abuse involve criminal behavior: the buying and selling of drugs, robbery or burglary as a means of obtaining money to purchase drugs, or involvement in a drug trafficking network that includes violent crime directed against rival drug dealers. There is considerable debate among criminologists over the relationship between drugs and crime.[44] There is no clear evidence that drug abuse is a direct cause of crime. Studies of crime and drugs have found mixed patterns: some individuals began their criminal activity before they started using drugs, whereas for others, drug use preceded involvement in crime. Moreover, some individuals "specialize" and either use (and/or sell) drugs but engage in no other criminal activity, or they commit crimes but do not use illegal drugs.[45]

Innovation involves an acceptance of society's goals but a rejection of the accepted means of attaining them—that is, some forms of innovation can be negative rather than positive. Crime is one mode of innovation. The person who embezzles money seeks material success but chooses an illegitimate (criminal) means of achieving it. Gang formation and drug trafficking are manifestations of entrepreneurship and neighborhood networking. Unfortunately, they lead to lawbreaking and often have destructive side effects (for example, gang-related shootings) rather than law obedience. These are examples of what Portes and Landolt refer to as the "downside" of social capital.[46] The person who steals to obtain money or things is seeking the external evidence of material success through illegal means.

Applying the Theory Social strain theory helps explain the high rates of delinquency and criminal behavior among racial and ethnic minorities in the United States. Criminal activity will be higher among those groups that are denied the opportunity to fulfill the American dream of individual achievement. The theory also explains far higher rates of retreatist (for example, drug abuse) and innovative (for example, criminal activity) responses. The high levels of economic inequality experienced by minorities, together with continuing discrimination based on race and ethnicity, mean that minorities are far less likely to be able to achieve approved social goals through conventional means.

Differential Association Theory

Edwin Sutherland's theory of differential association holds that criminal behavior is learned behavior. The more contact a person has with people who are already involved in crime, the more likely that person is to engage in criminal activity.[47]

Applying the Theory Given the structure of American communities, differential association theory has direct relevance to the disproportionate involvement of racial and ethnic minorities in the criminal justice system. Because of residential segregation based on income and race, a person who is poor and/or a racial or ethnic minority is more likely to have personal contact with people who are already involved in crime. The concentration of persons involved in crime in underclass neighborhoods produces enormous peer pressure to become involved in crime. In neighborhoods where gangs are prevalent, young people often experience tremendous pressure to join a gang simply as a means of personal protection. In schools where drug use is prevalent, juveniles will have more contact with drug users and are more likely to be socialized into drug use themselves. As noted earlier, Crutchfield argues that the secondary labor market brings together high concentrations of people with a weak attachment to their work and the future, who then socialize with each other and influence each other's propensity to commit crime.[48] Most parents have a basic understanding of differential association theory: they warn their children to avoid the "bad" kids in the neighborhood and encourage them to associate with the "good" kids.

Social Disorganization Theory

Followers of the Chicago school of urban sociology developed the social disorganization theory of crime.[49] Focusing on poor inner-city neighborhoods, this theory holds that the conditions of poverty undermine the institutions that socialize people into conventional, law-abiding ways of life. As a result, the values and behavior leading to delinquency and crime are passed on from one generation to another. The Chicago sociologists found that recent immigrants tended to have lower rates of criminality than the first American-born generation. They argued that immigrants were able to preserve old-world family structures that promoted stability and conventional behavior. These older values broke down in the new urban environment, however, which led to higher rates of criminality among the next generation. The Chicago sociologists noted the spatial organization of the larger metropolitan areas, with higher rates of criminal behavior in the poorer inner-city neighborhoods and lower rates in areas farther out.

The conditions of poverty contribute to social disorganization and criminality in several ways. Poverty and unemployment undermine the family, the primary unit of socialization, which leads to high rates of single-parent families. Lack of parental supervision and positive role models contributes to crime and delinquency. The concentration of the poor in certain neighborhoods means that individuals are subject to strong peer group influence tending toward nonconforming behavior. Poverty is also associated with inadequate prenatal care and malnutrition, which contribute to developmental and health problems that, in turn, lead to poor performance in schools.

Applying the Theory Social disorganization theory helps explain the high rates of crime and delinquency among racial and ethnic minorities. As our discussion of inequality suggests, minorities experience high rates of poverty and are geographically concentrated in areas with high rates of social disorganization.

Social disorganization theory is consistent with other theories of crime. It is consistent with social strain theory in that persons who are subject to conditions of social disorganization are far less likely to be able to achieve the dominant goals of society through conventional means and, therefore, are more likely to turn to crime. It is consistent with differential association theory in that neighborhoods with high levels of social disorganization will subject individuals, particularly young men, to strong influences tending toward delinquency and crime.

Culture Conflict Theory

Culture conflict theory holds that crime will be more likely to flourish in heterogeneous societies where there is a lack of consensus over society's values.[50] Human behavior is shaped by norms that are instilled through socialization and embodied in the criminal law. In any society, the majority not only defines social norms but controls the making and the administration of the criminal law. In some instances, certain groups do not accept the dominant social values. They may reject them on religious or cultural grounds or feel alienated from the majority because of discrimination or economic inequality. Conflict over social norms and the role of the criminal law leads to certain types of lawbreaking.

One example of religiously based culture conflict involves peyote, a cactus that has mild hallucinogenic effects when smoked and that some Native American religions use as part of their traditional religious exercises.[51] Today, many observers see national politics revolving around a "culture war" involving such issues as abortion, homosexuality, and religion in the public schools.[52] Some groups believe that abortion is murder and should be criminalized; others argue that it is a medical procedure that should be governed by the individual's private choice.

Applying the Theory Culture conflict theory helps explain some of the differential rates of involvement in American society, which is extremely heterogeneous, characterized by many different races, ethnic groups, religions, and cultural lifestyles. The theory encompasses the history of racial conflict—from the time of slavery, through the Civil War, to the modern civil rights movement—as one of the major themes in U.S. history. There is also a long history of ethnic and religious conflict. Americans of white, Protestant, and English background, for instance, exhibited strong prejudice against immigrants from Ireland and southern and eastern Europe, particularly Catholics and Jews.[53]

An excellent example of cultural conflict in American history is the long struggle over the consumption of alcohol that culminated in national Prohibition (1920–1933). The fight over alcohol was a bitter issue for nearly a hundred years before Prohibition. To a great extent, the struggle was rooted in ethnic and religious differences. Protestant Americans tended to take a very moralistic attitude toward alcohol, viewing abstinence as a sign of self-control and a means of rising to middle-class status. For many Catholic immigrant groups, particularly Irish and German, alcohol consumption was an accepted part of their cultural lifestyle. The long crusade to control alcohol use represented an attempt by middle-class Protestants to impose their lifestyle on working-class Catholics.[54]

Conflict Theory

Conflict theory holds that the administration of criminal justice reflects the unequal distribution of power in society.[55] The more powerful groups use the criminal justice system to maintain their dominant position and to repress groups or social movements that threaten it.[56] As Hawkins argues, conflict theory was developed primarily with reference to social class, with relatively little attention to race and ethnicity.[57]

The most obvious example of conflict theory in action was the segregation era in the South (1890s–1960s) when white supremacists instituted de jure segregation in public schools and other public accommodations.[58] The criminal justice system was used to maintain the subordinate status of African Americans. Because African Americans were disenfranchised as voters, they had no control or influence over the justice system. As a result, crimes by whites against African Americans went unpunished, and crimes by African Americans against whites were treated very harshly—including alleged or even completely fabricated offenses.[59] Meanwhile, outside of the South, discrimination also limited the influence of minorities over the justice system.

The civil rights movement has eliminated de jure segregation and other blatant forms of discrimination. Nonetheless, pervasive discrimination in society and the criminal justice system continues.

Applying the Theory Conflict theory explains the overrepresentation of racial and ethnic minorities in the criminal justice system in several ways. The criminal law singles out certain behavior engaged in primarily by the poor. Vagrancy laws are the classic example of the use of the criminal law to control the poor and other perceived "threats" to the social order. The criminal law has also been used against political movements challenging the established order: from sedition laws against unpopular ideas to disorderly conduct arrests of demonstrators. Finally, "street crimes" that are predominantly committed by the poor and disproportionately by racial and ethnic minorities are the target of more-vigorous enforcement efforts than are those crimes committed by the rich. The term *crime* refers more to robbery and burglary than to white-collar crime. In these ways, conflict theory explains the overrepresentation of racial and ethnic minorities among people arrested, convicted, and imprisoned.

Routine Activity Theory

Routine activity theory shifts the focus of attention from offenders to criminal incidents. Felson explains that the theory examines "how these incidents originate in the routine activities of everyday life."[60] Particularly important, the theory emphasizes the extent to which the daily routine creates informal social control that helps prevent crime or undermines those informal controls and leads to higher involvement in crime. (Informal social control includes, for example, the watchfulness of family, friends, and neighbors. Formal social control is exercised by the police and the rest of the criminal justice system.) Felson offers the example of parental supervision of teenagers. He cites data indicating that between 1940 and the 1970s, American juveniles spent an increasing amount of time away from the home with no direct parental supervision.[61] These changes are rooted in the changing nature of work and family life in contemporary society (as opposed to some kind of moral failing). These circumstances increase the probability that young people will engage in crime. To cite an earlier example, in the 1920s many people were alarmed that the advent of the automobile created the opportunity for young men and women to be alone together without direct parental supervision, with a resulting increase in premarital sexual behavior.

Applying the Theory Routine activity theory is particularly useful in explaining crime when it is integrated with other theories. If parental supervision represents an important informal social control, then family breakdown and single-parent households will involve less supervision and increase the probability of more involvement in crime. High rates of teenage unemployment will mean that more young people will have free time on their hands, and if unemployment is high in the neighborhood, they will have more association with other unemployed young people, including some who are already involved in crime.

The Limits of Current Theories

All of the theories discussed here attempt to explain the relationships among race, ethnicity, and crime in terms of social conditions. Hawkins argues that this approach represents the liberal political orientation that has dominated American sociology and criminology through most of this century.[62] He also believes that there are important limitations to this orientation. The liberal emphasis on social conditions arose out of a reaction to racist theories of biological determinism, which sought to explain high rates of crime among recent European immigrants and African Americans in terms of genetic inferiority. Herrnstein and Murray's controversial book, *The Bell Curve,* represents a recent version of this approach. The liberal emphasis on social conditions, however, tends to become a form of social determinism, as criminologists focus on the social pathologies of both minority communities and lower-class communities. Although consciously avoiding biologically based stereotypes, much of the research on social conditions has the unintended effect of perpetuating a different set of stereotypes about racial and ethnic minorities.

Hawkins suggests that if we seek a comprehensive explanation of the relationships among race, ethnicity, and crime, the most promising approach will be to combine the best insights from liberal criminology regarding social conditions, and conflict perspectives regarding both the administration of justice and intergroup relations.[63]

INEQUALITY AND SOCIAL REFORM

The most disturbing aspect of social inequality in America has been its persistence over 30 years despite a national effort to reduce or eliminate it. Peterson refers to this as the "poverty paradox": not just the persistence of poverty in the richest country in the world but its persistence in the face of a major attack on it.[64] The civil rights movement fought to eliminate racial discrimination, and several different government policies sought to create economic opportunity and eliminate poverty. In the 1960s, liberals adopted the War on Poverty and other Great Society programs; in the 1980s, conservative economic programs of reducing both taxes and government spending sought to stimulate economic growth and create job opportunities.

Not only has inequality persisted, but as Hacker, Orfield, and Ashkinaze argue, the gap between rich and poor and between whites and minorities has gotten worse in many respects. What happened? Did all the social and economic policies of the past generation completely fail?

There are four major explanations for the persistence of inequality, poverty, and the growth of the underclass.[65] Many liberals argue that it is the result of an inadequate welfare system. Social welfare programs in the United States are not nearly as comprehensive as those in other industrialized countries, lacking guaranteed health care, paid family leave, and comprehensive unemployment insurance. Other liberals argue that it is the result of the transformation of the national (and international) economy that has eliminated economic opportunities in the inner city and reduced earnings of many blue-collar jobs. Many conservatives argue that the persistence of poverty is the result of a "culture of poverty" that encourages attitudes and behavior patterns that keep people from rising out of poverty. Closely related to this view is the conservative argument that many government social and economic programs provide disincentives to work. These conservatives believe, for example, that the welfare system encourages people not to work and that the minimum wage causes employers to eliminate rather than create jobs.

The prominent African American social critic Cornell West argues that the traditional liberal–conservative debate on the relative importance of social structure versus individual character is unproductive. He points out that "structures and behavior are inseparable, that institutions and values go hand in hand."[66] In short, the problem of the persistence of inequality is extremely complex. The next section examines some of the major forces that have reshaped American life in the past generation and their impact on inequality.

The Impact of the Civil Rights Movement

The civil rights movement of the post–World War II years has been one of the most important events in U.S. history. The years between 1954 and 1965 witnessed nothing less than a revolution in American law, establishing equality as national policy.[67]

The legal assault on segregation, led by the NAACP, reached its apex in the landmark 1954 case of *Brown v. Board of Education*. The U.S. Supreme Court declared segregated public schools unconstitutional under the Fourteenth Amendment and invalidated the underlying doctrine of "separate but equal." Other cases invalidated other forms of race discrimination.[68] In 1967, for example, the Court declared unconstitutional a Virginia law barring interracial marriage.[69]

Legislation also attacked discrimination. The 1964 Civil Rights Act outlawed racial discrimination in employment, housing, public accommodations, and other areas of American life. In 1965, Congress passed the Voting Rights Act to eliminate racial discrimination in voting. President Lyndon Johnson issued Executive Order 11246 directing federal agencies to adopt affirmative action policies. Many states and municipalities, meanwhile, enacted their own civil rights statutes.

The following federal civil rights laws are particularly important:

1964 Civil Rights Act

1965 Voting Rights Act

1972 Equal Opportunity Act

1990 Americans with Disabilities Act

Impact on American Society The civil rights revolution had a profound impact on the American social structure. By outlawing overt or de jure racial discrimination, it "opened" society to a degree unprecedented in U.S. history. It also had a profound effect on the operations of every social institution, including the criminal justice system.

The most important changes occurred in the states of the South. The integration of the public schools between 1966 and 1973 was dramatic. In 1966, 80 percent of all minority students attended a school in which 90 percent or more of the students were also minorities. By 1973, the figure was only 25 percent. Public schools in the South went from being the most segregated to the most integrated in the entire country. At the same time, however, schools in the Northeast became more segregated between the 1960s and 1980s.[70]

The impact of the civil rights movement is also evident in electoral politics. African American voter registration, voter participation, and election of African American officials have dramatically increased. The change has been most profound in the South, where systematic disenfranchisement existed until the 1960s. In 1940, only 3.1 percent of voting-age African Americans were registered to vote; registration rose to 28.7 percent in 1960 and 66.9 percent in 1970.[71] The increase between 1960 and 1970 was clearly the result of the 1965 Voting Rights Act.

As a result of greater voter participation, the number of African American elected officials increased dramatically, from 33 nationwide in 1941 to 280 in 1965 and 8,896 in 1999. The number of African American members of the House of Representatives rose from 1 in 1940 to 4 in 1965, 20 in 1985, and 39 in 1999. The total number of Hispanic elected officials rose from 3,174 in 1985 to 5,205 in 2000. The number of Hispanic members of the House rose from 2 in 1941 to 17 in 1995.[72]

In 1999, there were 850 African American elected officials in Mississippi, including 8 elected sheriffs and 25 mayors. Throughout the Deep South, the Voting Rights Act has helped elect minorities as county commissioners, school board members, sheriffs, and officials in other important positions.[73] In Northern cities, African American mayors are common. In Cleveland in 1967, Carl Stokes was the first African American to be elected mayor of a major U.S. city. African Americans are serving or have recently served as mayors of New York, Chicago, Los Angeles, Philadelphia, Atlanta, New Orleans, Seattle, and many other cities.

The Civil Rights Movement and the Criminal Justice System The civil rights movement also transformed the criminal justice system. Again, the greatest changes occurred in the South. Under the old system of institutionalized segregation, the entire criminal justice system was an instrument for maintaining the subordination of African Americans. Disenfranchised as voters, African Americans did not serve on juries and had no voice in the election and appointment of officials who ran the criminal justice system.[74]

As a result, there were no African American police officers in the Deep South, and in the border states, the few African American officers who were hired were confined to policing the African American community and not allowed to arrest whites, no matter what their offense. Nor were there any African American sheriffs, prosecutors, judges, or correctional officials.

By the late 1970s, the South had become "integrated" into the national social structure. The distinctive racial caste system was abolished, and the problems facing Southern criminal justice agencies were essentially the same as those facing agencies in the North and West. However, problems persist with respect to police–community relations, but the situation in Atlanta or New Orleans is not fundamentally different from the situation in Boston or Seattle.[75] There is evidence of racial discrimination in criminal sentencing, but this problem has been found in states from all regions of the country.

The civil rights movement also had a profound effect on the criminal justice system outside the South. Racial discrimination was identified as a major problem in the justice system, and various reforms were undertaken to eliminate it. Police departments adopted police–community relations programs to improve relations with minority communities. The Supreme Court declared unconstitutional the practice of prosecutors or defense attorneys using peremptory challenges to exclude jurors because of race.[76] Racially segregated prisons were declared unconstitutional.[77]

African Americans and Hispanics, meanwhile, experienced increased employment in justice agencies and in a number of instances assumed positions of leadership. The percentage of all sworn police officers in city police departments who are African American increased from 3.6 percent in 1960 to 10 percent in 1997. Hispanics represented 4.1 percent of all municipal sworn officers in 1988 and 7 percent in 1997.[78]

The Attack on Economic Inequality

The economic policies of both liberal Democratic and conservative Republican presidents since the 1960s have attempted to stimulate the economy, create jobs, and eliminate poverty. The major liberal Democratic effort was the War on Poverty, begun in 1965 with the Economic Opportunity Act. The federal attack on poverty and inequality also included major programs related to health care, education, Social Security, food stamps, and other forms of government assistance. The major conservative Republican effort in the 1980s involved "Reaganomics" or "supply-side economics," which sought to stimulate the economy by lowering taxes and government spending. Conservatives also sought to reduce or eliminate many government assistance programs, arguing that they create disincentives to work.

The impact of these different measures is a matter of great controversy. Conservatives argue that the War on Poverty and other liberal policies of the 1960s not only failed to eliminate poverty but actually made things worse by impeding economic growth and removing the incentives for poor people to seek employment.[79] Liberals, meanwhile, argue that Reaganomics increased the gap between rich and poor, benefiting the wealthy and eliminating programs for the poor.

The data suggest that neither the economic policies of the liberals nor those of the conservatives have eliminated the structural inequalities in American society. As we have already suggested, the long-term trends have had contradictory effects. Some people have been able to take advantage of the new economic opportunities, whereas others have become even more deeply trapped in poverty—with the creation of a new underclass.

These trends have affected racial and ethnic minorities as well as whites. As Thernstrom and Thernstrom argue, many African Americans have been able to move into the middle class as a result of the elimination of job discrimination and the expansion of white-collar job opportunities.[80] These individuals are much better off than were their parents. For example, 75 percent of employed African American men in 1940 were either farm laborers or factory machine operators; 68 percent of the employed African American women were either domestic servants or farm laborers. By 1982, 20 percent of all employed African American men were in professional or managerial occupations, compared with only 6 percent in 1950.[81] Many Hispanic Americans have experienced similar social and economic progress.

Other members of minority communities, however, have been hit hard by the shrinking opportunities and are worse off than their parents were or even worse off than they themselves were 15 or 20 years earlier. These are the people who are trapped in the underclass. The National Research Council found a noticeable "contrast between blacks who have achieved middle-class status and those who have not."[82] As we discussed earlier, the conditions of poverty inhibit the transmission of human and social capital from one generation to another, thereby perpetuating poverty across generations.

The complex changes in the economy over the past three decades have directly impacted the racial and ethnic dimensions of crime and criminal justice. The persistence of severe inequality and the growth of the underclass have created conditions conducive to high rates of crime. The different theories of crime we discussed earlier—social strain theory, differential association theory, social disorganization theory, culture conflict theory, conflict theory, and routine activity theory—all would predict high rates of crime, given the changes in the economy that have occurred. Because racial and ethnic minorities have been disadvantaged by these economic trends, these theories of crime help explain the persistently high rates of crime among minorities.

It is important to note that the economic trends have coincided with the increased opportunities for minorities over the same period of time—at least for those able to take advantage of them. As we have already stated, some minorities have been able to move into the middle class. At the same time, the civil rights movement has resulted in greater political empowerment among minorities, as measured by voter participation, election of public officials, and employment in the criminal justice system.

Political empowerment by itself, however, is not sufficient to reduce criminal behavior. African Americans were elected as mayors in Cleveland, Detroit, Newark, Atlanta, Washington, D.C., and other cities at exactly the time when these cities faced the financial crisis resulting from the transformation of the economy. The financial crisis consisted of two parts: the tax base eroded as factories closed and middle-class people moved to the suburbs; at the same time, there were increased demands for public services in terms of welfare, police protection, and so forth.

In short, the civil rights movement has had a mixed effect on the inequalities in American social structure. It has opened the doors of opportunity for some racial and ethnic minorities. Often forgotten, these accomplishments are very substantial. The achievements of the civil rights movement, however, have not addressed the worsening economic conditions of the urban underclass.

CONCLUSION

The American social structure plays a major role in shaping the relationships among race, ethnicity, and crime. American society is characterized by deep inequalities related to race, ethnicity, and economics. There is persistent poverty, and minorities are disproportionately represented among the poor. In addition, economic changes have created a new phenomenon known as the urban underclass.

The major theories of crime explain the relationship between inequality and criminal behavior. In different ways, social strain, differential association, social disorganization, culture conflict, conflict, and routine activity theories all predict higher rates of criminal behavior among the poor and racial and ethnic minorities.

DISCUSSION QUESTIONS

1. Do you agree with the Kerner Commission's conclusion that we are "moving toward two societies, one black [and] one white"? Explain your answer.

2. Explain how residential discrimination contributes to crime.

3. What is meant by the concepts of human capital and social capital? How do they affect criminal behavior?

4. What has been the impact of the civil rights movement on crime and criminal justice?

5. Which theory of crime do you think best explains the prevalence of crime in the United States?

NOTES

1. Kerner Commission, *Report of the National Advisory Commission on Civil Disorders* (New York: Bantam Books, 1968), p. 1.

2. Andrew Hacker, *Two Nations: Black and White, Separate, Hostile, Unequal* (New York: Scribner's, 1992).

3. E. F. Borgatta and M. L. Borgatta, *Encyclopedia of Sociology,* Vol. 4 (New York: Macmillan, 1992), p. 1970.

4. Bureau of the Census, *Census of the Population, 2000.* Current estimates available at www.census.gov.

5. Gerald David Jaynes and Robin Williams Jr., eds., *A Common Destiny: Blacks and American Society* (Washington, DC: National Academy Press, 1989), p. 6.

6. Stephan Thernstrom and Abigail Thernstrom, *America in Black and White: One Nation, Indivisible* (New York: Simon & Schuster, 1997).

7. Bureau of the Census, *Household Net Worth and Asset Ownership: 1995* (Washington, DC: U.S. Government Printing Office, 2001).

8. Bureau of the Census, *Statistical Abstract of the United States, 2001* (Washington, DC: U.S. Government Printing Office, 2002), table 569.

9. Hacker, *Two Nations,* p. 105.

10. Bureau of the Census, *Statistical Abstract, 2001,* table 598.

11. Bureau of the Census, *Statistical Abstract, 2001,* p. 43, table 41.

12. Bureau of the Census, *Poverty in the United States: 2000* (Washington, DC: U.S. Government Printing Office, 2000).

13. Ibid.

14. Toby L. Parcel and Elizabeth G. Menaghan, *Parents' Jobs and Childrens'*

Lives (New York: Aldine deGruyter, 1994), p. 1.

15. "What Is Social Capital?" World Bank Group, PovertyNet. Available at www .worldbank.org/poverty.

16. Elliot Currie, *Confronting Crime* (New York: Pantheon Books, 1985), p. 243. The original study is by William McCord and Jose Sanchez, "The Treatment of Deviant Children: A Twenty-Five Year Follow-Up Study," *Crime and Delinquency* 29 (March 1983): 239–251.

17. Alejandro Portes and Patricia Landolt, "The Downside of Social Capital," *The American Prospect* 26 (May–June 1996): 18–21, 94.

18. Jaynes and Williams, *A Common Destiny,* p. 4.

19. Thernstrom and Thernstrom, *America in Black and White,* p. 17.

20. Ibid., p. 534.

21. Ibid., Chap. 7, "The Rise of the Black Middle Class," pp. 183–202.

22. U.S. Census Bureau, *Current Population Survey, March 1968–1999* (Washington, DC: U.S. Government Printing Office, 2000), table 2.

23. Bureau of Justice Statistics, *Criminal Victimization in the United States, 2000: Changes 1999–2000 with Trends 1993–2000* (Washington, DC: U.S. Government Printing Office, 2001).

24. William Julius Wilson, *The Truly Disadvantaged* (Chicago: University of Chicago Press, 1987); Christopher Jencks and Paul E. Peterson, eds., *The Urban Underclass* (Washington, DC: Brookings Institution, 1991); William Julius Wilson, ed., *The Ghetto Underclass* (Newbury Park, CA: Sage, 1993).

25. Hacker, *Two Nations,* p. 52.

26. Hacker, *Two Nations;* Andrew J. Win-nick, *Toward Two Societies: The Changing Distributions of Income and Wealth in the U.S. since 1960* (New York: Praeger, 1989); Gary Orfield and Carole Ashki-naze, *The Closing Door: Conservative Policy and Black Opportunity* (Chicago: University of Chicago Press, 1991).

27. Orfield and Ashkinaze, *The Closing Door,* p. xiii.

28. Jaynes and Williams, *A Common Destiny,* p. 321.

29. Robert D. Crutchfield, "Ethnicity, Labor Markets, and Crime," in *Ethnicity, Race, and Crime,* ed. D. F. Hawkins (Albany: State University Press of New York, 1995), p. 196.

30. Jaynes and Williams, *A Common Destiny,* pp. 78–79.

31. Bureau of Justice Statistics, *Criminal Victimization, 2000.*

32. Crutchfield, "Ethnicity, Labor Markets, and Crime," p. 196.

33. Wilson, *The Truly Disadvantaged,* pp. 137, 144; see also Bill E. Lawson, "Uplifting the Race: Middle-Class Blacks and the Truly Disadvantaged," in *The Underclass Question,* ed. Bill E. Lawson (Philadelphia: Temple University Press, 1992), pp. 90–113.

34. Wesley G. Skogan, *Disorder and Decline* (New York: Free Press, 1990), pp. 132–133.

35. James Q. Wilson and George Kelling, "Broken Windows: The Police and Neighborhood Safety," *Atlantic Monthly* 249 (March 1982): 29–38.

36. Wesley Skogan, "Fear of Crime and Neighborhood Change," in *Communities and Crime,* ed. A. Reiss and M. Tonry (Chicago: University of Chicago Press, 1986), pp. 215–220.

37. Wesley G. Skogan and Susan M. Hartnett, *Community Policing, Chicago Style* (New York: Oxford University Press, 1997).

38. The problem has been exaggerated in much of the news media coverage but is a serious problem nonetheless. See Dale Gieringer, "How Many Crack Babies?" in *Drug Prohibition and the Conscience of Nations,* ed. Arnold Trebach and Kevin B.

Zeese (Washington, DC: Drug Policy Foundation, 1990), pp. 71–75.

39. Peter Reuter, Robert MacCoun, and Patrick Murphy, *Money from Crime: A Study of the Economics of Drug Dealing in Washington, D.C.* (Santa Monica, CA: Rand Corporation, 1990).

40. Lawrence W. Sherman, "Police Crackdowns," in *Crime and Justice: An Annual Review of Research,* vol. 12, ed. Michael Tonry and Norval Morris (Chicago: University of Chicago Press, 1990).

41. Skogan, "Fear of Crime," p. 220.

42. Robert K. Merton, *Social Theory and Social Structure* (New York: Free Press, 1957).

43. Steven F. Messner and Richard Rosen-feld, *Crime and the American Dream,* 2d ed. (Belmont, CA: Wadsworth, 1997).

44. Michael Tonry and James Q. Wilson, eds., *Drugs and Crime, Crime and Justice: A Review of Research,* vol. 13 (Chicago: University of Chicago Press, 1990).

45. David N. Nurco, Timothy W. Kinlock, and Thomas E. Hanlon, "The Drugs–Crime Connection," in *Handbook of Drug Control in the United States,* ed. James A. Inciardi (New York: Greenwood, 1990), pp. 71–90.

46. Alejandro Portes and Patricia Landolt, "Unsolved Mysteries: The Tocqueville Files II," *The American Prospect* 7, 26 (May–June 1996): 10.

47. Edwin H. Sutherland, *Principles of Criminology,* 3d ed. (Philadelphia: Lippincott, 1939).

48. Crutchfield, "Ethnicity, Labor Markets, and Crime," p. 196.

49. W. I. Thomas and Florian Znaniecki, *The Polish Peasant in Europe and America* (Boston: Gorham, 1920); Clifford R. Shaw, Frederick M. Forbaugh, and Henry D. McKay, *Delinquency Areas* (Chicago: University of Chicago Press, 1929).

50. Thorsten Sellin, *Culture Conflict and Crime,* bulletin 41 (New York: Social Science Research Council, 1938).

51. Christopher Vecsey, ed., *Handbook of American Indian Religious Freedom* (New York: Crossroad, 1991).

52. James Davison Hunter, *Culture Wars: The Struggle to Define America* (New York: Basic Books, 1991).

53. Gustavus Myers, *History of Bigotry in the United States* (New York: Random House, 1943).

54. Joseph R. Gusfield, *Symbolic Crusade* (Urbana: University of Illinois Press, 1966).

55. Austin T. Turk, *Criminality and Legal Order* (Chicago: Rand McNally, 1969); Richard Quinney, *The Social Reality of Crime* (Boston: Little, Brown, 1970).

56. Allen E. Liska, ed., *Social Threat and Social Control* (Albany: State University Press of New York, 1992).

57. Darnell F. Hawkins, "Beyond Anomalies: Rethinking the Conflict Perspective on Race and Criminal Punishment," *Social Forces* 65 (March 1987): 719–745; Darnell F. Hawkins, "Ethnicity: The Forgotten Dimension of American Social Control," in *Inequality, Crime, and Social Control*, ed. George S. Bridges and Martha A. Myers (Boulder, CO: Westview, 1994), pp. 99–116.

58. C. Vann Woodward, *The Strange Career of Jim Crow*, 3d ed., rev. (New York: Oxford University Press, 1974).

59. Gunnar Myrdal, *An American Dilemma* (New York: Harper & Brothers, 1944).

60. Marcus Felson, *Crime and Everyday Life* (Thousand Oaks, CA: Pine Forge Press, 1994), p. xi.

61. Ibid., p. 104.

62. Darnell F. Hawkins, "Ethnicity, Race, and Crime: A Review of Selected Studies," in *Ethnicity, Race, and Crime*, pp. 31, 39–41.

63. Ibid.

64. Paul E. Peterson, "The Urban Underclass and the Poverty Paradox," in *The Urban Underclass*, pp. 3–27.

65. Summarized in Peterson, "The Urban Underclass and the Poverty Paradox," in *The Urban Underclass*, pp. 9–16.

66. Cornell West, *Race Matters* (Boston: Beacon, 1993), p. 12.

67. Donald G. Nieman, *Promises to Keep: African Americans and the Constitutional Order, 1776 to the Present* (New York: Oxford University Press, 1991), chap. 6, "The Civil Rights Movement and American Law, 1950–1969."

68. Richard Kluger, *Simple Justice* (New York: Vintage Books, 1977).

69. *Loving v. Virginia*, 388 U.S. 1 (1967).

70. Jaynes and Williams, *A Common Destiny*, pp. 76–77.

71. Ibid., p. 233.

72. Bureau of the Census, *Statistical Abstract, 2001,* tables 390, 399, 400.

73. Bureau of the Census, *Statistical Abstract, 2001,* p. 250, table 399.

74. Myrdal, *American Dilemma,* especially chap. 28, "The Police and Other Public Contacts."

75. Samuel Walker, "A Strange Atmosphere of Consistent Illegality: Myrdal on 'The Police and Other Public Contacts,'" in *An American Dilemma Revisited: Race Relations in a Changing World,* ed. Obie Clayton Jr. (New York: Russell Sage Foundation, 1996), pp. 226–246.

76. *Batson v. Kentucky,* 476 U.S. 79 (1986).

77. *Washington v. Lee,* 390 U.S. 266 (1968).

78. Bureau of Justice Statistics, *Law Enforcement Management and Administrative Statistics, 1997* (Washington, DC: U.S. Government Printing Office, 1999), p. ix; Samuel Walker and Charles M. Katz, *The Police in America: An Introduction,* 4th ed. (New York: McGraw-Hill, 2002), p. 389.

79. Charles Murray, *Losing Ground: American Social Policy, 1950–1980* (New York: Basic Books, 1984).

80. Thernstrom and Thernstrom, *America in Black and White*.

81. Jaynes and Williams, *A Common Destiny,* p. 312.

82. Ibid., p. 4.

4

Justice on the Street?

The Police and Racial and Ethnic Minorities

UNEQUAL JUSTICE?

Cincinnati has been torn by conflict between the police and the African American community: 15 African American men have been shot and killed by the police in recent years. A fatal shooting in April 2001 provoked a riot that resulted in significant property damage and a citywide curfew. At the same time, the police department was the subject of a lawsuit alleging racial profiling and investigated by the Civil Rights Division of the U.S. Justice Department. Exactly a year later, the city entered into a consent decree with the Justice Department, the American Civil Liberties Union (ACLU), and the local Black United Front that required sweeping reforms in the police department related to use of force by police officers, control of the canine unit, citizen complaints, and other issues.[1]

A survey of Cincinnati residents had previously found that nearly half (46.6 percent) of all African Americans said they had been personally "hassled" by the police, compared with only 9.6 percent of all whites. Hassled was defined as being "stopped or watched closely by a police officer, even when you had done nothing wrong."[2]

The events in Cincinnati, which resembled those in the turbulent 1960s, represent perhaps the worst single case of police–community relations problems. Nonetheless, similar tensions over shootings and excessive use of force by police are found in other cities as well.

The most controversial recent issue is racial profiling. Civil rights groups allege that police target African American drivers for traffic stops on the basis of

Percentage African American, 2000

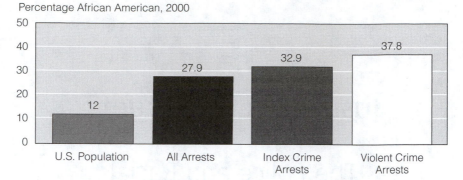

FIGURE 4.1 Disparities in Arrest

SOURCE: Federal Bureau of Investigation, Crime in the United States, 2000 (Washington, DC: U.S. GPO, 2001).

their race rather than for actual violations of the law. Robert Wilkins, an African American attorney, was stopped by the Maryland state police on Interstate 95 and subjected to a prolonged detention and illegal search. Wilkins's suit against the state police included observational data indicating that African Americans did not speed on I-95 at a higher rate than that of white drivers but constituted 73 percent of all drivers stopped for possible violations. Even worse, they represented 81 percent of all drivers whose cars were searched after being stopped.[3]

The issue of racial profiling in traffic stops is only part of a larger pattern of racial disparities in the criminal justice system. Racial and ethnic minorities are arrested, stopped and questioned, and shot and killed by the police out of proportion to their representation in the population. African Americans represent only 12 percent of the population but 27.9 percent of all arrests, 32.9 percent of all Index crime arrests, and 37.8 percent of all violent crime arrests (see Figure 4.1). They are shot and killed by police 3 times as often as whites, down from a ratio of 7:1 in the early 1970s.[4] Hispanic communities are often underserved by the police, as many people are reluctant to call the police for routine problems out of fear they will be subject to immigration law enforcement. Finally, Native American reservations face seriously inadequate law enforcement agencies.

A report by the Police Executive Research Forum (PERF) places the issue of racial profiling in a broader context. Racial bias does not occur just in traffic enforcement but can occur in any and all phases of law enforcement—traffic stops, arrests, failure to provide service, and so forth—and it is important to examine the full range of police activities to identify possible patterns of bias.[5]

Conflicting Evidence

Despite the evidence of disparate treatment of people of color by the police, a 2001 public opinion survey found that the vast majority of African Americans have "a great deal" (38 percent) or "some" (43 percent) confidence in the police. Only 19 percent expressed "very little" confidence, compared with 10 percent of whites.[6] These findings are consistent with other public opinion polls over the past 35 years. Clearly, there is much controversy and conflicting evidence about the interactions between the police and racial and ethnic minorities.

GOALS OF THE CHAPTER

This chapter explores the complex issues in the relationship between the police and racial and ethnic minority communities[7] and helps sort through the sometimes conflicting evidence on race, ethnicity, and criminal justice. The first section outlines a contextual approach that helps resolve the apparent contradictions in the available evidence. The second section examines public opinion about the police, comparing the attitudes of whites, African Americans, and Hispanics (unfortunately, there is little evidence on other racial and ethnic groups). The third section reviews the evidence on police behavior, beginning with the most serious action, use of deadly force, and proceeding through the less serious police activities. The fourth section deals with citizen complaints against the police, reviewing the evidence on the extent of misconduct and the ways police departments handle citizen complaints. The final section examines police employment practices. Particular attention is given to the law of employment discrimination and the historic problem of discrimination against racial and ethnic minorities.

A CONTEXTUAL APPROACH

This chapter adopts a contextual approach to help understand the complex and at times contradictory evidence related to police and racial and ethnic minorities. This approach disaggregates the general subject into distinct components.[8] There are four major contexts that affect relations between the police and minorities (see Table 4.1).

First, as noted in Chapter 1, we cannot talk about "minorities," or even "racial and ethnic minorities" as a homogeneous category. African Americans, Hispanics, Native Americans, and Asian Americans all have somewhat different experiences with the police. In 1999, the Bureau of Justice Statistics (BJS) conducted a national survey of citizen contacts with the police. Based on interviews with 80,000 citizens, this BJS police–citizen contact survey is the most systematic study of the subject. It found, for example, that Hispanics are far less likely to call the police than are whites or African Americans.[9] Nielsen argues that the Native American experience with the criminal justice system "cannot be understood without recognizing that it is just one of many interrelated issues that face Native peoples today," including "political power, land, economic development, [and] individual despair."[10]

Second, it is important to distinguish between different police departments. Some have much worse relations with minority communities than others. A 2001 survey by the *Washington Post* found that the rate of fatal shootings by po-

Table 4.1 Contexts of Policing

Different racial and ethnic groups
  African American
  Asian American
  Hispanic American
  Native American
  Non-Hispanic White Americans
Different police departments
  More professional departments
  Less professional departments
Different groups within each racial and ethnic group
  Upper class
  Middle class
  Lower class
Different police department units and tactics
  Patrol unit
    Aggressive patrol (e.g., many field stops)
    Community-oriented patrol (e.g., community input)
  Traffic unit
    Aggressive traffic enforcement
    Nonaggressive traffic enforcement
  Gang unit
    Enforcement oriented
    Prevention oriented

lice is 7 or 8 times higher in some cities than in others.[11] The 2001 riot in Cincinnati suggests that relations with the African American community in that city are much worse than in cities of similar size and diversity. The Boston Police Department, however, has been credited with developing improved relations with racial and ethnic minority communities, in particular by working through the Boston Ten Point Coalition, a group of community religious institutions.[12]

Third, it is important to recognize that there are different groups within racial and ethnic minority communities. Ronald Weitzer's research in Washington, D.C., found significant differences in perceptions of the police by low-income and middle-class African Americans in the city. Low-income and middle-class African Americans believe that race makes a difference in how police treat individuals, whereas middle-class respondents had a much more favorable view of police–community relations in their own neighborhood.[13] Not all African Americans and Hispanics are poor. All the public opinion surveys indicate that young men have a very different—and far more negative—experience with the police than do either adults or young women (discussed later).

Fourth, different police units and tactics have very different impacts on communities. Aggressive patrol tactics with frequent stops of citizens, for example, create resentment among young men. Drug enforcement efforts are disproportionately directed at minority communities. In some cities, the community policing officers may have good relations with residents, whereas the narcotics and gang unit members may have hostile relations.

In short, we cannot generalize about either racial or ethnic groups or the police. We have to focus on particular kinds of police actions and their effects on particular groups of people in society.

A LONG HISTORY OF CONFLICT

Conflict between the police and racial and ethnic minorities is nothing new. There have been three major eras of riots related to police abuse: 1917–1919, 1943, and 1964–1968. The Cincinnati riots of 2001 were only the latest chapter in a long history of conflict and violence.[14] The background to all these riots is depressingly similar. Noted African American psychologist Kenneth Clark told the Kerner Commission in 1967 that reading the reports of the earlier riots was like watching the same movie "re-shown over and over again, the same analysis, the same recommendations, and the same inaction."[15]

Alfredo Mirandé defines the long history of conflict between Hispanics and the police in terms of "gringo justice." Taking a broad historical and political perspective, he sees a fundamental "clash between conflicting and competing cultures, world views, and economic, political and judicial systems."[16] Conflict with the police is a product of the political and economic subordination of Hispanics, their concentration in distinct neighborhoods or barrios, and stereotyping of them as criminals.

The history of relations between the police and Hispanics is also punctuated by periodic riots, often provoked by police abuse. The so-called Zoot Suit Riot in Los Angeles in 1943 involved attacks on Hispanic men by white Navy personnel on shore leave and by police.[17] Major conflicts between the police and the Los Angeles Hispanic community also erupted in 1970 and 1971. More Hispanics than African Americans were arrested in the 1992 Los Angeles riots. A Rand report cited testimony that "both Latinos and blacks in Los Angeles feel powerless to change their position and have lost faith in the leaders and institutions of the community."[18]

THE POLICE AND
A CHANGING AMERICA

The changing face of the United States presents a special challenge for the police. The composition of the U.S. population is changing dramatically as a result of immigration. Between 1980 and 2000, the Hispanic population increased from 6.4 percent of the U.S. population to 11.8 percent. These changes create potential conflict related to race, ethnicity, cultural values, lifestyles, and political power. Many new American residents do not speak English and are not familiar with U.S. laws and police practices. Historically, the police have often aggravated conflicts with new arrivals and powerless people. The police have represented the established power structure, resisted change, and reflected the prejudices of the majority community.

A PERF report argues that, contrary to past practice, the police can "help prevent open conflict, mitigate intergroup tensions within a community and build meaningful partnerships among the diverse populace of modern cities."[19] The police can accomplish this by openly addressing issues related to racial and ethnic conflict and, through community policing, actively establishing positive relations among all the diverse groups in the community.

One starting point is for the police to develop language skills that enable them to communicate effectively with all segments of the community. One private firm (Network Omni Translation [www.networkomni.com]) provides translation services in a number of languages under contract with law enforcement agencies and other organizations. The Minneapolis Civilian Police Review Authority, which handles complaints against the police, publishes brochures explaining the complaint process in seven languages (English, Spanish, Lakota, Ojibway, Vietnamese, Cambodian, and Hmong).[20]

PUBLIC ATTITUDES ABOUT THE POLICE

Public attitudes about the police place the attitudes of people of color in context. Race and ethnicity are consistently the most important factors in shaping attitudes about the police. Yet, as Table 4.2 indicates, public attitudes are surprising. The vast majority of all Americans express confidence in the police. Among white Americans, 88 percent express either a "great deal" or "some" confidence, and only 10 percent express "very little" confidence. By comparison, nearly twice as many African Americans (19 percent) express "very little" confidence. In virtually every survey, Hispanic attitudes fall in between white and African American attitudes.[21]

At the same time, African Americans consistently report that they believe that the police treat African Americans unfairly or have experienced unfair treatment themselves. In a 2001 *Washington Post* survey, 37 percent said they had been "unfairly stopped by police," compared with only 4 percent of whites.[22] In another poll, over half of African Americans (58 percent) felt that the police in their community did not treat all races fairly, compared with only 20 percent of whites and 27 percent of Hispanics.[23]

The public opinion data contradict the popular image of total hostility between the police and minorities. The vast majority of African Americans and Hispanics are similar to most whites in their experience and attitudes: they are law-abiding people who rarely have contact with the police, and their major complaint is a lack of adequate police protection. When the Justice Department asked people to suggest improvements in policing, both whites and African Americans mainly indicated that they wanted more police protection.[24] Weitzer found that middle-class African Americans in Washington, D.C., had a

Table 4.2 Reported Confidence in the Police by Demographic Characteristics, United States, 2001

QUESTION: "I am going to read you a list of institutions in American society. Please tell me how much confidence you, yourself, have in each one—a great deal, quite a lot, some, or very little: the police?"

	Great Deal/ Quite a Lot	Some	Very Little	None
National	57%	31%	11%	1%
Sex				
Male	56	30	11	2
Female	58	31	11	
Race				
White	59	29	10	1
Black	38	43	19	0
Nonwhite	44	39	16	1
Age				
18 to 29 years	45	27	25	1
30 to 49 years	59	32	8	1
50 to 64 years	60	31	7	2
50 years and older	60	31	8	1
65 years and older	60	31	9	0

SOURCE: Bureau of Justice Statistics, *Source book as Criminal Justice Statistics, 2000* (Washington, DC: U.S. Government Printing Office, 2000), p. 109.

much more favorable view of relations with the police in their neighborhood than did poor African Americans. Their attitudes on this point, in fact, were much closer to those of white, middle-class Washington residents than of poor African Americans.[25]

Surveys over the past 30 years have found that public attitudes toward the police have been remarkably stable. In 1967, the President's Crime Commission reported that only 16 percent of nonwhites rated the police as "poor," and a 1977 survey found that only 19 percent of African Americans rated their police as "poor," compared with 9 percent of whites. A survey of 500 Hispanic residents of Texas found that only 15 percent rated their local police as "poor."[26]

Highly publicized controversial incidents have a short-term effect on public attitudes. In the immediate aftermath of the Rodney King beating, the percentage of white Los Angeles residents who said they "approve" of the Los Angeles police fell from more than 70 percent to 41 percent. The approval ratings by African Americans and Hispanics in the city, which were low to begin with, also fell. The approval ratings of all groups eventually returned to their previous levels, but white attitudes did so much more quickly than those of minority groups.

Age is the second most important factor in shaping attitudes toward the police. Young people, regardless of race, consistently have a more negative view of the police than do middle-aged and elderly people. This is not surprising. Young men are more likely to be out on the street, have contact with the police, and engage in illegal activity. At the same time, lower-income people have more negative attitudes toward the police than do upper-income people.

Hostile relations between the police and young, low-income men are partly a result of conflict over lifestyles. Werthman and Piliavin found that juvenile gang members in the early 1960s regarded their street corner hangouts as "a sort of 'home' or 'private place.'" They sought to maintain control over their space, particularly by keeping out rival gang members. Their standards of behavior for their space were different from what adults, especially middle-class adults, and the police considered appropriate for a public area.[27]

A contextual approach, in short, indicates that the heart of the conflict between police and racial and ethnic minorities involves young people, particularly young men, and especially those in low-income neighborhoods. The experiences of these individuals are not the same as those of older, middle-class members of minority neighborhoods.

POLICING RACIAL AND ETHNIC MINORITY COMMUNITIES

As already noted, it is not appropriate to talk about "racial and ethnic minorities" as a homogeneous group. These individuals have different types of experiences with the police.

The African American Community

Historically, the primary focus of police–community relations problems has involved the African American community. Thirty years ago, Bayley and Mendelsohn observed, "the police seem to play a role in the life of minority people out of all proportion to the role they play in the lives of the dominant white majority."[28] This is still true today and is the result of differences in income level, reported crime, and calls for police service.

African Americans are more likely than other Americans to be the victims of crime. The National Crime Victimization Survey (NCVS) reports that in 2000, the robbery rate for African Americans was more than twice that of whites (7.2 per 1,000 versus 2.7 per 1,000). African Americans also report crimes to the police at a slightly higher rate than whites do.[29] As previously noted, African Americans are shot and killed by the police at a much higher rate than the rate for whites and are more likely to be arrested than whites. Because of these factors, African American neighborhoods generally receive higher levels of police patrol than do white neighborhoods.

African Americans have much less favorable attitudes toward the police than does any other group, and they report higher levels of use of force against them (discussed later). A 1997 *New York Times* report found that some African American parents made special efforts to teach their children to be very respectful when confronted by a police officer, out of fear that their children (and particularly their sons) might be beaten or shot if they displayed any disrespect.[30]

The Hispanic Community

A report to the U.S. Justice Department concluded that "Latinos may have unique experiences with police which shape attitudes toward law enforcement officials."[31] The Hispanic community also experiences higher rates of crime than does the non-Hispanic white community. The robbery rate is about 13 percent higher for Hispanics than for non-Hispanics. Hispanics, however, are slightly less likely to report crimes than non-Hispanics (39 percent versus 41.8 percent for violent crimes).

The BJS survey of police–citizen contacts found that Hispanics initiate contact with the police *less* frequently (167 per 1,000 people) than either whites 221 per 1,000) or African Americans (189 per 1,000) and are also *less* likely to be stopped by the police for a traffic violation. One study found that the police did not stop many Hispanic drivers because officers decided that they probably would not be able to communicate with Spanish-speaking drivers, and therefore, nothing would result from the stop.[32]

Several factors help explain these differences in Hispanic–police contacts. Hispanics who do not speak English have difficulty communicating with the police and may not call. Some Hispanics fear that calling the police will expose members of their community to investigation regarding immigration status. Carter found that the Hispanic community's sense of family often regards intervention by an "outsider" (such as a police officer) as a threat to the family's integrity and, in the case of an arrest, as an attack on the father's authority.[33] (Other studies of Hispanic families, however, have found considerable variations that suggest that Carter employed inappropriate stereotypes.)

A series of focus groups in a Midwestern city found significant differences between how Hispanic, African American, and white residents would respond to an incident of police misconduct. Members of the predominantly Spanish-speaking group were far more fearful of the police, far less knowledgeable about the U.S. legal system, and less likely to file a complaint than either whites or African Americans. Much of the fear of the police was related to concern about possible immigration problems.[34]

The Native American Community

Native Americans occupy a unique legal status in the United States, which has an important effect on their relations with the police. Native American tribes are recognized as semisovereign nations with broad (although not complete) powers of self-government within the boundaries of the United States. There are over 500 federally recognized Native American tribes and about 330 federally recognized reservations, with approximately 200 have separate law enforcement agencies.[35]

This results in extremely complex problems related to the jurisdiction of tribal police agencies, county sheriff or city police departments, and federal authorities for particular crimes. In any specific case, jurisdiction depends on where the crime was committed, who committed the crime, and what crime was committed. Tribal police have jurisdiction only over crimes committed on

Indian lands by Native Americans. A crime committed by any other person on a reservation is the responsibility of the county sheriff. In addition, tribal authorities have jurisdiction only over less serious crimes. Murder and robbery, for example, are the responsibility of federal authorities.[36]

Native American policing is also complex because there are five different types of tribal law enforcement agencies: (1) Those operated and funded by the federal Bureau of Indian Affairs (BIA); (2) those federally funded but operated by the tribe under an agreement with the BIA (called PL 96-638 agencies); (3) those operated and funded by the tribes themselves; (4) those operated by tribes under the 1994 Indian Self-Determination Act; and (5) those operated by state and local governments under Public Law 280.[37]

A 2001 report to the National Institute of Justice (NIJ) found serious problems with policing on Indian lands. Not only has there been rising crime on reservations, but tribal police departments suffer from inadequate budgets and equipment, poor management, high levels of personnel turnover, and considerable political influence. Most tribal agencies are very small (10 or fewer sworn officers), and only half have a 911 emergency telephone service. About half (42.6 percent) cross-deputize their officers with the local county sheriff's department, meaning that their officers have law enforcement powers off the reservation. About two-thirds of all sworn officers employed by tribal departments are themselves Native Americans, and about 56 percent are members of the tribe they serve.

The NIJ report concludes that most of these problems are the legacy of federal Indian policy that has historically served the interests of the federal government rather than the goal of tribal autonomy and self-governance.

The Middle Eastern Community

The terrorist attack on the United States on September 11, 2001, raised fears of discrimination against Arab Americans on the basis of national origin, religion, or immigration status. The American-Arab Anti-Discrimination Committee (www.adc.org) reports increased incidents of discrimination following 9/11. There are about 4 million Arab Americans in the United States, who represent 2 percent of the population.

There are several policing issues that concern the Arab American community. The first is racial profiling, whereby the police, particularly federal authorities, identify individuals as suspects solely on the basis of their national origin. In the wake of 9/11, there were a number of incidents involving discrimination against Arab Americans attempting to fly on airlines. In some instances, the acts of discrimination were committed by private individuals or companies. A second issue involves hate crimes—people attack Arab Americans on the basis of their national origin or religion. Finally, there are issues related to the federal war on terrorism. Soon after 9/11, the FBI set out to interview 5,000 Arab American men in the United States, not as criminal suspects but simply as potential sources of information about possible terrorists. Many Arab Americans regarded this as intimidating and a form of racial profiling. The special issue of enforcing federal immigration laws—which affects Hispanics as well as Arab Americans—is discussed in the next section.

Special Issue: Enforcing Federal Immigration Laws

The enforcement of immigration laws represents a special problem for the Hispanic community—as well as for Asian, Middle Eastern, and African communities. Traditionally, local police have not enforced immigration laws because the laws are federal. The Immigration and Naturalization Service (INS) has been responsible for enforcement.

In the aftermath of 9/11, the federal government has proposed authorizing local law enforcement to enforce federal immigration laws. The terrorists who destroyed the World Trade Center and damaged the Pentagon were foreign nationals, some of whom were in the United States illegally. The Justice Department argues that local police involvement in immigration law enforcement would greatly increase the possibility of catching potential terrorists.

Many local police officials have objected to this new role. In the fall of 2001, the Portland, Oregon, police department and a few others refused to cooperate with the FBI in its effort to interview 5,000 men of Middle Eastern origin. The California Police Chiefs Association sent a letter to Attorney General Ashcroft opposing local police enforcement of immigration laws.[38] The Association and other local police officials fear that enforcing immigration laws will create conflict with immigrant communities with whom they want to develop good relations. As we have seen, Hispanics call the police at a lower rate than do other groups, in part because of fears of potential problems with immigration laws.[39]

POLICE USE OF DEADLY FORCE

The fatal shooting of an African American man by the Cincinnati police sparked the riots in that city in April 2001. Historically, police shootings have been the most explosive issue in police–community relations. In the 1970s, the police fatally shot eight African Americans for every one white person. By 1998, the ratio had been reduced to 4:1.[40] James Fyfe, one of the leading experts on the subject, asked whether the police have "two trigger fingers," one for whites and one for African Americans and Hispanics.[41]

On October 3, 1974, two Memphis police officers shot and killed Edward Garner, a 15-year-old African American. Garner was 5'4" tall, weighed 110 pounds, and was shot in the back of the head while fleeing with a stolen purse containing $10. The Memphis officers acted under the old *fleeing felon rule*, which allowed a police officer to shoot to kill, for the purpose of arrest, any fleeing suspected felon. The rule gave police officers very broad discretion, allowing them to shoot, for example, a juvenile suspected of stealing a bicycle worth only $50. Edward Garner's parents sued, and in 1985 the Supreme Court

Table 4.3 Citizens Shot and Killed, Memphis

	1969–1974		1985–1989	
	White	African American	White	African American
Armed & assaultive	5	7	6	7
Unarmed & assaultive	2	6	1	5
Unarmed & not assaultive	1	13	0	0
Totals, by race	8	26	7	12
Total		34		19

SOURCE: Adapted from Jerry R. Sparger and David J. Glacopassi, "Memphis Revisited: A Reexamination of Police Shootings after the Garner Decision," *Justice Quarterly* 9 (June 1992): 211–225.

declared the fleeing felon rule unconstitutional in *Tennessee v. Garner*. The Court ruled that the fleeing felon rule violated the Fourth Amendment protection against unreasonable searches and seizures, holding that shooting a person was a seizure.[42]

Police officers, of course, did not shoot every suspected fleeing felon. The data, however, suggest that they were much more likely to shoot African Americans than whites. Between 1969 and 1974, for example, police officers in Memphis shot and killed 13 African Americans in the "unarmed and not assaultive" category, but only one white person (see Table 4.3). In fact, half of all the African Americans shot were in that category.[43] The permissive fleeing felon rule allowed officers to act on the basis of prejudices and stereotypes. White officers were more likely to feel threatened by African American suspects than by white suspects in similar situations. Because the typical shooting incident occurs at night, in circumstances in which the officer has to make a split-second decision, it is often not clear whether the suspect has a weapon.

There are few studies of the shootings of Hispanics and none of Native Americans or Asian Americans. (The BJS report on deadly force trends from 1976 to 1991 does not include data on Hispanics.) Geller and Karales found that between 1974 and 1978, Hispanics were about twice as likely to be shot and killed by the Chicago police as whites, but only half as likely to be shot as African Americans.[44] One of the problems with studying this issue—as discussed in Chapter 1—is that criminal justice agencies have traditionally classified Hispanic's as "white," not distinguishing between Hispanics and non-Hispanic whites.

There are substantial differences among police departments regarding the number and rate of citizens shot and killed. Controlling for violent crime (an extremely relevant variable on this issue), Washington, D.C., police shot and killed almost 7 times as many citizens as did Boston police officers between 1990 and 2000 (6.35 per 10,000 violent crimes versus 0.91 per 10,000).[45] These variations highlight the importance of the contextual approach to police–community relations and the importance of differences in departmental policies and the enforcement of those policies and discipline of officers.

Disparity versus Discrimination in Police Shootings

The data on persons shot and killed by the police raises the question that pervades all studies of race, ethnicity, and criminal justice: When does evidence of a disparity indicate discrimination? The data clearly indicate a racial disparity in persons shot and killed by the police. Over the last 20 years, the ratio has been narrowed from 8:1 to 4:1.[46] Does the 4:1 ratio represent discrimination, or does it reflect a disparity that can be explained by factors other than race?

Geller and Karales addressed this question by controlling for the "at-risk" status of persons shot and killed by the Chicago police in the 1970s. People are not equally at risk of being shot by the police. Virtually all shooting victims are men rather than women; young men are also disproportionately represented compared with older men. Young men are more likely to engage in the behavior that places them at risk—namely, use of a weapon in street crime. Geller and Karales found when they controlled for at-risk status, defined in terms of arrest for "forcible felonies" (murder, rape, armed and strong-arm robbery, aggravated battery, aggravated assault, and burglary), the racial disparity disappeared. In fact, whites were shot and killed at a slightly higher rate.[47]

Controlling Police Shootings

One clear point emerges from the long-term data on police shootings: department policies can reduce the number of persons shot and killed by the police and in the process narrow the racial disparity. In the 1970s, in response to protests by civil rights groups, police departments began to adopt the *defense of life* rule, limiting shootings to situations that pose a threat to the life of the officer or some other person. Many departments also prohibit warning shots, shots to wound, and shots at or from moving vehicles. Officers are now required to fill out a report any time they discharge their weapon. These reports are then subject to an automatic review by supervisors.

Fyfe found that the defense of life rule reduced firearms discharges in New York City by almost 30 percent in just a few years. Across the country, the number of persons shot and killed by police declined from a peak of 559 in 1975 to 300 in 1987. Follow-up data on Memphis illustrate that the defense of life rule reduced the racial disparity in shootings. As Table 4.2 indicates, between 1985 and 1989, no people of either race were shot and killed in the fleeing felon category. The overall number of persons shot and killed fell significantly, and the racial disparity was cut in half.[48] The defense of life rule may not have changed police officer attitudes, but it did alter their behavior, curbing the influence of racial prejudice. Similar policies in departments across the country had the same effect. Nationally, the racial disparity between African Americans and whites declined from 8:1 in the 1970s to 4:1 by 1998.[49]

"POLICE BRUTALITY":
POLICE USE OF PHYSICAL FORCE

Q: Did you beat people up who you arrested?

A: No. We'd just beat people in general. If they're on the street, hanging around drug locations . . . .

Q: Why?

A: To show who was in charge.[50]

This exchange between the Mollen Commission and a corrupt New York City police officer in the mid-1990s dramatized the unrestrained character of police brutality in poor, high-crime neighborhoods in New York City. Police brutality has been a historic problem with U.S. police. In 1931, the Wickersham Commission reported that the "third degree," the "inflicting of pain, physical or mental, to extract confessions or statements is extensively practiced."[51] The 1991 Rodney King beating is probably the most notorious example of police use of excessive physical force. A 1998 report by Human Rights Watch concluded, "Race continues to play a central role in police brutality in the United States."[52]

The Mollen Commission defined brutality as the "threat of physical harm or the actual infliction of physical injury or pain."[53] Many people use an even broader definition. The President's Crime Commission found that 70.3 percent of African Americans included rudeness as police brutality, compared with 54.6 percent of whites.[54] The New York City Civilian Complaint Investigative Bureau classifies 16 specific police officer actions in the "force" category, including firing a gun, pointing a gun, using pepper spray, and using a police radio or flashlight as a club.[55]

The term *police brutality* is a political slogan with no precise meaning. We use the term *excessive force,* defined as any physical force that is more than reasonably necessary to accomplish a lawful police purpose. It is important to distinguish between *force* and *excessive force.* A police officer is legally justified in using force to protect himself or herself from physical attack or to subdue a suspect who is resisting arrest. Any amount of force in excess of that is improper.

There is much disagreement over the prevalence of police use of excessive force.[56] Critics of the police argue that it is a routine, nightly occurrence, whereas others believe that it is a rare event. The most systematic study of police use of force, the 1999 BJS police–citizen contact survey, found that police officers used force or threatened to use force in about 1 percent (0.96 percent) of all encounters with citizens.[57] This represents an estimated total of about

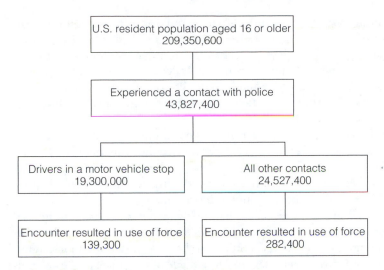

FIGURE 4.2 Police Use of Force

SOURCE: Bureau of Justice Statistics, *Contacts between Police and the Public: Findings from the 1999 National Survey* (Washington, DC: U.S. Government Printing Office, 2001), p. 1.

421,000 force incidents each year across the country (see Figure 4.2). The BJS report did not distinguish between justified and unjustified (or excessive) use of force. Observational studies, however, have estimated that about one-third of all uses of force are excessive or unjustified, which would translate into about 140,000 excessive force incidents per year nationally.[58]

There are substantial racial and ethnic disparities in police use of force, according to the BJS report. African Americans are nearly 3 times as likely to experience force or threatened force (2.06 percent of all encounters) than whites (0.72 percent). Hispanics were more likely than whites but less likely than African Americans to experience police use of force (1.85 percent). The BJS findings are roughly consistent with previous studies of use of force (which are systematically reviewed by Adams in *And Justice for All*).[59]

Some critics of the police have trouble believing the estimate that police use force only 1 percent of the time, arguing that use of force—and excessive force—is far more common. A contextual approach puts a different perspective on the 1 percent estimate for use of force and the one-third of 1 percent estimate for excessive force. Most contacts between citizens and the police involve situations of routine order maintenance and service. Certain situations, however, tend to be problematic. Studies consistently find that police use force 4 or 5 times more often against persons being arrested and are very likely to use force against people who challenge their authority. Some people believe that the police overreact to even legitimate questions from citizens. They refer to this police practice as "contempt of cop."[60] Reiss found that almost half of the victims of excessive force had either defied the officer's authority (39 percent of all cases) or resisted arrest (9 percent of all cases). Additionally, Black found that African Americans were more likely to be disrespectful than were whites after controlling for all other variables.[61] Police officers are also more likely to use force against people whose status or condition offends their moral beliefs, especially chronic alcoholics and homosexuals. Police officers apparently feel freer to use excessive force because they believe that these people are not likely to file a complaint about the incident.

Reiss concluded that race per se is not a determining factor in the use of excessive force: "Class rather than race determines police misconduct."[62] The typical victim of excessive force is a lower-class male, regardless of race. Other observers, however, disagree with this interpretation and see a systematic pattern of police use of force against young minority men.

The race or ethnicity of the officer has little apparent influence on the use of physical force. The majority of excessive force incidents are intraracial—that is, citizens are mistreated by a police officer of the same racial or ethnic group. In New York City, whites represented 68 percent of all officers in 2000 and 68 percent of all officers receiving citizen complaints; African Americans represented 14 percent of all officers and 12 percent of those receiving complaints; Hispanics represented 17 percent of all officers and 18 percent of those receiving complaints.[63] Worden found a very complex pattern of use of force, with African American officers somewhat more likely than white officers to use reasonable levels of force but less likely to use improper force.[64]

At the same time, however, police officers of different races have very different perceptions of how the police in general use force and treat people of color and the poor. A Police Foundation survey of officers nationwide found that 57 percent of African American officers agreed or strongly agreed with the statement "Police officers are more likely to use physical force against blacks and other minorities than against whites in similar situations," compared with only 5 percent of white officers. The responses to this statement reflected not what officers said they personally do, but what they perceived officers in general do (which probably means other officers in their own department).[65]

The data on officer involvement in excessive use of force parallel the data on the use of deadly force. In neither case is it a simple matter of white officers shooting or beating racial minority citizens. In both cases, officer behavior is heavily determined by the contextual or situational variables: location (high-crime versus low-crime precinct); the perceived criminal involvement of the citizen; the demeanor of the citizen; and in the case of physical force, the social status of the citizen.

Our contextual approach suggests that the use of physical force has special significance for racial minority communities. Even if the overall rate of use of force is only 1 percent of all encounters, incidents are concentrated among lower-class men and criminal suspects, which means they are disproportionately concentrated among racial and ethnic minorities. Reiss pointed out that incidents accumulate over time, creating a perception of systematic harassment.[66] A 1991 Gallup Poll reported that 45 percent of African Americans believed there was police brutality in their area, compared with only 33 percent of whites.[67] Finally, police use of force has special political significance for minorities. Because the police are the symbolic representatives of the established order, incidents of excessive force are perceived as part of the broader patterns of inequality and discrimination in society.

DISCRIMINATION IN ARRESTS?

Racial minorities are arrested far more often than whites. African Americans are only 12 percent of the population, but in 2000 they represented 27.9 percent of all arrests, 32.9 percent of arrests for Index crimes, and 37.8 percent of arrests for violent crimes (see Figure 4.1).[68] Tillman found that in California, 66 percent of all African American men were likely to be arrested before the age of 30, compared with only 34 percent of white men.[69] The FBI does not report data on ethnicity, so there are no national data on arrest rates for Hispanics. Native Americans represent 0.8 percent of the U.S. population but 1.1 percent of all persons arrested.[70]

The arrest data again raise the question of whether the racial disparities indicate a pattern of systematic racial discrimination or a disparity that is related to other factors such as involvement in crime (see Chapter 1, Box 1.3). In his study of arrest discretion, Donald Black found that police officers consistently underenforce the law, arresting only 58 percent of felony suspects and only 44 percent of misdemeanor suspects. The decision to arrest is primarily influenced by situational factors. Officers are more likely to arrest when (1) the evidence is strong; (2) the crime is of a more serious nature; (3) the complainant or victim requests an arrest; (4) the relationship between the victim and offender is distant (that is, strangers rather than acquaintances or spouses); and (5) the suspect is disrespectful toward the officer. In Black's study, the race of the suspect was not a major determinant of arrest decisions.[71]

Black did, however, find that African Americans were arrested more often than whites, mainly because they were more often disrespectful to police officers. This phenomenon represents a vicious circle in racial discrimination. Because of the broader patterns of racial inequality in U.S. society, young African American men have more negative attitudes toward the police (see discussion earlier in this chapter). Expressing their hostility toward police officers results in higher arrest rates, which only heightens their feelings of alienation and hostility. Klinger, however, questioned Black's interpretation of the impact of demeanor. He argued that the study did not specify when the hostile demeanor occurred. If it occurred after the actual arrest was made—and it is understandable that a person might express anger at that point—it did not cause the arrest.[72]

Another factor contributing to the racial disparity in arrests is the greater involvement of African Americans in the more serious crimes. The NCVS reports that victims perceived the offender to be African American in 46.5 percent of all single-offender robberies but only 22 percent of all assaults.[73] Because robbery is generally regarded as a more serious crime than assault, and because greater seriousness increases the probability of arrest, it follows that more African Americans will be arrested than whites.

Smith, Visher, and Davidson concluded that race does have an effect on arrest discretion. Analyzing 5,688 police–citizen encounters in 24 police departments in three major metropolitan areas, they found that police officers were more likely to arrest when the victim was white and the suspect was African American and more likely to comply with a white victim's request that the suspect be arrested. After controlling for all relevant variables, they concluded that "race does matter" and that African American suspects were more likely to be arrested than whites.[74]

Other studies have suggested that African Americans are more likely to be arrested on less stringent evidentiary criteria than whites.[75] Petersilia's study of racial disparities in California found that African American and Hispanic arrestees were more likely to be released by the police without the case going to the prosecutor and more likely to have the prosecutor reject the case. At first glance, it might appear that African Americans and Hispanics are being treated more leniently in these two postarrest decisions. Petersilia, however, suggested that racial and ethnic minorities are arrested more often on weaker evidence than whites, particularly in "on-view" situations rather than with a warrant. The weak evidence in on-view arrests is then more likely to result in a release or rejection later in the criminal process.[76] Nonetheless, an arrest, even one that does not lead to prosecution, represents a significant form of punishment and is often perceived as harassment.

The race of the officer does not appear to influence arrest decisions. African American, Hispanic, and white officers arrest people at similar rates and for generally the same reasons. Black found some evidence that African American officers were slightly more likely to arrest African American suspects, in part because these officers appeared to be more willing to comply with requests for arrests made by African American citizens. He admitted, however, that the subject has not been researched as thoroughly as it needs to be.[77]

Zero-Tolerance Policing

One of the important new developments in law enforcement is zero-tolerance or "quality of life" policing. Under this approach, the police concentrate on relatively minor crimes, such as public urination or loitering. In New York City, there was particular emphasis on "fare-beaters," individuals who try to cheat the subway system by jumping over the turnstile. People arrested for a minor crime often turn out to have an illegal gun in their possession or are wanted on outstanding warrants.[78] City officials, including the police, claim that the great reduction in crime in New York City in the 1990s was a result of quality of life policing. Other people, however, argue that this aggressive style of policing results in harassment of citizens, particularly young racial and ethnic minority men.[79] In fact, New York City experienced severe police–community relations problems in the 1990s as a result of several controversial shootings and the beating of Abner Louima in 1997. Most American cities experienced dramatic reductions in serious crime in the 1990s. Boston and San Diego, in particular, achieved lower crime rates without aggravating race relations.[80]

One of the important differences in policing styles is the extent to which an anticrime program is focused on suspected lawbreakers. The highly praised Boston Gun Project targets a specific list of known gang leaders and relies heavily on enforcement of probation and parole restrictions, which by definition are directed toward specific individuals. At the same time, the Ten Point Coalition involved active collaboration between the Boston police department and religious institutions, particularly in the African American community. By contrast, many police crackdowns in other cities have been indiscriminate: massive stops and frisks and arrests of young men in African American or Hispanic neighborhoods, without the benefit of information about actual gang members. Such indiscriminate crackdowns tend to sweep up innocent people and, in the process, aggravate police–community relations.

In sum, patterns of arrest by race are extremely complex. Racial minorities, especially African Americans, are arrested far more frequently than are whites. Much of this disparity, however, can be attributed to the greater involvement of minorities in serious crime. Greater disrespect for the police also contributes to arrest disparity. Even after all the relevant variables are controlled, however, some evidence of arrest discrimination against African Americans persists.

TRAFFIC STOPS: RACIAL PROFILING

A national controversy has been raging for several years over the issue of racial profiling. *Racial profiling* is defined as the use of race as an indicator in a profile of criminal suspects. In short, drivers are being stopped either entirely or in part because of their race or ethnicity. Civil rights leaders coined the term *driving while black* to describe this practice. Most Americans believe that racial profiling exists. In a July 2001 Gallup Poll, 83 percent of African Americans said they believe racial profiling is "widespread." Somewhat surprising, 55 percent of whites agree.[81]

There is tremendous debate over several related issues: Does racial profiling in fact occur? How can we measure police activity to determine whether or not racial profiling exists? If it does, what is the best method for eliminating it?[82]

Defining Racial Profiling

Several basic points need to be clarified. Most important, stopping someone *solely* because of race or ethnicity is illegal. In practice, however, traffic stops and arrests typically involve a complex mix of factors. There is no disagreement on this point. More controversial is stopping or arresting someone if race is only one of several factors. If race is one element in a general profile, a stop or arrest is probably illegal. A stop or arrest is legal, however, in a situation where race or ethnicity is one of several descriptors of a particular individual suspect (for example, male, young, tall, wearing baseball jacket and cap, and white).[83]

Profiling Contexts

Racial profiling occurs in at least three different contexts. One is the *War on Drugs,* where officers are targeting African Americans or Hispanics in the belief that they are very likely to be engaged in drug trafficking. This approach represents a profile of criminal suspects based on racial and ethnic stereotypes. The ACLU and others argue that the Drug Enforcement Administration (DEA) has encouraged racial profiling by state and local departments through its "Operation Pipeline." DEA training materials, they claim, stereotype African Americans and Hispanics as drug traffickers.[84]

A second context involves stopping citizens who appear to be *out of place:* an African American in a predominantly white neighborhood or a white in a predominantly African American neighborhood. This approach is also based on racial stereotypes, specifically the assumption that this person does not "belong" in this area and therefore must be engaged in some criminal activity. It ignores the fact that the African American in a white neighborhood may in fact live there, may have friends who live there, or may be visiting someone for business or professional purposes (for example, an insurance salesperson calling on a potential customer). Similarly, the white person in a predominantly African American neighborhood might have some legitimate personal or business-related reason for being there (for example, real estate sales).

A third context involves a *crackdown on crime.* In this case, the police department has decided to get tough on street crime through an aggressive stop, question, and frisk policy. It is likely to focus on a high-crime neighborhood, which, in turn, is likely to be an African American or Hispanic community. As a result, virtually all of the people stopped will be racial or ethnic minorities.

The Data on Traffic Stops

The BJS national survey of police–citizen contacts provides the best data on police traffic stop practices (see Table 4.4). The findings are extremely complex. First, traffic stops are the most common form of encounter between police officers and citizens, accounting for 52 percent of all encounters. Second, African American drivers are stopped more often than white drivers (12.3 percent and 10.4 percent, respectively). Somewhat surprising, Hispanic drivers were the least likely to be stopped (8.8 percent).[85]

The racial differences are even more pronounced with regard to more-specific traffic stop practices. Twice as many African American drivers as white drivers reported being stopped five or more times (3.4 percent compared with 1.6 percent). This clearly suggests that some African American drivers are being targeted by police. Whites were more likely to be stopped for speeding and drunk driving, whereas African Americans and Hispanics were more likely to be stopped for vehicle defects and record checks.

African American and Hispanic drivers were somewhat more likely to be ticketed than whites. Both African Americans and Hispanics were twice as

Table 4.4 Traffic Stop Experiences by Race and Ethnicity, 1999

Race or Ethnicity	PERCENTAGE OF ALL DRIVERS		PERCENTAGE OF DRIVERS STOPPED	
	Any Traffic Stop	Five or More Stops	Ticketed	Force Used in a Traffic Stop
White	10.4	1.6	51.8	0.6
African American	12.3	3.4	60.4	1.5
Hispanic	8.8	1.4	65.6	1.4

SOURCE: Bureau of Justice Statistics, *Contacts between Police and the Public: Findings from the 1999 National Survey* (Washington, DC: U.S. Government Printing Office, 2001), pp. 14, 16.

likely as whites to have force used against them in a traffic stop. These data support the view that, with regard to racial profiling, the greatest problems involve what happens *after* a traffic stop has been made.

Interpreting Traffic Stop Data

As is the case with the deadly force and physical force data, the traffic stop data raise difficult questions related to interpretation. There is a question of whether racial and ethnic disparities in traffic stops represent a pattern of discrimination. It is not clear what standard or baseline should be used to interpret the traffic stop data on the number and percentage of African Americans, Hispanics, and whites stopped by the police.

To date, most data collection efforts have used population data for the city (or county in the case of sheriff's departments). The report by the San Jose Police Department, for example, found that Hispanics represented 43 percent of all drivers stopped but only 31 percent of the San Jose population. These data clearly indicate a disparity in the percentage of Hispanics stopped by the police. But do these data indicate a pattern of discrimination? Proof of discrimination should be able to meet one of two tests or both: sufficient evidence to win a court case and/or to gain publication in a respected social science journal.[86]

Walker argues that population data are not a proper benchmark as they do not provide an accurate estimate of who is at risk of being stopped for a possible traffic violation. An at-risk estimate would take into account the percentage of a racial or ethnic group who are licensed drivers and who who actually drive and, most important, the percentage of actual traffic law violators who are members of various racial and ethnic groups.[87] In both the lawsuits against racial profiling in Maryland and New Jersey, the plaintiffs resolved these questions by conducting "rolling surveys" of the interstate highways. Observers drove on the highways and estimated the percentage of all drivers who were African American and the percentage of traffic law violators by race and ethnicity, and then measured these data against the racial breakdown of drivers actually stopped. In both Maryland and New Jersey, African Americans were not observed violating the law at a higher rate than white drivers were. These data provided convincing evidence that African American drivers were being stopped not because of their driving behavior or the condition of their cars but for some other reason—their race.[88]

The research strategy used in the lawsuits in Maryland and New Jersey was facilitated by the fact that it occurred on interstate highways. These are confined spaces with limited access where the police are performing only one task: traffic enforcement. However, this research strategy does not work for a metropolitan area. Cities are large geographic areas where citizens are moving about in many different ways and where the police are performing many different tasks: law enforcement, order maintenance, and service. In this constantly changing environment, it is difficult to estimate the number of traffic violators.[89]

Walker argues that a better approach to the problem of analyzing traffic stop data is to adapt the principles behind police early warning (EW) systems. EW systems are data-based management tools that collect and analyze police officer performance data (citizen complaints, officer use of force reports, and so on.) for the purpose of identifying those officers who have an unusually high number of indicators of problematic behavior. Identified officers are then subject to an intervention, either counseling or training, designed to improve their performance.[90]

EW systems operate by comparing officers' performance against that of their peers. The system does not depend on some a priori determination of the acceptable number of complaints or use of force incidents, but simply asks, "Who is far above the average?" Applying the EW approach to traffic stop data, officers would be compared with other officers having the same assignment (for example, same shift or same precinct or neighborhood). If the data indicated that two officers stopped far more drivers than officers working the same assignment—and even more suspiciously—stopped far more African American drivers than other officers did, they would be subject to intervention. The intervention could involve counseling, training over issues related to traffic stops or cultural diversity, or reassignment.

Controlling Bias in Traffic Stops

Several strategies have been developed to combat racial and ethnic bias in traffic stops. The principal strategy adopted by civil rights groups has been to demand that law enforcement agencies collect data on all traffic stops. Several states have passed laws requiring data collection, and a large number of departments have begun data collection voluntarily. A federal data collection law has been pending in Congress for several years.[91]

A second strategy has been to adopt policies to control officer handling of traffic stops. The consent decree in the Justice Department suit against the New Jersey State Police, for example, requires officers to notify their dispatcher when they are about to make a stop and to report the vehicle license number and the reason for the stop.[92] These requirements are designed to ensure that officers are accountable for each stop by documenting it. A related policy is to install video cameras in patrol cars and require that officers activate them for each traffic stop. Video cameras provide a visual record of the stop and can potentially document any inappropriate behavior by the officer or challenge false claims of officer misconduct raised by citizens.

The most comprehensive set of recommendations for handling traffic stops is contained in a PERF report, *Racially Biased Policing: A Principled Response*[93] The policy includes specific guidelines on when race (or ethnicity) may and may *not* be used in stopping citizens (see Box 4.1). It clearly states that race cannot be the sole or even the primary factor in determining whether or not to stop a citizen. Officers may, however, take race or ethnicity into account when it is information related to a "specific suspect or suspects" that links the suspect or suspects to a particular crime. Moreover, this information must come from a "trustworthy" source. In short, the police can use race as an indicator when they have a report of a robbery committed by a young male, white/African American/Hispanic, wearing a baseball cap and a red coat, and driving a white, late-model sedan. They cannot, however, begin stopping all white/African American/Hispanic males simply because police have reports of robberies committed by a male in one of those ethnic or racial categories. If they see an individual fitting the racial or ethnic category who also exhibits suspicious behavior, a stop would be justified.

The PERF policy then recommends specific steps that police officers should take to help reduce the perception of bias. Officers should "be courteous and professional"; when stopping a citizen, they should "state the reason for the stop as soon as practical"; they should "answer any questions the citizen may have" and "provide his or her name and badge number when requested"; and "apologize and/or explain if he or she determines that the reasonable suspicion was unfounded"[94]

Adoption of all the PERF recommendations by police departments could eliminate a major source of public dissatisfaction with the police among people of all racial and ethnic groups.

A Success Story: The Customs Bureau

The U.S. Customs Bureau represents a case study in how racial bias can be effectively controlled. A 2000 report on the Customs Bureau found significant disparities in searches of passengers entering the United States. African American women were more likely to be searched than either white women or African American males. Despite a high rate of intrusive searches, African American women were less likely to be found possessing contraband. A major problem was that Customs agents had almost unlimited discretion to choose whom to search. Additionally, the guidelines for identifying suspicious persons were extremely vague.[95]

In a series of reforms, the Customs Bureau developed a much shorter, more specific list of indicators that could justify a search and clear guidelines on agents' exercise of discretion, including requirements that they obtain supervisors' approval for particular kinds of searches. These reforms drastically reduced the number of searches, but the "hit rate," the percentage of times they found contraband, increased equally dramatically. At the same time, there were far fewer

---

BOX 4.1   Police Executive Research Forum (PERF) Recommended Policy on Traffic Stops

Title: Addressing Racially Biased Policing and the Perceptions Thereof

Purpose: This policy is intended to reaffirm this department's commitment to unbiased policing, to clarify the circumstances in which officers can consider race/ethnicity when making law enforcement decisions, and to reinforce procedures that serve to assure the public that we are providing service and enforcing laws in an equitable way.

Policy:

A. Policing Impartially
 1. Investigative detentions, traffic stops, arrests, searches, and property seizures by officers will be based on a standard of reasonable suspicion or probable cause in accordance with the Fourth Amendment of the U.S. Constitution. Officers must be able to articulate specific facts and circumstances that support reasonable suspicion or probable cause for investigative detentions, traffic stops, arrests, nonconsensual searches, and property seizures.

 Except as provided below, officers shall not consider race/ethnicity in establishing either reasonable suspicion or probable cause. Similarly, except as provided below, officers shall not consider race/ethnicity in deciding to initiate even those nonconsensual encounters that do not amount to legal detentions or to request consent to search.

 Officers may take into account the reported race or ethnicity of a specific suspect or suspects based on trustworthy, locally relevant information that links a person or persons of a specific race/ethnicity to a particular unlawful incident(s). Race/ethnicity can never be used as the sole basis for probable cause or reasonable suspicion.

---

unnecessary searches of innocent people, the vast majority of whom are people of color. In short, the Customs Bureau was "working smarter." [96] The lesson of the Customs Bureau experience is that racial bias in searches can be effectively reduced without harming effective law enforcement.

STREET STOPS AND FRISKS

Closely related to traffic stops is the police practice of stopping pedestrians on the street and either questioning or frisking them, or both. This practice has long been a source of police–community tensions and is often referred to as a field interrogation (FI). It is a crime-fighting policy designed to "emphasize to potential offenders that the police are aware of" them and to "reassure the general public that the patrol officers are actively engaged in protecting law-abiding citizens." Patrol officers have full discretion to conduct FIs. As we have seen with

BOX 4.1 *(continued)*

2. Except as provided above, race/ethnicity shall not be motivating factors in making law enforcement decisions.

B. Preventing Perceptions of Biased Policing
In an effort to prevent inappropriate perceptions of biased law enforcement, each officer shall do the following when conducting pedestrian and vehicle stops:

- Be courteous and professional.
- Introduce him- or herself to the citizen (providing name and agency affiliation), and state the reason for the stop as soon as practical, unless providing this information will compromise officer or public safety. In vehicle stops, the officer shall provide this information before asking the driver for his or her license and registration.
- Ensure that the detention is no longer than necessary to take appropriate action for the known or suspected offense, and that the citizen understands the purpose of reasonable delays.
- Answer any questions the citizen may have, including explaining options for traffic citation disposition, if relevant.
- Provide his or her name and badge number when requested, in writing or on a business card.
- Apologize and/or explain if he or she determines that the reasonable suspicion was unfounded (e.g., after an investigatory stop).

Compliance: Violations of this policy shall result in disciplinary action as set forth in the department's rules and regulations.

Supervision and Accountability: Supervisors shall ensure that all personnel in their command are familiar with the content of this policy and are operating in compliance with it.

SOURCE: Police Executive Research Forum, *Racially Biased Policing: A Principled Response* (Washington, DC: Author, 2001), pp. 51–53.

respect to deadly force, uncontrolled discretion opens the door for discriminatory practices. Some police departments employ an "aggressive preventive patrol" strategy to encourage FIs. Thirty-five years ago, the Kerner Commission found that such a strategy aggravated tensions with minority communities.[97]

Young African American and Hispanic men believe they are singled out for frequent and unjustified harassment in such actions. In Chicago, 71 percent of high school students surveyed reported that they had been stopped by the police, and 86 percent felt the police had been disrespectful.[98]

Studies of field interrogations have produced conflicting findings. In the San Diego Field Interrogation study from the 1970s, nearly half of all people stopped and questioned were African Americans, even though they represented only 17.5 percent and 4.8 percent of the population of the two precincts in the study. All of the people stopped and questioned were male, and about 60 percent were juveniles.[99] The San Diego study also found, however, that 75 percent of all the people stopped and questioned thought the officer had a right to stop them. In some respects, this seems to be a highly positive response.

On the other hand, if 25 percent of all people stopped and questioned did not feel that it was legitimate, there would be a significant number of unhappy or even angry people over the course of a year.[100]

A report by the Massachusetts attorney general found that "Boston police officers engaged in improper, and unconstitutional, conduct in the 1989–1990 period with respect to stops and searches of minority individuals."[101] Interviews with more than 50 individuals revealed a pattern of African American men and women being stopped and questioned without any basis for suspicion, threatened by the officers if they asked why they were being stopped, and subjected to highly intrusive and embarrassing strip searches in public.

The most sophisticated study of street stops was commissioned by the New York state attorney general. The study found that even after investigators had controlled for crime rates and the racial composition of particular neighborhoods, African Americans and Hispanics were stopped at rates that could not be explained by factors other than race and ethnicity. The data indicated that police actions were not explained by an effort to control disorder or to improve the quality of life in neighborhoods, but in terms of "policing poor people in poor places."[102]

An ethnographic study of a low-income, high-crime neighborhood in St. Louis found that police officers had deeply divided opinions about how to police the area. They wanted to establish close relations with residents and help them deal with their problems. At the same time, however, many officers wanted to "kick ass," meaning they wanted to be free to use their own judgment to deal with crime in the neighborhood. They did not engage in these tactics because of their fear of being disciplined by the department (being "written up").[103]

Special Issue: Stereotyping and Routine Police Work

An underlying problem in the traffic stop and stop-and-frisk issues is the tendency of police officers to stereotype certain kinds of people and to act on those stereotypes. Jerome Skolnick argued many years ago that stereotyping is built into police work. Officers are trained to be suspicious and look for criminal activity. As a result, they develop "a perceptual shorthand to identify certain kinds of people" as suspects, relying on visual "cues": dress, demeanor, context, gender, and age. Thus, a young, low-income man in a wealthy neighborhood presents several cues that trigger an officer's suspicion in a way that a middle-aged woman or even a young woman in the same context does not.[104]

Race is also often a "cue." A young, racial minority man in a white neighborhood is likely to trigger an officer's suspicion because he "looks out of place" —even though he could be an honors student who attends church regularly and has never committed a crime. By the same token, the presence of two middle-class, white men in a minority neighborhood known to have a high level of drug trafficking is likely to trigger the suspicion that they are seeking to purchase drugs. Because racial minority men are disproportionately arrested for robbery and burglary, police officers can fall into the habit of stereotyping all young, racial minority men as offenders. With traffic stops, certain types of vehicles also serve as "cues": officers believe that certain kinds of persons drive certain kinds of cars, with the result that vehicles are a proxy for race and class.

Harvard law professor Randall Kennedy asks the question, "Is it proper to use a person's race as a proxy for an increased likelihood of criminal conduct?"[105] That is, can the police stop an African American man simply because the suspect in a crime is in that category, or because of statistical evidence that young, African American men are disproportionately involved in crime, drug, or gang activity? He points out that the courts have frequently upheld this practice as long as race is one of several factors involved in a stop or an arrest and the stop is not done for purposes of harassment.

Kennedy then makes a strong argument that race should never be used as the basis for a police action "except in the most extraordinary of circumstances." First, if the practice is strictly forbidden, it will reduce the opportunity for the police to engage in harassment under the cloak of "reasonable" law enforcement measures. Second, the current practice of using race "nourishes powerful feelings of racial grievance against law enforcement authorities." Third, the resulting hostility to the police creates barriers to police–citizen cooperation in those communities "most in need of police protection." Fourth, permitting the practice contributes to racial segregation, as African Americans will be reluctant to venture into white neighborhoods for fear of being stopped by the police.[106]

VERBAL ABUSE

Verbal abuse by police officers is one of the more common complaints from citizens. In 1997, 13 percent of the complaints received by the Minneapolis Civilian Police Review Authority involved offensive language.[107] Verbal abuse demeans the citizen and is explicitly forbidden by many police departments. The Los Angeles Police Department policy states, "The deliberate or casual use of racially or ethnically derogatory language by Department employees is misconduct and will not be tolerated under any circumstances."[108]

Despite this prohibition, the Christopher Commission found a great deal of abusive language by police officers. It recovered computer messages between Los Angeles patrol officers containing racially offensive terms: "I'm back here in the project, pissing off the natives"; "we're huntin' wabbits . . . actually Muslim wabbits"; "just got mexercise for the night"; "don't transfer me any orientals . . . I had to already."[109] The contrast between the official departmental policy and actual officer behavior in Los Angeles dramatizes the problem of controlling verbal abuse.

Whether certain words are offensive depends on the specific context and how those words are perceived by the citizen. The mildest form of abuse is simple rudeness or discourtesy. An officer may speak in a sharp tone of voice or refuse to answer a citizen's question. Even if discourteous words do not have an explicit racial or ethnic component, they may be perceived as offensive in a certain context. Calling a citizen a name such as "asshole" or "scumbag" may not appear racially or ethnically motivated, but these words may be perceived as such in an encounter on the street between a white officer and a minority citizen.

Racial or ethnic slurs represent a more serious form of verbal abuse. They demean citizens, deny them equal treatment on the basis of their race or ethnicity, and aggravate police–community tensions. The San Francisco Office of Citizen Complaints regards racial, ethnic, or gender slurs to be so serious that complaints involving them are not eligible for mediation (that is, they are considered as serious as use of force complaints and have to be investigated in the same manner).[110]

For police officers, derogatory language is a control technique. White, Cox, and Basehart argue that profanity directed at citizens serves several functions: to get their attention; keep them at a distance; and label, degrade, dominate, and control them.[111] It is also often a moral judgment. As middle-class professionals, police officers often look down on people who do not live by their standards, including criminals, chronic alcoholics, and the homeless.

Verbal abuse is especially hard to control. The typical incident occurs on the street, often without any witnesses except other police officers or friends of the citizen, and leaves no tangible evidence (unlike a physical attack). Consequently, most complaints about verbal abuse become "swearing contests" in which the citizen says one thing and the officer says just the opposite. Only a small percentage of verbal abuse complaints are sustained. In 2000 and 2001, offensive language allegations represented only about 4 percent of all the complaints received by the New York City Civilian Complaint Review Board (CCRB), and only about half of those were race related.[112]

POLICE OFFICER
ATTITUDES AND BEHAVIOR

Are police officers prejudiced? What is the relationship between police officer attitudes and the behavior of police on the street? The evidence on these questions is extremely complex. As Smith, Graham, and Adams explain, "Attitudes are one thing and behavior is another."[113]

Bayley and Mendelsohn compared the attitudes of Denver police officers with those of the general public and found that police officers were prejudiced "but only slightly more so than the community as a whole." Eight percent of the officers indicated that they disliked Spanish-surnamed persons, compared with 6 percent of the general public. When asked about specific social situations (for example, "Would you mind eating together at the same table?" or "Would you mind having someone in your family marry a member of a minority group?"), the officers were less prejudiced against Spanish-surnamed persons than the general public was but more prejudiced against African Americans.[114]

Bayley and Mendelsohn's findings are consistent with other research indicating that police officers are not significantly different from the general population in terms of psychological makeup and attitudes, including attitudes about race and ethnicity. Police departments, in other words, do not recruit a distinct group of prejudiced or psychologically unfit individuals. Bayley and Mendelsohn found that on all personality scales, Denver police officers were "absolutely average people."[115]

The attitudes of officers are often contradictory, however. Smith et al. found that the overwhelming majority of police officers (79.4 percent) agreed or strongly agreed with the statement "Most people in this community respect police officers."[116] At the same time, however, most (44.2 percent) believed that the chances of being abused by a citizen were very high. The characteristics of an officer's assignment affect perception of the community. Officers assigned to racial or ethnic minority communities, high-crime areas, and poor neighborhoods thought they received less respect from the public than did officers working in other areas.

Reiss noted a significant contradiction between the attitudes and behavior of the officers observed in his study. About 75 percent of the officers were observed making racially derogatory remarks, yet they did not engage in systematic discrimination in arrest or use of physical force.[117] Attitudes do not translate directly into behavior for reasons related to the bureaucratic nature of police work. An arrest is reviewed first by a supervising officer and then by other criminal justice officials (prosecutor, defense attorney, and judge). News media coverage is also possible. The potentially unfavorable judgments of these people serve to control the officer's behavior. Verbal abuse, however, rarely comes to the attention of other officials and is therefore much harder to control.

Much of the research on police officer attitudes was conducted in the 1960s or early 1970s. Since then, police employment practices have changed substantially. Far more African American, Hispanic, female, and college-educated officers are employed today (discussed later). The earlier research, which assumed a disproportionately white, male police force, may no longer be valid.[118] In fact, the Police Foundation study of police abuse of authority found very striking differences in the attitudes of white and African American officers. African American officers, by a huge margin, are more likely to believe that police officers use excessive force and use excessive force more often against racial and ethnic minorities and the poor.[119]

Most police departments offer sensitivity or cultural diversity training programs for their officers. These programs typically cover the history of race relations, traditional racial and ethnic stereotypes, and explanations of different racial and ethnic cultural patterns. Questions have been raised about the effectiveness of these programs, however. Some critics fear that they may be counterproductive and serve only to reinforce negative attitudes, focus on attitudes rather than behavior, and fail to address departmental policies that may be the real cause of the problem.[120] Alpert, Smith, and Watters argued, "Mere class-room lectures . . . are insufficient," and emphasis needs to be placed on actual on-the-street behavior.[121]

MINORITIES AND POLICE CORRUPTION

Police corruption has a special impact on minority communities. Most police corruption involves vice activities—particularly drugs and gambling—that historically have been segregated in low-income and racial minority neighborhoods. In the 1970s, the Knapp Commission found that payoffs to New York City police officers were about $300 per month in midtown Manhattan, the central business district, and $1,500 in Harlem, the center of the African American community.[122] In the 1990s, the Mollen Commission exposed a pattern of corruption and violence in the poorest African American and Hispanic neighborhoods. Officers took bribes for protecting the drug trade, beat up drug dealers, broke into apartments, and stole drugs and money.[123]

Historically, police corruption has been concentrated in poor and racial minority neighborhoods because that is where illegal vice crimes have been concentrated. This pattern reflects a more general pattern of unequal law enforcement. The poor and minorities have not had the political power to demand the kind of law enforcement available to white and middle-class people. The result has been that vice and the resulting corruption are concentrated in poor and minority neighborhoods. The nonenforcement of the law is as much a form of discrimination as overenforcement.

Police corruption harms racial and ethnic minorities in several ways. First, allowing vice activities to flourish in low-income and minority communities represents an unequal and discriminatory pattern of law enforcement. Second, vice encourages secondary crime: the patrons of prostitutes are robbed; after-hours clubs are the scenes of robbery and assault; and competing drug gangs have shoot-outs with rival gangs. Third, community awareness of police corruption damages the reputation of the police. In 1993, 26 percent of African Americans thought the ethical standards of the police were "low" or "very low," compared with only 8 percent of whites.[124]

POLICE–COMMUNITY
RELATIONS PROGRAMS

In response to the riots of the 1960s, most big-city police departments established special police–community relations (PCR) programs to resolve racial and ethnic tensions. Most involved a separate PCR unit within the department. PCR unit officers spent most of their time speaking in schools or to community groups.[125] Some PCR units also staffed neighborhood storefront offices to make the department more accessible to community residents who either were intimidated by police headquarters or found it difficult to travel downtown. Another popular program was the "ride-along," which allowed citizens to ride in a patrol car and view policing from an officer's perspective.

PCR programs had a troubled history, and there is no evidence that they improved community relations. A Justice Department report concluded that PCR units "tended to be marginal to the operations of the police department," with little direct impact on patrol and other key operations.[126] Public education and ride-along programs reached people who already had a positive attitude toward the police. In the 1970s, most departments reduced or abolished their PCR programs.

Some of the original PCR activities have reappeared in community policing programs. The ambitious Chicago Alternative Police Services (CAPS) program includes a series of regular meetings between patrol beat officers and community residents.[127] The major difference is that under community policing, these meetings are designed to develop two-way communication, with citizens providing input into police policies. The old PCR programs mainly involved one-way communication from the police to the community—in short, a standard public relations effort where the organization attempts to sell itself to the public.

Reaching out to racial and ethnic minority communities also involves responding to specific concerns. In one of the best examples, the San Diego Police Department voluntarily decided to collect traffic stop data to determine if there was a pattern of racial profiling. San Diego was the first police department in the country to do voluntary data collection. San Jose, California, quickly followed suit, and many other departments across the country followed their example. In his introduction to the first traffic stop data report, San Jose police chief William Landsdowne explained that his department "prides itself upon being responsive to the needs and concerns of everyone who lives, works, learns, plays, and travels within San Jose."[128] Undertaking data collection—a difficult, time-consuming effort that is not popular with all the officers—indicates that the chief was willing to give real meaning to those words.

The Boston Police Department is widely credited with both reducing crime and improving relations with minority communities in the 1990s. The main program for reducing crime was the Boston Gun Project, a series of specific actions designed to reduce handgun violence among young people and gang members in particular. One of the main programs to improve police–community relations was the Ten Point Coalition, a partnership between the police department and the religious community. The Ten Point Coalition represents a combination of the principles underlying both community policing and problem-oriented policing. These principles include a recognition that the police cannot fight crime alone, that citizens are important "coproducers" of law enforcement services, and that police departments need to build working partnerships with established community groups. In African American communities, churches have historically been one of the most important institutions.[129]

The Ten Point Coalition established a number of specific efforts: "Adopt-a-Gang" programs where churches provide drop-in centers for young people, neighborhood crime-watch programs, partnerships with community health centers to provide counseling for families with problems, and rape crisis centers for battered women.[130]

CITIZEN COMPLAINTS
AGAINST THE POLICE

One of the greatest sources of tension between the police and minorities is the perceived failure of police departments to respond adequately to citizen complaints about police misconduct. The development of external citizen oversight agencies, which now exist in virtually all big cities, is a response to this problem.[131]

African Americans file a disproportionate number of all complaints against the police. In New York City, for example, African Americans made 52.2 percent of all complaints filed with the CCRB, even though they represent only 24.5 percent of the city's population (see Table 4.5).[132] Hispanics, on the other hand, are less likely to file complaints against the police for several reasons. Language barriers are a problem for Hispanics who do not speak English, and many police departments do not provide information or complaint forms in Spanish (or Asian languages). Many recent immigrants, do not understand the nature of the citizen complaint process and assume that they need an attorney. Also, many recent immigrants from Mexico or other Latin American countries are extremely fearful of the police because complaining about an officer in those countries can result in serious retaliation, even death.

Racial and ethnic minorities allege that police departments fail to adequately investigate complaints and do not discipline officers who are guilty of misconduct. There is a widespread belief that the complaint review process is just a "cover-up."[133] Most people who feel they are victims of police abuse do not even file a formal complaint. One study found that only 30 percent of those people who felt they had a reason to complain about a police officer took any kind of action, and only some of them contacted the police department. Most people called someone else (a friend or some other government official).[134]

Historically, some departments have actively discouraged citizen complaints. The Kerner Commission found evidence of this in the 1960s.[135] In the 1990s, the Christopher Commission found that officers at Los Angeles police stations discouraged people from filing complaints and sometimes even threatened them with arrest. Additionally, officers frequently did not complete Form 1.81, which records an official complaint.[136] In response to criticisms about how it handled complaints, the Los Angeles Police Department established a special 800 number as a complaint hotline. A study by the ACLU in Los Angeles, however, found that only 13 percent of the people calling local police stations were given the 800 number. Other callers (71.9 percent) were told that either there

Table 4.5 Citizen Complaints, New York City, January 2001–June 2002

RACE AND ETHNICITY OF COMPLAINANTS COMPARED
WITH THE POPULATION OF NEW YORK CITY

	Complainants	New York City Population
White[a]	16.6%	35.0%
Black	52.5	24.5
Latino	26.3	27.0
Asian	2.1	9.8
Others	2.5	3.7

SOURCE: New York City Civilian Complaint Review Board, *Status Report, January–June 2002* (New York: Author, 2002), p. 48.

[a]Racial and ethnic categories used by the New York City Civilian Complaint Review Board (CCRB).

was no such number or that the officer could not give it out, or they were put on hold indefinitely.[137]

Internal affairs (IA) units have traditionally handled citizen complaints. The police subculture is very strong, however, and IA officers tend to protect their colleagues and the department against external criticism. Westley found that the police subculture emphasizes "silence, secrecy, and solidarity." Under the informal "code of silence," officers are often willing to lie to cover up misconduct by fellow officers.[138] The Christopher Commission concluded that in Los Angeles, "the greatest single barrier to the effective investigation and adjudication of complaints is the officers' unwritten 'code of silence.'" The code "consists of one simple rule: an officer does not provide adverse information against a fellow officer."[139] The Mollen Commission investigating police corruption in New York City found the "pervasiveness" of the code of silence "alarming." The Commission asked one officer, "Were you ever afraid that one of your fellow officers might turn you in?" He answered, "Never," because "cops don't tell on cops."[140]

As a result, most citizen complaints become "swearing contests": The citizen alleges one thing, and the officer denies it. Few citizen complaints are sustained by police investigators. The Police Foundation found that city police departments sustain only 10.4 percent of all complaints.[141]

One alternative to traditional complaint investigation is to mediate complaints. Mediation is a voluntary process in which the complainant and the officer meet face-to-face (usually for about an hour) with a professional mediator supervising the session. The point of mediation is not to establish guilt but to foster a dialogue that leads to better understanding on both sides of the issue. The end result is often simply an agreement that each side has listened to and understands what the other person's point of view is. Vivian Berger, an experienced mediator in New York City, argues that mediation is particularly appropriate for complaints when the officer and the complainant are of different races or ethnic groups. She explains that many complaints are not formally about race (for example, the allegation is discourtesy) but that "they are really about race." That is, the complaint is the result of misunderstandings that are rooted in racial or cultural differences. Mediation provides a structured process in which both sides have to listen to each other. In many cases, this can help bridge the racial divide.[142]

Citizen Oversight of the Police

To ensure better handling of complaints against the police, civil rights groups have demanded external or citizen oversight of complaints. Citizen oversight is based on the idea that persons who are not police officers will be more independent and objective in investigating complaints. Despite strong opposition from police unions, citizen review has spread rapidly in recent years. By 2001, there were over 100 oversight agencies in the United States, covering almost all of the big cities and many smaller cities.[143]

Some citizen oversight procedures investigate complaints themselves (for example, the San Francisco Office of Citizen Complaints). Others provide some citizen input into investigations conducted by IA officers (for example, the Kansas City Office of Citizen Complaints). Some procedures systematically audit the performance of the IA unit (for example, the Portland Independent Police Review Office, which is located in the office of the city auditor).[144]

There is some evidence that citizen review enhances public confidence in the complaint process. In 1991, for example, San Francisco had 5 times as many complaints per officer as Los Angeles. Some observers argue that San Francisco generates more complaints because its civilian review procedure enhances citizens feelings that their complaints will receive a fair hearing, whereas the Los Angeles Police Department (before recent reforms) was actively discouraging complaints.[145]

POLICE EMPLOYMENT PRACTICES

Discrimination in the employment of racial and ethnic minorities as police officers has been a long-standing problem. During the Segregation Era (1890s–1960s), Southern cities did not hire any African American officers, and police departments in Northern states engaged in systematic employment discrimination.[146] In 1967, for example, African Americans made up 23 percent of the population in Oakland but only 2.3 percent of the police officers.[147] Employment discrimination occurs in three different areas of policing: recruitment, promotion to supervisory ranks, and assignment to shifts and specialized units.

The Boston police commissioner recognizes the need for a diverse workforce in terms of practical law enforcement:" I know that having African American and Hispanic and Vietnamese officers, people of different backgrounds and cultures who can conduct comfortable interviews with crime victims and can infiltrate crime rings that aren't white—I know the need for that is just common sense."[148]

Trends in Racial Minority Employment

Since the 1960s, some progress has been made in the employment of racial and ethnic minority police officers (see Figure 4.3). In 1960, an estimated 3.6 percent of all sworn officers in the United States were African Americans; by 1990, the figure had risen to 10.5 percent. Hispanics represented about 5.2 percent of all sworn officers in city police departments in 1990 (little data exist on Hispanic officers for earlier years).[149]

The aggregate figures on employment are misleading because, as noted in Chapter 1, the racial and ethnic minority groups are not evenly distributed across the country. It is more useful to look at particular police departments to see whether they represent the communities they serve. The accreditation standards for law enforcement agencies require that "the agency has minority group and female employees in the sworn law enforcement ranks in approximate proportion to the makeup of the available work force in the law enforcement agency's service community."[150]

The Equal Employment Opportunity (EEO) Index provides a representative measure. The EEO Index compares the percentage of minority group officers with the percentage of that group in the local population. If, for example, a community is 40 percent African American and 30 percent of the officers are African American, the EEO Index is 0.75.[151] The EEO Index offers some interesting comparisons across police departments. New York City had an EEO Index of only 0.40 for African Americans in 1992: 11.4 percent of the officers and 28.7 percent of the city population. This was one of the lowest rates for any big city. Even worse, the New York City EEO Index had been 0.40 in 1983. Thus, the department had made almost no progress in the employment of African Americans in 10 years. The Cleveland Police Department, on the other hand, made significant gains in the employment of African Americans. Its EEO Index rose from 0.26 in 1983 to 0.56 in 1992. This progress resulted from an active recruitment effort and was achieved despite the fact that the number of sworn officers in the department decreased from 2,091 to 1,668 [152]

The Boston Police Department provides an example of how an employer can take active steps to increase racial and ethnic minority employment. Police Commissioner Paul Evans found that the local civil service rules made exceptions for job candidates with special skills. Because Boston has a significant Haitian population, Evans was able to use these rules to hire officers who could speak French Creole and thus could communicate better with Haitian residents. Evans then extended this practice to include job applicants who could speak Spanish, Vietnamese, or Chinese.[153]

Los Angeles offers another interesting perspective on minority employment. In 1992, the police department had a perfect EEO Index (1.00) for African Americans (14 percent of both the population and the sworn officers). Yet, the Rodney King incident revealed that the department had a serious race relations problem. The Christopher Commission found a racist climate within

Percentage of full-time sworn personnel

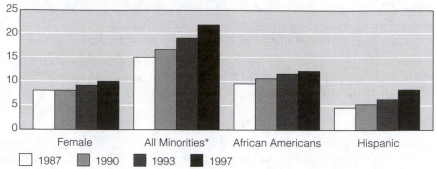

*Includes African Americans, Hispanics, Asians, Pacific Islanders,
Native Americans, and Alaska Natives.

FIGURE 4.3 Female and Minority Local Police Officers, 1987, 1990, 1993, and 1997

SOURCE: Bureau of Justice Statistics, *Local Police Departments, 1997* (Washington, DC: U.S. Government Printing Office, 2000), p. 4.

the department, with officers making racist comments over the department's computerized message system.[154] In short, merely employing racial minority officers does not automatically eliminate police–community relations problems. The quality of policing is largely determined by the organizational culture of the department, which is the combined product of leadership by the chief, formal policies on critical issues such as the use of force, and rank-and-file officer peer culture.

In some police departments, white officers are now the minority: only about 25 percent of the officers in Washington, DC, and 20 percent in Miami. The Miami–Dade Police Department is 46 percent white, 35 percent Hispanic, and 17 percent African American.[155]

Recent immigration trends have heightened the importance of having bilingual officers who can communicate in Spanish or Asian languages. The Christopher Commission found that in 1991 in the heavily Hispanic communities of Los Angeles, often no Spanish-speaking officers were available to take citizen complaints.[156] Similar problems arise in communities with significant Asian American populations, representing different nationalities and languages.

A study of police and Hispanic citizen interactions in a Midwestern city found that even though language barriers did not create any major crises (even violent incidents arising from an inability to communicate), they did create delays in the delivery of services and some frustration on the part of officers. When handling a situation in which the citizens did not speak English, officers either found a family member or bystander who could translate or simply "muddled through" with "street Spanish."[157]

Relatively few Native Americans and Asian Americans are employed as sworn police officers in departments other than tribal law enforcement agencies (where Native Americans are about 56 percent of all officers). The Justice

Department's report *Law Enforcement Management and Administrative Statistics* provides the most systematic set of data. A few police departments do have a significant number of Asian American officers. They represent 12 percent of the officers in San Francisco, for example, and 7 percent of the Seattle police. Native Americans, on the other hand, are substantially underrepresented, even in states with the largest Native American populations. They are only 1 percent of the sworn officers in Albuquerque, New Mexico, for example.[158]

The Law of Employment Discrimination

Employment discrimination based on race or ethnicity is illegal. The Fourteenth Amendment to the U.S. Constitution provides that "No state shall . . . deny to any person . . . the equal protection of the laws." Title VII of the 1964 Civil Rights Act prohibits employment discrimination based on race, color, national origin, religion, or sex. The 1972 Equal Employment Opportunity Act extended the coverage of Title VII to state and local governments. In addition, state civil rights laws prohibit employment discrimination on the basis of race or ethnicity. According to Section 703, "It shall be an unlawful employment practice for an employer . . . to fail or refuse to hire or to discharge any individual, or otherwise to discriminate against any individual with respect to his compensation, terms, conditions, or privileges of employment, because of such individual's race, color, religion, sex, or national origin."[159]

The most controversial aspect of employment discrimination is the policy of affirmative action. The Office of Federal Contract Compliance defines affirmative action as "results-oriented actions [taken] to ensure equal employment opportunity [which may include] goals to correct under-utilization . . . [and] backpay, retroactive seniority, makeup goals and timetables." Affirmative action originated in 1966 when President Lyndon Johnson issued Executive Order 11246 directing all federal contractors to have affirmative action programs. Some affirmative action programs are voluntary, whereas others are court ordered; some have general goals, whereas others have specific quotas.

An affirmative action program consists of several steps. The first is a census of employees to determine the number and percentage of racial minorities and women in different job categories. The data are then used to identify underutilization. *Underutilization* exists where the percentage of employees in a particular job category is less than the percentage of potentially qualified members of that group in the labor force.

If underutilization exists, the employer is required to develop a plan to eliminate it. Recruitment programs typically include active outreach to potential minority applicants, mainly through meetings with community groups and leaders. The New Haven, Connecticut, police department successfully increased the representation of racial minority officers from 22 percent in 1991 to 40 percent by 2000. The department recognized that its traditional methods of recruiting, such as placing ads in the newspaper, were not working effectively for groups other than whites. To overcome this problem, the department worked closely with community groups, holding focus groups to discuss the issue, for example. These sessions generated ideas about which messages were most effective with different racial and ethnic groups, and focus group members later helped with the recruitment effort. Also, police officer recruiters were carefully selected on the basis of their enthusiasm, communication skills, and ability to relate to different groups.[160]

An employer may voluntarily adopt an affirmative action plan with quotas. In 1974, the Detroit Police Department adopted a voluntary quota of promoting one African American officer for each white officer promoted. As a result, by 1992, half of all the officers at the rank of sergeant or above were African American. Most affirmative action plans have been court ordered, as a result of discrimination suits under Title VII of the 1964 Civil Rights Act. A 1980 consent decree settling the suit against the Omaha, Nebraska, police department, for example, established a long-term goal of having 9.5 percent African American officers in the department within 7 years. At the time of the suit, African Americans were only 4 percent of the sworn officers, and the figure had been declining. To achieve the 9.5 percent goal, the court ordered a three-stage recruitment plan: African Americans would be 40 percent of all new recruits until they were 6 percent of the department, 33 percent of recruits until they were 8 percent, and then 25 percent of recruits until the final 9.5 percent goal was reached. The city reached the goals of the court order ahead of schedule, and by 1992, African American officers were 11.5 percent of the police department.

Discrimination in Assignment

Discrimination also occurs in the assignment of police officers. In the South during the Segregation Era, African American officers were not assigned to white neighborhoods and were not permitted to arrest whites.[161] Many Northern cities also confined minority officers to minority neighborhoods. Reiss found that some police departments dumped their incompetent white officers on racial minority neighborhoods.[162] Seniority rules that govern the assignment in most departments today make blatant discrimination difficult. Officers with the most seniority, regardless of race, ethnicity, or gender, have first choice for the most desirable assignments. Seniority rules can have an indirect race effect, however. In a department that has only recently hired a significant number of racial or ethnic minorities, these officers will be disproportionately assigned to high-crime areas because of their lack of seniority. Fyfe found that this seniority-based assignment pattern explained why African American officers in New York City fired their weapons more often than white officers did (although the rates were virtually the same for all officers assigned to the high-crime areas, regardless of race).[163]

There is also discrimination in assignment to special and desirable units. The special counsel to the Los Angeles County Sheriff Department identified two categories of desirable positions. "Coveted" positions were those that officers sought because they are interesting, high paying, or convenient (in terms of work schedule). In the Los Angeles Sheriff Department, these included the Special Enforcement Bureau, the Narcotics Bureau, and precinct station detective assignments. "High-profile" positions, on the other hand, are those likely to lead to promotion and career advancement. These include operations deputy, the Recruitment Training Bureau, and field training officer positions.[164]

An investigative study by the *New York Times* found that African American male officers were seriously underrepresented in the elite units of the New York City Police Department (NYPD). The 124-officer mounted patrol unit had only 3 African Americans, and there were only 2 in the 159-officer harbor patrol unit. It is well understood in the NYPD that selection for an elite unit depends on having a friend who will sponsor you—a "hook" or a "rabbi" in the slang of the NYPD. With few people in high command and in elite units, African American officers often find their career paths blocked in those areas.[165]

The assignment of African American officers to plainclothes detective work has created a new problem. In 1992, an African American transit police officer in New York City wearing plain clothes was shot and seriously wounded by a white officer who mistook him for a robber.[166] Similar incidents have occurred in other cities. The *New York Times* report found that in New York City, virtually all of the many of African American officers interviewed had at some time been stopped and questioned—sometimes at gunpoint—by white officers.[167]

The Impact of Diversity

Civil rights leaders and police reformers have fought for increased employment of racial and ethnic minorities with three different goals in mind. First, employment discrimination is illegal and must be eliminated for that reason alone. Second, some reformers believe that minority officers will behave in different ways than white officers on the street and be less likely to discriminate in making arrests or using physical force.[168] Third, many experts argue that police departments should reflect the communities they serve to create a positive public image.

With respect to the first objective, increased minority employment means that the agency is complying with the law of equal employment opportunity. Obeying the law is an important consideration, regardless of any other effects of minority employment. Along these lines, failure to hire an adequate number of racial or ethnic minorities frequently results in an employment discrimination suit, which is expensive and tends to create organizational turmoil.

With respect to the second goal, there is no clear evidence that white, African American, or Hispanic police officers behave in different ways on the job (see the Focus on an Issue: Would It Make a Difference? on p. 132). That is, they arrest and use physical and deadly force in similar fashions. For the most part, they are influenced by situational factors: the seriousness of the offense, the demeanor of the suspect, and so forth.

There is increased recognition of the importance of having officers with skills in languages other than English. Common sense suggests that officers who can communicate effectively in Spanish or Cambodian will be better able to serve people who speak those languages.[169] At present, however, there are no studies that would confirm this hypothesis.

Focus on an Issue
Would It Make a Difference?
Assigning African American Officers
to African American Neighborhoods

Some civil rights activists argue that police departments should assign African American officers exclusively to African American neighborhoods. They believe that these officers would be more sensitive to community needs, more polite and respectful to neighborhood residents, and less likely to act in a discriminatory manner.

Is this a good idea? Would it, in fact, improve the quality of policing in minority neighborhoods? The evidence does not support this proposal.

First, as we have already seen, no evidence suggests that African American, Hispanic, and white officers behave in significantly different ways. Fyfe's (1981) research on deadly force found that officers assigned to high-crime precincts fired their weapons at similar rates, regardless of race. Reiss (1968) found that white and African American officers used excessive physical force at about the same rate.

Black (1980) found no significant differences in the arrest patterns of white and African American officers. It is worth noting that male and female officers have also been found to behave in roughly similar ways. Thus, most experts on the police argue that situational and departmental factors, not race or gender, influence police officer behavior (Sherman, 1980).

Second, assigning only African American officers to African American neighborhoods, or Hispanic officers to Hispanic neighborhoods, would discriminate against the officers themselves. It would "ghettoize" them and deny them the variety of assignments and experience that helps lead to promotion. The policy would also perpetuate racial stereotypes by promoting the idea that only African American officers could handle the African American community.

Finally, the proposal is based on a faulty assumption about the nature of American urban communities. Although there are all-white, all–African American, and all-Hispanic neighborhoods, there are also many mixed neighborhoods. It is impossible to draw a clear line between the "white" and the "black" communities. Under the proposed policy, which officers would be assigned to mixed neighborhoods? Moreover, the racial and ethnic composition of neighborhoods is constantly changing (Reiss, 1971). Today's all-white neighborhood is tomorrow's multiracial and multiethnic neighborhood. Any attempt to draw precinct boundaries based on race or ethnicity would be quickly outdated.

Diversifying a police department does have an impact on the police subculture, bringing in people with different attitudes. African American and Hispanic officers have formed their own organizations at both the local and national levels. The National Black Police Officers Association and the Guardians, for example, represent African American officers. Hispanic officers have formed the National Latino Peace Officers Association and the Hispanic American Command Officers Association. These organizations offer a different perspective on police issues from the one presented by white police officers. After the Rodney King incident, for example, members of the African American Peace Officers Association in Los Angeles stated, "Racism is widespread in the department."[170] This was a very different point of view than that expressed by white Los Angeles officers. In this respect, minority employment breaks down the solidarity of the police subculture.

The National Black Police Officers Association published a brochure titled *Police Brutality: A Strategy to Stop the Violence,* urging officers to report brutality by other officers. This brochure represents a sharp break with the traditional norms of the police subculture, which emphasize protecting other officers from outside investigations.[171] The Police Foundation's national survey of police officers found that African American officers are far more likely to believe that officers in their department use excessive force than are white officers.[172] Finally, an evaluation of community policing in Chicago found that African American officers were more receptive to change—including community policing—than were white officers.[173]

In short, minority officers do have a different perspective on policing and police problems than white officers. The extent to which these attitudes are translated into different behavior on the street is not clear, however.

At the same time, differences in attitudes among officers of different race and ethnicity can cause conflict within the department. In a number of departments, race relations have been strained when African American officers file employment discrimination suits and white officers file countersuits challenging affirmative action programs. In a study of a Midwestern police department, Robin Haarr found little daily interaction between white and African American officers. In particular, she asked officers who they would seek out if they had a problem or question that needed answering.[174] In short, the racial divisions that exist in society at large are reproduced within police departments.

With respect to the third goal, improved police–community relations, there is only limited evidence that increased minority employment improves public opinion about the police. A survey of Chicago residents found a small but significant number of people who felt that the Chicago Police Department has improved because of increased numbers of minority officers in supervisory positions. Significantly, no respondents felt that the department had gotten worse because of increased minority employment.[175] A study in Detroit found that, unlike in all other surveys, African American residents rated the police department more favorably than did white residents, suggesting that this more favorable rating was due to the significant African American representation in city government, including the police department.[176] As already mentioned, having bilingual officers on the force may improve the ability of the police to serve communities of recent immigrants and in that respect improve police–community relations with those groups.

Minorities as Supervisors and Chief Executives

Promotion African American and Hispanic officers are also seriously under-represented in supervisory ranks. In 1992, African Americans were 11.5 percent of all sworn officers in New York City but only 6.6 percent of the officers at the rank of sergeant and above. In Los Angeles, Hispanics were 22.3 percent of all sworn officers but only 13.4 percent of those at the rank of sergeant and above.[177]

Female African American and Hispanic officers encounter both race and gender discrimination. Women, regardless of race or ethnicity, are significantly underrepresented among all sworn officers and even more underrepresented in the supervisory ranks. A 1992 survey found that white female officers were being promoted at a faster rate than either African American or Hispanic female officers. In Chicago, for example, there were 73 white females, 37 African American females, and 2 Hispanic females above the rank of sergeant in a department of 12,291 sworn officers.[178] The data contradict the popular belief that minority women enjoy a special advantage because employers count them in two affirmative action categories. Hispanic women, in fact, were almost completely unrepresented at the rank of sergeant and above.

Chief Executives Racial and ethnic minorities have been far more successful in achieving the rank of police chief executive. In recent years, African Americans have served as chief executive in many of the largest police departments in the country: New York City, Los Angeles, Chicago, Philadelphia, Atlanta, and New Orleans, among others. Several African American individuals have established distinguished careers as law enforcement chief executives. Lee P. Brown served as sheriff of Multnomah County, Oregon, and then police chief in Atlanta, Houston, and New York City. In 1993, he became President Clinton's director of the Office of Drug Control Policy and later was elected mayor of Houston. Hubert Williams served as police commissioner in Newark, New Jersey, and then became president of the Police Foundation, a private police research organization. Charles Ramsey was appointed superintendent of the Washington, D.C., police department in 1998 after directing the Chicago Police Department's community policing program.

CONCLUSION

Significant problems persist in the relations between police and racial and ethnic communities in the United States. African Americans and Hispanics rate the police lower than do white Americans. There is persuasive evidence that minorities are more likely than white Americans to be shot and killed, arrested, and victimized by excessive physical force. Although some progress has been made in recent years in controlling police behavior, particularly with respect to the use of deadly force, significant racial and ethnic disparities remain. In addition, there is evidence of misconduct directed against racial and ethnic minorities and of police departments failing to discipline officers who are guilty of misconduct. Finally, police department employment discrimination continues.

With reference to the discrimination–disparity continuum we discussed in Chapter 1, the evidence about the police suggests a combination of three of the different patterns. Some disparities are institutionalized discrimination resulting from the application of neutral criteria (as in the greater likelihood of arrest for the more serious crimes). Some represent contextual discrimination (as in the greater likelihood of arrest of minorities suspected of crimes against whites). And some are individual acts of discrimination by prejudiced individuals. There is no basis for saying that a situation of pure justice exists or that racism is a "myth," as William Wilbanks argued.

The evidence supports the conflict perspective regarding the police and racial and ethnic minorities. The data suggest that police actions such as arrest, use of deadly force, and verbal abuse reflect the broader patterns of social and economic inequality in U.S. society that we discussed in detail in Chapter 3. Those inequalities are both racial and economic. Thus, the injustices suffered by racial and ethnic minorities at the hands of the police are a result of both discrimination against ethnic and racial minorities and the disproportionate representation of minorities among the poor.

The evidence also supports Hawkins's call for a modified conflict perspective that takes into account evident complexities and contingencies. Some of the evidence we have reviewed, for example, indicates that in certain situations, African Americans receive less law enforcement protection than do whites. Discrimination can result from too little policing as well as excessive policing. Other evidence suggests that the race of the suspect must be considered in conjunction with the race of the complainant.

Finally, the evidence indicates significant changes in some important areas of policing with respect to racial and ethnic minorities. On the positive side, the number of persons shot and killed by the police has declined. On the negative side, the War on Drugs has been waged most heavily against racial and ethnic minorities. In terms of employment, some slow but steady progress has been made in the employment of African Americans and Hispanics as police officers.

DISCUSSION QUESTIONS

1. What is meant by a contextual approach to examining policing, race, and ethnicity?
2. How is policing in Native American communities different from policing in the rest of the United States?
3. When does police use of force become "excessive" or "unjustified"? Give a definition of *excessive force*.
4. Are there any significant differences between how Hispanics and African Americans interact with the police? Explain.
5. Is there racial or ethnic discrimination in arrests? What is the evidence on this question?

6. Define the concept of *affirmative action*. Do you support or oppose affirmative action in the employment of police officers? Do you think affirmative action is more important in policing than in other areas of life? Explain.

NOTES

1. The Cincinnati consent decree and other consent decrees can be found at the U.S. Civil Rights Division Web site http://www.usdoj.gov/crt/split/.

2. Sandra Lee Browning, Francis T. Cullen, Liqun Cao, Renee Kopache, and Thomas J. Stevenson, "Race and Getting Hassled by the Police: A Research Note," *Police Studies* 17, no. 1 (1994): 1–11.

3. David Harris, *Profiles in Injustice: Why Racial Profiling Won't Work* (New York: New Press, 2001); for the latest news, reports, and legislation on racial profiling, see Harris's Web site: www.profilesininjustice.com; ACLU, *Driving While Black* (New York: Author, 1999).

4. Bureau of Justice Statistics, *Policing and Homicide, 1976–98: Justifiable Homicide by Police, Police Officers Murdered by Felons,* NCJ 180987 (Washington, DC: U.S. Government Printing Office, 2001). Available at www.ncjrs.org.

5. Police Executive Research Forum, *Racially Biased Policing: A Principled Response* (Washington, DC: Author, 2001).

6. Gallup Poll data cited in Bureau of Justice Statistics, *Sourcebook of Criminal Justice Statistics, 2000,* p. 109. Online edition available at www.albany.edu.

7. It is drawn heavily from Samuel Walker and Charles M. Katz, *The Police in America: An Introduction,* 4th ed. (New York: McGraw-Hill, 2002), chap. 9.

8. Samuel Walker, *Police Interactions with Racial and Ethnic Minorities: Assessing the Evidence and Allegations* (Washington, DC: Police Executive Research Forum, 2000).

9. Bureau of Justice Statistics, *Contacts between Police and the Public: Findings from the 1999 National Survey,* NCJ 184057 (Washington, DC: U.S. Government Printing Office, 2001). Available at www.ncjrs.org.

10. Marianne O. Nielsen, "Contextualization for Native American Crime and Criminal Justice Involvement," in *Native Americans, Crime, and Justice,* ed. Marianne O. Nielsen and Robert A. Silverman (Boulder, CO: Westview, 1996), p. 10.

11. "Officers Killed with Impunity," *Washington Post* (July 1, 2001), p. 1.

12. U.S. Department of Justice, *Youth Violence: A Community-Based Response: One City's Success Story* (Washington, DC: U.S. Department of Justice, 1996).

13. Ronald Weitzer, "Racialized Policing: Residents' Perceptions in Three Neighborhoods," *Law and Society Review* 34, no. 1 (2000): 129–156.

14. Walker and Katz, *Police in America* chap. 2.

15. National Advisory Commission on Civil Disorders [Kerner Commission], *Report* (New York: Bantam Books, 1968).

16. Alfredo Mirandé, *Gringo Justice* (Notre Dame, IN: University of Notre Dame Press, 1987).

17. A video documentary, *Zoot Suit Riots,* along with supporting educational material, can be found on the Public Broadcasting System Web site at www.pbs.org.

18. Joan Petersilia and Allan Abrahamse, *The Los Angeles Riot of Spring, 1992: A Profile of Those Arrested* (Santa Monica, CA: Rand Corporation, 1993); see also U.S. Civil Rights Commission, *Mexican-Americans and the Administration of Justice* (Washington, DC: U.S. Government Printing Office, 1970).

19. Henry I. DeGeneste and John P. Sullivan, *Policing a Multicultural Community* (Washington, DC: Police Executive Research Forum, 1997), p. 15.

20. Minneapolis Civilian Review Authority, *How to File a Complaint* (Minneapolis MN: CRA, n.d.).

21. Gallup Poll data cited in Bureau of Justice Statistics, *Sourcebook, 2000,* p. 109.

22. "Discrimination in America," *Washington Post* (June 21, 2001).

23. Harris Poll data, reported in Bureau of Justice Statistics, *Sourcebook, 2000,* p. 119.

24. U.S. Department of Justice, *The Police and Public Opinion* (Washington, DC: U.S. Government Printing Office, 1977), pp. 39–40.

25. Ronald Weitzer, "Racialized Policing," pp. 129–156.

26. A comprehensive overview of public opinion trends is in Steven A. Tuch and Ronald Weitzer, "Racial Differences in Attitudes toward the Police," *Public Opinion Quarterly* 61 (1997): 643–663.

27. Carl Werthman and Irving Piliavin, "Gang Members and the Police," in *The Police: Six Sociological Essays,* ed. David J. Bordua (New York: Wiley, 1967), p. 58.

28. David H. Bayley and Harold Mendelsohn, *Minorities and the Police: Confrontation in America* (New York: Free Press, 1969), p. 109.

29. Bureau of Justice Statistics, *Criminal Victimization 2000: Changes 1999–2000 with Trends 1993–2000,* NCJ 187007 (Washington, DC: U.S. Government Printing Office, 2001). Available at www.ncjrs.org.

30. "From Some Parents, Warnings about Police," *New York Times* (October 23, 1997), p. A18.

31. Cynthia Perez McCluskey, *Policing the Latino Community* (East Lansing, MI: Julian Samora Research Institute, 1998), p. 3.

32. Leigh Herbst and Samuel Walker, "Language Barriers in the Delivery of Police Services: A Study of Police and Hispanic Interactions in a Midwestern City," *Journal of Criminal Justice* 29, no. 4 (2001): 329–340.

33. David L. Carter, "Hispanic Perceptions of Police Performance: An Empirical Assessment," *Journal of Criminal Justice* 13 (1985): 487–500.

34. Samuel Walker, "Complaints against the Police: A Focus Group Study of Citizen Perceptions, Goals, and Expectations,"

Criminal Justice Review 22, no. 2 (1997): 207–225.

35. Stewart Wakeling, Miriam Jorgensen, Susan Michaelson, and Manley Begay, *Policing on American Indian Reservations: A Report to the National Institute of Justice,* NCJ 188095 (Washington, DC: U.S. Government Printing Office, 2001). Available at www.ncjrs.org.

36. Ibid., p. 9. Much information about Native Americans and criminal justice can be found at the U.S. Department of Justice Web site: www.usdoj.gov.otj.

37. Wakeling et al., *Policing on American Indian Reservations,* p. 7.

38. California Police Chiefs Association, letter to Attorney General John Ashcroft (April 10, 2002).

39. "Police Departments Balk at Idea of Becoming 'Quasi-INS Agents,'" *USA Today* (May 7, 2002), p. 8a.

40. Bureau of Justice Statistics, *Policing and Homicide, 1976–98.*

41. James J. Fyfe, "Reducing the Use of Deadly Force: The New York Experience," in *Police Use of Deadly Force,* U.S. Department of Justice (Washington, DC: U.S. Government Printing Office, 1978), p. 29.

42. *Tennessee v. Garner,* 471 U.S. 1 (1985).

43. James J. Fyfe, "Blind Justice: Police Shootings in Memphis," *Journal of Criminal Law and Criminology* 73, no. 2 (1982): 707–722.

44. William A. Geller and Kevin J. Karales, *Split-Second Decisions* (Chicago: Chicago Law Enforcement Study Group, 1981), p. 119.

45. "Officers Killed with Impunity," p. 1.

46. Bureau of Justice Statistics, *Policing and Homicide, 1976–98.*

47. Geller and Karales, *Split-Second Decisions.*

48. Jerry R. Sparger and David J. Giacopassi, "Memphis Revisited: A Reexamination of Police Shootings after the Garner Decision," *Justice Quarterly* 9 (June 1992): 211–225.

49. James J. Fyfe, "Administrative Interventions on Police Shooting Discretion," *Journal of Criminal Justice* 7 (winter 1979):

309–323; Bureau of Justice Statistics, *Policing and Homicide, 1976–98.*

50. City of New York, Commission to Investigate Allegations of Police Corruption [Mollen Commission], *Commission Report* (New York: Author, 1994), p. 48.

51. National Commission on Law Observance and Enforcement, *Lawlessness in Law Enforcement* (Washington, DC: U.S. Government Printing Office, 1931), p. 4.

52. Human Rights Watch, *Shielded from Justice: Police Brutality and Accountability in the United States* (New York: Author, 1998), p. 39.

53. City of New York, *Commission Report,* p. 44, n. 4.

54. President's Commission on Law Enforcement and Administration of Justice, *Field Surveys,* vol. 5: *A National Survey of Police and Community Relations* (Washington, DC: U.S. Government Printing Office, 1967), p. 151.

55. New York City Civilian Complaint Review Board, *Status Report, January–December 2001* (New York: Author, 2002), p. 38.

56. The best review of the available studies is in Kenneth Adams, "Measuring the Prevalence of Police Abuse of Force," in *And Justice for All,* ed. William A. Geller and Hans Toch (Washington, DC: Police Executive Research Forum, 1995), pp. 61–98; see also Anthony M. Pate and Lorie Fridell, *Police Use of Force,* 2 vols. (Washington, DC: Police Foundation, 1993).

57. Bureau of Justice Statistics, *Contacts between Police and the Public.*

58. Summarized in Adams, "Measuring the Prevalence of Police Abuse of Force."

59. Ibid, pp. 92–97.

60. Robert E. Worden, "The 'Causes' of Police Brotality: Theory and Evidence on Police Use of Force," In *And Justice for All,* pp. 31–59; Human Rights Watch, *Shielded from Justice,* p. 51.

61. Albert Reiss, *The Police and the Public* (New Haven, CT: Yale University Press, 1971); Donald Black, "The Social Organization of Arrest," in *The Manners and Customs of the Police,* ed. Donald Black (New York: Academic Press, 1980), pp. 85–108.

62. Reiss, *The Police and the Public,* pp. 149, 155.

63. New York City Civilian Complaint Review Board, *Status Report, 2001,* p. 48.

64. Worden, "The 'Causes' of Police Brutality," pp. 52–53.

65. David Weisburd, Rosann Greenspan, Edwin E. Hamilton, Kellie A. Bryant, and Hubert Williams, *The Abuse of Police Authority: A National Study of Police Officers' Attitudes* (Washington, DC: Police Foundation, 2001).

66. Reiss, *The Police and the Public,* p. 151.

67. George Gallup Jr., *The Gallup Poll Monthly* (March 1991) p. 1.

68. Bureau of Justice Statistics, *Sourcebook, 2000,* Table 4.10.

69. Robert Tillman, "The Size of the Criminal Population: The Prevalence and Incidence of Adult Arrest," *Criminology* 25 (August 1987): 561–579.

70. U.S. Census Bureau, *Statistical Abstract of the United States: 2001* (Washington, DC: U.S. Government Printing Office, 2001), table 10, 308.

71. Black, "The Social Organization of Arrest," pp. 85–108.

72. David A. Klinger, "Demeanor or Crime? Why 'Hostile' Citizens Are More Likely to Be Arrested," *Criminology* 32, no. 3 (1994): 475–493.

73. Bureau of Justice Statistics, *Criminal Victimization in the United States, 1999,* (Washington, DC: U.S. Government Printing Office, 2001), table 40.

74. Douglas A. Smith, Christy Visher, and Laura A. Davidson, "Equity and Discretionary Justice: The Influence of Race on Police Arrest Decisions," *Journal of Criminal Law and Criminology* 75 (spring 1984): 234–249; Douglas A. Smith and Christy A. Visher, "Street-Level Justice: Situational Determinants of Police Arrest Decisions," *Social Problems* 29 (December 1981): 167–177.

75. John R. Hepburn, "Race and the Decision to Arrest: An Analysis of Warrants Issued," *Journal of Research in Crime and Delinquency* 15 (1978): 54–73.

76. Joan Petersilia, *Racial Disparities in the Criminal Justice System* (Santa Monica, CA: Rand Corporation, 1983), pp. 21–26.

77. Black, *The Manners and Customs of the Police*, p. 108.

78. George L. Kelling and Catherine M. Coles, *Fixing Broken Windows* (New York: Free Press, 1996).

79. New York Civil Liberties Union, *Deflecting Blame* (New York: Author, 1998), p. 48.

80. John E. Eck and Edward R. Maguire, "Have Changes in Policing Reduced Violent Crime?: An Assessment of the Evidence," in *The Crime Drop in America,* ed. Alfred Blumstein and Joel Wallman (New York: Cambridge University Press, 2000), pp. 224–228.

81. The Gallup Organization, *Black-White Relations in the United States: 2001 Update* (Princeton, NJ: Author, 2001).

82. Harris, *Profiles in Injustice;* ACLU, *Driving While Black.*

83. Police Executive Research Forum, *Racially Biased Policing.*

84. ACLU, *Driving While Black;* Harris, *Profiles in Injustice.*

85. Bureau of Justice Statistics, *Contacts between Police and the Public;* Bureau of Justice Statistics, *Characteristics of Drivers Stopped by Police, 1999,* NCJ 191548 (Washington, DC: U.S. Government Printing Office, 2002).

86. San Jose Police Department, *Vehicle Stop Demographic Study: First Report* (San Jose: Author, 1999).

87. Samuel Walker, "Searching for the Denominator: Problems with Police Traffic Stop Data and an Early Warning System Solution," *Justice Research and Policy* 3 (spring 2001): 63–95.

88. Harris, *Profiles in Injustice.*

89. Walker, "Searching for the Denominator."

90. Ibid. Samuel Walker, Geoffrey P. Alpert, and Dennis J. Kenney, *Early Warning Systems: Responding to the Problem Police Officer,* NCJ 188565, Research in Brief (Washington, DC: U.S. Government Printing Office, 2001).

91. Current information about data collection laws and data reports is available at www.profilesininjustice.com.

92. *United States v. State of New Jersey.* This decree and others are available on the U.S. Department of Justice Web site: http://www.usdoj.gov/crt/split.

93. Police Executive Research Forum, *Racially Biased Policing.*

94. Ibid., pp. 51–53.

95. General Accounting Office, *U.S. Customs Service: Better Targeting of Airline Passengers for Personal Searches Could Produce Better Results,* GAO/GGD-00-38 (March 2000).

96. Harris, *Profiles in Injustice.*

97. National Advisory Commission, Report, pp. 301, 304–305.

98. Warren Friedman and Marsha Hott, *Young People and the Police* (Chicago: Chicago Alliance for Neighborhood Safety, 1995), p. 111.

99. John E. Boydston, *San Diego Field Interrogation: Final Report* (Washington, DC: Police Foundation, 1975), pp. 16, 62.

100. Boydston, *San Diego Field Interrogation,* p. 62.

101. Massachusetts Attorney General, *Report of the Attorney General's Civil Rights Division on Boston Police Department Practices* (Boston: Attorney General's Office, 1990).

102. Jeffrey Fagan and Garth Davies, "Street Stops and Broken Windows: *Terry,* Race, and Disorder in New York City," *Fordam Urban Law Journal,* 28 (2001): 457–504.

103. Carolyn M. Ward, "Policing in the Hyde Park Neighborhood, St. Louis: Racial Bias, Political Pressure, and Community Policing," *Crime, Law and Social Change* 26 (1997): 171–172.

104. Jerome Skolnick, *Justice without Trial: Law Enforcement in a Democratic Society,* 3d ed. (New York: Macmillan, 1994), pp. 44–47.

105. Randall Kennedy, *Race, Crime, and the Law* (New York: Vintage Books, 1998), p. 137.

106. Ibid., pp. 151, 153.

107. Minneapolis Civilian Police Review Authority, *1997 Annual Report* (Minneapolis, MN: Author, 1998), exhibit F.

108. Christopher Commission, *Report of the Independent Commission on the Los Angeles Police Department* (Los Angeles: Author, 1991), p. 73.

109. Ibid., pp. 72–73.

110. Samuel Walker, Carol Archbold, and Leigh Herbst, *Mediating Citizen Complaints against Police Officers: A Guide for Police and Community Leaders* (Washington, DC: Office of Community Oriented Policing Services, 2002). Available at www.cops .usdoj.gov.

111. Mervin F. White, Terry C. Cox, and Jack Basehart, "Theoretical Considerations of Officer Profanity and Obscenity in Formal Contacts with Citizens," in *Police Deviance,* 2d ed., ed. Thomas Barker and David L. Carter (Cincinnati, OH: Anderson, 1991), pp. 275–297; John Van Maanen, "The Asshole," in *Policing: A View from the Street,* ed. John Van Maanen and Peter Manning (Santa Monica, CA: Goodyear, 1978), pp. 221–238.

112. New York City Civilian Complaint Review Board, *Status Report, 2001,* pp. 37, 44.

113. Douglas A. Smith, Nanette Graham, and Bonney Adams, "Minorities and the Police: Attitudinal and Behavioral Questions," in *Race and Criminal Justice,* ed. Michael J. Lynch and E. Britt Patterson (New York: Harrow & Heston, 1991), p. 31.

114. Bayley and Mendelsohn, *Minorities and the Police,* p. 144.

115. Ibid., pp. 15–18.

116. Smith et al., "Minorities and the Police," p. 28.

117. Reiss, *The Police and the Public,* p. 147.

118. Samuel Walker, "Racial-Minority and Female Employment in Policing: The Implications of 'Glacial' Change," *Crime and Delinquency* 31 (October 1985): 555–572.

119. Weisburd et al., *The Abuse of Police Authority.*

120. Jerome L. Blakemore, David Barlow, and Deborah L. Padgett, "From the Classroom to the Community: Introducing Process in Police Diversity Training," *Police Studies* 18, no. 1 (1995): 71–83.

121. Geoffrey P. Alpert, William C. Smith, and Daniel Watters, "Law Enforcement: Implications of the Rodney King Beating," *Criminal Law Bulletin* 28 (September–October 1992): 477.

122. New York City, *The Knapp Commission Report on Police Corruption* (New York: Braziller, 1972), p. 1.

123. City of New York, *Commission Report.*

124. Bureau of Justice Statistics, *Sourcebook of Criminal Justice Statistics, 1993,* p. 165.

125. Fred A. Klyman and Joanna Kruckenberg, "A National Survey of Police–Community Relations Units," *Journal of Police Science and Administration* 7 (March 1979): 74.

126. Ibid., p. 74.

127. Wesley G. Skogan and Susan M. Hartnett, *Community Policing: Chicago Style* (New York: Oxford University Press, 1997).

128. San Jose Police Department, *Vehicle Stop Demographic Study.*

129. PolicyLink, *Community-Centered Policing: A Force for Change* (Oakland, CA: Author, 2001), pp. 16–20.

130. U.S. Department of Justice, *Youth Violence.*

131. Samuel Walker, *Police Accountability: The Role of Citizen Oversight* (Belmont, CA: Wadsworth, 2001).

132. New York City Civilian Complaint Review Board, *Status Report, 2001,* p. 1.

133. Human Rights Watch, *Shielded from Justice.* pp. 63–65.

134. Samuel Walker and Nanette Graham, "Citizen Complaints in Response to Police Misconduct: The Results of a Victimization Survey," *Police Quarterly* 1 (1998): 65–89.

135. National Advisory Commission, *Report.*

136. Christopher Commission, *Report of the Independent Commission,* pp. 153–161.

137. ACLU of Southern California, *The Call for Change Goes Unanswered* (Los Angeles: Author, 1992), p. 23.

138. William A. Westley, *Violence and the Police* (Cambridge, MA: MIT Press, 1970).

139. Christopher Commission, *Report of the Independent Commission,* p. 168.

140. City of New York, *Commission Report,* p. 53.

141. Pate and Fridell, *Police Use of Force,* vol. 1, p. 118. A discussion of the reasons why so few complaints are sustained is in Walker, *Police Accountability,* pp. 121–137.

142. Walker, Archbold, and Herbst, *Mediating Citizen Complaints.*

143. Walker, *Police Accountability,* p. 6.

144. Information about different citizen oversight agencies is available at www.policeaccountability.org.

145. Walker, *Police Accountability,* p. 122.

146. W. Marvin Dulaney, *Black Police in America* (Bloomington: Indiana University Press, 1996).

147. President's Commission on Law Enforcement and Administration of Justice, *Task Force Report: The Police* (Washington, DC: U.S. Government Printing Office, 1967), p. 168.

148. "From Court Order to Reality: A Diverse Boston Police Force," *New York Times* (April 4, 2001), p. 1.

149. Summarized in Walker and Katz, *Police in America,* chap. 11.

150. Commission on Accreditation for Law Enforcement Agencies, *Standards for Law Enforcement Agencies,* 3d ed., standard 31–2 (Fairfax, VA: Author, 1994).

151. Samuel Walker and K. B. Turner, *A Decade of Modest Progress* (Omaha: University of Nebraska at Omaha, 1992).

152. The EEO Index is described in Walker and Turner, *A Decade of Modest Progress,* p. 1.

153. "From Court Order to Reality," p. 1.

154. Christopher Commission, *Report of the Independent Commission.*

155. Bureau of Justice Statistics, *Law Enforcement Management and Administrative Statistics, 1999* (Washington, DC: U.S. Government Printing Office, 2001).

156. Christopher Commission, *Report of the Independent Commission.*

157. Herbst and Walker, "Language Barriers in the Delivery of Police Services."

158. Wakeling et al., *Policing on American Indian Reservations.*

159. U.S. Department of Labor, Office of Federal Contract Compliance, *Employment Standards Administration* (n.d.).

160. PolicyLink, *Community-Centered Policing,* p. 33.

161. Gunnar Myrdal, "Police and Other Public Contacts," in *An American Dilemma* (New York: Harper & Brothers, 1944); W. Marvin Dulaney, *Black Police in America* (Bloomington: Indiana University Press, 1996).

162. Reiss, *The Police and the Public,* p. 167.

163. James J. Fyfe, "Who Shoots?: A Look at Officer Race and Police Shooting," *Journal of Police Science and Administration* 9, no. 4 (1981): 367–382.

164. Merrick J. Bobb, Special Counsel, *9th Semiannual Report* (Los Angeles: Los Angeles County, 1998), pp. 59–61.

165. "For Black Officers, Diversity Has Its Limits," *New York Times* (April 2, 2001), p. 1.

166. "Alone, Undercover, and Black: Hazards of Mistaken Identity," *New York Times* (November 22, 1992), p. A1.

167. "Alienation Is a Partner for Black Officers," *New York Times* (April 3, 2001), p. 1.

168. The Kerner Commission, for example, argued that "Negro officers can also be particularly effective in controlling disorders"; National Advisory Commission, *Report,* p. 315.

169. PolicyLink, *Community-Centered Policing,* pp. 36–37.

170. "Los Angeles Force Accused from Within," *New York Times* (March 29, 1991), p. A18.

171. National Black Police Officers Association, *Police Brutality: A Strategy to Stop the Violence* (Washington, DC: Author, nd).

172. Weisburd et al., *The Abuse of Police Authority.*

173. Skogan and Hartnett, *Community Policing.*

174. Robin N. Haarr, "Patterns of Interaction in a Police Patrol Bureau: Race and Gender Barriers to Integration," *Justice Quarterly* 14 (March 1997): 53–85.

175. Samuel E. Walker and Vincent J. Webb, "Public Perceptions of Racial and

Minority Employment and Its Perceived Impact on Police Service," paper presented at the American Society of Criminology Annual Meeting, 1997.

176. Frank et al., "Reassessing the Impact of Race on Citizens' Attitudes toward the Police."

177. Walker and Turner, *A Decade of Modest Progress.*

178. Samuel Walker, Susan E. Martin, and K. B. Turner, "Through the Glass Ceiling? Promotion Rates for Minority and Female Police Officers," paper presented at the American Society of Criminology, November 1994.

5

The Courts

A Quest for Justice during the Pretrial Process

[I]t is clear to me that if America ever is to eradicate racism, lawyers will have to lead. We must cleanse the justice system, because until the justice system is truly colorblind, we cannot have any genuine hope for the elimination of bias in the other segments of American life.

—PHILIP S. ANDERSON, PRESIDENT, AMERICAN BAR ASSOCIATION[1]

In March 1931, nine African American teenage boys were accused of raping two white girls on a slow-moving freight train traveling through Alabama. They were arrested and taken to Scottsboro, Alabama, where they were indicted for rape, a capital offense. One week later, the first case was called for trial. When the defendant appeared without counsel, the judge hearing the case simply appointed all members of the local bar to represent him and his co-defendants. An out-of-state lawyer also volunteered to assist in the defense, but the judge appointed no counsel of record.

The nine defendants were tried and convicted, and eight were sentenced to death. They appealed their convictions, arguing that their right to counsel had been denied. In 1932, the U.S. Supreme Court issued its ruling in the case of *Powell v. Alabama,*[2] one of the most famous Supreme Court cases in U.S. history. The Court reversed the defendants' convictions and ruled that due process of law required the appointment of counsel for young, inexperienced, illiterate, and indigent defendants in capital cases.

The Supreme Court's ruling in *Powell* provided the so-called Scottsboro Boys with only a short reprieve. They were quickly retried, reconvicted, and resentenced to death, even though one of the alleged victims had recanted and questions were raised about the credibility of the other victim's testimony. Once again, the defendants appealed their convictions, this time contending that their right to a fair trial by an impartial jury had been denied. All of the defendants had been tried by all-white juries. They argued that the jury selection procedures used in Alabama were racially biased. Although African Americans who were registered to vote were eligible for jury service, they were excluded in practice because state officials refused to place their names on the lists from which jurors were chosen. In 1935, the Supreme Court, noting that the exclusion of all African Americans from jury service deprived African American defendants of their right to the equal protection of the laws guaranteed by the Fourteenth Amendment, again reversed the convictions.[3]

The Supreme Court's decision was harshly criticized in the South. The *Charleston News and Courier,* for example, stated that racially mixed juries were "out of the question" and asserted that the Court's decision "can and will be evaded."[4] Southern sentiment also strongly favored yet another round of trials. Thomas Knight Jr., the attorney who prosecuted the Scottsboro cases the second time, noted, "Approximately ninety jurors have been found saying the defendants were guilty of the offense with which they are charged and for which the penalty is death." Knight reported that he had been "retained by the State to prosecute the cases and [would] prosecute the same to their conclusion."[5]

Less than eight months after the Supreme Court's decision, a grand jury composed of 13 whites and one African American returned new indictments against the nine defendants. Haywood Patterson, the first defendant to be retried, again faced an all-white jury. Although there were 12 African Americans among the 100 potential jurors, 7 of the 12 asked to be excused, and the prosecutor used his peremptory challenges to remove the remaining five. In his closing argument, the prosecutor also implied that an acquittal would force the women of Alabama "to buckle six-shooters about their middles" in order to protect their "sacred secret parts." He pleaded with the jurors, "Get it done quick and protect the fair womanhood of this great State."[6]

Patterson was convicted and sentenced to 75 years in prison. The sentence, although harsh, represented "a victory of sorts."[7] As the *Birmingham Age-Herald* noted, the decision "represents probably the first time in the history of the South that a Negro has been convicted of a charge of rape upon a white woman and has been given less than a death sentence."[8]

Three of the remaining eight defendants were tried and convicted in July 1937. One of the three, Clarence Norris, was sentenced to death; the other two received prison sentences of 75 and 99 years. Shortly thereafter, Ozie Powell pled guilty to assaulting an officer after the State agreed to dismiss the rape charge. That same day, in an unexpected and controversial move, the State dropped all charges against the remaining four defendants. In a prepared statement, Attorney General Thomas Lawson asserted that the State was "convinced beyond any question of doubt . . . that the defendants that have been tried are guilty." However, "after careful consideration of all the testimony, every lawyer connected with the prosecution is convinced that the defendants Willie Roberson and Olen Montgomery are not guilty." Regarding the remaining two defendants, who were twelve and thirteen years old when the crime occurred, Dawson stated that "the ends of justice would be met at this time by releasing these two juveniles on condition that they leave the State, never to return."[9]

The State's decision to drop charges against four of the nine defendants led editorial writers for newspapers throughout the United States to call for the immediate release of the defendants who previously had been convicted. The *Richmond Times-Dispatch* stated that the State's action "serves as a virtual clincher to the argument that all nine of the Negroes are innocent," and the *New York Times* called on the State to "do more complete justice later on."[10]

Clarence Norris's death sentence was commuted to life imprisonment in 1938, but the Alabama Pardon and Parole Board repeatedly denied the five defendants' requests for parole. One of the defendants finally was granted parole in 1943, and by 1950 all of them had gained their freedom. Collectively, the nine Scottsboro Boys served 104 years in prison for a crime that many believe was "almost certainly, a hoax."[11]

THE SITUATION TODAY

The infamous Scottsboro case illustrates overt discrimination directed against African American criminal defendants. However, those events took place in the 1930s and 1940s, and much has changed since then. Legislative reforms and Supreme Court decisions protecting the rights of criminal defendants, coupled with changes in attitudes, have made it less likely that criminal justice officials will treat defendants of different races differently. Racial minorities are no longer routinely denied bail and then tried by all-white juries without attorneys to assist them in their defense. They are no longer brought into court in chains and shackles. They no longer receive "justice" at the hands of white lynch mobs.

Despite these reforms, inequities persist. Racial minorities, and particularly those suspected of crimes against whites, remain the victims of unequal justice. In 1983, for example, Lenell Geter, an African American man, was charged with the armed robbery of a Kentucky Fried Chicken restaurant in Balch Springs, Texas. Despite the absence of any physical evidence to connect him to the crime and despite the prosecution's failure to establish his motive for the crime, Geter was convicted by an all-white jury and sentenced to life in prison.

Geter's conviction was particularly surprising given the fact that he had an ironclad alibi. Nine of his coworkers, all of whom were white, testified that Geter was at work on the day of the crime. His supervisor testified that there was no way Geter could have made the 50-mile trip from work to the site of the crime by 3:20 P.M., the time when the robbery occurred. According to one coworker, "Unless old Captain Kirk dematerialized him and beamed him over there, he couldn't have made it back by then. He was here at work. There's no question in my mind—none at all."[12]

Prosecutors in the county where Geter was tried denied that race played a role in his conviction. As one of them put it, "To say this is a conviction based on race is as far out in left field as you can get."[13] Geter's coworkers disagreed; they argued that Geter and his codefendant (who also was African American) would not have been charged or convicted if they had been white.

Events that occurred following the trial suggest that Geter's coworkers were right. Another man arrested for a series of armed robberies eventually was linked to the robbery of the Kentucky Fried Chicken restaurant. Geter's conviction and sentence were overturned after the employees who originally identified Geter picked this suspect out of a lineup. Geter served over a year in prison for a crime he did not commit.

Like Lenell Geter, James Newsome, an African American sentenced to life in prison for the armed robbery and murder of a white man, also had an alibi. At his trial for the 1979 murder of Mickey Cohen, the owner of Mickey's Grocery Store in Chicago, Newsome's girlfriend and her two sisters testified that he was with them at the time of the murder. The prosecutor trying the case argued that Newsome's girlfriend, who was a convicted burglar, was not a credible witness. He also introduced the testimony of three eyewitnesses who identified Newsome as Cohen's killer.[14]

Despite the fact that there was no physical evidence linking Newsome to the crime and that Newsome's fingerprints were not found on the items in the store handled by the killer, the jury hearing the case found Newsome guilty. Although Cook County prosecutors had sought the death penalty, the jury recommended life in prison.

Newsome, who steadfastly maintained his innocence, spent the next 15 years appealing his conviction. With the help of Norval Morris, a University of Chicago Law School professor, and two noted Chicago defense attorneys, Newsome was able to convince the Cook County Circuit Court to order that the fingerprints obtained from the crime scene be run through the police department's computerized fingerprint database to see if they matched any of those on file. The tests revealed that the fingerprints matched those of Dennis Emerson, a 45-year-old Illinois death row inmate who, at the time of Cohen's murder, was out on parole after serving three years for armed robbery.

Two weeks later, Newsome was released from prison. Shortly thereafter, Illinois governor Jim Edgar pardoned Newsome and ordered his criminal record expunged. Following his release, James Newsome, who spent 15 years in prison for a crime he did not commit, said, "I finally felt vindicated. I had defeated a criminal justice giant. Fifteen years ago, they told me that I would never walk the streets again in my life. What did I do? I slayed a giant—a criminal justice giant."[15] Like Geter, Newsome contended that race played a role in his arrest and conviction. "In the most [racially] polarized city in the world," Newsome stated, "racism was a factor. I was a suspect and I was convenient."[16]

Race also played a role in the case of Clarence Brandley, an African American who was sentenced to death for the rape and murder of Cheryl Dee Fergeson, a white student at a high school north of Houston where Brandley worked as a janitor. Brandley and a coworker found the body and were the initial suspects in the case. Brandley's coworker, who was white, reported that during their interrogation one of the police officers stated, "One of you two is going to hang for this." Then he turned to Brandley and said, "Since you're the nigger, you're elected." The police investigating the case claimed that three hairs found on the victim implicated Brandley. Although the hairs were never forensically tested, the police claimed that they were identical "in all observable characteristics" to Brandley's.[17]

Brandley was indicted by an all-white grand jury and tried before an all-white jury, which hung 11 to 1 in favor of conviction. He was retried by a second all-white jury after the district attorney trying the case used his peremptory challenges to strike all of the prospective African American jurors. During his closing argument, the district attorney referred to Brandley as a "necrophiliac" and a "depraved sex maniac." This time, the jurors found Brandley guilty and recommended a death sentence, which the judge imposed.

Brandley spent six years on death row before a Texas district court, citing misconduct on the part of police and prosecutors, threw out his conviction. The judge, who noted that there was strong evidence that the crime was committed by two white men, stated that "the color of Clarence Brandley's skin was a substantial factor which pervaded all aspects of the State's capital prosecution against him, and was an impermissible factor which significantly influenced the investigation, trial and post-trial proceedings of [Brandley's] case."[18]

These three recent cases, of course, do not prove that there is a pattern of *systematic* discrimination directed against racial minorities in courts throughout the United States. One might argue, in fact, that these three cases are simply exceptions to the general rule of impartiality. As we explained in Chapter 1, the validity of the discrimination thesis rests not on anecdotal evidence but on the results of empirical studies of criminal justice decision making.

GOALS OF THE CHAPTER

In this chapter and in Chapter 6, we discuss the treatment of racial minorities in court. The focus in this chapter is on pretrial decision making. Our goal is to determine whether people of color are more likely than whites to be tried without adequate counsel to represent them or to be denied bail or detained in jail prior to trial. In addition, we review research on prosecutors' charging and plea bargaining decisions for evidence of differential treatment of racial minorities and whites. We argue that recent reforms adopted voluntarily by the states or mandated by court decisions have reduced, but not eliminated, racial discrimination in the criminal court system.

DECISIONS REGARDING COUNSEL AND BAIL

As we explained in Chapter 3, racial minorities are at a disadvantage in court both because of their race and because they are more likely than whites to be poor. This "double jeopardy" makes it more difficult for minority defendants to obtain competent attorneys or secure release from jail prior to trial. This, in turn, hinders their defense and may increase the odds that they will be convicted and sentenced harshly. Given these consequences, decisions regarding provision of counsel and bail obviously are important.

Racial Minorities and the Right to Counsel

The Sixth Amendment to the U.S. Constitution states, "In all criminal prosecutions, the accused shall enjoy the right to have the assistance of counsel for his defense." Historically, this meant simply that if a defendant had an attorney, he could bring the attorney along to defend him. The problem, of course, was that this was of no help to the majority of defendants, and particularly minority defendants, who were too poor to hire their own attorneys.

The U.S. Supreme Court, recognizing that defendants could not obtain fair trials without the assistance of counsel, began to interpret the Sixth Amendment as requiring the appointment of counsel for indigent defendants. The process began in 1932 when the Court ruled in *Powell v. Alabama* that states must provide attorneys for indigent defendants charged with capital crimes (see the earlier discussion of the Scottsboro case).[19] The Court's decision in a 1938 case, *Johnson v. Zerbst,* required the appointment of counsel for all indigent defendants in federal criminal cases,[20] but the requirement was not extended to the states until *Gideon v. Wainwright* was decided in 1963.[21] In that 1963 decision, Justice Black's majority opinion stated:

> [R]eason and reflection require us to recognize that in our adversary system of criminal justice, any person haled into court, who is too poor to hire a lawyer, cannot be assured a fair trial unless counsel is provided for him . . . . The right of one charged with crime to counsel may not be deemed fundamental and essential to fair trials in some countries, but it is in ours.

In subsequent decisions, the Court ruled that "no person may be imprisoned, for any offense, whether classified as petty, misdemeanor, or felony, unless he was represented by counsel,"[22] and that the right to counsel is not limited to trial, but applies to all "critical stages" in the criminal justice process.[23] As a result of these rulings, most defendants must be provided with counsel from arrest and interrogation through sentencing and the appellate process. As illustrated in Box 5.1, the Supreme Court has also ruled that defendants are entitled to *effective* assistance of counsel.[24]

At the time the *Gideon* decision was handed down, 13 states had no statewide requirement for appointment of counsel except in capital cases.[25] Other states relied on members of local bar associations to defend indigents, often on a pro bono basis. Following *Gideon,* it became obvious that other procedures would be required if all felony defendants were to be provided attorneys.

States moved quickly to implement the constitutional requirement articulated in *Gideon,* either by establishing public defender systems or by appropriating money for court-appointed attorneys. The number of public defender systems grew rapidly. In 1951, there were only seven public defender organizations in the United States; in 1964, there were 136, and by 1973, the total had risen to 573.[26] A recent national survey of indigent defense services among all U.S. prosecutorial districts found that 21 percent used a public defender program, 19 percent used an assigned counsel system, and 7 percent used a con-

---

BOX 5.1   The Supreme Court and "Effective" Assistance of Counsel

In 1984, the Supreme Court articulated constitutional standards for determining whether a defendant had ineffective assistance of counsel. The Court ruled, in the case of *Strickland v. Washington* (466 U.S. 668 [1984], at 687), that to establish ineffectiveness, a defendant must prove:

- First, "that counsel's performance was deficient. This requires showing that counsel made errors so serious that counsel was not functioning as the 'counsel' guaranteed the defendant by the Sixth Amendment."
- Second, "that the deficient performance prejudiced the defense. This requires showing that counsel's errors were so serious as to deprive the defendant of a fair trial, a trial whose result is reliance."

The Court also stated that to establish ineffectiveness, a "defendant must show that counsel's representation fell below an objective standard of reasonableness." To establish prejudice, a defendant "must show that there is a reasonable probability that, but for counsel's unprofessional errors, the result of the proceeding would have been different."

The Court revisited this issue in 2000, ruling that Terry Williams had been denied effective assistance of counsel in *Williams v. Taylor* (529 U.S. 420 [2000]). Williams was convicted of robbery and murder and sentenced to death after a Virginia jury concluded that he had a high probability of future dangerousness.

At the sentencing hearing, Williams's lawyer failed to introduce evidence that Williams was borderline mentally retarded and did not advance beyond sixth grade. He also failed to introduce the testimony of prison officials, who described Williams as among the inmates "least likely to act in a violent, dangerous, or provocative way." Instead, Williams's lawyer spent most of his time explaining that he realized it would be difficult for the jury to find a reason to spare Williams's life. His comments included the following: "I will admit too that it is very difficult to ask you to show mercy to a man who maybe has not shown much mercy himself . . . . Admittedly, it is very difficult to . . . ask that you give this man mercy when he has shown so little of it himself. But I would ask that you would."

The Supreme Court ruled that Williams's right to effective assistance of counsel had been violated. According to the Court, "There was a reasonable probability that the result of the sentencing proceeding would have been different if competent counsel had presented and explained the significance of all the available evidence."

---

tract attorney system; the remaining districts (43 percent) reported that a combination of methods was used.[27] A survey of inmates incarcerated in state and federal prisons in 1997 revealed that about 73 percent of the state inmates and 60 percent of the federal inmates were represented by a public defender or assigned counsel. This survey also revealed that African Americans and Hispanics were more likely than whites to be represented by a public defender or assigned counsel. Among state prison inmates, for example, 77 percent of the African Americans, 73 percent of the Hispanics, and 69 percent of the whites reported that they were represented by a publicly funded attorney.[28]

Quality of Legal Representation As a result of Supreme Court decisions expanding the right to counsel and the development of federal and state policies implementing these decisions, African Americans and other racial minorities are no longer routinely denied legal representation at trial or at any of the other critical stages in the process. Questions have been raised, however, about the quality of legal representation provided to indigent defendants by public defenders. A recent article in the *Harvard Law Review,* for example, claimed:

> Nearly four decades after *Gideon,* the states have largely, and often outrageously, failed to meet the Court's constitutional command. The widespread, lingering deficiencies in the quality of indigent counsel have led some to wonder whether this right, so fundamental to a fair and accurate adversarial criminal process, is unenforceable.[29]

According to this author, the fact that most criminal defendants are indigent, coupled with the "low quality of indigent defense," raises fundamental questions about the "overall fairness of the criminal justice system."[30]

There is evidence suggesting that defendants share this view. In fact, one of the most often quoted statements about public defenders is the answer given by an unidentified prisoner in a Connecticut jail to the question of whether he had a lawyer when he went to court. "No," he replied, "I had a public defender."[31] Some social scientists echo this negative assessment, charging that public defenders, as part of the courtroom workgroup, are more concerned with securing guilty pleas as efficiently and as expeditiously as possible than with aggressively defending their clients.[32] As Weitzer notes (and as the examples in Box 5.2 confirm), "In many jurisdictions, public defenders and state-appointed attorneys are grossly underpaid, poorly trained, or simply lack the resources and time to prepare for a case—a pattern documented in cases ranging from the most minor to the most consequential, capital crimes."[33]

Other social scientists disagree. Citing studies showing that criminal defendants represented by public defenders do not fare worse than those represented by private attorneys,[34] these researchers suggest that critics "have tended to underestimate the quality of defense provided by the public defender."[35] Wice concluded that the public defender is able to establish a working relationship with prosecutors and judges "in which the exchange of favors, so necessary to greasing the squeaky wheel of justice, can directly benefit the indigent defendant."[36] As part of the courtroom workgroup, in other words, public defenders are in a better position than private attorneys to negotiate favorable plea bargains and thus to mitigate punishment.

A recent report by the Bureau of Justice Statistics (BJS) revealed that case outcomes for state and federal defendants represented by public attorneys do not differ dramatically from those represented by private counsel.[37] There were only very slight differences in the conviction rates of defendants represented by public and private attorneys, but somewhat larger differences in the incarceration rates. At the federal level, 87.6 percent of the defendants represented by public attorneys were sentenced to prison, compared to 76.5 percent of the defendants with private attorneys. The authors of the report attributed this to the

---

Box 5.2   Are Indigent Capital Defendants Represented by Incompetent Attorneys?

In "Judges and the Politics of Death," Stephen Bright and Patrick Keenan (1995, p. 800) claimed, "Judges often fail to enforce the most fundamental protection of an accused, the Sixth Amendment right to counsel, by assigning an inexperienced or incompetent lawyer to represent the accused." In support of their assertion, they offered the following examples:

- A capital defendant who was represented by a lawyer who had passed the bar exam only 6 months earlier, had not taken any classes in criminal law or criminal procedure, and had never tried a jury or a felony trial.
- An attorney who described his client as "a little old nigger boy" during the penalty phase of the trial.

- A judge in Harris County, Texas, who responded to a capital defendant's complaints about his attorney sleeping during the trial with the assertion "The Constitution doesn't say the lawyer has to be awake."
- A Florida attorney who stated during the penalty phase of a capital case, "Judge, I'm at a loss. I really don't know what to do in this type of proceeding. If I'd been through one, I would, but I've never handled one except this time."
- A study of capital cases in Philadelphia that found that "even officials in charge of the system say they wouldn't want to be represented in Traffic Court by some of the people appointed to defend poor people accused of murder."

---

fact that public counsel represented a higher percentage of violent, drug, and public-order offenders, whereas private attorneys represented a higher percentage of white-collar defendants. Felony defendants in state courts also faced lower odds of incarceration if they were represented by private attorneys (53.9 percent) rather than by public defenders (71.3 percent). In both state and federal court, on the other hand, defendants represented by private attorneys got shorter sentences than those represented by public defenders. At the federal level, the mean sentences were 58 months (public attorneys) and 62 months (private attorneys); at the state level, they were 31.2 months (public attorneys) and 38.3 months (private attorneys).[38]

Race, Type of Counsel, and Case Outcome   The data presented thus far do not address the question of racial discrimination in the provision of counsel. Although it is true that African American and Hispanic defendants are more likely than white defendants to be represented by public defenders, it does not necessarily follow that racial minorities will be treated more harshly than whites as their cases move through the criminal justice system. As we have noted, studies have not consistently shown that defendants represented by public defenders fare worse than defendants represented by private attorneys.

Most studies have not directly compared the treatment of African American, Hispanic, and white defendants represented by public defenders and private attorneys. It is possible that racial minorities represented by public defenders re-

Table 5.1 Race/Ethnicity and Type of Attorney in Chicago, Miami, and Kansas City

Race of Defendant	PERCENTAGE REPRESENTED BY A PRIVATE ATTORNEY		
	Chicago	Miami	Kansas City
White	22.5	34.5	37.8
Black	6.9	23.4	24.8
Hispanic	21.2	27.3	NA[a]

[a]There were only 47 Hispanic defendants in Kansas City.

ceive more punitive sentences than whites represented by public defenders, or that whites who hire their own attorneys receive more lenient sentences than racial minorities who hire their own attorneys. That is, hiring an attorney could provide more benefits to whites than to racial minorities, and representation by a public defender could have more negative consequences for racial minorities than for whites.

Holmes, Hosch, Daudistel, Perez, and Graves found evidence supporting these possibilities in one of the two Texas counties where they explored the interrelationships among race/ethnicity, legal resources, and case outcomes.[39] The authors of this study found that in Bexar County (San Antonio), both African American and Hispanic defendants were significantly less likely than white defendants to be represented by a private attorney, even after such things as the seriousness of the crime, the defendant's prior criminal record, and the defendant's gender, age, and employment status were taken into account. The authors also found that defendants who retained a private attorney were more likely to be released prior to trial and received more lenient sentences than those represented by a public defender.[40] In this particular jurisdiction, then, African American and Hispanic defendants were less likely than whites to be represented by a private attorney, and, as a result, they received more punitive treatment than whites.

An examination of the sentences imposed on defendants convicted of felonies in three large urban jurisdictions in 1993 and 1994 produced somewhat different results. Spohn and DeLone compared the proportions of white, African American, and Hispanic defendants who were represented by a private attorney in Chicago, Miami, and Kansas City.[41] As shown in Table 5.1, in all three jurisdictions whites were substantially more likely than African Americans to have private attorneys. In Chicago, 22.5 percent of white defendants, but only 6.9 percent of African American defendants, had a private attorney. In Miami, Hispanics were also less likely than whites to be represented by a private attorney.

Although the data presented in Table 5.1 reveal that smaller proportions of racial minorities than whites had access to the services of a private attorney, they do not provide evidence of differential treatment based on either type of

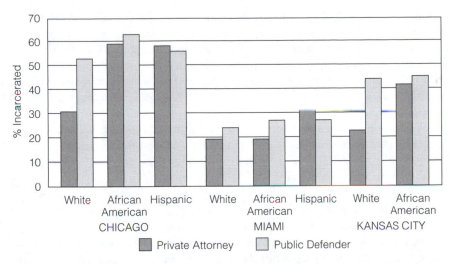

FIGURE 5.1 Race/Ethnicity, Type of Attorney, and Incarceration Rates in Chicago, Miami, and Kansas City

attorney or race/ethnicity. In fact, when Spohn and DeLone examined the sentences imposed on racial minorities and whites in each jurisdiction, they found an interesting pattern of results. As shown in Figure 5.1, in Chicago and Kansas City, only whites benefited from having a private attorney. Among African Americans, the incarceration rates for defendants represented by private attorneys were only slightly lower than for those represented by public defenders; among Hispanics in Chicago, the rate for defendants with private attorneys was actually somewhat *higher* than for those with public defenders. In Miami, both whites and African Americans benefited from representation by private counsel, but Hispanics with private attorneys were sentenced to prison at a slightly *higher* rate than Hispanics represented by public defenders.

The incarceration rates displayed in Figure 5.1 do not take into account differences in the types of cases handled by private attorneys and public defenders. It is certainly possible that the incarceration rates for defendants represented by private attorneys generally are lower than for those represented by public defenders, not because private attorneys are more experienced, more competent, and more zealous, but because the types of cases they handle are less serious or because the defendants they represent have less serious prior criminal records. If private attorneys, in other words, typically represent first offenders charged with relatively minor crimes, whereas public defenders represent recidivists as well as first offenders and violent offenders as well as nonviolent offenders, we would expect the sentences imposed on defendants with private attorneys to be less severe than those imposed on defendants with public defenders, irrespective of the quality of representation provided by the attorney.

To test this possibility, Spohn and DeLone analyzed the relationship between race/ethnicity, type of attorney, and the likelihood of incarceration, controlling for several indicators of the seriousness of the crime and for the offender's prior criminal record, age, gender, and employment status. They found that, with one exception, the type of attorney had no effect on the odds of incarceration for any racial/ethnic group in any jurisdiction. The only exception was in Miami, where African Americans represented by private attorneys faced significantly lower odds of incarceration than African Americans represented by public defenders.

These results cast doubt on assertions that racial minorities are disadvantaged by their lack of access to private counsel. At least in these three jurisdictions, public defenders do not appear to "provide a lower caliber defense than what private attorneys offer."[42]

In summary, although it would be premature to conclude on the basis of research conducted to date either that decisions concerning the provision of counsel are racially neutral or that the consequences of these decisions for racial minorities are unimportant, significant changes have occurred since the 1930s. It is clear that scenes from the infamous Scottsboro case will not be replayed in the 1990s. The Supreme Court has consistently affirmed the importance of the right to counsel and has insisted that states provide attorneys to indigent criminal defendants at all critical stages in the criminal justice process. Although some critics have questioned the quality of legal services afforded indigent defendants, particularly in capital cases where the stakes are obviously very high, the findings of a number of methodologically sophisticated studies suggest that "indigent defenders get the job done and done well."[43] In short, it is no longer true that racial minorities "are without a voice"[44] in courts throughout the United States.

Racial Minorities and Bail Decision Making

Critics of the traditional money bail system, in which defendants either pay the amount set by the judge or pay a bail bondsman to post bond for them, argue that the system discriminates against poor defendants. They also charge that the system discriminates, either directly or indirectly, against racial minorities. Critics contend that historically African American and Hispanic defendants have been more likely than white defendants to be detained prior to trial, either because the judge refused to set bail or because the judge set bail at an unaffordable level.[45] "As a result," according to one commentator, "the country's jails are packed to overflowing with the nation's poor—with red, brown, black, and yellow men and women showing up in disproportionate numbers."[46]

Bail Reform Concerns about the rights of poor defendants and about the consequences of detention prior to trial led to the first bail reform movement, which emerged in the 1960s and emphasized reducing pretrial detention. Those who lobbied for reform argued that the purpose of bail was to ensure the defendant's appearance in court and that bail therefore should not exceed the amount necessary to guarantee that the defendant would show up for all court proceedings. Proponents of this view asserted that whether a defendant was released or detained prior to trial should not depend on his or her economic

Focus on an Issue
Racial Minorities and the Legal Profession

In the early 1930s, one of the defendants in the Scottsboro case described the courtroom where he was convicted and sentenced to death as "one big smiling white face" (Carter, 1969, p. 302). With the exception of the defendants themselves, no racial minorities were present in the courtroom.

Although the situation obviously has changed since then, racial minorities still represent a very small proportion of the lawyers and judges in the United States. Among those enrolled in law schools in 1999, for example, 7.4 percent were African American, 5.7 percent were Hispanic, 6.3 percent were Asian American, and less than 1 percent were Native American (American Bar Association, 2000, Table 4). In 1998, 7 percent of all lawyers, but only 3 percent of all partners in law firms, were racial minorities (Tables 2 and 19).

Racial minorities make up an even smaller proportion of the judiciary. In 1997, 2.8 percent of all judges in the United States were African American, 2.2 percent were Hispanic, and less than 1 percent were Asian American or Native American. The situation was somewhat more positive at the federal level, where 11.3 percent of all district court judges and 6.9 percent of all court of appeals judges were African American. Hispanics composed 5.0 percent of the district court bench and 6.2 percent of the appellate court bench. There were, on the other hand, very few Asian Americans or Native Americans on the federal bench (Tables 42 and 46). Most of the racial minorities on the federal bench were men. Among district court judges, there were 54 African American men but only 16 African American women; there were 26 Hispanic men and 5 Hispanic women (Table 44).

The American Bar Association's 2000 report on the progress of minorities in the legal profession concluded that minority entry into the profession had stalled and that the obstacles to minority entry into the profession had grown more formidable. The report noted that the campaign to end affirmative action in law school admissions, which had spread rapidly throughout the United States, threatened "to stifle minority entry and advancement in the profession for years to come" (p. 28). According to the ABA, "the legal profession—already one of the least integrated professions in the country—threatens to become even less representative of the citizens and society it serves" (p. x).

THE PERCEPTIONS OF AFRICAN AMERICAN AND WHITE LAWYERS: DIVIDED JUSTICE?

A 1998 survey of African American and white lawyers commissioned by the *ABA Journal* and the *National Bar Association Magazine* revealed stark racial differences in perceptions of the justice system (ABA, 1999). When asked about the amount of racial bias that currently exists in the justice system, over half of the African American lawyers, but only 6.5 percent of the white lawyers, answered "very much." In fact, 29.6 percent of the white lawyers stated that they believed there was "very little" racial bias in the justice system.

Responses to other questions also varied by race:

(continued)

(*continued*)

- How does the amount of racial bias in the justice system compare with other segments of society?

	African Americans	Whites
More	22.7%	5.7%
Same	69.6	40.5
Less	5.9	45.8

- Have you witnessed an example of racial bias in the justice system in the past three years?

	African Americans	Whites
Yes	66.9%	15.1%
No	31.1	82.4

- What is your assessment of the ability of the justice system to eliminate racial bias in the future?

	African Americans	Whites
Hopeful	59.1%	80.7%
Pessimistic	38.2	15.1

- Should police be allowed to create profiles of likely drug dealers or other criminals as a way to combat crime?

	African Americans	Whites
Yes	17.8%	48.6%
No	74.6	36.9

- Should race be a factor in creating the profiles?

	African Americans	Whites
Race OK	5.5%	19.5%
Race Not OK	91.2	67.9

- Have you seen an attempt to skew a jury racially because of the race of the defendant?

	African Americans	Whites
Yes	51.7%	22.4%
No	45.8	73.6

- Are minority women lawyers treated less fairly than white women lawyers in hiring and promotion?

	African Americans	Whites
Yes	66.5%	10.9%
No	14.3	60.4

As these results clearly suggest, African American lawyers are substantially more likely than white lawyers to believe that the justice system is racially biased. As the author of the study noted, "Though they have made the justice system their life's work, many black lawyers believe the word 'justice' has a white spin that says 'just us'" (Carter, 1999, p. 42).

status or race. They also cited research demonstrating that the type and amount of bail imposed on the defendant and the time spent by the defendant in pretrial detention affected the likelihood of a guilty plea, the likelihood of conviction at trial, and the severity of the sentence.[47]

Arguments such as these prompted state and federal reforms designed to reduce pretrial detention. Encouraged by the results of the Manhattan Bail Project, which found that the majority of defendants released on their own recognizance did appear for trial,[48] local jurisdictions moved quickly to reduce reliance on monetary bail and to institute programs modeled after the Manhattan Bail Project. Many states revised their bail laws, and in 1966 Congress passed the Bail Reform Act, which proclaimed release on recognizance the presumptive bail decision in federal cases.

Then, as Walker noted, "the political winds shifted."[49] The rising crime rate of the 1970s generated a concern for crime control and led to a reassessment of bail policies. Critics challenged the traditional view that the only function of bail was to assure the defendant's appearance in court. They argued that guaranteeing public safety was also a valid function of bail and that pretrial detention should be used to protect the community from "dangerous" offenders.

These arguments fueled the second bail reform movement, which emerged in the 1970s and emphasized preventive detention. Conservative legislators and policymakers lobbied for reforms allowing judges to consider "public safety" when making decisions concerning the type and amount of bail.[50] Thirty-four states had enacted legislation by 1984 giving judges the right to deny bail to defendants deemed dangerous.[51] Also in 1984, Congress passed a law authorizing preventive detention of dangerous defendants in federal criminal cases.[52]

The Effect of Race on Bail Decision Making Proponents of bail reform argued that whether a defendant was released or detained prior to trial should not depend on his or her economic status or race. They argued that bail decisions should rest either on assessments of the likelihood that the defendant would appear in court or on predictions of the defendant's dangerousness.

The problem, of course, is that there is no way to guarantee that judges will not take race into account in making these assessments and predictions. As Mann asserted, even the seemingly objective criteria used in making these decisions "may still be discriminatory on the basis of economic status or skin color."[53] If judges stereotype African Americans and Hispanics as less reliable and more prone to violence than whites, they will be more inclined to detain people of color and release whites, irrespective of their more objective assessments of risk of flight or dangerousness.

Studies examining the effect of race on bail decisions have yielded contradictory findings. Some researchers conclude that judges' bail decisions are based primarily on the seriousness of the offense and the defendant's prior criminal record and ties to the community; race has no effect once these factors are taken into consideration.[54] Other researchers contend that the defendant's economic status, not race, determines the likelihood of pretrial release.[55] If this is the case, one could argue that bail decision making reflects *indirect* racial discrimination, as African American and Hispanic defendants are more likely than white defendants to be poor.

A number of studies document *direct* racial discrimination in bail decisions. A study by Bridges of bail decision making in King County, Washington, for example, examined the effect of race/ethnicity on four bail outcomes: whether the defendant was released on his or her own recognizance, whether the Court set monetary bail, what amount of bail was required, and whether the defendant was held in custody pending trial.[56] As shown in Table 5.2, he found that racial minorities were less likely than whites to be released on their own recognizance and were more likely than whites to have bail set. Racial minorities were also held in pretrial detention at higher rates than whites. The detention rate was 55 percent for Native Americans, 54 percent for Hispanics, 36 percent

Table 5.2 Race/Ethnicity and Bail Outcomes in King County, Washington

	Whites	All Racial Minorities	African Americans	Hispanics	Native Americans	Asian Americans
Released on personal recognizance	25%	14%	14%	10%	8%	18%
Monetary bail set	34%	56%	46%	60%	60%	50%
Median bail amount	$10,000	$10,000	$10,000	$10,000	$10,000	$15,000
In custody prior to trial	28%	39%	36%	54%	55%	35%

SOURCE: George S. Bridges, *A Study on Racial and Ethnic Disparities in Superior Court Bail and Pre-Trial Detention Practices in Washington* (Olympia: Washington State Minority and Justice Commission, 1997), table 1.

for African Americans, and 28 percent for whites. There were, on the other hand, no differences in the median amount of bail required.

Bridges noted that although "at face value these differences may seem alarming,"[57] they might be due to legitimate factors that criminal justice officials take into consideration when establishing the conditions of pretrial release: the defendant's ties to the community, the perceived dangerousness of the defendant, and any previous history of the defendant's failure to appear at court proceedings. When he controlled for these legally relevant variables and for the defendant's age and gender, however, he found that the race effects did not disappear. Racial minorities and men were less likely than whites and women to be released on their own recognizance and more likely than whites and women to be required to pay bail as a condition of release. For both of these decisions, the prosecutor's recommendation regarding the type and amount of bail was the strongest predictor of outcome. In contrast, race had no effect on the likelihood of pretrial detention once the bail conditions and the amount of bail set by the judge were taken into account.

Interviews with King County criminal justice officials revealed that most of them believed the racial differences in bail outcomes could be attributed to three factors: racial minorities' lack of resources and consequent inability to retain a private attorney, the tendency of judges to follow the recommendations of prosecutors, and cultural differences and language barriers that made it difficult to contact the defendant's references or verify information provided by the defendant. Because racial minorities were more likely than whites to be poor, they were more likely to be represented by public defenders with large caseloads and limited time to prepare for bail hearings. Resource constraints similarly limited the amount of time that judges and pretrial investigators were able to devote to bail decisions, which led to reliance on the recommendations proffered by the prosecutor. Although Bridges stressed that his study produced no evidence "that disparities are the product of overt, prejudicial acts by courts officials," he nonetheless concluded that "race and ethnicity matter in the dis-

Table 5.3 Probability of Pretrial Release for Typical White, African American, and Hispanic Defendants in Chicago, Miami, and Kansas City

Race of Defendant	PROBABILITY OF PRETRIAL RELEASE		
	Chicago	Miami	Kansas City
White	.48	.63	.50
African American	.38	.56	.47
Hispanic	.50	.54	NA

NOTE: These probabilities were calculated for male defendants who were 30 years old, charged with one count of possession of narcotics with intent, had one prior prison term of more than one year, were not on probation at the time of the current offense, and were represented by a public defender.

position of criminal cases."[58] He added that this "is a serious concern for the courts in Washington," as it "implies that, despite the efforts of judges and others dedicated to fairness in the administration of justice, justice is not administered fairly."[59]

Other evidence of direct racial discrimination is found in an analysis of the likelihood of pretrial release in Chicago, Miami, and Kansas City. Using data on offenders convicted of felonies in 1993 and 1994, Spohn and DeLone compared the odds of pretrial release for white, African American, and Hispanic defendants.[60] They controlled for the seriousness of the charges against the defendant, the number of charges the defendant was facing, representation of the defendant by a private attorney or a public defender, and the defendant's prior record, gender, and age. They found that in Chicago, African Americans were less likely than whites to be released pending trial, whereas in Miami, both African Americans and Hispanics were significantly less likely than whites be to released prior to trial. In Kansas City, on the other hand, the difference in the likelihood of pretrial release for whites and African Americans was not statistically significant.

The data presented in Table 5.3 illustrate these differences. Spohn and DeLone used the results of their multivariate analysis to calculate the probability of pretrial release for "typical" white, African American, and Hispanic defendants in each jurisdiction. In Chicago, the probability of pretrial release was 50 percent for Hispanics and 48 percent for whites, but only 38 percent for African Americans. In Miami, the probabilities for African Americans and Hispanics (56 percent and 54 percent, respectively) were lower than the probability for whites (63 percent). There was only a 3 percentage-point difference in the likelihood of pretrial release for whites and African Americans adjudicated in Kansas City.

There is also evidence that defendant race interacts with other variables related to bail severity. Farnworth and Horan, for example, found that the amount of bail imposed on white defendants who retained private attorneys was less than the amount imposed on African American defendants who retained private attorneys.[61] Chiricos and Bales similarly found that the likelihood of pretrial detention was greatest for African American defendants who were unemployed.[62]

A study of bail decision making in 10 federal district courts also found evidence of an indirect relationship between race/ethnicity and bail decisions. This study revealed that race did not have a direct effect on bail outcomes but did interact with a number of other variables to produce harsher bail outcomes for some types of African American defendants.[63] More specifically, the authors found that having a prior felony conviction had a greater negative effect on bail severity for African American defendants than for white defendants, and having more education or a higher income had a greater positive effect for whites than for African Americans.

Bail and Case Outcomes Concerns about discrimination in bail decision making focus on two facts: African American and Hispanic defendants who are presumed to be innocent are jailed prior to trial *and* those who are detained prior to trial are more likely to be convicted and receive harsher sentences than those who are released pending trial. These concerns focus, in other words, on the possibility that discrimination in bail decision making has "spillover" effects on other case processing decisions.

A recent analysis of pretrial release of felony defendants by the BJS attests to the validity of these concerns.[64] Using data from 1998, the BJS compared the conviction rates for released and detained defendants in the 75 largest counties in the United States. They found that 78 percent of those who were detained prior to trial, but only 63 percent of those who were released, were convicted. There were similar disparities for each of the four types of offenses analyzed. Among offenders charged with violent crimes, for example, the conviction rates were 70 percent for those who were detained and 50 percent for those who were released; the figures for drug offenders were 83 percent (detained offenders) and 67 percent (released offenders). A BJS study using data from 1992 revealed that pretrial status also affected the likelihood of incarceration: 50 percent of the detained defendants were sentenced to prison, compared to only 19 percent of those who were released prior to trial.[65]

Although these data suggest that pretrial release does have important spillover effects on case outcomes, the higher conviction and imprisonment rates for defendants who were detained pending trial could be due to the fact that defendants who are held in jail prior to trial tend to be charged with more serious crimes, have more serious prior criminal histories, and have a past history of nonappearance at court proceedings. The BJS study, for example, found that defendants charged with murder had the lowest release rate and that defendants with more serious prior records or a history of nonappearance were more likely to be detained prior to trial.[66] Given these findings, it is possible that the relationship between pretrial status and case outcomes would disappear once controls for case seriousness and prior criminal record were taken into consideration.

Table 5.4 The Effect of Pretrial Detention on Incarceration Rates for Typical Felony Offenders in Chicago and Kansas City

	% SENTENCED TO PRISON	
	Detained Prior to Trial	Released Prior to Trial
Chicago		
African American male	73	23
Hispanic male	72	22
White male	63	16
African American female	53	11
Hispanic female	55	11
White female	42	7
Kansas City		
African American male	29	16
White male	24	13
African American female	13	6
White female	10	5

NOTE: These probabilities were calculated for defendants who were 30 years old, were charged with one count of possession of narcotics with intent, had one prior felony conviction, were not on probation at the time of the current offenses, were represented by a public defender, and pled guilty.

Data collected for the three–city study described earlier were used to explore this possibility.[67] Spohn and DeLone found that the offender's pretrial status was a strong predictor of the likelihood of imprisonment, even after other relevant legal and extralegal variables were taken into account. In all three cities, offenders who were released prior to trial faced substantially lower odds of a prison sentence than did offenders who were detained pending trial. Further analysis of sentences imposed by judges in Chicago and Kansas City revealed that pretrial detention had a similar effect on incarceration for each racial/ethnic group and for males and females.[68] As shown in Table 5.4, among both males and females, African American, Hispanic, and white defendants who were detained prior to trial faced substantially greater odds of incarceration than African American, Hispanic, and white defendants who were released pending trial. In Chicago, the highest incarceration rates were found for African American (73 percent), Hispanic (72 percent), and white (63 percent) males; the lowest rates for were found for African American (11 percent), white (7 percent), and Hispanic (11 percent) females.

The results of this study suggest that defendants who are detained prior to trial, regardless of their race, receive more punitive sentences than those who are released. This does not mean, however, that African American and white defendants are *equally likely* to be sentenced to prison. Earlier, we noted that this study showed that African Americans were more likely than whites to be detained prior to trial in Chicago and that both African Americans and Hispanics faced a greater likelihood of pretrial detention than whites in Miami.

Because they are detained more often than whites in the first place, African American and Hispanic defendants are more likely than whites to suffer both the pains of imprisonment prior to trial and the consequences of pretrial detention at sentencing.

Although the findings are somewhat contradictory, it thus appears that the reforms instituted since the 1960s have not produced racial equality in bail decision making. It is certainly true that racial minorities are no longer routinely jailed prior to trial because of judicial stereotypes of dangerousness or because they are too poor to obtain their release. Nevertheless, there is evidence that judges in some jurisdictions continue to take race into account in deciding on the type and amount of bail. There is also evidence that race interacts with factors such as prior record or employment status to produce higher pretrial detention rates for African American defendants than for white defendants. Given the consequences of pretrial detention, these findings are an obvious cause for concern.

CHARGING AND PLEA BARGAINING DECISIONS

> Regrettably, the evidence is clear that prosecutorial discretion is systematically exercised to the disadvantage of black and Hispanic Americans. Prosecutors are not, by and large, bigoted. But as with police activity, prosecutorial judgment is shaped by a set of self-perpetuating racial assumptions.[69]

Thus far we have examined criminal justice decisions concerning appointment of counsel and bail for evidence of racial discrimination. We have shown that, despite reforms mandated by the Supreme Court or adopted voluntarily by the states, inequities persist. African Americans and Hispanics who find themselves in the arms of the law continue to suffer discrimination in these important court processing decisions.

In this section, we examine prosecutors' charging and plea bargaining decisions for evidence of differential treatment of minority and white defendants. We argue that there is compelling evidence of racial *disparity* in charging and plea bargaining. We further contend that this disparity frequently reflects racial *discrimination*.

Prosecutors' Charging Decisions

Prosecutors exercise broad discretion in deciding whether to file formal charges against individuals suspected of crimes and in determining the number and seriousness of the charges to be filed. According to the Supreme Court, "So long as the prosecutor has probable cause to believe that the accused committed an offense defined by statute, the decision whether or not to prosecute, and what charge to file or bring before a grand jury, generally rests entirely in his discretion."[70] As Justice Jackson noted in 1940, "The prosecutor has more control over life, liberty, and reputation than any other person in America."[71]

The power of the prosecutor is reflected in the fact that in most states, from one-third to one-half of all felony cases are dismissed by the prosecutor prior to a determination of guilt or innocence.[72] Prosecutors can reject charges at the initial screening, either because they believe the suspect is innocent or, more typically, because they believe the suspect is guilty but a conviction would be unlikely. Prosecutors can also reject charges if they feel it would not be in the "interest of justice" to continue the case—because the crime is too trivial, because of a perception that the suspect has been punished enough, or because the suspect has agreed to provide information about other, more serious, cases.[73] Finally, prosecutors can reject charges as felonies but prosecute them as misdemeanors.

If a formal charge is filed by the prosecutor, it still can be reduced to a less serious felony or to a misdemeanor during plea bargaining. It can also be dismissed by the court on a recommendation by the prosecutor. This typically happens when the case "falls apart" prior to trial. A witness may refuse to cooperate or may fail to appear at trial, or the judge may rule that the confession or other essential evidence is inadmissible. Unlike the prosecutor's initial decision to reject the charge, the decision to dismiss a charge already filed requires official court action.

The Effect of Race on Charging Decisions Although the prosecutor's discretion is broad, it is not unlimited. The Supreme Court, in fact, has ruled that the decision to prosecute may not be "deliberately based upon an unjustifiable standard such as race, religion, or other arbitrary classification."[74] The prosecutor, in other words, cannot legitimately take the race of the suspect into account in deciding whether to file charges or not or in deciding on the seriousness of the charge to be filed.

Gunnar Myrdal, a Swedish social scientist and author of a book examining the "Negro problem" in the United States in the late 1930s and early 1940s, found substantial discrimination against African Americans in the decision to charge or not. As Myrdal noted:

> State courts receive indictments for physical violence against Negroes in an infinitesimally small proportion of the cases. It is notorious that practically never have white lynching mobs been brought to court in the south, even when the killers are known to all in the community and are mentioned by name in the local press. When the offender is a Negro, indictment is easily obtained, and no such difficulty at the start will meet the prosecution of the case.[75]

Only a few studies have examined the effect of race on prosecutorial charging decisions, and they reached contradictory conclusions. Some researchers found either that race did not affect charging decisions at all,[76] or that race played a very minor role in the decision to prosecute or not.[77] The authors of these studies concluded that the decision to prosecute was based primarily on the strength of evidence in the case.

Table 5.5 The Effect of Race and Gender on Prosecutors' Charging Decisions

	ADJUSTED MEANS[a]		
Group	Rejected at Screening	Dismissed by Court	Fully Prosecuted
African American male	46%	34%	39%
African American female	57	42	30
Hispanic male	46	33	42
Hispanic female	54	43	31
White male	54	33	26
White female	59	42	19

SOURCE: Table adapted from Cassia Spohn, John Gruhl, and Susan Welch, "The Impact of the Ethnicity and Gender of Defendants on the Decision to Reject or Dismiss Felony Charges," *Criminology* 25 (1987): 175–191.

[a]Means have been adjusted for the effect of four independent variables: age of the defendant, prior record of the defendant, seriousness of the charge, and whether the defendant used a weapon.

Several studies concluded that prosecutors' charging decisions *are* affected by race. An analysis of the decision to reject or dismiss charges against felony defendants in Los Angeles County, for example, revealed a pattern of discrimination in favor of female defendants and against African American and Hispanic defendants.[78] The authors controlled for the defendant's age and prior criminal record, the seriousness of the charge against the defendant, and whether or not the defendant used a weapon in committing the crime. As shown in Table 5.5, they found that Hispanic males were most likely to be prosecuted fully, followed by African American males, white males, and females of all ethnic groups.

The authors of this study speculated that prosecutors took both race and gender into account in deciding whether to file charges in "marginal cases." They reasoned that strong cases would be prosecuted and weak cases dropped regardless of the race or gender of the suspect. In marginal cases, on the other hand,

> prosecutors may simply feel less comfortable prosecuting the dominant rather than the subordinate ethnic groups. They might feel the dominant groups are less threatening. Or they might believe they can win convictions more often against blacks and Hispanics than against Anglos.[79]

Similar results surfaced in a study of prosecutors' charging decisions in King County, Washington.[80] When the authors of this study examined the prosecutors' decisions to file felony charges (rather than file misdemeanor charges or decline to prosecute the case), they found that prosecutors were substantially more likely to file felony charges against racial minorities than against whites. These differences were especially pronounced for violent crimes and drug offenses. Moreover, the racial disparities did not disappear when the authors controlled for the seriousness of the crime, the defendant's prior criminal record, and the defendant's age and gender. Even taking these factors into account, Native Americans were 1.7 times more likely than whites to be charged with a felony, and African Americans were 1.15 times more likely than whites to face felony charges.[81]

Crutchfield, Weis, Engen, and Gainey stressed that these racial differences were not "necessarily the result of individuals making biased decisions."[82] Rather, the differences probably reflected race-linked legal, economic, and social factors that prosecutors take into account in deciding whether to charge or not, as well as officials' focus on drug offenses involving crack cocaine. As we have repeatedly emphasized, however, this type of subtle or indirect discrimination is problematic. It is difficult to disentangle the effects of race/ethnicity, social class, employment history, and family situation. Even if criminal justice officials are justified in taking these social and economic factors into account, doing so will necessarily produce unintended race effects.

The Effect of Offender Race and Victim Race on Charging Decisions

The research discussed thus far suggests that the race/ethnicity of the offender affects prosecutors' charging decisions. There is also evidence that charging decisions vary depending on the race of the offender and the the race of the victim. LaFree, for example, found that African Americans arrested for raping white women were more likely to be charged with felonies than were either African Americans arrested for raping African American women or whites arrested for raping white women.[83] Another study found that defendants arrested for murdering whites in Florida were more likely to be indicted for first-degree murder than those arrested for murdering African Americans.[84]

Research on sexual assault case processing decisions in Detroit reached a different conclusion. Spohn and Spears used data on sexual assaults bound over for trial in Detroit Recorder's Court to examine the effect of offender race, victim race, and other case characteristics on the decision to dismiss the charges against the defendant (versus the decision to fully prosecute the case).[85] Building on previous research demonstrating that African Americans who murder or rape whites receive more punitive treatment than other victim/offender racial combinations, they hypothesized that black-on-white sexual assaults would be less likely than either black-on-black or white-on-white sexual assaults to result in the dismissal of all charges. They found just the opposite: the likelihood of charge dismissal was significantly *greater* for cases involving African American offenders and white victims than for the other two groups of offenders. They also found that African Americans prosecuted for assaulting whites were *less* likely to be convicted than whites charged with sexually assaulting whites.[86]

Spohn and Spears concluded that their "unexpected findings" suggest that black-on-white sexual assaults with weaker evidence are less likely to be screened out during the preliminary stages of the process.[87] Police and prosecutors, in other words, may regard sexual assaults involving African American men and white women as inherently more serious than intraracial sexual assaults; consequently, they may be more willing to take a chance with a reluctant victim or a victim whose behavior at the time of the incident was questionable. According to the authors of this study,

The police may be willing to make an arrest and the prosecutor may be willing to charge, despite questions about the procedures used to obtain physical evidence or about the validity of the defendant's confession. If this is true, then cases involving black offenders and white victims will be more likely than other types of cases to "fall apart" before or during trial.[88]

A study of charging decisions in California reached a similar conclusion. Petersilia found that white suspects were *more* likely than African American or Hispanic suspects to be formally charged.[89] Her analysis of the reasons given for charge rejection led her to conclude that the higher dismissal rates for nonwhite suspects reflected the fact that "blacks and Hispanics in California are more likely than whites to be arrested under circumstances that provide insufficient evidence to support criminal charges."[90] (See Chapter 4 for further discussion of this finding.) Prosecutors were more reluctant to file charges against racial minorities than against whites, in other words, because they viewed the evidence against racial minorities as weaker and the odds of convicting them as lower.

Race, Drugs, and Selective Prosecution   The results of Petersilia's study in Los Angeles and Spohn and Spears's study in Detroit provide evidence suggestive of a pattern of *selective prosecution*. That is, cases involving racial minorities, or certain types of racial minorities, are singled out for prosecution, whereas similar cases involving whites are either screened out very early in the process or never enter the system in the first place.

This argument has been made most forcefully with respect to drug offenses. In *Malign Neglect,* for example, Michael Tonry argues, "Urban black Americans have borne the brunt of the War on Drugs."[91] More specifically, he charges that "the recent blackening of America's prison population is the product of malign neglect of the war's effects on black Americans."[92] Miller similarly asserts that "from the first shot fired in the drug war African-Americans were targeted, arrested, and imprisoned in wildly disproportionate numbers."[93]

There is ample evidence that the War on Drugs is being fought primarily in African American and Hispanic communities. In 1997, for example, racial minorities were nearly three-quarters of all offenders prosecuted in federal district courts for drug trafficking: 25 percent of these offenders were white, 33 percent were African American, and 41 percent were Hispanic.[94] These figures are inconsistent with national data on use of drugs, which reveal that whites are more likely than either African Americans or Hispanics to report having "ever" used a variety of drugs, including cocaine, PCP, LSD, and marijuana.[95]

Some commentators cite evidence of a different type of selective prosecution in drug cases (see Box 5.3 for the U.S. attorney general's memorandum regarding racial neutrality in federal prosecution). Noting that the penalties for use of crack cocaine mandated by the federal sentencing guidelines are substantially harsher than the penalties provided under many state statutes, these critics suggest that state prosecutors are more likely to refer crack cases involving racial minorities to the federal system for prosecution. Berk and Campbell, for example, compared the racial makeup of defendants arrested for sale of crack co-

---

BOX 5.3   The U.S. Attorney General and Racial Neutrality in Prosecution

In January 1999, Janet Reno, attorney general of the United States, issued a memorandum titled "Ensuring Racial Neutrality in Prosecution Practices" to all United States Attorneys. Excerpts from the memo include the following:

- Each United States Attorney should examine his or her office's practices and procedures and take all necessary measures to ensure the use of race-neutral policies in the exercise of prosecutorial discretion within a district. Absent compelling, specific law enforcement imperatives there is ordinarily no justification for differing policies and practices within a district with respect to similarly situated defendants. Moreover, any race-neutral policy that has a disparate racial impact should be carefully reviewed to determine whether the disparity is justified by law enforcement necessity and not the product of conscious or unconscious racial bias.

- Care must be taken to ensure that race plays no part in the Government's decision whether to file a substantial assistance motion or the amount of any recommended reduction.

- As the chief federal law enforcement officer in the district, the United States Attorney should take a leadership role in ensuring that all agencies within the district are aware of issues of racial disparity . . . . [O]ur constant vigilance will ensure that there is no perception of racial disparity in the discharge of our duties. The public recognition that our policies are administered in a race-neutral fashion is as important as the reality that we do so administer them.

SOURCE: memorandum available at http:/www .usdoj.gov/ag/readingroom/.

---

caine in Los Angeles to that of defendants charged with sale of crack cocaine in state and federal courts. They found that the racial makeup of arrestees was similar to the racial makeup of those charged with violating state statutes. However, African Americans were overrepresented in federal cases; in fact, over a 4-year period, no whites were prosecuted for the sale of crack cocaine in federal court.[96] (See Box 5.4 for a discussion of a different type of selective prosecution.)

This issue was addressed by the Supreme Court in 1996. The five defendants in the case of *United States v. Armstrong et al.* alleged that they were selected for prosecution in federal court (the U.S. District Court for the Central District of California) rather than in state court because they were African American.[97] They further alleged that this decision had serious potential consequences. Christopher Armstrong, for example, faced a prison term of 55 years to life under federal statutes, compared to 3 to 9 years under California law. Another defendant, Aaron Hampton, faced a maximum term of 14 years under California law but a mandatory life term under federal law.

Following their indictment for conspiring to possess with intent to distribute more than 50 grams of crack cocaine, the defendants filed a motion for discovery of information held by the U.S. Attorney's Office regarding the race of

BOX 5.4   Are African American Pregnant Women Who Abuse Drugs Singled Out for Prosecution under Child Abuse/Neglect Statutes?

Prosecution of Pregnant Women Who Abuse Drugs

In 1989, Jennifer Clarise Johnson, a 23-year-old African American crack addict, became the first woman in the United States to be convicted for exposing a baby to illegal drugs during pregnancy. The Florida court gave Johnson 15 to 20 years probation and required her to enter drug treatment and report subsequent pregnancies to her probation officer. According to the prosecutor who filed charges against Johnson, "We needed to make sure this woman does not give birth to another cocaine baby." (Humphries et al., 1995, p. 169).

Other prosecutions and convictions in other state courts followed; by 1992, over 100 women in 24 states had been charged with abusing an unborn child through illegal drug use during pregnancy.

Many of these cases were appealed and, until 1997, all of the appeals resulted in the dismissal of charges. Then in October 1997, the South Carolina Supreme Court became the first court in the United States to rule that a viable fetus could be considered a person under child abuse laws and that a pregnant woman who abused drugs during the third trimester of pregnancy therefore could be charged with child abuse or other, more serious, crimes (*Whitner v. State of South Carolina* [Davis Adv. Sh.

No. 19 S. E. 2d 1996]). Two months later, Talitha Renee Garrick, a 27-year-old African American woman who admitted that she smoked crack cocaine an hour before she gave birth to a stillborn child, pled guilty to involuntary manslaughter in a South Carolina courtroom.

Do Prosecutors "Target" Pregnant African American Women?

A number of commentators contend that prosecutors' charging decisions in these types of cases reflect racial discrimination. Humphries et al. (1995), for example, asserted, "The overwhelming majority of prosecutions involve poor women of color" (p. 173). Roberts (1991) similarly argued, "Poor Black women are the primary targets of prosecutors, not because they are more likely to be guilty of fetal abuse, but because they are Black and poor" (p. 1432).

To support her allegations, Roberts cited evidence documenting that most of the women who have been prosecuted have been African American; she notes that the 52 women prosecuted through 1990 included 35 African Americans, 14 whites, 2 Hispanics, and 1 Native American. Ten out of 11 cases in Florida, and 17 out of 18 cases in South Carolina, were brought against African American women (p. 1421, n.6). According to Roberts, these glaring disparities cre-

persons prosecuted by that office. In support of their motion, they offered a study showing that all of the defendants in the crack cocaine cases closed by the Federal Public Defender's Office in 1991 were African American.

The U.S. District Court ordered the U.S. Attorney's Office to provide the data requested by the defendants. When federal prosecutors refused to do so, noting that there was no evidence that they had refused to prosecute white or Hispanic crack defendants, U.S. District Court Judge Consuelo Marshall dis-

BOX 5.4   (*continued*)

ate a presumption of racially selective prosecution.

Randall Kennedy, an African American professor of law at Harvard University and the author of *Race, Crime, and the Law*, acknowledged that Roberts's charges of selective prosecution and racial misconduct "are surely plausible." As he noted, "Given the long and sad history of documented, irrefutable racial discrimination in the administration of criminal law . . . no informed observer should be shocked by the suggestion that some prosecutors treat black pregnant women more harshly than identically situated white pregnant women" (Kennedy, 1997, p. 354).

Kennedy claimed, however, that Roberts's contention that prosecutors target women "*because* they are black and poor," (p. 35) although plausible, is not persuasive. He noted that Roberts relied heavily on evidence from a study designed to estimate the prevalence of alcohol and drug abuse among pregnant women in Pinellas County, Florida. This study revealed that there were similar rates of substance abuse among African American and white women, but that African American women were 10 times more likely than white women to be reported to public health authorities (as Florida law required).

Kennedy argued that the Florida study does not provide conclusive evidence of racial bias. He noted, in fact, that the authors of the study themselves suggested that the disparity in reporting rates might reflect either the fact that newborns who have been exposed to cocaine exhibit more severe symptoms at birth or the fact that African American pregnant women are more likely than white pregnant women to be addicted to cocaine (rather than to alcohol, marijuana, or some other drug). Kennedy asserted that Roberts failed to address these alternative hypotheses and simply insisted "that 'racial prejudice and stereotyping must be a factor' in the racially disparate pattern of reporting" (p. 360).

Kennedy also contended that Roberts's analysis failed to consider the problem of underprotection of the law. Imagine, he asked, what the reaction would be if the situation were reversed and prosecutors brought child abuse charges solely against drug-abusing white women. "Would that not rightly prompt suspicion of racially selective devaluation of black babies on the grounds that withholding prosecution deprives black babies of the equal *protection* of the laws?" (p. 363)

What do you think? Do prosecutors "target" pregnant women who are poor and African American? What would the reaction be (among whites? among African Americans?) if only white women were prosecuted?

missed the indictments. The Ninth Circuit U.S. Court of Appeals affirmed Judge Marshall's dismissal of the indictments. The appellate court judges stated that they began with "the presumption that people of all races commit all types of crimes—not with the premise that any type of crime is the exclusive province of any particular racial or ethnic group."[98] They stated that the defendant's evidence showing that all 24 crack defendants were African American required some response from federal prosecutors.

The U.S. Supreme Court disagreed. In an eight-to-one decision that did not settle the issue of whether the U.S. Attorney's Office engaged in selective prosecution, the Court ruled that federal rules of criminal procedure regarding discovery do not require the government to provide the information requested by the defendants. Although prosecutors *are* obligated to turn over documents that are "material to the preparation of the . . . defense," this applies *only* to documents needed to mount a defense against the government's "case-in-chief" (that is, the crack cocaine charges) and not to documents needed to make a selective prosecution claim. Further, the Court ruled that "for a defendant to be entitled to discovery on a claim that he was singled out for prosecution on the basis of his race, he must make a threshold showing that the Government declined to prosecute similarly situated suspects of other races."[99]

Justice Stevens, the lone dissenter in the case, argued that the evidence of selective prosecution presented by the defendants "was sufficiently disturbing to require some response from the United States Attorney's Office." According to Stevens,

> If a District Judge has reason to suspect that [the United States Attorney for the Central District of California], or a member of her staff, has singled out particular defendants for prosecution on the basis of their race, it is surely appropriate for the Judge to determine whether there is a factual basis for such a concern.[100]

Stevens added that the severity of federal penalties imposed for offenses involving crack cocaine and the documented racial patterns of enforcement "give rise to a special concern about the fairness of charging practices for crack offenses." His concerns are echoed by U.S. District Court Judge Consuelo B. Marshall, who observed, "We do see a lot of these [crack] cases and one does ask why some are in state court and some are being prosecuted in federal court . . . and if it's not based on race, what's it based on?"[101]

Race and Plea Bargaining Decisions

There has been relatively little research focusing explicitly on the effect of race on prosecutors' plea bargaining decisions. Few studies have asked if prosecutors take the race of the defendant into consideration in deciding whether to reduce or drop charges in exchange for a guilty plea. Moreover, the studies that have been conducted have reached contradictory conclusions.

Research reveals that prosecutors' plea bargaining decisions are strongly determined by the strength of evidence against the defendant, by the defendant's prior criminal record, and by the seriousness of the offense.[102] Prosecutors are more willing to offer concessions to defendants who commit less serious crimes and have less serious prior records. They are also more willing to alter charges when the evidence against the defendant is weak or inconsistent.

A number of studies conclude that white defendants are offered plea bargains more frequently and get better deals than racial minorities. A study of the charging process in New York, for example, found that race did not affect charge reductions if the case was disposed of at the first presentation. Among defendants who did not plead guilty at the first opportunity, on the other hand, African Americans received less substantial reductions than whites.[103] An analysis of 683,513 criminal cases in California concluded that "Whites were more successful in getting charges reduced or dropped, in avoiding 'enhancements' or extra charges, and in getting diversion, probation, or fines instead of incarceration."[104]

A recent analysis of plea bargaining under the federal sentencing guidelines also concluded that whites receive better deals than racial minorities.[105] This study, which was conducted by the United States Sentencing Commission, examined sentence reductions for offenders who provided "substantial assistance" to the government. According to § 5K1.1 of the *Guidelines Manual*, if an offender assists in the investigation and prosecution of another person who has committed a crime, the prosecutor can ask the court to reduce the offender's sentence. Because the guidelines do not specify either the types of cooperation that "count" as substantial assistance or the magnitude of the sentence reduction that is to be given, this is a highly discretionary decision.

The Sentencing Commission estimated the effect of race/ethnicity on both the probability of receiving a substantial assistance departure and the magnitude of the sentence reduction. They controlled for other variables such as the seriousness of the offense, use of a weapon, the offender's prior criminal record, and other factors deemed relevant under the sentencing guidelines. They found that African Americans and Hispanics were less likely than whites to receive a substantial assistance departure; among offenders who did receive a departure, whites received a larger sentence reduction than either African Americans or Hispanics.[106] According to the Commission's report, "the evidence consistently indicated that factors that were associated with either the making of a § 5K1.1 motion and/or the magnitude of the departure were not consistent with principles of equity."[107]

Similar results were reported by Albonetti, who examined the effect of guideline departures on sentence outcomes for drug offenders.[108] She found that guideline departures (most of which reflected prosecutors' motions to reduce the sentence in return for the offender's "substantial assistance") resulted in larger sentence reductions for white drug offenders than for African American or Hispanic drug offenders. A guideline departure produced a 23 percent reduction in the probability of incarceration for white offenders, compared to a 14 percent reduction for Hispanic offenders and a 13 percent reduction for African American offenders.[109] Albonetti concluded that her findings "strongly suggest that the mechanism by which the federal guidelines permit the exercise of discretion operates to the disadvantage of minority defendants."[110]

Two studies found that race did not affect plea bargaining decisions in the predicted way. An examination of the guilty plea process in nine counties in Illinois, Michigan, and Pennsylvania revealed that defendant race had no effect on four measures of charge reduction.[111] The authors of this study concluded that "the allocation of charge concessions did not seem to be dictated by blatantly discriminatory criteria or punitive motives."[112] A study of charge reductions in two jurisdictions found that racial minorities received more *favorable* treatment than whites. In one county, African Americans received more favorable charge reductions than whites; in the other county, Hispanics were treated more favorably than whites.[113] The authors of this study speculated that these results might reflect devaluation of minority victims. As they noted, "If minority victims are devalued because of racist beliefs, such sentiments could, paradoxically, produce more favorable legal outcomes for minority defendants." The authors also suggested that the results might reflect overcharging of minority defendants by the police; prosecutors may have been forced "to accept pleas to lesser charges from black defendants because of the initial overcharging."[114]

In sum, although the evidence concerning the effect of race on prosecutors' charging and plea bargaining decisions is both scanty and inconsistent, a number of studies have found that African American and Hispanic suspects are more likely than white suspects to be charged with a crime and prosecuted fully. There is also evidence supporting charges of selective prosecution of racial minorities, especially for drug offenses. The limited evidence concerning the effect of race on plea bargaining is even more contradictory. Given the importance of these initial charging decisions, these findings "call for the kind of scrutiny in the pretrial stages that has been so rightly given to the convicting and sentencing stages."[115]

CONCLUSION

The court system that tried and sentenced the Scottsboro Boys in 1931 no longer exists, in the South or elsewhere. Reforms mandated by the U.S. Supreme Court or adopted voluntarily by the states have eliminated much of the blatant racism directed against racial minorities in court. African American and Hispanic criminal defendants are no longer routinely denied bail and then tried by all-white juries without attorneys to assist them in their defense. They are not consistently prosecuted and convicted with less-than-convincing evidence of guilt.

Implementation of these reforms, however, has not produced equality of justice. As shown in the preceding sections of this chapter, there is evidence that defendant race/ethnicity continues to affect decisions regarding bail, charging, and plea bargaining. Some evidence suggests that race has a direct and obvious effect on these pretrial decisions; other evidence suggests that the effect of race is indirect and subtle. It is important to note, however, that discriminatory treatment during the pretrial stage of the criminal justice process can have profound consequences for racial minorities at trial and sentencing. If racial minorities are more likely than whites to be represented by incompetent attorneys or detained in jail prior to trial, they may, as a result of these differences, face greater odds of conviction and harsher sentences. Racially discriminatory charging decisions have similar spillover effects at trial.

DISCUSSION QUESTIONS

1. Some commentators have raised questions about the quality of legal representation provided to the poor. They have also suggested that racial minorities, who are more likely than whites to be poor, are particularly disadvantaged. Is this necessarily the case? Are racial minorities represented by public defenders or assigned counsel treated more harshly than those represented by private attorneys? If you were an African American, Hispanic, or Native American defendant and could choose whether to be represented by a public defender or a private attorney, which would you choose? Why?

2. Racial minorities make up a very small proportion of the lawyers and judges in the United States. What accounts for this? What difference, if any, would it make if more of the lawyers representing criminal defendants were racial minorities?

3. Assume that racial minorities *are* more likely than whites to be detained prior to trial. Why is this a matter for concern? What are the consequences of pretrial detention? How could the bail system be reformed to reduce this disparity?

4. Randall Kennedy, the author of *Race, Crime, and the Law,* argues that it is sometimes difficult to determine "whether, or for whom, a given disparity is harmful" (p. 10). Regarding the prosecution of pregnant women who abuse drugs, he states, "Some critics attack as racist prosecutions of pregnant drug addicts on the grounds that such prosecutions disproportionately burden blacks." But, he asks, "On balance, are black communities *hurt* by prosecutions of pregnant women for using illicit drugs harmful to their unborn babies or *helped* by intervention which may at least plausibly deter conduct that will put black unborn children at risk?" How would you answer this question?

5. Assume that there is evidence that prosecutors in a particular jurisdiction offer more favorable plea bargains to racial minorities than to whites— that is, they are more willing to reduce the charges and/or to recommend a sentence substantially below the maximum permitted by law if the defendant is a racial minority. What would explain this seemingly "anomalous" finding?

6. What evidence would the defendants in *United States v. Armstrong et al.,* the Supreme Court case in which five black defendants challenged their prosecution for drug offenses in federal rather than state court, need to prove that they had been the victims of unconstitutional selective

prosecution? How would they obtain this evidence? Has the Supreme Court placed an unreasonable burden on defendants alleging selection prosecution?

NOTES

1. Philip S. Anderson, "Striving for a Just Society," *ABA Journal* (February 1999): 66.

2. *Powell v. Alabama,* 287 U.S. 45 (1932).

3. *Norris v. Alabama,* 294 U.S. 587 (1935).

4. Dan T. Carter, *Scottsboro: A Tragedy of the American South* (Baton Rouge: Louisiana State University Press, 1969), p. 326.

5. Ibid., p. 328.

6. Ibid., pp. 344–345.

7. Ibid., p. 347.

8. *Birmingham Age-Herald* (January 24, 1936), quoted in Carter, *Scottsboro,* p. 347.

9. Carter, *Scottsboro,* pp. 376–377.

10. Ibid., p. 377.

11. Randall Kennedy, *Race, Crime, and the Law* (New York: Vintage Books, 1997), p. 104.

12. Peter Applebome, "Facts Perplexing in Texas Robbery," *New York Times* (December 19, 1983), p. 17.

13. Ibid., p. 17.

14. *Chicago Tribune* (August 9, 1995), sec. 5, pp. 1–2.

15. Ibid., p. 2.

16. Ibid.

17. Available at the Justice Project Web site: http://www.justice.policy.net/cjreform/profiles.

18. Kennedy, *Race, Crime, and the Law,* p. 127.

19. *Powell v. Alabama,* 287 U.S. 45 (1932).

20. *Johnson v. Zerbst,* 304 U.S. 458 (1938).

21. *Gideon v. Wainwright,* 372 U.S. 335 (1963).

22. *Argersinger v. Hamlin,* 407 U.S. 25 (1972).

23. A defendant is entitled to counsel at every stage "where substantial rights of the accused may be affected" that require

the "guiding hand of counsel" (*Mempa v. Rhay,* 389 U.S. 128 [1967]). These critical stages include arraignment, preliminary hearing, entry of a plea, trial, sentencing, and the first appeal.

24. *Strickland v. Washington,* 466 U.S. 668 (1984).

25. Anthony Lewis, *Gideon's Trumpet* (New York: Vintage Books, 1964).

26. Lisa J. McIntyre, *The Public Defender: The Practice of Law in the Shadows of Repute* (Chicago: University of Chicago Press, 1987).

27. Bureau of Justice Statistics, *Defense Counsel in Criminal Cases* (Washington, DC: U.S. Department of Justice, 2000), table 5.

28. Ibid., tables 16 and 19.

29. "Notes: Gideon's Promise Unfulfilled: The Need for Litigated Reform of Indigent Defense," *Harvard Law Review* 113 (2000): 2062.

30. Ibid., p. 2065.

31. Jonathan D. Casper, "Did You Have a Lawyer When You Went to Court? No, I Had a Public Defender," *Yale Review of Law & Social Action* 1 (1971): 4–9.

32. See, for example, Abraham S. Blumberg, "The Practice of Law as a Confidence Game: Organizational Cooptation of a Profession," *Law & Society Review* 1 (1967): 15–39; David Sudnow, "Normal Crimes: Sociological Features of the Penal Code in the Public Defender's Office," *Social Problems* 12 (1965): 255–277.

33. Ronald Weitzer, "Racial Discrimination in the Criminal Justice System: Findings and Problems in the Literature," *Journal of Criminal Justice* 24 (1996): 313.

34. Jonathan D. Casper, *Criminal Courts: The Defendant's Perspective* (Englewood Cliffs, NJ: Prentice-Hall, 1978); Martin

A. Levin, *Urban Politics and the Criminal Courts* (Chicago: University of Chicago Press, 1977); McIntyre, *The Public Defender: The Practice of Law in the Shadow of Repute*; Dallin H. Oaks and Warren Lehman, "Lawyers for the Poor," in *The Scales of Justice,* ed. Abraham S. Blumberg (Chicago: Aldine, 1970); Lee Silverstein, *Defense of the Poor* (Chicago: American Bar Foundation, 1965); Gerald R. Wheeler and Carol L. Wheeler, "Reflections on Legal Representation of the Economically Disadvantaged: Beyond Assembly Line Justice," *Crime and Delinquency* 26 (1980): 319–332.

35. Jerome Skolnick, "Social Control in the Adversary System," *Journal of Conflict Resolution* 11 (1967): 67.

36. Paul B. Wice, *Chaos in the Courthouse: The Inner Workings of the Urban Municipal Courts* (New York: Praeger, 1985).

37. Bureau of Justice Statistics, *Defense Counsel in Criminal Cases.*

38. Ibid.

39. Malcolm D. Holmes, Harmon M. Hosch, Howard C. Daudistel, Dolores A. Perez, and Joseph B. Graves, "Ethnicity, Legal Resources, and Felony Dispositions in Two Southwestern Jurisdictions," *Justice Quarterly* 13 (1996): 11–30.

40. Ibid., p. 24.

41. The findings reported in this chapter are unpublished. For a discussion of the overall conclusions of this study, see Cassia Spohn and Miriam DeLone, "When Does Race Matter? An Examination of the Conditions under Which Race Affects Sentence Severity," *Sociology of Crime, Law, and Deviance* 2 (2000): 3–37.

42. Weitzer, "Racial Discrimination in the Criminal Justice System," p. 313.

43. Roger A. Hanson and Brian J. Ostrom, "Indigent Defenders Get the Job Done and Done Well," in *Criminal Justice: Law and Politics,* 6th ed., ed. George Cole (Belmont, CA: Wadsworth, 1993).

44. Gunnar Myrdal, *An American Dilemma: The Negro Problem and Modern Democracy* (New York: Harper & Brothers, 1944), p. 547.

45. Myrdal, *An American Dilemma,* p. 548.

46. Haywood Burns, "Black People and the Tyranny of American Law," *The Annals of the American Academy of Political and Social Sciences* 407 (1973): 161.

47. Celesta A. Albonetti, "An Integration of Theories to Explain Judicial Discretion," *Social Problems* 38 (1991): 247–266; Ronald A. Farrell and Victoria L. Swigert, "Prior Offense Record as a Self-Fulfilling Prophecy," *Law & Society Review* 12 (1978): 437–453; Caleb Foote, "Compelling Appearance in Court: Administration of Bail in Philadelphia," *University of Pennsylvania Law Review* 102 (1954): 1031–1079; Joan Petersilia, *Racial Disparities in the Criminal Justice System* (Santa Monica, CA: Rand Corporation, 1978); Wheeler and Wheeler, "Reflections on Legal Representation of the Economically Disadvantaged."

48. Wayne Thomas, *Bail Reform in America* (Berkeley: University of California Press, 1976).

49. Samuel Walker, *Taming the System: The Control of Discretion in Criminal Justice, 1950–1990* (New York: Oxford University Press, 1993).

50. J. Austin, B. Krisberg, and P. Litsky, "The Effectiveness of Supervised Pretrial Release," *Crime and Delinquency* 31 (1985): 519–537; John S. Goldkamp, "Danger and Detention: A Second Generation of Bail Reform," *The Journal of Criminal Law and Criminology* 76 (1985): 1–74; Walker, *Taming the System.*

51. Goldkamp, "Danger and Detention."

52. This law was upheld by the U.S. Supreme Court in *United States v. Salerno,* 481 U.S. 739 (1987).

53. Coramae Richey Mann, *Unequal Justice: A Question of Color* (Bloomington: Indiana University Press, 1993), p. 168.

54. R. Stryker, Ilene Nagel, and John Hagan, "Methodology Issues in Court Research: Pretrial Release Decisions for Federal Defendants," *Sociological Methods and Research* 11 (1983): 460–500; Charles M. Katz and Cassia Spohn, "The Effect of Race and Gender on Bail Outcomes: A Test of an Interactive Model," *American Journal of Criminal Justice* 19 (1995): 161–184.

55. S. H. Clarke and G. G. Koch, "The Influence of Income and Other Factors on Whether Criminal Defendants Go to Prison," *Law & Society Review* 11 (1976): 57–92.

56. George S. Bridges, *A Study on Racial and Ethnic Disparities in Superior Court Bail and Pre-Trial Detention Practices in Washington* (Olympia: Washington State Minority and Justice Commission, 1997).

57. Ibid., p. 54.

58. Ibid., p. 98.

59. Ibid.

60. The findings reported here are unpublished. See Spohn and DeLone, "When Does Race Matter?" for a discussion of the overall conclusions of their study.

61. Margaret Farnworth and Patrick Horan, "Separate Justice: An Analysis of Race Differences in Court Processes," *Social Science Research* 9 (1980): 381–399.

62. Theodore G. Chiricos and William D. Bales, "Unemployment and Punishment: An Empirical Assessment," *Criminology* 29 (1991): 701–724.

63. Celesta A. Albonetti, Robert M. Hauser, John Hagan, and Ilene H. Nagel, "Criminal Justice Decision Making as a Stratification Process: The Role of Race and Stratification Resources in Pretrial Release," *Journal of Quantitative Criminology* 5 (1989): 57–82.

64. Bureau of Justice Statistics, *Felony Defendants in Large Urban Counties, 1998* (Washington, DC: U.S. Department of Justice, 2001), table 24.

65. Bureau of Justice Statistics, *Pretrial Release of Felony Defendants, 1992* (Washington, DC: U.S. Department of Justice, 1994), pp. 13–14.

66. Bureau of Justice Statistics, *Felony Defendants in Large Urban Counties, 1998,* tables 13 and 18.

67. Spohn and DeLone, "When Does Race Matter?" table 2.

68. Spohn and DeLone, unpublished data.

69. Leadership Conference on Civil Rights, *Justice on Trial: Racial Disparities in the American Criminal Justice System* (Washington, DC: Author, 2000).

70. *Bordenkircher v. Hayes,* 434 U.S. 357, 364 (1978).

71. Kenneth Culp Davis, *Discretionary Justice* (Baton Rouge: Louisiana State University Press, 1969), p. 190.

72. Barbara Boland (INSLAW Inc.), *The Prosecution of Felony Arrests* (Washington, DC: Bureau of Justice Statistics, 1983); Kathleen B. Brosi, *A Cross-City Comparison of Felony Case Processing* (Washington, DC: Institute for Law and Social Research, 1979); Vera Institute of Justice, *Felony Arrests: Their Prosecution and Disposition in New York City's Courts* (New York: Longman, 1981).

73. Charles E. Silberman, *Criminal Violence, Criminal Justice* (New York: Random House, 1978), p. 271.

74. *Bordenkircher v. Hayes,* 434 U.S. 357, 364.

75. Myrdal, *An American Dilemma,* pp. 552–553.

76. Ilene Nagel Bernstein, William R. Kelly, and Patricia A. Doyle, "Societal Reaction to Deviants: The Case of Criminal Defendants," *American Sociological Review* 42 (1977): 743–755; Malcolm M. Feeley, *The Process Is the Punishment: Handling Cases in a Lower Criminal Court* (New York: Russell Sage Foundation, 1979); John Hagan, "Parameters of Criminal Prosecution: An Application of Path Analysis to a Problem of Criminal Justice," *Journal of Criminal Law and Criminology* 65 (1975): 536–544.

77. Celesta A. Albonetti, "Criminality, Prosecutorial Screening, and Uncertainty: Toward a Theory of Discretionary Decision Making in Felony Case Processing, *Criminology* 24 (1986): 623–644; Martha A. Myers, *The Effects of Victim Characteristics in the Prosecution, Conviction, and Sentencing of Criminal Defendants,* unpublished Ph.D. dissertation (Bloomington: Indiana University, 1977).

78. Cassia Spohn, John Gruhl, and Susan Welch, "The Impact of the Ethnicity and Gender of Defendants on the Decision to Reject or Dismiss Felony Charges," *Criminology* 25 (1987): 175–191.

79. Ibid., p. 186.

80. Robert D. Crutchfield, Joseph G. Weis, Rodney L. Engen, and Randy R.

Gainey, *Racial and Ethnic Disparities in the Prosecution of Felony Cases in King County* (Olympia Washington State Minority and Justice Commission, 1995).

81. Ibid., p. 32.

82. Ibid., p. 58.

83. Gary D. LaFree, "The Effect of Sexual Stratification by Race on Official Reactions to Rape," *American Sociological Review* 45 (1980): 842–854.

84. Michael L. Radelet, "Racial Characteristics and the Imposition of the Death Penalty," *American Sociological Review* 46 (1981): 918–927.

85. Cassia Spohn and Jeffrey Spears, "The Effect of Offender and Victim Characteristics on Sexual Assault Case Processing Decisions," *Justice Quarterly* 13 (1996): 649–679.

86. Ibid., pp. 661–662.

87. Ibid., p. 673.

88. Ibid., p. 674.

89. Petersilia, *Racial Disparities in the Criminal Justice System.*

90. Ibid., p. 26.

91. Michael Tonry, *Malign Neglect: Race, Crime, and Punishment in America* (New York: Oxford University Press, 1995), p. 105.

92. Ibid., p. 115.

93. Jerome Miller, *Search and Destroy: African-American Males in the Criminal Justice System* (Cambridge: Cambridge University Press, 1996), p. 80.

94. United States Sentencing Commission, *1997 Sourcebook of Federal Sentencing Statistics* (Washington, DC: Author, 1998), table 4.

95. U.S. Department of Health and Human Services, Substance Abuse and Mental Health Services Administration, *National Household Survey on Drug Abuse: Population Estimates 1994* (Rockville, MD: Author, 1995).

96. Richard Berk and Alec Campbell, "Preliminary Data on Race and Crack Charging Practices in Los Angeles," *Federal Sentencing Reporter* 6 (1993): 36–38.

97. *United States v. Armstrong et al.*, 517 U.S. 456 (1996).

98. 48 F.3d 1508 (9th Cir. 1995).

99. *United States v. Armstrong et al.*, 517 U.S. 456 (1996).

100. Ibid. (Stevens, J., dissenting).

101. Leadership Conference on Civil Rights, *Justice on Trial,* p. 14.

102. Lynn M. Mather, *Plea Bargaining or Trial?* (Lexington, MA: Heath, 1979).

103. Ilene Nagel Bernstein, Edward Kick, Jan T. Leung, and Barbara Schultz, "Charge Reduction: An Intermediary State in the Process of Labelling Criminal Defendants," *Social Forces* 56 (1977): 362–384.

104. Weitzer, "Racial Discrimination in the Criminal Justice System," p. 313.

105. Linda Drazga Maxfield and John H. Kramer, *Substantial Assistance: An Empirical Yardstick Gauging Equity in Current Federal Policy and Practice* (Washington, DC: United States Sentencing Commission, 1998).

106. Ibid., pp. 14–19.

107. Ibid., p. 21.

108. Celesta A. Albonetti, "Sentencing under the Federal Sentencing Guidelines: Effects of Defendant Characteristics, Guilty Pleas, and Departures on Sentence Outcomes for Drug Offenses, 1991–92," *Law & Society Review* 31 (1997): 789–822.

109. Ibid., p. 813.

110. Ibid., p. 818.

111. Peter F. Nardulli, James Eisenstein, and Roy B. Flemming, *The Tenor of Justice: Criminal Courts and the Guilty Plea Process* (Chicago: University of Chicago Press, 1988).

112. Ibid., p. 238.

113. Malcolm D. Holmes, Howard C. Daudistel, and Ronald A. Farrell, "Determinants of Charge Reductions and Final Dispositions in Cases of Burglary and Robbery," *Journal of Research in Crime and Delinquency* 24 (1987): 233–254.

114. Ibid., pp. 248–249.

115. Spohn et al., "The Impact of the Ethnicity and Gender of Defendants" p. 189.

6

Justice on the Bench?

Trial and Adjudication in Criminal Court

> In our courts, when it's a white man's word against a black man's,
> the white man always wins. They're ugly but those are the facts of life.
> The one place where a man ought to get a square deal is a courtroom,
> be he any color of the rainbow, but people have a way of carrying
> their resentments right into a jury box.
>
> —HARPER LEE, *TO KILL A MOCKINGBIRD*[1]

We began the previous chapter with a discussion of the Scottsboro case, a case involving nine young African American males who were convicted of raping two white girls in the early 1930s. We noted that the defendants were tried by all-white juries and that the Supreme Court overturned their convictions because of the systematic exclusion of African Americans from the jury pool.

However, the Scottsboro Boys were tried in the 1930s, and much has changed since then. Race relations have improved, and decisions handed down by the Supreme Court have made it increasingly difficult for court systems to exclude African Americans from jury service. Nevertheless, "racial prejudice still sometimes seems to sit as a 'thirteenth juror.'"[2] All-white juries continue to convict African American defendants on less-than-convincing evidence. Despite persuasive evidence of guilt, all-white juries continue to acquit whites who victimize African Americans. And police and law enforcement officials sometimes bend the law in their zeal to obtain a conviction. Consider the following recent cases:

1987 Robert Bacon Jr. was sentenced to death by an all-white jury in North Carolina. Bacon, an African American, was convicted of killing his girlfriend's estranged husband; both his girlfriend and her husband were white. Only four of the 42 potential jurors questioned at his trial were African American; the trial judge dismissed two of them as unqualified to serve, and the prosecutor used his peremptory challenges to eliminate the other two. The North Carolina Supreme Court threw out the death sentence and ordered a new sentencing hearing. Forty-six of the 48 jurors summoned for the hearing were white. The prosecutor used his peremptory challenges to dismiss the two nonwhites, and an all-white jury resentenced Bacon to death. In October 2001, North Carolina governor Mike Easley commuted Bacon's sentence to life in prison without the possibility of parole.[3]

1987   A jury of 10 whites and two blacks acquitted Bernie Goetz, the so-called subway vigilante, of all but one relatively minor charge in the shooting of four young men on a New York City subway. Goetz, a white man, was accused of shooting and seriously wounding four African American youths who Goetz said had threatened him. A man outside the courtroom held up a sign reading, "Congratulations! Bernie Goetz wins one for the good guys."

1991   Four white Los Angeles police officers were charged in the beating of Rodney King, an African American man stopped for a traffic violation. A videotape of the incident, which showed the officers hitting King with their batons and kicking him in the head as he lay on the ground, was introduced as evidence at the trial. Los Angeles exploded in riots after a jury composed of 10 whites, one Asian American, and one Hispanic acquitted the officers on all charges.

1997   Orange County (California) superior court judge Everett Dickey reversed Geronimo Pratt's 1972 conviction for first-degree murder, assault with intent to commit murder, and robbery.[4] Pratt, a decorated Vietnam War veteran and a leader in the Black Panther Party, was accused of killing Caroline Olsen and shooting her ex-husband Kenneth Olsen on the Lincoln Park tennis court in Santa Monica. Pratt, who claimed he had been in Oakland on Panther business at the time of the crime, was convicted based in large part on the testimony of another member of the Black Panther Party, Julius Butler. It was later revealed that Butler had been a paid police informant and that police and prosecutors in Los Angeles conspired to keep this information from the jury hearing Pratt's case. Over the next 25 years, Pratt's lawyers filed a series of appeals, arguing that Pratt's conviction "was based on false testimony knowingly presented by the prosecution."[5] Their requests for a rehearing were repeatedly denied by California courts, and the Los Angeles District Attorney's Office refused to reopen the case. Then, in May 1997, Judge Dickey granted Pratt's petition for a writ of habeas corpus and reversed his conviction. Citing errors by the district attorney who tried the case, Judge Dickey stated, "The evidence which was withheld about Julius Butler and his activities could have put the whole case in a different light, and failure to timely disclose it undermines confidence in the verdict."[6] Geronimo Pratt, who spent 25 years in prison—including eight years in solitary confinement—was released on June 10, 1997. In April 2000, Pratt's lawsuit for false imprisonment and violation of his civil rights was settled out of court: the City of Los Angeles agreed to pay Pratt $2.75 million, and the federal government agreed to pay him $1.75 million. Pratt's attorney, Johnnie Cochran Jr., described the settlement as "unprecedented" and praised Pratt for "the relentless pursuit of justice." Cochran also stated that the settlement puts "to rest a matter that has dragged on for more than three decades."[7]

GOALS OF THE CHAPTER

In this chapter, we focus on trial and adjudication in criminal court. We begin with an examination of race and the jury selection process. We focus on both the procedures used to select the jury pool and the process of selecting the jurors for a particular case. We also discuss the issue of "playing the race card" in a criminal trial. We end the chapter by summarizing the scholarly debate surrounding the issue of racially based jury nullification.

SELECTION OF THE JURY POOL

> Three facts about jury discrimination are largely undisputed. First, the all-white jury has been a staple of the American criminal justice system for most of our history. Second, the Supreme Court has long condemned discrimination in jury selection. And third, race discrimination in jury selection remains a pervasive feature of our justice system to this day. The interesting question is how all of these facts can be true at the same time.
>
> —DAVID COLE, *NO EQUAL JUSTICE*[8]

The jury plays a critically important role in the criminal justice system. Indeed, "the jury is the heart of the criminal justice system."[9] Although it is true that most cases are settled by plea and not by trial, many of the cases that do go to trial involve serious crimes in which defendants are facing long prison terms, or even the death penalty. In these serious—and highly publicized—cases, the jury serves as the conscience of the community and, in the words of the U.S. Supreme Court, as "an inestimable safeguard against the corrupt or overzealous prosecutor and against the compliant, biased, or eccentric judge."[10] As the Court has repeatedly emphasized, the jury also serves as "the criminal defendant's fundamental 'protection of life and liberty against race or color prejudice.'"[11]

The Supreme Court first addressed the issue of racial discrimination in jury selection in its 1880 decision of *Strauder v. West Virginia*.[12] The Court ruled that a West Virginia statute limiting jury service to white males violated the equal protection clause of the Fourteenth Amendment and therefore was unconstitutional. The Court concluded that the statute inflicted two distinct harms. The first was a harm that affected the entire African American population. According to the Court,

> The very fact that colored people are singled out and expressly denied by a statute all right to participate in the administration of the law, as jurors, because of their color . . . is practically a brand upon them affixed by the law, an assertion of their inferiority, and a stimulant to that race prejudice which is an impediment to securing to individuals of the race that equal justice which the law aims to secure to all others.[13]

The Court stated that the West Virginia statute inflicted a second harm that primarily hurt African American defendants, who were denied even the *chance* to have people of their own race on their juries. "How can it be maintained," the justices asked, "that compelling a man to submit to trial for his life by a jury drawn from a panel from which the State has expressly excluded every man of his race, because of his color alone, however well qualified in other respects, is not a denial to him of equal legal protection?"[14] The Court added that this was precisely the type of discrimination the equal protection clause was designed to prevent.

After *Strauder v. West Virginia,* it was clear that states could not pass laws excluding African Americans from jury service. This ruling, however, did not prevent states, and particularly Southern states, from developing techniques designed to preserve the all-white jury. In Delaware, for example, local jurisdictions used lists of taxpayers to select "sober and judicious" persons for jury service. Under this system, African American taxpayers were eligible for jury service but were seldom, if ever, selected for the jury pool. The state explained this result by noting that few of the African Americans in Delaware were intelligent, experienced, or moral enough to serve as jurors. As the chief justice of the Delaware Supreme Court concluded: "That none but white men were selected is in nowise remarkable in view of the fact—too notorious to be ignored—that the great body of black men residing in this State are utterly unqualified by want of intelligence, experience, or moral integrity to sit on juries."[15]

The U.S. Supreme Court refused to accept this explanation. In *Neal v. Delaware,* decided two years after *Strauder,* the court ruled that the practice had systematically excluded African Americans from jury service and was therefore a case of purposeful—and unconstitutional—racial discrimination.[16] Justice Harlan, writing for the Court, stated that it was implausible "that such uniform exclusion of [Negroes] from juries, during a period of many years, was solely because . . . the black race in Delaware were utterly disqualified, by want of intelligence, experience, or moral integrity."[17]

These early court decisions did not eliminate racial discrimination in jury selection, particularly in the South. Gunnar Myrdal's analysis of the "Negro problem" in the United States in the late 1930s and early 1940s concluded that the typical jury in the South was composed entirely of whites.[18] He noted that some courts had taken steps "to have Negroes on the jury list and call them in occasionally for service."[19] He added, however, that many Southern courts, and particularly those in rural areas, had either ignored the constitutional requirement or had developed techniques "to fulfill legal requirements without using Negro jurors."[20] As a result, as Wishman noted, "For our first hundred years, blacks were explicitly denied the right to be jurors, which meant that if a black defendant was not lynched on the spot, an all-white jury would later decide what to do with him."[21]

Since the mid-1930s, the Supreme Court has made it increasingly difficult for court systems to exclude African Americans or Hispanics from the jury pool. It consistently has struck down the techniques used to circumvent the requirement of racial neutrality in the selection of the jury pool. The Court, for example, ruled that it was unconstitutional for a Georgia county to put the names of white potential jurors on white cards, the names of African American potential jurors on yellow cards, and then "randomly" draw cards to determine who would be summoned.[22] Similarly, the Court struck down the "random" selection of jurors from tax books in which the names of white taxpayers and African American taxpayers were in separate sections.[23] As the Justices stated in *Avery v. Georgia,* "The State may not draw up its jury lists pursuant to neutral procedures but then resort to discrimination at other stages in the selection process."[24]

The states' response to the Supreme Court's increasingly vigilant oversight of the jury selection process was not always positive.[25] The response in some Southern jurisdictions "was a new round of tokenism aimed at maintaining as much of the white supremacist status quo as possible while avoiding judicial intervention."[26] These jurisdictions, in other words, included a token number of racial minorities in the jury pool in an attempt to head off charges of racial discrimination. The Supreme Court addressed this issue as late as 1988.[27] The Court reversed the conviction of Tony Amadeo, who was sentenced to death for murder in Putnam County, Georgia, after it was revealed that the Putnam County district attorney asked the jury commissioner to limit the number of African Americans and women on the master lists from which potential jurors were chosen.

Although these Supreme Court decisions have made it more difficult for states to discriminate overtly on the basis of race, the procedures used to select the jury pool are not racially neutral. Many states obtain the names of potential jurors from lists of registered voters, automobile registrations, or property tax rolls. The problem with this seemingly objective method is that in some jurisdictions, racial minorities are less likely than whites to register to vote or to own automobiles or taxable property. As a result, racial minorities are less likely than whites to receive a jury summons. Further compounding the problem is the fact that "for a number of reasons, from skepticism and alienation to the inability to take time off from their jobs, minorities and the poor are also less likely to respond to those summonses they receive."[28] The result is a jury pool that overrepresents white middle- and upper-class persons and underrepresents racial minorities and those who are poor (see Box 6.1).

BOX 6.1 Excerpts from Massachusetts Jury Selection Statute

Juror Service

Juror service in the participating counties shall be a duty which every person who qualifies under this chapter shall perform when selected. All persons selected for juror service on grand and trial juries shall be selected at random from the population of the judicial district in which they reside. All persons shall have equal opportunity to be considered for juror service. All persons shall serve as jurors when selected and summoned for that purpose except as hereinafter provided. No person shall be exempted or excluded from serving as a grand or trial juror because of race, color, religion, sex, national origin, economic status, or occupation. Physically handicapped persons shall serve except where the court finds such service is not feasible. This court shall strictly enforce the provisions of this section.

Disqualification from Juror Service

As of the date of receipt of the juror summons, any citizen of the United States, who is a resident of the judicial district or who lives within the judicial district more than fifty per cent of the time, whether or not he is registered to vote in any state or federal election, shall be qualified to serve as a grand or trial juror in such judicial district unless one of the following grounds for disqualification applies:

1. Such person is under the age of eighteen years.

2. Such person is seventy years of age or older and indicates on the juror confirmation form an election not to perform juror service.

3. Such person is not able to speak and understand the English language.

4. Such person is incapable by reason of a physical or mental disability of rendering satisfactory juror service.

5. Such person is solely responsible for the daily care of a permanently disabled person living in the same household and the performance of juror service would cause a substantial risk of injury to the health of the disabled person.

6. Such person is outside the judicial district and does not intend to return to the judicial district and does not intend to return to the judicial district at any time during the following year.

7. Such person has been convicted of a felony within the past seven years or is defendant in pending felony cases or is in the custody of a correctional institution.

8. Such person has served as a grand or trial juror in any state or federal court within the previous three calendar years or the person is currently scheduled to perform such service.

SOURCE: 234A M.6.L.A. § 1 et seq.

Techniques for Increasing Racial Diversity

State and federal jurisdictions have experimented with a number of techniques for increasing the racial diversity of the jury pool. When officials in Hennepin County (St. Paul), Minnesota, which is 9 percent nonwhite, discovered that most grand juries were all white, they instituted a number of reforms designed to make jury service less burdensome. They doubled the pay for serving, provided funding to pay jurors' day-care expenses, and included a round-trip bus pass with each jury summons.[29] As a result of these measures, the number of racial minorities selected for grand juries increased.

A more controversial approach involves "race-conscious jury selection."[30] Some jurisdictions, for example, send a disproportionate number of summonses to geographic areas with large populations of racial minorities. Others attempt to select a more representative jury pool by subtracting the names of white prospective jurors until the proportion of racial minorities in the pool matches the proportion in the population. A more direct effort to ensure racial diversity involves setting aside a certain number of seats for racial minorities. Although no jurisdiction has applied this approach to the selection of trial jurors, judges in Hennepin County are required to select two minority grand jurors for every grand jury.[31]

Opinions regarding these techniques are divided. Randall Kennedy argued that "officials should reject proposals for race-dependent jury reforms."[32] Although he acknowledged that these proposals are well intentioned, Kennedy maintained that they would have unintended consequences (for example, jurors selected because of their race might believe they are expected to act as representatives of their race during deliberations) and would be difficult to administer (for example, officials would be required to determine the race of potential jurors and defendants, which would inevitably result in controversies over racial identification). Kennedy also suggested that the more direct techniques may be unconstitutional. As he noted, "Over the past decade, the U.S. Supreme Court has become increasingly hostile to race-dependent public policies, even when they have been defended as efforts to include historically oppressed racial minorities in networks of economic opportunity and self-government."[33] Although the Supreme Court has not yet addressed this issue, in 1998 the U.S. Court of Appeals for the Sixth Circuit ruled that subtracting nonwhites from jury panels so that all panels matched the racial makeup of the community violated the equal protection rights of white jurors.[34]

Those on the other side contend that race-conscious plans that create representative jury pools should be allowed because they reduce the likelihood that people of color will be tried by all-white juries. Albert Alschuler, an outspoken advocate of racial quotas for juries, asserted that "few statements are more likely to evoke disturbing images of American criminal justice than this one: 'the defendant was tried by an all-white jury.'"[35] He and other critics of jury selection procedures contend that lack of participation by racial minorities on juries that convict the African Americans and Hispanics who fill court dockets in many jurisdictions leads to questions regarding the legitimacy of their verdicts. Advocates of race-conscious plans also argue that the inclusion of greater numbers of racial minorities will counteract the cynicism and distrust that minorities feel toward their government. As David Cole, a professor at Georgetown University Law Center, wrote, "If the criminal justice system is to be accepted by the black community, the black community must be represented on juries. The long history of excluding blacks from juries is one important reason why blacks as a class are more skeptical than whites about the fairness of the criminal justice system."[36]

THE PEREMPTORY CHALLENGE: RACIAL PROFILING IN THE COURTROOM?

The Supreme Court consistently has ruled that a jury should be drawn from a representative cross section of the community and that race is not a valid qualification for jury service. These requirements, however, apply only to the selection of the jury pool. They do not apply to the selection of individual jurors for a particular case. In fact, the Court has repeatedly stated that a defendant is *not* entitled to a jury "composed in whole or in part of persons of his own race."[37] Thus, prosecutors and defense attorneys can use their peremptory challenges—"challenges without cause, without explanation, and without judicial scrutiny"[38]—as they see fit (for evidence of this, see Box 6.2). They can use their peremptory challenges in a racially discriminatory manner.

It is clear that lawyers do take the race of the juror into consideration during the jury selection process. Prosecutors assume that racial minorities will side with minority defendants, and defense attorneys assume that racial minorities will be more inclined than whites to convict white defendants. As a result of these assumptions, both prosecutors and defense attorneys have used their peremptory challenges to strike racial minorities from the jury pool. Kennedy, in fact, characterized the peremptory challenge as "a creature of unbridled discretion that, in the hands of white prosecutors and white defendants, has often been used to sustain racial subordination in the courthouse."[39]

Dramatic evidence of this surfaced recently in Philadelphia. In April 1997, Lynne Abraham, Philadelphia's district attorney, released a 1986 videotape made by Jack McMahon, a former assistant district attorney and her electoral opponent. In the hour-long training video, McMahon advised fellow prosecutors that "young black women are very bad for juries" and that "blacks from the low-income areas are less likely to convict." He also stated, "There's a resentment for law enforcement. There's a resentment for authority. And as a result, you don't want those people on your jury."[40] A Philadelphia defense attorney characterized the videotape as "an abuse of the office," noting, "It was unconstitutional then, and it's unconstitutional now. You don't teach young attorneys to exclude poor people, or black people or Hispanic people."[41]

These comments notwithstanding, there is compelling evidence that prosecutors do use their peremptory challenges to strike racial minorities from the jury pool. As a result, African American and Hispanic defendants are frequently tried by all-white juries. In 1964, for example, Robert Swain, a 19-year-old African American, was sentenced to death by an all-white jury for raping a white woman in Alabama. The prosecutor had used his peremptory challenges to

BOX 6.2   Selecting a Jury: Stereotypes and Prejudice

A 1973 Texas prosecutors' manual for jury selection provided the following advice:

- You are not looking for a fair juror, but rather a strong, biased and sometimes hypocritical individual who believes that defendants are different from them in kind, rather than degree. You are not looking for any member of a minority group which may subject him to oppression—they almost always empathize with the accused. You are not looking for free thinkers or flower children.
- Observation is worthwhile. . . . Look for physical afflictions. These people usually sympathize with the accused.
- I don't like women jurors because I can't trust them. They do, however, make the best jurors in cases involving crimes against children.
- Extremely overweight people, especially women and young men, indicate a lack of self-discipline

and oftentimes instability. I like the lean and hungry look.

- If the veniremen have not lived in the county long, ask where they were born and reared. People from small towns and rural areas generally make good State's jurors. People from the east or west coasts often make bad jurors.
- Intellectuals such as teachers, etc. generally are too liberal and contemplative to make good State's jurors.
- Ask veniremen their religious preference. Jewish veniremen generally make poor State's jurors. Jews have a history of oppression and generally empathize with the accused. Lutherans and Church of Christ veniremen usually make good State's jurors.

SOURCE: Albert W. Alschuler, "The Supreme Court and the Jury: Voir Dire, Peremptory Challenges, and the Review of Jury Verdicts," *University of Chicago Law Review* 56 (1989): 153. Available at http://www.lexis-nexis.com/universe.

strike all six African Americans on the jury panel. In 1990, the State used all of its peremptory challenges to eliminate African Americans from the jury that would try Marion Barry, the African American mayor of Washington, DC, on drug charges.

The Supreme Court and the Peremptory Challenge: From *Swain* to *Batson*

The Supreme Court initially was reluctant to restrict the prosecutor's right to use peremptory challenges to excuse jurors on the basis of race. In 1965, the Court ruled in *Swain v. Alabama* that the prosecutor's use of peremptory challenges to strike all six African Americans in the jury pool did not violate the equal protection clause of the Constitution.[42] The Court reasoned,

> The presumption in any particular case must be that the prosecutor is using the State's challenges to obtain a fair and impartial jury. . . . The presumption is not overcome and the prosecutor therefore subjected to examination by allegations that in the case at hand all Negroes were

removed from the jury or that they were removed because they were Negroes.[43]

The Court went on to observe that the Constitution did place some limits on the use of the peremptory challenge. The justices stated that a defendant could establish a prima facie case of purposeful racial discrimination by showing that the elimination of African Americans from a particular jury was part of a pattern of discrimination in that jurisdiction.

The problem, of course, was that the defendants in *Swain* and in the cases that followed, could not meet this stringent test. As Wishman observed, "A defense lawyer almost never has the statistics to prove a pattern of discrimination, and the state under the *Swain* decision is not required to keep them."[44] The ruling, therefore, provided no protection to the individual African American defendant deprived of a jury of his peers by the prosecutor's use of racially discriminatory strikes. As Supreme Court Justice William Brennan later wrote,

> With the hindsight that two decades affords, it is apparent to me that *Swain*'s reasoning was misconceived. . . . *Swain* holds that the state may presume in exercising peremptory challenges that only white jurors will be sufficiently impartial to try a Negro defendant fairly. . . . Implicit in such a presumption is profound disrespect for the ability of individual Negro jurors to judge impartially. It is the race of the juror, and nothing more, that gives rise to the doubt in the mind of the prosecutor.[45]

Despite harsh criticism from legal scholars and civil libertarians,[46] who argued that *Swain* imposed a "crushing burden . . . on defendants alleging racially discriminatory jury selection,"[47] the decision stood for twenty-one years. It was not until 1986 that the Court, in *Batson v. Kentucky*,[48] rejected *Swain*'s systematic exclusion requirement and ruled "that a defendant may establish a prima facie case of purposeful discrimination in selection of the petit jury solely on evidence concerning the prosecutor's exercise of peremptory challenges at the defendant's trial."[49] The justices added that once the defendant makes a prima facie case of racial discrimination, the burden shifts to the State to provide a racially neutral explanation for excluding African American jurors. (See Box 6.3 for a discussion of the use of the peremptory challenge to exclude African American jurors in cases involving white defendants.)

Interpreting and Applying the *Batson* Standard Although *Batson* seemed to offer hope that the goal of a representative jury was attainable, an examination of cases decided since 1986 suggests otherwise. State and federal appellate courts have ruled, for example, that leaving one or two African Americans on the jury precludes any inference of purposeful racial discrimination on the part of the prosecutor[50] and that striking only one or two jurors of the defendant's race does not constitute a "pattern" of strikes.[51]

Trial and appellate courts have also been willing to accept virtually any explanation offered by the prosecutor to rebut the defendant's inference of purposeful discrimination.[52] As Kennedy noted, "Judges tend to give the benefit of the doubt to the prosecutor."[53] Kennedy cited as an example *State v. Jackson*,

BOX 6.3   White Defendants and the Exclusion of Black Jurors

The Equal Protection Clause of the Fourteenth Amendment declares, "No State shall . . . deny to any person within its jurisdiction the equal protection of the law." Enacted in the wake of the Civil War, the Fourteenth Amendment was designed to protect the rights of the newly freed slaves. As Congressman Stevens, one of the amendment's sponsors stated, "Whatever law punishes a white man for a crime shall punish the black man precisely in the same way and to the same degree. Whatever law protects the white man shall afford 'equal' protection to the black man" (Mason & Beancy, 1972, p. 379).

The Supreme Court has interpreted the equal protection clause to prohibit prosecutors from using their peremptory challenges in a racially discriminatory manner—that is, to forbid prosecutors from striking African Americans or Hispanics from the pool of potential jurors in cases involving African American and Hispanic defendants. But what about cases involving white defendants? Are prosecutors prohibited from using their challenges to strike racial minorities when the defendant is white?

The Supreme Court has ruled that white defendants *can* challenge the exclusion of racial minorities from the jury. In 1991, for example, the Court ruled that "a criminal defendant may object to the race-based exclusion of jurors effected through peremptory challenges regardless of whether the defendant and the excluded juror share the same race" (*Powers v. Ohio*, 499 U.S. 400 [1991]). This case involved a white criminal defendant on trial for

homicide who objected to the prosecutor's use of peremptory challenges to remove African Americans from the jury. In 1998, the Court handed down a similar decision regarding the grand jury, ruling that whites who are indicted by grand juries from which African Americans have been excluded can challenge the constitutionality of the indictment (*Campbell v. Louisiana*, 523 U.S. 392 [1998]).

In both of these cases, the Court stated that a white defendant has the right to assert a violation of equal protection on behalf of excluded African American jurors. According to the Court, the discriminatory use of peremptory challenges by the prosecution "casts doubt upon the integrity of the judicial process and places the fairness of the criminal proceeding in doubt." And while an individual juror does not have the right to sit on any particular jury, "he or she does possess the right not to be excluded from one on account of race." As the Court stated, "Both the excluded juror and the criminal defendant have a common interest in eliminating racial discrimination from the courtroom." Because it is unlikely that the excluded juror will challenge the discriminatory use of the peremptory challenge, the defendant can assert this right on his or her behalf (*Powers v. Ohio*, 499 U.S. 400 [1991]).

What do you think? Should a white defendant be allowed to challenge the prosecutor's use of peremptory challenges to exclude African Americans and other racial minorities from his or her jury?

a case in which the prosecutor used her peremptory challenges to strike four African Americans in the jury pool. According to Kennedy,

> The prosecutor said that she struck one black prospective juror because she was unemployed and had previously served as a student counselor at a university, a position that bothered the prosecution because it was "too liberal a background." The prosecution said that it struck another black prospective juror because she, too, was unemployed, and, through her demeanor, had displayed hostility or indifference. By contrast, two whites who were unemployed were seated without objection by the prosecution.[54]

Although Kennedy acknowledged that "one should give due deference to the trial judge who was in a position to see directly the indescribable subtleties," he stated that he "still has difficulty believing that, had these prospective jurors been white, the prosecutor would have struck them just the same."[55] Echoing these concerns, Serr and Maney conclude, "The cost of forfeiting truly peremptory challenges has yielded little corresponding benefit, as a myriad of 'acceptable' explanations and excuses cloud any hope of detecting racially based motivations."[56]

The validity of their concerns is illustrated by a recent Supreme Court case, *Purkett v. Elem.*[57] Jimmy Elem, an African American on trial for robbery in Missouri, objected to the prosecutor's use of peremptory challenges to strike two African American men from the jury panel. The prosecutor provided the following racially neutral explanation for these strikes:

> I struck [juror] number twenty-two because of his long hair. He had long curly hair. He had the longest hair of anybody on the panel by far. He appeared to me to not be a good juror for that fact, the fact that he had long hair hanging down shoulder length, curly, unkempt hair. Also, he had a mustache and a goatee type beard. And juror number twenty-four also has a mustache and goatee type beard. Those are the only two people on the jury . . . with the mustache and goatee type beard. . . . And I don't like the way they looked, with the way the hair is cut, both of them. And the mustaches and the beards look suspicious to me.[58]

The U.S. Court of Appeals for the Eighth Circuit ruled that the prosecutor's reasons for striking the jurors were not legitimate race-neutral reasons because they were not plausibly related to "the person's ability to perform his or her duties as a juror."[59] Thus, the trial court had erred in finding no intentional discrimination.

The Supreme Court reversed the circuit court's decision, ruling that *Batson v. Kentucky* required only "that the prosecution provide a race-neutral justification for the exclusion, not that the prosecution show that the justification is plausible." Noting that neither a beard nor long, unkempt hair is a characteristic peculiar to any race, the Court stated that the explanation offered by the prosecutor, although it may have been "silly or superstitious," was race neutral. The trial court, in other words, was required to evaluate the *genuineness* of the prosecutor's explanation, not its *reasonableness*. As the Court noted, "At this step of the inquiry, the issue is the facial validity of the prosecutor's explanation. Unless a discriminatory intent is inherent in the prosecutor's explanation, the reason offered will be deemed race neutral."[60]

The two dissenting judges—Justice Stevens and Justice Breyer—were outraged. They argued that the Court in this case actually overruled a portion of the opinion in *Batson v. Kentucky*. They stated that, the majority's conclusions notwithstanding, *Batson* clearly required that the explanation offered by the prosecutor must be "related to the particular case to be tried." According to Justice Stevens,

> In my opinion, it is disrespectful to the conscientious judges on the Court of Appeals who faithfully applied an unambiguous standard articulated in one of our opinions to say that they appear to have seized on our admonition in *Batson* . . . that the reason must be "related to the particular case to be tried." Of course, they "seized on" that point because *we told them to*. The Court of Appeals was following *Batson*'s clear mandate. To criticize those judges for doing their jobs is singularly inappropriate.[61]

Justice Stevens went on to say, "Today, without argument, the Court replaces the *Batson* standard with the surprising announcement that any neutral explanation, no matter how 'implausible or fantastic,' even if it is 'silly or superstitious,' is sufficient to rebut a prima facie case of discrimination."

Critics of *Batson* and its progeny maintain that until the courts articulate and apply a more meaningful standard or eliminate peremptory challenges altogether, "peremptory strikes will be color-blind in theory only"[62] (see the Focus on an Issue).

There is incontrovertible evidence that the reforms implemented since the Scottsboro Boys were tried, convicted, and sentenced to death by all-white juries have reduced racial discrimination in the jury selection process. Decisions handed down by the Supreme Court have made it difficult, if not impossible, for courts to make "no pretense of putting Negroes on jury lists, much less calling or using them in trials."[63] However, the jury selection process remains racially biased. Prosecutors continue to use the peremptory challenge to exclude African American and Hispanic jurors from cases with African American and Hispanic defendants,[64] and appellate courts continue to rule that their "racially neutral" explanations adequately meet the standards articulated in *Batson*. Supreme Court decisions notwithstanding, the peremptory challenge remains an obstacle to impartiality.

PLAYING THE "RACE CARD" IN A CRIMINAL TRIAL

In 1994, O. J. Simpson, an African American actor and former all-American football star, was accused of murdering his ex-wife, Nicole Brown Simpson, and Ronald Goldman, a friend of hers. On October 4, 1995, a jury composed

Focus on an Issue
Should We Eliminate the Peremptory Challenge?

In theory, the peremptory challenge is used to achieve a fair and impartial jury. The assumption is that each side will "size up" potential jurors and use its challenges "to eliminate real or imagined partiality or bias that may be based only on a hunch, an impression, a look, or a gesture" (Way, 1980, p. 344). Thus, a prosecutor may routinely strike "liberal" college professors, and a defense attorney may excuse "prosecution-oriented" business executives. The result of this process, at least in principle, is a jury that will decide the case based on the evidence alone.

The reality is that both sides use their peremptory challenges to "stack the deck" (Levine, 1992, p. 51). The prosecutor attempts to pick a jury that will be predisposed to convict, whereas the defense attorney attempts to select jurors who will be inclined to acquit. Rather than choose open-minded jurors who will withhold judgment until they have heard all of the evidence, in other words, each attorney attempts to pack the jury with sympathizers. According to one attorney, "Most successful lawyers develop their own criteria for their choices of jurors. Law professors, experienced lawyers, and a number of technical books suggest general rules to help select *favorable jurors*" [emphasis added] (Wishman, 1986, p. 105).

DO PROSECUTORS USE PEREMPTORY CHALLENGES IN A RACIALLY DISCRIMINATORY MANNER?

The controversy over the use of the peremptory challenge has centered on the prosecution's use of its challenges to eliminate African Americans from juries trying African American defendants. It centers on what Justice Marshall called "the shameful practice of racial discrimination in the selection of juries" (*Batson v. Kentucky,* 479 U.S. 79 [1986]). Critics charge that the process reduces minority participation in the criminal justice system and makes it difficult, if not impossible, for racial minorities to obtain a "jury of their peers." They assert that peremptory challenges "can transform even a representative venire into a white, middle-class jury," thereby rendering "meaningless the protections provided to the venire selection process by *Strauder* and its progeny" (Serr & Maney, 1988, pp. 7–8).

There is substantial evidence that prosecutors exercise peremptory challenges in a racially discriminatory manner. A study of challenges issued in Calcasieu Parish, Louisiana, from 1976 to 1981, for example, found that prosecutors excused African American jurors at a disproportionately high rate (Turner, Lovell, Young, & Denny, 1986, pp. 61–69). Although the authors also found that defense attorneys tended to use their challenges to excuse whites, they concluded, "Because black prospective jurors are a minority in many jurisdictions, the exclusion of most black prospective jurors by prosecution can be accomplished more easily than the similar exclusion of Caucasian prospective jurors by defense" (Turner et al., 1986, p. 68; Hayden, Senna, & Siegel, 1978).

African American defendants challenging their convictions by all-white juries also have produced evidence of racial bias. One defendant, for example, showed that Missouri prosecutors challenged 81 percent of the African American

(continued)

(continued)
ican jurors available for trial in 15 cases
with African American defendants
(*United States v. Carter,* 528 F. 2d 844,
848 [CA 8 1975]). Another defendant
presented evidence indicating that in
53 Louisiana cases involving African
American defendants, federal prosecutors used over two-thirds of their challenges against African Americans, who
made up less than one-fourth of the
jury pool (*United States v. McDaniels,*
379 F. Supp. 1243 [ED La. 1974]). A
third defendant showed that South Carolina prosecutors challenged 82 percent
of the African American jurors available
for 13 trials involving African American
defendants (*McKinney v. Walker,* 394 F.
Supp. 1015, 1017–1018 [SC 1974]).
Evidence such as this supports Justice
Marshall's contention (in a concurring
opinion in *Batson v. Kentucky*) that "misuse of the peremptory challenge to exclude black jurors has become both
common and flagrant" (*Batson v. Kentucky,* 106 S.Ct. 1712, 1726 [1986]
[Marshall, J., concurring]).

ARE ALL-WHITE JURIES INCLINED TO CONVICT AFRICAN AMERICAN DEFENDANTS?

Those who question the prosecutor's
use of peremptory challenges to eliminate African Americans from the jury
pool argue that African American defendants tried by all-white juries are disproportionately convicted. They assert
that white jurors take the race of the defendant and the race of the victim into
account in deciding whether to convict
the defendant.

Researchers have examined jury verdicts in actual trials and in mock jury
studies for evidence of racial bias. Kalven and Zeisel (1966), for example,

asked the presiding judge in more than
1,000 cases if he or she agreed with the
jury's verdict. Judges who disagreed
with the verdict were asked to explain
the jury's behavior. Judges disagreed
with the jury's decision to convict the
defendant in 22 cases; in four of these
cases, they attributed the jury's conviction to prejudice against African American defendants involved in interracial
sex. Kalven and Zeisel also found that
juries were more likely than judges
to acquit African American defendants who victimized other African
Americans.

Johnson (1985) argued, "Mock jury
studies provide the strongest evidence
that racial bias frequently affects the determination of guilt" (p. 1625). She reviewed nine mock jury studies in which
the race of the defendant was varied
while other factors were held constant.
According to Johnson, white "jurors"
in all of the studies were more likely to
convict minority-race defendants than
they were to convict white defendants
(p. 1626).

One mock jury study found evidence of racial bias directed at both the
defendant and the victim (Klein &
Creech, 1982, p. 21). In this study,
white college students read two tran-
scripts of four crimes in which the race
of the male defendant and the race of
the female victim were varied; they
then were asked to indicate which defendant was more likely to be guilty.
For the crime of rape, the probability
that the defendant was guilty ranged
from 70 percent for crimes with African American offenders and white
victims to 68 percent for crimes with
white offenders and white victims,
52 percent for crimes with African
American offenders and African American victims, and 33 percent for crimes
with white offenders and African American victims (Klein & Creech, 1982,
p. 24).

SHOULD THE PEREMPTORY CHALLENGE BE ELIMINATED?

Defenders of the peremptory challenge, although admitting that there is inherent tension between peremptory challenges and the quest for a representative jury, argue that the availability of peremptories ensures an *impartial* jury. Defenders of the process further argue that restricting the number of peremptory challenges or requiring attorneys to provide reasons for exercising them would make selection of an impartial jury more difficult. Those who advocate elimination of the peremptory challenge assert that prosecutors and defense attorneys can use the challenge for cause to eliminate biased or prejudiced jurors (Levin, 1988). They argue that because prosecutors exercise their peremptory challenges in a racially discriminatory manner, African American defendants are often tried by all-white juries predisposed toward conviction.

In a concurring opinion in the *Batson* case, Justice Marshall called on the Court to ban the use of peremptory challenges by the prosecutor and to allow states to ban their use by the defense (*Batson v. Kentucky,* 106 S.Ct. 1712, 1726 [1986] [Marshall, J., concurring]). Marshall argued that the remedy fashioned by the Court in *Batson* was inadequate to eliminate racial discrimination in the use of the peremptory challenge. He noted that a black defendant could not attack the prosecutor's discriminatory use of peremptory challenges at all unless the abuse was "so

flagrant as to establish a prima facie case," and that prosecutors, when challenged, "can easily assert racially neutral reasons for striking a juror" (*Batson v. Kentucky,* at 1727).

Other commentators, who acknowledge that the solution proposed in *Batson* is far from ideal and that reform is needed, propose more modest reforms. Arguing that the chances for abolition of the peremptory challenge are slim, they suggest that a more feasible alternative would be to limit the number of challenges available to each side. As one legal scholar noted, "Giving each side fewer challenges will make it more difficult to eliminate whole groups of people from juries" (Note, "*Batson v. Kentucky,*" 1988, p. 298). Another argued that courts must "enforce the prohibition against racially discriminatory peremptory strikes more consistently and forcefully than they have done thus far" (Kennedy, 1997, p. 230). Another, more radical, suggestion is to allow each side to designate one or two prospective jurors who cannot be challenged peremptorily (see, for example, Ramirez, 1998, p. 161).

Those who lobby for reform of the peremptory challenge maintain that the system would be fairer without it. As Morris B. Hoffman (2000) put it, "Imagine a jury selection process that sends the message to all 50 prospective jurors in the courtroom that this is a rational process. That we have rules for deciding who is fair and not fair, just as we have rules for deciding who prevails in the end and who does not."

---

of seven African American women, two white women, one Hispanic man, and one African American man acquitted Simpson of all charges. Many commentators attributed Simpson's acquittal at least in part to the fact that his attorney, Johnnie L. Cochran Jr., had "played the race card" during the trial. In fact, another of Simpson's attorneys, Robert Shapiro, charged that Cochran not only played the race card, but he "dealt it from the bottom of the deck."[65]

Cochran was criticized for attempting to show that Mark Fuhrman, a Los Angeles police officer who found the bloody glove that linked Simpson to the crime, was a racist who planted the evidence in an attempt to frame Simpson. He was also harshly criticized for suggesting during his closing argument that the jurors would be justified in nullifying the law by acquitting Simpson. Cochran encouraged the jurors to take Fuhrman's racist beliefs into account during their deliberations. He urged them to "send a message" to society that "we are not going to take that anymore."[66]

Although appeals to racial sentiment—that is, "playing the race card"—are not unusual in U.S. courts, they are rarely used by defense attorneys representing African Americans accused of victimizing whites. Much more typical are *prosecutorial* appeals to bias. Consider the following examples:

- An Alabama prosecutor declared, "Unless you hang this Negro, our white people living out in the country won't be safe."[67]

- A prosecutor in North Carolina dismissed as implausible the claim of three African American men that the white woman they were accused of raping had consented to sex with them. The prosecutor stated that "the average white woman abhors anything of this type in nature that had to do with a black man."[68]

- A prosecutor in a rape case involving an African American man and a white woman asked the jurors, "Gentlemen, do you believe that she would have had intercourse with this black brute?"[69]

- A prosecutor in a case involving the alleged kidnapping of a white man by two African American men said in his closing argument that "not one *white* witness has been produced" to rebut the victim's testimony [emphasis added].[70]

- A prosecutor stated during the penalty phase of a capital case involving Walter J. Blair, an African American man charged with murdering a white woman, "Can you imagine [the victim's] state of mind when she woke up at 6 o'clock that morning, staring into the muzzle of a gun held by this black man?"[71]

All of these appeals to racial sentiment, with the exception of the last, resulted in reversal of the defendants' convictions. A federal court of appeals, for example, ruled in 1978 that the North Carolina prosecutor's contention that a white woman would never consent to sex with an African American man was a "blatant appeal to racial prejudice." The court added that when such an appeal involves an issue as "sensitive as consent to sexual intercourse in a prosecution for rape . . . the prejudice engendered is so great that automatic reversal is required."[72]

A federal court of appeals, on the other hand, refused to reverse Walter Blair's conviction and death sentence. Its refusal was based on the fact that Blair's attorney failed to object at trial to the prosecutor's statement. The sole dissenter in the case suggested that the court should have considered whether the defense attorney's failure to object meant that Blair had been denied effective assistance of counsel. He also vehemently condemned the prosecutor's statement, which he asserted "played upon white fear of crime and the tendency of white people to associate crime with blacks."[73]

According to Harvard law professor Randall Kennedy, playing the race card in a criminal trial is "virtually always morally and legally wrong." He asserted that doing so encourages juries to base their verdicts on irrelevant considerations and loosens the requirement that the state prove the case beyond a reasonable doubt. As he noted, "Racial appeals are not only a distraction but a menace that can distort interpretations of evidence or even seduce jurors into believing that they should vote in a certain way irrespective of the evidence."[74]

Race-Conscious Jury Nullification:
Black Power in the Courtroom?

In a provocative essay published in the *Yale Law Journal* shortly after O. J. Simpson's acquittal, Paul Butler, an African American professor of law at George Washington University Law School, argued for "racially based jury nullification."[75] That is, he urged African American jurors to refuse to convict African American defendants accused of nonviolent crimes, regardless of the strength of the evidence mounted against them. According to Butler, "It is the moral responsibility of black jurors to emancipate some guilty black outlaws."[76]

Jury nullification, which has its roots in English common law, occurs when a juror believes that the evidence presented at trial establishes the defendant's guilt, but nonetheless votes to acquit. The juror's decision may be motivated either by a belief that the law under which the defendant is being prosecuted is unfair or by an objection to the application of the law to a particular defendant. In the first instance, a juror might refuse to convict a defendant tried in federal court for possession of more than 50 grams of crack cocaine, based on the juror's belief that the draconian penalties mandated by the law are unfair. In the second instance, a juror might vote to acquit a father charged with child endangerment after his 2-year-old daughter, who was not restrained in a child safety seat, was thrown from the car and killed when he lost control of his car on an icy road. In this case, the juror does not believe that the law itself is unfair, but rather that the defendant has suffered enough and that nothing will be gained by additional punishment.

Jurors clearly have the power to nullify the law and to vote their conscience. If a jury votes unanimously to acquit, the double jeopardy clause of the Fifth Amendment prohibits reversal of the jury's decision. The jury's decision to acquit, even in the face of overwhelming evidence of guilt, is final and cannot be reversed by the trial judge or by an appellate court. In most jurisdictions, however, jurors do not have to be told that they have the right to nullify the law.[77]

Butler's position on jury nullification is that the "black community is better off when some nonviolent lawbreakers remain in the community rather than go to prison."[78] Arguing that there are far too many African American men in prison, Butler suggested that there should be "a presumption in favor of nullification" in cases involving African American defendants charged with *non-*

violent, victimless, crimes like possession of drugs.[79] Butler claimed that enforcement of these laws has a disparate effect on the African American community and does not "advance the interest of black people."[80] He also suggested that white racism, which "creates and sustains the criminal breeding ground which produces the black criminal," is the underlying cause of much of the crime committed by African Americans.[81] He thus urged African American jurors to "nullify without hesitation in these cases."[82]

Butler did not argue for nullification in all types of cases. In fact, he asserted that defendants charged with violent crimes like murder, rape, and armed robbery should be convicted if there is proof of guilt beyond a reasonable doubt. He contended that nullification is not morally justifiable in these types of cases because "people who are violent should be separated from the community, for the sake of the nonviolent."[83] Violent African American offenders, in other words, should be convicted and incarcerated in order to protect potential innocent victims. Butler was willing to "write off" this type of offender based on his belief that the "black community cannot afford the risks of leaving this person in its midst."[84]

The more difficult cases, according to Butler, involve defendants charged with nonviolent property offenses or with more serious drug trafficking offenses. He discussed two hypothetical cases, one involving a ghetto drug dealer and the other involving a thief who burglarizes the home of a rich family. His answer to the question "Is nullification morally justifiable here?" is "It depends."[85] Although he admitted that "encouraging people to engage in self-destructive behavior is evil,"[86] and that therefore most drug dealers should be convicted, he argued that a juror's decision in this type of case might rest on the particular facts in the case. Similarly, although he is troubled by the case of the burglar who steals from a rich family because the behavior is "so clearly wrong,"[87] he argued that the facts in the case—for example, a person who steals to support a drug habit—might justify a vote to acquit. Nullification, in other words, may be a morally justifiable option in both types of cases.

Randall Kennedy's Critique Randall Kennedy raised a number of objections to Butler's proposal, which he characterized as "profoundly misleading as a guide to action."[88] Although he acknowledged that Butler's assertion that there is racial injustice in the administration of the criminal law is correct, Kennedy nonetheless objected to Butler's portrayal of the criminal justice system as a "one-dimensional system that is totally at odds with what black Americans need and want, a system that unequivocally represents and unrelentingly imposes 'the white man's law.'"[89] Kennedy faulted Butler for his failure to acknowledge either the legal reforms implemented as a result of struggles *against* racism or the significant presence of African American officials in policymaking positions and the criminal justice system. The problems inherent in the criminal justice system, according to Kennedy, "require judicious attention, not a campaign of defiant sabotage."[90]

Kennedy objected to the fact that Butler expressed more sympathy for nonviolent African American offenders than for "the law-abiding people compelled by circumstances to live in close proximity to the criminals for whom he is willing to urge subversion of the legal system." [91] He asserted that law-abiding African Americans "desire *more* rather than *less* prosecution and punishment for *all* types of criminals" [92] and suggested that, in any case, jury nullification "is an exceedingly poor means for advancing the goal of a racially fair administration of criminal law." [93] He claimed that a highly publicized campaign of jury nullification carried on by African Americans will not produce the social reforms that Butler demands. Moreover, such a campaign might backfire. Kennedy suggested that it might lead to increased support for proposals to eliminate the requirement that the jury be unanimous in order to convict, restrictions on the right of African Americans to serve on juries, or widespread use of jury nullification by white jurors in cases involving white-on-black crime.

According to Kennedy, the most compelling reason to oppose Butler's call for racially based jury nullification is that it is based on "an ultimately destructive sentiment of racial kinship that prompts individuals of a given race to care more about 'their own' than people of another race." [94] He objected to the implication that it is proper for African American jurors to be more concerned about the fate of African American defendants than of white defendants, more disturbed about the plight of African American communities than of white communities, and more interested in protecting the lives and property of African Americans than of white citizens. "Along that road," according to Kennedy, "lies moral and political disaster." Implementation of Butler's proposal, Kennedy insisted, would not only increase, but legitimize, "the tendency of people to privilege in racial terms 'their own.'" [95]

CONCLUSION

In Chapter 5, we concluded that the reforms implemented during the past few decades have substantially reduced racial discrimination during the pretrial stages of the criminal justice process. Our examination of the jury selection process suggests that a similar conclusion is warranted. Reforms adopted voluntarily by the states or mandated by appellate courts have made it increasingly unlikely that African American and Hispanic defendants will be tried by all-white juries. An important caveat, however, concerns the use of racially motivated peremptory challenges. Supreme Court decisions notwithstanding, prosecutors still manage to use the peremptory challenge to eliminate African Americans and Hispanics from juries trying African American and Hispanic defendants. More troubling, prosecutors' "racially neutral" explanations for strikes alleged to be racially motivated continue to be accepted at face value. Coupled with anecdotal evidence that prosecutors are not reluctant to "play the race card" in a criminal trial, these findings regarding jury selection suggest that the process of adjudication, like the pretrial process, is not free of racial bias.

Based on the research reviewed in this chapter and the previous one, we conclude that contemporary court processing decisions are not characterized by *systematic* discrimination against racial minorities. This may have been true at the time that the Scottsboro Boys were tried, but it is no longer true. As we have shown, the U.S. Supreme Court has consistently affirmed the importance of protecting the rights of criminal defendants and has insisted that the race of the defendant not be taken into consideration in making case processing decisions. Coupled with reforms adopted voluntarily by the states, these decisions make systematic racial discrimination unlikely.

We are not suggesting, however, that these reforms have produced an equitable, or color-blind, system of justice. We are not suggesting that contemporary court processing decisions reflect *pure justice*. Researchers have demonstrated that court processing decisions in some jurisdictions reflect racial discrimination, whereas decisions in other jurisdictions are racially neutral. Researchers have also shown that African Americans and Hispanics who commit certain types of crimes are treated more harshly than whites, and that being unemployed, having a prior criminal record, or being detained prior to trial may have a more negative effect on court outcomes for people of color than for whites.

These findings lead us to conclude that discrimination against African Americans and other racial minorities is not universal but is confined to certain types of cases, certain types of settings, and certain types of defendants. We conclude that the court system of today is characterized by *contextual discrimination*.

DISCUSSION QUESTIONS

1. The Supreme Court has repeatedly asserted that a defendant is not entitled to a jury "composed in whole or in part of persons of his own race." Although these rulings establish that states are not *obligated* to use racially mixed juries, they do not *prohibit* states from doing so. In fact, a number of policymakers and legal scholars have proposed reforms that use racial criteria to promote racial diversity on American juries. Some have suggested that the names of majority race jurors be removed from the jury list (thus ensuring a larger proportion of racial minorities); other have suggested that a certain number of seats on each jury be set aside for racial minorities. How would you justify these reforms to a state legislature? How would an opponent of these reforms respond? Overall, are these good ideas or bad ideas?

2. Evidence suggesting that prosecutors use their peremptory challenges to preserve all-white juries in cases involving African American or Hispanic defendants has led some commentators to call for the elimination of the peremptory challenge. What do you think is the strongest argument in favor of eliminating the peremptory challenge? In favor of retaining it?

3. Given that the Supreme Court is unlikely to rule that the peremptory challenge violates the right to a fair trial and is therefore unconstitutional, are there any remedies or reforms that could be implemented?

4. Should a white defendant be allowed to challenge the prosecutor's use of peremptory challenges to exclude African Americans and other racial minorities from his or her jury? Why or why not?

5. In this chapter, we present a number of examples of lawyers who "played the race card" in a criminal trial. Almost all of them involved prosecutors who appealed to the racist sentiments of white jurors. But what about defense attorneys representing African American defendants who attempt to appeal to the racial sentiments of African American jurors? Does this represent misconduct? How should the judge respond?

6. Why does Paul Butler advocate "racially based jury nullification"? Why does Randall Kennedy disagree with him?

NOTES

1. Harper Lee, *To Kill a Mockingbird* (New York: Warner Books, 1960), p. 220.

2. James P. Levine, *Juries and Politics* (Pacific Grove, CA: Brooks/Cole, 1992), p. 106.

3. Available at http://www.spectator online.com.

4. For an excellent discussion of this case, see Jack Olsen, *Last Man Standing: The Tragedy and Triumph of Geronimo Pratt* (New York: Doubleday, 2000).

5. Ibid., p. 367.

6. Ibid., p. 465.

7. Jeremy Engel, "Federal Judge Approves $4.5 Million Settlement in Pratt Case," *Metropolitan News-Enterprise, Capitol News Service* (May 1, 2000).

8. David Cole, *No Equal Justice: Race and Class in the American Criminal Justice System* (New York, New Press, 1999), p. 103.

9. Ibid., p. 101.

10. *Duncan v. Louisiana,* 391 U.S. 145 (1968).

11. *McCleskey v. Kemp,* 481 U.S. 279 (1987) (quoting *Strauder v. West Virginia,* 100 U.S. 303 [1880].

12. *Strauder v. West Virginia,* 100 U.S. 303 (1880).

13. Ibid. at 307–308.

14. Ibid. at 309.

15. *Neal v. Delaware,* 103 U.S. 370, 394, at 393–394 (1881).

16. Ibid.

17. Ibid. at 397.

18. Gunnar Myrdal, *An American Dilemma: The Negro Problem and Modern Democracy* (New York: Harper & Brothers, 1944), p. 549.

19. Ibid.

20. Ibid.

21. Seymour Wishman, *Anatomy of a Jury: The System on Trial* (New York: Times Books, 1986), p. 54.

22. *Avery v. Georgia,* 345 U.S. 559 (1953).

23. *Whitus v. Georgia,* 385 U.S. 545 (1967).

24. *Avery v. Georgia,* 345 U.S. 559, 562 (1953).

25. Randall Kennedy, *Race, Crime, and the Law,* (New York: Vintage, 1997), p. 179.

26. Ibid.

27. *Amadeo v. Zant,* 486 U.S. 214 (1988).

28. Cole, *No Equal Justice,* pp. 104–105.

29. Michael Higgins, "Few Are Chosen," *ABA Journal* (February 1999): 50–51.

30. Kennedy, *Race, Crime, and the Law,* p. 239.

31. Albert W. Alschuler, "Racial Quotas and the Jury," *Duke Law Journal* 44 (1995): 44.

32. Kennedy, *Race, Crime, and the Law,* p. 253.

33. Ibid., p. 255.

34. *United States v. Ovalle,* 136 F.3d 1092 (1998).

35. Alschuler, "Racial Quotas and the Jury," p. 704.

36. Cole, *No Equal Justice,* p. 126.

37. *Strauder v. West Virginia,* 100 U.S. 303 (1880), at 305; *Batson v. Kentucky,* 476 U.S. 79, 85 (1986).

38. *Swain v. Alabama,* 380 U.S. 202, 212 (1965).

39. Kennedy, *Race, Crime, and the Law,* p. 214.

40. "Former Philadelphia Prosecutor Accused of Racial Bias in Election Year," *New York Times* (April 3, 1997).

41. Ibid.

42. *Swain v. Alabama,* 380 U.S. 202 (1965).

43. Ibid. at 222.

44. Wishman, *Anatomy of a Jury,* p. 115.

45. Justice Brennan, dissenting from denial of certiorari in *Thompson v. United States,* 105 S.Ct., at 445.

46. See Comment, "*Swain v. Alabama,* A Constitutional Blueprint for the Perpetuation of the All-White Jury," *Virginia Law Review* 52 (1966): 1157; Note, "Rethinking Limitations on the Peremptory Challenge," *Columbia Law Review* 85 (1983): 1357.

47. Brian J. Serr and Mark Maney, "Racism, Peremptory Challenges, and the Democratic Jury: The Jurisprudence of a Delicate Balance," *Journal of Criminal Law and Criminology* 79 (1988): 13.

48. *Batson v. Kentucky,* 476 U.S. 79, 93–94 (1986).

49. Ibid. at 96.

50. *United States v. Montgomery,* 819 F.2d (CA 8 1987), at 851. The 11th Circuit, however, rejected this line of reasoning in *Fleming v. Kemp,* 794 F.2d 1478 (11th Cir. 1986), and *United States v. David,* 803 F.2d 1567 (11th Cir. 1986).

51. *United States v. Vaccaro,* 816 F.2d 443, 457 (9th Cir. 1987); *Fields v. People,* 732 P.2d 1145, 1158 n.20 (Colo. 1987).

52. Serr and Maney, "Racism, Peremptory Challenges, and the Democratic Jury," pp. 43–47.

53. Kennedy, *Race, Crime, and the Law,* p. 211.

54. Ibid., p. 213.

55. Kennedy, *Race, Crime, and the Law,* p. 214.

56. Serr and Maney, "Racism, Peremptory Challenges, and the Democratic Jury," p. 63.

57. *Purkett v. Elem,* 115 S.Ct. 1769 (1995). Available at http://www.lexis-nexis.com/universe.

58. Ibid.

59. *Purkett v. Elem,* 25 F. 3d 679, 683 (1994).

60. *Purkett v. Elem,* 115 S.Ct. 1769 (1995).

61. Ibid. (Stevens, J., dissenting).

62. Cole, *Unequal Justice,* p. 124.

63. Myrdal, *An American Dilemma,* pp. 547–548.

64. A study of peremptory challenges issued from 1976 to 1981 in Calcasieu Parish, Louisiana, for example, found that prosecutors excused African American jurors at a disproportionately high rate. See Billy M. Turner, Rickie D. Lovell, John C. Young, and William F. Denny, "Race and Peremptory Challenges during Voir Dire: Do Prosecution and Defense Agree?" *Journal of Criminal Justice* 14 (1986): 61–69.

65. "Shapiro Lashes Out at Cochran over 'Race Card,'" *USA Today* (October 4, 1995).

66. Kennedy, *Race, Crime, and the Law,* pp. 286–290.

67. *Moulton v. State,* 199 Ala. 411 (1917).

68. *Miller v. North Carolina,* 583 F.2d 701 (CA 4 1978).

69. *State v. Washington,* 67 So. 930 (La. Sup. Ct. 1915).

70. *Withers v. United States,* 602 F.2d 124 (CA 6 1976).

71. *Blair v. Armontrout,* 916 F.2d 1310 (CA 8 1990).

72. *Miller v. North Carolina,* 583 F.2d 701 (CA 4 1978), at 708.

73. *Blair v. Armontrout,* 916 F.2d 1310 (CA 8 1990), at 1351.

74. Kennedy, *Race, Crime, and the Law,* pp. 256–257.

75. Paul Butler, "Racially Based Jury Nullification: Black Power in the Criminal Justice System," *Yale Law Journal* 105 (1995): 677–725.

76. Ibid., p. 679.

77. See, for example, *United States v. Dougherty*, 473 F.2d 1113 (D.C. Cir. 1972).

78. Butler, "Racially Based Jury Nullification," p. 679.

79. Ibid., p. 715.

80. Ibid., p. 714.

81. Ibid., p. 694.

82. Ibid., p. 719.

83. Ibid., p. 716.

84. Ibid., p. 719.

85. Ibid.

86. Ibid.

87. Ibid., p. 720.

88. Kennedy, *Race, Crime, and the Law,* p. 299.

89. Ibid.

90. Ibid., p. 301.

91. Ibid., p. 305.

92. Ibid., pp. 305–306.

93. Ibid., p. 301.

94. Ibid., p. 310.

95. Ibid.

7

Race and Sentencing

In Search of
Fairness and Justice

In 1990, The Sentencing Project reported that nearly one-fourth (23 percent) of all African American males aged 20–29 were under some form of criminal justice supervision—in prison, in jail, on probation, or on parole.[1] Over the next four years, this rate, which the author of the report labeled "shockingly high," continued to increase. By 1994, almost one in three (32 percent) young African American men was under criminal justice supervision.[2] This figure was substantially higher than the rate for young Hispanic men (12.3 percent) and more than four times greater than that for young white men (6.7 percent). The authors of the report concluded that the high rates for young African American men "attest to the gravity of the crisis facing the African American community."[3]

Explanations for the disproportionate number of African American and Hispanic males under the control of the criminal justice system are complex. As discussed in more detail in Chapter 9, a number of studies have concluded that most—but not all—of the racial disparity in incarceration rates can be attributed to racial differences in offending patterns and prior criminal records. Young African American and Hispanic males, in other words, face greater odds of incarceration than young white males primarily because they commit more serious crimes and have more serious prior criminal records. The National Research Council's Panel on Sentencing Research concluded in 1983 that "factors other than racial discrimination in the sentencing process account for most of the disproportionate representation of black males in U.S. prisons."[4]

Not all of the racial disparity, however, can be explained away in this fashion. Many scholars contend that at least some of the overincarceration of racial minorities is due to racially discriminatory sentencing policies and practices. As one commentator noted, "A conclusion that black overrepresentation among prisoners is not primarily the result of racial bias does not mean that there is no racism in the system."[5] The National Academy of Sciences Panel similarly concluded that evidence of racial discrimination in sentencing may be found in some jurisdictions or for certain types of crimes.

Underlying this controversy are questions concerning discretion in sentencing. To be fair, a sentencing scheme must allow the judge or jury discretion to shape sentences to fit individuals and their crimes. The judge or jury must be free to consider all *relevant* aggravating and mitigating circumstances. To be consistent, on the other hand, a sentencing scheme requires the evenhanded application of objective standards. The judge or jury must take only relevant considerations into account and must be precluded from determining sentence severity based on prejudice or whim.

Critics of the sentencing process argue that judges, jurors, and other members of the courtroom workgroup sometimes exercise their discretion inappropriately. Although they acknowledge that some degree of sentence disparity is to be expected in a system that attempts to individualize punishment, these critics suggest that there is *unwarranted* disparity in the sentences imposed on similarly situated offenders convicted of similar crimes. More to the point, they assert that judges impose harsher sentences on African American and Hispanic offenders than on white offenders.

Other scholars contend that judges' sentencing decisions are not racially biased, that disparity in sentencing is due to legitimate differences between individual cases, and that racial disparities disappear once these differences are taken into consideration. These scholars argue, in other words, that judges' sentencing decisions are both fair and consistent.

GOALS OF THE CHAPTER

In this chapter, we address the issue of racial disparity in sentencing. Our purpose is not simply to add another voice to the debate over the *existence* of racial discrimination in the sentencing process. Although we do attempt to determine whether racial minorities are sentenced more harshly than whites, we believe that this is a theoretically unsophisticated and incomplete approach to a complex phenomenon. It is overly simplistic to assume that racial minorities will receive harsher sentences than whites regardless of the nature of the crime, the seriousness of the offense, the culpability of the offender, or the characteristics of the victim. The more interesting issue is "when does race matter?" It is this question that we attempt to answer.

RACIAL DISPARITY IN SENTENCING

There is clear and convincing evidence of two types of racial *disparity* in sentencing. The first type is derived from national statistics on prison admissions and prison populations (discussed in detail in Chapter 9), which reveal that the incarceration rates for African Americans and Hispanics are much higher than the rate for whites. In June 2001, for example, 4,848 of every 100,000 African American men, 1,668 of every 100,000 Hispanic men, and 705 of every 100,000 white men were incarcerated in a state or federal prison or local jail. The incarceration rates for women, although much lower than the rates for men, revealed a similar pattern: 380 of 100,000 for African Americans, 119 of 100,000 for Hispanics, and 67 of 100,000 for whites. Among males between the ages of 25 and 29, the disparities were even larger: 13,391 of every 100,000 African Americans, 4,140 of every 100,000 Hispanics, and 1,821 of every 100,000 whites were incarcerated.[6]

The second type comes from studies of judges' sentencing decisions. These studies, which are the focus of this chapter, reveal that African American and Hispanic offenders are more likely than white offenders to be sentenced to prison; those who are sentenced to prison receive longer terms than whites. Consider the following statistics:

- African American and Hispanic offenders sentenced under the federal sentencing guidelines in 1989 and 1990 received harsher sentences than white offenders. The incarceration rate was 85 percent for Hispanics, 78 percent for African Americans, and 72 percent for whites. Among those sentenced to prison, the average sentence was 71 months for African Americans, 50 months for whites, and 48 months for Hispanics.[7]

- Among offenders convicted of drug offenses in federal district courts in 1997 and 1998, the mean sentence length was 82 months for African Americans and 52 months for whites. For drug offenses with mandatory minimum sentences, the mean sentences were 136 months for African Americans and 82 months for whites.[8]

- Sixty-five percent of the African American offenders convicted of violent crimes in state courts in 1996 were sentenced to prison, compared with 51 percent of the white offenders. The figures for offenders convicted of drug offenses were 43 percent for African Americans and 27 percent for whites.[9]

- African American and Hispanic offenders convicted of felonies in Chicago, Miami, and Kansas City faced greater odds of incarceration than whites. In Chicago, 66 percent of the African Americans, 59 percent of the Hispanics, and 51 percent of the whites were incarcerated. In Miami, 51 percent of the African Americans, 40 percent of the Hispanics, and 35 percent of the whites were incarcerated. In Kansas City, 46 percent of the African Americans, 40 percent of the Hispanics, and 36 percent of the whites were incarcerated.[10]

Four Explanations for Racial Disparities in Sentencing

These statistics provide compelling evidence of racial disparity in sentencing. They indicate that the sentences imposed on African American and Hispanic offenders are different than—that is, harsher than—the sentences imposed on

---

BOX 7.1   Four Explanations for Racial Disparities in Sentencing

African Americans and Hispanics are sentenced more harshly than whites for the following reasons:

1. They commit more serious crimes and have more serious prior criminal records than whites.

   Conclusion: racial disparity but not racial discrimination

2. They are more likely than whites to be poor; being poor is associated with a greater likelihood of pretrial detention and unemployment, both of which may lead to harsher sentences.

   Conclusion: indirect (that is, economic) discrimination

3. Judges are biased or have prejudiced against racial minorities.

   Conclusion: direct racial discrimination

4. The disparities occur in some contexts but not in others.

   Conclusion: subtle (that is, contextual) racial discrimination

---

white offenders. These statistics, however, do not tell us *why* this occurs nor whether the racial disparities in sentencing reflect racial discrimination and, if so, whether that discrimination is institutional or contextual. We suggest that there are at least four possible explanations for racial disparity in sentencing, only three of which reflect racial discrimination. Box 7.1 summarizes these explanations.

First, the differences in sentence severity could be due to the fact that African Americans and Hispanics commit more serious crimes and have more serious prior criminal records than whites. Studies of sentencing decisions have consistently demonstrated the importance of these two "legally relevant" factors (see Box 7.2 for an alternative interpretation). Offenders who are convicted of more serious offenses, who use a weapon to commit the crime, or who seriously injure the victim receive harsher sentences, as do offenders who have prior felony convictions. The more severe sentences imposed on African Americans and Hispanics might reflect the influence of these legally prescribed factors rather than the effect of racial prejudice on the part of judges or other members of the courtroom workgroup who participate in the sentencing process. In this case, the racial disparities in sentencing would not reflect racial discrimination.

Second, the differences could result from economic discrimination. As explained in Chapter 5, poor defendants are not as likely as middle- or upper-class defendants to have a private attorney or to be released prior to trial. They are also more likely to be unemployed. All of these factors may be related to sentence severity. Defendants represented by private attorneys or released prior to trial may receive more lenient sentences than those represented by public defenders or held in custody prior to trial. Defendants who are unemployed may be sentenced more harshly than those who are employed. Because African American and Hispanic defendants are more likely than white defendants to be poor, economic discrimination amounts to *indirect* racial discrimination.

BOX 7.2   Are Crime Seriousness and Prior Criminal Record "Legally Relevant" Variables?

Most policymakers and researchers assume that the seriousness of the conviction charge and the offender's prior criminal record are legally relevant to the sentencing decision. They assume that judges who base sentence severity primarily on crime seriousness and prior record are making legitimate, and racially neutral, sentencing decisions. But are they?

Some scholars argue that crime seriousness and prior criminal record are "race-linked" variables. If, for example, sentencing schemes consistently mandate the harshest punishments for the offenses for which racial minorities are most likely to be arrested (such as, robbery and drug offenses involving crack cocaine), the imposition of punishment is not necessarily racially neutral.

Similarly, if prosecutors routinely file more serious charges against racial minorities than against whites who engage in the same type of criminal conduct, or offer less attractive plea bargains to racial minorities than to whites, the more serious conviction charges for racial minorities will re-

flect these racially biased charging and plea bargaining decisions. An African American defendant who is convicted of a more serious crime than a white defendant, in other words, may not necessarily have engaged in more serious criminal conduct than his white counterpart.

Prior criminal record may also be race linked. If police target certain types of crimes (for example, selling illegal drugs) or patrol certain types of neighborhoods (for example, inner-city neighborhoods with large African American or Hispanic populations) more aggressively, racial minorities will be more likely than whites to "accumulate" a criminal history that then can be used to increase the punishment for the current offense. Racially biased charging and convicting decisions would have a similar effect.

If crime seriousness and prior criminal record are, in fact, race linked in the ways just outlined, it is misleading to conclude that sentences based on these two variables are racially neutral.

Third, the differences could be due to overt or *direct* racial discrimination on the part of judges and other participants in the sentencing process. Judges might take the race or ethnicity of the offender into account in determining the appropriate sentence, and prosecutors might consider the offender's race or ethnicity in deciding whether to plea bargain and in making sentence recommendations to the judge. If so, this implies that judges and prosecutors who are confronted with similarly situated African American, Hispanic, and white offenders treat racial minorities more harshly than whites. It also implies that these criminal justice officials, the majority of whom are white, stereotype African American and Hispanic offenders as more violent, more dangerous, and less amenable to rehabilitation than white offenders.

Fourth, the sentencing disparities could reflect both equal treatment and discrimination, depending on the nature of the crime, the racial composition of the victim–offender dyad, the type of jurisdiction, the age and gender of the offender, and so on. It is possible, in other words, that racial minorities who commit certain types of crimes (such as forgery) are treated no differently than whites who commit these crimes, whereas those who commit other types of crimes (such as sexual assault) are sentenced more harshly than their white counterparts. Similarly, it is possible that racial discrimination in sentencing offenders convicted of sexual assault is confined to the South or to cases involving African American offenders and white victims. It is possible, in other words, that the type of discrimination found in the sentencing process is contextual discrimination.

EMPIRICAL RESEARCH ON RACE AND SENTENCING

Researchers have conducted dozens of studies to determine which of the four explanations for racial disparity in sentencing is more correct and to untangle the complex relationship between race and sentence severity. In fact, as Zatz has noted, this issue "may well have been the major research inquiry for studies of sentencing in the 1970s and early 1980s."[11] The studies that have been conducted vary considerably in theoretical and methodological sophistication. They range from simple bivariate comparisons of incarceration rates for whites and racial minorities to methodologically more rigorous multivariate analyses designed to identify direct race effects to even more sophisticated designs incorporating tests for indirect race effects and for interaction between race and other predictors of sentence severity. The findings generated by these studies and the conclusions drawn by their authors also vary.

Reviews of Recent Research

Studies conducted from the 1930s through the 1960s generally concluded that racial disparities in sentencing reflected overt racial discrimination. For example, the author of one of the earliest sentencing studies, published in 1935, claimed that "equality before the law is a social fiction."[12] Reviews of these early studies, however, found that most of them were methodologically flawed.[13] They typically used simple bivariate statistical techniques and failed to control adequately for crime seriousness and prior criminal record.

The conclusions of these early reviews, coupled with the findings of its own review of sentencing research,[14] led the National Research Council's Panel on Sentencing Research to state in 1983 that the sentencing process was not characterized by "a widespread systematic pattern of discrimination."[15] Rather, "some pockets of discrimination are found for particular judges, particular crime types, and in particular settings."[16] Marjorie Zatz, who reviewed the results of four waves of race and sentencing research conducted from the 1930s through the early 1980s, reached a somewhat different conclusion.[17] Although she acknowledged that "it would be misleading to suggest that race/ethnicity is *the* major determinant of sanctioning," Zatz nonetheless asserted that "race/ethnicity is *a* determinant of sanctioning, and a potent one at that."[18]

The two most recent reviews of research on race and sentencing confirm Zatz's assertion. Chiricos and Crawford reviewed 38 studies published between 1979 and 1991 that included a test for the direct effect of race on sentencing decisions in noncapital cases.[19] Their review differed from previous reviews by distinguishing results involving the decision to incarcerate or not from those involving the length of sentence decision. Chiricos and Crawford also considered whether the effect of race varied depending on structural or contextual conditions. They asked whether the impact of race would be stronger "in southern jurisdictions, in places where there is a higher percentage of Blacks in the population or a higher concentration of Blacks in urban areas, and in places with a higher rate of unemployment."[20] Noting that two-thirds of the studies they examined had been published subsequent to the reviews published in the mid–1980s (which generally concluded that race did not play a prominent role in sentencing decisions), Chiricos and Crawford stated that their assessment "provides a fresh look at an issue that some may have considered all but closed."[21]

The authors' assessment of the findings of these 38 studies revealed "significant evidence of a *direct* impact of race on imprisonment."[22] This effect, which persisted even after the effects of crime seriousness and prior criminal record were controlled, was found only for the decision to incarcerate or not and not for the decision on length of sentence. The authors also identified a number of structural contexts that conditioned the race/imprisonment relationship. African American offenders faced significantly greater odds of incarceration than white offenders in the South, in places where African Americans composed a larger percentage of the population, and in places where the unemployment rate was high.

Spohn's[23] review of noncapital sentencing research using data from the 1980s and 1990s also highlighted the importance of attempting to identify "the structural and contextual conditions that are most likely to result in racial discrimination."[24] Spohn reviewed 40 studies examining the relationship between race, ethnicity, and sentencing, including 32 studies of sentencing decisions at the state level and 8 at the federal level. Consistent with the conclusions of Chiricos and Crawford, Spohn reported that many of these studies found a *direct race effect.* At both the state and federal levels, there was evidence that African Americans and Hispanics were more likely than whites to be sentenced to prison; at the federal level, there was also evidence that African Americans received longer sentences than whites.[25]

Noting that "[e]vidence concerning direct racial effects . . . provides few clues to the circumstances under which race matters,"[26] Spohn also evaluated the 40 studies included in her review for evidence of indirect or contextual discrimination. Although she acknowledged that some of the evidence was contradictory—for example, some studies revealed that racial disparities were confined to offenders with less serious prior criminal records, whereas others reported such disparities only among offenders with more serious criminal histories—Spohn nonetheless concluded that the studies revealed four "themes" or "patterns" of contextual effects. Box 7.3 summarizes these themes.

The first theme or pattern revealed was that the combination of race/ethnicity and other legally irrelevant offender characteristics produces greater sen-

> ## BOX 7.3 Race, Ethnicity, and Sentencing Decisions: Contextual Effects
>
> Spohn's review of recent studies analyzing the effect of race and ethnicity on state and federal sentencing decisions identified four themes or patterns of contextual effects.
>
> 1. Racial minorities are sentenced more harshly than whites if they
>
>   are young and male,
>
>   are unemployed,
>
>   are male and unemployed,
>
>   are young, male, and unemployed,
>
>   have lower incomes,
>
>   have less education.
>
> 2. Racial minorities are sentenced more harshly than whites if they
>
>   are detained in jail prior to trial,
>
>   are represented by a public defender rather than a private attorney,
>
>   are convicted at trial rather than by plea,
>
>   have more serious prior criminal records.
>
> 3. Racial minorities who victimize whites are sentenced more harshly than other race-of-offender/race-of-victim combinations.
>
> 4. Racial minorities are sentenced more harshly than whites if they are
>
>   convicted of less serious crimes,
>
>   convicted of drug offenses or more serious drug offenses.
>
> SOURCE: Cassia Spohn, "Thirty Years of Sentencing Reform: A Quest for a Racially Neutral Sentencing Process," in *Policies, Processes, and Decisions of the Criminal Justice System*, vol. 3, *Criminal Justice 2000* (Washington, DC: U.S. Department of Justice, 2000).

tence disparity than race/ethnicity alone. That is, the studies demonstrated that certain types of racial minorities—males, the young, the unemployed, the less educated—are singled out for harsher treatment. Some studies found that each of these offender characteristics, including race/ethnicity, had a direct effect on sentence outcomes but that the combination of race/ethnicity and one or more of the other characteristics was a more powerful predictor of sentence severity than any characteristic individually. Other studies found that race/ethnicity had an effect only if the offender was male, young, and/or unemployed.[27]

The second pattern of indirect/interaction effects was that a number of process-related factors conditioned the effect of race/ethnicity on sentence severity.[28] Some of the studies revealed, for example, that pleading guilty, hiring a private attorney, or providing evidence or testimony in other cases resulted in greater sentence discounts for white offenders than for African American or Hispanic offenders. Other studies showed that racial minorities paid a higher penalty—in terms of harsher sentences—for being detained prior to trial or for having a serious prior criminal record. As Spohn noted, these results demonstrate that race and ethnicity influence sentence outcomes through their relationships with earlier decisions and suggest that these process-related determinants of sentence outcomes do not operate in the same way for racial minorities and whites.

The third theme or pattern revealed concerned an interaction between the race of the offender and the race of the victim. Consistent with research on the death penalty (discussed in Chapter 8), two studies found that African Americans who sexually assaulted whites were sentenced more harshly than either African Americans who sexually assaulted other African Americans or whites who sexually assaulted whites. Thus, "punishment is contingent on the race of the victim as well as the race of the offender."[29]

The final pattern of indirect/interaction effects, which Spohn admitted was "less obvious" than the other three, was that the effect of race/ethnicity was conditioned by the nature of the crime.[30] Some studies found that racial discrimination was confined to less serious—and thus more discretionary—crimes. Other studies revealed that racial discrimination was most pronounced for drug offenses or, alternatively, that harsher sentencing of racial minorities was found only for the most serious drug offenses.[31]

The fact that a majority of the studies reviewed by Chiricos and Crawford and by Spohn found that African Americans and Hispanics were more likely than whites to be sentenced to prison, even after taking crime seriousness and prior criminal record into account, suggests that racial discrimination in sentencing is not a thing of the past. Although the contemporary sentencing process may not be characterized by "a widespread systematic pattern of discrimination,"[32] it is not racially neutral.

Race/Ethnicity, Sentence Outcomes, and Conflict Theory Spohn's conclusion that race/ethnicity interacts with or is conditioned by other predictors of sentence severity is consistent with the arguments put forth by Peterson and Hagan. They asserted that the contradictory findings of early research exploring the effect of race on sentencing resulted in part from an oversimplification of conflict theory, the principal theoretical model used in studies of race and criminal punishment (see Chapter 3 for a detailed discussion of conflict theory).[33] Most researchers simply test the hypothesis that racial minorities will be sentenced more harshly than whites, assuming, either explicitly or implicitly, that racial minorities will receive more severe sentences than whites regardless of the characteristics of the offender, the nature of the crime, the race of the victim, or the relationship between the victim and the offender.

As Hawkins notes, however, conflict theory "does not support a simplistic expectation of greater punishment for blacks than whites under all circumstances."[34] Rather, conflict theorists argue that "the probability that criminal sanctions will be applied varies according to the extent to which the behaviors of the powerless conflict with the interests of the power segments."[35] Crimes that threaten the power of the dominant class will therefore produce harsher penalties for African Americans who commit those crimes, and crimes that pose relatively little threat to the system of white authority will not necessarily result in harsher sanctions for African Americans.[36] According to this view, African Americans who murder, rape, or rob whites will receive harsher sentences than African Americans who victimize members of their own race. As Peterson and Hagan note,

> When black offenders assault or kill black victims, the devalued status of
> the black victims and the paternalistic attitudes of white authorities can

justify lenient treatment. . . . When blacks violate white victims, the high sexual property value attached to the white victims and the racial fears of authorities can justify severe treatment.[37]

Criminal justice scholars have proposed revising the conflict perspective on race and sentencing to account for the possibility of interaction between defendant race and other predictors of sentence severity. Hawkins, for example, argues for the development of a more comprehensive conflict theory that embodies race-of-victim and type-of-crime effects.[38] Similarly, Peterson and Hagan argue for research "that takes context-specific conceptions of race into account."[39]

As Spohn's review of recent research demonstrates, researchers examining the linkages between race and sentence severity have begun to heed these suggestions. They have begun to conduct research designed to identify the circumstances under which African Americans will be sentenced more harshly than whites and to design studies that attempt to determine "when race matters."

WHEN DOES RACE MATTER?

Research conducted during the past two decades clearly demonstrates that race/ethnicity interacts with or is conditioned by (1) other legally irrelevant offender characteristics, (2) process-related factors, (3) the race of the victim, and (4) the nature and seriousness of the crime. A comprehensive review of these studies is beyond the scope of this book. Instead, we summarize the findings of a few key studies. We begin by summarizing the results of a study that found both direct and indirect racial effects and then review the findings of a series of studies that explore the relationship among race, gender, age, employment status, and sentence severity. We review studies that examine differential treatment of interracial and intraracial crime and then discuss the findings of one study that examined the effect of race on sentencing for different types of crimes and the findings of a number of studies that focus explicitly on the relationship between race and sentence severity for drug offenders. Our purpose is to illustrate the subtle, complex ways in which race influences the sentencing process.

Sentencing in Three Urban Jurisdictions:
Direct and Indirect Race Effects

A number of methodologically sound studies have concluded that African American and Hispanic offenders are sentenced more harshly than whites. Spohn and DeLone, for example, compared the sentences imposed on African American, Hispanic, and white offenders convicted of felonies in Chicago, Kansas City, and Miami in 1993 and 1994.[40] They controlled for the legal and extralegal variables that affect judges' sentencing decisions: the offender's age, gender, and prior criminal record; whether the offender was on probation at the time of the current offense; the seriousness of the conviction charge; the

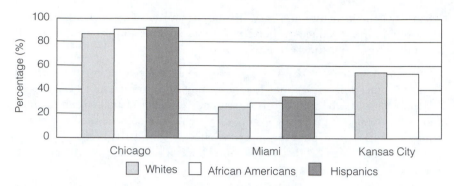

FIGURE 7.1 Estimated Probabilities of Incarceration for Offenders Convicted of Burglary

number of conviction charges; the type of attorney representing the offender; whether the offender was detained or released prior to trial; and whether the offender pled guilty or went to trial.

Spohn and DeLone found evidence of racial discrimination in the decision to incarcerate or not in two of the three jurisdictions. Although race had no effect on the likelihood of incarceration in Kansas City, both African Americans and Hispanics were more likely than whites to be sentenced to prison in Chicago, and Hispanics (but not African Americans) were more likely than whites to be incarcerated in Miami. The data presented in Figure 7.1 illustrate these results more clearly. The authors used the results of their multivariate analyses to calculate the estimated probability of imprisonment for a "typical" white, African American, and Hispanic offender who was convicted of burglary in each of the three cities.[41]

These estimated probabilities confirm that offender race had no effect on the likelihood of incarceration in Kansas City; 55 percent of the whites and 54 percent of the African Americans convicted of burglary were sentenced to prison. In Chicago, there was about a 4 percentage-point difference between white offenders and African American offenders and between white offenders and Hispanic offenders. In Miami, the difference between white offenders and Hispanic offenders was somewhat larger; even after the other legal and extralegal variables were taken into consideration, 34 percent of the Hispanics, but only 26 percent of the whites, received a prison sentence.

Spohn and DeLone also compared the sentences imposed on offenders who were incarcerated. They found that race/ethnicity had no effect on the length of the prison sentence in Chicago or Miami. In Kansas City, on the other hand, African Americans convicted of drug offenses received sentences that were 14 months longer than those of whites convicted of drug offenses; African Americans convicted of property crimes received sentences that were nearly 7 months longer than those of whites convicted of these crimes.

Consistent with the explanations presented in Box 7.1, Spohn and DeLone also found evidence of economic discrimination. When they analyzed the likelihood of pretrial detention, controlling for crime seriousness, the offender's prior criminal record, and other factors associated with the type and amount of bail required by the judge, they found that African Americans and Hispanics faced significantly higher odds of pretrial detention than whites in Chicago and Miami, and that African Americans were more likely than whites to be detained in Kansas City. They also found that pretrial detention was a strong predictor of the likelihood of incarceration following conviction. Because African American and Hispanic defendants were more likely than whites to be detained prior to trial, they were substantially more likely than those who were released to be incarcerated.

The authors of this study were careful to point out that the race effects they uncovered, although statistically significant, were "rather modest"[42] and that the seriousness of the offense and the offender's prior criminal record were the primary determinants of sentence outcomes. They noted, however, that the fact that offender race/ethnicity had both direct and indirect effects, coupled with the fact that female offenders and those who were released prior to trial received substantially more lenient sentences than male offenders and those who were detained before trial, suggests that "judges' sentencing decisions are not guided *exclusively* by factors of explicit legal relevance."[43] They concluded that judges' sentencing decisions reflect "stereotypes of dangerousness and culpability that rest, either explicitly or implicitly, on considerations of race, gender, pretrial status, and willingness to plead guilty."[44] (See Box 7.4 for a discussion of sentencing outcomes for Native Americans.)

Race/Ethnicity, Gender, Age, and Employment: A Volatile Combination?

In a recent article exploring the "convergence of race, ethnicity, gender, and class on court decisionmaking," Zatz urged researchers to consider the ways in which offender (and victim) characteristics jointly affect case outcomes.[45] As she noted, "Race, gender, and class are the central axes undergirding our social structure. They intersect in dynamic, fluid, and multifaceted ways."[46]

The findings of a series of studies conducted by Darrell Steffensmeier and his colleagues at Pennsylvania State University illustrate these "intersections." Research published by these teams of researchers during the early 1990s concluded that race,[47] gender,[48] and age[49] each played a role in the sentencing process in Pennsylvania. However, it is interesting to note, especially in light of their later research findings,[50] that their initial study of the effect of race on sentencing concluded that race contributed "very little" to our understanding of judges' sentencing decisions.[51] Although the incarceration (jail or prison) rate for African Americans was 8 percentage points higher than the rate for whites, there was only a 2 percentage-point difference in the rates at which African Americans and whites were sentenced to prison. Race also played "a very small role in decisions about sentence length."[52] The average sentence for African American defendants was only 21 days longer than the average sentence for white defendants. These findings led Kramer and Steffensmeier to conclude

BOX 7.4   Native Americans and Sentencing Disparity

Most studies investigating the effect of race on sentence outcomes focus exclusively on African Americans and whites. There are relatively few studies that include Hispanics and even fewer that include other racial minorities, such as Native Americans.

Young (1990) asserted that the failure of criminal justice researchers to address issues relating to Native Americans "means that Native Americans are viewed in terms of narrow ethnocentric stereotypes (e.g., drunken savage)" (p. 59). Lujan (1998) similarly contended that the stereotype of the "drunken Indian" makes Native Americans more vulnerable to arrest for alcohol-related offenses and that stereotypical perceptions of reservation life as unstable and conducive to crime may lead to longer sentences for Native Americans.

The few studies that do examine sentence outcomes for Native Americans have produced mixed results. Some studies found that Native Americans and whites are sentenced similarly once crime seriousness, prior record, and other legally relevant variables are taken into account (Feimer, Pommersheim, & Wise, 1990; Pommersheim & Wise, 1989). Other studies concluded that Native Americans adjudicated in federal (Swift & Bickel, 1974) and state (Alvarez & Bachman, 1996; Hall & Simkins, 1975) courts are sentenced more harshly than similarly situated whites or that Native Americans serve significantly more of their prison sentence before parole or release than whites do (Bachman, Alvarez, & Perkins, 1996; Bynum & Paternoster, 1984).

In a recent study, Alvarez and Bachman (1996) used data on offenders incarcerated in Arizona state correctional facilities in 1990 to compare sentence lengths for Native Americans and whites. They found that whites received longer sentences than Native Americans for homicide, but Native Americans received longer sentences than whites for burglary and robbery.

Alvarez and Bachman speculated that these findings may reflect the fact that homicide tends to be intraracial, whereas burglary and robbery are more likely to be interracial. Whites may have received longer sentences for homicide because their victims were also likely to be white, whereas the victims of Native Americans were typically other Native Americans. As the authors note, "Because the lives of American Indian victims may not be especially valued by U.S. society and the justice system, these American Indian defendants may receive more lenient sentences for their crime." Similarly, Native Americans convicted of burglary or robbery may have received harsher sentences than whites convicted of these crimes because their victims were more likely to be "higher-status Caucasians" (p. 558).

Alvarez and Bachman concluded that their study demonstrates "the need for more crime-specific analyses to investigate discriminatory practices in processing and sentencing minority group members, especially American Indians" (p. 558).

that "if defendants' race affects judges' decisions in sentencing . . . it does so very weakly or intermittently, if at all."[53]

This conclusion is called into question by Steffensmeier, Ulmer, and Kramer's more recent research, which explores the ways in which race, gender, and age interact to influence sentence severity.[54] They found that each of the three legally irrelevant offender characteristics had a significant direct effect on both the likelihood of incarceration and the length of the sentence: African Americans were sentenced more harshly than whites, younger offenders were sentenced more harshly than older offenders, and males were sentenced more harshly than females. More important, they found that the three factors interacted to produce substantially harsher sentences for one particular category of offenders—young, African American males—than for any other age–race–gender combination. According to the authors, their results illustrate the "high cost of being black, young, and male."[55]

Although the research conducted by Steffensmeier and his colleagues provides important insights into the judicial decision-making process, their findings also suggest the possibility that factors other than race, gender, and age may interact to affect sentence severity. If, as the authors suggest, judges impose harsher sentences on offenders perceived to be more deviant, more dangerous, and more likely to recidivate, and if these perceptions rest, either explicitly or implicitly, on "stereotypes associated with membership in various social categories,"[56] then offenders with constellations of characteristics other than "young, black, and male" may also be singled out for harsher treatment.

The validity of this assertion is confirmed by the results of a recent replication and extension of the Pennsylvania study. Spohn and Holleran examined the sentences imposed on offenders convicted of felonies in Chicago, Miami, and Kansas City.[57] Their study included Hispanics as well as African Americans and tested for interactions between race, ethnicity, gender, age, and employment status. They found that none of the five offender characteristics had a significant effect on the length of the sentence in any of the three jurisdictions, but that each characteristic had a significant effect on the decision to incarcerate or not in at least one of the jurisdictions. As shown in Part A of Table 7.1, in Chicago, African American offenders were 12.1 percent more likely than white offenders to be incarcerated; Hispanics were 15.3 percent more likely than whites to be incarcerated. In Miami, the difference in the probabilities of incarceration for Hispanic offenders and white offenders was 10.3 percent. Male offenders were over 20 percent more likely than female offenders to be sentenced to prison in Chicago and Kansas City, and unemployed offenders faced significantly higher odds of incarceration than employed offenders (+9.3 percent) in Kansas City. In all three jurisdictions, offenders aged 21–29 were about 10 percent more likely than offenders aged 17–20 to be sentenced to prison.[58] Race, ethnicity, gender, age, and employment status, then, each had a direct effect on the decision to incarcerate or not.

Like Steffensmeier and his colleagues, Spohn and Holleran found that various combinations of race/ethnicity, gender, age, and employment status were better predictors of incarceration than any variable alone. As shown in Part B of Table 7.1, young African American and Hispanic males were consistently more likely than middle-aged white males to be sentenced to prison. These offenders, however, were not the only ones singled out for harsher treatment. In Chicago, young African American and Hispanic males and middle-aged African American males faced higher odds of incarceration than middle-aged white males. In Miami, young African American and Hispanic males and older His-

Table 7.1 Do Young, Unemployed African American and Hispanic Males Pay a Punishment Penalty?

DIFFERENCES IN THE PROBABILITIES OF INCARCERATION: THE EFFECT OF RACE, ETHNICITY, GENDER, AGE, AND EMPLOYMENT STATUS

A. Probability Differences	Chicago	Miami	Kansas City
African Americans versus whites	+12.1%	not significant	not significant
Hispanics versus whites	+15.3%	+10.3%	(not applicable)
Males versus females	+22.8%	not significant	+21.1%
Unemployed versus employed	not significant	(not applicable)	+9.3%
Age 21–29 versus age 17–20	+10.0%	+9.5%	+10.8%

DIFFERENCES IN THE PROBABILITIES OF INCARCERATION: MALE OFFENDERS ONLY

B. Probability Differences between Whites aged 30–39 and	Chicago	Miami	Kansas City
African Americans, 17–29	+18.4%	+14.7%	+12.7%
Hispanics, 17–29	+25.1%	+18.2%	(not applicable)
Whites, 17–29	not significant	not significant	+14.4%
African Americans, 30–39	+23.3%	not significant	not significant
Hispanics, 30–39	not significant	+18.5%	(not applicable)

C. Probability Differences between Employed Whites and			
Unemployed African Americans	+16.9%	(not applicable)	+13.0%
Unemployed Hispanics	+23.5%	(not applicable)	(not applicable)
Unemployed Whites	not significant	(not applicable)	not significant
Employed African Americans	not significant	(not applicable)	not significant
Employed Hispanics	not significant	(not applicable)	(not applicable)

SOURCE: Cassia Spohn and David Holleran, "The Imprisonment Penalty Paid by Young, Unemployed Black and Hispanic Male Offenders," *Criminology* 38 (2000): tables 3, 5, and 6.

panic males were incarcerated more often than middle-aged white males. And in Kansas City, both young African American males and young white males faced higher odds of incarceration than middle-aged white males. These results led Spohn and Holleran to conclude that "in Chicago and Miami the combination of race/ethnicity and age is a more powerful predictor of sentence severity than either variable individually, while in Kansas City age matters more than race." [59]

The findings of the studies conducted by Steffensmeier and his colleagues and by Spohn and Holleran confirm Richard Quinney's assertion, made nearly 30 years ago, that "judicial decisions are not made uniformly. Decisions are made according to a host of extra-legal factors, including the age of the offender, his race, and social class." [60] Their findings confirm that dangerous or problematic populations are defined "by a mix of economic *and* racial . . . references." [61] African American and Hispanic offenders who are also male, young, and unemployed may pay a higher punishment penalty than either white offenders or other types of African American and Hispanic offenders.

Why Do Young, Unemployed Racial Minorities Pay a Punishment Penalty? The issue is *why* young, unemployed racial minorities are punished more severely than other types of offenders—why "today's prevailing criminal predator has become a euphemism for young, black males."[62]

A number of scholars suggest that certain categories of offenders are regarded as more dangerous and more problematic than others and thus more in need of formal social control. Spitzer, for example, used "social dynamite" to characterize that segment of the deviant population that is viewed as particularly threatening and dangerous;[63] he asserted that social dynamite "tends to be more youthful, alienated and politically volatile" and contended that those who fall into this category are more likely than other offenders to be formally processed through the criminal justice system.[64] Building on this point, Box and Hale argued that unemployed offenders who are also young, male, and members of a racial minority will be perceived as particularly threatening to the social order and thus will be singled out for harsher treatment.[65] Judges, in other words, regard these types of "threatening" offenders as likely candidates for imprisonment "in the belief that such a response will deter and incapacitate and thus defuse this threat."[66]

Steffensmeier and his colleagues advanced a similar explanation for their finding "that young black men (as opposed to black men as a whole) are the defendant subgroup most at risk to receive the harshest penalty."[67] They interpreted their results using the "focal concerns" theory of sentencing. According to this perspective, judges' sentencing decisions reflect their assessment of the blameworthiness or culpability of the offender, their desire to protect the community by incapacitating dangerous offenders or deterring potential offenders, and their concerns about the practical consequences, or social costs, of sentencing decisions. Because judges rarely have enough information to accurately determine an offender's culpability or dangerousness, they develop a "perceptual shorthand" based on stereotypes and attributions that are themselves linked to offender characteristics such as race, gender, and age. Thus, according to these researchers,

> Younger offenders and male defendants appear to be seen as more of a threat to the community or not as reformable, and so also are black of-fenders, particularly those who also are young and male. Likewise, concerns such as "ability to do time" and the costs of incarceration appear linked to race-, gender-, and age-based perceptions and stereotypes.[68]

The conclusions proffered by Spohn and Holleran, who noted that their results are consistent with the focal concerns theory of sentencing, are very similar. They suggested that judges, who generally have limited time in which to make decisions and incomplete information about offenders, "may resort to stereotypes of deviance and dangerousness that rest on considerations of race, ethnicity, gender, age, and unemployment."[69] Young, unemployed African

American and Hispanic males, in other words, are viewed as more dangerous, more threatening, and less amenable to rehabilitation; as a result, they are sentenced more harshly.

Differential Treatment of
Interracial and Intraracial Sexual Assault

There is compelling historical evidence that interracial and intraracial crimes have been treated differently. Gunnar Myrdal's examination of the Southern court system in the 1930s, for example, revealed that African Americans who victimized whites received the harshest punishment, whereas African Americans who victimized other African Americans were often "acquitted or given a ridiculously mild sentence."[70] Myrdal also noted that "it is quite common for a white criminal to be set free if his crime was against a Negro."[71]

These patterns are particularly pronounced for the crime of sexual assault. As Brownmiller has noted, "No single event ticks off America's political schizophrenia with greater certainty than the case of a black man accused of raping a white woman."[72] Evidence of this can be found in pre–Civil War statutes that prescribed different penalties for African American and white men convicted of sexual assault. As illustrated in Box 7.5, these early laws also differentiated between the rape of a white woman and the rape of an African American woman.

Differential treatment of interracial and intraracial sexual assaults continued even after passage of the Fourteenth Amendment, which outlawed the types of explicit statutory racial discrimination previously discussed. In the first half of this century, African American men accused of, or even suspected of, sexually assaulting white women often faced white lynch mobs bent on vengeance. As Wriggens noted, "The thought of this particular crime aroused in many white people an extremely high level of mania and panic."[73] In a 1907 Louisiana case, the defense attorney stated:

> Gentlemen of the jury, this man, a nigger, is charged with breaking into the house of a white man in the nighttime and assaulting his wife, with the intent to rape her. Now, don't you know that, if this nigger had committed such a crime, he never would have been brought here and tried; that he would have been lynched, and if I were there I would help pull on the rope.[74]

African American men who escaped the mob's wrath were almost certain to be convicted, and those who were convicted were guaranteed a harsh sentence. Many, in fact, were sentenced to death; 405 of the 453 men executed for rape in the United States from 1930 to 1972 were African Americans.[75] According to Brownmiller, "Heavier sentences imposed on blacks for raping white women is an incontestable historic fact."[76] As we show, it is not simply a historic fact. Research conducted during the past two decades illustrates that African American men convicted of raping white women continue to be singled out for harsher treatment.

**BOX 7.5   Pre–Civil War Statutes on Sexual Assault:
Explicit Discrimination against African American
Men Convicted of Raping White Women**

Virginia Code of 1819
The penalty for the rape or attempted rape of a white woman by a slave, African American, or mulatto was death; if the offender was white, the penalty was 10–21 years.

Georgia Penal Code of 1816
The death penalty was given for rape or attempted rape of a white woman by slaves or free persons of color. A term of not more than 20 years was given for the rape of a white woman by a white man. A white man convicted of raping an African American woman could be fined or imprisoned at the court's discretion.

Pennsylvania Code of 1700
The penalty for the rape of a white woman by an African American man was death; the penalty for attempted rape was castration. The penalty for a white man was 1–7 years in prison.

Kansas Compilation of 1855
An African American man convicted of raping a white woman was to be castrated at his own expense. The maximum penalty for a white man convicted of raping a white woman was 5 years in prison.

SOURCE: Jennifer Wriggins, "Rape, Racism, and the Law," *Harvard Women's Law Journal* 6 (1983): 103–141.

Offender–Victim Race and Sentences for Sexual Assault Researchers analyzing the impact of race on sentencing for sexual assault have argued that focusing only on the race of the defendant and ignoring the race of the victim will produce misleading conclusions about the overall effect of race on sentencing. They contend that researchers may incorrectly conclude that race does not affect sentence severity if only the race of the defendant is taken into consideration. Table 7.2 presents a hypothetical example to illustrate how this might occur. Assume that 460 of 1,000 African American men (46 percent) and 440 of 1,000 white men (44 percent) convicted of sexual assault in a particular jurisdiction were sentenced to prison. A researcher who focused only on the race of the offender would therefore conclude that the incarceration rates for the two groups were nearly identical.

Assume now that the 1,000 cases involving African American men included 800 cases with African American victims and 200 cases with white victims, and that 320 of the 800 cases with African American victims and 140 of the 200 cases with white victims resulted in a prison sentence. As shown in Table 7.2, although the overall incarceration rate for African American offenders is 46 percent, the rate for crimes involving African American men and white women is 70 percent, whereas the rate for crimes involving African American men and African American women is only 40 percent. A similar pattern—an incarceration rate of 50 percent for cases with white victims but only 30 percent for cases with African American victims—is found for sexual assaults involving white offenders. The similar incarceration rates for African American and white offenders mask large differences based on the race of the victim.

Table 7.2 Incarceration of Offenders Convicted of Sexual Assault: A Hypothetical Example of the Effect of Offender–Victim Race

Example: 2,000 men convicted of sexual assault. Analysis reveals that incarceration rate for African Americans is very similar to the rate for whites.

1,000 convicted African American offenders	460 incarcerated = 46% incarceration rate
1,000 convicted white offenders	440 incarcerated = 44% incarceration rate

Problem: Similarities are masking differences based on the race of the victim.

1,000 African American Offenders	460 incarcerated (46%)
800 cases with African American victims	320 incarcerated (40%)
200 cases with white victims	140 incarcerated (70%)
1,000 White Offenders	440 incarcerated (44%)
300 cases with African American victims	90 incarcerated (30%)
700 cases with white victims	350 incarcerated (50%)

Thus, the incarceration rate varies from 30% (for whites who assaulted African Americans) to 70% (for African Americans who assaulted whites).

The findings of recent empirical research suggest that the scenario just described is not simply hypothetical. LaFree, for example, examined the impact of offender–victim race on the disposition of sexual assault cases in Indianapolis.[77] He found that African American men who assaulted white women were more likely than other offenders to be sentenced to prison and to receive longer prison sentences.

LaFree concluded that his results highlighted the importance of examining the racial composition of the offender–victim pair. Because the law was applied *most* harshly to African Americans charged with raping white women but *least* harshly to African Americans charged with raping African American women, simply examining the overall disposition of cases with African American defendants would have produced misleading results.

Walsh reached a similar conclusion. When he examined the sentences imposed on offenders convicted of sexual assault in a metropolitan Ohio county, he found that neither the offender's race nor the victim's race influenced the length of the sentence. In addition, the incarceration rate for white defendants was *higher* than the rate for African American defendants. Further analysis, however, revealed that African Americans convicted of assaulting whites received more severe sentences than those convicted of assaulting members of their own race. This was true for those who assaulted acquaintances as well as for those who assaulted strangers.[78] As Walsh noted, "The leniency extended to blacks who sexually assault blacks provides a rather strong indication of disregard for minority victims of sexual assault."[79]

Somewhat different results were reported by Spohn and Spears, who analyzed a sample of sexual assaults bound over for trial from 1970 through 1984 in Detroit Recorder's Court.[80] Unlike previous researchers, who controlled only for offender–victim race and other offender and case characteristics, the authors of this study also controlled for a number of victim characteristics: the age of the victim, the relationship between the victim and the offender, evidence of risk-taking behavior on the part of the victim, and the victim's behavior at the time of the incident. They compared the incarceration rates and the maximum sentences imposed on three combinations of offender–victim race: African American–African American, African American–white, and white–white.

In contrast to LaFree and Walsh, Spohn and Spears found that the race of the offender–victim pair did not affect the likelihood of incarceration. The sentences imposed on African Americans who assaulted whites, on the other hand, were significantly longer than the sentences imposed on whites who assaulted whites or African Americans who assaulted African Americans. The average sentence for black-on-white crimes was over 4 years longer than the average sentence for white-on-white crimes and over 3 years longer than the average sentence for black-on-black crimes. These results, according to the authors, reflected discrimination based on the offender's race and the victim's race.[81]

To explain the fact that offender–victim race affected the length of sentence but had no effect on the decision to incarcerate or not, the authors suggested that judges confronted with offenders convicted of sexual assault may have relatively little discretion in deciding whether to incarcerate. As they noted, "Because sexual assault is a serious crime . . . the 'normal penalty' may be incarceration. Judges may have more latitude, and thus more opportunities to consider extralegal factors such as offender/victim race, in deciding on the length of the sentence."[82]

Spohn and Spears also tested a number of hypotheses about the interrelationships among offender race, victim race, and the relationship between the victim and the offender. Noting that previous research has suggested that crimes between intimates are perceived as less serious than crimes between strangers, they hypothesized that sexual assaults involving strangers would be treated more harshly than assaults involving intimates or acquaintances regardless of the offender's or the victim's race. Contrary to their hypothesis, they found that the offender–victim relationship came into play only when both the offender and the victim were African American. African Americans convicted of assaulting African American strangers received harsher sentences than African Americans convicted of assaulting African American intimates or acquaintances; they were more likely to be incarcerated, and those who were incarcerated received longer sentences.[83]

The data presented in Figure 7.2 illustrate these differences. The authors used the results of their multivariate analysis of sentence length to calculate adjusted sentence means for each of the six relationship combinations of offender race–victim race. These adjusted rates take all of the other independent variables into account and show that three types of offenders received substantially longer sentences than the other three types. The harshest sentences were imposed on African Americans who victimized whites (strangers or nonstrangers) and on African Americans who victimized African American strangers. More

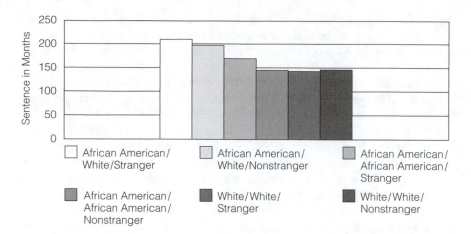

FIGURE 7.2 Offender's Race, Victim's Race, Relationship, and Length of Sentence

SOURCE: Cassia Spohn and Jeffrey Spears, "The Effect of Offender and Victim Characteristics on Sexual Assault Case Processing Decisions," *Justice Quarterly* 3 (1996): 649–679.

lenient sentences were imposed on African Americans who assaulted African American nonstrangers and on whites who assaulted whites (strangers or non-strangers).

As the authors noted, these results suggest that judges consider the offender's race, but not the relationship between the victim and offender, in determining the appropriate sentence for offenders convicted of assaulting whites. Regardless of the relationship between the victim and the offender, African Americans who victimized whites received longer sentences than whites who victimized whites. However, judges do consider the relationship between the victim and offender in determining the appropriate sentence for African Americans convicted of sexually assaulting other African Americans. Judges apparently believe that African Americans who sexually assault African American strangers deserve harsher punishment than those who sexually assault African American friends, relatives, or acquaintances.

Considered together, the results of these studies demonstrate that criminal punishment is contingent on the race of the victim as well as on the race of the offender. They demonstrate that *"the meaning of race varies, and that, despite simplistic interpretations of conflict theory, both differential severity and leniency are possible."*[84] The harshest penalties will be imposed on African Americans who victimize whites and the most lenient penalties on African Americans who victimize other African Americans.

The Effect of Race on Sentencing
for Various Types of Crimes

The studies summarized thus far highlight the importance of testing for interaction between offender race/ethnicity and other factors, such as the age, gender, and employment status of the offender and the race of the victim. The importance of "rethinking the conflict perspective on race and criminal punishment"[85] is also demonstrated by the results of studies examining the effect of race on sentence severity for various types of crimes. Some researchers, building on Kalven and Zeisel's "liberation hypothesis,"[86] assert that African Americans will be sentenced more harshly than whites only in less serious cases.

The liberation hypothesis suggests that jurors deviate from their fact-finding mission in cases in which the evidence against the defendant is weak or contradictory. Jurors' doubts about the evidence, in other words, liberate them from the constraints imposed by the law and free them to consider their own sentiments or values. When Kalven and Zeisel examined jurors' verdicts in rape cases, for example, they found that jurors' beliefs about the victim's behavior were much more likely to influence their verdicts if the victim had been raped by an unarmed acquaintance rather than by a stranger armed with a gun or a knife.

The liberation hypothesis suggests that in more serious cases, the appropriate sentence is strongly determined by the seriousness of the crime and by the defendant's prior criminal record. In these types of cases, judges have relatively little discretion and thus few opportunities to consider legally irrelevant factors such as race. In less serious cases, the appropriate sentence is not clearly indicated by the features of the crime or the defendant's criminal record, which may leave judges more disposed to bring extralegal factors to bear on the sentencing decision.

Consider, for example, a case of sexual assault in which the offender, who has a prior conviction for armed robbery, raped a stranger at gunpoint. This case clearly calls for a severe sentence; all defendants who fall into this category, regardless of their race or their victim's race, will be sentenced to prison for close to the maximum term.

The appropriate sentence for a first-time offender who assaults an acquaintance with a weapon other than a gun, however, is not necessarily obvious. Some defendants who fall into this category will be incarcerated, but others will not. This opens the door for judges to consider the race of the defendant or the race of the victim in determining the appropriate sentence.

Spohn and Cederblom used data on defendants convicted of violent felonies in Detroit to test the hypothesis that racial discrimination in sentencing is confined to less serious criminal cases.[87] Although they acknowledged that all of the cases included in their data file are by definition "serious cases," they argued that some are more serious than others. Murder, rape, and robbery are more serious than assault; crimes in which the defendant used a gun are more serious than those in which the defendant did not use a gun; and crimes in which the defendant had a prior felony conviction are more serious than those in which the defendant did not have prior convictions.

As shown in Table 7.3, which summarizes the results of their analysis of the likelihood of incarceration (controlling for other variables linked to sentence severity), the authors found convincing support for their hypothesis. With only one exception, race had a significant effect on the decision to incarcerate or not only in less serious cases. African Americans convicted of assault were incarcerated at a higher rate than whites convicted of assault; there were no racial differences for the three more serious offenses. Similarly, race affected the like-

Table 7.3 The Effect of Race on the Likelihood of Incarceration for Various Types of Cases in Detroit

	Effect of Race on Incarceration Statistically Significant?
Most serious conviction charge	
Murder	No
Robbery	No
Rape	No
Other sex offenses	No
Assault	Yes
Prior criminal record	
Violent felony conviction	No
No violent felony conviction	Yes
Relationship between offender and victim	
Strangers	No
Acquaintances	Yes
Use of a weapon	
Offender used a gun	No
Offender did not use a gun	Yes
Injury to victim	
Offender injured victim	Yes
Offender did not injure victim	Yes

SOURCE: Adapted from Cassia Spohn and Jerry Cederblom, "Race and Disparities in Sentencing: A Test of the Liberation Hypothesis," *Justice Quarterly* 8 (1991): 305–327.

lihood of incarceration for defendants with no violent felony convictions, but not for those with a prior conviction; for defendants who victimized acquaintances, but not for those who victimized strangers; and for defendants who did not use a gun to commit the crime, but not for those who did use a gun.

Spohn and Cederblom concluded that their results provided support for Kalven and Zeisel's liberation hypothesis, at least with respect to the decision to incarcerate or not, and that their findings offered important insights into judges' sentencing decisions. According to the authors,

> When the crime is serious and the evidence strong, judges' sentencing decisions are determined primarily by factors of explicit legal relevance —the seriousness of the conviction charge, the number of conviction charges, the nature of the defendant's prior criminal record, and so on. Sentencing decisions in less serious cases, on the other hand, reflect the influence of extralegal as well as legal factors.[88]

These results demonstrate that the criteria used by judges to determine the appropriate sentence will vary depending on the nature of the crime and the defendant's prior criminal record. More to the point, they demonstrate that *the effect of race on sentence severity will vary.* Judges impose harsher sentences on African Americans than on whites under some circumstances and for some types of crime; they impose similar sentences under other circumstances and for other types of crime. The fact that race does not affect sentence severity for *all* cases, in other words, does not mean that judges do not discriminate in *any* cases.

Sentencing and the War on Drugs

The task of assessing the effect of race on sentencing is complicated by the War on Drugs, which critics contend has been fought primarily in minority communities. Tonry, for example, argued that "urban black Americans have borne the brunt of the War on Drugs."[89] More specifically, he charged that "the recent blackening of America's prison population is the product of malign neglect of the war's effects on black Americans."[90] Miller similarly asserted, "The racial discrimination endemic to the drug war wound its way through every stage of the processing—arrest, jailing, conviction, and sentencing."[91] Mauer's criticism is even more pointed. He asserted that "the drug war has exacerbated racial disparities in incarceration while failing to have any sustained impact on the drug problem."[92]

Comments such as these suggest that racial minorities will receive more punitive sentences than whites for drug offenses. This expectation is based in part on recent theoretical discussions of the "moral panic" surrounding drug use and the War on Drugs.[93] Moral panic theorists argue that society is characterized by a variety of commonsense perceptions about crime and drugs that result in community intolerance for such behaviors and increased pressure for punitive action.[94] Many theorists argue that this moral panic can become ingrained in the judicial ideology of sentencing judges, resulting in more severe sentences for those—that is, African Americans and Hispanics—believed to be responsible for drug use, drug distribution, and drug-related crime.[95]

Racial Disparities in Sentences Imposed for Drug Offenses As demonstrated in earlier chapters and summarized in what follows, there is ample evidence that the War on Drugs has been fought primarily in minority communities. In May 2000, Human Rights Watch, a New York–based watchdog organization, issued a report titled *Punishment and Prejudice*.[96] The report analyzed nationwide prison admission statistics and presented the results of the first state-by-state analysis of the impact of drug offenses on prison admissions for African Americans and whites. The authors of the report alleged that the War on Drugs, which is "ostensibly color blind," has been waged "disproportionately against black Americans." As they noted, "The statistics we have compiled present a unique—and devastating—picture of the price black Americans have paid in each state for the national effort to curtail the use and sale of illicit drugs." The following statistics from the report support this conclusion.

- African Americans constituted 62.6 percent of all drug offenders admitted to state prisons in 1996; in certain states, the disparity was much greater—in Maryland and Illinois, for example, 90 percent of all persons admitted to state prisons for drug offenses were African American.

- Nationwide, the rate of drug admissions to state prison for African American men was 13 times greater than the rate for white men; in 10 states, the rates for African American men were 26 to 57 times greater than those for white men.

- Drug offenders accounted for 38 percent of all African American prison admissions, but only 24 percent of all white prison admissions; in New

Hampshire, drug offenders accounted for 61 percent of all African American prison admissions.

- The disproportionate rates at which African Americans are sentenced to prison for drug offenses "originate in racially disproportionate rates of arrest." From 1979 to 1998, the percentage of drug users who were African American did not vary appreciably; however, among those arrested for drug offenses, the percentage of African Americans rose significantly. In 1979, African Americans made up 10.8 percent of all drug users and 21.8 percent of all drug arrests; in 1998, African Americans made up 16.9 percent of all drug users and 37.3 percent of all drug arrests.

The authors of the report stated that their purpose was "to bring renewed attention to extreme racial disparities in one area of the criminal justice system —the incarceration of drug law offenders." They also asserted that although the high rates of incarceration for all drug offenders are a cause for concern, "the grossly disparate rates at which blacks and whites are sent to prison for drug offenses raise a clear warning flag concerning the fairness and equity of drug law enforcement across the country, and underscore the need for reforms that would minimize these disparities without sacrificing legitimate drug control objectives."

Critics of the report's conclusions, which they branded "inflammatory," argued that the statistics presented did not constitute evidence of racial discrimination. "There will be inevitably, inherently, disparities of all sorts in the enforcement of any kind of law," said Todd Graziano, a senior fellow in legal studies at the Heritage Foundation.[97] Critics noted that because the illegal drug trade flourishes in inner-city, minority neighborhoods, the statistics presented in the report could simply indicate that African Americans commit more drug crimes than whites.

There are relatively few studies that focus on racial disparities in sentences imposed on drug offenders and even fewer that have been conducted since the War on Drugs began. Moreover, the results of these studies are somewhat inconsistent. Some researchers find that African American and Hispanic drug offenders are sentenced more harshly than white drug offenders;[98] other researchers conclude either that there are few if any racial differences[99] or that racial minorities convicted of certain types of drug offenses are sentenced more leniently than their white counterparts.[100]

We summarize the results of two studies comparing the sentences imposed on African American, Hispanic, and white drug offenders. Both of these studies used data on offenders sentenced since the initiation of the War on Drugs. The first study used data on offenders sentenced in state courts;[101] the second analyzed data on offenders sentenced under the federal sentencing guidelines.[102]

Sentencing of Drug Offenders in State Courts Spohn and Spears used data on offenders convicted of felony drug offenses in Chicago, Kansas City, and Miami in 1993 and 1994 to test the hypothesis that African Americans and Hispanics would be sentenced more harshly than whites. They found that Hispanics, but not African Americans, faced greater odds of incarceration than

Table 7.4 Predicted Probabilities of Incarceration and Adjusted Sentences for African American, Hispanic, and White Drug Offenders in Three Cities

	Chicago	Miami	Kansas City
Probability of prison sentence			
African American	.796	.177	.370
Hispanic	.789	.227	NA
White	.765	.111	.341
Probability of a jail or prison sentence: Miami			
African American		.812	
Hispanic		.804	
White		.774	
Adjusted prison sentence (in months)			
African American	38.61	46.73	73.11
Hispanic	47.03	58.49	NA
White	41.35	56.51	58.12

SOURCE: Adapted from Cassia Spohn and Jeffrey Spears, "Sentencing of Drug Offenders in Three Cities: Does Race/Ethnicity Make a Difference?" in *Crime Control and Criminal Justice: The Delicate Balance,* ed. Darnell F. Hawkins, Samuel L. Meyers Jr., and Randolph N. Stone (Westport, CT: Greenwood, 2002).

whites in Miami, but that racial minorities and whites were sentenced to prison at about the same rate in Chicago and Kansas City. Similarly, they found that African Americans received longer sentences than whites in Kansas City, but that the sentences imposed on racial minorities and whites were very similar in Chicago and Miami.

These similarities and differences are illustrated by the estimated probabilities of incarceration and the adjusted mean sentences for each racial group in each jurisdiction (see Table 7.4). The estimated probabilities of incarceration are calculated for a "typical" offender (that is, male, 30 years old, convicted of one count of an offense involving cocaine, one prior felony conviction) and take all of the other independent variables included in the analysis into account. They reveal substantial interjurisdictional variation in the likelihood of a prison sentence. They also confirm that race/ethnicity affected the probability of a prison sentence only in Miami.

The data presented in Table 7.4 reveal that the typical drug offender faced much higher odds of imprisonment in Chicago than in Kansas City or Miami. Three of every four offenders, regardless of race, were sentenced to prison in Chicago, compared with only one of every three, again regardless of race, in Kansas City. In Miami, in contrast, the odds of a prison sentence were much lower, particularly for white drug offenders. In this jurisdiction, the typical Hispanic drug offender was twice as likely as the typical white offender to be sentenced to prison.

The authors explained that the low rate of imprisonment in Miami reflects the fact that those convicted of less serious drug offenses normally were sentenced to the Dade County jail rather than to state prison. As shown in Table 7.4, in Miami the odds of incarceration (in either jail or prison) were very similar to the odds of imprisonment in Chicago. When the authors used overall incarceration, rather than imprisonment, they found that the predicted probabilities for African American, Hispanic, and white drug offenders were very similar. As they noted, "In Miami, then, judges appear to take the offender's ethnicity into account in deciding between prison and either jail or probation, but not in deciding between some form of incarceration and probation."[103]

The data presented in Table 7.4 also illustrate the authors' finding that judges in Kansas City imposed much longer sentences on African American than on white drug offenders. The mean sentence for African Americans was 73.11 months, compared with only 58.12 months for white offenders. In Chicago and Miami, the mean sentences imposed on whites were very similar to those imposed on African Americans and Hispanics. There were, however, more substantial differences in the sentences imposed on African American and Hispanic offenders. Hispanics received sentences that were almost 15 months longer than those of African Americans in Miami and over 8 months longer than those of African Americans in Chicago. In all three jurisdictions, one group of offenders received significantly longer sentences—African Americans in Kansas City and Hispanics in Miami and Chicago.

The authors of this study admitted that they were "somewhat puzzled" by their finding that Hispanics were sentenced more harshly than African Americans in Miami and Chicago.[104] They explained that they expected the "moral panic" surrounding drug use, drug distribution, and drug-related crime[105] to produce harsher sentences for both African Americans and Hispanics, who make up the majority of drug offenders in each jurisdiction. According to Spohn and Spears,

> The fact that harsher treatment was reserved for Hispanics in Miami, while unexpected, is not particularly surprising; arguably, the most enduring perception about drug importation and distribution in Miami is that these activities are dominated by Hispanics of various nationalities. This explanation, however, is less convincing with regard to our finding that Hispanics received longer sentences than blacks in Chicago.[106]

Further analysis of the sentences imposed in Chicago revealed that only certain types of Hispanic offenders—those convicted of the most serious drug offenses, convicted of a prior felony, and unemployed at the time of arrest—received longer sentences than African American offenders. The authors stated that this pattern of results suggests that judges in Chicago "may be imposing more severe sentences on offenders characterized as particularly problematic."[107] It suggests that Chicago judges use ethnicity, offense seriousness, prior record, and employment status to define what might be called a "dangerous class" of drug offenders.[108] The Hispanic drug offender who manufactures or sells large quantities of drugs, who is a repeat offender, or who has no legitimate means of financial support may be perceived as particularly dangerous, particularly likely to recidivate.

Sentencing of Drug Offenders in the Federal Courts Albonetti examined sentences imposed on drug offenders under the federal sentencing

Focus on an Issue
Penalties for Crack and Powder Cocaine

Federal sentencing guidelines for drug offenses differentiate between crack and powder cocaine. In fact, the guidelines treat crack cocaine as being 100 times worse than powder cocaine. Possession of 500 grams of powder cocaine, but only 5 grams of crack, triggers a mandatory minimum sentence of 5 years. Critics charge that this policy, although racially neutral on its face, discriminates against African American drug users and sellers, who prefer crack cocaine to powder cocaine. Over 90 percent of the offenders sentenced for crack offenses in federal courts are African American. Those who defend the policy, on the other hand, suggest that it is not racially motivated; as Randall Kennedy (1994, 1997), an African American professor at Harvard Law School, contends, the policy is a sensible response "to the desires of law-abiding people—including the great mass of black communities—for protection against criminals preying on them" (1994, p. 1278).

In 1993, Judge Lyle Strom, the chief judge of the United States District Court in Nebraska, sentenced four African American crack dealers to significantly shorter prison terms than called for under the guidelines. In explanation, Strom wrote, "Members of the African American race are being treated unfairly in receiving substantially longer sentences than Caucasian males who traditionally deal in powder cocaine" (*Omaha World Herald,* April 17, 1993, p. 1).

Strom's decision was overturned by the Eighth Circuit Court of Appeals in 1994. The three-judge panel ruled that even if the guidelines are unfair to African Americans, that is not enough to justify a more lenient sentence than called for under the guidelines. Other federal appellate courts have upheld the 100-to-1 rule, holding that the rule does not violate the equal protection clause of the Fourteenth Amendment (see, for example, *United States v. Thomas,* 900 F.2d 37 [4th Cir. 1990]; *United States v. Frazier,* 981 F.2d 92 [3d Cir. 1992]; and *United States v. Latimore,* 974 F2d 971 [8th Cir. 1992]).

In 1996, the U.S. Supreme Court ruled eight to one that African Americans who allege that they have been singled out for prosecution under the crack cocaine rule must first show that whites in similar circumstances were not prosecuted (*United States v. Armstrong,* 116 S. Ct. 1480 [1996]). The case was brought by five African American defendants from Los Angeles who claimed that prosecutors were systematically steering crack cocaine cases involving African Americans to federal court, where the 100-to-1 rule applied, but steering cases involving whites to state court, where lesser penalties applied. The Court stated that a defendant who claimed that he or she was a victim of selective prosecution "must demonstrate that the federal prosecutorial policy had a discriminatory effect and that it was motivated by a discriminatory purpose."

The U. S. Sentencing Commission has recommended that the penalties for crack and powder cocaine offenses be equalized. In 1995, the Commission recommended that the 100-to-1 ratio be changed to a 1-to-1 ratio. Both Congress and President Clinton rejected this amendment. In May 2002, the Commission "unanimously and firmly" reiterated its earlier position that "the various congressional objectives can be achieved more effectively by decreasing substantially the 100-to-1 drug quantity

(*continued*)

(*continued*)
ratio" (U. S. Sentencing Commission, 2002, p. viii). The Commission recommended increasing the quantity levels that trigger the mandatory minimum penalties for crack cocaine. They recommended that the 5-year mandatory minimum threshold be increased to at least 25 grams and that the 10-year mandatory minimum threshold be increased to at least 250 grams. The Commission also recommended that Congress repeal the mandatory minimum sentence for simple possession of crack cocaine.

The Commission's 2002 report also noted that the majority (85 percent in 2000) of offenders subject to the harsh penalties for drug offenses involving crack cocaine were African American. Although the Commissioners acknowledged that this did not necessarily prove that "the current penalty structure promotes unwarranted disparity based on race," they cautioned that "even the perception of racial disparity [is] problematic because it fosters disrespect for and lack of confidence in the criminal justice system"(p. viii).

---

guidelines for evidence of bias against racial minorities.[109] Although the federal guidelines were designed to reduce judicial discretion in sentencing and, as a result, to eliminate "unwarranted sentencing disparity among defendants with similar records who had been found guilty of similar criminal conduct,"[110] both judges and prosecutors retain some discretion. Albonetti was particularly interested in determining the degree to which prosecutorial charging and plea bargaining decisions work to the disadvantage of racial minorities. As she noted, "Under the federal guidelines, a prosecuting attorney can circumvent the guideline-defined sentence through charging, guilty plea negotiations, and motions for a sentence that is a departure from the guideline sentence."[111]

Albonetti used 1991–1992 data on drug offenders sentenced in federal district courts to test a number of hypotheses concerning the relationship between the offender's race/ethnicity, the prosecutor's "process-related decisions,"[112] and sentence severity. Her first hypothesis was that African American and Hispanic offenders will be sentenced more harshly than similarly situated white offenders. Her second hypothesis was that African American and Hispanic offenders "will receive less benefit"[113] from pleading guilty and from guideline departures[114] than will white offenders. White offenders, in other words, will receive greater sentence reductions than either African American or Hispanic offenders if they plead guilty or if the judge accepts the prosecutor's motion for a departure from the guidelines.

In support of her first hypothesis, Albonetti found that both African American and Hispanic drug offenders received more severe sentences than white drug offenders. These results were obtained after all of the legally relevant variables (offense severity, criminal history, type of drug offense, and number of counts) and process-related factors (whether the defendant pled guilty and whether the defendant's sentence was a departure from the guidelines) were taken into consideration.

Regarding her second hypothesis, Albonetti found that pleading guilty produced a similar reduction in sentence severity for all three groups of offenders.

The effect of a guideline departure varied among the three groups, with whites receiving a significantly greater benefit than either African Americans or Hispanics. Among white defendants, a guideline departure produced a 23 percent reduction in the probability of incarceration; the comparable figures for African Americans and Hispanics were 13 percent and 14 percent, respectively. According to the author, "These findings strongly suggest that the mechanism by which the federal guidelines permit the exercise of discretion operates to the disadvantage of minority defendants."[115]

Albonetti also found that white offenders received a larger sentence reduction than African American or Hispanic offenders as a result of being convicted for possession of drugs rather than drug trafficking, and that whites benefited more from educational achievements than did racial minorities. She concluded that the pattern of results found in her study suggests that "the federal sentencing guidelines have not eliminated sentence disparity linked to defendant characteristics for defendants convicted of drug offenses in 1991–92."[116] (As detailed in the Focus on an Issue, there is considerable controversy regarding the sentences mandated for offenses involving crack and powder cocaine.)

SENTENCING REFORM: THE QUEST FOR A "JUST" PUNISHMENT SYSTEM

Concerns about disparity, discrimination, and unfairness in sentencing led to a "remarkable burst of reform"[117] that began in the mid-1970s and continues today. The initial focus of reform efforts was the indeterminate sentence, in which the judge imposed a minimum and maximum sentence and the parole board determined the date of release. The parole board's determination of when the offender should be released rested on its judgment of whether the offender had been rehabilitated or had served enough time for the particular crime. Under indeterminate sentencing, sentences were tailored to the individual offender, and discretion was distributed both to the criminal justice officials who determined the sentence and to corrections officials and the parole board. The result of this process was "a system of sentencing in which there was little understanding or predictability as to who would be imprisoned and for how long."[118]

Both liberal and conservative reformers challenged the principles underlying the indeterminate sentence and called for changes designed to curb discretion, reduce disparity and discrimination, and achieve proportionality and parsimony in sentencing. Liberals and civil rights activists argued that indeterminate sentencing was arbitrary and capricious and therefore violated defendants' rights to equal protection and due process of law.[119] They charged that indeterminate sentences were used to incapacitate those who could not be rehabilitated and that offenders' uncertainty about their date of release contributed to prison unrest. Liberal critics were also apprehensive about the potential for racial bias under indeterminate sentencing schemes. They asserted that "racial discrimination in the criminal justice system was epidemic, that judges, parole boards, and corrections officials could not be trusted, and that tight controls on officials' discretion offered the only way to limit racial disparities."[120]

Political conservatives, on the other hand, argued that the emphasis on rehabilitation too often resulted in excessively lenient treatment of offenders who had committed serious crimes or had serious criminal histories.[121] They also charged that sentences that were not linked to crime seriousness and offender culpability were unjust,[122] and they championed sentencing reforms designed to establish and enforce more punitive sentencing standards. Their arguments were bolstered by research findings demonstrating that most correctional programs designed to rehabilitate offenders and reduce recidivism were ineffective.[123]

After a few initial "missteps," in which jurisdictions attempted to *eliminate* discretion altogether through flat-time sentencing,[124] states and the federal government adopted structured sentencing proposals designed to *control* the discretion of sentencing judges. A number of states adopted determinate sentencing policies that offered judges a limited number of sentencing options and included enhancements for use of a weapon, presence of a prior criminal record, or infliction of serious injury. Other states and the federal government adopted sentence guidelines that incorporated crime seriousness and prior criminal record into a sentencing "grid" that judges were to use in determining the appropriate sentence. Other reforms enacted at both the federal and state levels included mandatory minimum penalties for certain types of offenses (especially drug and weapons offenses), "three-strikes-and-you're-out" laws that mandated long prison sentences for repeat offenders, and truth-in-sentencing statutes that required offenders to serve a larger portion of the sentence before being released.

This process of experimentation and reform revolutionized sentencing in the United States. Thirty years ago every state and the federal government had an indeterminate sentencing system, and "the word 'sentencing' generally signified a slightly mysterious process which . . . involved individualized decisions that judges were uniquely qualified to make."[125] The situation today is much more complex. Sentencing policies and practices vary considerably on a number of dimensions, and there is no longer anything that can be described as the "American" approach.

The reforms enacted during the past 30 years clearly were *designed* to ameliorate discrimination in sentencing. Sentencing guidelines explicitly prohibit consideration of the offender's race, gender, or social class; they shift the focus of sentencing away from the personal characteristics of the offender to the nature and seriousness of the offense and the culpability of the offender. Mandatory minimum sentence statutes and three-strikes laws are applicable to *all* offenders—regardless of race, gender, or social class—whose offense conduct and prior record qualify them for these sentence enhancements. If these laws are applied as intended, legally irrelevant offender characteristics should not affect sentencing decisions in jurisdictions with sentencing guidelines; likewise, offender characteristics should not affect the application of mandatory minimum penalties or three-strikes provisions.

Focus on an Issue
Does It Make a Difference? A Comparison of the Sentencing Decisions of African American, Hispanic, and White Judges

Historically, most state and federal judges have been white males. Although the nation's first African American judge was appointed in 1852, by the mid-1950s there were only a handful of African Americans presiding over state or federal courts. During the 1960s and 1970s, civil rights leaders lobbied for increased representation of African Americans at all levels of government, including the courts. By 1989, there were nearly 500 African American judges on the bench nationwide.

Those who champion the appointment of racial minorities argue that African American and Hispanic judges could make a difference. They contend that increasing the number of racial minorities on state and federal courts will alter the character of justice and the outcomes of the criminal justice system. Because the life histories and experiences of African Americans and Hispanics differ dramatically from those of whites, the beliefs and attitudes they bring to the bench will also differ. Justice A. Leon Higginbotham Jr., an African American who retired from the U.S. Court of Appeals for the Third Circuit in 1993, wrote, "The advantage of pluralism is that it brings a multitude of different experiences to the judicial process" (Washington, 1994, p. 11). More to the point, he stated that "someone who has been a victim of racial injustice has greater sensitivity of the court's making sure that racism is not perpetrated, even inadvertently" (pp. 11–12). Judge George Crockett's assessment of the role of the black judge was even more pointed: "I think a black judge . . . has got to be a reformist—he cannot be a member of the club. The

whole purpose of selecting him is that the people are dissatisfied with the status quo and they want him to shake it up, and his role is to shake it up" (Crockett, 1984, p. 393).

Assuming that African American judges agree with Judge Crockett's assertion that their role is to "shake it up," how would this affect their behavior on the bench? One possibility is that African American (and Hispanic) judges might attempt to stop—or at least slow—the flow of young African American (and Hispanic) men into state and federal prisons. If African American judges view the disproportionately high number of young African American males incarcerated in state and federal prisons as a symptom of racial discrimination, they might be more willing than white judges to experiment with alternatives to incarceration for offenders convicted of nonviolent drug and property crimes. Welch, Combs, and Gruhl (1988) make an analogous argument. Noting that African American judges tend to view themselves as liberal rather than conservative, they speculate that African American judges might be "more sympathetic to criminal defendants than white judges are, since liberal views are associated with support for the underdog and the poor, which defendants disproportionately are" (p. 127). Other scholars similarly suggest that increasing the number of African American judges would reduce racism in the criminal justice system and produce more equitable treatment of African American and white defendants (Crockett, 1984; Welch et al., 1988).

Statements made by African Amer-
(continued)

(*continued*)

ican judges suggest that they might bring a unique perspective to the courts. Smith's (1983) survey of African American judges throughout the United States revealed that these judges believed that their presence on the bench reduced racial discrimination and promoted equality of justice. A Philadelphia judge, for instance, stated that the mere presence of African American judges "has done more than anything I know to reduce police brutality and to reduce illegal arrests and things of that sort" (cited in Smith, 1983, p. 80). Nearly half of the respondents stated that African American judges should exercise their powers to protect the rights of African American defendants. One Michigan judge remarked that African American judges should state that "everybody's going to get equal justice," by saying that "you're going to give blacks something that they haven't been getting in the past" (cited in Smith, 1983, p. 81).

DECISION MAKING BY AFRICAN AMERICAN AND WHITE FEDERAL JUDGES

As more African Americans have been appointed or elected to state and federal trial courts, it has become possible to compare their decisions with those of white judges. Two studies examined the consequences of the affirmative action policies of President Carter, who appointed a record number of African Americans to the federal courts. (Carter appointed 258 judges to the federal district courts and courts of appeals; 37 [14 percent] of those appointed were African Americans. In contrast, only 7 of the 379 [1.8 percent] persons appointed to the federal bench by President Reagan were African American.)

Walker and Barrow (1985) compared decisions handed down by the Af-

rican American and white district court judges appointed by President Carter. They asked, "Did it make a difference that President Carter appointed unprecedented numbers of women and minorities to the bench as opposed to filling vacancies with traditional white, male candidates?" (pp. 613–614). The authors found no differences in criminal cases or in four other types of cases. In criminal cases, African American judges ruled in favor of the defense 50 percent of the time; white judges ruled in favor of the defense 48 percent of the time. These similarities led the authors to conclude that African American judges do not view themselves as advocates for the disadvantaged or see themselves as especially sympathetic to the policy goals of minorities.

Gottschall (1983) examined decisions in the U.S. Courts of Appeals in 1979 and 1981. He compared the decisions of African American and white judges in terms of "attitudinal liberalism," which he defined as "a relative tendency to vote in favor of the legal claims of the criminally accused and prisoners in criminal and prisoner's rights cases and in favor of the legal claims of women and racial minorities in sex and race discrimination cases" (p. 168).

In contrast to Walker and Barrow, Gottschall found that the judge's race had a "dramatic impact" on voting in cases involving the rights of criminal defendants and prisoners. African American male judges voted to support the legal claims of defendants and prisoners 79 percent of the time, compared to only 53 percent for white male judges. African American judges, however, did not vote more liberally than white judges in race or sex discrimination cases. Gottschall concluded that "affirmative action for blacks *does* appear to influence voting on the courts of appeals in cases involving the rights of the accused and prisoners, where black voting is markedly more liberal than is that of whites" (p. 173).

DECISION MAKING BY AFRICAN AMERICAN AND WHITE STATE JUDGES

Research comparing the sentencing decisions of African American and white state court judges has also yielded mixed results. Most researchers have found few differences and have concluded that the race of the judge is not a strong predictor of sentence severity (Engle, 1971; Spohn, 1990; Uhlman, 1978). Two early studies, for example, found few differences in the sentencing behavior of African American and white judges. Engle (1971) analyzed Philadelphia judges' sentencing decisions and found that although the judge's race had a statistically significant effect, nine other variables were stronger predictors of sentence outcomes. He concluded that the race of the judge exerted "a very minor influence" overall (pp. 226–227). Uhlman's (1979) study of convicting and sentencing decisions in "Metro City" reached a similar conclusion. African American judges imposed somewhat harsher sentences than white judges, but the differences were relatively small. And both African American and white judges imposed harsher sentences on African American defendants than on white defendants. Moreover, there was more "behavioral diversity" among the African American judges than between African American and white judges. Some of the African American judges imposed substantially harsher sentences than the average sentence imposed by all judges, whereas other African American judges imposed significantly more lenient sentences. These findings led Uhlman to conclude

that "black and white judges differ little in determining both guilt and the punishment a defendant 'deserves' for committing a crime in Metro City" (p. 71).

A later study of sentencing decisions in Metro City reached a different conclusion. Welch et al. (1988) found that African American judges were more likely than white judges to send white defendants to prison. Further analysis led them to conclude that this difference reflected African American judges' tendency to incarcerate African American and white defendants at about the same rate and white judges' tendency to incarcerate African American defendants more often than white defendants. They also found, however, that African American judges, but not white judges, favored defendants of their own race when determining the length of the prison sentence. These results led them to conclude that "black judges provide more than symbolic representation" (p. 134). According to these authors, "To the extent that they equalize the criminal justice system's treatment of black and white defendants, as they seem to for the crucial decision to incarcerate or not, [black judges] thwart discrimination against black defendants. In fact, the quality of justice received by both black and white defendants may be improved" (p. 134).

A study of sentencing decisions by African American and white judges on the Cook County (Chicago) Circuit Court reached a similar conclusion (Spears, 1999). Spears found that African American judges sentenced white, African American, and Hispanic offenders to prison at about the same rate, whereas white judges sentenced both African American and Hispanic offenders to prison at a significantly higher rate than white offenders. In fact, compared to white offenders sentenced by white judges, African American of

(continued)

(*continued*)

fenders sentenced by white judges had a 13 percent greater probability of imprisonment; for Hispanic offenders sentenced by white judges, the difference was 15 percent. Like the Metro City study, this study found that white judges sentenced racial minorities more harshly than whites and concluded that having African American judges on the bench "does provide more equitable justice" (p. 135).

Spohn's (1990) analysis of the sentences imposed on offenders convicted of violent felonies in Detroit Recorder's Court produced strikingly different results and led to very different conclusions. Like Engle and Uhlman, Spohn uncovered few meaningful differences between African American and white judges. She found that African American judges were somewhat more likely than white judges to sentence offenders to prison, but that judicial race had no effect on the length of sentence. Like Engle, she concluded that "the effect of judicial race, even where significant, was clearly overshadowed by the effect of the other independent variables" (p. 1206). Spohn also tested for interaction between the race of the judge, the race of the offender, and the race of the victim. She attempted to determine, first, if African American and white judges treated African American and white offenders differently and, second, if African American and white judges imposed different sentences on African American offenders who victimized other African Americans, African American offenders who victimized whites, white offenders who victimized other whites, and white offenders who victimized African Americans.

Spohn's research highlighted the similarities in the sentences imposed by African American and white judges. African American judges incarcerated

72.9 percent of African American offenders, whereas white judges incarcerated 74.2 percent, a difference of fewer than 2 percentage points. The adjusted figures for white offenders were 65.3 percent (African American judges) and 66.5 percent (white judges), again a difference of fewer than 2 percentage points. More important, these data reveal that both African American and white judges sentenced African American defendants more harshly than white defendants. For both African American and white judges, the adjusted incarceration rates for African American offenders were 7 percentage points higher than for white offenders. Moreover, African American judges sentenced offenders to prison at about the same rate as white judges, regardless of the racial makeup of the offender–victim pair. These findings led Spohn to conclude that there was "remarkable similarity" in the sentencing decisions of African American and white judges (p. 1211). They also led her to question the assumption that discrimination against African American defendants reflects prejudicial or racist attitudes on the part of white criminal justice officials. As she noted, "Contrary to expectations, both black and white judges in Detroit imposed harsher sentences on black offenders. Harsher sentencing of black offenders, in other words, cannot be attributed solely to discrimination by white judges" (pp. 1212–1213). Spohn suggested that her findings contradicted the widely held assumption that African Americans do not discriminate against other African Americans, as well as conventional wisdom about the role of African American judges. She concluded "that we should be considerably less sanguine in predicting that discrimination against black defendants will decline as the proportion of black judges increases" (p. 1213).

To explain her unexpected finding that both African American and white judges sentenced African American defendants more harshly than white defendants, Spohn suggested that African American and white judges might perceive African American offenders as more threatening and more dangerous than white offenders. Alternatively, she speculated that at least some of the discriminatory treatment of African American offenders might be due to concern for the welfare of African American victims. African American judges "might see themselves not as representatives of black defendants but as advocates for black victims. This, coupled with the fact that black judges might see themselves as potential victims of black-on-black crime, could help explain the harsher sentences imposed on black offenders by black judges" (p. 1214).

Spohn acknowledged that because we do not know with any degree of certainty what goes through a judge's mind during the sentencing process, these explanations were highly speculative. As she explained, "We cannot know precisely how the race of the offender is factored into the sentencing equation. Although the data reveal that both black and white judges sentence black offenders more harshly than white offenders, the data do not tell us *why* this occurs" (p. 1214).

DECISION MAKING BY HISPANIC AND WHITE STATE JUDGES

Although most research examining the effect of judicial characteristics on sentencing has focused on the race of the sentencing judge, there is one study that compares the sentencing decisions of white and Hispanic judges in two South-

western jurisdictions (Holmes, Hosch, Daudistel, Perez, & Graves, 1993). Holmes and his colleagues found that Hispanic judges sentenced white and Hispanic offenders similarly, whereas white judges sentenced Hispanics more harshly than whites. In fact, the sentences imposed on Hispanic offenders by Hispanic and white judges were very similar to the sentences imposed by Hispanic judges on white offenders. What was different, according to these researchers, was that white judges sentenced white offenders more leniently. Thus, "Anglo judges are not so much discriminating against Hispanic defendants as they are favoring members of their ethnic groups" (p. 502).

REASONS FOR SIMILARITIES IN DECISION MAKING

Although there is some evidence that African American and Hispanic judges sentence racial minorities and whites similarly, whereas white judges give preferential treatment to white offenders, the bulk of the evidence suggests that judicial race/ethnicity makes very little difference. The fact that African American, Hispanic, and white judges decide cases similarly is not particularly surprising. Although this conclusion challenges widely held presumptions about the role of African American and Hispanic criminal justice officials, it is not at odds with the results of other studies comparing African American and white decision makers. As noted in Chapter 4, studies have documented similarities in the behavior of African American and white police officers.

Similarities in judicial decision making can be attributed in part to the judicial recruitment process, which produces a more or less homogeneous judi-

(continued)

(*continued*)
ciary. Most judges recruited to state courts are middle or upper class and were born and attended law school in the state in which they serve. African American and white judges apparently even share similar background characteristics. Studies indicate that "both the black and white benches appear to have been carefully chosen from the establishment center of the legal profession" (Uhlman, 1978, p. 893). The judicial recruitment process, in other words, may screen out candidates with unconventional views.

These similarities are reinforced by the judicial socialization process, which produces a subculture of justice and encourages judges to adhere to prevailing norms, practices, and precedents. They are also reinforced by the courtroom workgroup—judges, prosecutors, and defense attorneys who work together day after day to process cases as efficiently as possible. Even unconventional or maverick judges may be forced to conform. As one African American jurist noted, "No matter how 'liberal' black judges may believe themselves to be, the law remains essentially a conservative doctrine, and those who practice it conform" (Wright, 1973, pp. 22–23).

Race/Ethnicity and the Federal Sentencing Guidelines

The findings of a comprehensive review of recent federal and state sentencing research suggests that the sentencing reforms have not achieved their goal of eliminating unwarranted racial disparity.[126] Spohn reviewed eight methodologically sophisticated studies of sentences imposed under the federal sentencing guidelines.[127] She found that each of these studies revealed that racial minorities were sentenced more harshly than whites, either for all offenses or for some types of offenses. Moreover, racial disparities were not confined to the decision to incarcerate or not and the length of the prison sentence. Compared to whites, African Americans and Hispanics were less likely to be offered a sentence reduction for acceptance of responsibility[128] or for providing substantial assistance in the prosecution of another offender.[129] Among those who did receive a departure for substantial assistance, the sentence discount that African Americans and Hispanics received was less than the discount that whites received.[130] African Americans and Hispanics were more likely than whites to be sentenced at or above the minimum sentence indicated by applicable mandatory minimum sentencing provisions.[131]

The fact that significant racial differences were found for each of the various alternative measures of sentence severity is interesting. Although the federal sentencing guidelines severely constrain judges' discretion in deciding between prison and probation and in determining the length of the sentence, they place only minimal restrictions on the ability of judges (and prosecutors) to reduce sentences for substantial assistance or acceptance of responsibility. Mandatory minimum sentences can also be avoided through charge manipulation. Albonetti notes that "these process-related decisions offer potential avenues through which prosecutors [and judges] can circumvent guideline-defined sentence outcomes."[132] The validity of this assertion is confirmed by the fact that each of the six federal-level studies that examined an alternative measure of sentence severity found evidence of direct discrimination against both African American and Hispanic offenders.

These findings are confirmed by a recent study of federal sentencing decisions.[133] Using data on male offenders convicted of drug and nondrug offenses from 1993 to 1996, Steffensmeier and Demuth compared sentence outcomes for four groups of offenders: whites, African Americans, white Hispanics, and African American Hispanics. As shown in Part A of Table 7.5, which presents descriptive data on sentence outcomes, the likelihood of incarceration was substantially longer and the mean prison sentence significantly shorter for white offenders than for racial minorities. Whites were also more likely than racial minorities to receive a downward departure and a departure for providing substantial assistance.

These differences did not disappear when the authors controlled for offense seriousness, prior criminal record, and other relevant predictors of sentence severity. As shown in Part B of Table 7.5, which presents the differences in the likelihood of incarceration and the mean prison sentence for racial minorities compared to whites, racial minorities were sentenced more harshly than whites. The differences were particularly pronounced for drug offenses. African American Hispanics were 20 percent more likely than whites to be sentenced to prison, and their sentences averaged 23 months longer than those imposed on whites. Similarly, white Hispanics faced a 16 percent greater likelihood of incarceration and 19 months longer in prison than whites. African Americans were 11 percent more likely than whites to be sentenced to prison; those who were incarcerated received sentences that averaged 16 months longer than those imposed on whites.[134]

Further analysis revealed that a considerable amount of the differential treatment of Hispanics was due to the fact that they were less likely than whites to receive either downward departures or substantial assistance departures. These findings led Steffensmeier and Demuth to conclude that "the ethnic disparities found in our analysis are real and meaningful—they support our theoretical hypotheses and they also raise some concerns about the equal application of the law and the wherewithal of the sentencing guidelines in reducing sentencing disparities of any kind."[135]

Race/Ethnicity and State Sentencing Reforms

Evidence concerning the impact of state sentencing reforms is inconsistent. Petersilia's analysis of California's determinate sentencing system found that African Americans and Hispanics were more likely than whites to be sentenced to prison; racial minorities who were incarcerated also received longer sentences and served a longer time in prison.[136] An examination of sentences imposed by judges in Minnesota before and after the implementation of guidelines showed that the impact of race and socioeconomic status declined but did not disappear.[137] The authors also found that race affected sentencing indirectly through

Table 7.5 Race/Ethnicity and Sentence Outcomes: Male Offenders in U.S. District Courts, 1993–1996

A. Descriptive Data

	NONDRUG OFFENSES		HISPANIC		DRUG OFFENSES		HISPANIC	
	White	African American	White	African American	White	African American	White	African American
Percentage imprisoned	67.1	78.1	73.2	75.2	88.1	96.7	95.7	97.2
Mean sentence (months)	44.0	70.6	53.4	77.2	70.5	122.6	78.2	95.3
Downward departure (%)	9.0	5.4	7.7	4.0	5.4	4.8	6.8	6.0
Substantial assistance departure (%)	114.1	10.4	12.8	6.7	38.0	31.2	28.0	26.1

B. Differences in the Probability of Incarceration and Mean Prison Sentence

	NONDRUG OFFENSES		HISPANIC		DRUG OFFENSES		HISPANIC	
	White	African American	White	African American	White	African American	White	African American
Probability of incarceration		+5%	+7%	+6%		+11%	+16%	+20%
Mean prison sentence (difference in months)		+1	+4	+16		+16	+19	+23

SOURCE: Darrell Steffensmeier and Stephen Demuth, "Ethnicity and Sentencing Outcomes in U.S. Federal Courts: Who Is Punished More Harshly?" *American Sociological Review* 65 (2000).

its effect on prior criminal record and use of a weapon. They concluded that disparities under the guidelines "are slightly more subtle, but no less real."[138] Dixon's study of sentencing under the Minnesota guidelines, on the other hand, found that offender race was unrelated to sentence severity.[139]

A series of studies examining sentencing under Pennsylvania's guidelines demonstrates the subtle ways in which race/ethnicity can affect sentence outcomes.[140] The sentencing guidelines found in Pennsylvania are "looser" than those found in Minnesota or in the federal system; judges in Pennsylvania have considerably more discretion and thus more opportunities to consider extralegal factors than do judges in other jurisdictions.

One study used Pennsylvania data to explore the effect of race/ethnicity on the likelihood that the judge would depart from the guidelines.[141] Kramer and Ulmer examined both dispositional departures, in which the guidelines call for incarceration but the judge chooses an alternative to incarceration, and durational departures, in which the judge imposes a jail or prison term that is longer or shorter than the term specified by the guidelines. They found that African American offenders were less likely than white offenders to receive a dispositional departure; the downward durational departures given to African Americans were also smaller than those given to whites. The authors found similar results when they compared the sentences imposed on Hispanic and white offenders.

When Kramer and Ulmer examined the reasons given by judges for departures, they found evidence suggesting that race-linked stereotypes affected these decisions. The most common reasons given for departures were that the defendant expressed remorse or appeared to be a good candidate for rehabilitation, the defendant pled guilty, the defendant was caring for dependents, the defendant was employed, and the defendant's prior record was less serious than his or her criminal history score suggested. As the authors noted, "When these reasons are given by judges, they are given more often for women, whites, and (obviously) those who pleaded guilty."[142]

In discussing the ways in which these reasons reflected race-linked stereotypes, the authors state:

Although these judges do not explicitly mention factors such as race or gender, it is plausible that the process of "sizing up" a defendant's "character and attitude" in terms of whether he or she is a candidate for a departure below guidelines may involve the use of race and gender stereotypes and the behavioral expectations they mobilize.[143]

Kramer and Ulmer conclude that "departures below guidelines are an important locus of race and gender differences in sentencing."[144]

Have Sentencing Guidelines Increased the Likelihood of Racial Discrimination?

Michael Tonry suggested that sentence guidelines actually may have exacerbated the problem of racial disparity in sentencing. His critique of sentence guidelines focuses on the prohibition against consideration of offenders' "spe-

---

BOX 7.6   The Illusion of Like-Situated Offenders

Michael Tonry suggested that those who call for proportionality in punishment mistakenly assume that it is possible to place individuals into a manageable number of categories composed of "like-situated offenders." He suggested that this is an "illusion," as "neither offenders nor punishments come in standard cases."

> Consider a minority offender charged with theft who grew up in a single-parent, welfare-supported household, who has several siblings in prison, and who was formerly drug-dependent, but who has been living in a common-law marriage for five years, has two children whom he supports, and who has worked steadily for three years at a service station—first as an attendant, then an assistant mechanic, and now a mechanic. None of these personal characteristics was supposed to influence the sentencing decision, and certainly not to justify imposing a noncusto-

dial sentence on a presumed prison-bound offender.

Tonry also objected to the fact that sentence guidelines do not take account of the "collateral effects" of punishment.

> Incarceration for a drug crime for a woman raising children by herself may result in the breakup of her family and the placement of her children in foster homes or institutions or in homes of relatives who will not be responsible care providers. Incarceration of an employed father and husband may mean loss of the family's income and car, perhaps the breakup of a marriage.

According to Tonry, "To ignore that collateral effects of punishments vary widely among seemingly like-situated offenders is to ignore things that most people find important."

SOURCE: Michael Tonry, *Malign Neglect* (New York: Oxford University Press, 1995), pp. 155–157.

---

cial circumstances."[145] Under sentence guidelines, the harshness of the sentence depends on the severity of the offense and the offender's prior criminal record; judges are not supposed to consider factors such as the offender's employment status, marital status, family situation, or education.

Although Tonry acknowledged that these restrictions were designed to prevent unduly lenient sentences for affluent offenders and unduly harsh sentences for poor offenders, he argued that in reality they have harmed "disadvantaged and minority offenders, especially those who have to some degree overcome dismal life chances."[146] Tonry characterized these restrictions as "mistakes":

> They may have been necessary mistakes that showed us how to protect against aberrantly severe penalties and exposed the injustices that result when sentencing shifts its focus from the offender to the offense. Mistakes they were, however, and we now know how to do better.[147]

"Doing better," according to Tonry, means allowing judges to consider factors other than the offender's crime and prior criminal record. Tonry argued that "neither offenders nor punishments come in standard cases"[148] and stated that a just punishment system would require judges to consider the offender's personal circumstances, as well as the effects of punishment on the offender and the offender's family (see Box 7.6). He asserted that a just system would allow judges to mitigate sentences for disadvantaged inner-city youth, who face greater temptations to commit crimes than do affluent suburban youth. It would also allow judges to mitigate sentences for "offenders from deprived backgrounds who have achieved some personal successes."[149] The problem is that current federal and state sentencing guidelines typically do not allow judges to make these distinctions.

It thus appears that reformers' hopes for determinate sentencing and sentencing guidelines have not been fully realized. Although overt discrimination against African Americans is less likely, discrimination in sentencing has not disappeared. As Zatz has concluded, the sentencing procedures currently being used "are less blatantly biased than were their predecessors, and are cloaked with the legitimacy accruing from formalized rules. . . . Differential processing and treatment is now veiled by legitimacy, but it is a legitimacy in which certain biases have become rationalized and institutionalized."[150]

CONCLUSION

Despite dozens of studies investigating the relationship between defendant race and sentence severity, a definitive answer to the question "Are racial minorities sentenced more harshly than whites?" remains elusive. Although a number of studies have uncovered evidence of racial discrimination in sentencing, others have found that there are no significant racial differences.

The failure of research to produce uniform findings of racial discrimination in sentencing has led to conflicting conclusions. Some researchers assert that racial discrimination in sentencing has declined over time and contend that the predictive power of race, once relevant legal factors are taken into account, is quite low. Other researchers claim that discrimination has not declined or disappeared but simply has become more subtle and difficult to detect. These researchers argue that discrimination against racial minorities is not universal but is confined to certain types of cases, settings, and defendants.

We assert that the latter explanation is more convincing. We suggest that although the sentencing process in most jurisdictions today is not characterized by overt or systematic racism, racial discrimination in sentencing has not been eliminated. We argue that sentencing decisions in the 1990s reflect *contextual discrimination*. Judges in some jurisdictions continue to impose harsher sentences on racial minorities who murder or rape whites and more lenient sentences on racial minorities who victimize members of their own racial or ethnic group. Judges in some jurisdictions continue to impose racially biased sentences in less serious cases; in these "borderline cases," racial minorities get prison, and whites get probation. In jurisdictions with sentencing guidelines, judges depart from the presumptive sentence less often when the offender is African American or Hispanic than when the offender is white. Judges, in other words, continue to take race into account, either explicitly or implicitly, when determining the appropriate sentence.

It thus appears that although flagrant racism in sentencing has been eliminated, equality under the law has not been achieved. Today, whites who commit crimes against racial minorities are not beyond the reach of the criminal justice system, African Americans suspected of crimes against whites do not receive "justice" at the hands of white lynch mobs, and racial minorities who victimize other racial minorities are not immune from punishment. Despite these significant changes, inequities persist. Racial minorities who find themselves in the arms of the law continue to suffer discrimination in sentencing.

DISCUSSION QUESTIONS

1. Why is evidence of racial disparity in sentencing not necessarily evidence of racial discrimination in sentencing? What are the alternative explanations?

2. Some researchers argue that racial stereotypes affect the ways in which decision makers, including criminal justice officials, evaluate the behavior of racial minorities. What are the stereotypes associated with African Americans? Hispanics? Native Americans? Asian Americans? How might these stereotypes affect judges' sentencing decisions?

3. Do you agree or disagree with the argument (see Box 7.2) that crime seriousness and prior criminal record are not legally relevant variables?

4. Based on Spohn's (2000) review of research on race and sentencing, "Thirty Years of Sentencing Reform: A Quest for a Racially Neutral Sentencing Process," how would you answer the question, when does race matter?

5. Research reveals that young, unemployed African American and Hispanic males pay a higher punishment penalty than other types of offenders. What accounts for this?

6. Spohn and Spears's study of sentencing decisions in sexual assault cases revealed that judges imposed the harshest sentences on African Americans who sexually assaulted whites (strangers or nonstrangers) and on African Americans who sexually assaulted African American strangers. They imposed much more lenient sentences on African Americans who sexually assaulted African American friends, relatives, and acquaintances and on whites who victimized others (strangers or nonstrangers). How would you explain this pattern of results?

7. The federal sentencing guidelines currently mandate a 5-year minimum prison sentence for possession of 5 grams of crack cocaine or 500 grams of powder cocaine. Is this policy racially biased? Should the 100-to-1 ratio be reduced? Eliminated?

8. Those who champion the appointment/election of racial minorities to the bench argue that African American and Hispanic judges could make a difference. Why? Does research comparing the sentencing decisions of white judges to those of African American or Hispanic judges confirm or refute this assumption?

9. The sentencing reforms adopted during the past three decades were designed to structure discretion and eliminate unwarranted disparity in sentence outcomes. Has this goal been achieved?

NOTES

1. Marc Mauer, *Young Black Men and the Criminal Justice System: A Growing National Problem* (Washington, DC: The Sentencing Project, 1990).

2. Marc Mauer and Tracy Huling, *Young Black Americans and the Criminal Justice System: Five Years Later* (Washington, DC: The Sentencing Project, 1995).

3. Ibid., p. 2.

4. Alfred Blumstein, Jacqueline Cohen, Susan E. Martin, and Michael Tonry, *Research on Sentencing: The Search for Reform*, Vol. 1 (Washington, DC: National Academy Press, 1983), p. 13.

5. Michael Tonry, *Malign Neglect: Race, Crime, and Punishment in America* (New York: Oxford University Press, 1995), p. 49.

6. Bureau of Justice Statistics, *Prison and Jail Inmates at Midyear 2001* (Washington, DC: U.S. Department of Justice, 2002), table 15.

7. Douglas C. McDonald and Kenneth E. Carlson, *Sentencing in the Federal Courts: Does Race Matter?* (Washington, DC: U.S. Department of Justice, 1993).

8. Paula Kautt and Cassia Spohn, "Cracking Down on Black Drug Offenders? Testing for Interactions among Offenders' Race, Drug Type, and Sentencing Strategy in Federal Drug Sentences," *Justice Quarterly* 19 (2002): 2–35.

9. Bureau of Justice Statistics, *State Court Sentencing of Convicted Felons, 1996* (Washington, DC: U.S. Department of Justice, 2000).

10. Cassia Spohn and Miriam DeLone, "When Does Race Matter? An Analysis of the Conditions under Which Race Affects Sentence Severity," *Sociology of Crime, Law, and Deviance* 2 (2000): 3–37.

11. Marjorie Zatz, "The Changing Forms of Racial/Ethnic Biases in Sentencing," *Journal of Research in Crime and Delinquency* 25 (1987): 69.

12. Thorsten Sellin, "Race Prejudice in the Administration of Justice," *American Journal of Sociology* 41 (1935): 217.

13. John Hagan, "Extra-legal Attributes and Criminal Sentencing: An Assessment of a Sociological Viewpoint," *Law & Society Review* 8 (1974): 357–383; Gary Kleck, "Racial Discrimination in Sentencing: A Critical Evaluation of the Evidence with Additional Evidence on the Death Penalty," *American Sociology Review* 43 (1981): 783–805.

14. John Hagan and Kristin Bumiller, "Making Sense of Sentencing: A Review and Critique of Sentencing Research," in *Research on Sentencing: The Search for Reform,* ed. Alfred Blumstein, Jacqueline Cohen, Susan Martin, and Michael Tonry (Washington, DC: National Academy Press, 1983).

15. Blumstein et al. *Research on Sentencing,* p. 93.

16. Ibid.

17. Zatz, "The Changing Forms of Racial/Ethnic Biases in Sentencing."

18. Ibid., p. 87.

19. Theodore G. Chiricos and Charles Crawford, "Race and Imprisonment: A Contextual Assessment of the Evidence," in *Ethnicity, Race, and Crime: Perspectives across Time and Place,* ed. Darnell F. Hawkins (Albany: State University of New York Press, 1995).

20. Ibid., p. 282.

21. Ibid., p. 300.

22. Ibid.

23. Cassia Spohn, "Thirty Years of Sentencing Reform: A Quest for a Racially Neutral Sentencing Process" in *Policies, Processes, and Decisions of the Criminal Justice System,* vol. 3, *Criminal Justice 2000* (Washington, DC: U.S. Department of Justice, 2000).

24. Hagan and Bumiller, "Making Sense of Sentencing," p. 21.

25. Spohn, "Thirty Years of Sentencing Reform," pp. 455–456.

26. Ibid., p. 458.

27. Ibid., pp. 460–461.

28. Ibid., pp. 466–467.

29. Ibid., p. 469.

30. Ibid., p. 461.

31. Ibid., pp. 469–473.

32. Blumstein et al., *Research on Sentencing,* vol. 1, p. 93.

33. Darnell F. Hawkins, "Beyond Anomalies: Rethinking the Conflict Perspective on Race and Criminal Punishment," *Social Forces* 65 (1987): 719–745.

34. Ibid., p. 724.

35. Richard Quinney, *The Social Reality of Crime* (Boston: Little, Brown, 1970), p. 18.

36. Hawkins, "Beyond Anomalies," p. 736.

37. Ruth Peterson and John Hagan, "Changing Conceptions of Race: Toward an Account of Anomalous Findings in Sentencing Research," *American Sociological Review* 49 (1984): 57.

38. Hawkins, "Beyond Anomalies."

39. Peterson and Hagan, "Changing Conceptions of Race," p. 69.

40. Spohn and DeLone, "When Does Race Matter?"

41. These estimated probabilities are adjusted for the effects of the other legal and extralegal variables included in the multivariate analysis. See Spohn and DeLone, "When Does Race Matter?" for a description of the procedures used to calculate the probabilities.

42. Spohn and DeLone, "When Does Race Matter?" p. 29.

43. Ibid.

44. Ibid., p. 30.

45. Marjorie Zatz, "The Convergence of Race, Ethnicity, Gender, and Class on Court Decisionmaking: Looking toward the 21st Century," in *Policies, Processes, and Decisions of the Criminal Justice System,* vol. 3, *Criminal Justice 2000* (Washington, DC: U.S. Department of Justice, 2000).

46. Ibid., p. 540.

47. John H. Kramer and Darrell Steffensmeier, "Race and Imprisonment Decisions," *The Sociological Quarterly* 34 (1993): 357–376.

48. Darrell Steffensmeier, John Kramer, and Cathy Streifel, "Gender and Imprisonment Decisions," *Criminology* 31 (1993): 411–446.

49. Darrell Steffensmeier, John Kramer, and Jeffery Ulmer, "Age Differences in Criminal Sentencing," *Justice Quarterly* 12 (1995): 701–719.

50. Darrell Steffensmeier, Jeffery Ulmer, and John Kramer, "The Interaction of Race, Gender, and Age in Criminal Sentencing: The Punishment Cost of Being Young, Black, and Male," *Criminology* 36 (1998): 363–397.

51. Kramer and Steffensmeier, "Race and Imprisonment Decisions," p. 370.

52. Ibid., p. 368.

53. Ibid., p. 373.

54. Ibid.

55. Ibid., p. 789.

56. Ibid., p. 768.

57. Cassia Spohn and David Holleran, "The Imprisonment Penalty Paid by Young, Unemployed Black and Hispanic Male Offenders," *Criminology* 38 (2000): 281–306.

58. Ibid., pp. 291–293.

59. Ibid., p. 301.

60. Quinney, *The Social Reality of Crime,* p. 142.

61. Dario Melossi, "An Introduction: Fifty Years Later, Punishment and Social Structure in Contemporary Analysis," *Contemporary Crises* 13 (1989): 317.

62. Gregg Barak, "Between the Waves: Mass-Mediated Themes of Crime and Justice," *Social Justice* 21 (1994): 137.

63. Steven Spitzer, "Toward a Marxian Theory of Deviance," *Social Problems* 22 (1975): 645.

64. Ibid., p. 646.

65. Steven Box and Chris Hale, "Unemployment, Imprisonment, and Prison Overcrowding," *Contemporary Crises* 9 (1985): 209–228.

66. Ibid., p. 217.

67. Steffensmeier, Ulmer, and Kramer, "The Interaction of Race, Gender, and Age in Criminal Sentencing," p. 789.

68. Ibid., p. 787.

69. Spohn and Holleran, "The Imprisonment Penalty Paid by Young, Unemployed Black and Hispanic Male Offenders," p. 301.

70. Gunnar Myrdal, *An American Dilemma: The Negro Problem and Modern Democracy* (New York: Harper & Brothers, 1944), p. 551.

71. Ibid., p. 553.

72. Susan Brownmiller, *Against Our Will: Men, Women and Rape* (New York: Bantam Books, 1975).

73. Jennifer Wriggens, "Rape, Racism, and the Law," *Harvard Women's Law Journal* 6 (1983), p. 104.

74. Ibid., p. 109.

75. Marvin E. Wolfgang and Marc Reidel, "Race, Judicial Discretion and the Death Penalty," *Annals of the American Academy* 407 (1973): 119–133; Marvin E. Wolfgang and Marc Reidel, "Rape, Race and the Death Penalty in Georgia, " *American Journal of Orthopsychiatry* 45 (1975): 658–668.

76. Brownmiller, *Against Our Will,* p. 237.

77. Gary D. LaFree, *Rape and Criminal Justice: The Social Construction of Sexual Assault* (Belmont, CA: Wadsworth, 1989).

78. Anthony Walsh, "The Sexual Stratification Hypothesis and Sexual Assault in Light of the Changing Conceptions of Race," *Criminology* 25 (1987): 153–173.

79. Ibid., p. 167.

80. Cassia Spohn and Jeffrey Spears, "The Effect of Offender and Victim Characteristics on Sexual Assault Case Processing Decisions," *Justice Quarterly* 13 (1996): 649–679.

81. Ibid., p. 663.

82. Ibid., p. 675.

83. Ibid., p. 665.

84. Peterson and Hagan, "Changing Conceptions of Race," p. 67.

85. Ibid., p. 719.

86. Harry Kalven Jr. and Hans Zeisel, *The American Jury* (Boston: Little, Brown, 1966).

87. Cassia Spohn and Jerry Cederblom, "Racial Disparities in Sentencing: A Test of the Liberation Hypothesis," *Justice Quarterly* 8 (1991): 305–327.

88. Ibid., p. 323.

89. Michael Tonry, *Malign Neglect,* p. 105.

90. Ibid., p. 115.

91. Jerome G. Miller, *Search and Destroy: African-American Males in the Criminal Justice System* (Cambridge: Cambridge University Press, 1996), p. 83.

92. Marc Mauer, *Race to Incarcerate* (New York: New Press, 1999), p. 143.

93. William J. Chambliss, "Crime Control and Ethnic Minorities: Legitimizing Racial Oppression by Creating Moral Panics," in *Ethnicity, Race, and Crime: Perspectives across Time and Place,* ed. Darnell F. Hawkins (Albany: State University of New York Press, 1995); Tonry, *Malign Neglect.*

94. Phillip Jenkins, "'The Ice Age:' The Social Construction of a Drug Panic," *Justice Quarterly* 11 (1994): 7–31.

95. For a review of this research, see Theodore G. Chiricos and Miriam DeLone, "Labor Surplus and Punishment: A

Review and Assessment of Theory and Evidence," *Social Problems* 39: 421–446.

96. Human Rights Watch, *Punishment and Prejudice: Racial Disparities in the War on Drugs,* Vol. 12, No. 2 (G) (May 2000) Available at http://www.hrw.org/reports/2000/usa/.

97. Ibid.

98. Theodore G. Chiricos and William D. Bales, "Unemployment and Punishment: An Empirical Assessment," *Criminology* 29 (1991): 701–724; Kramer and Steffensmeier, "Race and Imprisonment Decisions"; Martha Myers, "Symbolic Policy and the Sentencing of Drug Offenders," *Law & Society Review* 23 (1989): 295–315; James D. Unnever, "Direct and Organizational Discrimination in the Sentencing of Drug Offenders," *Social Problems* 30 (1982): 212–225. Note that Unnever found significant differences between African Americans and whites, but not between Hispanics and whites.

99. Cassia Spohn and Jeffrey Spears, "Sentencing of Drug Offenders in Three Cities: Does Race/Ethnicity Make a Difference?" in *Crime Control and Criminal Justice: The Delicate Balance,* ed. Darnell F. Hawkins, Samuel L. Meyers Jr., and Randolph N. Stone (Westport, CT: Greenwood, 2002); Unnever, "Direct and Organizational Discrimination in the Sentencing of Drug Offenders."

100. See the earlier discussion of Peterson and Hagan, "Changing Conceptions of Race."

101. Spohn and Spears, "Sentencing of Drug Offenders in Three Cities."

102. Celesta A. Albonetti, "Sentencing under the Federal Sentencing Guidelines: Effects of Defendant Characteristics, Guilty Pleas, and Departures on Sentence Outcomes for Drug Offenses, 1991–1992," *Law & Society Review* 31 (1997): 789–822.

103. Spohn and Spears, "Sentencing of Drug Offenders in Three Cities," p. 29.

104. Ibid.

105. See Chambliss, "Crime Control and Ethnic Minorities," and Tonry, *Malign Neglect.*

106. Spohn and Spears, "Sentencing of Drug Offenders in Three Cities," p. 29.

107. Ibid., pp. 29–30.

108. Jeffrey S. Adler, "The Dynamite, Wreckage, and Scum in our Cities: The Social Construction of Deviance in Industrial America," *Justice Quarterly* 11 (1994): 33–49.

109. Albonetti, "Sentencing under the Federal Sentencing Guidelines."

110. 28 U.S.C. 991(b)(1)(B) (Supp. 1993).

111. Albonetti, "Sentencing under the Federal Sentencing Guidelines," p. 790.

112. Ibid.

113. Ibid., p. 780.

114. Albonetti noted (p. 817) that most of the departures in these cases were "judicial decisions to comply with prosecutorial motions based on the defendant having provided substantial assistance to the government in the prosecution of others."

115. Ibid., p. 818.

116. Ibid., pp. 818–819.

117. Samuel Walker, *Taming the System: The Control of Discretion in Criminal Justice, 1950–1990* (New York: Oxford University Press, 1993), p. 112.

118. U.S. Department of Justice, Bureau of Justice Assistance, *National Assessment of Structured Sentencing* (Washington, DC: U.S. Government Printing Office, 1996), p. 6.

119. American Friends Service Committee, *Struggle for Justice: A Report on Crime and Punishment in America* (Boston: Little, Brown, 1971); Kenneth C. Davis, *Discretionary Justice: A Preliminary Inquiry* (Baton Rouge: Louisiana State University Press, 1969); Marvin Frankel, *Criminal Sentences: Law without Order* (New York: Hill & Wang, 1972).

120. Tonry, *Malign Neglect,* p. 164.

121. See, for example, Ernest van den Haag, *Punishing Criminals: Confronting a Very Old and Painful Question* (New York: Basic Books, 1975); James Q. Wilson, *Thinking about Crime* (New York: Basic Books, 1975).

122. Andrew von Hirsch, *Doing Justice: The Choice of Punishments* (New York: Hill & Wang, 1976).

123. Robert Martinson, "What Works? Questions and Answers about Prison Reform," *Public Interest* 24 (1974): 22–54.

124. Walker, *Taming the System*, p. 123.

125. Michael Tonry, *Sentencing Matters* (New York: Oxford University Press, 1996), p. 3.

126. Spohn, "Thirty Years of Sentencing Reform."

127. The eight studies of federal sentencing decisions included in the review were Albonetti, "Sentencing under the Federal Sentencing Guidelines"; Ronald S. Everett and Barbara C. Nienstedt, "Race, Remorse, and Sentence Reduction: Is Saying You're Sorry Enough?" *Justice Quarterly* 16 (1999): 99–122; Patrick Langan, "Sentence Reductions for Drug Traffickers for Assisting Federal Prosecutors" (unpublished manuscript); Linda D. Maxfield and John H. Kramer, *Substantial Assistance: An Empirical Yardstick Gauging Equity in Current Federal Policy and Practice* (Washington, DC: U.S. Sentencing Commission, 1998); Douglas C. McDonald and Kenneth E. Carlson, *Sentencing in Federal Courts: When Does Race Matter?* (Washington, DC: U.S. Department of Justice, 1993); Brent L. Smith and Kelly R. Damphouse, "Punishing Political Offenders: The Effect of Political Motive on Federal Sentencing Decisions," *Criminology* 34 (1996): 289–321; U.S. Sentencing Commission, *Special Report to the Congress: Mandatory Minimum Penalties in the Federal Criminal Justice System* (Washington, DC: Author, 1991); U.S. Sentencing Commission, *Substantial Assistance Departures in the United States Courts* (Washington, DC: Author 1995).

128. Everett and Nienstedt, "Race, Remorse, and Sentence Reduction."

129. Langan, "Sentence Reductions for Drug Traffickers for Assisting Federal Prosecutors"; Maxfield and Kramer, *Substantial Assistance;* U.S. Sentencing Commission, *Substantial Assistance Departures in the United States Courts.*

130. Maxfield and Kramer, *Substantial Assistance.*

131. U.S. Sentencing Commission, *Special Report to the Congress.*

132. Albonetti, "Sentencing under the Federal Sentencing Guidelines," p. 790.

133. Darrell Steffensmeier and Stephen Demuth, "Ethnicity and Sentencing Outcomes in U.S. Federal Courts: Who Is Punished More Harshly?" *American Sociological Review* 65 (2000): 705–729.

134. Ibid., p. 718.

135. Ibid., p. 725.

136. Joan Petersilia, *Racial Disparities in the Criminal Justice System* (Santa Monica, CA: Rand Corporation, 1983).

137. Terance D. Miethe and Charles A. Moore, "Socioeconomic Disparities under Determinate Sentencing Systems: A Comparison of Preguideline and Postguideline Practices in Minnesota," *Criminology* 23 (1985): 337–363.

138. Ibid., p. 358.

139. Jo Dixon, "The Organizational Context of Criminal Sentencing," *American Journal of Sociology* 100 (1995): 1157–1198.

140. Kramer and Steffensmeier, "Race and Imprisonment Decisions"; John H. Kramer and Jeffery T. Ulmer, "Sentencing Disparity and Departures from Guidelines," *Justice Quarterly* 13 (1996): 81–106; Jeffery T. Ulmer and John H. Kramer, "Court Communities under Sentencing Guidelines: Dilemmas of Formal Rationality and Sentencing Disparity," *Criminology* 34 (1996): 383–408.

141. Kramer and Ulmer, "Sentencing Disparity and Departures from Guidelines."

142. Ibid., p. 99.

143. Ibid.

144. Ibid., p. 101.

145. Tonry, *Malign Neglect,* pp. 170–172.

146. Ibid.

147. Ibid., p. 190.

148. Ibid., p. 155.

149. Ibid., p. 160.

150. Zatz, "The Changing Forms of Racial/Ethnic Biases in Sentencing," p. 87.

8

⚘

The Color of Death

Race and the Death Penalty

> We may not be capable of devising procedural or substantive rules to
> prevent the more subtle and often unconscious forms of racism from
> creeping into the system . . . discrimination and arbitrariness could not be
> purged from the administration of capital punishment without sacrificing the
> equally essential component of fairness—individualized sentencing.
>
> —SUPREME COURT JUSTICE HARRY BLACKMUN[1]

In February 1994, Supreme Court Justice Harry A. Blackmun announced that
he would "no longer tinker with the machinery of death."[2] In an opinion
dissenting from the Court's order denying review in a Texas death penalty
case, Blackmun charged the Court with coming "perilously close to murder"
and announced that he would vote to oppose all future death sentences. He also
stated that the death penalty was applied in an arbitrary and racially discriminatory manner. "Rather than continue to coddle the Court's delusion that the
desired level of fairness has been achieved and the need for regulation eviscer-
ated," Blackmun wrote, "I feel morally and intellectually obligated simply to
concede that the death penalty experiment has failed."[3]

Justice Blackmun is not alone in his assessment. Legal scholars, civil libertarians, and state and federal policymakers have also questioned the fairness of
the process by which a small proportion of convicted murderers are sentenced
to death and an even smaller proportion are eventually executed.[4] As a lawyer
who defends individuals charged with capital crimes explained, "You are dealing with a group of people who are in this situation not so much because of
what they did, but because of who they are. And who they are has a lot to do
with the color of their skin and their socio-economic status."[5] Echoing Justice
Blackmun, these critics contend that "the most profound expression of racial
discrimination in sentencing occurs in the use of capital punishment."[6]

Concerns about the fairness of the death penalty process, coupled with evidence of wrongful conviction of some of those on death row, led a number of
commentators and policymakers to suggest that it was time to rethink the death

penalty. In July 2001, Supreme Court Justice Sandra Day O'Connor, a conservative voice on death penalty issues, said that there were "serious questions" about the fairness of the death penalty process. She stated, "If statistics are any indication, the system may well be allowing some innocent defendants to be executed."[7] Rudolph J. Gerber, a former Arizona Court of Appeals judge, raised similar concerns, noting that "our capital punishment system falls disproportionately on minorities . . . and sweeps some innocent defendants . . . in its wide nets."[8] Opinions such as these prompted calls for reform of the death penalty process. By 2002, legislation requiring a moratorium on executions had been introduced in over a third of the states; similar legislation had been introduced in both houses of Congress.

As these events demonstrate, controversy continues to swirl around the use of the death penalty in the United States. Although issues other than race and class animate this controversy, these issues clearly are central. The questions asked and the positions taken by those on each side of the controversy mimic to some extent the issues that dominate discussions of the noncapital sentencing process. Supporters of capital punishment contend that the death penalty is administered in an evenhanded manner on those who commit the most heinous murders; they also argue that the restrictions contained in death penalty statutes and the procedural safeguards inherent in the process preclude arbitrary and discriminatory decision making. Opponents contend that the capital sentencing process, which involves a series of highly discretionary charging, convicting, and sentencing decisions, is fraught with race- and class-based discrimination and that the appellate process is unlikely to uncover, much less remedy, these abuses.

GOALS OF THE CHAPTER

In this chapter, we address the issue of racial discrimination in the application of the death penalty. We begin with a discussion of Supreme Court decisions concerning the constitutionality of the death penalty and then discuss racial differences in attitudes toward capital punishment. We present statistics on death sentences and executions and summarize the results of empirical studies examining the effect of race on the application of the death penalty. We then discuss *McCleskey v. Kemp,*[9] the Supreme Court case that directly addressed the question of racial discrimination in the imposition of the death penalty, and conclude with a discussion of recent calls for a moratorium on the death penalty and legislation intended to reform the capital sentencing process.

THE CONSTITUTIONALITY
OF THE DEATH PENALTY

The Eighth Amendment to the U.S. Constitution prohibits "cruel and unusual punishments." The determination of which punishments are cruel and unusual, and thus unconstitutional, has been left to the courts. According to the Supreme Court,

Punishments are cruel when they involve torture or lingering death; but the punishment of death is not cruel, within the meaning of that word as used in the Constitution. It implies there something inhuman and barbarous, something more than the mere extinguishment of life.[10]

Whatever the arguments may be against capital punishment, both on moral grounds and in terms of accomplishing the purposes of punishment—and they are forceful—the death penalty has been employed throughout our history, and, in a day when it is still widely accepted, it cannot be said to violate the constitutional concept of cruelty.[11]

Although the Supreme Court has stated consistently that punishments of torture violate the Eighth Amendment, the Court has never ruled that the death penalty itself is a cruel and unusual punishment.

 *Furman v. Georgia*

In 1972, the Supreme Court ruled in *Furman v. Georgia* that the death penalty, as it was being administered under then-existing statutes, was unconstitutional.[12] The five-to-four decision, in which nine separate opinions were written, did not hold that the death penalty per se violated the Constitution's ban on cruel and unusual punishment. Rather, the majority opinions focused on the procedures by which convicted defendants were selected for the death penalty. The justices ruled that because the statutes being challenged offered no guidance to juries charged with deciding whether or not to sentence convicted murderers or rapists to death, there was a substantial risk that the death penalty would be imposed in an arbitrary and discriminatory manner.

Although all of the majority justices were concerned about the arbitrary and capricious application of the death penalty, the nature of their concerns varied. Justices Brennan and Marshall wrote that the death penalty was inherently cruel and unusual punishment. Justice Brennan argued that the death penalty violated the concept of human dignity, and Justice Marshall asserted that the death penalty served no legitimate penal purpose. These justices concluded that the death penalty would violate the Constitution under any circumstances.

The other three justices in the majority concluded that capital punishment as it was then being administered in the United States was unconstitutional. These justices asserted that the death penalty violated both the Eighth Amendment's ban on cruel and unusual punishment and the Fourteenth Amendment's requirement of equal protection under the law. Justice Douglas stated that the procedures used in administering the death penalty were "pregnant with discrimination." Justice Stewart focused on the fact that the death penalty was "so wantonly and so freakishly imposed." Justice White found "no meaningful basis for distinguishing the few cases in which [the death penalty] is imposed from the many cases in which it is not."[13]

The central issue in the *Furman* case was the meaning of the Eighth Amendment's prohibition of cruel and unusual punishment, but the issue of racial discrimination in the administration of the death penalty was raised by three of the five justices in the majority. Justices Douglas and Marshall cited evidence of discrimination against defendants who were poor, powerless, or African American. Marshall, for example, noted that giving juries "untrammeled discretion" to impose a sentence of death was "an open invitation to discrimination."[14] Justice Stewart, although asserting that "racial discrimination has not been proved," stated that Douglas and Marshall "have demonstrated that, if any basis can be discerned for the selection of these few to be sentenced to die, it is the constitutionally impermissible basis of race."[15]

The Impact of *Furman* The impact of the *Furman* decision was dramatic. The Court's ruling "emptied death rows across the country" and "brought the process that fed them to a stop."[16] Many commentators argued that *Furman* reflected the Supreme Court's deep-seated concerns about the fairness of the death penalty process; they predicted that the Court's next step would be the abolition of capital punishment. Instead, the Court defied these predictions, deciding to regulate capital punishment rather than abolish it.

Also as a result of the *Furman* decision, the death penalty statutes in 39 states were invalidated. Most of these states responded to *Furman* by adopting new statutes designed to narrow discretion and thus to avoid the problems of arbitrariness and discrimination identified by the justices in the majority.

These statutes were of two types. Some required the judge or jury to impose the death penalty if a defendant was convicted of first-degree murder. Others permitted the judge or jury to impose the death penalty on defendants convicted of certain crimes, depending on the presence or absence of aggravating and mitigating circumstances. These "guided-discretion" statutes typically required a bifurcated trial in which the jury first decided guilt or innocence and then decided whether to impose the death penalty or not. They also provided for automatic appellate review of all death sentences.

Post-*Furman* Decisions

The Supreme Court ruled on the constitutionality of the new death penalty statutes in 1976. The Court held that the mandatory death penalty statutes enacted by North Carolina and Louisiana were unconstitutional,[17] both because they provided no opportunity for consideration of mitigating circumstances and because the jury's power to determine the degree of the crime (conviction for first-degree murder or for a lesser included offense) opened the door to the type of "arbitrary and wanton jury discretion" condemned in *Furman*.[18] The Justices stated that the central problem of the mandatory statutes was their treatment of all defendants "as members of a faceless, undifferentiated mass to be subjected to the blind infliction of the penalty of death."[19]

In contrast, the Supreme Court ruled that the guided-discretion death penalty statutes adopted by Georgia, Florida, and Texas did not violate the Eighth Amendment's prohibition of cruel and unusual punishment.[20] In *Gregg v. Georgia*, the Court held that Georgia's statute—which required the jury to consider and weigh 10 specified aggravating circumstances (see Box 8.1), allowed the jury to consider mitigating circumstances, and provided for automatic appellate review—channeled the jury's discretion and thereby reduced the likelihood

---

BOX 8.1   Georgia's Guided-Discretion Death Penalty Statute

Under Georgia law, if the jury finds at least one of the following aggravating circumstances, it may, but need not, recommend death:

1. The offense was committed by a person with a prior record of conviction for a capital felony or by a person who has a substantial history of serious assaultive criminal convictions.
2. The offense was committed while the offender was engaged in the commission of another capital felony, or aggravated battery, or burglary or arson in the first degree.
3. The offender knowingly created a great risk of death to more than one person in a public place by means of a weapon or device which would normally be hazardous to the lives of more than one person.
4. The offender committed the offense of murder for himself or another, for the purpose of receiving money or any other thing of monetary value.
5. The murder of a judicial officer, former judicial officer, district attorney or solicitor or former dis-

trict attorney or solicitor during or because of the exercise of his official duty.
6. The offender caused or directed another to commit murder or committed murder as an agent or employee of another person.
7. The offense was outrageously or wantonly vile, horrible or inhuman in that it involved torture, depravity of mind, or an aggravated battery to the victim.
8. The offense was committed against any peace officer, corrections employee or fireman while engaged in the performance of his official duties.
9. The offense was committed by a person in, or who has escaped from, the lawful custody of a peace officer or place of lawful confinement.
10. The murder was committed for the purpose of avoiding, interfering with, or preventing a lawful arrest or custody in a place of lawful confinement, of himself or another.

SOURCE: Georgia Code Ann. § 27-2534.1 (Supp. 1975).

---

that the jury would impose arbitrary or discriminatory sentences.[21] According to the Court,

> No longer can a jury wantonly and freakishly impose the death sentence; it is always circumscribed by the legislative guidelines. In addition, the review function of the Supreme Court of Georgia affords additional assurance that the concerns that prompted our decision in *Furman* are not present to any significant degree in the Georgia procedure applied here.[22]

Since 1976, the Supreme Court has handed down additional decisions on the constitutionality of the death penalty. With the exception of *McCleskey v. Kemp*, which we address later, these decisions do not focus on the question of racial discrimination in the application of the death penalty. The Court has ruled that the death penalty cannot be imposed on a defendant convicted of the crime of rape,[23] that the death penalty can be imposed on an offender convicted of felony murder if the offender played a major role in the felony and displayed "reckless indifference to the value of human life,"[24] and that the Eighth Amendment does not prohibit the execution of offenders who are mentally retarded[25] or youths who commit crimes at age 16 or older.[26] In 2002, the Supreme Court was reviewing cases involving the execution of mentally retarded offenders and the imposition of the death penalty by a judge (or a panel of judges) following conviction by a jury.

ATTITUDES TOWARD CAPITAL PUNISHMENT

In *Gregg v. Georgia,* the seven justices in the majority noted that both the public and state legislatures had endorsed the death penalty for murder. The Court stated that "it is now evident that a large proportion of American society continues to regard it as an appropriate and necessary criminal sanction." Public opinion data indicates that the Court was correct in its assessment of the level of support for the death penalty. In 1976, the year that *Gregg* was decided, 66 percent of the respondents to a nationwide poll said that they favored the death penalty for persons convicted of murder.[27] By 1997, three-quarters of those polled voiced support for the death penalty. Although the exoneration of death row inmates and subsequent calls for a moratorium on executions (discussed later) led to a decline in support, in July 2001, 67 percent of Americans still reported that they favored the death penalty for persons convicted of murder.[28]

The reliability of these figures has not gone unchallenged. In fact, Supreme Court Justices themselves have raised questions about the reliability and meaning of public opinion data derived from standard "do you favor or oppose?" polling questions. Justice Marshall observed in his concurring opinion in *Furman* that Americans were not fully informed about the ways in which the death penalty was used or about its potential for abuse. According to Marshall, the public did not realize that the death penalty was imposed in an arbitrary manner or that "the burden of capital punishment falls upon the poor, the ignorant, and the underprivileged members of society."[29] Marshall suggested that public opinion data demonstrating widespread support for the death penalty should therefore be given little weight in determining whether capital punishment is consistent with "evolving standards of decency." In what has become known as the "Marshall Hypothesis,"[30] he stated that "the average citizen" who knew "all the facts presently available regarding capital punishment would . . . find it shocking to his conscience and sense of justice."[31]

Researchers have also raised questions about the poll results,[32] suggesting that support for the death penalty is not absolute but depends on such things as the circumstances of the case, the character of the defendant, or the alternative punishments that are available. Bowers, for example, challenged the conclusion that "Americans solidly support the death penalty" and suggested that the poll results have been misinterpreted.[33] He argued that instead of reflecting a "deep-seated or strongly held commitment to capital punishment," expressed public support for the death penalty "is actually a reflection of the public's desire for a genuinely harsh but meaningful punishment for convicted murderers."[34]

In support of this proposition, Bowers presented evidence from surveys of citizens in a number of states and from interviews with capital jurors in three states. He found that support for the death penalty plummeted when respondents were given an alternative of life in prison without parole plus restitution to the victim's family; moreover, a majority of the respondents in every state preferred this alternative to the death penalty. Bowers also found that about three-quarters of the respondents, and 80 percent of jurors in capital cases, agreed that "the death penalty is too arbitrary because some people are executed and others are sent to prison for the very same crimes." Bowers concluded that the results of his study "could have the critical effect of changing the perspectives of legislators, judges, the media, and the public on how people think about capital punishment."[35]

Consistent with Bowers's results, recent public opinion polls reveal that most Americans believe that innocent people are sometimes convicted of murder. These polls also suggest that respondents' beliefs about the likelihood of wrongful convictions affect their views of the death penalty. A Harris poll conducted in July 2001 found that 94 percent of those polled believed that innocent people are "sometimes" convicted of murder; only 3 percent stated that this "never happens."[36] When respondents were asked, "If you believed that quite a substantial number of innocent people are convicted of murder, would you then believe in or oppose the death penalty for murder?" 53 percent said that they would oppose the death penalty, compared to 36 percent who stated that they would continue to support it.

It is also clear that there are significant racial differences in support for the death penalty. The 2001 Harris poll, for example, found that 73 percent of whites and 63 percent of Hispanics expressed support for the death penalty, compared to only 46 percent of African Americans.[37] In fact, as shown in Figure 8.1, since 1976 the percentage of respondents who report that they support the death penalty has been consistently higher among whites than among African Americans. Estimates of the number of innocent persons convicted of murder also vary by race and ethnicity. African American respondents estimated that 22 of every 100 persons convicted of murder were innocent. In contrast, the estimate was 15 of every 100 for Hispanic respondents, and 10 of every 100 for white respondents.[38]

Researchers have advanced a number of explanations to account for these consistent racial differences. Some attribute African American opposition to perceptions of racial bias in the application of the death penalty.[39] Others contend that white support is associated with racial prejudice.[40] One study, for example, found that antipathy to African Americans (which was measured by two items asking respondents to indicate their attitudes toward living in a majority–African American neighborhood or having a family member marry an African American) and belief in racial stereotypes (believing that African Americans are lazy, unintelligent, violent, and poor) predicted white respondents' support for the death penalty.[41] As the authors noted, "Simply put, many White

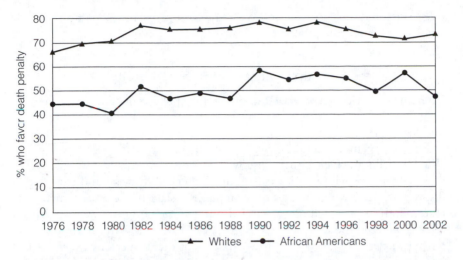

FIGURE 8.1 African American and White Attitudes toward Capital Punishment for Persons Convicted of Murder, 1970–2002

SOURCE: Data from Bureau of Justice Statistics, *Sourcebook of Criminal Justice Statistics, 1996* (Washington, DC: U.S. Government Printing Office, 2001). Data for 2002 from Harris poll. Available at www.harrisinteractive.com/harris_poll/index.asp?PID=252, table 6.

people are both prejudiced against Blacks and are more likely to favor capital punishment." [42] The authors concluded that their finding of an association between racial prejudice and support for the death penalty suggests "that public sentiment may be an unacceptable indicator of contemporary standards of appropriate punishment for persons convicted of homicide." [43]

RACE AND THE DEATH PENALTY: THE EMPIRICAL EVIDENCE

The Supreme Court's decisions regarding the constitutionality of the death penalty have been guided by a number of assumptions. In the *Furman* decision, the five justices in the majority assumed that the absence of guidelines and procedural rules in then-existing death penalty statutes opened the door to arbitrary, capricious, and discriminatory decision making. In *Gregg*, the Court affirmed the guided-discretion statutes on their face and assumed that the statutes would eliminate the problems condemned in *Furman*. The Court assumed, in other words, that racial discrimination was a potential problem under the statutes struck down in *Furman* but would not be a problem under the statutes approved in *Gregg* and the companion cases.

In this section, we address the validity of these assumptions. We begin by presenting statistics on the application of the death penalty and then discuss the results of pre-*Furman* and post-*Furman* studies investigating the relationship between race and the death penalty. We also examine recent research on the federal capital sentencing process.

Statistical Evidence of Racial Disparity

There is clear evidence of racial disparity in the application of the death penalty. Despite the fact that African Americans make up only 13 percent of the U.S. population, they have been a much larger proportion of offenders sentenced to death and executed, both historically and during the post-*Gregg* era. There is also compelling evidence that those who murder whites, and particularly African Americans who murder whites, are sentenced to death and executed at disproportionately high rates. For example, the state of Georgia, which generated both *Furman* and *Gregg,* carried out 18 executions between 1976 and 1994. Twelve of those executed were African Americans; 6 of the 12 were sentenced to death by all-white juries. Sixteen of the 18 persons executed had killed whites.[44]

The pattern found in Georgia casts doubt on the Supreme Court's assertion in *Gregg* that the disparities that prompted their decision in *Furman* will not be present "to any significant degree" under the guided-discretion procedures.[45] Other evidence also calls this into question. Consider the following statistics:

- Of the persons under sentence of death in the United States at the end of 2000, 1,535 (42.7 percent) were African Americans; of the 54 females on death row, 16 (33.3 percent) were African Americans.[46]

- African Americans make up approximately half of the death row populations in North Carolina, South Carolina, Ohio, Delaware, Mississippi, and Virginia; they constitute nearly two-thirds of those on death row in Pennsylvania, Illinois, and Louisiana.[47]

- Eighteen of the 26 offenders sentenced to death by the federal courts from 1993 through April 2002 were African Americans, five were whites, two were Hispanics, and one was Asian American.[48]

- Of the 749 prisoners executed from 1976 through 2001, 417 (56 percent) were whites, 265 (35 percent) were African Americans, 48 (6 percent) were Hispanics, and 18 (2 percent) were Native Americans or Asian Americans.[49]

- Of the 1,156 victims of those executed from 1977 through 2001, 934 (81 percent) were whites, 157 (14 percent) were African Americans, 39 (3 percent) were Hispanics, and 26 (2 percent) were Native Americans or Asian Americans. During this period, approximately 50 percent of all murder victims were African Americans.[50]

- From 1977 through 2001, 52 percent of the prisoners executed were whites convicted of killing other whites, 23 percent were African Americans convicted of killing whites, 10 percent were African Americans convicted of killing other African Americans, and less than 2 percent were whites convicted of killing African Americans.[51]

- Among those executed from 1930 through 1972 for the crime of rape, 89 percent (405 of the 455) were African Americans.[52] During this period, Louisiana, Mississippi, Oklahoma, Virginia, West Virginia, and the District of Columbia executed 66 African American men, but not a single white man, for the crime of rape.[53]

- Among those sentenced to death for rape in North Carolina from 1909 to 1954, 56 percent of the African Americans, but only 43 percent of the whites, were eventually executed.[54]

- Twenty percent of the whites, but only 11 percent of the African Americans, sentenced to death for first-degree murder in Pennsylvania between 1914 and 1958 had their sentences commuted to life in prison.[55]

These statistics clearly indicate that African Americans have been sentenced to death and executed "in numbers far out of proportion to their numbers in the population."[56] They document racial disparity in the application of the death penalty, both prior to *Furman* and following *Gregg*.[57] As we have noted frequently throughout this book, however, disparities in the treatment of racial minorities and whites do not necessarily constitute evidence of racial discrimination. Racial minorities may be sentenced to death at a disproportionately high rate not because of discrimination in the application of the death penalty but because they are more likely than whites to commit homicide, the crime most frequently punished by death. As illustrated by the hypothetical examples presented in Box 8.2, the appropriate comparison is not the number of African Americans and whites sentenced to death during a given year or over time, but the percentage of death-eligible homicides involving African Americans and whites that result in a death sentence.

The problem with the hypothetical examples presented in Box 8.2 is that there are no national data on the number of death-eligible homicides or on the race of those who commit or who are arrested for such crimes. Kleck, noting that most homicides are intraracial, used the number of African American and white homicide *victims* as a surrogate measure.[58] He created an indicator of "execution risk" by dividing the number of executions (for murder) of persons of a given race in a given year by the number of homicide victims of that race who died in the previous year.[59] Using data from 1930 through 1967, Kleck found that the risk of execution was somewhat greater for whites (10.43 executions per 1,000 homicides) than for African Americans (9.72 executions per 1,000 homicides) for the United States as a whole, but that African Americans faced a greater likelihood of execution than whites in the South (10.47 for African Americans versus 8.39 for whites).[60] He concluded that the death penalty "has not generally been imposed for murder in a fashion discriminatory toward blacks, except in the South."[61]

None of the statistics cited here, including the execution rates calculated by Kleck, prove that the death penalty has been imposed in a racially discriminatory manner, in the South or elsewhere, either before the *Furman* decision or after the *Gregg* decision. As we pointed out earlier, conclusions of racial discrimination in sentencing rest on evidence indicating that African Americans are

---

BOX 8.2   Discrimination in the Application of the Death Penalty: Hypothetical Examples

Example 1
- 210 death-eligible homicides with African American offenders: 70 offenders (30 percent) receive the death penalty.
- 150 death-eligible homicides with white offenders: 50 offenders (30 percent) receive the death penalty.
- Conclusion: No evidence of discrimination, despite the fact that a disproportionate number of African Americans are sentenced to death.

Example 2
- 210 death-eligible homicides with African American offenders: 90 offenders (43 percent) receive the death penalty.
- 150 death-eligible homicides with white offenders: 30 offenders (20 percent) receive the death penalty.
- Conclusion: Possibility of discrimination, as African Americans are more than twice as likely as whites to be sentenced to death.

Table 8.1 Criminal History Profile of Prisoners under Sentence of Death in the United States, 2000

	RACE OF PRISONER		
	African American (N = 1,520)	Hispanic (N = 339)	White (N = 1,679)
Prior felony conviction (%)	68.1 (951)	58.9 (188)	61.7 (962)
Prior homicide conviction (%)	8.5 (126)	6.9 (23)	8.0 (132)
On parole at time of capital offense (%)	18.7 (255)	24.4 (76)	15.3 (233)

SOURCE: Department of Justice, Bureau of Justice Statistics, *Capital Punishment 2000* (Washington, DC: U.S. Government Printing Office, 1997), table 9.

---

sentenced more harshly than whites after other legally relevant predictors of sentence severity are taken into account.

Even if it can be shown that African Americans face a greater risk of execution than whites, we cannot necessarily conclude that this reflects racial prejudice or racial discrimination. The difference might be due to legitimate legal factors—the heinousness of the crime or the prior criminal record of the offender, for example—that juries and judges consider in determining whether to sentence the offender to death. If African Americans are sentenced to death at a higher rate than whites because they commit more heinous murders than whites or because they are more likely than whites to have a prior conviction for murder, then we cannot conclude that criminal justice officials or juries are making racially discriminatory death penalty decisions.

The data presented in Table 8.1 provide some evidence in support of this possibility. Among prisoners under sentence of death in 2000, African Americans were more likely than either Hispanics or whites to have a prior felony conviction. African Americans and Hispanics were also more likely than whites to have been on parole when they were arrested for the capital offense. There were, on the other hand, very few differences in the proportions of whites and racial minorities who had a prior homicide conviction.

Just as the presence of racial disparity does not necessarily signal the existence of racial discrimination, the absence of disparity does not necessarily indicate the absence of discrimination. Even if it can be shown that African Americans generally face the same risk of execution as whites, in other words, we cannot conclude that the capital sentencing process operates in a racially neutral manner. Assume, for example, that the crimes for which African Americans are sentenced to death are less serious than those for which whites are sentenced to death. If this is the case, apparent equality of treatment may be masking race-linked assessments of crime seriousness. Moreover, as we noted in our discussion of the noncapital sentencing process, it is important to consider not only the race of the offender but also the race of the victim. If African Americans who murder whites are sentenced to death at a disproportionately high rate and African Americans who murder other African Americans are sentenced to death at a disproportionately low rate, the overall finding of "no difference" in the death sentence rates for African American and white offenders may be masking significant differences based on the race of the victim. As Johnson wrote in 1941,

> If caste values and attitudes mean anything at all, they mean that offenses by or against Negroes will be defined not so much in terms of their intrinsic seriousness as in terms of their importance in the eyes of the dominant group. Obviously, the murder of a white person by a Negro and the murder of a Negro by a Negro are not at all the same kind of murder from the standpoint of the upper caste's scale of values . . . instead of two categories of offenders, Negro and white, we really need four offender–victim categories, and they would probably rank in seriousness from high to low as follows: (1) Negro versus white, (2) white versus white, (3) Negro versus Negro, and (4) white versus Negro.[62]

Evidence in support of Johnson's rankings is presented in Box 8.3, which focuses on the "anomalous" cases in which whites have been executed for crimes against African Americans. According to Radelet, "The scandalous paucity of these cases, representing less than two-tenths of 1% of known executions, lends further support to the evidence that the death penalty in this country has been discriminatorily applied."[63]

There is now a substantial body of research investigating the relationship between race and the death penalty. Most, but not all, of the research tests for both race-of-defendant and race-of-victim effects. Some of these studies are methodologically sophisticated, both in terms of the type of statistical analysis employed and in terms of the number of variables taken into consideration in the analysis. Other studies use less sophisticated statistical techniques and include fewer control variables.

**BOX 8.3   Executions of Whites for Crimes against
African Americans: Exceptions to the Rule?**

Since 1608, there have been about 16,000 executions in the United States (Radelet [1989, p. 531]; Radelet noted that the best source of information on executions is the archive developed by Watt Espy, who has obtained information on 15,978 executions carried out in American jurisdictions since 1608). Of these, only 30, or about two-tenths of 1 percent, were executions of whites for crimes against African Americans. Historically, in other words, there has been one execution of a white for a crime against an African American for every 533 recorded executions.

Michael Radelet (1989) believes that these white offender–African American victim cases, which would appear to be "theoretically anomalous" based on the proposition that race is an important determinant of sentencing, are not really "exceptions to the rule" (p. 533). Although acknowledging that each case is in fact anomalous if *race alone* is used to predict the likelihood of a death sentence, Radelet suggests that these cases are consistent with a more gen-

eral theoretical model that uses the *relative social status* of defendants and victims to explain case outcomes. These cases, in other words, are consistent with "the general rule that executions almost always involve lower status defendants who stand convicted for crimes against victims of higher status" (p. 536).

Radelet's examination of the facts in each case revealed that 10 of the 30 cases involved white men who murdered slaves, and 8 of the 10 involved men convicted of murdering a slave who belonged to someone else. The scenario of Case 13, for example, read as follows:

> June 2, 1854. Texas. James Wilson (a.k.a. Rhode Wilson). Wilson had been on bad terms with a powerful white farmer, and had threatened to kill him on several occasions. One day Wilson arrived at the farm with the intention of carrying out the threats. The farmer was not home, so Wilson instead murdered the farmer's favorite slave (male) (p. 538).

We summarize the results of these studies—presenting the results of the pre-*Furman* studies first and then the results of the post-*Furman* studies. Our purpose is to assess the validity of the Supreme Court's assumptions that race played a role in death penalty decisions prior to *Furman*, but that the guided discretion statutes enacted since 1976 have removed arbitrariness and discrimination from the capital sentencing process.

Pre-*Furman* Studies

We noted in our discussion of the Supreme Court's decision in *Furman v. Georgia* that three of the five justices in the majority mentioned the problem of racial discrimination in the application of the death penalty. Even two of the dissenting justices—Chief Justice Burger and Justice Powell—acknowledged the existence of historical evidence of discrimination against African Americans. Justice Powell also stated, "If a Negro defendant, for instance, could demonstrate

BOX 8.3   (*continued*)

According to Radelet, cases such as this are really "economic crimes" in which the true victim is not the slave, but the slave's owner. As he notes, "Slaves are property, the wealth of someone else, and their rank should be measured accordingly" (p. 534). James Wilson was sentenced to death not because he killed a slave but because he destroyed the property of someone of higher status than himself. Similarly, the death sentences imposed on the two men who killed their own slaves were meant to discourage such brutality, which might threaten the legitimacy of the institution of slavery.

The 20 remaining cases of whites who were executed for crimes against African Americans involved either

- an African American victim of higher social status than his white murderer (five cases);
- a defendant who was a marginal member of the white community—a tramp, a recent immigrant, a hard drinker (four cases);

- a defendant with a long record of serious criminality (seven cases); or
- murders that were so heinous that they resulted in "an unqualified disgust and contempt for the offender unmitigated by the fact of his or the victim's race" (pp. 534–535).

Based on his analysis of these 30 cases, Radelet concluded that "it was not primarily outrage over the violated rights of the black victim or the inherent value of the victim's life that led to the condemnation" (p. 536). Rather, the 30 white men executed for crimes against African Americans were sentenced to death because the crimes threatened the institution of slavery, involved a victim of higher social status than the defendant, or involved a defendant who was a very marginal member of the community. As Radelet noted, "The data show that the criminal justice system deems the executioner's services warranted not simply for those who *do something*, but who also *are someone*" (p. 536 [emphasis in original]).

that members of his race were being singled out for more severe punishment than others charged with the same offense, a constitutional violation might be established." [64]

Several studies suggest that African Americans, and particularly African Americans who murdered or raped whites, were "singled out for more severe punishment" in the pre-*Furman* era. [65] Most of these studies were conducted in the South. Researchers found, for example, that African Americans indicted for murdering whites in North Carolina from 1930 to 1940 faced a disproportionately high risk of a death sentence, [66] that whites sentenced to death in nine Southern and border states during the 1920s and 1930s were less likely than African Americans to be executed, [67] and that African Americans sentenced to death in Pennsylvania were less likely than whites to have their sentences commuted to life in prison and more likely than whites to be executed. [68]

Garfinkel's study of the capital sentencing process in North Carolina during the 1930s revealed the importance of taking the race of both the offender

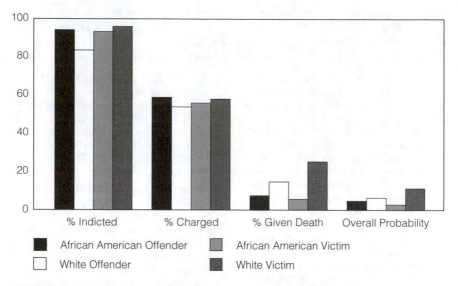

FIGURE 8.2 Death Penalty Decisions in North Carolina, by Race of Offender and Victim, 1930–1940

SOURCE: Data obtained from Harold Garfinkel, "Research Note on Inter- and Intra-Racial Homicides," *Social Forces* 27 (1949), tables 2 and 3.

and the victim into account.[69] Garfinkel examined three separate decisions: the grand jury's decision to indict for first-degree murder; the prosecutor's decision to go to trial on a first-degree murder charge (in those cases in which the grand jury returned an indictment for first-degree murder); and the judge or jury's decision to convict for first-degree murder (and thus to impose the mandatory death sentence).

As shown in Figure 8.2, which summarizes the movement of death-eligible cases from one stage to the next, there were few differences based on the race of the offender. In fact, among defendants charged with first-degree murder, white offenders were *more* likely than African American offenders to be convicted of first-degree murder and thus to be sentenced to death; 14 percent of the whites, but only 9 percent of the African Americans, received a death sentence. In contrast, there were substantial differences based on the race of the victim, particularly in the decision to convict the defendant for first-degree murder. Only 5 percent of the defendants who killed African Americans were convicted of first-degree murder and sentenced to death, compared to 24 percent of the defendants who killed whites.

The importance of considering the race of both the offender and the victim is further illustrated by the data presented in Figure 8.3. Garfinkel's analysis revealed that African Americans who killed whites were more likely than any of the other race-of-offender—race-of-victim groups to be indicted for, charged with, or convicted of first-degree murder. Again, the differences were particularly pronounced at the trial stage of the process. Among offenders charged

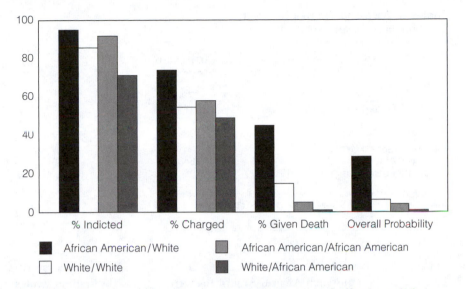

FIGURE 8.3 Death Penalty Process in North Carolina, by Race of Offender and Victim

SOURCE: Data obtained from Harold Garfinkel, "Research Note on Inter- and Intra-Racial Homicides," *Social Forces* 27 (1949), tables 2 and 3.

with first-degree murder, the rate of conviction ranged from 43 percent for African Americans who killed whites to 15 percent for whites who killed whites, to 5 percent for African Americans who killed African Americans, to 0 percent for whites who killed African Americans. The overall probability of a death sentence (that is, the probability that an indictment for homicide would result in a death sentence) revealed similar disparities.

The results of Garfinkel's study suggest that there were pervasive racial differences in the administration of capital punishment in North Carolina during the 1930s. Although Garfinkel did not control for the possibility that the crimes committed by African Americans and the crimes committed against whites were more serious, and thus more likely to deserve the death penalty, the magnitude of the differences "cast[s] doubt on the possibility that legally relevant factors are responsible for these differences."[70]

Studies of the use of capital punishment for the crime of rape also reveal overt and pervasive discrimination against African Americans. These studies reveal that "the death penalty for rape was largely used for punishing blacks who had raped whites."[71] One analysis of sentences for rape in Florida from 1940 through 1964, for example, revealed that 54 percent of the African Americans convicted of raping whites received the death penalty, compared to only 5 percent of the whites convicted of raping whites. Moreover, none of the eight whites convicted of raping African Americans were sentenced to death.[72]

Wolfgang and Reidel's study of the imposition of the death penalty for rape in 12 Southern states from 1945 through 1965 uncovered a similar pattern.[73] As shown in Table 8.2, they found that 13 percent of the African Americans,

Table 8.2 Race and the Death Penalty for Rape in the South, 1945–1965

	SENTENCED TO DEATH		NOT SENTENCED TO DEATH	
	N	%	*N*	%
Race of offender				
African American	110	13	713	87
White	9	2	433	98
Race of offender/victim				
African American/white	113	36	204	64
All other combinations	19	2	902	98

SOURCE: Marvin E. Wolfgang and Marc Reidel, "Race, Judicial Discretion, and the Death Penalty," *Annals of the American Academy* 407 (1973): 129, tables 1 and 2.

but only 2 percent of the whites, were sentenced to death. Further analysis revealed that cases in which African Americans were convicted of raping whites were 18 times more likely to receive a death penalty than were cases with any other racial combinations.

These differences did not disappear when Wolfgang and Reidel controlled for commission of a contemporaneous felony or for other factors associated with the imposition of the death penalty. According to the authors, "All the nonracial factors in each of the states analyzed 'wash out,' that is, they have no bearing on the imposition of the death penalty in disproportionate numbers upon blacks. The only variable of statistical significance that remains is race."[74]

Critics of the pre-*Furman* research note that most researchers did not control for the defendant's prior criminal record, for the heinousness of the crime, or for other predictors of sentence severity. Kleck, for example, although admitting that additional controls probably would not eliminate "the huge racial differentials in use of the death penalty" for rape, asserts that the more modest differences found for homicide might disappear if these legal factors were taken into consideration.[75]

A handful of more methodologically sophisticated studies of capital sentencing in the pre-*Furman* era control for these legally relevant factors. An analysis of death penalty decisions in Georgia, for example, found that African American defendants and defendants who murdered whites received the death penalty more often than other equally culpable defendants.[76] These results were limited, however, to borderline cases in which the appropriate sentence (life in prison or death) was not obvious.

An examination of the capital sentencing process in pre-*Furman* Texas also found significant racial effects.[77] Ralph, Sorensen, and Marquart controlled for legal and extralegal factors associated with sentence severity. They found that offenders who killed during a felony had a higher probability of receiving the death penalty, as did nonwhite offenders and offenders who killed whites. Their analysis revealed that the race of the victim was the most important extralegal variable; those who killed whites were 25.2 percent more likely to be sentenced to death than those who killed nonwhites. The authors concluded, "Overall we found a significant race-linked bias in the death sentencing of non–Anglo-American murderers; the victim's race, along with legal factors taken together, emerged as the pivotal element in sentencing."[78]

The results of these studies reveal that the Supreme Court was correct in its assumption of the potential for racial discrimination in the application of the death penalty in the pre-*Furman* era. The death penalty for rape was primarily reserved for African Americans who victimized whites. The evidence with respect to homicide, although less consistent, also suggests that African Americans, and particularly African Americans who murdered whites, were sentenced to death at a disproportionately high rate. We now turn to an examination of the capital sentencing process in the post-*Furman* era.

Post-*Furman* Studies

In *Gregg v. Georgia,* the Supreme Court upheld Georgia's guided-discretion death penalty statute and stated that "the concerns that prompted our decision in *Furman* are not present to any significant degree in the Georgia procedure applied here."[79] The Court, in essence, predicted that race would not affect the capital sentencing process in Georgia or in other states with similar statutes. Critics of the Court's ruling were less optimistic. Wolfgang and Reidel, for example, noted that the post-*Furman* statutes narrowed, but did not eliminate, discretion. They suggested that "it is unlikely that the death penalty will be applied with greater equity when substantial discretion remains in these post-*Furman* statutes."[80]

Other commentators predicted that the guided-discretion statutes would simply shift discretion, and thus the potential for discrimination, to earlier stages in the capital sentencing process. They suggested that discretion would be transferred to charging decisions made by the grand jury and the prosecutor. Thus, according to Bowers and Pierce, "under post-*Furman* capital statutes, the extent of arbitrariness and discrimination, if not their distribution over stages of the criminal justice process, might be expected to remain essentially unchanged."[81]

Compelling evidence supports this hypothesis. (See also Box 8.4.) Studies conducted during the past two decades document substantial discrimination in the application of the death penalty under post-*Furman* statutes. A recent report by the U.S. General Accounting Office (GAO) concluded that there was "a pattern of evidence indicating racial disparities in the charging, sentencing, and imposition of the death penalty after the *Furman* decision."[82]

The GAO evaluated the results of 28 post-*Furman* empirical studies of the capital sentencing process and found that the race of the victim had a statistically significant effect in 23 of the 28 studies. Those who murdered whites were more likely to be charged with capital murder and to be sentenced to death than those who murdered African Americans. The authors of the report noted that the race of the victim affected decisions made at all stages of the criminal justice process. They concluded that these differences could not be explained

---

**BOX 8.4   Discrimination in the Georgia Courts:
The Case of Wilburn Dobbs**

Statistical evidence of racial disparities in the use of the death penalty, although important, cannot illustrate the myriad ways in which racial sentiments influence the capital sentencing process.

Consider the case of Wilburn Dobbs, an African American on death row in Georgia for the murder of a white man (case described in Bright, 1995, pp. 912–915). The judge trying his case referred to him in court as "colored" and "colored boy," and two of the jurors who sentenced him to death admitted after trial that they used the racial epithet "nigger." Moreover, the court-appointed lawyer assigned to his case, who also referred to Dobbs as "colored," stated on the morning of the trial that he was "not prepared to go to trial" and that he was "in a better position to prosecute the case than defend it." He also testified before the federal court hearing Dobbs's appeal that he believed that African Americans were uneducated and less intelligent than whites and admitted that he used the word "nigger" jokingly (pp. 912–913).

The federal courts that heard Dobbs's appeals ruled that neither the racial attitudes of the trial judge or the defense attorney nor the racial prejudice of the jurors required that Dobbs's death sentence be set aside. The Court of Appeals, for instance, noted that although several of the jurors made statements reflecting racial prejudice, none of them "viewed blacks as more prone to violence than whites or as morally inferior to whites" (*Dobbs v. Zant*, 963 F.2d 1403, 1407 [11th Cir. 1991], cited in Bright, 1995, n. 7).

The Court's reasoning in this case led Stephen Bright to conclude that "racial discrimination which would not be acceptable in any other area of American life today is tolerated in criminal courts" (p. 914).

---

by the defendant's prior criminal record, the heinousness of the crime, or other legally relevant variables.

With respect to the effect of the race of the defendant, the GAO report concluded that the evidence was "equivocal."[83] The report noted that about half of the studies found that the race of the defendant affected the likelihood of being charged with a capital crime or receiving the death penalty; most, but not all, of these studies found that African Americans were more likely than whites to be sentenced to death. The authors of the report also stated that although some studies found that African Americans who murdered whites faced the highest odds of receiving the death penalty, "the extent to which the finding was influenced by race of victim rather than race of defendant was unclear."[84]

A comprehensive review of the post-*Furman* research is beyond the scope of this book.[85] Instead, we summarize the results of two studies. The first, a study of the capital sentencing process in Georgia, is one of the most sophisticated studies conducted to date and figured prominently in the Supreme Court's decision in *McCleskey v. Kemp*.[86] The second is a study of capital sentencing patterns in eight states.[87] We then discuss recent research on the federal capital sentencing process.

Table 8.3 Death Penalty Decisions in Post-*Furman* Georgia

Offender and Victim Race	Overall Death-Sentencing Rate	Prosecutor's Decision to Seek Death Penalty	Jury's Decision to Impose Death Penalty
African American/White	.35 (45/130)	.58 (72/125)	.58 (45/77)
White/White	.22 (51/230)	.38 (85/224)	.56 (51/91)
African American/African American	.06 (17/232)	.15 (34/231)	.40 (14/35)
White/African American	.14 (2/14)	.21 (3/14)	.67 (2/3)

SOURCE: David C. Baldus, George G. Woodworth, and Charles A. Pulaski Jr., *Equal Justice and the Death Penalty* (Boston: Northeastern University Press, 1990), tables 30 and 34.

Race and the Death Penalty in Georgia David Baldus and his colleagues analyzed the effect of race on the outcomes of over 600 homicide cases in Georgia from 1973 through 1979.[88] Their examination of the raw data revealed that the likelihood of receiving a death sentence varied by the race of both the offender and the victim. The first column of Table 8.3 shows that 35 percent of the African Americans charged with killing whites were sentenced to death, compared to only 22 percent of the whites who killed whites, 14 percent of the whites who killed African Americans, and 6 percent of the African Americans who killed other African Americans.

Baldus and his coauthors also discovered that the race of the victim played an important role in both the prosecutor's decision to seek the death penalty and the jury's decision to impose the death penalty (see columns 2 and 3, Table 8.3). The victim's race was a particularly strong predictor of the prosecutor's decision to seek or waive the death penalty. In fact, Georgia prosecutors were nearly 4 times more likely to request the death penalty for African American offenders convicted of killing whites than for African American offenders convicted of killing African Americans. The effect of the race of the victim was less pronounced when the offender was white: prosecutors sought the death penalty in 38 percent of the cases with white offenders and white victims, but only 21 percent of the cases with white offenders and African American victims.

The authors of this study then controlled for over 200 variables that might explain these disparities; they included detailed information on the defendant's background and prior criminal record, information concerning the circumstances and the heinousness of the crime, and measures of the strength of evidence against the defendant. They found that inclusion of these controls did not eliminate the racial differences. Although the race of the offender was only a weak predictor of death penalty decisions once these legal factors were taken into consideration, the race of the victim continued to exert a strong effect on both the prosecutor's decision to seek the death penalty and the jury's decision to impose the death penalty. In fact, those who killed whites were over four times as likely to be sentenced to death as those who killed African Americans.

Further analysis revealed that the effects of race were not uniform across the range of homicide cases included in the analysis. Not surprising, race had little effect on decision making in the least aggravated cases, in which virtually no one received the death penalty, or in the most heinous cases, in which a high percentage of murderers, regardless of their race or the race of their victims, were sentenced to death. Rather, race played a role primarily in the midrange of cases where decision makers could decide either to sentence the offender to life in prison or impose the death penalty. In these types of cases, the death-sentencing rate for those who killed whites was 34 percent, compared to only 14 percent for those who killed African Americans.

These findings led Baldus and his colleagues to conclude that the race of the victim was "a potent influence in the system" [89] and that the state of Georgia was operating a "dual system" for processing homicide cases. According to the authors, "Georgia juries appear to tolerate greater levels of aggravation without imposing the death penalty in black victim cases; and, as compared to white victim cases, the level of aggravation in black victim cases must be substantially greater before the prosecutor will even seek a death sentence." [90]

Anthony Amsterdam's analysis was even more blunt. [91] Noting that 9 of the 11 murderers executed by Georgia between 1973 and 1988 were African American and that 10 of the 11 had white victims, Amsterdam asked, "Can there be the slightest doubt that this revolting record is the product of some sort of racial bias rather than a pure fluke?" [92]

Some commentators would be inclined to answer this question in the affirmative, arguing that the statistics included in the Baldus study are not representative of death penalty decisions in the United States as a whole, but rather are peculiar to Southern states such as Georgia, Texas, Florida, and Mississippi. A recent study by Gross and Mauro addressed this possibility.

Death Penalty Decisions in Eight States Gross and Mauro examined death penalty decisions in eight states—Arkansas, Florida, Georgia, Illinois, Mississippi, North Carolina, Oklahoma, and Virginia. They found that the risk of a death sentence was much lower for defendants charged with killing African Americans than for defendants charged with killing whites in each of the eight states included in their study. [93] In Georgia, for example, those who killed whites were nearly 10 times as likely to be sentenced to death as those who killed African Americans. The ratios for the other states included in the study were 10:1 (Mississippi), 8:1 (Florida), 7:1 (Arkansas), 6:1 (Illinois, Oklahoma, and North Carolina), and 5:1 (Virginia).

The authors also discovered that African Americans who killed whites faced the greatest odds of a death sentence. Figure 8.4 presents the percentages of death sentences by race of offender and race of victim for the three states with the largest number of death-eligible cases. In Georgia, 20.1 percent of the African Americans who killed whites were sentenced to death, compared to only 5.7 percent of the whites who killed whites, 2.9 percent of the whites who killed African Americans, and less than 1 percent (0.8 percent) of the African Americans who killed African Americans. There were similar disparities in

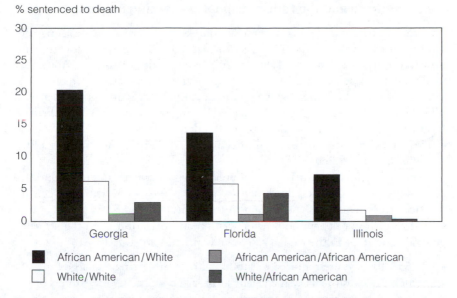

% sentenced to death

FIGURE 8.4 Death Sentence Rates in Post-*Furman* Era, by Race of Offender and Victim

SOURCE: Data obtained from Samuel R. Gross and Robert Mauro, *Death & Discrimination; Racial Disparities in Capital Sentencing* (Boston: Northeastern University Press, 1989).

Florida and Illinois. In fact, in these three states, only 32 of the 4,731 cases with African American defendants and African American victims resulted in a death sentence, compared to 82 of the 621 cases involving African American defendants and white victims.

These racial disparities did not disappear when Gross and Mauro controlled for other legally relevant predictors of sentence severity. According to the authors,

> The major factual finding of this study is simple: there has been racial discrimination in the imposition of the death penalty under post–*Furman* statutes in the eight states that we examined. The discrimination is based on the race of the victim, and it is a remarkably stable and consistent phenomenon. . . . The data show "a clear pattern, unexplainable on grounds other than race."[94]

These results, coupled with the strong evidence of victim-based discrimination documented by the Baldus study, suggest that the issues raised by the Supreme Court in *Furman* have not been resolved. According to Austin Sarat, professor of jurisprudence and political science at Amherst College, "The post-*Furman* effort to rationalize death sentences has utterly failed; it has been replaced by a policy that favors execution while trimming away procedural protection for capital defendants. This situation only exacerbates the incompatibility of capital punishment and legality."[95]

Race and the Federal Capital Sentencing Process

As noted earlier, state legislatures moved quickly to revise their death penalty statutes in the wake of the 1972 *Furman* decision. The federal government, however, did not do so until 1988, when passage of the Anti-Drug Abuse Act made the death penalty available for certain serious drug-related offenses. The number of federal offenses for which the death penalty is an option increased substantially as a result of legislation passed during the mid-1990s. The Federal Death Penalty Act of 1994 added over 40 federal offenses to the list of capital crimes, and the Antiterrorism and Effective Death Penalty Act of 1996 added an additional four offenses.[96]

The Department of Justice has adopted a set of standards and procedures—commonly known as the "death penalty protocol"—to govern death penalty decisions in federal cases. According to this protocol, a U.S. Attorney cannot seek the death penalty without prior written authorization from the attorney general. The steps in the capital case review process are as follows:[97]

- U.S. Attorneys are required to submit all cases involving a charge for which the death penalty is a legally authorized sanction—regardless of whether the attorney recommends seeking the death penalty—to the Capital Case Unit of the Criminal Division for review;

- The Capital Case Unit reviews the case and prepares an initial analysis and recommendation regarding the death penalty;

- The case is forwarded to the attorney general's Capital Case Review Committee, which is composed of senior Justice Department lawyers—the members of the committee meet with the U.S. Attorney and defense counsel responsible for the case, review documents submitted by all parties, and make a recommendation to the attorney general;

- The attorney general makes the final decision regarding whether to seek the death penalty.

According to the Department of Justice, these procedures are designed to ensure that the federal capital sentencing process is fair and equitable: "Both the legal rules and the administrative procedures that currently govern federal capital cases incorporate extensive safeguards against any influence of racial or ethnic bias or prejudice."[98]

The Department of Justice has conducted two studies of the federal capital sentencing process. The first, released in 2000, revealed that from 1995 to 2000, U.S. Attorneys forwarded for review 682 death-eligible cases. Eighty percent of the defendants in these cases were racial minorities: 324 (48 percent) were African American; 195 (29 percent) were Hispanic; and 29 (4 percent) were Native American, Asian American, and other races.[99] This study also revealed, however, that participants in the review process were less likely to recommend (or to seek) the death penalty if the defendant was a racial minority. As shown in Table 8.4, U.S. Attorneys recommended the death penalty in 36 percent of

Table 8.4 Race/Ethnicity and the Federal Death Penalty: 1995–2000

			RACE OF THE DEFENDANT		
	Total	**White**	**African American**	**Hispanic**	**Other**
Number (% of total) of cases submitted for review	682	134 (20%)	324 (47%)	195 (29%)	29 (4%)
Rate at which U.S. Attorneys recommended seeking the death penalty	.27	.36	.25	.20	.52
Rate at which the Review Committee recommended seeking the death penalty	.30	.40	.27	.25	.50
Rate at which the attorney general approved filing of notice of intent to seek the death penalty	.27	.38	.25	.20	.46
Rate at which the Department of Justice sought the death penalty	.23	.33	.22	.16	.41

SOURCE: U.S. Department of Justice, *The Federal Death Penalty System: A Statistical Survey (1988–2000)* (Washington, DC: Author), pp. 10–11.

the cases involving white defendants, compared with 25 percent of those involving African American defendants and 20 percent of those involving Hispanic defendants. There was a similar pattern of results for the Capital Case Unit's recommendation (to the attorney general) to request the death penalty, the attorney general's decision to authorize the U.S. Attorney to file a notice of intent to seek the death penalty, and the Department of Justice's final decision to seek the death penalty.

The data in Table 8.4 demonstrate that although the Justice Department's study did not find racial bias in the decisions that followed the U.S. Attorney's initial decision to submit the case for review, it did find that a significant majority of the cases that were submitted for review involved African American and Hispanic defendants. The attorney general at the time, Janet Reno, stated that she was "sorely troubled" by these findings, adding that "we must do all we can in the federal government to root out bias at every step." Reno's concerns were echoed by U.S. Deputy Attorney General Eric Holder, an African American prosecutor who oversaw the study. He said that he was "both personally and professionally disturbed by the numbers." [100] Publication of the report also led President Clinton to grant a 6-month reprieve to Juan Raul Garza, a Mexican American from Texas who was scheduled to be executed in January 2001. In granting the reprieve, Clinton stated that "the examination of possible racial and regional bias should be completed before the United States goes forward with an execution in a case that may implicate the very questions raised by the Justice Department's continuing study." [101]

Attorney General Reno ordered the Department of Justice to gather additional data about the federal capital sentencing process. The results of this study,
which was overseen by Janet Reno's successor, John Ashcroft, were released in
2001.[102] Unlike the first study, which examined only those cases that were
charged as capital crimes and submitted for review, this study included an
analysis of cases in which the facts would have supported a capital charge but
the defendants were not charged with a capital crime (and thus the case was not
submitted for review). The results of the second study were generally similar to
those of the first. Within the larger pool of cases examined in the follow-up
study, which included 973 defendants, 17 percent (166) were white, 42 percent
(408) were African American, and 36 percent (350) were Hispanic. Consistent
with the results of the 2000 study, "potential capital cases involving Black or
Hispanic defendants were less likely to result in capital charges and submission
of the case to the review procedure . . . likewise [these cases] were less likely to
result in decisions to seek the death penalty." [103]

The 2001 report, which noted that the proportion of racial minorities in
federal capital cases was substantially greater than the proportion of racial minorities in the general population, concluded that "the cause of this disproportion is not racial or ethnic bias, but the representation of minorities in the pool
of potential federal capital cases." [104] The report attributed the overrepresentation of African Americans and Hispanics in the federal capital case pool to a
number of factors, including the fact that federal law enforcement officers focused their attention on drug trafficking and related criminal violence. According to the report,

> In areas where large-scale, organized drug trafficking is largely carried out
> by gangs whose membership is drawn from minority groups, the active
> federal role in investigating and prosecuting these crimes results in a high
> proportion of minority defendants in federal cases, including a high pro-
> portion of minority defendants in potential capital cases arising from the
> lethal violence associated with the drug trade. This is not the result of any
> form of bias, but reflects the normal factors that affect the division of fed-
> eral and state prosecutorial responsibility.[105]

Opponents of the death penalty criticized the 2001 report, and the Justice
Department's interpretation of the data, on a number of grounds. The American Civil Liberties Union (ACLU), for example, asserted that there were a number of problems with the study, which it characterized as "fatally flawed." [106]
The ACLU noted that the report did not address questions regarding the prosecution of cases in the federal system rather than the state system or examine
whether race/ethnicity played a role in these decisions or in U.S. Attorneys'
decisions to enter into plea bargains. The ACLU asserted that Attorney General Ashcroft reached a "premature" conclusion that "racial bias has not played
a role in who is on federal death row in America," adding that "this remarkable conclusion is not only inaccurate, but also dangerous, because it seeks to

give Americans the impression that our justice system is fair when in fact there is substantial evidence that it is not."[107]

On June 11, 2001, Timothy McVeigh, who was convicted on a number of counts stemming from the 1995 Oklahoma City bombing, became the first federal offender since 1963 to be put to death. The execution of Juan Raul Garza, a Texas marijuana distributor who was sentenced to death in 1993 for the murder of three other drug traffickers, followed eight days later. By April 2002, there were 26 offenders on federal death row: 18 African Americans, five whites, two Hispanics, and one Asian American.[108]

Explanations for Disparate Treatment

Researchers have advanced two interrelated explanations for the higher death penalty rates for homicides involving African American offenders and white victims and the lower rates for homicides involving African American offenders and African American victims.

The first explanation builds on conflict theory's premise that the law is applied to maintain the power of the dominant group and to control the behavior of individuals who threaten that power.[109] It suggests that crimes involving African American offenders and white victims are punished most harshly because they pose the greatest threat to "the system of racially stratified state authority".[110] Some commentators further suggest that in the South, the death penalty may be imposed more often on African Americans who kill whites "because of a continuing adherence to traditional southern norms of racial etiquette."[111]

The second explanation emphasizes the race of the victim rather than the racial composition of the victim—offender dyad. This explanation suggests that crimes involving African American victims are not taken seriously and/or that crimes involving white victims are taken very seriously. It also suggests that the lives of African American victims are devalued relative to the lives of white victims. Thus, crimes against whites will be punished more severely than crimes against African Americans regardless of the offender's race. Some commentators suggest that these beliefs are encouraged by the media, which plays up the murders of wealthy whites but ignores those involving poor African Americans and Hispanics. The publicity accorded crimes involving middle-class and wealthy white victims also influences prosecutors to seek the death penalty more often in these types of cases than in cases involving poor racial minorities. According to David Baldus, "If the victim is black, particularly if he's an unsavory character, a drug dealer, for example, prosecutors are likely to say, 'No jury would return a death verdict.'"[112]

Most researchers have failed to explain adequately *why* those who victimize whites are treated more harshly than those who victimize African Americans. Gross and Mauro suggest that the explanation, at least in capital cases, may hinge on the degree to which jurors are able to identify with the victim.[113] The authors argue that jurors take the life-or-death decision in a capital case very seriously. To condemn a murderer to death thus requires something more than sympathy for the victim. Jurors will not sentence the defendant to death unless they are particularly horrified by the crime, and they will not be particularly horrified by the crime unless they can identify or empathize with the victim. According to Gross and Mauro,

> In a society that remains segregated socially if not legally, and in which the great majority of jurors are white, jurors are not likely to identify with black victims or to see them as family or friends. Thus jurors are more likely to be horrified by the killing of a white than of a black, and more likely to act against the killer of a white than the killer of a black.[114]

Bright offers a somewhat different explanation.[115] He contends that the unconscious racism and racial stereotypes of prosecutors, judges, and jurors, the majority of whom are white, "may well be 'stirred up'" in cases involving an African American offender and a white victim.[116] In these types of cases, officials' and jurors' beliefs that African Americans are violent or morally inferior, coupled with their fear of African Americans, might incline them to seek or to impose the death penalty. Bright also asserts that black-on-white murders generate more publicity and evoke greater horror than other types of crimes. As he notes, "Community outrage, . . . the social and political clout of the family in the community, and the amount of publicity regarding the crime are often far more important in determining whether death is sought than the facts of the crime or the defendant's record and background."[117]

MCCLESKEY V. KEMP: THE SUPREME COURT AND RACIAL DISCRIMINATION IN THE APPLICATION OF THE DEATH PENALTY

Empirical evidence of racial discrimination in the capital sentencing process has been used to mount constitutional challenges to the imposition of the death penalty. African American defendants convicted of raping or murdering whites have claimed that the death penalty is applied in a racially discriminatory manner in violation of both the equal protection clause of the Fourteenth Amendment and the cruel and unusual punishment clause of the Eighth Amendment.

These claims have been consistently rejected by state and federal appellate courts. The case of the Martinsville Seven, a group of African American men who were sentenced to death for the gang-rape of a white woman, was the first case in which defendants explicitly argued that the death penalty was administered in a racially discriminatory manner.[118] It was also the first case in which lawyers presented statistical evidence to prove systematic racial discrimination in capital cases. As explained in more detail in the Focus on an Issue, "The Case of the Martinsville Seven," the defendants' contention that the Virginia rape statute had "been applied and administered with an evil eye and an unequal hand"[119] was repeatedly denied by Virginia appellate courts.

The question of racial discrimination in the application of the death penalty has also been addressed in federal court. In a series of decisions, the Courts of Appeals ruled that the empirical studies used to document systematic racial discrimination did not take every variable related to capital sentencing into account and that the evidence presented did not demonstrate that the appellant's *own* sentence was the product of discrimination.[120]

The Supreme Court directly addressed the issue of victim-based racial discrimination in the application of the death penalty in the case of *McCleskey v. Kemp*.[121] Warren McCleskey, an African American, was convicted and sentenced to death in Georgia for killing a white police officer during the course of an armed robbery. McCleskey claimed that the Georgia capital sentencing process was administered in a racially discriminatory manner. In support of his claim, he offered the results of the study conducted by Baldus and his colleagues.[122] As noted earlier, this study found that African Americans convicted of murdering whites had the greatest likelihood of receiving the death penalty.

The Supreme Court rejected McCleskey's Fourteenth and Eighth Amendment claims. Although the majority accepted the validity of the Baldus study, they nonetheless refused to accept McCleskey's argument that the disparities documented by Baldus signaled the presence of unconstitutional racial discrimination. Justice Powell, writing for the majority, argued that the disparities were "unexplained" and stated, "At most, the Baldus study indicates a discrepancy that appears to correlate with race."[123] The Court stated that the Baldus study was "clearly insufficient to support an inference that any of the decision-makers in McCleskey's case acted with discriminatory purpose."[124]

The Court also expressed its concern that accepting McCleskey's claim would open a Pandora's box of litigation. "McCleskey's claim, taken to its logical conclusion," Powell wrote, "throws into serious question the principles that underlie our entire criminal justice system . . . if we accepted McCleskey's claim that racial bias impermissibly tainted the capital sentencing decision, we would soon be faced with similar claims as to other types of penalty."[125] A ruling in McCleskey's favor, in other words, would open the door to constitutional challenges to the legitimacy of both the capital sentencing process and sentencing in general.

The four dissenting justices were outraged. Justice Brennan, who was joined in dissent by Justices Blackmun, Marshall, and Stevens, wrote, "The Court today holds that Warren McCleskey's sentence was constitutionally imposed. It finds no fault with a system in which lawyers must tell their clients that race casts a large shadow on the capital sentencing process." Brennan also characterized the majority's concern that upholding McCleskey's claim would encourage other groups—"even women"[126]—to challenge the criminal sentencing process "as a fear of too much justice" and "a complete abdication of our judicial role."[127]

Focus on an Issue
The Case of the Martinsville Seven

Just after dark on January 8, 1949, Ruby Floyd, a 32-year-old white woman, was assaulted and repeatedly raped by several men as she walked in a predominantly African American neighborhood in Martinsville, Virginia (Rise, 1995, p. 122). Within a day and a half, seven African American men had been arrested; when confronted with incriminating statements made by their co-defendants, all of them confessed. Two months later, a grand jury composed of four white men and three African American men indicted each defendant on one count of rape and six counts of aiding and abetting a rape by the other defendants.

The defendants were tried in the Seventh Judicial Circuit Court, located in Martinsville. Before the legal proceedings began, Judge Kennon Caithness Whittle, who presided over all of the trials, called the prosecutors and defense attorneys into his chambers to remind them of their duty to protect the defendants' right to a fair trial and to plead with them to "downplay the racial overtones" of the case. He emphasized that the case "must be tried as though both parties were members of the same race" (p. 30).

Although prosecutors took Judge Whittle's admonitions to heart and emphasized the seriousness of the crime and the defendants' evident guilt rather than the fact that the crime involved the rape of a white woman by African American men, the "racial overtones" of the case inevitably surfaced. Defense attorneys, for example, moved for a change of venue, arguing that inflammatory publicity about the case, coupled with widespread community sentiment that the defendants were guilty and "ought to get the works" (p. 32) meant

that the defendants could not get a fair trial in Martinsville. Judge Whittle, who admitted that it might be difficult to find impartial jurors and acknowledged that some jurors might be biased against the defendants because of their race, denied the motion, asserting that "no mass feeling about these defendants" had surfaced (p. 35). Later, prosecutors used their peremptory challenges to exclude the few African Americans who remained in the jury pool after those who opposed the death penalty had been excused for cause. As a result, each case was decided by an all-white jury. The result of each day-long trial was the same: all seven defendants were found guilty of rape and sentenced to death. On May 3, 1949, less than 4 months after the assault on Ruby Floyd, Judge Whittle officially pronounced sentence and announced that four of the defendants were to be executed on July 15, the remaining three on July 22. Noting that this gave the defendants more than 60 days to appeal, he stated, "If errors have been made I pray God they may be corrected" (p. 48).

The next 19 months witnessed several rounds of appeals challenging the convictions and death sentences of the Martinsville Seven. The initial petition submitted by attorneys for the NAACP Legal Defense Fund, which represented the defendants on appeal, charged the trial court with four violations of due process. Although none of the charges focused directly on racially discriminatory practices, allegations of racial prejudice were interwoven with a number of the arguments. Appellants noted, for example, that prior to 1866, Virginia law specified that the death penalty for rape could be imposed only on African American men convicted of raping white women; even after the law was repealed, virtually all of those sentenced to death for rape had been African American. They also stated that the trial judge's questioning of prospective jurors about capital punishment and subsequent exclusion of those who were opposed to the imposition of the death penalty sent the unmistakable message that "only one penalty would be appropriate for the offenders" (p. 85).

These appeals failed at both the state and federal levels. The Virginia Supreme Court of Appeals voted unanimously to affirm the convictions. Chief Justice Edward W. Hudgins, who wrote the opinion, vehemently denied appellants' assertions that the death penalty was reserved for African Americans, noting that there was not "a scintilla of evidence" to support it (*Hampton v. Commonwealth*, 58 S.E.2d 288, 298 [Va. Sup. Ct., 1950]). Hudgins also chastised the defendants' attorneys for even raising the issue, contending that it was nothing more than "an abortive attempt to inject into the proceedings racial prejudice" (*Hampton v. Commonwealth*).

The defendants appealed the decision to the U.S. Supreme Court, but the Court declined to review the case. This prompted the NAACP attorneys to adopt a radically different strategy for the next round of appeals. Rather than challenge the defendants' convictions and death sentences on traditional due process grounds, the attorneys mounted a direct attack on the discriminatory application of the death penalty in Virginia. Martin Martin and Samuel Tucker, the NAACP attorneys who argued in support of the defendants' habeas corpus petition, presented statistical evidence documenting a double stan-

dard of justice in Virginia rape cases. Noting that 45 African Americans, but not a single white, had been executed for rape since 1908, Tucker stated that African Americans were entitled to the same protection of the law as whites and concluded that "if you can't equalize upward [by executing more whites], we must equalize downward" (Rise, 1995, p. 121).

In an opinion that foreshadowed the Supreme Court's decision in *McCleskey v. Kemp* a quarter of a century later, Judge Doubles, who was presiding over the Hustings Court of the City of Richmond, denied the petition. Judge Doubles stated that there was no evidence of racial discrimination in the actions of the six juries that sentenced the Martinsville Seven to death or in the performance of other juries in similar cases. He then concluded that even if one assumed that those juries had been motivated by racial prejudice, "the petitioners could not demonstrate that an official policy of discrimination, rather than the independent actions of separate juries, resulted in the death verdicts" (p. 124). As a result, there was no violation of the Constitution.

The case was then appealed to the Virginia Supreme Court and, when that appeal failed, to the U.S. Supreme Court. In January 1951, the Supreme Court again declined to review the case. Last-minute efforts to save the Martinsville Seven failed. Four of the men were executed on February 2, the remaining three on February 5. "After two years, six trials, five stays of execution, ten opportunities for judicial review, and two denials of executive clemency, the legal odyssey of the Martinsville Seven had ended" (p. 148).

Legal scholars were similarly outraged. Anthony Amsterdam, who was the lead attorney in a 1968 U.S. Court of Appeals case in which an African American man challenged his death sentence for the rape of a white woman,[128] wrote:

> I suggest that any self-respecting criminal justice professional is obliged to speak out against this Supreme Court's conception of the criminal justice system. We must reaffirm that there can be no justice in a system which treats people of color differently from white people, or treats crimes against people of color differently from crimes against white people.[129]

Randall Kennedy's analysis was similarly harsh. He challenged Justice Powell's assertion that the Baldus study indicated nothing more "than a discrepancy that appears to correlate with race," which he characterized as "a statement as vacuous as one declaring, say, that 'at most' studies on lung cancer indicate a discrepancy that appears to correlate with smoking."[130] Bright characterized the decision as "a badge of shame upon America's system of justice."[131] Gross and Mauro concluded, "The central message of the *McCleskey* case is all too plain; de facto racial discrimination in capital sentencing is legal in the United States."[132] (See Box 8.5 for a discussion of the possible remedies for racial discrimination in the application of the death penalty.)

The Execution of Warren McCleskey

The Court's decision in *McCleskey v. Kemp* did not mark the end of Warren McCleskey's odyssey through the appellate courts. He filed another appeal in 1987, alleging that the testimony of a jailhouse informant, which was used to rebut his alibi defense, was obtained illegally. Offie Evans testified at McCleskey's trial in 1978 that McCleskey admitted to and boasted about killing the police officer. McCleskey argued that the state placed Evans in the jail cell next to his and instructed Evans to try to get him to talk about the crime. He contended that because he did not have the assistance of counsel at the time he made the incriminating statements, they could not be used against him.

In 1991, the Supreme Court denied McCleskey's claim, asserting that the issue should have been raised in his first appeal.[133] The Court stated that McCleskey would have been allowed to raise a new issue if he had been able to demonstrate that the alleged violation resulted in the conviction of an innocent person. However, according to the Court, "the violation, if it be one, resulted in the admission at trial of truthful inculpatory evidence which did not affect the reliability of the guilt determination. The very statement that McCleskey now embraces confirms his guilt."[134]

After a series of last-minute appeals, requests for clemency, and requests for commutation were denied, Warren McCleskey was strapped into the electric chair at the state prison in Jacksonville, Georgia. He was pronounced dead at 3:13 A.M., September 26, 1991.

Justice Thurgood Marshall, one of three dissenters from the Supreme Court's decision not to grant a stay of execution, wrote, "In refusing to grant a stay to review fully McCleskey's claims, the court values expediency over human life.

BOX 8.5 Racial Discrimination in Capital Sentencing: The Problem of Remedy

A number of commentators have suggested that the Court's reluctance to accept McCleskey's claim reflected its anxiety about the practical consequences of ruling that race impermissibly affected the capital sentencing process (Baldus, Woodworth, & Pulaski, 1990, pp. 384–387; Gross & Mauro, 1989, Chap. 11; Kennedy, 1998, pp. 340–345). The Court's decision, in other words, reflected its concern about the appropriate remedy if it found a constitutional violation.

The remedies that have been suggested include the following:

1. *Abolish the death penalty, and vacate all existing death sentences nationwide.* The problem with this remedy, of course, is that it is impractical, given the level of public support for the death penalty and the current emphasis on crime control. As Gross and Mauro (1989, p. 216) note, "Although abolition is a perfectly practical solution to the problems of capital punishment . . . it is not a serious option in America now."

2. *Vacate all death sentences in each state where there is compelling evidence of racial disparities in the application of the death penalty.* Although this state-by-state approach would not completely satisfy the abolitionists, according to Kennedy (1998, p. 341), it would place "a large question mark over the legitimacy of any death penalty system generating unexplained racial disparities of the sort at issue in *McCleskey*.

3. *Limit the class of persons eligible for the death penalty to those who commit the most heinous and the most aggravated homicides.* As Justice Stevens suggested in his dissent in *McCleskey*, the Court could narrow the class of death-eligible defendants to those "categories of extremely serious crimes for which prosecutors consistently seek, and juries consistently impose, the death penalty without regard to the race of the victim or the race of the offender" (*McCleskey v. Kemp*, at 1806). Although not an "ideal" solution for a number of reasons, this would, as Baldus, Woodworth, and Pulaski (1990, p. 385) contend, impart "a greater degree of rationality and consistency into state death-sentencing systems than any of the other procedural safeguards that the Supreme Court has heretofore endorsed."

4. *Reinstate mandatory death sentences for certain crimes.* This remedy would, of course, require the Supreme Court to retract its invalidation of mandatory death penalty statutes. Kennedy (1998, p. 341) contends that this would not solve the problem because prosecutors could refuse to charge the killers of African Americans with a capital crime and juries could decline to convict those who killed African Americans of crimes that triggered the mandatory death sentence.

5. *Opt for the "level-up solution," which would require courts to purposely impose more death sentences on those who murdered African Americans* (Kennedy, 1998, p. 344). According to Kennedy, states in which there are documented racial disparities in the use of the death penalty could be given a choice: either condemn those who kill African Americans to death at the same rate at those who kill whites or "relinquish the power to put anyone to death" (p. 344).

Repeatedly denying Warren McCleskey his constitutional rights is unacceptable. Executing him is inexcusable."[135]

The Aftermath of *McCleskey*

Opponents of the death penalty viewed the issues raised in *McCleskey v. Kemp* as the only remaining challenge to the constitutionality of the death penalty. They predicted that the Court's decision, which effectively closed the door to similar appeals, would speed up the pace of executions. Data on the number of persons executed since 1987 provide support for this. Although only 25 persons were executed in 1987 and only 14 were executed in 1991, the numbers began to increase in 1992. Figure 8.5 shows that the number of persons put to death jumped from 31 in 1992 to 98 in 1999; the number of executions declined to 85 in 2000 and to 66 in 2001.[136]

The increase in executions since 1991 no doubt reflects the impact of two recent Supreme Court decisions sharply limiting death row appeals. As noted earlier, in 1991 the Court ruled that, with few exceptions, death row inmates and other state prisoners must raise constitutional claims on their first appeals.[137] This ruling, coupled with a 1993 decision stating that "late claims of innocence" raised by death row inmates who have exhausted other federal appeals do not automatically qualify for a hearing in federal court,[138] severely curtailed the ability of death row inmates to pursue multiple federal court appeals.

The U.S. House of Representatives responded to the Supreme Court's ruling in *McCleskey v. Kemp* by adding the Racial Justice Act to the 1994 Omnibus Crime Bill. A slim majority of the House voted for the provision, which would have allowed condemned defendants to challenge their death sentences by showing a *pattern* of racial discrimination in the capital sentencing process in their jurisdictions. Under this provision, the defendant would not have to show that criminal justice officials acted with discriminatory purpose in his or her case; rather, the defendant could use statistical evidence indicating that a disproportionate number of those sentenced to death in the jurisdiction were African Americans or had killed whites. Once this pattern of racial discrimination had been established, the State would be required to prove that its death penalty decisions were racially neutral. The State might rebut an apparent pattern of racial discrimination in a case involving an African American convicted of killing a white police officer, for example, by showing a consistent pattern of seeking the death penalty for defendants, regardless of race, who were accused of killing police officers.

Opponents of the Racial Justice Act argued that it would effectively abolish the death penalty in the United States. As Senator Orrin Hatch remarked, "The so-called Racial Justice Act has nothing to do with racial justice and everything to do with abolishing the death penalty."[139] The provision was a source of heated debate before it was eventually eliminated from the 1994 Omnibus Crime Bill.

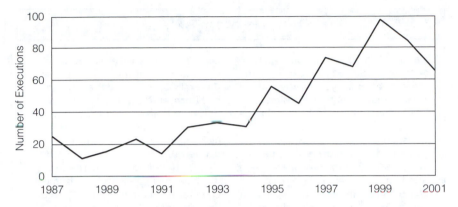

FIGURE 8.5 Executions in the United States, 1987–2001

SOURCE: Criminal Justice Project of the NAACP Legal Defense and Educational Fund, Inc., *Death Row USA: Winter 2002.* Available at http://www.deathpenaltyinfo.org/DEATHROWUSArecent.pdf.

THE DEATH PENALTY
IN THE 21ST CENTURY

Opponents of the death penalty assumed that the Supreme Court's decision in *McCleskey v. Kemp,* coupled with the defeat of the Racial Justice Act, sounded a death knell for attempts to abolish the death penalty. They predicted that these decisions would quiet—if not extinguish—the controversy surrounding the death penalty. Contrary to their predictions, the controversy did not die down. In fact, a series of events at the turn of the century pushed the issue back on the public agenda:

- In February 1997, the American Bar Association (ABA) went on record as being formally opposed to the current capital sentencing system and called for an immediate moratorium on executions in the United States. The ABA report cited the following concerns: lack of adequate counsel in death penalty cases, restrictions on access to appellate courts, and racial disparities in the administration of capital punishment.[140]

- In January 2000, George Ryan, the governor of Illinois, issued a moratorium on the use of the death penalty in that state. His decision was motivated by the fact that since the death penalty had been reinstated in Illinois, 12 persons had been executed, but 13 had been exonerated. Governor Ryan called for a "public dialogue" on "the question of the fairness of the application of the death penalty in Illinois" and stated that he favored a moratorium because of his "grave concerns about our state's shameful record of convicting innocent people and putting them on death row."[141]

- In May 2000, the New Hampshire legislature voted to repeal the death penalty. One legislator—a Republican and a longtime supporter of the

---

BOX 8.6   Death and Discrimination in Texas

On June 5, 2000, the U.S. Supreme Court set aside Victor Saldano's death sentence after lawyers for the State of Texas admitted that the decision had been based in part on the fact that he is Hispanic (Saldano v. Texas, 99-8119). Saldano kidnapped Paul Green at gunpoint from a grocery store parking lot, took him to an isolated area, shot him five times, and stole his watch and wallet. At Saldano's sentencing hearing, a psychologist testified about Saldano's "future dangerousness." He noted that African Americans and Hispanics were overrepresented in prison and stated that the fact that Saldano was Hispanic was an indicator of his future dangerousness. The Texas Court of Criminal Appeals upheld Saldano's death sentence, stating that allowing his ethnicity to be used as an indicator of dangerousness was not a "fundamental error."

In his appeal to the U.S. Supreme Court, Saldano disagreed with that conclusion. He stated that it is "fundamentally unfair for the prosecution to use racial and ethnic stereotypes in order to obtain a death penalty." The Texas attorney general conceded Saldano's point. He admitted that the State had erred and joined Saldano in asking the Supreme Court to order a new sentencing hearing. After the

Court's decision was announced, a spokesperson for the Texas Attorney General's Office stated that an audit had uncovered eight additional cases that might raise similar issues regarding testimony linking race and ethnicity to assessments of future dangerousness.

Questions about the fairness of the Texas death penalty process have been raised in other forums. During the summer of 2000, for example, the *Chicago Tribune* (June 11 and 12, 2000) published a two-part series that focused on the 131 executions carried out during Texas governor George W. Bush's tenure. Since 1977, Texas has executed 218 persons, which is more than 3 times the number executed by any other state (BJS, 2000). The *Tribune* report noted that in 40 of the 131 cases, the defense attorney either presented no mitigating evidence at all or called only one witness during the sentencing hearing. In 43 of the cases, the defendant was represented by an attorney who had been (or was subsequent to the trial) publicly sanctioned for misconduct by the State Bar of Texas. One attorney, for example, had been practicing for only 17 months when he was appointed to represent Davis Losada, who was accused of rape and murder. Losada was found guilty and sentenced to death

---

death penalty—justified his vote for repeal by saying, "There are no millionaires on death row. Can you honestly say that you're going to get equal justice under the law when, if you've got the money, you are going to get away with it?"[142] Although the legislation was subsequently vetoed by the governor, it was the first time in more than two decades that a state legislature had voted to repeal the death penalty.

- In October 2000, the Texas Civil Rights Project (TCRP) released a report on the death penalty in Texas (see Box 8.6, "Death and Discrimination in Texas"). The report identified six critical issues, including the competency of attorneys appointed to represent defendants charged with capital

---

BOX 8.6 *(continued)*

after the attorney delivered a "disjointed and brief argument" in which he told the jury: "The System. Justice. I don't know. But that's what y'all are going to do." He later admitted that he had a conflict of interest in the case (he previously had represented the key witness against his client), and in 1994 he was disbarred for stealing money from his clients.

Other problems cited in the *Tribune* report included the use of unreliable evidence, such as testimony by jailhouse informants; the use of questionable testimony from a psychiatrist, nicknamed "Dr. Death," regarding the potential dangerousness of capital offenders; and the refusal of the Texas Court of Criminal Appeals to order new trials or sentencing hearings despite allegations of fundamental violations of defendants' rights. The report noted that since Governor Bush took office in 1995, the Court of Criminal Appeals had affirmed 270 capital convictions, granted new trials eight times, and ordered new sentencing hearings only six times.

In September 2000, the Texas Civil Rights Project (TCRP) issued a comprehensive report, "The Death Penalty in Texas," that identified many of the same problems. The authors of the report stated that there were "six areas where the probability of error and the probability of wrongful execution grow dramatically" (p. i): appointment of counsel to represent indigent defendants; the prosecutor's decision to seek the death penalty; the jury selection process; the sentencing process; the appellate process; and the review of cases by the Board of Pardons and Parole. The report emphasized that the issue was not "a possible break at one juncture, but a probable break at two or more critical junctures" (p. i).

To remedy these deficiencies, the TCRP recommended that Governor Bush call for a moratorium on the death penalty in Texas. The TCRP also recommended that Governor Bush appoint a commission to review the convictions of those currently on death row; the commission would be charged with determining whether the defendant's rights to due process had been violated and whether race and/or social class affected the death penalty process (p. iv). According to the report, "If the State of Texas is going to continue to take the lives of people, then it needs to repair the system." The report concluded that "the frightening truth of the matter is that Texas is at greater risk than at anytime since it resumed executions in 1982 of killing innocent people" (p. ii).

---

murder, that "decrease due process for low-income death penalty defendants and increase the probability of wrongful convictions." The report called on Governor Bush to institute a moratorium on the death penalty pending the results of two studies, one of which would determine whether race and social class influenced the use of the death penalty in Texas.[143]

- During 2001, two Supreme Court Justices—Sandra Day O'Connor and Ruth Bader Ginsburg—gave speeches in which they criticized the handling of death penalty cases. O'Connor stated that "some innocent defendants have been convicted and sentenced to death," and Ginsburg noted that she "had yet to see a death case . . . in which the defendant was well represented at trial."[144]

As these examples illustrate, concerns about the fairness and accuracy of the capital sentencing process led many to conclude that it was time to rethink the death penalty. This period of "rethinking" spawned two distinct movements, one for reform of the capital sentencing process and one for abolishing the death penalty.

The Movement to Reform the Death Penalty

Advocates of reform contend that the capital sentencing process can be "fixed." Although acknowledging that the system is not infallible, they argue that the enactment of reforms designed to ensure that innocent persons are not convicted and sentenced to death will remedy the situation. The proposed reforms include increasing access to postconviction DNA testing and providing funding to pay for DNA tests requested by indigent inmates; banning the execution of mentally retarded offenders; and establishing standards on qualifications and experience for defense counsel in death penalty cases.

Typical of this approach is the Innocence Protection Act of 2001, a package of criminal justice reforms that was introduced in both houses of Congress. The Act, which had 216 cosponsors in the House of Representatives and 24 cosponsors in the Senate, would (1) allow a person convicted of a federal crime to obtain DNA testing to support a claim of innocence, (2) prohibit states from denying applications for DNA testing made by death row inmates if specified conditions apply, (3) encourage states to develop minimum standards for capital representation, and (4) provide funding to ensure that indigent defendants have access to lawyers who meet those minimum standards.[145] William D. Delahunt, the Act's chief sponsor in the Senate, stated that "the impact of these measures will be felt far beyond the confines of death penalty cases. By raising standards we can help restore public confidence, not just in the fairness and reliability of capital trials, but in the integrity of the American justice system as a whole."[146]

The bipartisan commission appointed by Illinois Governor George Ryan after he halted executions in January 2000 took a similar approach. The commission's report was issued in April 2002 and recommended 85 changes in the capital sentencing process in Illinois. Included were proposals to prohibit the imposition of the death penalty based solely on the testimony of a single eyewitness, a jailhouse informant, or an accomplice; to videotape interrogations of suspects; to establish an independent forensics laboratory; and to establish a state panel to review prosecutors' decisions to seek the death penalty. The report also proposed eliminating several categories of capital crimes, including murder committed in the course of a felony. The cochair of the commission, Thomas P. Sullivan, a former federal prosecutor, stated that the options were to "repair or repeal" the death penalty. "Fix the capital punishment system or abolish it," he said. "There is no other principled recourse."[147]

The Movement to Abolish the Death Penalty

In contrast to those who advocate reform of the capital sentencing system, proponents of abolishing the death penalty contend that the system is fatally flawed. To support their position, these "new abolitionists"[148] cite mounting evidence of wrongful conviction of those on death row (see Box 8.7), as well as evidence that the death penalty is administered in an arbitrary and discriminatory manner. Like former Supreme Court Justice Harry Blackmun, they argue that it is futile to continue to "tinker with the machinery of death."[149]

Whereas traditional abolitionists base their opposition to the death penalty on the immorality of state killing, the sanctity of human life, or the inherent cruelty of death as a punishment, the new abolitionists claim that the death penalty "has not been, and cannot be, administered in a manner that is compatible with our legal system's fundamental commitments to fair and equal treatment."[150] They contend that the implementation of procedural rules, such as those proposed by the advocates of reform, has not solved—indeed, cannot solve—the problems inherent in the capital sentencing process: the post-*Furman* reforms notwithstanding, "the death penalty remains fraught with arbitrariness, discrimination, caprice, and mistake."[151] Like Justice Blackmun, the advocates of abolition insist that "no combination of procedural rules or substantive regulations ever can save the death penalty from its inherent constitutional deficiencies."[152]

Concerns about fairness and discrimination in the capital sentencing process prompted death penalty opponents to call not for procedural reforms but for a moratorium on executions in the United States. Although these resolutions typically call for a cessation of executions until reforms designed to ensure due process and equal protection have been implemented, Sarat maintains that they "amount to a call for the abolition, not merely the cessation, of capital punishment."[153]

Sarat contends that the reforms needed to "fix" the capital sentencing process—provision of competent counsel for all capital defendants, expansion of death row inmates' rights to appeal, guaranteed access to DNA testing, and review of prosecutors' decisions to seek the death penalty—although feasible, are "hardly a likely or near-term possibility."[154] He notes, for example, that one of the reasons cited by the ABA in its call for a moratorium on the death penalty is the "longstanding patterns of racial discrimination . . . in courts around the country."[155] To address this problem, the ABA calls for the development of "effective mechanisms" to eliminate racial discrimination in capital cases. Similarly, the National Death Penalty Moratorium Act of 2001, which has been introduced in both houses of Congress, would set up a National Commission on the Death Penalty; the commission would be charged with "establishing guidelines and procedures which . . . ensure that the death penalty is not administered in a racially discriminatory manner."[156] The problem, according to Sarat, is that it is not clear that any such "mechanisms," "guidelines," or "procedures" exist. As he contends,

> The pernicious effects of race in capital sentencing are a function of the
> persistence of racial prejudice throughout society combined with the

BOX 8.7   The Death Penalty and Wrongful Convictions

Opponents of the death penalty consistently note the possibility that an individual will be sentenced to death for a crime that he or she did not commit. Bedau and Radelet (1987) have identified 350 cases in which defendants were wrongfully convicted of a homicide for which they could have received the death penalty or of a rape in which the death penalty was imposed. Of these individuals, 139 were sentenced to die; 23 eventually were executed. Another 22 persons came within 72 hours of being executed.

These wrongful convictions include a number of persons sentenced to death in the post-*Furman* era. In 1987, for example, Walter McMillian, an African American man who was dating a white woman, was charged with the death of an 18-year-old white female store clerk in Alabama. In spite of testimony from a dozen witnesses, who swore he was at home on the day of the murder, and despite the lack of any physical evidence, McMillian was convicted after a trial that lasted only a day and a half. His conviction hinged on the testimony of Ralph Myers, a 30-year-old with a long criminal record. The jury recommended life in prison without parole, but the judge hearing the case, citing the "vicious and brutal killing of a young lady in the full flower of adulthood," sentenced McMillian to death (*Omaha World Herald,* March 3, 1993).

Six years later, Myers recanted his testimony. He said he had been pressured by law enforcement officials to accuse McMillian and to testify against him in court. McMillian was freed in March 1993, after prosecutors conceded that his conviction was based on perjured testimony and that evidence had been withheld from his lawyers. He had spent 6 years on death row for a crime he did not commit.

A similar fate awaited Rolando Cruz, a Hispanic American who, along with codefendant Alejandro Hernandez, was convicted of the 1983 kidnapping, rape, and murder of 10-year-old Jeanine Nicarico in DuPage County (Illinois) Circuit Court. Cruz was twice convicted and condemned to death for the crime, but both verdicts were overturned by appellate courts because of procedural errors at trial. He spent nearly 10 years on death row before he was acquitted at a third trial in November 1995. Hernandez was also convicted twice and sentenced to death once before his case was dropped following the acquittal of Cruz (articles in the *Chicago Tribune,* 1995–1998).

This case attracted national attention for what many believed was the "railroading" of Cruz and Hernandez.

wide degree of discretion necessary to afford individualized justice in capital prosecutions and capital trials. Prosecutors with limited resources may be inclined to allocate resources to cases that attract the greatest public attention, which often will mean cases where the victim was white and his or her assailant black. Participants in the legal system—whether white or black—demonize young black males, seeing them as more deserving of death as a punishment because of their perceived danger. These cultural effects are not remediable in the near term.[157]

Because it may be impossible to ensure that the capital sentencing process is operated in a racially neutral manner, Sarat and others who embrace the new abolitionism maintain that the only solution is to abolish the death penalty.

BOX 8.7 *(continued)*

Prosecutors presented no physical evidence or eyewitness testimony linking the two to the crime but relied almost exclusively on the testimony of jailhouse informants who stated that the defendants had admitted the crime and on questionable testimony regarding a dream about the crime that Cruz allegedly described to sheriff's deputies. They also ignored compelling evidence that another man, Brian Dugan, had committed the crime. According to Eric Zorn, a reporter for the *Chicago Tribune* (October 18, 1995), "The crime had been 'solved' by cobbling together a shabby case against Rolando Cruz and Alex Hernandez of Aurora and presenting it to a jury that convicted them and sent them to Death Row."

On November 3, 1995, Judge Ronald Mehling, who was presiding at Cruz's third trial, acquitted Cruz of the charges. In a strongly worded address from the bench, Mehling stated that the murder investigation was "sloppy" and that the government's case against Cruz was "riddled with lies and mistakes." As reported in the *Chicago Tribune* on November 4, 1995, he also sharply criticized prosecutors for their handling of the "vision statement" and suggested that investigators had lied about the statement and about other evidence. "What troubles me in this case," Mehling said, "is what the evidence does not show." Cruz was set free that day; Hernandez was released several weeks later.

One year later, a grand jury handed down a 47-count indictment against three of the prosecutors and four of the sheriff's deputies involved in the case. On April 9, 1998, the *Chicago Tribune* reported that the indictment charged the deputies with repeated acts of perjury and alleged that prosecutors knowingly presented perjured testimony and buried the notes of an interview with Dugan that could have exonerated Cruz. The defendants, dubbed the "DuPage Seven," were acquitted of all charges in 1999. Lawyers for Rolando Cruz, Alejandro Hernandez, and Stephen Buckley (a third defendant who had been charged in the crime) then filed a federal civil rights suit. In October 2000, the DuPage County state's attorney agreed to pay the defendants an out-of-court settlement of $3.5 million.

These two cases are not isolated incidents. In April 2002, Ray Krone, who was convicted and sentenced to death for the murder of a cocktail waitress in 1991, became the 100th former death row prisoner to be exonerated since 1973. Krone was freed after DNA tests revealed that he was not the killer.

CONCLUSION

The findings of research examining the effect of race on the capital sentencing process are consistent. Study after study has demonstrated that those who murder whites are much more likely to be sentenced to death than those who murder African Americans. Many of these studies have also shown that African Americans convicted of murdering whites receive the death penalty more often than whites who murder other whites.

These results suggest that racial disparities in the application of the death penalty reflect racial discrimination. Some might argue that these results signal contextual, rather than systematic, racial discrimination. As noted earlier, although research consistently has revealed that those who murder whites are sentenced to death at a disproportionately high rate, not all studies have found that African American offenders are more likely than white offenders to be sentenced to death.

We contend that the type of discrimination found in the capital sentencing process falls closer to the systematic end of the discrimination continuum presented in Chapter 1. Racial discrimination in the capital sentencing process is not limited to the South, where historical evidence of racial bias would lead one to expect differential treatment, but is applicable to other regions of the country as well. It is not confined to one stage of the decision-making process but affects decisions made by prosecutors as well as juries. Also, it is not confined to the pre-*Furman* era, when statutes offered little or no guidance to judges and juries charged with deciding whether to impose the death penalty or not, but is found under the more restrictive guided-discretion statutes enacted since *Furman*. Moreover, this effect does not disappear when legally relevant predictors of sentence severity are taken into consideration.

With respect to the capital sentencing process, then, empirical studies suggest that the Supreme Court was overly optimistic in predicting that the statutory reforms adopted since *Furman* would eliminate racial discrimination. To the contrary, these studies document "a clear pattern unexplainable on grounds other than race."[158]

DISCUSSION QUESTIONS

1. Do you agree or disagree with the so-called Marshall Hypothesis—that is, that the average citizen who knew "all the facts presently available regarding capital punishment would . . . find it shocking to his conscience and sense of justice?"

2. In *Gregg v. Georgia,* the Supreme Court assumed that racial discrimination would not be a problem under the guided-discretion statutes enacted in the wake of the *Furman* decision. Does the empirical evidence support or refute this assumption?

3. Explain why Michael Radelet believes that the handful of executions of whites for crimes against African Americans are not really "exceptions to the rule."

4. The procedures adopted by the Department of Justice to govern death penalty decisions in federal cases (the so-called death penalty protocol) are designed to ensure that the federal capital sentencing process is fair and equitable. But studies conducted by the Department of Justice revealed that racial minorities were overrepresented in federal capital criminal cases and among those sentenced to death in U.S. District Courts. How did the Justice Department interpret these findings? Why did the American Civil Liberties Union conclude that the 2001 study was "fatally flawed"?

5. In the case of the Martinsville Seven, a series of state and federal court rulings rejected the defendants' allegations regarding racial discrimination in the application of the death penalty; Judge Doubles, for instance, ruled that there was no evidence of racial discrimination in the actions of the six juries that sentenced the seven men to death. In *McCleskey v. Kemp,* the U.S. Supreme Court similarly ruled that there was insufficient evidence "to support an inference that any of the decisionmakers in McCleskey's case acted with discriminatory purpose." Assume that you are the lawyer representing an African American offender who has been sentenced to death. What types of evidence would you need to convince the appellate courts that decision makers in your client's case had "acted with discriminatory purpose"? Is it realistic to assume that any offender can meet this burden of proof?

6. Consider the five remedies for racial discrimination in capital sentencing (see Box 8.5). Which do you believe is the appropriate remedy? Why?

7. In 1994, Supreme Court Justice Harry Blackmun stated that it was futile to continue to "tinker with the machinery of death." Although those who advocate abolishing the death penalty agree with this assessment, advocates of reform contend that the death penalty can be "fixed." Summarize the arguments of those who advocate reform.

8. Do you agree or disagree with our conclusion that "the type of discrimination found in the capital sentencing process falls closer to the systematic end of the discrimination continuum presented in Chapter 1"? Why?

NOTES

1. *Callins v. Collins,* 510 U.S. 1141, 1154–155 (1994).

2. Ibid., at 1145.

3. Ibid.

4. For a discussion of the "new abolitionist policies," see Austin Sarat, "Recapturing the Spirit of *Furman:* The American Bar Association and the New Abolitionist Politics," *Law and Contemporary Problems* 61 (1998): 5–28; and Austin Sarat, *When the State Kills: Capital Punishment and the American Condition* (Princeton, NJ: Princeton University Press, 2001), chap. 9.

5. Cited in Sarat, "Recapturing the Spirit of *Furman,* p. 14.

6. Clyde E. Murphy, "Racial Discrimination in the Criminal Justice System," *North Carolina Central Law Journal* 17 (1988): 171–190.

7. Death Penalty Information Center, *The Death Penalty in 2001: Year-End Report* (Washington, DC: Author, 2001), p. 3.

8. Ibid.

9. *McCleskey v. Kemp,* 481 U.S. 279 (1987).

10. *In re Kemmler,* 136 U.S. 436, 447 (1890).

11. *Trop v. Dulles,* 356 U.S. 86, 99 (1958).

12. *Furman v. Georgia,* 408 U.S. 238 (1972).

13. Ibid. at 257 (Douglas, J., concurring), at 310 (Stewart, J., concurring), at 313 (White, J., concurring).

14. Ibid. at 257 (Marshall, J., concurring).

15. Ibid. at 310 (Stewart, J., concurring).

16. Samuel R. Gross and Robert Mauro, *Death & Discrimination: Racial Disparities in*

Capital Sentencing (Boston: Northeastern University Press, 1989), p. 215.

17. *Woodson v. North Carolina,* 428 U.S. 280 (1976); *Roberts v. Louisiana,* 428 U.S. 325 (1976).

18. *Woodson v. North Carolina,* 428 U.S. 280, 303 (1976).

19. Ibid. at 305.

20. *Gregg v. Georgia,* 428 U.S. 153 (1976); *Proffitt v. Florida,* 428 U.S. 242 (1976); *Jurek v. Texas,* 428 U.S. 262 (1976).

21. *Gregg v. Georgia,* 428 U.S. 153 (1976).

22. Ibid. at 206–207.

23. *Coker v. Georgia,* 433 U.S. 584, 592 (1977).

24. *Tison v. Arizona,* 107 S.Ct. 1676 (1987).

25. *Penry v. Lynaugh,* 109 S.Ct. 2934 (1989).

26. *Stanford v. Kentucky,* 109 S.Ct. 1969 (1989).

27. National Opinion Research Center, *General Social Surveys, 1972–94, General Social Surveys, 1996* (Storrs, CT: The Roper Center for Public Opinion Research, University of Connecticut, 1997).

28. Humphrey Taylor, "Support for Death Penalty Still Very Strong in Spite of Widespread Belief That Some Innocent People Are Convicted of Murder," Harris Interactive. Available at www .harrisinteractive.com/harris_poll/index .asp?PID=252.

29. *Furman v. Georgia,* 408 U.S. 238, 365–366 (1972) (Marshall, J., concurring).

30. Raymond Paternoster, *Capital Punishment in America* (New York: Lexington Books, 1991), p. 72.

31. *Furman v. Georgia,* 408 U.S. 238, 369, 1972 (Marshall, J., concurring).

32. See, for example, Robert M. Bohm, "American Death Penalty Opinion, 1936–1986: A Critical Examination of the Gallup Polls," in *The Death Penalty in America: Current Research,* ed. Robert M. Bohm (Cincinnati, OH: Anderson, 1991); William Bowers, "Capital Punishment and Contemporary Values: People's Misgivings and the Court's Misperceptions," *Law & Society Review* 27 (1993): 157–175; James

Alan Fox, Michael L. Radelet, and Julie L. Bonsteel, "Death Penalty Opinion in the Post-*Furman* Years," *New York University Review of Law and Social Change* 18 (1990–1991): 499–528; Philip W. Harris, "Over-Simplification and Error in Public Opinion Surveys on Capital Punishment, *Justice Quarterly* 3 (1986): 429–455; Austin Sarat and Neil Vidmar, "Public Opinion, the Death Penalty, and the Eighth Amendment: Testing the Marshall Hypothesis," in *Capital Punishment in the United States,* ed. Hugo A. Bedau and Chester M. Pierce (New York: AMS Publications, 1976).

33. Bowers, "Capital Punishment and Contemporary Values," p. 162.

34. Ibid.

35. Ibid., p. 172.

36. Taylor, "Support for Death Penalty Still Very Strong," table 6.

37. Ibid.

38. Ibid.

39. Tom W. Smith, "A Trend Analysis of Attitudes toward Capital Punishment, 1936–1974," in *Studies of Social Change since 1948,* vol. 2, ed. James E. Davis (Chicago: National Opinion Research Center, 1975), pp. 257–318.

40. Steven E. Barkan and Steven F. Cohn, "Racial Prejudice and Support for the Death Penalty by Whites," *Journal of Research in Crime and Delinquency* 31 (1994): 202–209; Robert L. Young, "Race, Conceptions of Crime and Justice, and Support for the Death Penalty," *Social Psychological Quarterly* 54 (1991): 67–75.

41. Barkan and Cohn, "Racial Prejudice and Support for the Death Penalty by Whites."

42. Ibid., p. 206.

43. Ibid., p. 207.

44. Stephen B. Bright, "Discrimination, Death and Denial: The Tolerance of Racial Discrimination in Infliction of the Death Penalty," *Santa Clara Law Review* 35 (1995): 901–950.

45. *Gregg v. Georgia,* 428 U.S. 153, 207 (1976).

46. U.S. Department of Justice, Bureau of Justice Statistics, *Capital Punishment 2000*

(Washington, DC: U.S. Government Printing Office, 2001), pp. 6–7.

47. Ibid., p. 6.

48. NAACP Legal Defense and Educational Fund, *Death Row USA: Winter 2002*. Available at http://www.deathpenaltyinfo.org/DEATHROWUSArecent.pdf.

49. Ibid.

50. Ibid.

51. Ibid.

52. U.S. Department of Justice, Bureau of Justice Statistics, *Capital Punishment 1991* (Washington, DC: U.S. Government Printing Office), p. 8.

53. Marvin E. Wolfgang and Marc Riedel, "Race, Judicial Discretion, and the Death Penalty," *The Annals of the American Academy of Political and Social Science* 407 (1973): 123.

54. Elmer H. Johnson, "Selective Factors in Capital Punishment," *Social Forces* 36 (1957): 165.

55. Marvin E. Wolfgang, Arlene Kelly, and Hans C. Nolde, "Comparisons of the Executed and the Commuted among Admissions to Death Row," *Journal of Criminal Law, Criminology, and Police Science* 53 (1962): 301.

56. Gary Kleck, "Racial Discrimination in Criminal Sentencing: A Critical Evaluation of the Evidence with Additional Evidence on the Death Penalty," *American Sociological Review* 46 (1981): 793.

57. For example, according to Raymond Fosdick, who studied U.S. police departments shortly before the country's entry into World War I, Southern police departments had three classes of homicide. One official told Fosdick, "If a nigger kills a white man, that's murder. If a white man kills a nigger, that's justifiable homicide. If a nigger kills another nigger, that's one less nigger." See Raymond Fosdick, *American Police Systems* (1920; reprint, Montclair, NJ: Patterson Smith Reprint Series, 1972), p. 45.

58. Kleck, "Racial Discrimination in Criminal Sentencing," p. 793.

59. Ibid.

60. Ibid., p. 796.

61. Ibid., p. 798.

62. Guy Johnson, "The Negro and Crime," *Annals of the American Academy* 217 (1941): 98.

63. Michael L. Radelet, "Executions of Whites for Crimes against Blacks: Exceptions to the Rule?" *The Sociological Quarterly* 30 (1989): 535.

64. *Furman v. Georgia*, 408 U.S. 238, 449 (1972) (Powell, J., dissenting).

65. Harold Garfinkel, "Research Note on Inter- and Intra-Racial Homicides," *Social Forces* 27 (1949): 369–381; Johnson, "The Negro and Crime"; Charles S. Mangum Jr., *The Legal Status of the Negro* (Chapel Hill: North Carolina Press, 1940); Paige H. Ralph, Jonathan R. Sorensen, and James W. Marquart, "A Comparison of Death-Sentenced and Incarcerated Murderers in Pre-*Furman* Texas," *Justice Quarterly* 9 (1992): 185–209; Wolfgang et al., "Comparison of the Executed and Commuted among Admissions to Death Row"; Marvin E. Wolfgang and Marc Riedel, "Race, Judicial Discretion, and the Death Penalty," *Annals of the American Academy* 407 (1973): 119–133; Marvin E. Wolfgang and Marc Riedel, "Rape, Race, and the Death Penalty in Georgia," *American Journal of Orthopsychiatry* 45 (1975): 658–668.

66. Johnson, "The Negro and Crime."

67. Mangum, *The Legal Status of the Negro*.

68. Wolfgang et al., "Comparisons of the Executed and Commuted among Admissions to Death Row."

69. Garfinkel, "Research Note on Inter- and Intra-Racial Homicides."

70. William Bowers and Glenn L. Pierce, "Arbitrariness and Discrimination under Post-*Furman* Capital Statutes," *Crime and Delinquency* 74 (1980): 1067–1100.

71. Kleck, "Racial Discrimination in Criminal Sentencing," p. 788.

72. Florida Civil Liberties Union, *Rape: Selective Electrocution Based on Race* (Miami: Author, 1964).

73. Wolfgang and Reidel, "Race, Judicial Discretion, and the Death Penalty."

74. Ibid., p. 133.

75. Kleck, "Racial Discrimination in Criminal Sentencing," p. 788.

76. David C. Baldus, George Wood-worth, and Charles A. Pulaski, *Equal Justice and the Death Penalty: A Legal and Empirical Analysis* (Boston: Northeastern University Press, 1990).

77. Ralph et al., "A Comparison of Death-Sentenced and Incarcerated Murderers in Pre-*Furman* Texas."

78. Ibid., p. 207.

79. Ibid., pp. 206–207.

80. Wolfgang and Reidel, "Rape, Race and the Death Penalty in Georgia," p. 667.

81. Bowers and Pierce, "Arbitrariness and Discrimination," p. 587.

82. U.S. General Accounting Office, *Death Penalty Sentencing: Research Indicates Pattern of Racial Disparities* (Washington, DC: Author, 1990), p. 5.

83. Ibid., p. 6.

84. Ibid.

85. Studies that find either a race-of-victim or race-of-defendant effect include (but are not limited to) Stephen Arkin, "Discrimination and Arbitrariness in Capital Punishment: An Analysis of Post-*Furman* Murder Cases in Dade County, Florida, 1973–1976," *Stanford Law Review* 33 (1980): 75–101; William Bowers, "The Pervasiveness of Arbitrariness and Discrimination under Post-*Furman* Capital Statutes," *Journal of Criminal Law & Criminology* 74 (1983): 1067–1100; Bowers and Pierce, "Arbitrariness and Discrimination under Post-*Furman* Capital Statutes"; Sheldon Ekland-Olson, "Structured Discretion, Racial Bias, and the Death Penalty: The First Decade after *Furman* in Texas," *Social Science Quarterly* 69 (1988): 853–873; Thomas Keil and Gennaro Vito, "Race and the Death Penalty in Kentucky Murder Trials: An Analysis of Post-*Gregg* Outcomes," *Justice Quarterly* (1990): 189–207; Raymond Paternoster, "Prosecutorial Discretion in Requesting the Death Penalty: A Case of Victim-Based Racial Discrimination," *Law & Society Review* 18 (1984): 437–478; Michael L. Radelet, "Racial Characteristics and the Imposition of the Death Penalty," *American Sociological Review* 46 (1981): 918–927; Michael L. Radelet and Glenn L. Pierce,

"Race and Prosecutorial Discretion in Homicide Cases," *Law & Society Review* 19 (1985): 587–621; and Dwayne M. Smith, "Patterns of Discrimination in Assessments of the Death Penalty: The Case of Louisiana," *Journal of Criminal Justice* 15 (1987): 279–286.

86. Baldus et al., *Equal Justice and the Death Penalty*.

87. Gross and Mauro, *Death & Discrimination*.

88. Baldus et al., *Equal Justice and the Death Penalty*.

89. Ibid., p. 185.

90. David Baldus, Charles Pulaski, and George Woodworth, "Comparative Review of Death Sentences: An Empirical Study of the Georgia Experience," *The Journal of Criminal Law & Criminology* 74 (1983): 709–710.

91. Anthony Amsterdam, "Race and the Death Penalty," *Criminal Justice Ethics* 7 (1988): 2, 84–86.

92. Ibid., p. 85.

93. Gross and Mauro, *Death & Discrimination,* chaps. 4 and 5.

94. Ibid., pp. 109–110.

95. Sarat, "Recapturing the Spirit of *Furman*," p. 27.

96. U.S. Department of Justice, *The Federal Death Penalty System: A Statistical Survey (1988–2000)* (Washington, DC: Author, 2000), p. 4.

97. U.S. Department of Justice, *The Federal Death Penalty System: Supplementary Data, Analysis and Revised Protocols for Capital Case Review* (Washington, DC: Author, 2001), pp. 6–7.

98. Ibid., p. 5.

99. U.S. Department of Justice, *The Federal Death Penalty System: A Statistical Survey (1988–2000),* p. 9.

100. Marc Lacey and Raymond Bonner, "Reno Troubled by DP Stats," *New York Times,* September 12, 2000, p. A17.

101. American Civil Liberties Union, *Federal Death Row: Is It Really Color-Blind? Analysis of June 6 Department of Justice Report on the Death Penalty.* Available at

http://www.aclu.org/Congress/10614la.htm.

102. U.S. Department of Justice, *The Federal Death Penalty System: Supplementary Data, Analysis and Revised Protocols for Capital Case Review.*

103. Ibid., p. 9.

104. Ibid., p. 3.

105. Ibid.

106. American Civil Liberties Union, *Federal Death Row.*

107. Ibid.

108. NAACP, *Death Row USA.*

109. Richard Quinney, *The Social Reality of Crime* (Boston: Little, Brown, 1970); Austin Turk, *Criminality and Legal Order* (New York: Rand McNally, 1969).

110. Darnell F. Hawkins, "Beyond Anomalies: Rethinking the Conflict Perspective on Race and Criminal Punishment," *Social Forces* 65 (1987): 726.

111. Keil and Vito, "Race and the Death Penalty in Kentucky Murder Trials," p. 204.

112. Quoted in Stephen Wissink, "Race and the Big Needle," *Spectator Online.* Available at http://www.spectatoronline.com/2001-03-07/news_cover.html.

113. Gross and Mauro, *Death & Discrimination.*

114. Ibid., p. 113.

115. Bright, "Discrimination, Death and Denial," pp. 903–905.

116. Ibid. pp. 904–905.

117. Ibid., p. 921.

118. For an excellent and detailed discussion of this case, see Eric W. Rise, *The Martinsville Seven: Race, Rape, and Capital Punishment* (Charlottesville: University Press of Virginia, 1995).

119. Ibid., p. 122.

120. See, for example, *Maxwell v. Bishop,* F.2d 138 (8th Cir. 1968); *Spinkellink v. Wainwright,* 578 F.2d 582 (5th Cir. 1978); *Shaw v. Martin,* 733 F.2d 304 (4th Cir. 1984); and *Prejean v. Blackburn,* 743 F.2d 1091 (5th Cir. 1984).

121. *McCleskey v. Kemp,* 481 U.S. 279, 107 S.Ct. 1756 (1987).

122. David C. Baldus, George W. Woodworth, and Charles A. Pulaski, "Monitoring and Evaluating Contemporary Death Penalty Systems: Lessons from Georgia," *University of California at Davis Law Review* 18 (1985): 1375–1407.

123. *McCleskey v. Kemp,* 107 S.Ct. 1756, 1777 (1987).

124. Ibid. at 1769.

125. *McCleskey v. Kemp,* 481 U.S. 279, 315 (1987) (Brennan, J., dissenting).

126. Ibid. at 316–317.

127. Ibid.

128. *Maxwell v. Bishop,* 398 F.2d 138 (CA 8 1968).

129. Amsterdam, "Race and the Death Penalty," p. 86.

130. Randall Kennedy, *Race, Crime, and the Law* (New York: Vintage Books, 1998).

131. Bright, "Discrimination, Death and Denial," p. 947.

132. Gross and Mauro, *Death & Discrimination,* p. 212.

133. *McCleskey v. Zant,* 111 S. Ct. 1454 (1991).

134. Ibid.

135. *New York Times,* September 26, 1991, p. A10.

136. NAACP, *Death Row USA.*

137. *McCleskey v. Zant,* 111 S.Ct. 1454 (1991).

138. *Herrera v. Collins,* 113 S.Ct. 853 (1993).

139. *Congressional Record,* S4602 (April 21, 1994).

140. Alex J. Hurder, "Whatever You Think about the Death Penalty, a System That Will Take Life Must First Give Justice: A Report from the Individual Rights and Responsibilities Death Penalty Committee," *Human Rights Magazine* 24: 22.

141. Press release, January 31, 2000. Available at http://www.state.il.us/gov/press/00/Jan/morat.htm.

142. John Kifner, "A State Votes to End Its Death Penalty," *New York Times,* May 19, 2000, p. A8.

143. Press release, September 20, 2000. Available at http://www.igc.org/tcrp/press/HRR/death_penalty.htm.

144. Cited in Kenneth Jost, "Rethinking the Death Penalty," *CQ Researcher* 11 (November 16, 2001), p. 962.

145. Innocence Protection Act of 2001, 107th Congress, H.R. 912.

146. United States Senate, Committee on the Judiciary, Testimony of the Honorable William D. Delahunt of Massachusetts in support of the Innocence Protection Act of 2001, June 27, 2001.

147. Jodi Wilgoren, "Few Death Sentences or None under Overhaul Proposed by Illinois Panel," *The New York Times on the Web* (April 16, 2002). Available at http://www.nytimes.com.

148. Sarat, *When the State Kills,* pp. 246–260.

149. *Callins v. Collins,* 510 U.S. 1141, 1145 (1994).

150. Sarat, *When the State Kills,* p. 251.

151. *Callins v. Collins,* 510 U.S. 1141, 1144 (1994) (Blackmun, J., dissenting).

152. Ibid. at 1145.

153. Sarat, *When the State Kills,* p. 255.

154. Ibid., p. 256.

155. Ibid.

156. National Death Penalty Moratorium Act of 2001, S. 223, H.R. 1038.

157. Sarat, *When the State Kills,* p. 257.

158. Gross and Mauro, *Death & Discrimination,* pp. 109–110.

9

Corrections versus College: Minorities in Society

A Picture in Black, Brown, and White

The number of people under correctional supervision in the United States has risen substantially in the last 30 years, often outpacing population growth. During the same period, the number of people attending college also increased. In the United States in 2000, there were 6.5 million people under some form of correctional supervision (prison, jail, probation, or parole)[1] and over 15 million people pursuing some form of higher education.[2] The United States currently has the highest incarceration rates per population than any other country in the world[3] and one of the highest rates for people pursuing higher education.[4]

Whereas roughly 3 percent of the adult U.S. population is under correctional supervision, nearly 6 percent is attending college.[5] This profile of incarceration versus education differs by race, ethnicity, and gender; but essentially, more African American and Hispanic males are under some form of correctional supervision than are attending college. However, less than half as many white males are in prison as in college. Specifically, nearly 20 percent of African American males and 8 percent of Hispanic males are under correctional supervision, compared to less than 3 percent of white males.[6] Estimates of college attendance, however, indicate that 8 percent of African American males, less than 6 percent of Hispanic males, and roughly 7 percent of white males were attending college in 2000.[7]

GOALS OF THE CHAPTER

This chapter describes various disparities in the ethnic and racial makeup of American correctional populations. It examines which groups are overrepresented in situations of incarceration and supervision in the community. The extent of minority overrepresentation is also explored in relation to gender distinctions, federal versus state populations, and historical fluctuations.

This descriptive information is supplemented by a discussion of current research on discrimination in the correctional setting. Finally, the inmate social system, which reflects key aspects of prison life, is discussed. This section will focus on the influence of minority group status on prison subcultures and religion.

THE INCARCERATED:

PRISON AND JAIL POPULATIONS

Describing incarcerated populations in the United States is a complicated task. The answer to the question "Who is locked up?" depends on what penal institution and which inmates we are discussing. Prison population figures are descriptive counts taken on one day, midyear. These figures are used to describe disparity and are not standardized rates (see later discussion). There are a number of important distinctions between prisons and jails, male and female inmates, and state and federal populations. In addition, important changes occur over time.

Prisons are distinct from jails because they serve different functions in the criminal justice system.[8] These differences may result in different levels of minority overrepresentation, so jails and prisons are discussed separately. Gender differences are also important when discussing incarceration; therefore, we also explore the issues of the racial and ethnic composition of male and female prisoner populations. State and federal prison populations must be examined separately because of the differences in state and federal crime.[9]

Minority Overrepresentation

The primary observation to be made about the racial and ethnic composition of the prison population in the United States (see Table 9.1, column 1) is that African Americans are strikingly overrepresented compared to their presence in the general population. Hispanics are also overrepresented, but not as markedly. African Americans are less than 15 percent of the U.S. population but nearly 50 percent of all incarcerated offenders. Hispanics are roughly 12 percent of the U. S. population; however, they represent over 16 percent of the prison population. Conversely, whites (non-Hispanic) are underrepresented compared to their presence in the population: over 70 percent of the general population but just over one-third (35.7 percent) of the prison population.

Table 9.1 Racial and Ethnic Profile of State and Federal Prison Populations by Gender, at Midyear 2000

	Combined	Male	Female
White (non-Hispanic)	35.7%	35.3%	41.2%
African American (non-Hispanic)	46.2	46.3	44.7
Hispanic	16.4	16.7	12.0
Other (Native American/ Alaskan Native, Asian/ Pacific Islander)	1.7	1.4	2.1

SOURCE: Allen J. Beck and Paige M. Harrison, *Prisoners in 2000* (Washington, DC: Department of Justice, 2001). Available at www.ojp.usdoj.gov/bjs/.

Hispanics have represented the fastest-growing minority group being imprisoned in recent years. They were 10.5 percent of the prison population in 1985, 15.5 percent in 1995, and 16.4 percent in 2000.[10] These increases reflect a rate twice as high as the increase for African American and white inmates.[11] Little information is available about the number of Asian/Pacific Islander, Alaskan Native/Native American prisoners, as they are generally represented as a single group. The representation of Asians and Pacific Islanders does not appear substantially greater than their representation in the general population. However, Native American and Alaska Natives are overrepresented compared to their representation in the U.S. population (see Focus on an Issue on page 306).

Racial and Ethnic Female Prisoners The picture of the racial and ethnic composition of prison populations changes slightly when focusing on gender (see Table 9.1, columns 2 and 3). Because women make up less than 7 percent of federal and state prisoners,[12] we should not generalize patterns from predominantly male populations to females. For example, whereas prison populations have increased markedly in the last several years, the increase for female inmates is more rapid than for male inmates from 1990 to 2000. Over this 10-year period, female prison populations have increased 108 percent, and male populations have increased 77 percent.[13] Among female prisoners, similarities and differences exist when comparing their racial and ethnic makeup to the overall (predominantly male) prison population. African American women make up the largest group of female prisoners (44.7 percent). This figure is slightly lower than the African American male prison population (46.7 percent). The percentage of Hispanic female prisoners is lower than the percentage of Hispanic male prisoners (12.0 percent versus 16.7 percent). Correspondingly, the percentage of the white female prisoner population is larger than that of the white male prisoner population (41.2 percent versus 35.3 percent).

Racial and Ethnic Federal Prisoners Although state prison populations account for the majority (nearly 90 percent) of incarcerated offenders, a look at

**Table 9.2 Racial and Ethnic Profile
of Federal Prison Population, 2000**

	Percentage
Race	
White	57.6
African American	39.2
Other	3.2
Ethnicity (of any race)	
Hispanic	32.3
Non-Hispanic	67.7

SOURCE: Bureau of Justice Statistics, *Sourcebook of Criminal Justice Statistics, 2000* (Washington, DC: U.S. Department of Justice, 2001). Available at www.albany.edu/sourcebook/.

the racial and ethnic percentages of federal populations separately is warranted. Just as state and federal laws differ, so will state and federal prison populations, as they present different offenses and unique sentencing practices (see Chapter 7). An important implication for federal prisoners is that they can expect to serve up to 50 percent more of their original sentence than state inmates do.[14]

Comparisons between state and federal prison populations with regard to racial composition present a challenge. The Bureau of Justice Statistics sources used to estimate the racial and ethnic composition of federal and state prison populations in Table 9.1 reflect the convention of using racial and ethnic status combined (white, non–Hispanic; African American, non–Hispanic; Hispanic, other); however, similar to the U.S. census, the Federal Bureau of Prisons uses the convention of measuring race and ethnicity as separate concepts.

The descriptive profile of the federal inmate population presented in Table 9.2 suggests an important correction in the magnitude of racial and ethnic differences in state versus federal prison populations.[15] African Americans do not appear as severely overrepresented in the federal prison population as they do in the profile of state and federal prison populations combined. In short, when the federal population is considered separately, African Americans represent less than 40 percent of the population, whereas state and federal populations combined reveal that more than 46 percent are African American.

Perhaps the most startling contrast appears with the Hispanic population. When Hispanics are identified as being of any race, they represent nearly one-third (32.2 percent) of the federal prison population, compared to less than 20 percent of the combined prison population. These data suggest that the overrepresentation of Hispanics in federal prison populations is hidden in the description of the racial and ethnic composition. Also, the underrepresentation of whites in prison is inflated by the extraction of Hispanics (who are predominantly white) from the calculation of demographic percentages.

These differences in disparity among racial and ethnic groups are explained in large part by different patterns of offending. Whites are relatively more likely to commit and be convicted of federal offenses. African Americans, however, are

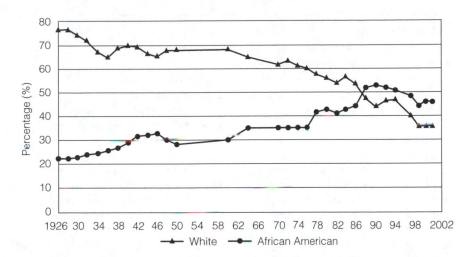

FIGURE 9.1 Admissions to State and Federal Prison by Race, 1926–2001

SOURCES: Bureau of Justice Statistics, *Race of Prisoners Admitted to State and Federal Institutions, 1926–86* (Washington, DC: U.S. Government Printing Office, 1991); Bureau of Justice Statistics, *Correctional Populations in the United States, 1996* (Washington, DC: U.S. Government Printing Office, 1997); Bureau of Justice Statistics, *Correctional Populations in the United States, 1997* (Washington, DC: U.S. Government Printing Office, 1998); Allen J. Beck, *Prison and Jail Inmates, 1999* (Washington, DC: U.S. Department of Justice, 2000); Allen J. Beck and Jennifer C. Karberg, *Prison and Jail Inmates at Midyear 2000* (Washington, DC: U.S. Department of Justice, 2001); Allen J. Beck, Jennifer C. Karberg, and Paige M. Harrison, *Prison and Jail Inmates at Midyear 2001* (Washington, DC: U.S. Department of Justice, 2002). All sources available at www.ojp.usdoj/bjs/.

relatively more likely to be arrested and convicted for Index crimes, which are generally state offenses. Hispanics are consistently overrepresented among convicted drug offenders at the federal level and among immigration law offenders.[16]

Differences in the magnitude of racial disparity among the various racial and ethnic groups in prison offer more support that the impact of race and ethnicity is not a constant. That is, the impact of overrepresentation in incarceration settings varies in magnitude and quality. The racial and ethnic profile of prison inmates is to some extent conditioned by how the concepts *race* and *ethnicity* are measured. One of the important implications of the more extreme overrepresentation of Hispanic offenders in federal prison is that they will serve longer sentences than those offenders sentenced to state prisons, given that federal prisoners can expect to serve 50 percent more of their original sentence than state inmates do.[17] In short, this detrimental aspect of imprisonment for Hispanics would not have been known if we had examined only the demographic profile offered in Table 9.1.

Historical Trends

The overrepresentation of African Americans in state and federal prisons is not a new phenomenon. Figure 9.1 provides a graphic illustration of the changing demographic composition of the prison population from 1926 to 2001. Reviewing this figure, we can document a disproportionate number of African

---

Focus on an Issue
Correctional Personnel: Similarities and Differences on the Basis of Race

---

Currently, federal and state prisons have fairly equitable African American representation among correctional officers and supervisors, compared to the general population, but Hispanic representation among correctional personnel is still lacking (American Correctional Association, 1993). There are important reasons for achieving equitable minority representation. Ensuring fair employment practices in government hiring is one goal; others champion the importance of minority decision makers as having a beneficial (and perhaps less discriminatory) impact on the treatment of minority populations.

Author's (1994) review of the research in the area of attitudes and beliefs of correctional officers toward inmates and punishment ideologies suggests that respondents' views do appear to differ in many ways on the basis of race. In particular, he noted that African American officers appear to have more positive attitudes toward inmates than white officers do. However, others have found that African American officers express a preference for greater distance between

officers and inmates than white officers do. Additionally, neither white nor African American correctional officers reflect an ability to correctly identify the self-reported needs of prison inmates.

In relation to ideological issues, African American officers are more often supportive of rehabilitation than their white counterparts. African American officers also appear to be more ambivalent about the current punitive nature of the criminal justice system, indicating that the court system is often too harsh.

In short, current research does not offer a definitive answer to the question of whether minority and white correctional officers make different decisions on the basis of race. Assuming that differential decision making by correctional officers could be both a positive and negative exercise of discretion, at what point are differential decisions beneficial to inmates rather than unprofessional or unjust? What research could be done to resolve the issue of the presence or absence of differential decision making by correctional officers on the basis of race?

Americans in the prison population since 1926 (the beginning of national-level data collection on prison populations). In 1926, African Americans represented 9 percent of the population and 21 percent of the prison population.[18] Over time, the proportion of the prison population of African Americans has increased steadily, reaching 30 percent in the 1940s, 35 percent in 1960, 44 percent in 1980, peaking at slightly over 50 percent in the mid-1990s, and leveling off at about 45 percent in the late 1990s. The representation of African Americans in the general population has never exceeded 15 percent. The ratio of African American prisoner population to white prisoner population was 2.5:1 in 1926 but is currently 4:1.

Impact of the War on Drugs

Dramatic increases in the overrepresentation of African Americans in the prison population have occurred in a context of generally increasing prison population totals and rising incarceration rates since the early 1970s. The increasing incarceration levels seem to be slowing in the first years of the 21st century but remain at a level of approximately 2 million people incarcerated in state and federal jails and prisons. Although the increased level surely has multiple sources, it may reflect an impact of the War on Drugs. Tonry, for example, argues that the War on Drugs has had a particularly detrimental effect on African American males.[19] Evidence of this impact, he argues, can be seen by focusing on the key years affected by the War on Drugs: 1980 to 1992. During this period, the number of white males incarcerated in state and federal prisons increased by 143 percent; for African American males, the number increased by 186 percent.[20]

Statisticians for the BJS argue that the sources of growth for prison populations differ for white and African American inmates. Specifically, drug offenses and violent offenses account for the largest source of growth among state prison inmates. During the 10-year period from 1985 to 1995, "the increasing number of drug offenders accounted for 42 percent of the total growth of black inmates and 26 percent of the growth among white inmates."[21] The number of black inmates serving time for violent offenses rose by 37 percent, whereas growth among white inmates was at a higher 47 percent.[22]

As we discussed in Chapters 2 and 4, the differential impact of the War on Drugs may be due more to the enforcement strategies of law enforcement than higher patterns of minority of drug use. Critics argue that whereas the police are *reactive* in responding to robbery, burglary, and other Index offenses, they are *proactive* in dealing with drug offenses. There is evidence to suggest that they target minority communities—where drug dealing is more visible and where it is thus easier to make arrests—and tend to give less attention to drug activities in other neighborhoods.

Incarceration Rates

Another way to describe the makeup of U.S. prisons is to examine incarceration rates. The information offered by incarceration rates expands the picture of the prison inmate offered in population totals and percentages (given earlier) and presents the most vivid picture of the overrepresentation of African Americans in prison populations. Rates allow for the standardization of population figures that can be calculated over a particular target population. For example, the general incarceration rate in 2001 was 690 per 100,000 population.[23] This number can be further explored by calculating rates that reflect the number of one race group in the prison population relative to the number of that population in the overall U.S. population.

As shown in Table 9.3, over the last decade, African Americans and Hispanics were substantially more likely than whites to be incarcerated in state and federal prisons. Although rates for all groups are increasing over time, the current rate for African American males remains the highest, which is 6 to 7 times

Table 9.3 Incarceration Rates by Race/Ethnicity and Gender (per 100,000 Population)

	MALE			FEMALE		
	White	African American	Hispanic	White	African American	Hispanic
1990	339	2,376	817	19	125	43
1995	461	3,250	1,174	27	176	57
2001	705	4,848	1,668	67	380	119

SOURCES: Allen J. Beck, Jennifer C. Karberg, and Paige Harrison, *Prison and Jail Inmates at Midyear 2001* (Washington, DC: U.S. Department of Justice, 2002); Christopher J. Mumola and Allen J. Beck, *Prisoners, 1996* (Washington, DC: U.S. Department of Justice, 1997).

BOX 9.1   International Comparisons

In the international arena, the United States has one of the highest incarceration rates in the world. According to the Sentencing Project (Maur, 1994), in 1993 there were 519 people incarcerated in jails and prisons in the United States for every 100,000 people in the general population, second only to Russia (558 persons per 100,000 population). The next closest country was South Africa with the substantially lower rate of 368. European countries have much lower rates: England/Wales at 93, Germany at 80, and Sweden at 69. The Sentencing Project calculated that the U.S. incarceration rate in 2001 surpassed that of Russia (690 per 100,000 versus 679 per 100,000).

The Sentencing Project also calculated that the incarceration rate for African American males in the United States is more than 4 times the rate in South Africa in the last years of apartheid. That is, in 1993, the U.S. incarceration rate for African American males was 3,822 per 100,000 compared to the South African rate of 815 per 100,000 (Maur, 1994). In 2001, the incarceration rate for African American males soared to 4,848 per 100,000 (see Table 9.3).

The racial disparity in the nation's prison populations is revealed even more dramatically by data from the Sentencing Project (2001) that estimates that at some point in their lives, African American males have a 29 percent chance of serving time in prison or jail. Hispanic males have a lower lifetime risk at 16 percent, and white males have a 4 percent chance of being incarcerated at some time during their lives.

---

higher than that for white males. Rates for Hispanic males are also higher than for white males, but lower than for African American males. Note that female rates of incarceration are substantially lower than male rates, but they are increasing over time. In 2001, rates of incarceration for African American females were over 5 times higher than for white females and 3 times higher than for Hispanics females.[24] Additionally, Hispanic females have an incarceration rate 2 times that of white females.[25] United States incarceration rates are placed in an international context in Box 9.1.

JAILS AND MINORITIES

The Role of Jail

Jail populations are significantly different from prison populations. Because jails serve a different function in the criminal justice system, they are subject to different dynamics in terms of admissions and releases. The Annual Survey of Jails reveals that just over half of the daily population of all jail inmates are being detained while awaiting trial (56 percent), and just under half are convicted offenders.[26] Those awaiting trial are in jail because they are denied bail or were unable to raise bail. The other inmates are convicted offenders who have been sentenced to serve time in jail. Although the vast majority of these inmates have been convicted of misdemeanors, some convicted felons are given a "split sentence" involving jail followed by probation. Also, a small number of inmates have been sentenced and are in jail awaiting transfer to state or federal prison facilities.

Because of the jail's role as a pretrial detention center, there is a high rate of turnover among the jail population. The data used in Table 9.4 represent a static 1–day count rather than an annual total of all people who pass through the jail system. Thus, *daily* population of jails is lower than that of prisons, but the *annual* total of people incarcerated in jails is higher.

Minority Overrepresentation

As Table 9.4 indicates, whites make up the largest proportion of inmates in jails around the country. However, African Americans are overrepresented in jail populations (40.6 percent) and whites are underrepresented (43.0 percent) compared to their representation in the general population. Hispanics (14.7 percent) are a slightly higher percentage of the jail population than their representation in the general population. These percentages change slightly from year to year. Sometimes African Americans make up the largest proportion of jail inmates,

Table 9.4 Percentage of Jail Inmates by Race and Ethnicity, 2001

Race/Ethnicity	Percentage
White (non-Hispanic)	43.0
African American (non-Hispanic)	40.6
Hispanic	14.7
Other (Native American/ Alaskan Native, Asian/ Pacific Islander)	1.6

SOURCE: Allen J. Beck, Jennifer C. Karberg, and Paige M. Harrison, *Prison and Jail Inmates at Midyear, 2001* (Washington, DC: U.S. Department of Justice, 2002).

Focus on an Issue
Jails on Tribal Lands

In the year 2001, nearly 50,000 Native Americans were under correctional supervision (prison, jail, probation, or parole) in the United States (federal, state, local, and tribal authorities combined). The U.S. population is approximately 1 percent Native American; however, the incarceration rate for Native Americans in prison and jail facilities was 19 percent higher than the incarceration rate for all other races combined (849 per 100,000 Native Americans compared to 690 persons per 100,000 U.S. residents of all other races combined).

The description of jails on tribal lands is presented by the BJS report "Survey of Jails in Indian Country" (SJIC). Most recently conducted in 2001, the survey reflects the statutory meaning of "Indian Country" (18 U.S.C. 1151): all lands within an Indian reservation; dependent Indian Communities; and Indian Trust allotments. Federal regulations limit the ju-

risdiction and incarceration powers of tribal governments to "crime committed by Indians in Indian Country. Sentences are limited to 1 year and a $5,000 fine per offense or both" (25 U.S.C. 1153). The SJIC reveals that a total of 2,030 persons were incarcerated in 68 confinement facilities. This population is smaller than the number of Native Americans held in locally operated city/county jails, which was estimated at 6,000 for the year 2001.

Nearly half of the tribal inmate population is held in 10 jails. The largest Native American tribal jail population is in the Pine Ridge Correctional Facility in South Dakota. However, Arizona has the largest Native American jail population and has 7 of the 10 largest jail populations.

SOURCE: Todd D. Minton, *Jails in Indian Country, 2001* (Washington, DC: U.S. Department of Justice, 2002). Available at www.ojp.usdoj.gov/bjs/.

---

so over time, there is roughly the same percentage of African Americans and whites in jail. The overrepresentation of Hispanics has been higher in some years than in 2001 (for example, 15.5 percent in 1996), indicating a more serious disparity than reflected in Table 9.4. Overall, the picture of disparity depicted by these percentages of jail inmates is essentially similar to the reflection of race and ethnicity in prison populations.

Because of the jail's function as a pretrial detention center, jail population is heavily influenced by bail decisions. If more people are released on nonfinancial considerations, the number of people in jail will be lower. This raises the questions of racial discrimination in bail setting, which we discussed in Chapter 5. As noted in that chapter, there is evidence that judges impose higher bail—or are more likely to deny bail altogether—if the defendant is a racial minority.

PAROLE: EARLY RELEASE FROM PRISON

Parole is a form of early release from prison under supervision in the community. Prison inmates are released to one of two forms of parole: discretionary parole or mandatory parole. The U.S. Department of Justice defines *discretion-*

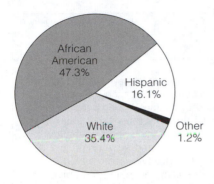

FIGURE 9.2 State Parole Populations by Race and Ethnicity, 1999

SOURCE: Timothy A. Hughes, Doris James Wilson, and Allen J. Beck, *Trends in State Parole, 1999–2000* (Washington, DC: Department of Justice, 2001). Available at www.ojp.usdoj.gov/bjs/.

ary parole as a decision made by a parole board to "conditionally release prisoners based on a statutory or administrative determination of eligibility," whereas *mandatory parole* "occurs in jurisdictions using determinate sentencing statutes. Inmates are conditionally released from prison after serving a portion of their original sentence minus any good time earned."[27] Not surprising, therefore, parole populations are similar in racial and ethnic distribution to federal and state prison populations. In 2000 (see Figure 9.2), 35.4 percent of the inmates released on parole were white, 47.3 percent were African American, 16.1 percent were Hispanic, and approximately 1 percent were other races.[28]

The benevolent side of this picture of probation is that African Americans and Hispanics are making the transition to parole (arguably a positive move) in proportions similar to prison population figures. However, parole revocation figures require a closer look.

Success and Failure on Parole

A parolee "succeeds" on parole if he or she completes the terms of supervision without violations. A parolee can "fail" in one of two ways: either by being arrested for another crime or by violating one of the conditions of parole release (such as using drugs, possessing a weapon, or violating curfew). In either case, parole authorities can revoke parole and send the person back to prison.

Parole revocation, therefore, is nearly equivalent to the judge's power to sentence an offender in the first place because it can mean that offender will return to prison. The decision to revoke parole is discretionary; parole authorities may choose to overlook a violation and not send the person back to prison. This use of discretion opens the door for possible discrimination.

Most parolees are released from state prisons. Currently, nearly 80 percent of inmates will be released to parole supervision rather than simply be released at the expiration of their sentence. In 1999, 42 percent of all parolees at the state level successfully completed parole.[29] The success rate varied somewhat by racial/ethnic group: 40.0 percent of whites, 39.0 percent of African Americans, 50.6 percent of Hispanics, and 42.2 percent of other races.[30] The percentage of parole violators by race in the year 1999 indicates that the majority of those violating parole were African American (51.8 percent), with whites representing less than one-third of violators (27.5 percent) and Hispanics approximately one-fifth of violators (18.3 percent).[31]

BOX 9.2 Supervision in the Community: An Uneven Playing Field?

Both parole and probation involve supervision in the community under a set of specific provisions for client behavior. One of the most common provisions is the requirement of employment. Not being able to attain or retain employment may lead to a violation of supervision conditions and unsuccessful discharge of an individual from probation or parole. Essentially, a person could be sent to prison for being unemployed. It is possible that the employment provision creates disparate hardships for minorities. In 1999, the unemployment rate was 3.7 percent for whites, 8.0 percent for African Americans, and 6.4 percent for Hispanics (U.S. Census Bureau, 2000). Unemployment rates also vary by age: people between the ages of 16 and 24 have higher unemployment rates than the general population does. Young people have unemployment rates 2 to 3 times higher, with the highest unemployment rates found for young (aged 16–19) African American males at 27.9 percent and young Hispanics at 18.6 percent, and the lowest for young white males at 12.0 percent (U.S. Census Bureau, 2000). In short, ethnic- and race-specific unemployment rates vary substantially, showing the disadvantaged status of minorities in the labor market. Does this aspect of the general economy adversely impact minorities on probation and parole? If yes, could this be seen as a form of institutional discrimination? What should be done about this?

A small number of federal inmates are still eligible for parole consideration.[32] Recent data on federal parole reveal that approximately 78 percent of federal parole discharges were from successful completion of parole conditions.[33] Once again, these rates vary by minority group status. Whites and other races had the highest successful completion rate of 76 percent, followed by Hispanics at 68 percent and African Americans at 53 percent.[34] Similarly, African Americans had the highest return rate to prison (36 percent), with all other groups exhibiting a return rate of lower than 20 percent.[35] Issues of success and failure on parole (and probation) are often linked to employment stability. These issues are addressed as a potential avenue of discrimination in Box 9.2.

PROBATION: A CASE OF SENTENCING DISCRIMINATION?

Probation is an alternative to incarceration, a sentence to supervision in the community. The majority of all the people under correctional supervision are on probation, totaling nearly 4 million.[36]

The racial demographics in Figure 9.3 offer a picture of the probation population with race and ethnicity presented separately. These figures indicate that African Americans are overrepresented (34 percent) in the probation pop-

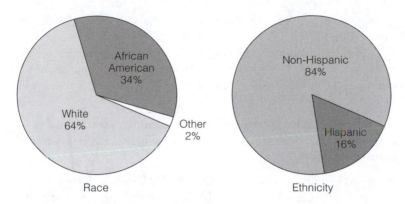

FIGURE 9.3 Probation Populations by Race and Ethnicity, 2000

SOURCE: U.S. Department of Justice, "News Release: National Correctional Population Reaches New High" (August 26, 2001). Available at www.ojp.usdoj/bjs/abstract/oous000.htm.

ulation relative to their presence in the general population.[37] Correspondingly, whites are underrepresented at 64 percent of all probationers.[38] The ethnic breakdown of those under sentence of probation reveals Hispanics are again overrepresented compared to non-Hispanics (16 percent versus 84 percent).[39]

It is immediately apparent that the racial disparity for probation is not as great as it is for the prison population, however. Given that probation is a less severe sentence than prison, this difference may indicate that the advantage of receiving the less severe sentence of probation is reserved for whites. In a study of sentencing in California, Petersilia found that 71 percent of whites convicted of a felony were granted probation, compared with 67 percent of African Americans and 65 percent of Hispanics.[40] Similarly, Spohn and colleagues found that in "borderline cases" in which judges could impose either a long probation sentence or a short prison sentence, whites were more likely to get probation, and African Americans were more likely to get prison. (We discuss the issue of discrimination in sentencing in Chapter 7.)

PERSPECTIVES ON THE
RACIAL DISTRIBUTION OF
CORRECTIONAL POPULATIONS

Several theoretical arguments are advanced to explain the overwhelming overrepresentation of African Americans in the correctional system. The most fundamental question is whether prison populations reflect discrimination in the criminal justice system or other factors. One view is that the overrepresentation reflects widespread discrimination; the alternative view is that the overrepresentation results from a disproportionate involvement in criminal activity on the part of minorities. Mann argues that there is systematic discrimination based on color,[41] whereas Wilbanks contends that the idea of systematic discrimination is a "myth."[42]

The work of Alfred Blumstein offers a benchmark to explore the results of such research. Focusing on 1979 prison population data, Blumstein sought to isolate the impact of discrimination from other possible factors. The key element of his research is the following formula:[43]

X = ratio of expected black-to-white incarceration rates based only on arrest disproportionality/ratio of black-to-white incarceration rates actually observed.

Essentially, this formula compares the expected black–white disparity (X) in state prison populations based on recorded black–white disparity in arrest rates (numerator) over the observed black–white disparity in incarceration rates (denominator). Thus, accepting the argument that arrest rates are not a reflection of discrimination, Blumstein's formula calculates the portion of the prison population left unexplained by the disproportionate representation of African Americans at the arrest stage. In short, this figure is the amount of actual racial disproportionality in incarceration rates that is open to an explanation or charge of discrimination.

Overall, Blumstein found that 20 percent of the racial disparity in incarceration rates is left unexplained by the overrepresentation of African Americans at the arrest stage. Crime-specific rates indicate that results vary by crime type:[44]

Offense	*Percentage*
All offenses	20.0
Homicide	2.8
Aggravated assault	5.2
Robbery	15.6
Rape	26.3
Burglary	33.1
Larceny/auto theft	45.6
Drugs	48.9

Arguably, the main implication of this list is that the level of unexplained disproportionality is "directly related to the discretion permitted or used in handling each of the offenses, which tends to be related to offense seriousness—the less serious the offenses (and the greater discretion), the greater the amount of the disproportionality in prison that must be accounted for on grounds other than differences in arrest."[45]

This observation is particularly salient in the context of drug offenses. Recall the arguments from Chapter 4 contending that drug arrest decisions are subject to more proactive enforcement than most other offenses. Combine this observation with the fact that during the recent surge of incarceration rates (1980–1996), drug offenses have had the greatest impact on new commitments to prison. In short, the offense category indicated to suffer from the broad use of discrimination and the most opportunity for discrimination is the fastest-growing portion of new commitments to prison. Thus, Blumstein's findings, although generally not an indictment of the criminal justice system, ominously suggest the presence of discrimination during the era of the War on Drugs.

Langan reexamined Blumstein's argument, contending that he relied on an inappropriate data set.[46] Langan argued that prison admissions offered a more appropriate comparison to arrest differentials than prison populations. Langan also incorporated victim identification data as a substitute for arrest data to circumvent the biases associated with arrest. In addition to altering Blumstein's formula, he looked at 3 years of data (1973, 1979, and 1982) across five offense types (robbery, aggravated assault, simple assault, burglary, and larceny). Even after making these modifications, Langan confirmed Blumstein's findings: about 20 percent of the racial overrepresentation in prison admissions was left unexplained.

In an updated analysis with 1990 prison population data, Blumstein found that the amount of unexplained variation in racially disproportionate prison populations on the basis of arrest data increased from 20 to 24 percent. In addition, the differentials discussed earlier on the basis of discretion and seriousness increased for drug crimes and less serious crimes, decreasing only for homicide and robbery.[47] This seems to confirm the argument that the War on Drugs has increased the racial disparities in prison populations.

Tonry challenged Blumstein's work on several grounds.[48] He argued, first, that it is a mistake to assume that official UCR arrest statistics accurately reflect offending rates. As discussed in Chapter 4, there is evidence of race discrimination in arrests. This is particularly true with respect to drug arrests, which account for much of the dramatic increase in the prison populations in recent years. Second, Tonry pointed out that Blumstein's analysis used national-level data. Aggregating in this fashion can easily mask evidence of discrimination in certain areas of the country.

Tonry's third criticism was that Blumstein's approach could easily hide "off-setting forms of discrimination that are equally objectionable but not observable in the aggregate."[49] One example would be sentencing African American offenders with white victims more harshly, and at the same time punishing African American offenders with African American victims less harshly (see Chapter 7 for a more detailed discussion). The former represents a bias against African American offenders and the latter, a bias against African American victims. If we aggregate the data, as Blumstein did, neither pattern is evident.

Hawkins and Hardy spoke to the possibility of regional differences by looking at state-specific imprisonment rates.[50] They found a wide variation across the 50 states in the extent of the differential in African American imprisonment rates left unexplained by disproportionate African American arrest rates. The "worst state" was New Mexico, with only 2 percent of the difference explained by the expected impact of arrest; the "best state" was Missouri, with 96 percent of the incarceration rates of African Americans explained by differential arrest rates. Hawkins and Hardy concluded that "Blumstein's figure of 80 percent would not seem to be a good approximation for all states."[51]

In an attempt to look past systematic racial discrimination in the criminal justice system, researchers have begun to explore the intricacies of contextual discrimination. A review by Chiricos and Crawford reveals that researchers have started to study the impact of social context on the racial composition of imprisonment rates by investigating such issues as the population's racial composition, the percentage of unemployed African Americans, and the region (South versus non-South).[52]

The first two issues reflect the theoretical argument that communities, and thus decision makers, will be apprehensive under certain conditions and become more punitive. Specific conditions of apprehension (or threat) are related to racial mass. For example, large concentrations of African Americans will be associated with a higher fear of crime and a need to be more punitive. Michalowski and Pearson found that racial composition of African Americans in a state was positively associated with general incarceration rates.[53] However, the impact of racial composition on race-specific incarceration rates is less clear. Hawkins and Hardy discovered that states with smaller percentages of African Americans were associated with more racial disparity in incarceration rates than could be accounted for by arrest rates.[54] In contrast, Bridges and Crutchfield found that states with higher percentages of African Americans in the general population were associated with lower levels of racial disparity in incarceration rates.[55] DeLone and Chiricos argued that this inconsistency is due to an improper level of analysis.[56] They argued that looking at state-level imprisonment and racial composition rates can be deceiving. The proper level of analysis is the level of the sentencing court. In their study of county-level incarceration rates, they found that higher percentages of African Americans led to higher levels of general incarceration and of African American incarceration rates.

Race-specific unemployment rates reflect the idea that idle (or surplus) populations are crime prone and in need of deterrence. This line of reasoning requires a more punitive response, with higher incarceration rates when the perceived crime-prone population is idle.[57] Generally, this "threat" is measured by the unemployment rate of the perceived crime-prone population—young African American males. DeLone and Chiricos have found that at the county level, high unemployment rates for young African American males are not associated with higher general incarceration rates but are predictive of higher incarceration rates for young African American males.[58] Box 9.3 offers several additional explanations for African American incarceration rates.

Adjustment to Prison

Research on the adjustment of men to life in prison has been available for many years, beginning with Clemmer's *The Prison Community*[59] and including Sykes's *The Society of Captives*[60] and Irwin and Cressey's "Thieves, Convicts and Inmate Culture."[61] Jacobs argued that without exception these studies disregarded the issue of race, even though the prison populations in the institutions under study were racially diverse.[62] Consequently, according to Jacobs, the prevailing concept of the "prison subculture" needs to be revised. Jacobs argued that race is the defining factor of the prison experience: racial and ethnic identity defines

---

BOX 9.3   Additional Explanations for the Racial Distribution of U.S. Prison Populations

Historically, some have argued that prison replaced the social control of slavery in the South after the end of the Civil War. Given the criminalization of vagrancy and the operation of the convict lease system, a de facto slavery system was invoked on those African Americans who did not leave the South and who refused to offer their labor to former plantation owners who needed it (Du Bois, 1901; Myers, 1999).

Others have argued that prison has always been used to supplement the needs of capitalism as a mechanism to control surplus populations in times of high unemployment (Michalowski & Carlson, 1999). Specifically, African American males, who have the highest unemployment rates, have been viewed as socially dangerous surplus populations (for a review of this literature, see Chiricos & DeLone, 1992).

In the context of the War on Drugs, some have argued that the rising African American male prison populations are a response to a moral panic about drugs that stems from the association of crime and drug use with this population almost exclusively (Chiricos, 1995).

---

the social groupings in prisons, the operation of informal economic systems, the organization of religious activities, and the reasons for inmate misconduct. In other words, white inmates tend to associate with white inmates, African American inmates with African Americans, and so on. In this respect, the racial and ethnic segregation in prison mimics society on the outside.

Goodstein and MacKenzie supported Jacobs's observations and argued that their own "exploratory study of race and inmate adjustment to prison demonstrates that the experience of imprisonment differs for African Americans and whites."[63] They reported that although African Americans may develop more antiauthoritarian attitudes and are more likely to challenge prison officials, they appear to have fewer conflicts with fellow inmates.

Wright explored the relationship between "race and economic marginality" to explain adjustment to prison.[64] He explored the apparently commonsense assumption that African Americans, because of their experience in the "modern urban ghetto" (see "underclass," Chapter 3), will be more "resilient" to the pains of imprisonment. In short, "ghetto life supposedly socializes the individual to engage in self-protection against the hostile social environment of the slum and the cold and unpredictable prison setting."[65] Using multiple indicators of adaptation to the prison environment, Wright found that although economic marginality does appear to influence the ease of adjustment to prison, this appears to be the case regardless of race.

Other research on male prison populations also indicates that race may not always explain institutional behavior. Research on the effects of race on levels of institutional misconduct reveals an inconsistent picture. Whereas some researchers find nonwhites overrepresented in inmate misconduct, Petersilia and Honig's study of three state prison systems found three different patterns in re-

Focus on an Issue
Life in Prison: Segregation by Law or Choice?

A series of court decisions have declared de jure racial segregation in prisons to be unconstitutional. As late as the 1970s, prisons in the South and even some in Northern states such as Nebraska segregated prisoners according to race as a matter of official policy. Even though such policies have been outlawed, inmates often self-segregate along racial and ethnic lines as a matter of choice.

This poses a difficult problem for correctional administrators. Should inmates be forced to have integrated work, housing, and education assignments? Or should administrators allow them to make decisions on the basis of personal preference, even if these decisions result in self-segregation? Racial tensions are a serious problem in most prisons; forcing white and African

American inmates to share cells when they are actively hostile to each other could bring these tensions to a boil. In one instance, a white inmate felt so threatened by the politicized racial atmosphere in his prison that he filed suit asking a federal court to reverse the integration requirement and return to segregation (Jacobs, 1983).

On the other hand, if correctional administrators bowed to the wishes of inmates on this matter, they would create two problems. They would be actively promoting racial segregation, which is illegal, and they would undermine their own authority by acknowledging that inmates could veto policy they did not like.

What is the best strategy for administrators in this difficult situation? You decide.

lationships between race and rule infractions.[66] In Michigan, there was no relationship between race and rule infractions; in California, whites had significantly higher rule infractions; and in Texas, African Americans had significantly higher rule infractions.

Flanagan found similarly inconsistent results.[67] He argued that inmates' age at commitment, history of drug use, and current incarceration offense are most predictive of general misconduct rates. He did find, however, that race is an important predictor for older inmates with no drug history and sentenced for an offense other than homicide. Flanagan suggested that race (among other predictors) is a variable that is inappropriate to use in assisting with the security classification of inmates, due to its low predictive power in relation to institutional misconduct.

Recent research of federal prison inmates by Harer and Steffensmeier offers support for the importation model of prison violence, indicating that African American inmates are significantly more likely to receive disorderly conduct reports for violence than white inmates, but lower levels of alcohol and drug misconduct reports than whites.[68] This picture reflects the differential levels of violence and drug behavior between African Americans and whites reflected in arrest figures and assumed to characterize the general behavior patterns of these groups in U.S. society (see Chapter 2).

Many correctional observers say that even with the numerical dominance of African Americans in correctional facilities, they are still at a disadvantage in terms of the allocation of resources. For example, Thomas argues that race operates in prison culture to guide behavior, allocate resources, and elevate white groups to a privileged status even when they are not numerically dominant.[69]

Race and Religion Religion often emerges as a source of solidarity among prison inmates, as well as a mechanism for inmates to adjust to the frustrations of the prison environment. Although religion may be seen as a benign, or even a rehabilitative influence, some religious activities in prison have been met with criticism by correctional officials and have been accepted only with federal court intervention. Concern arises when religious tenets seem to espouse the supremacy of one racial group over another.

Jacobs argued that the Black Muslim movement in U.S. prisons was a response to active external proselytizing by the church.[70] The most influential Muslim movement was the Nation of Islam, founded by Elijah Muhammad. Conley and Debro pointed out that although the Nation of Islam was not particularly competitive with Christianity in the nonprison population, "it had special appeal to incarcerated Black males. In contrast to the various religious denominations, which preached religious repentance and submission and obedience to the U.S. justice system . . . the Nation of Islam preached Black pride and resistance to white oppression."[71] Prison administrators overtly resisted the movement for several years. The American Correctional Association issued a policy statement in 1960 refusing to recognize the legitimacy of the Muslim religion, based on arguments that it was a "cult" that disrupted prison operations. Jacobs noted that "prison officials saw in the Muslims not only a threat to prison authority, but also a broader revolutionary challenge to American society" that led to challenges of the white correctional authority.[72]

Consequently, prison officials tried to suppress Muslim religious activities by such actions as banning the Koran. This led to lawsuits asserting the Muslims' right to the free exercise of religion. In 1962, however, the U.S. Supreme Court in *Fulwood v. Clemmer* ordered the District of Columbia Department of Corrections to "stop treating the Muslims differently from other religious groups."[73] This decision paved the way for the Black Muslim movement to be seen as a legitimate religion and to be taken seriously as a vehicle of prison change through such avenues as litigation.

One example of the rise and subsequent influence of Native American religious groups can be found in Nebraska. The Native American Cultural and Spiritual Awareness group (NASCA) is composed of Native American inmates who seek to build solidarity and appreciation of Native American values.[74] This group also pursues change in the prison environment through litigation. The elements of inmate-on-inmate violence and guard assaults characteristic of other groups are not apparent here.

As the direct result of litigation, Native American inmates won the right to have a sweat lodge on prison grounds and to have medicine men and women visit to perform religious ceremonies. This concession is significant because it occurred 4 years before federal legislation dictated the recognition and acceptance of Native American religions.

Other religious movements are of concern to prison officials and social commentators due to the movements' apparent assertions of racial supremacy. The impact of such values in a closed environment such as a prison is obvious, but concerns have surfaced that the impact of these subcultures may reach outside prison walls. Are groups emerging, under the guise of religions, that promote tenets of racial hatred?

The Five Percent and Asatru movements are two such groups; the former is made up of African Americans and the latter, of whites, each emphasizing tenets of racial purity. Currently, six states censor the teachings of the Five Percenters, and other states label all followers as gang members.[75] The movement began in Harlem in 1964 and has spread across the country, claiming thousands of followers. Teachings include the rejection of "history, authority and organized religion," and members call themselves a nation of Gods (men) and Earths (women).[76] Although the group advocates peace and rejects drinking and drugs, correctional officials have linked Five Percenters to violence in some state institutions. Similar to the beliefs of the Nation of Islam, the beliefs of Five Percenters stress that "blacks were the original beings and must separate from white society."[77]

The Asatru followers practice a form of pagan religion based on principles of pre-Christian Nordic traditions. This religion was officially recognized in Iceland in 1972 and professes nine noble virtues, including courage, honor, and perseverance. However, prison officials claim that as this group has grown in popularity in American prisons, so has racial violence. Some critics charge "that while Asatru is a genuine religion to some followers, these modern pagan groups have been a breeding ground for right-wing extremists" and attract white supremacists.[78] Some state prison systems have taken steps to ban Asatru groups, stating security concerns. Some Asatru followers have surfaced in connection with acts of racial violence. Most notable perhaps is the recent case of John William King, a white male convicted of the dragging death of an African American man in Jasper, Texas. While serving a prison sentence prior to this crime, King is said to have joined an Odinist group, an Asatru variant. From this affiliation, he has tattoos depicting an African American man lynched on a cross and the words *Aryan Pride*.[79]

Prison Gangs

Currently, prison gangs are an integral part of understanding the prison environment and the inmate social system. Little systematic information on prison gangs (or security threat groups) is available. However, from the states that do document such subcultures, evidently prison gangs cover the racial and ethnic spectrum. Some of these gangs have networks established between prisons, across states, and most recently, with street gangs.

Focus on an Issue
Indigenous Justice Paradigm

In "Traditional and Contemporary Tribal Justice," Melton (1998) observed that in many contemporary tribal communities, "a dual justice system exists, one based on an American paradigm of justice and the other based on an indigenous paradigm." The American justice paradigm is characterized by an adversarial system and stands apart from most religious tenets. Crimes are viewed as actions against the state, with little attention to the needs of the victim or community. The focus is on the defendant's individual rights during adjudication. Punishing the offender is generally governed by a retributive philosophy and removal from society.

In contrast, tribal justice is based on a holistic philosophy and not easily divorced from the religious and spiritual realms of everyday life. Melton attempts to distill the characteristic elements of a number of diverse American tribal justice ideologies into an Indigenous Justice Paradigm. The holistic philosophy is the key element of this paradigm and supports a "circle of justice" where "the center of the circle represents the underlying problems and issues that need to be resolved to attain peace and harmony for the individuals and the community" (p. 66). The corresponding values of restorative and reparative justice prescribe the actions the offender must perform to be forgiven. These values reflect the importance of the victim and the community in restoring harmony.

The influence of the American justice paradigm on Native American communities has a long and persistent history (Zatz, Lujan, & Snyder-Joy, 1991). However, the values of restorative and reparative justice are emerging in a number of programs off the reservation. In particular, the restorative justice practices of the Navajo Nation have influenced a number of new offender rehabilitation programs, including many supported by the Presbyterian Church.

The Texas prison system offers an example of the variety of gangs present in prisons today. As of 1990, the Texas prison system documented eight well-established prison gangs: two were white, two were African American, and four were Hispanic.[80] Here are some representative examples:

Texas Syndicate: This group has its origins in the California Department of Corrections. Once released, these individuals returned to Texas and entered the Texas Department of Corrections as the result of continuing criminal activity. The membership is predominantly Hispanic, with the occasional acceptance of white inmates. This group is structured along paramilitary lines, has a documented history of prison violence, and will enforce rule breaking with death.[81]

Texas Mafia: The membership of this group is predominantly white, with occasional acceptance of Hispanic members. These inmates have ties to motorcycle gangs and are implicated in the production and sale of illicit drugs.[82]

Focus on an Issue
Civil Rights of Convicted Felons

Individuals convicted of felonies in the United States may experience a range of sentences from incarceration to probation. Such sentences, in effect, limit the civil rights of the convicted. No longer do we live in a society that views the convicted felon from the legal status of civil death, literally a slave of the state, but some civil rights restrictions endure after the convicted offender serves a judicially imposed sentence. *Collateral consequences* is a term used to refer to the statutory restrictions imposed by a legislative body on a convicted felon's rights. Such restrictions vary by state but include restrictions on employment, carrying firearms, holding public office, and voting.

According to the Sentencing Project (2002), 49 states and the District of Columbia restrict the rights of all prisoners to vote, 28 states restrict the right to vote for offenders on probation, and 32 states limit this right while on parole. In most states, the right to vote can be restored (automatically or by petition) after completion of the sentence (or within a fixed number of years). However, in 8 states the legal prohibition on voting is permanent. The Sentencing Project reports that although some states allow for the restoration of voting rights to felony offenders who have served out their sentences, the process is not easy. On March 3, 1999, the *Omaha World Herald* reported that in Nebraska, the offender has to apply to the Pardons Board for reinstatement, in Alabama, "ex-offenders are required to provide a DNA sample to the Alabama Department of Forensic Sciences as part of the process of regaining the right to vote" (The Sentencing Project, 2002).

Given the current increases in incarceration rates across the country, the additional penalty of disenfranchisement for convicted felons becomes an increasing concern. In short, the permanence of this measure may have unanticipated consequences. As reported in the *Omaha World Herald,* the overrepresentation of African American males in our prisons means that "significant proportions of the black population in some states have been locked out of the voting booth" (p. 22). For example, in Florida, which denies voting rights permanently to convicted felons, nearly one-third of the African American male population is not eligible to vote (p. 22). Arguably, laws such as these, which have the effect of barring a substantial portion of the minority population from voting, fail to promote a racially diverse society. Should convicted offenders be allowed to earn back their right to vote as a recognition of their efforts at rehabilitation? Should we change laws that have a racial impact, even if the intent is not racially motivated?

Aryan Brotherhood of Texas: This group emerged in the early 1980s, and membership is dominated by white, racist inmates. The group is implicated in prison violence as well as illegal activities on the outside.[83]

Mandingo Warriors: This group is made up of African Americans and came into existence after most of the Hispanic and white groups. These members are involved in prison violence and the sub-rosa economic system but appear to be less organized than the other racial and ethnic groups.[84]

Women in Prison

Studies addressing the imprisonment of women are less numerous than those for men, but they are increasing in number. Within this growing body of research, the issue of race is not routinely addressed. When race is assessed, the comparisons are generally limited to African Americans and whites. The evidence is mixed on the issue of whether race affects the adjustment of women to prison life.

MacKenzie explained the behaviors (conflicts and misconduct reports) of women in prison on the basis of age and attitudes (anxiety, fear of victimization).[85] She commented that the four prisons she examined are similar in racial composition, but failed to comment on whether she explored differences by race in relation to attitudes and aggressive behavior. Such research ignores the possibility that race may influence one's perception of prison life, tendencies toward aggression, age of inmate, or length of time in prison.

MacKenzie, Robinson, and Campbell, in later works, did address race in the demographic description of the incarcerated women.[86] In a study of one women's prison in Louisiana, for example, they found that nonwhite women were severely overrepresented among all prisoners and even more likely to be serving long sentences. Their findings indicated unique adjustment problems for long-term inmates, but they failed to incorporate race into their explanatory observations about institutional misconduct. This omission seems contrary to the observation that nonwhite women are more likely to have longer sentences.

Race has specifically been recognized as a factor in research addressing the issue of sexual deprivation among incarcerated women. Leger identified racial dimensions to several key explanatory factors in the participation of female prisoners in lesbianism.[87] First, the demographic information reveals that most lesbian relationships are intraracial and that no distinctions emerged by race in participation in the gay or straight groups. Second, once dividing the group by the characteristics of previous confinements (yes or no) and age at first gay experience, the pattern of even representation of whites and African Americans changed. African American females were overrepresented in the group indicating previous confinement, and the information about age at first arrest indicated that African American females were more likely to have engaged in their first lesbian act prior to their first arrest.

CONCLUSION

The picture of the American correctional system is most vivid in black and white but also has prominent images of brown. Such basic questions as who is in prison and how individuals survive in prison cannot be divorced from the issues of race and ethnicity. The most salient observation about minorities and corrections is the striking overrepresentation of African Americans in prison populations. In addition, this overrepresentation is gradually increasing in new court commitments and population figures. Explanations for this increasing overrepresentation are complex.

The most obvious possibility is that African American criminality is increasing. This explanation has been soundly challenged by Tonry's work, which compares the stability of African American arrest rates since the mid-1970s to the explosive African American incarceration rates of the same period.[88] He argues that a better explanation may be the racial impact of the War on Drugs.

Blumstein's analysis offers another clue to the continuing increase in the African American portion of the prison population that links discretion and the War on Drugs.[89] His work suggests that the racial disparities in incarceration rates for drug offenses are not well explained by racial disparities in drug arrest rates. Thus, the War on Drugs and its impact on imprisonment may be fostering the "malign neglect" Tonry charges.

DISCUSSION QUESTIONS

1. What must a researcher do to advance a description of disparity to an argument of discrimination? In the case of prison populations, how do you advance from the demographic description of the overrepresentation of African Americans in prison to a causal analysis of discrimination by the criminal justice system?

2. In what way are Blumstein's findings about the wide variation of unexplained racial disparity in prison populations according to type of offense similar to the liberation hypothesis discussed in the chapter on sentencing (Chapter 7)?

3. What correctional policies can be created from the principles of restorative justice (based on indigenous justice principles)? Are these values more compatible with some offenses than others? More appropriate for some types of offenders than others?

4. Do you think prison gang formation is influence most by external forces and the gang affiliations offenders bring to prison from the street or by the internal forces of the prison environment, such as racial composition? What arguments can you offer to support your position?

NOTES

1. U.S. Department of Justice, "News Release: National Correctional Population Reaches New High" (August 26, 2001). Available at www.ojp.usdoj/bjs/abstract/oous000.htm.

2. U.S. Census Bureau, *United States Statistical Abstract, 2000* (Washington, DC:

U.S. Government Printing Office). Available at www.census.gov/population/socdemo/school/ppl-148/tab01.text.

3. Marc Maur, *Americans behind Bars: A Comparison of International Rates of Incarceration* (Washington, DC: The Sentencing Project, 1991).

4. National Center for Education Statistics (June 2002). Available at http://nces.ed.gov/pubs2001/digest/.

5. U.S. Census Bureau, *United States Statistical Abstract, 2000.*

6. Estimates calculated from U.S. Department of Justice, "News Release"; Allen J. Beck and Paige M. Harrison, *Prisoners in 2000* (Washington, DC: U.S. Department of Justice, 2001). Available at www.ojp.usdoj.gov/bjs/.

7. U.S. Census Bureau, *United States Statistical Abstract, 2000.*

8. Harry E. Allen and Clifford E. Simonson, *Corrections in America: An Introduction,* 7th ed. (Englewood Cliffs, NJ: Prentice-Hall, 1995).

9. Ibid.

10. Beck and Harrison, *Prisoners in 2000.*

11. Ibid.

12. Ibid.

13. Ibid.

14. Bureau of Justice Statistics, *Comparing State and Federal Inmates, 1991* (Washington, DC: U.S. Government Printing Office, 1993).

15. Bureau of Justice Statistics, *Sourcebook of Criminal Justice Statistics, 2000* (Washington, DC: U.S. Government Printing Office, 2001), p. 524. Available at www.albany.edu/sourcebook/.

16. Bureau of Justice Statistics, *Comparing State and Federal Inmates, 1991.*

17. Ibid.

18. Margaret Werner Cahalan, *Historical Corrections Statistics in the United States, 1850–1984* (Washington, DC: U.S. Government Printing Office, 1986), pp. 65–66.

19. Michael Tonry, *Malign Neglect* (New York: Oxford University Press, 1995).

20. Ibid.

21. Ibid., p. 21.

22. Ibid.

23. Allen J. Beck, Jennifer C. Karberg, and Paige M. Harrison, *Prison and Jail Inmates at Midyear, 2001* (Washington, DC: U.S. Department of Justice, 2002).

24. Ibid.

25. Ibid.

26. The Sentencing Project: Facts about Prison and Prisoners (June 2002). Available at www.sentencingproject.org.

27. Timothy A. Hughes, Doris James Wilson, and Allen J. Beck, *Trends in State Parole, 1990–2000* (Washington, DC: U.S. Department of Justice, 2001), p ? Available at www.ojp.usdoj.gov/bjs/.

28. Bureau of Justice Statistics, *Trends in State Parole, 1990–2000* (Washington, DC: Department of Justice, 2001). Available at www.ojp.usdoj.gov/bjs/.

29. Ibid.

30. Ibid.

31. Ibid.

32. Federal parole was eliminated in 1987 when the federal sentencing guidelines were implemented. Anyone sentenced prior to this is still eligible for parole consideration.

33. The Sentencing Project: Facts about Prison and Prisoners (2001). Available at www.sentencingproject.org.

34. Ibid.

35. Ibid.

36. U.S. Department of Justice, "News Release" (August 26, 2001).

37. Ibid.

38. Ibid.

39. Ibid.

40. Joan Petersilia, *Racial Disparities in the Criminal Justice System* (Santa Monica, CA: Rand Corporation, 1983), p. 28.

41. Coramae Richey Mann, *Unequal Justice: A Question of Color* (Bloomington: Indiana University Press, 1993).

42. William Wilbanks, *The Myth of the Racist Criminal Justice System* (Monterey, CA: Brooks/Cole, 1987).

43. Alfred Blumstein, "On the Disproportionality of United States Prison Populations," *Journal of Criminal Law and Criminology* 73 (1982): 1259–1281.

44. Ibid., p. 1274.

45. Ibid.

46. Patrick Langan, "Racism on Trial: New Evidence to Explain the Racial Composition of Prisons in the United

States," *Journal of Criminal Law and Criminology* 76 (1985): 666–683.

47. Alfred Blumstein, "Racial Disproportionality in U.S. Prisons Revisited," *University of Colorado Law Review* 64 (1993): 743–760.

48. Tonry, *Malign Neglect,* p. 67–68.

49. Ibid.

50. Darnell F. Hawkins and Kenneth A. Hardy, "Black-White Imprisonment Rates: A State-by-State Analysis," *Social Justice* 16 (1989): 75–94.

51. Ibid., p. 79.

52. Theodore G. Chiricos and Charles Crawford, "Race and Imprisonment: A Contextual Assessment of the Evidence," in *Ethnicity, Race and Crime,* ed. Darnell F. Hawkins (Albany: State University of New York Press, 1995).

53. Raymond J. Michalowski and Michael A. Pearson, "Punishment and Social Structure at the State Level: A Cross-Sectional Comparison of 1970 and 1980," *Journal of Research in Crime and Delinquency* 27 (1990): 52–78.

54. Hawkins and Hardy, "Black-White Imprisonment Rates."

55. George S. Bridges and Robert D. Crutchfield, "Law, Social Standings and Racial Disparities in Imprisonment," *Social Forces* 66 (1988): 699–724.

56. Miriam A. DeLone and Theodore G. Chiricos, "Young Black Males and Incarceration: A Contextual Analysis of Racial Composition," paper presented at the annual meeting of the American Society of Criminology, 1994.

57. Dario Melossi, "An Introduction: Fifty Years Later, Punishment and Social Structure in Comparative Analysis," *Contemporary Crises* 13 (1989): 311–326.

58. DeLone and Chiricos, "Young Black Males and Incarceration."

59. Donald Clemmer, *The Prison Community* (New York: Holt, Rinehart and Winston, 1940).

60. Gresham M. Sykes, *The Society of Captives* (Princeton, NJ: Princeton University Press, 1958).

61. John Irwin and Donald Cressey, "Thieves, Convicts and Inmate Culture," *Social Problems* 10 (1962): 142–155.

62. James Jacobs, *New Perspectives on Prison and Imprisonment* (Ithaca, NY: Cornell University Press, 1983).

63. Lynne Goodstein and Doris Layton MacKenzie, "Racial Differences in Adjustment Patterns of Prison Inmates—Prisonization, Conflict, Stress and Control," in *The Criminal Justice System and Blacks,* ed. Daniel Georges-Abeyie (New York: Clark Boardman, 1984).

64. Kevin N. Wright, "Race and Economic Marginality," *Journal of Research in Crime and Delinquency* 26 (1989): 67–89.

65. Ibid, p. 67.

66. Joan Petersilia and P. Honig, *The Prison Experiences of Career Criminals* (Santa Monica, CA: Rand Corporation, 1980).

67. Timothy Flanagan, "Correlates of Institutional Misconduct among Prisoners," *Criminology* 21 (1983): 29–39.

68. Miles D. Harer, and Darrell J. Steffensmeier, "Race and Prison Violence," *Criminology* 34 (1996): 323–355.

69. Jim Thomas, "Racial Codes in Prison Culture: Snapshots in Black and White," in *Race and Criminal Justice,* ed. Michael Lynch and Britt Patterson (New York: Harrow & Heston, 1991).

70. Jacobs, *New Perspectives on Prison and Imprisonment.*

71. Darlene Conley and Julius Debro, "Black Muslims in California Prisons: The Beginning of a Social Movement for Black Prisoners in the United States," in *Race, Class, Gender and Justice in the United States,* ed. Charles E. Reasons, Darlene J. Conley, and Julius Debro (Boston: Allyn & Bacon, 2002), p. 279.

72. Jacobs, *New Perspectives on Prison and Imprisonment,* p. 65.

73. Ibid.

74. Elizabeth S. Grobsmith, *Indians in Prison* (Lincoln: University of Nebraska Press, 1994).

75. *Omaha World Herald* (December 6, 1998), p. 19-A.

76. Ibid.

77. Ibid.

78. *Omaha World Herald* (February 28, 1999), p. 1.

79. Ibid.

80. Robert Fong, Ronald Vogel, and Salvador Buentello, "Prison Gang Dynamics: A Look inside the Texas Department of Corrections," in *Corrections: Dilemmas and Directions,* ed. Peter J. Benekos and Alida V. Merlo (Highland Heights, KY: Academy of Criminal Justice Sciences; Cincinnati, OH: Anderson, 1992).

81. Buentello Salvador, "Combatting Gangs in Texas," *Corrections Today* (July 1992): 58–60.

82. Ibid.

83. Ibid.

84. Fong et al., "Prison Gang Dynamics."

85. Doris L. MacKenzie, "Age and Adjustment to Prison: Interactions with Attitudes and Anxiety," *Criminal Justice and Behavior* 14 (1987): 427–447.

86. Doris L. MacKenzie, James Robinson, and Carol Campbell, "Long-Term Incarceration of Female Offenders: Prison Adjustment and Coping," *Criminal Justice and Behavior* 16 (1989): 223–238.

87. Robert G. Leger, "Lesbianism among Women Prisoners: Participants and Nonparticipants," *Criminal Justice and Behavior* 14 (1987): 448–467.

88. Tonry, *Malign Neglect.*

89. Blumstein, "On the Disproportionality of the United States Prison Populations" and "Racial Disproportionality in U.S. Prisons Revisited."

10

✖

Minority Youth and Crime

Minority Youth in Court

In June 2001, Lionel Tate, an African American boy who was 12 years old when he killed a 6-year-old family friend while demonstrating a wrestling move he had seen on television, was sentenced to life in prison without the possibility of parole. Tate, who claimed that the death was an accident, was tried as an adult in Broward County, Florida, and convicted of first-degree murder. One month later, Nathaniel Brazill, a 14-year-old African American, was sentenced by a Florida judge to 28 years in prison without the possibility of parole. Brazill was 13 years old when he shot and killed Barry Grunow, a popular 30-year-old seventh-grade teacher at a middle school in Lake Worth, Florida. Although Brazill did not deny that he fired the shot that killed his teacher, he claimed that he had only meant to scare Grunow and that the shooting was an accident. Like Tate, Brazill was tried as an adult; he was convicted of second-degree murder.

These two cases raised a storm of controversy regarding the prosecution of children as adults. Those on one side argue that children who commit adult crimes, such as murder, should be treated as adults; they should be prosecuted as adults and sentenced to adult correctional institutions. As Marc Shiner, the prosecutor in Brazill's case, put it, "This was a heinous crime committed by a young man with a difficult personality who should be behind bars. Let us not forget a man's life has been taken away."[1] Those on the other side contend that prosecuting children as adults is "unwarranted and misguided." They assert that children who commit crimes of violence typically suffer from severe mental and emotional problems and that locking kids up in adult jails does not deter crime or rehabilitate juvenile offenders. Although they acknowledge that juvenile offenders should be punished for their actions, they claim that incarcerating them in adult prisons for the rest of their lives "is an outrage."[2] According to Vincent Schiraldi, president of the Justice Policy Institute, "In adult prisons, Brazill will never receive the treatment he needs to reform himself. Instead, he will spend his time trying to avoid being beaten, assaulted, or raped in a world where adults prey on, rather than protect, the young."[3]

GOALS OF THE CHAPTER

The prosecution of children as adults, and the potential for racial bias in the decision to "waive" youth to adult court, is one of the issues we address in this chapter. We discuss racial/ethnic patterns in victimization of juveniles and in offending by juveniles, as well as the treatment of juveniles by the police. We end the chapter with a discussion of the treatment of minority youth by the juvenile justice system. Consistent with the approach taken in previous chapters, our goals are to (1) explore the myths and realities about victimization of and crime by minority youth; (2) examine the relationship between the police and racial and ethnic minority youth; and (3) review recent research on racial disparities in the juvenile justice system.

YOUNG RACIAL MINORITIES
AS VICTIMS AND OFFENDERS

Juveniles as Victims of Crime

In Chapter 2, we showed that, regardless of age, African Americans have higher personal theft and violent victimization rates than other racial/ethnic groups and Hispanics generally have higher victimization rates than non–Hispanics. However, information concerning the racial and ethnic trends in victimization for juveniles is scarce. In this section, we examine National Crime Victimization Survey (NCVS) data, supplemented by National Incident Based Reporting System (NIBRS) data and Supplemental Homicide Reports (SHR) from the FBI. We first discuss property victimization, followed by violent victimization and homicide victimization.

Property Victimization Using information from the 1996 and 1997 NCVS, the Office of Juvenile Justice and Delinquency Prevention released a brief titled "Juvenile Victims of Property Crimes."[4] Their findings indicated that one of every six juveniles (defined as youth aged 12–17) had been the victim of property crime.[5] This rate was 40 percent higher than the property crime victimization rate for adults.[6]

Table 10.1 offers a comparison of juvenile and adult property crime victimization rates by race and ethnicity. A ratio of juvenile to adult rates higher than

Table 10.1 Juvenile and Adult Property Victimization Rates by Race and Ethnicity, 1996 and 1997 Combined

	PROPERTY CRIME RATE (PER 1,000 POPULATION)		Property Crime Ratio (Juvenile/ Adults)
	Juvenile	Adult	
Victim race			
White	162	114	1:4*
African American	194	151	1:3*
Other	155	108	1:4*
Victim ethnicity			
Hispanic	143	133	1:1
Non-Hispanic	170	117	1:5*

SOURCE: Office of Juvenile Justice and Delinquency Prevention, "Juvenile Victims of Property Crimes" (Washington, DC: U.S. Department of Justice, 2000). Available at www.ncjrs.org/html/ojjdp.

*Juvenile rate versus adult rate; significant difference at the .05 level or below.

1:1 indicates that the juvenile victimization rate is higher than the adult rate. The ratio of 1:4 for whites, for example, indicates that the property crime victimization rate for white juveniles is higher than for white adults; moreover, the differences are statistically significant. This pattern is found for all three racial categories. Hispanic property crime victimization rates, however, do not vary significantly between juveniles and adults, but non-Hispanic rates do vary.

Looking at the victimization rates for juveniles only in Table 10.1, we see that African American youth have the highest property crime victimization rates, followed by white youth, and youth of other races (Native American/Alaskan Native and Asian/Pacific Islander). The racial pattern of property crime victimization among juveniles, in other words, mirrors the overall pattern for all ages combined (see Chapter 2); both comparisons show the highest rates for African Americans. The victimization rates of Hispanic and non-Hispanic juveniles (higher rates for non-Hispanics), on the other hand, differ from the rates for all age groups combined (higher rates for Hispanics).[7]

The FBI also collects information about crime victims through the NIBRS. These data do not represent the entire U.S. population, but they do provide substantial information on the victims of crime in the jurisdictions covered. Using this information, researchers estimate that juveniles with the following characteristics have a relatively high risk for property crime victimization: "African American juveniles, juveniles in urban areas, and juveniles in the West."[8] In short, these victimization patterns closely mirror "the higher risk for adults in these categories."[9]

Violent Victimization In general, violent victimization rates are higher for younger than for older age groups. For example, in 2000, the violent victimization rate for youth 15 to 19 years old was 64.3 victimizations for every 1,000 persons in that age group; in contrast, the rate for those 20 to 24 years old was 49.4.[10]

Table 10.2 Juvenile Homicide Victimization Rates by Race and Gender (per 100,000 Population, Ages 14–17)

	1990	1995	1999
White male	7.5	8.7	5.0
White female	2.5	2.7	1.7
African American male	59.1	63.2	31.0
African American female	10.3	11.9	6.9

SOURCE: James Allen Fox and Marianne W. Zawitz, "Homicide Trends in the United States" (Washington, DC: U.S. Department of Justice, 2001). Available at www.ojp.usdoj.gov/bjs.

A recent analysis of violent victimization trends by age and race indicates that young African American males are particularly at risk. For African American males aged 12–15, 1 out of every 14 was the victim of a violent crime; for those aged 16–19, the rate was 1 out of 6; for those aged 20–24, the rate was 1 out of 8.[11] Moreover, the violent victimization rate for African American males between the ages of 16 and 19 was two times the rate for white males and three times the rate for white females.[12] The majority of these incidents involved serious violent crimes—rapes, robberies, and aggravated assaults.

Young African American males were also more likely to be victims of crimes involving weapons, particularly handguns. From 1987 to 1992, the average annual rate (per 1,000 population) of handgun victimization was 39.7 for African Americans in the 16–19 age group and 29.4 for those in the 20–24 age group. The comparable rates for white males were 9.5 (aged 16–19) and 9.2 (aged 20–24).[13]

Homicide Victimization In 1999, one in every eight murder victims was under the age of 18.[14] Although homicide events are fairly rare (15,533 in 1999), racial patterns and trends by age are available. The SHR collected by the FBI indicate that there are important racial patterns found in homicide trends. As discussed in Chapter 2, African Americans generally are overrepresented both as homicide victims and offenders. Whereas the highest homicide rates, regardless of race and age, are found among 18- to 24-year-olds, youth between the ages of 14 and 17 have rates that are similar to those for the group aged 25 and older.[15]

Table 10.2 presents the homicide victimization rates for 14- to 17-year-olds, which indicate that homicide rates varied substantially from 1990 to 1999. For each of the four groups—white males, white females, African American males, and African American females—the rates peaked in 1995 and declined substantially by 1999. Aside from the changes over time, the most startling finding revealed by the data concerns the differences in homicide victimization rates by race. Regardless of gender, African American juveniles have higher victimization rates than white juveniles. In 1999, for example, the rate for African American females was four times greater than the rate for white females, and the rate for African American males was six times greater than the rate for white males. In fact, the homicide victimization rate for African American females was higher than the rate for white males.

It seems clear that African American youth are overrepresented as homicide victims in the United States. The picture of the juvenile homicide victim is similar to that of the juvenile homicide offender, which is discussed in the following section.

Juveniles as Offenders

Creating a profile of the juvenile offender is not an easy task. Much of the available data relies on arrest statistics and/or the perceptions of crime victims. Some critics argue that the portrait of the offender based on these data is biased and suggest that the picture of the typical offender should be taken from a population of adjudicated offenders. We discuss this alternative picture of the juvenile offender in the section on juveniles in the correctional system later in this chapter.

Juvenile Arrests The UCR arrest data presented in Table 10.3 are available by race and age. The racial differences in arrest statistics for offenders under 18 years of age are similar to those for offenders in all age groups. The overrepresentation of African American youth for violent crimes is notable; African Americans made up 42 percent of all arrests for violent Index crimes. Among young offenders arrested for both homicide and robbery, African Americans constituted 50 percent of all arrestees. African American juveniles are also overrepresented among arrests for serious property crimes (Part 1/Index crimes), but the proportions are smaller than for violent crime (27.3 percent for serious property crime versus 42.1 percent for violent crime).

Native American youth make up less than 1 percent of the juvenile population; they are slightly overrepresented in juvenile arrest figures for Index offenses (1.2 percent of all arrestees), especially property offenses (1.3 percent of all arrestees). Asian/Pacific Islander youth, who make up less than 3 percent of the U.S. population, are not overrepresented for any Part 1/Index offenses.

The data presented in Table 10.3 reveal more variability in the race of juveniles arrested for the less serious Part 2 offenses. White juveniles are overrepresented for driving under the influence, liquor law violations, and drunkenness; they represent over 90 percent of arrestees in each category. African Americans represent less than 8 percent of juveniles arrested for these offenses. A similar pattern is found for vandalism, where the racial makeup of arrestees is consistent with the racial makeup of the general population. African American juveniles are overrepresented among arrestees for a number of offenses, including other assaults (32.7 percent), fraud (33.9 percent), embezzlement (34.7 percent), offenses involving stolen property (37.2 percent), prostitution (39.3 percent), gambling (86.4 percent of all arrests), and disorderly conduct (32.4 percent).

Native American youth are overrepresented for two of the liquor-related Part 2 offenses: DUI and liquor law violations. They make up 2.8 percent of all arrests for liquor law violations and 1.5 percent of all arrests for driving under the influence. Asian/Pacific Islander youth are overrepresented only for the

Table 10.3 Percentage Distribution of Arrests by Race, 2000 (under 18 Years of Age)

	% White	% African American	% Native American	% Asian
Total	72.1	25.1	1.2	1.7
Part 1/Index crimes	67.1	29.7	1.3	2.0
Murder and nonnegligent manslaughter	47.1	49.8	0.5	2.6
Forcible rape	63.1	34.4	0.8	0.7
Robbery	41.4	56.1	0.7	1.8
Aggravated assault	60.9	36.6	1.0	1.5
Burglary	72.9	24.6	1.0	1.5
Larceny-theft	70.2	26.2	1.4	2.2
Motor vehicle theft	55.3	41.3	1.3	2.1
Arson	79.5	18.4	1.0	1.1
Violent crime	55.4	42.1	0.9	1.6
Property crime	69.4	27.3	1.3	2.0
Part 2/non-Index crimes				
Other assaults	64.9	32.7	1.2	1.0
Forgery and counterfeiting	77.2	20.0	0.6	2.3
Fraud	63.4	33.9	0.8	1.8
Embezzlement	62.0	34.7	0.8	1.5
Stolen property: buying, receiving, possessing	60.2	37.2	0.9	1.7
Vandalism	81.8	15.8	1.2	1.2
Weapons: carrying, possessing, etc.	67.0	30.6	0.8	1.6
Prostitution and commercialized vice	57.4	39.3	1.7	1.5
Sex offenses (except forcible rape and prostitution)	70.9	26.9	0.8	1.4
Drug abuse violations	70.2	28.1	0.7	1.0
Gambling	11.7	86.4	0.3	1.6
Offenses against family and children	77.5	19.8	0.8	2.0
DUI	92.9	4.7	1.5	1.0
Liquor law violations	91.9	4.6	2.8	0.7
Drunkenness	91.2	7.5	0.6	0.7
Disorderly conduct	65.9	32.4	0.9	0.8
Vagrancy	73.9	24.6	0.6	0.6
All other offenses (except traffic)	75.1	22.3	1.1	1.5
Suspicion	72.5	25.2	0.4	1.9
Curfew and loitering law violations	72.2	24.7	1.1	2.0
Runaways	76.3	17.9	1.4	4.4

SOURCE: Federal Bureau of Investigation, *Crime in the United States, 2000* (Washington, DC: U.S. Department of Justice, 2001).

Table 10.4 Juvenile Homicide Offenders and Offending Rates by Race and Gender, 1999 (per 100,000 Population, Aged 14–17)

| | OFFENDERS | | Offender |
	Numbers	Percentage	Rate
White males	643	40.2	10.2
White females	72	4.5	1.2
African American males	823	51.4	67.3
African American females	63	3.9	5.3

SOURCE: James Allen Fox and Marianne W. Zawitz, "Homicide Trends in the United States" (Washington, DC: U.S. Department of Justice, 2001). Available at www.ojp.usdoj.gov/bjs.

status offense of running away and are significantly underrepresented for offenses such as liquor law violations and drug abuse violations.

Homicide Offenders Data on homicide offenders reveal that offending peaks at around age 18, that males are overrepresented as offenders, that roughly 50 percent of all homicides are committed by offenders known to the victim (nonstrangers), and that the victim and the offender typically come from the same age group and racial category. The FBI SHR data can be used to calculate approximate rates of homicide offending by age, race, and gender. We consider these approximate rates because the data come from reports filled out by police agencies investigating homicides, rather than from convicted offenders. As a consequence, these data may reflect a number of biases and should be viewed with caution.

The SHR data indicate that offending rates vary by age group and that the pattern is similar to that found for victimization rates: the 18- to 24-year-old group has the highest offending rate, followed by the 14- to 17-year-old group, and those 25 and older have the lowest offending rates.[16] Table 10.4 displays homicide offending rates for 1999 for white males, white females, African American males, and African American females aged 14–17. (It should be noted that persons in the 14- to 17-year-old group make up less than 10 percent of those identified as offenders.)[17] Over 90 percent of all homicide offenders are male; African American males are 51.4 percent of these offenders, and white males, 40.2 percent. The homicide offending rate for African American males (67.3 per 100,000 population) is more than six times higher than the rate for white males (10.2 per 100,000 population). Although the homicide offending rate of young African American females is low, it is four times higher than the rate for young white females (5.3 versus 1.2 per 100,000 population).

The intraracial pattern identified in Chapter 2 for all homicides—that is, most homicides involve victims and offenders of the same race—is found for juvenile homicides as well. However, interracial homicides are more common among young perpetrators.[18] (See Box 10.1 for a discussion of the media's presentation of crime.)

BOX 10.1   Race, Crime, and the Media

In a recent review of over 70 studies focusing on crime in the news, Lori Dorfman and Vincent Schiraldi of the Berkeley Media Studies Group asked the following questions: Does news coverage reflect actual crime trends? How does news coverage depict minority crime? Does news coverage disproportionately depict youth of color as perpetrators of crime?

The authors of the report concluded that "the studies taken together indicate that depictions of crime in the news are not reflective of the rate of crime generally, the proportion of crime that is violent, the proportion of crime committed by people of color, or the proportion of crime that is committed by youth. The problem is not the inaccuracy of individual stories, but the cumulative choices of what is included in the news—or not included—present the public with a false picture of higher frequency and severity of crime than is actually the case."

Dorfman and Schiraldi noted that although crime dropped 20 percent from 1990 to 1998, crime news coverage increased by over 80 percent. Moreover, 75 percent of the studies found that minorities were overrepresented as perpetrators; over 80 percent of the studies found that more attention was paid to white victims than to minority victims. The authors concluded that the studies revealed that a "misinformation synergy" occurs in the way crime news is presented in the media. The result is a message that crime is constantly on the increase, the offenders are young minority males, and their victims are white.

SOURCE: Lori Dorfman and Vincent Schiraldi, "Off Balance: Youth, Race and Crime in the News," Executive Summary (Berkeley Media Studies Group, 2001), pp. 1–56. Available at www.buildingblocksforyouth.org/media/.

JUVENILES OF COLOR AND THE POLICE

The racial/ethnic patterns found in data on arrests of juveniles raise questions about the general pattern of relations between the police and juveniles. We have previously discussed this subject in Chapter 4, but it is useful to review the major points here.

First, juveniles have a high level of contact with the police, and juveniles of color have particularly high rates of contact. Several factors explain this pattern. Most important, young people tend to be out on the street more than adults, which is simply a matter of lifestyle related to the life cycle. Low-income juveniles are even more likely to be out in public than middle-class youth because middle-class and wealthy people have more opportunities for indoor recreation: family rooms, large backyards, and so on. A study of juvenile gangs in the 1960s found that gang members regarded the street corner as, in effect, their private space.[19] At the same time, juveniles are more likely to be criminal offenders than middle-aged persons, as criminal activity peaks between ages 14 and 24. For this reason, the police are likely to pay closer attention to juveniles—and to stop and question them on the street—than to older persons.

Second, in large part because of the higher levels of contact, juveniles consistently have less favorable attitudes toward the police. Age and race, in fact, are the two most important determinants of public attitudes. As Chapter 4 explains, the attitudes of Hispanics are less favorable than those of non-Hispanic whites but not as negative as those of African Americans. When age and race are combined, the result is that young African Americans have the most negative attitudes toward the police.[20]

Attitudes—and behavior that reflects negative attitudes—can have a significant impact on arrest rates. In his pioneering study of arrest patterns, Donald Black found that the demeanor of the suspect was one of the important determinants of an officer's decision to make an arrest. With other factors held constant, individuals who are less respectful or more hostile are more likely to be arrested. Black then found that African Americans were more likely to be less respectful of the police and consequently more likely to be arrested. Thus, the general state of poor relations leads to hostility in individual encounters with the police, which, in turn, results in higher arrest rates.[21]

RACE/ETHNICITY AND
THE JUVENILE JUSTICE SYSTEM

One particularly troubling aspect of juvenile justice as it has been
constructed throughout the 20th Century is its disproportionate
involvement, in an aggregate social sense, with youths from the
lowest socioeconomic strata, who at least in the latter half of the
20th Century overwhelmingly have been children of color.[22]

Although most research on the effect of race on the processing of criminal defendants has focused on adults, researchers have also examined the juvenile justice system for evidence of racial discrimination. Noting that the juvenile system, with its philosophy of *parens patriae*,[23] is more discretionary and less formal than the adult system, researchers suggest that there is greater potential for racial discrimination in the processing of juveniles than in the processing of adults. In cases involving juveniles, in other words, criminal justice officials are more concerned about rehabilitation than retribution, and they have discretion to decide whether to handle a case formally or informally. As a result, they have more opportunities than those who handle cases involving adults to take extralegal factors such as race/ethnicity and gender into consideration during the decision-making process.

There is compelling evidence that racial minorities are overrepresented in the juvenile justice system. In 1997, for example, African Americans made up 15 percent of the U.S. population aged 10–17 but 31 percent of all youth in the juvenile justice system. Whites constituted approximately 80 percent of the youth population but only 66 percent of all offenders in juvenile court.[24] African American juveniles were involved in 37 percent of person offense cases (murder, rape, robbery, and assault), 26 percent of property offense cases, and 32 percent of drug offense cases. Stated another way, for most offenses, African

Focus on an Issue
The Past, Present, and Future of the Juvenile Court

The traditional view of the emergence of the juvenile court in America describes the "child savers" as a liberal movement of the late 19th century made up of benevolent, civic-minded, middle-class Americans who worked to help delinquent, abused, and neglected children who were suffering from the negative impact of the rapid growth of industrialization. Although the emergence of the juvenile court is most often described as the creation of a welfare agency for the humane treatment of children, Platt (1977) highlighted the movement's social control agenda as well. According to Platt, the "child saving movement" did little to humanize the justice system for children, but rather "helped create a system that subjected more and more juveniles to arbitrary and degrading punishments" (p. xvii).

Platt contended that the attention of the juvenile court was originally focused on a select group of at-risk youth: court personnel focused on the children of urban, foreign-born, poor families as moral reclamation projects (p. xvii). Feld (1999) argued that in modern times, the juvenile court continues to intervene disproportionately in the lives of minority youth. He asserted that the persistent overrepresentation of minor-

ity youth at all stages of the system is largely the consequence of the juvenile court's unstable foundation of trying to reconcile social welfare and social control agendas. This conceptual contradiction allows "public officials to couch their get-tough policy changes in terms of 'public safety' rather than racial oppression" (p. 6).

Feld argued that the social welfare and social control aims of the juvenile court are irreconcilable and that attempts to pursue and reconcile these two competing agendas have left the contemporary juvenile court in crisis. He called it "a conceptually and administratively bankrupt institution with neither a rationale nor a justification" (pp. 3–4). He also contended that the juvenile court today offers a "second-class criminal court for young people" rather than a welfare agency (p. 4). Feld suggested that the distinction between adult and juvenile courts should be eliminated and that social welfare agencies should be used to address the needs of youth. His suggestion would make age a mitigating factor in our traditional, adjudicatory (adult) court system.

Would this policy suggestion ease the oppressive element of the juvenile court's intervention in the lives of racial and ethnic minorities? Why or why not?

American juveniles were referred to juvenile court at a rate more than double that for whites.[25]

There is also evidence of racial disparity in the treatment of juvenile offenders. Table 10.5 presents nationwide data on juvenile court outcomes in 1998 and shows that African Americans were treated more harshly than whites at several stages in the juvenile justice process. African Americans were more likely than whites to be detained prior to juvenile court disposition, to be petitioned to juvenile court for further processing, and to be waived to adult court. Among those adjudicated delinquent, African Americans were more likely than whites

Table 10.5 Juvenile Court Case Outcomes, 1998

	Whites (%)	African Americans (%)
Delinquent cases		
Detained prior to juvenile court disposition	16.8	22.8
Petitioned to juvenile court	53.8	64.9
Petitioned Cases		
Adjudicated delinquent	65.0	60.0
Waived to adult court	0.7	1.0
Adjudicated cases		
Placed out of home	24.1	29.5
Placed on probation	58.0	57.2
Dismissed	5.0	5.8

SOURCE: U.S. Department of Justice, Bureau of Justice Statistics, *Sourcebook of Criminal Justice Statistics, 2000* (Washington, DC: U.S. Government Printing Office, 2001).

to be placed in a juvenile facility but somewhat less likely than whites to be placed on probation. White youth, on the other hand, were more likely than African American youth to be adjudicated delinquent, and the dismissal rate was slightly higher for African Americans than for whites.

Much of the criticism of the treatment of racial minorities by the juvenile justice system focuses on the fact that racial minorities are more likely than whites to be detained in secure facilities prior to adjudication and sentenced to secure confinement following adjudication. Since 1988, the Juvenile Justice and Delinquency Prevention Act has required states to determine whether the proportion of minorities in confinement exceeds their proportion in the general population. If there is disproportionate minority confinement, the state must develop and implement policies to reduce it. In the United States as a whole, racial minorities made up 34 percent of the population of cases referred to juvenile court in 1997; they accounted for 62 percent of all juveniles detained pending adjudication and 67 percent of all juveniles committed to public detention facilities. In seven states and the District of Columbia, more than 80 percent of the youth placed in public detention facilities were racial minorities.[26]

Detention prior to adjudication was most likely for African American youth charged with drug offenses (40 percent) and least likely for white youth charged with property offenses (11 percent). African American juveniles made up 33 percent of all drug offenders processed in juvenile court but 59 percent of all drug offenders who were detained.[27] There was a similar pattern for residential placement following adjudication. African Americans made up 40 percent of all juveniles in residential placement; Hispanics, 18 percent; and whites, 37 percent. African American youth accounted for 64 percent of all residential

placements for drug trafficking, 54 percent of all placements for other drug offenses, and 55 percent of all placements for robbery. The comparable figures for
Hispanic youth were 21 percent (drug trafficking), 18 percent (other drug offenses), and 24 percent (robbery).[28] The custody rate for African American juveniles (1,018 per 100,000 juveniles in the population) was nearly double the
rate for Hispanic juveniles (515 per 100,000); it was nearly 5 times the rate for
white juveniles (204 per 100,000 population).[29]

The figures presented in Table 10.6 and the statistics on disproportionate
minority confinement do not take racial differences in crime seriousness, prior
juvenile record, or other legally relevant criteria into consideration. If racial
minorities are referred to juvenile court for more serious offenses or have more
serious criminal histories than whites, the observed racial disparities in case
processing might diminish or disappear once these factors are taken into consideration. Like research on sentencing in adult court, studies of juvenile court
outcomes consistently reveal that judges base their decisions primarily on the
seriousness of the offense and the offender's prior record.[30] Thus, "real differences in rates of criminal behavior by black youths account for part of the disparities in justice administration."[31]

Research conducted during the past 20 years reveals that racial differences
in past and current involvement in crime do not account for all of the differential treatment of racial minorities in juvenile court. Pope and Feyerherm, for
example, reviewed 46 studies published in the 1970s and 1980s.[32] They discovered that two-thirds of the studies they examined found evidence that racial
minorities were treated more harshly, even after offense seriousness, prior record, and other legally relevant factors were taken into account. A recent review
of 14 studies published during the 1990s found a similar pattern of results.[33]
The Panel on Juvenile Crime concluded that these more recent studies revealed
that "both behavior and biases contribute to the racial disparities." An analysis
of disproportionate minority confinement reached the same conclusion. According to Huizinga and Elliot, "Even if the slightly higher rates for more serious offenses among minorities were given more importance than is statistically indicated, the relative proportions of whites and minorities involved in
delinquent behavior could not account for the observed differences in incarceration rates."[34]

The studies conducted to date also find evidence of what is referred to as
"cumulative disadvantage"[35] or "compound risk." [36] That is, they reveal that
small racial differences in outcomes at the initial stages of the process "accumulate and become more pronounced as minority youths are processed further
into the juvenile justice system."[37] The Panel on Juvenile Crime, for example,
calculated the likelihood that a youth at one stage in the juvenile justice process
would reach the next stage (the transitional probability), as well as the proportion of the total population under age 18 that reached each stage in the juvenile justice process (the compound probability).[38] The Panel did this separately
for African American and white youth and then used these probabilities to calculate the African American-to-white relative risk and the African American-
to-white compound risk. As shown in Table 10.6, 7.2 percent of the African

Table 10.6 Juvenile Justice Outcomes for African Americans and Whites: Compound Risk

Outcome	TRANSITIONAL PROBABILITY[a]		COMPOUND PROBABILITY[b]		AFRICAN AMERICAN-TO-WHITE RISK	
	African Americans	Whites	African Americans	Whites	Relative Risk[c]	Compound Risk[d]
Arrested	.072	.036	.072	.036	2.00:1.00	2.00:1.00
Referred to juvenile court	.690	.580	.050	.021	1.19:1.00	2.38:1.00
Case handled formally	.620	.540	.031	.011	1.15:1.00	2.82:1.00
Adjudicated delinquent/ found guilty	.550	.590	.0168	.0067	0.93:1.00	2.51:1.00
Placed in residential facility	.320	.260	.0053	.0017	1.23:1.00	3.12:1.00

SOURCE: Adapted from The Panel on Juvenile Justice, *Juvenile Crime Juvenile Justice* (Washington, DC: National Academy Press, 2001), fig. 6.3 and table 6.5.

[a]The transitional probability = the proportion of youth at one stage who proceed to the next stage.

[b]The compound probability = the proportion of the population under age 18 that reaches each stage in the process.

[c]The relative risk = the ratio of the African American transitional probability to the white transitional probability.

[d]The compound risk = the ratio of the African American compound probability to the white compound probability.

American population under age 18, but only 3.6 percent of the white population under age 18, was arrested. African Americans, in other words, were twice as likely as whites to be arrested. Of those arrested, 69 percent of the African Americans and 58 percent of the whites were referred to juvenile court. Taking these differences into account resulted in a compound probability—that is, the proportion of the total youth population referred to juvenile court—of 5.0 percent for African American youth and 2.1 percent for white youth. Thus, African Americans were 2.38 times more likely than whites to be referred to juvenile court. These differences in outcomes, as Table 10.6 shows, meant that at the end of the process, African Americans were more than 3 times as likely as whites to be adjudicated delinquent and confined in a residential facility. The Panel pointed out that "at almost every stage in the juvenile justice process the racial disparity is clear, but not extreme. However, because the system operates cumulatively the risk is compounded and the end result is that black juveniles are three times as likely as white juveniles to end up in residential placement."[39]

In the sections that follow, we summarize the findings of four recent, methodologically sophisticated studies. The first is a comparison of outcomes for African Americans and whites in Florida. The second is an analysis of outcomes for African American, Hispanic, and white youth in Pennsylvania; and the third, which also examines the treatment of juveniles in Pennsylvania, is an exploration of the degree to which outcomes are affected by the urbanization of the jurisdiction and the youth's family situation. The fourth study is an examination of outcomes for white and African American youth in Georgia, which analyzes the degree to which admitting guilt affects adjudication and disposition. We also discuss evidence concerning racial disparities in waivers to adult criminal court.

Race/Ethnicity and Juvenile Court
Outcomes in Four Jurisdictions

Processing Juveniles in Florida Bishop and Frazier examined the processing of African American and white juveniles in Florida.[40] In contrast to previous researchers, most of whom focused on a single stage of the juvenile justice process, these researchers followed a cohort of 54,266 youth through the system from intake to disposition. They examined the effect of race on five stages in the process: (1) the decision to refer the case to juvenile court for formal processing (rather than close the case without further action or handle the case informally); (2) the decision to place the youth in detention prior to disposition; (3) the decision to petition the youth to juvenile court; (4) the decision to adjudicate the youth delinquent (or hold a waiver hearing in anticipation of transferring the case to criminal court); and (5) the decision to commit the youth to a residential facility (or transfer the case to criminal court).

Table 10.7 displays the outcomes for African American and white youth, as well as the proportion of African Americans in the cohort at each stage in the process. These data indicate that African Americans were substantially more likely than whites to be recommended for formal processing (59.1 percent ver-

Table 10.7 Race and Juvenile Justice Processing in Florida, 1979–1981

	Recommended for Formal Processing	Detained	Petitioned to Juvenile Court	Adjudicated Delinquent	Incarcerated/ Transferred
African Americans	59.1%	11.0%	47.3%	82.5%	29.6%
Whites	45.6	10.2	37.8	80.0	19.5
Proportion African American	34.0	30.0	32.4	33.3	43.1

SOURCE: Adapted from Donna M. Bishop and Charles E. Frazier, "The Influence of Race in Juvenile Justice Processing," *Journal of Research in Crime and Delinquency* 25 (1988): 250.

sus 45.6 percent), petitioned to juvenile court (47.3 percent versus 37.8 percent), and either incarcerated in a residential facility or transferred to criminal court (29.6 percent versus 19.5 percent). As the cohort of offenders proceeded through the juvenile justice system, the proportion that was African American increased from 34.0 percent (among those recommended for formal processing) to 43.1 percent (among those committed to a residential facility or transferred to criminal court). As Bishop and Frazier pointed out, however, these differences could reflect the fact that the African American youths in their sample were arrested for more serious crimes and had more serious prior criminal records than white youths. If this were the case, the differences would reflect racial disparity but not racial discrimination.

When the authors controlled for crime seriousness, prior record, and other predictors of juvenile justice outcomes, they found that the racial differences did not disappear. Rather, African Americans were more likely than whites to be recommended for formal processing, referred to juvenile court, and adjudicated delinquent. They also received harsher sentences than whites. These findings led Bishop and Frazier to conclude that "race is a far more pervasive influence in processing than much previous research has indicated."[41]

A follow-up study using more recent Florida data (1985–1987) produced similar results.[42] As shown in Figure 10.1, Frazier and Bishop found that outcomes for "typical" white and nonwhite youth varied significantly. They defined a typical youth as "a 15-year-old male arrested for a misdemeanor against person (e.g., simple battery), with a prior record score consistent with having one prior referral for a misdemeanor against property (e.g., criminal mischief)."[43] Compared to his white counterpart, the typical nonwhite youth was substantially more likely to be recommended for formal processing, held in secure detention prior to disposition, and committed to a residential facility or transferred to criminal court. They also found that being detained had a significant effect on subsequent outcomes; youth who were detained were significantly more likely than those who were released to be referred to juvenile court and, if adjudicated delinquent, to be committed to a residential facility or transferred to criminal court. Thus, nonwhite youth, who were more likely than

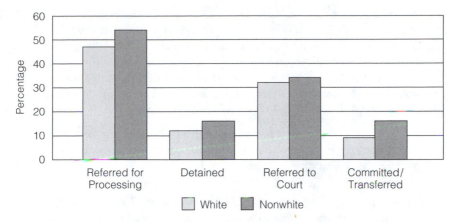

FIGURE 10.1 Juvenile Court Outcomes for "Typical" Florida Youth, 1985–1987

SOURCE: Adapted from Charles E. Frazier and Donna M. Bishop, "Reflections on Race Effects in Juvenile Justice," in *Minorities in Juvenile Justice,* ed. Kimberly Kempf Leonard, Carl E. Pope, and William H. Feyerherm (Thousand Oaks, CA: Sage, 1995).

white youth to be detained, were sentenced more harshly both because of their race (a direct effect) and because of their custody status (an indirect effect).

Frazier and Bishop also conducted interviews with criminal justice officials. During the interview, the respondent was asked whether the findings of harsher treatment of nonwhites "were consistent with their experiences in Florida's juvenile justice system between 1985 and 1987."[44] Most of the intake supervisors and public defenders stated that they believed juvenile justice dispositions were influenced by the race of the youth. In contrast, only 25 percent of the prosecutors and 33 percent of the judges believed that nonwhites were treated more harshly than similarly situated whites.

Although some of the racial differentials in treatment were attributed to racial bias—that is, to prejudiced individuals or a biased system of juvenile justice—a number of respondents suggested that the race effects actually reflected differences in economic circumstances or family situations. As one prosecutor observed, "The biggest problem is the lack of money and resources. Blacks don't have the resources. Whites are more likely to have insurance to pay for treatment. The poor I saw were always poor, but the black poor were poorer yet." Other respondents cited the fact that white parents were more likely than African American parents to be able to hire a private attorney and, as a result, got more favorable plea bargains. Some officials mentioned the role played by family considerations, noting that youth from single-parent families or families perceived to be incapable of providing adequate supervision were treated more harshly than those from intact families. Although they acknowledged that this practice had a disparate effect on minority youth, most officials defended it as "fair and appropriate." As one judge stated, "Inadequate family and bad neighborhood correlate with race and ethnicity. It makes sense to put kids from these circumstances in residential facilities."[45]

Frazier and Bishop concluded that the results of their study "leave little doubt that juvenile justice officials believe race is a factor in juvenile justice processing."[46] They noted that because some officials believed that race directly affected juvenile justice outcomes, whereas others thought that the effect of race was subtle and indirect, "policies aimed at eradicating discrimination must focus both on individual racism and on racism in its most subtle institutional forms."[47] They offered the following recommendations:[48]

- States should establish procedures for all the agencies comprising the juvenile justice system to require reporting, investigating, and responding to professionals whose decisions appear to have been influenced by racial or ethnic bias.

- State legislatures should mandate the development of a race, ethnic, and cultural diversity curriculum that personnel at every level of the juvenile justice system should be required to complete.

- Intake policies and practices should be altered so that youths referred for screening are not rendered ineligible for diversion and other front-end programs if their parents or guardians (a) cannot be contacted, (b) are contacted but are unable to be present for an intake interview, or (c) are unable to participate in family-centered programs.

- In any situation in which persons with economic resources (e.g., income or insurance benefits) are allowed to arrange for private care as a means of diversion from the juvenile justice system or less harsh formal dispositions, precisely the same treatment services should be made available at state expense to serve the poor—whether minority or majority race youths.

Frazier and Bishop acknowledged that these "fairly modest proposals" were unlikely to eliminate racial discrimination that had "survived for generations in a legal environment that expressly forbids it." Nonetheless, they were "cautiously optimistic" that their recommendations would have some effect. As they stated, "If implemented with a genuine interest in their success, such policies will both help reduce discriminatory actions and promote equal justice."[49]

Processing Juveniles in Pennsylvania Leonard and Sontheimer explored the effect of race and ethnicity on juvenile justice case outcomes in Pennsylvania.[50] Although African Americans and Hispanics accounted for only 19 percent and 4 percent, respectively, of the general youth population in the 14 counties included in the study, they constituted 46 percent (African Americans) and 7 percent (Hispanics) of all referrals to juvenile court.[51]

Like the two studies discussed earlier, this study used a multivariate model to examine the effect of race/ethnicity on a series of juvenile justice outcomes. Leonard and Sontheimer found that both African American and Hispanic youth "were more likely than whites with similar offenses, prior records, and school problems to have their cases formally processed, especially in nonrural court settings."[52] They also found that minority youth were significantly more likely than whites to be detained prior to adjudication and that detention was a strong predictor of subsequent outcomes. African American and Hispanic youth, in other words, were detained more frequently than whites and, as a result, were more likely than whites to be adjudicated delinquent and to be placed in a residential facility following adjudication.

Leonard and Sontheimer suggested that their findings have important policy implications. In particular, they recommended that

> [The] criteria used by individual intake officers should be evaluated to determine whether factors that may more often negatively affect minorities are accorded importance. Racially neutral criteria in detention decisions should be established. . . . Cultural bias, including value judgments not based on fact (such as notions that minority parents may not provide adequate supervision for their children or that certain neighborhoods are not conducive to growing up well) must not influence detention.[53]

Intake and Disposition Decisions in Pennsylvania A second study of juvenile justice decision making in Pennsylvania focused on two stages in the process: the decision to formally refer a youth to the juvenile court rather than handle the case informally and the decision to place the youth in a secure detention facility following adjudication.[54] As shown in Table 10.8, which displays the bivariate relationships between the two outcomes and the legal and extralegal variables that may affect those outcomes, DeJong and Jackson found that African American and Hispanic youth were more likely than white youth to be referred to juvenile court and more likely to be committed to a detention facility. The likelihood of a formal referral was also greater for youth with the following characteristics: male, aged 15 and older, living in a single-parent (mother only) family, not in school, charged with a drug offense, charged with a felony, and with two or more prior arrests. A similar pattern of results was found for the decision to place the youth in a secure facility.

Further analysis of the data using multivariate techniques led DeJong and Jackson to conclude that race/ethnicity did not have a significant effect on either outcome once the other variables were taken into consideration. Although Hispanics were significantly more likely than whites and African Americans to be formally referred to juvenile court, the referral rates for African American and white youth did not differ. Neither Hispanics nor African Americans faced greater odds than whites of commitment to a secure facility. The race of the youth, however, did affect these outcomes indirectly. In particular, white youth who lived with both parents were less likely than those who lived in single-parent families to be formally referred to juvenile court or placed in secure confinement following disposition. Among African American youth, on the other hand, living with both parents rather than in a single-parent household did not have these positive effects. As DeJong and Jackson pointed out, "Black youths are treated the same whether they are living with parents or with their mothers only; for these youths, family status does not protect against [formal referral or] incarceration."[55] In addition, African American youth, but not white youth, were treated more harshly in rural counties than in urban or suburban counties.

Table 10.8 The Characteristics of Youth Formally Referred to Juvenile Court and Placed in Secure Confinement following Disposition

	Formally Referred (%)	Placed in Secure Facility (%)
Race/ethnicity		
White	49.5	14.9
African American	61.4	17.8
Hispanic	59.4	22.9
Gender		
Male	57.5	17.1
Female	38.4	12.9
Age		
12 and below	43.7	11.8
13	50.0	14.3
14	51.9	17.5
15	56.9	12.7
16	58.6	21.0
17 and above	54.7	17.1
Living with mother only	65.9	17.8
Living with both parents	55.1	10.7
In school	61.0	15.8
Not in school	68.2	22.6
Charge type		
Property	66.2	16.1
Violent	61.2	15.9
Drug	71.6	23.7
Other	29.6	15.6
Charge seriousness		
Felony	78.5	19.5
Misdemeanor	35.8	12.5
Number of prior arrests		
None	48.7	10.5
One	64.7	22.9
Two	70.1	32.2
Three or more	76.4	35.8

SOURCE: Adapted from Christina DeJong and Kenneth C. Jackson, "Putting Race into Context: Race, Juvenile Justice Processing, and Urbanization," *Justice Quarterly* 15 (1998): 487–504, table 2.

DeJong and Jackson speculated that the fact that family status did not affect outcomes for African American youth might be due to juvenile justice officials' stereotyped beliefs about African American families. That is, officials "may view all black fathers as absentee" or "may view the black family structure as weak."[56] If this is the case, African American youth who live in two-parent families would not be regarded as better candidates for diversion or for treatment within the community than those who live in single-parent families. This type of subtle discrimination may be more common than the overt discrimination that characterized the system previously.[57]

Adjudication and Disposition Decisions in Georgia A study of juvenile court outcomes in Georgia focused on the interaction between the race of the juvenile and admitting or denying the crime.[58] Ruback and Vardaman posited two opposing effects for admitting/denying guilt, one based on the youth's potential for rehabilitation and the other based on due process considerations. They asserted that if the primary goal of the juvenile justice system was rehabilitation, then indicators of amenability to rehabilitation should be important predictors of case disposition. Because admitting guilt signals that the youth accepts responsibility for his or her actions and feels remorse and also indicates that the youth may be a good candidate for treatment rather than punishment, an admission of guilt should—again, if rehabilitation is the goal—lead to more lenient treatment. On the other hand, if the goal of the court is to punish the guilty, *denial* of guilt might lead to more lenient treatment. This might be particularly true, according to Ruback and Vardaman, in large urban jurisdictions with heavy caseloads. If the youth denies guilt, the court must hold an evidentiary hearing and prove the charges. Prosecutors might prefer to dismiss the case rather than use their limited resources to secure a conviction.

Ruback and Vardaman found that whereas African Americans were overrepresented in juvenile court populations in the 16 Georgia counties they examined, white youth were treated more harshly than African American youth.[59] White juveniles (43 percent) were more likely than African American juveniles (39 percent) to be adjudicated delinquent, and African American juveniles (29 percent) were more likely than white juveniles (23 percent) to have their cases dismissed. The authors also found that white youth were substantially more likely to admit the crimes they were accused of committing: 66 percent of the whites, compared to only 51 percent of the African Americans, admitted their guilt.

When Ruback and Vardaman compared adjudication outcomes for African American and white youth, controlling for crime seriousness, prior record, whether the case was heard in an urban or rural county, whether the youth admitted guilt, and the youth's age and gender, they found that race had no effect. Admitting guilt, on the other hand, had a strong effect on the likelihood of being adjudicated delinquent. The odds of being adjudicated delinquent were also higher in rural than in urban counties.

The authors of the study concluded that the harsher treatment of white youth could be attributed to two factors. First, whites were more likely than African Americans to admit guilt, and admitting guilt led to a higher likelihood of being adjudicated delinquent. Second, cases involving whites were more likely than those involving African Americans to be processed in rural courts, where the odds of being adjudicated delinquent were higher.[60] They also suggested that their results might reflect judges' beliefs that white youths would be more likely to benefit from the interventions and services available to the court:

> An intervention by the court may be deemed more likely to affect the future behavior of white juveniles (who generally have shorter legal histories), while the same intervention with Black juveniles (who generally

have longer legal histories) may be perceived as wasted effort. It may be . . . that only white juveniles are believed to be worth investing resources in so as to reduce the chances of their committing future crimes.[61]

Ruback and Vardaman maintained that this might also explain why white youth admitted their guilt at a higher rate than African American youth did. That is, juvenile justice officials might have urged whites to admit the crime so that they could receive an informal adjustment and court intervention.

In summary, the results of the studies reviewed here suggest that the effect of race/ethnicity on juvenile court outcomes is complex. Some researchers concluded that race and ethnicity have direct or overt effects on case outcomes. Research conducted in Florida and Pennsylvania, for example, found that racial minorities were treated more harshly than whites at several stages in the juvenile justice process, including detention, and that detention had significant spillover effects on subsequent adjudication and disposition decisions. Other researchers concluded that the effect of race/ethnicity is indirect rather than direct. Research conducted in Pennsylvania, for instance, found that living in a two-parent family benefited whites but not African Americans, whereas research in Georgia found that the *harsher* treatment of white youth reflected their higher rates of admitting guilt and a greater likelihood of being prosecuted in rural rather than urban jurisdictions.

These studies also suggest that the effect of race on juvenile justice outcomes may vary from one jurisdiction to another and highlight the importance of conceptualizing decision making in the juvenile justice system as a process. According to Secret and Johnson, "In examining for racial bias in juvenile justice system decisions, we must scrutinize each step of the process to see whether previous decisions create a racial effect by changing the pool of offenders at subsequent steps."[62] The importance of differentiating among racial and ethnic groups is also clear. As one author noted, "Circumstances surrounding the case processing of minority youths not only may be different from those for whites, but also may vary among minority groups."[63]

Transfer of Juveniles to Criminal Court

In 1998, youth under age 15 accounted for 2 percent of all arrests for murder/manslaughter, 6 percent of all arrests for forcible rape, and 9 percent of all arrests for robbery; youth between the ages of 15 and 17 made up 17 percent of all murder/manslaughter arrests, 16 percent of all forcible rape arrests, and 32 percent of all robbery arrests.[64] More striking, juvenile arrest rates increased 100 percent between 1985 and 1994. Juvenile arrests for *violent* crimes increased from 66,976 in 1985 to 117,200 in 1994 (an increase of 75 percent), and arrests for *murder* increased from 1,193 to 2,982 (an increase of 150 percent).

Statistics such as these, coupled with highly publicized cases of very young children accused of murder and other violent crimes, prompted a number of states to alter procedures for handling certain types of juvenile offenders. In 1995, for example, Illinois lowered the age of admission to prison from 13 to

10. This change was enacted after two boys, ages 10 and 11, dropped a 5–year–old boy out of a 14th–floor window of a Chicago public housing development. In 1996, a juvenile court judge ordered that both boys, who were then 12 and 13, be sent to a high–security juvenile penitentiary; her decision made the 12–year–old the nation's youngest inmate at a high–security prison.[65]

Other states responded to the increase in serious juvenile crime by either lowering the age when children can be transferred from juvenile court to criminal court and/or expanding the list of offenses for which juveniles can be waived to criminal court. A report by the GAO indicated that 44 states passed new laws between 1978 and 1995 regarding the waiver of juveniles to criminal court; in 24 of these states, the new laws increased the population of juveniles that potentially could be sent to criminal court.[66] California, for example, changed the age at which juveniles could be waived to criminal court from 16 to 14 (for specified offenses); Missouri reduced the age at which children could be certified to stand trial as adults from 14 to 12.

The GAO report also noted that the percentage of delinquency cases waived to criminal court (the judicial waiver rate) increased from 1.2 percent in 1988 to 1.6 percent in 1992; the number of cases waived increased from 7,000 to just under 12,000.[67] The 1992 judicial waiver rate was highest for drug offenses (3.1 percent), followed by person offenses (2.4 percent), and property offenses (1.3 percent). The number of delinquency cases transferred to criminal court peaked in 1994 (at 12,100 cases waived). Between 1994 and 1998, the number waived declined by one–third, to about 8,000 cases. In 1998, waived cases involving property offenses (3,200) outnumbered those involving person offenses (2,800) or drug offenses (1,300).[68]

The GAO report provided some data on the race of juveniles waived to criminal court. Nationally, 50 percent of juveniles whose cases were waived were African American, 47 percent were white, and 3 percent were of other races.[69] These figures mirror almost exactly the racial makeup of arrests of persons under age 18 for violent crime: 50 percent were African American, 48 percent were white, and 2 percent were of other races. These similarities suggest that racial disparities in the judicial waiver rate do not reflect racial discrimination on the part of juvenile court judges. They suggest, in other words, that African American youth are overrepresented among those waived to criminal court because they are overrepresented among those arrested for violent crimes.

The validity of this explanation is called into question by Table 10.9, which presents judicial waiver rates by race and type of offense for six states. (Because of the small number of cases for each offense, the GAO was unable to simultaneously control for legally relevant criteria such as the type of offense, prior referrals, and age at referral.) Among offenders arrested for violent crimes, the waiver rate for African Americans was higher than the rate for whites in all six states. Among offenders arrested for drug offenses, the African American waiver rate was higher than the white rate in all but one of the six states. In four states (Arizona, Florida, Missouri, and South Carolina), African Americans were more likely to have their cases waived for each of the three types of offenses. The dif-

Table 10.9 Waiver Rates by Race and Type of Offense, 1990–1991

	WAIVER RATE (%)		
	Violent Crimes	Property Crimes	Drug Offenses
Arizona			
African Americans	9.1	2.6	10.9
Whites	5.1	1.3	0.8
California			
African Americans	1.3	0.1	0.2
Whites	0.5	0.1	0.4
Florida			
African Americans	2.3	0.8	3.0
Whites	1.0	0.7	1.2
Missouri			
African Americans	7.4	1.8	7.5
Whites	2.4	1.6	3.3
Pennsylvania			
African Americans	3.0	1.6	3.9
Whites	1.4	1.6	1.6
South Carolina			
African Americans	4.4	0.4	3.8
Whites	1.6	0.2	0.0

SOURCE: U.S. General Accounting Office, *Juvenile Justice: Juveniles Processed in Criminal Court and Case Dispositions* (Washington, DC: Author, 1995), tables 11.3, 11.6, 11.9, 11.12, 11.15, and 11.18.

ferences were particularly pronounced in Arizona, where African American juveniles had waiver rates that were twice as high as white rates for violent offenses and property crimes and 13.6 times higher than white rates for drug offenses.

Although additional research incorporating other legally relevant criteria obviously is needed before definitive conclusions can be drawn, the data displayed in Table 10.9 suggest that the decision to transfer a juvenile offender to adult court is not racially neutral. At least in the six states included in the GAO's analysis, African Americans faced substantially higher odds than whites of being transferred into the more punitive adult court system.

Explaining Disparate Treatment of Juvenile Offenders

The studies discussed here provide compelling evidence that African American and Hispanic juveniles are treated more harshly than similarly situated white juveniles. The question, of course, is why this occurs. Secret and Johnson suggested that juvenile court judges may attribute positive or negative characteristics to offenders based on their race/ethnicity.[70] Judges, in other words, may use extralegal characteristics such as race to create "a mental map of the accused person's underlying character" and to predict his or her future behavior.[71] As Mann noted, officials' attitudes "mirror the stereotype of minorities as typically violent, dangerous, or threatening."[72] Alternatively, according to Secret and Johnson, the harsher treatment of African American and Hispanic juveniles might reflect both class and race biases on the part of juvenile court judges. As conflict theory posits, "the individual's economic and social class and the color of his skin . . . determine his relationship to the legal system."[73]

These speculations regarding court officials' perceptions of minority and white youth have not been systematically tested. Researchers assume that findings of differential treatment of racial minorities signal the presence of race-linked stereotypes or racially prejudiced attitudes, but there have been few attempts to empirically verify either the existence of differing perceptions of white and minority youth or the degree to which these perceptions can account for racial disparities in the juvenile justice system.

A recent study by Bridges and Steen addressed this issue by examining 233 narrative reports written by juvenile probation officers in three counties in the state of Washington during 1990 and 1991.[74] The narratives, which were used by the court in determining the appropriate disposition of the case, were based on interviews with the youth and the youth's family and on written documents such as school records and juvenile court files. Each narrative included the probation officer's description of the youth's crime and assessment of the factors that motivated the crime, as well as an evaluation of the youth's background and assessment of his or her likelihood of recidivism. The information gleaned from these narratives was used "to explore the relationship between race; officials' characterizations of youths, their crimes, and the causes of their crimes; officials' assessments of the threat of future crime by youths; and officials' sentence recommendations."[75]

Bridges and Steen's review of the narratives revealed that probation officers described African American and white youth and their crimes differently. They tended to attribute crimes committed by whites to negative environmental factors (poor school performance, delinquent peers, dysfunctional family, use of drugs or alcohol), but to attribute crimes committed by African Americans to negative personality traits and "bad attitudes" (refusal to admit guilt, lack of remorse, failure to take offense seriously, lack of cooperation with court officials). They also found that probation officers judged African American youth to have a significantly higher risk of reoffending than white youth.

Further analysis, which controlled for the juvenile's age, gender, prior criminal history, and seriousness of the current offense, confirmed these findings. As the authors noted, "Being black significantly reduces the likelihood of negative *external* attributions by probation officers and significantly increases the likelihood of negative *internal* attributions, even after adjusting for severity of the presenting offense and the youth's prior involvement in criminal behavior."[76] To illustrate these differences, the authors discussed the narratives written for two very similar cases of armed robbery, one involving an African American youth and one involving a white youth. The African American youth's crime was described as "very dangerous" and as "premeditated and willful," and his criminal behavior was attributed to an amoral character, lack of remorse, and no desire to change. In contrast, the white youth was portrayed as an "emaciated little boy" whose crime was attributed to a broken home, association with delinquent peers, and substance abuse.

Bridges and Steen's examination of the factors related to probation officers' assessments of the risk of reoffending revealed that youth who committed more serious crimes or had more serious criminal histories were judged to be at higher risk of future offending. Although none of the offender's demographic characteristics, including race, were significantly related to assessments of risk, probation officers' attributions of delinquency did affect these predictions. Youth whose delinquency was attributed to negative internal causes were judged to be at higher risk of future delinquency than youth whose crimes were attributed to negative external factors. According to Bridges and Steen, "This suggests that youths whose crimes are attributed to internal causes are more likely to be viewed as 'responsible' for their crimes, engulfed in a delinquent personality and lifestyle, and prone to committing crimes in the future."[77]

The authors of this study concluded that race influenced juvenile court outcomes indirectly. Probation officers were substantially more likely to attribute negative internal characteristics and attitudes to African American youth than to white youth; these attributions, in turn, shaped their assessments of dangerousness and their predictions of future offending. As Bridges and Steen stated, "Insofar as officials judge black youths to be more dangerous than white youths, they do so because they attribute crime by blacks to negative personalities or their attitudinal traits and because black offenders are more likely than white offenders to have committed serious offenses and have histories of prior involvement in crime."[78]

The results of this study illustrate the "mechanisms by which officials' perceptions of the offender as threatening develop or influence the process of legal decision-making."[79] They suggest that perceptions of threat and, consequently, predictions about future delinquency are influenced by criminal justice officials' assessments of the causes of criminal behavior. Thus, "officials may perceive blacks as more culpable and dangerous than whites in part because they believe the etiology of their crimes is linked to personal traits" that are "not as amenable to the correctional treatments the courts typically administer."[80]

JUVENILES UNDER CORRECTIONAL SUPERVISION

As the previous section illustrates, the racial makeup of juveniles at key stages of the juvenile justice system varies by decision type. Generally, nonwhite youth (the majority of whom are African American) are overrepresented at every stage of decision making. Nonwhite youth are also at greater risk of receiving harsher sanctions than white youth. For example, nonwhite youth are detained in secure custody prior to their juvenile court hearing at rates that exceed those for white youth, regardless of the seriousness of the delinquency offense. In 1997, 27 percent of African American youth and 19 percent of other minori-

Table 10.10 Racial and Ethnic Profile of Juvenile Offenders in Residential Placement, 1997

	ALL OFFENSES		STATUS OFFENSES	
	Male (%)	Female (%)	Male (%)	Female (%)
White (non-Hispanic)	36	49	57	61
African American (non-Hispanic)	41	33	31	28
Hispanic	19	13	7	8
Native American/Alaska Native	1	2	2	2
Asian/Pacific Islander	2	1	1	1

SOURCE: Office of Juvenile Justice and Delinquency Prevention, *OJJDP Statistical Briefing Book*. Available at http://www.ojjdp.ncjrs.org/ojstatbb/html/qa331.html.

ties were detained, compared with 15 percent of white youth.[81] Recently, there has been a decline in the proportion of white youth detained but an increase in the proportion of African American youth in custody.[82]

Table 10.10 presents data on the racial and ethnic makeup of juvenile offenders who are placed in a secure residential facility after being adjudicated delinquent. The percentages vary by race and ethnicity, as well as by gender and offense type.[83] White and Asian youth are underrepresented among youth in residential placement, whereas African American, Hispanic, and Native American/Alaska Native youth generally are overrepresented. Among male offenders, African American youth accounted for the largest proportion (41 percent) of offenders in residential placement. In contrast, among females, white youth made up the largest proportion (nearly half) of offenders who were placed in a residential facility. Whereas the overrepresentation of Hispanic youth is more pronounced for male than for female offenders, the overrepresentation of Native American/Alaska Native youth is higher for females than for males. For status offenses (that is, running away from home and truancy), whites make up the largest proportion of offenders placed in secure confinement; this pattern is found for both male and female offenders.

Another way to gauge the extent of overrepresentation of racial and ethnic groups placed in residential facilities by the juvenile court is to examine custody rates calculated for each racial and ethnic group (see Table 10.11).[84] Consistent with the results discussed earlier, important differences exist across race, ethnicity, and gender. African American male juveniles have the highest custody rate of any group examined; in fact, their rate is more than five times higher than the rate for white males. Hispanic, Native American/Alaska Native, and Asian/Pacific Islander males all have higher custody rates than the rate for white males but lower rates than the rate for African American males. The custody rate of African American females is nearly four times the rate for white females and is similar to the rate for white males. Interestingly, Native American/Alaska Native youth have the highest custody rate among females. Hispanic females have a custody rate only slightly higher than that of their white

Table 10.11 Juvenile Male and Female Custody Rates by Racial and Ethnic Categories (per 100,000 Population), 1997

	Male	Female
Overall	620	102
White (non-Hispanic)	327	75
African American (non-Hispanic)	1,776	234
Hispanic	902	100
Native American/Alaska Native	817	424
Asian/Pacific Islander	361	39

SOURCE: Office of Juvenile Justice and Delinquency Prevention, *OJJDP Statistical Briefing Book*. Available at http://ojjdp.ncjrs.org/ojstatbb/html/qa335(&6).html.

counterparts, and the rate for Asian/Pacific Islander females is only about half that of white females.

CONCLUSION

The victimization and offending patterns for juveniles mirror those for adults. Juveniles of color, and particularly African American males, face a higher risk of victimization than white juveniles. This pattern is found for property crime, violent crime, and homicide. In fact, the homicide victimization rate for young African American females is higher than the rate for young white males.

Although the common perception of the juvenile offender is that he or she is a person of color,[85] the data discussed in this chapter indicate that whites constitute the majority of juvenile offenders for most crimes. The notable exceptions (among the more serious Index offenses) are robbery, where over half of those arrested are African American, and murder and nonnegligent manslaughter, where African American youth make up nearly half of all arrestees. The overrepresentation of African American juveniles in arrest statistics is not a constant, however. The most pronounced disparities are found for violent crimes, where from one-third to one-half of all arrestees are African American. There is less racial disparity for property offenses; for these crimes, between one-fourth and one-third of those arrested are African American. Further, whites are overrepresented among arrestees for many of the drug and alcohol offenses.

The results of studies examining the effect of race/ethnicity on juvenile justice processing decisions suggest that the juvenile justice system, like the criminal justice system for adults, is not free of racial bias. There is compelling evidence that racial minorities are treated more harshly than whites at various points in the juvenile justice process. Most important, minority youth are substantially more likely than white youth to be detained pending disposition, adjudicated delinquent, and waived to adult court. They are also sentenced more harshly than their white counterparts, at least in part because of the tendency of criminal justice officials to attribute their crimes to internal (personality) rather than external (environmental) causes.

DISCUSSION QUESTIONS

1. Describe the characteristics of juvenile victims of crime. Are they similar to or different from the characteristics of adult victims of crime?

2. There is a common perception that the typical juvenile offender is a person of color. Is this an accurate perception?

3. What explains the fact that juveniles of color have higher rates of contact with the police than white youth do?

4. Why is there greater potential for racial discrimination in the juvenile justice system than in the adult justice system?

5. Studies of the juvenile justice system reveal that racial minorities are subject to "cumulative disadvantage" or "compound risk." Explain what this means and why it is a cause for concern.

6. We suggest that preliminary evidence indicating that African American juveniles are more likely than white juveniles to be waived to adult court should be confirmed by additional research that incorporates legally relevant criteria other than the seriousness of the offense. What other variables should be taken into consideration?

7. Although studies reveal that African American, Hispanic, and Native American youth are treated more harshly than white youth at several stages of the juvenile justice process (even after the seriousness of the offense and the offender's prior juvenile record are taken into consideration), they do not tell us why these disparities occur. How would you explain these differences? How do Bridges and Steen account for them?

NOTES

1. Kate Randall, "Another Florida Teenager Receives Harsh Adult Prison Sentence." Available at http://www.wsws.org/articles/2001/aug2001.

2. "Juvenile Justice Experts Decry Severity of Life in Adult Prison for Nathaniel Brazill" (May 15, 2001). Available at http://www.cjcj.org.

3. Ibid.

4. Office of Juvenile Justice and Delinquency Prevention, "Juvenile Victims of Property Crimes" (Washington, DC: U.S. Department of Justice, 2000). Available at http://www.unh.edu/ccrc/propertycrime.pdf

5. Ibid.

6. Office of Juvenile Justice and Delinquency Prevention, "Juvenile Victims of Property Crimes."

7. Ibid., p. 5.

8. Ibid.

9. Ibid.

10. Callie Marie Rennison, *Criminal Victimization 2000: Changes 1999–2000 with Trends 1993–2000* (Washington, DC: U.S. Department of Justice, 2001). Available at www.ojp.usdoj.gov/bjs/.

11. Bureau of Justice Statistics, *Young Black Male Victims* (Washington, DC: U.S. Department of Justice, 1994).

12. Ibid.

13. Ibid.

14. James Allen Fox and Marianne W. Zawitz, *Homicide Trends in the United States* (Washington, DC: U.S. Department of Justice, 2001). Available at www.ojp.usdoj .gov/bjs.

15. Ibid.

16. Ibid.

17. Ibid.

18. Ibid.

19. Carl Werthman and Irving Piliavin, "Gang Members and the Police," in *The Police: Six Sociological Essays,* ed. David J. Bordua (New York: Wiley, 1967), p. 58.

20. Gallup Poll data, reported in Bureau of Justice Statistics, *Sourcebook of Criminal Justice Statistics, 2000,* table 2.16. Available at www.albany.edu/sourcebook.

21. Donald Black, "The Social Organization of Arrest," in *The Manners and Customs of the Police,* ed. Donald Black (New York: Academic Press, 1980).

22. Philip W. Harris, Wayne N. Welsh, and Frank Butler, "A Century of Juvenile Justice," in *Criminal Justice 2000. The Nature of Crime: Continuity and Change,* Vol. 1 (Washington, DC: National Institute of Justice, 2000), p. 360.

23. Literally translated as "father of the country," this phrase refers to the government's right and obligation to act on behalf of a child (or a person who is mentally ill).

24. Office of Juvenile Justice and Delinquency Prevention, *Offenders in Juvenile Court, 1997* (Washington, DC: U.S. Department of Justice, 2000).

25. Office of Juvenile Justice and Delinquency Prevention, *Delinquency Cases in Juvenile Courts, 1997* (Washington, DC: U.S. Department of Justice, 2000).

26. Office of Juvenile Justice and Delinquency Prevention, *Minorities in the Juvenile Justice System* (Washington, DC: U.S. Department of Justice, 1999). The states were California (81%), Connecticut (83%), Hawaii (89%), Louisiana (81%), New Jersey (88%), New Mexico (81%), and New York (87%), and the District of Columbia (100%).

27. Ibid., pp. 9–10.

28. Ibid., p. 11.

29. Ibid., p. 14.

30. See, for example, Donna M. Bishop and Charles S. Frazier, "Race Effects in Juvenile Justice Decision-Making: Findings of a Statewide Analysis," *Journal of Criminal Law and Criminology* 86 (1996): 392–413.

31. Barry C. Feld, *Bad Kids: Race and the Transformation of the Juvenile Court* (London and New York: Oxford University Press, 1999), p. 266.

32. Carl E. Pope and William H. Feyerherm, "Minority Status and Juvenile Justice Processing: An Assessment of the Research Literature (Part I)," *Criminal Justice Abstracts* 22 (1990): 327–335.

33. Panel on Juvenile Crime, *Juvenile Crime Juvenile Justice* (Washington, DC: National Academy Press, 2001), p. 254.

34. David Huizinga and Delbert S. Elliot, "Juvenile Offenders: Prevalence, Offender Incidence, and Arrest Rates by Race," *Crime and Delinquency* 33 (1987): 212.

35. Donna M. Bishop and Charles E. Frazier, "The Influence of Race in Juvenile Justice Processing," *Journal of Research in Crime and Delinquency* 25 (1988): 242–263.

36. Panel on Juvenile Crime, *Juvenile Crime Juvenile Justice,* p. 254.

37. Pope and Feyerherm, "Minority Status and Juvenile Justice Processing," p. 334.

38. Panel on Juvenile Crime, *Juvenile Crime Juvenile Justice,* pp. 254–258.

39. Ibid., p. 257.

40. Bishop and Frazier, "The Influence of Race in Juvenile Justice Processing."

41. Ibid., p. 258.

42. Charles E. Frazier and Donna M. Bishop, "Reflections on Race Effects in Juvenile Justice," in *Minorities in Juvenile Justice,* ed. Kimberly Kempf Leonard, Carl E. Pope, and William H. Feyerherm (Thousand Oaks, CA: Sage, 1995).

43. Ibid., p. 25.

44. Ibid., p. 28.

45. Ibid., p. 35.

46. Ibid., p. 40.

47. Ibid., p. 41.

48. Ibid., pp. 41–45.

49. Ibid., p. 45.

50. Kimberly Kempf Leonard and Henry Sontheimer, "The Role of Race in Juvenile Justice in Pennsylvania," in *Minorities in Juvenile Justice,* ed. Kimberly Kempf Leonard, Carl E. Pope, and William H. Feyerherm (Thousand Oaks, CA: Sage, 1995).

51. Ibid., p. 108.

52. Ibid., p. 119.

53. Ibid., pp. 122–123.

54. Christina DeJong and Kenneth C. Jackson, "Putting Race into Context: Race, Juvenile Justice Processing, and Urbanization," *Justice Quarterly* 15 (1998): 487–504.

55. Ibid., p. 501.

56. Ibid., p. 502.

57. A study of juvenile justice outcomes in Ohio also found evidence of indirect discrimination. This study revealed that African American youth whose families were receiving welfare benefits were more likely than African American youth whose families were not on welfare to be placed in secure confinement following adjudication. The same pattern was not observed for whites. According to the authors, this suggests that "only minority families on welfare are regarded as unsuitable for supervising their delinquent children." Bohsiu Wu and Angel Ilarraza Fuentes, "The Entangled Effects of Race and Urban Poverty," *Juvenile and Family Court Journal* 49 (1998): 49.

58. R. Barry Ruback and Paula J. Vardaman, "Decision Making in Delinquency Cases: The Role of Race and Juveniles'

Admission/Denial of the Crime," *Law and Human Behavior* 21 (1997): 47–69.

59. Ibid., p. 52.

60. Ibid., p. 59.

61. Ibid., p. 67.

62. Philip E. Secret and James B. Johnson, "The Effect of Race on Juvenile Justice Decision Making in Nebraska: Detention, Adjudication, and Disposition, 1988–1993," *Justice Quarterly* 14 (1997): 445–478.

63. Ibid., p. 274.

64. U.S. Department of Justice, Federal Bureau of Investigation, *Crime in the United States, 1994* (Washington, DC: U.S. Government Printing Office, 1995), pp. 227–228.

65. "Chicago Boy, 12, Will Be Youngest in U.S. Prison," *Omaha World Herald* (January 31, 1996).

66. U.S. General Accounting Office, *Juvenile Justice: Juveniles Processed in Criminal Court and Case Dispositions* (Washington, DC: Author, 1995), p. 2.

67. Ibid., p. 10.

68. Office of Juvenile Justice and Delinquency Prevention, *Delinquency Cases Waived to Criminal Court, 1989–1998* (Washington, DC: U.S. Department of Justice, 2001).

69. U.S. General Accounting Office, *Juvenile Justice,* p. 12.

70. Secret and Johnson, "The Effect of Race on Juvenile Justice Decision Making in Nebraska."

71. Ibid., p. 450.

72. Coramae Richey Mann, *Unequal Justice: A Question of Color* (Bloomington: Indiana University Press, 1993), p. 255.

73. R. Lefcourt, "The Administration of Criminal Law," in *Criminal Justice in America,* ed. Richard Quinney (Boston: Little, Brown, 1974).

74. George S. Bridges and Sara Steen, "Racial Disparities in Official Assessments of Juvenile Offenders: Attributional Stereotypes as Mediating Mechanisms," *American Sociological Review* 63 (1998): 554–570.

75. Ibid., p. 558.

76. Ibid., pp. 563–564.

77. Ibid., p. 564.

78. Ibid., p. 567.

79. Ibid.

80. Ibid.

81. Office of Juvenile Justice and Delinquency Prevention, *Offenders in Juvenile Court, 1997.*

82. Ibid.

83. Office of Juvenile Justice and Delinquency Prevention, *OJJDP Statistical Briefing Book.*

84. Ibid.

85. Jeffrey Reiman, *The Rich Get Richer and the Poor Get Prison* (Boston: Allyn & Bacon, 1995).

11

·人·

The Color of Justice

There is no escaping the fact that race, crime, and justice are inextricably linked in the minds of most Americans. Perceptions of the nature of this linkage vary, however. Many Americans view crime and the criminal justice system through a lens distorted by racial stereotypes and prejudice. They equate crime with African American crime but refuse to acknowledge that this perception might produce racially discriminatory criminal justice practices and policies. Although admitting that some individuals within the criminal justice system make racially biased decisions, they insist that there is no evidence of widespread or systematic racial discrimination.

Other Americans take a different but equally extreme position. They believe that it is inaccurate and misleading to suggest that crime is synonymous with African American crime and argue that our current crime control policies—which emphasize more police, higher bail, and harsher sentences—have a disparate effect on African Americans and Hispanics. These critics also believe that those who argue that the solution to the crime problem is to "lock 'em up and throw away the key" typically visualize the faces behind the bars as black, brown, and red. They suggest that racism permeates the criminal justice system and insist that racially biased decisions are the norm, not the exception to the general rule of impartiality.

The current controversy over racial profiling illustrates these different perspectives on crime and criminal justice. Advocates of "tough" law enforcement, particularly with respect to drugs, believe that a high rate of traffic stops of people of color is justified because they are more likely to be involved in criminal activity, particularly drug trafficking. To support this view, these advocates often cite the high arrest rates of African Americans and Hispanics. Critics, however, point out that this is circular reasoning: racial and ethnic stereotypes are used to justify higher arrest rates, which, in turn, are used to justify higher rates of traffic stops.

It is our position that the truth lies somewhere between these two extremes. The first position ignores many of the complexities of crime in the United States and presents an overly optimistic view of the treatment of racial minorities who find themselves in the arms of the law. The second position glosses over some of the realities of crime in the United States and paints an unrealistically pessimistic picture of the treatment of racial minorities.

We believe that the criminal justice system is characterized by obvious disparities based on race and ethnicity. It is impossible to ignore the disproportionate number of minorities arrested, imprisoned, and placed on death row. Some of the decisions that produce these results involve discrimination. The question with which we have wrestled in this book, however, is whether there is *systematic* racial and ethnic discrimination. After considering all of the evidence, we conclude that the U.S. criminal justice system is characterized by *contextual* discrimination.

RACE, CRIME, AND JUSTICE

The overriding goal of this book is to separate fact from fiction and myth from reality. We have shown that it is inaccurate and misleading to equate crime with African American crime and to characterize the typical victim as white, the typical offender as African American, and the typical crime as an interracial act of violence. Victimization data consistently reveal that African Americans and Hispanics are more likely than whites to fall victim to household and personal crime. The racial differences are particularly pronounced for crimes of violence, especially murder and robbery. Crime statistics also reveal that intraracial crimes occur more often than interracial crimes.

It is less clear that the picture of the typical offender as African American is inaccurate. Certainly more whites than racial minorities are arrested each year, but this is a consequence of the fact that whites make up 75 percent of the U.S. population and people of color, only 25 percent, rather than a reflection of a more pronounced propensity toward crime among whites. If we examine arrest rates, the picture changes: African Americans are arrested at a disproportionately high rate.

Although criminal justice scholars and policymakers continue to debate the meaning of the disproportionately high African American arrest rate—with some arguing that it reflects a higher offending rate and others that it signals selective enforcement of the law—there is no denying the fact that African Americans are arrested more often than one would expect, particularly for crimes of violence, such as murder, rape, and robbery. The explanation for this overrepresentation is complex, incorporating social, economic, and political factors.

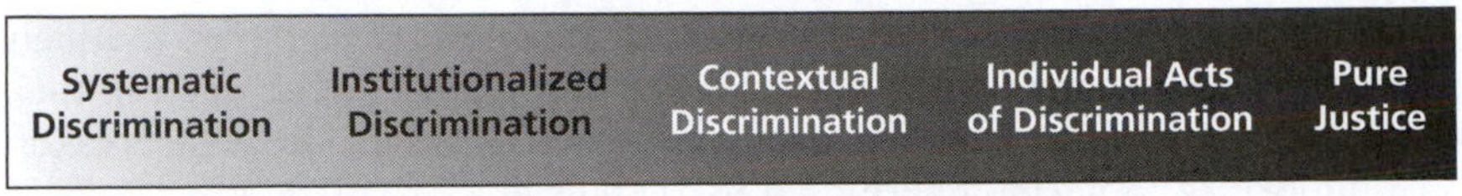

Systematic Discrimination	Institutionalized Discrimination	Contextual Discrimination	Individual Acts of Discrimination	Pure Justice

FIGURE 11.1 Discrimination Continuum

It thus seems clear that one cannot paint an accurate picture of crime in the United States without relying to some extent on race and ethnicity. Race and crime *are* linked, although not necessarily in the ways that most Americans assume.

We have also shown that the criminal justice system is neither completely free of racial bias nor systematically racially biased. In Chapter 1, we suggested that there are different types and degrees of racial discrimination (see Figure 11.1). At one end of the discrimination continuum is pure justice, which means that there is no discrimination at any time, place, or point in the criminal justice system. At the other end is systematic discrimination, which means that discrimination prevails at all stages of the criminal justice system, in all places, and at all times.

We suggest that the U.S. criminal justice system falls between the two ends of the continuum. More specifically, we suggest that the system is characterized by contextual discrimination. Racial minorities are treated more harshly than whites at some stages of the criminal justice process (for example the decision to seek or impose the death penalty) but no differently than whites at other stages of the process (for example, the selection of the jury pool). The treatment accorded racial minorities is more punitive than that accorded whites in some regions or jurisdictions but is no different than that accorded whites in other regions or jurisdictions. For example, some police departments tolerate excessive force directed at racial minorities or the use of racial profiling, and others do not. Racial minorities who commit certain types of crimes (such as drug offenses or violent crimes against whites) or who have certain types of characteristics (for example they are young, male, and unemployed) are treated more harshly than whites who commit these crimes or have these characteristics.

We are not arguing that the U.S. criminal justice system *never* has been characterized by systematic racial discrimination. In fact, the evidence discussed in earlier chapters suggests just the opposite. The years preceding the civil rights movement (pre-1960s) were characterized by blatant discrimination directed against African Americans and other racial minorities at all stages of the criminal justice process. This pattern of widespread discrimination was not limited to the South but was found throughout the United States.

Until fairly recently, crimes against African Americans and calls for help from minority communities were often ignored by the police. Racial minorities suspected of crimes, and particularly those suspected of crimes against whites, were more likely than whites to be harassed by the police or subject to racial profiling. They were also more likely than whites to be arrested, to be subjected to excessive force, and to become the victims of deadly force.

Also until rather recently, racial minorities who were arrested were routinely denied bail, tried by all-white juries without attorneys to assist them in their defense, and prosecuted and convicted on less-than-convincing evidence. Racial minorities convicted of crimes were sentenced more harshly than whites. They were more likely than whites to be incarcerated and sentenced to death and executed.

Our analysis of current research on race and the criminal justice system leads us to conclude that the situation today is somewhat different. Although the contemporary criminal justice system is not characterized by pure justice, many of the grossest racial inequities have been reduced, if not eliminated. Reforms mandated by the U.S. Supreme Court or adopted voluntarily by the states have tempered the blatant racism directed against racial minorities by criminal justice officials.

The Supreme Court consistently has affirmed the importance of protecting criminal suspects' rights. The Court has ruled, for example, that searches without warrants generally are unconstitutional, that confessions cannot be coerced, that suspects must be advised of their rights and provided with attorneys to assist them in their defense, that jurors must be chosen from a representative cross section of the population, and that the death penalty cannot be administered in an arbitrary and capricious manner.

Most of these decisions reflect the Court's concern with general procedural issues rather than racial discrimination. The Court, in other words, was attempting to safeguard the rights of *all* criminal defendants. Nevertheless, some observers argue that the Supreme Court's consideration of these procedural issues often was "influenced by the realization that in another case they might affect the posture of a Negro in a hostile southern court."[1]

Even when the Court did not explicitly address the question of racial discrimination in the criminal justice system, its rulings on general procedural issues did lead to improvements in the treatment of racial minorities. By insisting that the states protect the rights of all defendants—racial minorities as well as whites—the Supreme Court rulings discussed earlier led indirectly to the elimination of racially biased criminal justice practices and policies. Coupled with reforms adopted voluntarily by the states, these decisions made systematic racial discrimination unlikely.

We want to reiterate that we are not suggesting that racial discrimination has been completely eliminated from the U.S. criminal justice system. It is certainly true that in the year 2003, whites who commit crimes against African Americans are not beyond the reach of the criminal justice system, African Americans suspected of crimes against whites do not receive "justice" at the hands of white lynch mobs, and African Americans who victimize other African Americans are not immune from punishment. Despite these significant changes, racial inequities persist. As we have shown in the preceding chapters, African Americans and other racial minorities continue to suffer both overt and subtle discrimination within the criminal justice system. Persuasive evidence indicates that racial minorities suffer discrimination at the hands of the police. They are subject to racial profiling and are more likely than whites to be shot and killed, arrested, and victimized by excessive physical force. In addition, there is evidence of police misconduct directed at racial minorities, as well as evidence that police departments fail to discipline officers found guilty of misconduct.

Compelling evidence also points to discrimination within the court system. Supreme Court decisions and statutory reforms have not eliminated racial bias in decisions regarding bail, charging, plea bargaining, jury selection, and juvenile justice processing. Discrimination in sentencing also persists. Judges in some jurisdictions continue to impose harsher sentences on African American offenders who murder or rape whites and more lenient sentences on African Americans who victimize other African Americans. Judges also impose racially biased sentences in less serious cases; in these "borderline cases," people of color are more likely to get prison, whereas whites more typically get probation. Partly as a consequence of these discriminatory sentencing practices, the number of African Americans incarcerated in U.S. jails and prisons has swelled; African Americans now are a majority of those incarcerated.

We are particularly troubled by the persistence of racial discrimination at two of the most critical stages in the criminal justice process—police use of deadly force and the application of the death penalty. The effect of racial bias in these irrevocable life-or-death decisions is profound. The fact that it persists is deeply disturbing.

Court rulings and policy changes designed to regulate deadly force and death penalty decisions have made racial discrimination less likely. Studies reveal that the ratio of African Americans to whites killed by the police has dropped from approximately 7:1 to 3:1. Studies also reveal that the gross racial disproportions that characterized death penalty decisions earlier in this century, and particularly those that characterized decisions to impose the death penalty for the crime of rape, no longer exist.

This clearly is progress. However, we cannot ignore the fact that discrimination remains in these two critical decisions—both of which involve the ultimate decision to take the life of another person. Moreover, the fact that discrimination persists in the face of legal efforts to eradicate it suggests that decision making in these two areas reflects racial stereotypes and deeply buried racial prejudices. It suggests that police officers' definitions of dangerousness, and thus their willingness to use deadly force, depend to some degree on the race of the suspect. It suggests that judges' and jurors' assessments of the heinousness of a crime, and thus their willingness to impose the death penalty, are influenced by the race of the offender and the race of the victim.

Our analysis of race and crime in the United States suggests that those who conclude that "the criminal justice system is not racist"[2] are misinformed. Although reforms have made systematic racial discrimination—discrimination in all stages, in all places, and at all times—unlikely, the U.S. criminal justice system has never been, and is not now, color-blind.

NOTES

1. Archibald Cox, *The Warren Court* (Cambridge, MA: Harvard University Press, 1968), p. 6.

2. William Wilbanks, *The Myth of a Racist Criminal Justice System* (Belmont, CA: Wadsworth, 1987), p. 10.

Selected Bibliography

Albonetti, Celesta A. "Criminality, Prosecutorial Screening, and Uncertainty: Toward a Theory of Discretionary Decision Making in Felony Case Processing." *Criminology* 24 (1986): 623–644.

———. "Sentencing under the Federal Sentencing Guidelines: Effects of Defendant Characteristics, Guilty Pleas, and Departures on Sentencing Outcomes for Drug Offenses, 1991–1992." *Law & Society Review* 31 (1997): 789–822.

Albonetti, Celesta A., Robert M. Hauser, John Hagan, and Ilene H. Nagel. "Criminal Justice Decision Making as a Stratification Process: The Role of Race and Stratification Resources in Pretrial Release." *Journal of Quantitative Criminology* 5 (1989): 57–82.

Allen, James Paul, and Eugene James Turner. *We the People: An Atlas of America's Ethnic Diversity.* New York: Macmillan, 1988.

Alschuler, Albert W. "Racial Quotas and the Jury." *Duke Law Journal* 44 (1995): 44.

Alvarez, Alexander, and Ronet D. Bachman. "American Indians and Sentencing Disparity: An Arizona Test." *Journal of Criminal Justice* 24 (1996): 549–561.

American Bar Association. *Race and the Law: Special Report.* Chicago: American Bar Association, 1999.

American Bar Association Commission on Racial and Ethnic Diversity in the Profession. *Miles to Go 2000: Progress of Minorities in the Legal Profession.* Chicago: American Bar Association, 2000.

American Civil Liberties Union. *Driving While Black.* New York: ACLU, 1999.

———. *Federal Death Row: Is It Really Color-Blind? Analysis of June 6 Department of Justice Report on the Death Penalty.* Available at www.aclu.org/Congress/106141a.htm.

American Correctional Association. *1993 Directory of Juvenile and Adult Correctional Departments, Institutions, Agencies and Paroling Authorities.* Laurel, MD: American Correctional Association, 1993.

American Friends Service Committee. *Struggle for Justice: A Report on Crime and Punishment in America.* Boston: Little, Brown, 1971.

Amsterdam, Anthony. "Race and the Death Penalty." *Criminal Justice Ethics* 7 (1988): 84–86.

Author, John A. "Correctional Ideology of Black Correctional Officers." *Federal Probation* 58 (1994): 57–65.

Bachman, Ronet D., Alexander Alvarez, and C. Perkins. "The Discriminatory Imposition of the Law: Does It Affect Sentence Outcomes for American Indians?" In *Native Americans, Crime and Justice,* edited by Marianne O. Nielsen and Robert A. Silverman. Boulder, CO: Westview Press, 1996.

Baldus, David C., Charles Pulaski, and George Woodworth. "Comparative Review of Death Sentences: An Empirical Study of the Georgia Experience." *Journal of Criminal Law & Criminology* 74 (1983): 661–673.

Baldus, David C., George Woodworth, and Charles A. Pulaski. *Equal Justice and the Death Penalty: A Legal and Empirical Analysis.* Boston: Northeastern University Press, 1990.

Barak, Gregg, Jeanne M. Flavin, and Paul S. Leighton. *Class, Race, Gender and Crime: Social Realities of Justice in America.* Los Angeles: Roxbury, 2001.

Barkan, Steven E., and Steven F. Cohn. "Racial Prejudice and Support for the Death Penalty by Whites." *Journal of Research in Crime and Delinquency* 31 (1994): 202–209.

Bayley, David H., and Harold Mendelsohn. *Minorities and the Police: Confrontation in America.* New York: Free Press, 1969.

Bedau, Hugo A., and Michael L. Radelet. "Miscarriages of Justice in Potentially Capital Cases." *Stanford Law Review* 40 (1987): 21–179.

Bing, Robert. "Politicizing Black-on-Black Crime: A Critique of Terminological Preference." In *Black-on-Black Crime,* edited by P. Ray Kedia. Bristol, IN: Wyndham Hall Press, 1994.

Bishop, Donna M., and Charles E. Frazier. "The Influence of Race in Juvenile Justice Processing." *Journal of Research in Crime and Delinquency* 25 (1988): 242–263.

Black, Donald. *The Manners and Customs of the Police.* New York: Academic Press, 1980.

Blumberg, Abraham S. "The Practice of Law as a Confidence Game: Organizational Cooptation of a Profession." *Law & Society Review* 1 (1967): 15–39.

Blumstein, Alfred. "On the Disproportionality of United States' Prison Populations." *Journal of Criminal Law & Criminology* 73 (1982): 1259–1281.

Blumstein, Alfred, Jacqueline Cohen, Susan E. Martin, and Michael Tonry. *Research on Sentencing: The Search for Reform.* Vol. 1. Washington, DC: National Academy Press, 1983.

Bowers, William. "The Pervasiveness of Arbitrariness and Discrimination under Post-*Furman* Capital Statutes." *Journal of Criminal Law & Criminology* 74 (1983): 1067–1100.

Bridges, George S., and Robert D. Crutchfield. "Law, Social Standing and Racial Disparities in Imprisonment." *Social Forces* 66 (1988): 699–724.

Bridges, George S., and Sara Steen. "Racial Disparities in Official Assessments of Juvenile Offending: Attributional Stereotypes as Mediating Mechanisms." *American Sociological Review* 65 (1998): 554–570.

Bright, Stephen B. "Discrimination, Death and Denial: The Tolerance of Racial Discrimination in the Infliction of the Death Penalty." *Santa Clara Law Review* 35 (1995): 901–950.

Bright, Stephen B., and Patrick J. Keenan. "Judges and the Politics of Death: Deciding between the Bill of Rights and the Next Election in Capital Cases." *Boston University Law Review* 75 (1995): 759–835.

Browning, Sandra Lee, Francis T. Cullen, Liqun Cao, Renee Kopache, and Thomas J. Stevenson. "Race and Getting Hassled by the Police: A Research

Note." *Police Studies* 17, no. 1 (1994): 1–11.

Building Blocks for Youth. *Donde Está la Justicia?* East Lansing: Michigan State University, 2002.

Bureau of Justice Statistics. *Black Victims.* Washington, DC: U.S. Government Printing Office, 1990.

———. *Hispanic Victims.* Washington, DC: U.S. Government Printing Office, 1990.

———. *Capital Punishment 1991.* Washington, DC: U.S. Department of Justice, 1992.

———. *Police Use of Force: Collection of National Data.* Washington, DC: U.S. Government Printing Office, 1997.

———. *Contacts between Police and the Public: Findings from the 1999 National Survey,* NCJ 184057. Washington, DC: U.S. Government Printing Office, 2001. Available at www.ncjrs.org.

———. *Policing and Homicide, 1976–98: Justifiable Homicide by Police, Police Officers Murdered by Felons.* Washington, DC: U.S. Government Printing Office, 2001.

———. *Prison and Jail Inmates at Midyear 2001.* Washington, DC: U.S. Department of Justice, 2002.

Butler, Paul. "Racially Based Jury Nullification: Black Power in the Criminal Justice System." *Yale Law Journal* 105 (1995): 677–725.

Bynum, Timothy S., and Raymond Paternoster. "Discrimination Revisited: An Exploration of Frontstage and Backstage Criminal Justice Decision Making." *Sociology and Social Research* 69 (1984): 90–108.

Cahalan, Margaret Werner. *Historical Corrections Statistics in the United States, 1850–1984.* Washington, DC: U.S. Government Printing Office, 1986.

Campbell, Anne. *Girls in the Gang: A Report from New York City.* Oxford: Basil Blackwell, 1984.

———. *The Girls in the Gang.* 2d ed. Cambridge, MA: Basil Blackwell, 1991.

Carter, Dan T. *Scottsboro: A Tragedy of the American South.* Baton Rouge: Louisiana State University Press, 1969.

Carter, David L. "Hispanic Interaction with the Criminal Justice System in Texas: Experiences, Attitudes, and Perceptions." *Journal of Criminal Justice* 11 (1983): 213–227.

Carter, Terry. "Divided Justice." *ABA Journal* (February 1999): 42–45.

Casper, Jonathan D. *Criminal Courts: The Defendant's Perspective.* Englewood Cliffs, NJ: Prentice-Hall, 1978.

Chambliss, William J. "Crime Control and Ethnic Minorities: Legitimizing Racial Oppression by Creating Moral Panics." In *Ethnicity, Race, and Crime: Perspectives across Time and Place,* edited by Darnell F. Hawkins. Albany: State University of New York Press, 1995.

Chin, Ko-Lin, Jeffrey Fagan, and Robert J. Kelly. "Patterns of Chinese Gang Extortion." *Justice Quarterly* 9 (1992): 625–646.

Chiricos, Theodore G. "The Moral Panic of the Drug War." In *Race and Criminal Justice,* edited by Michael J. Lynch and E. Britt Patterson. New York: Harrow & Heston, 1995.

Chiricos, Theodore G., and William D. Bales. "Unemployment and Punishment: An Empirical Assessment." *Criminology* 29 (1991): 701–724.

Chiricos, Theodore G., and Charles Crawford. "Race and Imprisonment: A Contextual Assessment of the Evidence." In *Ethnicity, Race and Crime,* edited by Darnell F. Hawkins. Albany: State University of New York Press, 1995.

Chiricos, Theodore G., and Miriam A. DeLone. "Labor Surplus and Punishment: A Review and Assessment of Theory and Evidence." *Social Problems* 39 (1992): 421–446.

Cole, David. *No Equal Justice: Race and Class in the American Criminal Justice System.* New York: New Press, 1999.

Covey, Herbert C., Scott Menard, and Robert J. Franzese. *Juvenile Gangs.* Springfield, IL: Charles C. Thomas, 1992.

Crockett, George. "The Role of the Black Judge." In *The Criminal Justice System and Blacks,* edited by D. Georges-

Abeyie. New York: Clark Boardman, 1984.

Davis, Kenneth Culp. *Discretionary Justice.* Baton Rouge: Louisiana State University Press, 1969.

Death Penalty Information Center. *The Death Penalty in 2001: Year-End Report.* Washington, DC: Death Penalty Information Center, 2001.

Decker, David L., David Shichor, and Robert M. O'Brien. *Urban Structure and Victimization.* Lexington, MA: D. C. Heath, 1982.

Decker, Scott H. "Citizen Attitudes toward the Police: A Review of Past Findings and Suggestions for Future Policy." *Journal of Police Science and Administration* 9 (1981): 80–87.

DeJong, Christina, and Kenneth C. Jackson. "Putting Race into Context: Race, Juvenile Justice Processing, and Urbanization." *Justice Quarterly* 15 (1998): 487–504.

Dixon, Jo. "The Organizational Context of Criminal Sentencing." *American Journal of Sociology* 100 (1995): 1157–1198.

Dorfman, Lori, and Vincent Schiraldi. "Off Balance: Youth, Race and Crime in the News." Executive Summary. Berkeley Media Studies Group, 2001. Available at www .buildingblocksforyouth.org/media/.

Du Bois, W. E. B. "The Spawn of Slavery: The Convict-Lease System in the South." *The Missionary Review of the World* 14 (1901): 373–745.

Dulaney, W. Marvin. *Black Police in America.* Bloomington: Indiana University Press, 1996.

Elliot, Delbert, David Huizinga, Brian Knowles, and Rachel Canter. *The Prevalence and Incidence of Delinquent Behavior: 1976–1980: National Estimates of Delinquent Behavior by Sex, Race, Social Class and Other Selected Variables.* Boulder, CO: Behavioral Research Institute, 1983.

Engle, Charles Donald. *Criminal Justice in the City: A Study of Sentence Severity and Variation in the Philadelphia Court System.* Ph.D. diss., Temple University, 1971.

Esbensen, Finn-Aage, and David Huizinga. "Gangs, Drugs and Delinquency." *Criminology* 31 (1993): 565–590.

Everett, Ronald S., and Barbara C. Nienstedt. "Race, Remorse, and Sentence Reduction: Is Saying You're Sorry Enough?" *Justice Quarterly* 16 (1999): 99–122.

Fagan, Jeffrey. "The Social Organization of Drug Use and Drug Dealing among Urban Gangs." *Criminology* 27 (1989): 633–666.

Farnworth, Margaret, and Patrick Horan. "Separate Justice: An Analysis of Race Differences in Court Processes." *Social Science Research* 9 (1980): 381–399.

Feeley, Malcolm M. *The Process Is the Punishment: Handling Cases in a Lower Criminal Court.* New York: Russell Sage Foundation, 1979.

Feimer, Steve, Frank Pommersheim, and Steve Wise. "Marking Time: Does Race Make a Difference? A Study of Disparate Sentencing in South Dakota." *Journal of Crime and Justice* 13 (1990): 86–102.

Feld, Barry C. *Bad Kids, Race and the Transformation of the Juvenile Court.* New York: Oxford University Press, 1999.

Flowers, Ronald Barri. *Minorities and Criminality.* Westport, CT: Greenwood Press, 1988.

Fong, Robert, Ronald Vogel, and Salvador Buentello. "Prison Gang Dynamics: A Look Inside the Texas Department of Corrections." In *Corrections: Dilemmas and Directions,* edited by Peter J. Benekos and Alida V. Merlo. Highland Heights, KY: Anderson Publishing Co. and Academy of Criminal Justice Sciences, 1992.

Frankel, Marvin. *Criminal Sentences: Law without Order.* New York: Hill & Wang, 1972.

Frazier, Charles E., and Donna M. Bishop. "Reflections on Race Effects in Juvenile Justice." In *Minorities in Juvenile Justice,* edited by Kimberly Kempf Leonard, Carl E. Pope, and William H. Feyerherm. Thousand Oaks, CA: Sage, 1995.

Fyfe, James J. "Who Shoots? A Look at Officer Race and Police Shooting." *Journal of Police Science and Administration* 9 (1981): 367–382.

————. "Blind Justice: Police Shootings in Memphis." *Journal of Criminal Law and Criminology* 73 (1982): 707–722.

Garfinkel, Harold. "Research Notes on Inter- and Intra-Racial Homicides." *Social Forces* 27 (1949): 369–381.

Geller, William A., and Michael S. Scott. *Deadly Force: What We Know.* Washington, DC: Police Executive Research Forum, 1992.

Geller, William A., and Hans Toch, eds. *And Justice for All.* Washington, DC: Police Executive Research Forum, 1995.

Gilliard, Darrell K., and Allen Beck. *Prisoners, 1993.* Washington, DC: U.S. Department of Justice, 1994.

Goodstein, Lynne, and Doris Layton MacKenzie. "Racial Differences in Adjustment Patterns of Prison Inmates— Prisonization, Conflict, Stress and Control." In *The Criminal Justice System and Blacks,* edited by Daniel Georges-Abeyie. New York: Clark Boardman, 1984.

Gottschall, Jon. "Carter's Judicial Appointments: The Influence of Affirmative Action and Merit Selection on Voting on the U.S. Courts of Appeals." *Judicature* 67 (1983): 165–173.

Greenfeld, Lawrence, and Steven K. Smith. *American Indians and Crime.* Washington, DC: Bureau of Justice Statistics, 1999.

Grobsmith, Elizabeth S. *Indians in Prison.* Lincoln: University of Nebraska Press, 1994.

Gross, Samuel R., and Robert Mauro. *Death & Discrimination: Racial Disparities in Capital Sentencing.* Boston: Northeastern University Press, 1989.

Hacker, Andrew. *Two Nations: Black and White, Separate, Hostile, Unequal.* New York: Scribners, 1992.

Hagan, John. "Extra-Legal Attributes and Criminal Sentencing: An Assessment of a Sociological Viewpoint." *Law & Society Review* 8 (1974): 357–383.

Hagedorn, John M. *People and Folks.* Chicago: Lake View Press, 1989.

Hall, Edwin L., and Albert A. Simkins. "Inequality in the Types of Sentences Received by Native Americans and Whites." *Criminology* 13: 199–222.

Hamm, Mark S. *American Skinheads.* Westport, CT: Praeger, 1994.

Harris, David. *Profiles in Injustice: Why Racial Profiling Doesn't Work.* New York: New Press, 2002.

Harris, Mary G. *Cholas: Latino Girls in Gangs.* New York: AMS Press, 1988.

Harris, Philip W., Wayne N. Welsh, and Frank Butler. "A Century of Juvenile Justice." In *Criminal Justice 2000, The Nature of Crime: Continuity and Change.* Vol. 1. Washington, DC: National Institute of Justice, 2000.

Hawkins, Darnell F. "Beyond Anomalies: Rethinking the Conflict Perspective on Race and Criminal Justice." *Social Forces* 65 (1987): 719–745.

————. "Ethnicity: The Forgotten Dimension of American Social Control." In *Inequality, Crime, and Social Control,* edited by George S. Bridges and Martha A. Myers. Boulder, CO: Westview Press, 1994.

————, ed. *Ethnicity, Race, and Crime.* Albany: State University of New York Press, 1995.

Hawkins, Darnell F., and Kenneth A. Hardy. "Black-White Imprisonment Rates: A State-by-State Analysis." *Social Justice* 16 (1989): 75–94.

Hayden, George, Joseph Senna, and Larry Siegel. "Prosecutorial Discretion in Peremptory Challenges: An Empirical Investigation of Information Use in the Massachusetts Jury Selection Process." *New England Law Review* 13 (1978): 768–790.

Herbst, Leigh, and Samuel Walker. "Language Barriers in the Delivery of Police Services: A Study of Police and Hispanic Interactions in a Midwestern City." *Journal of Criminal Justice* 29, no. 4 (2001): 329–340.

Hindelang, Michael J. "Race and Involvement in Common Law Personal

Crimes." *American Sociological Review* 43 (1978): 93–109.

Hoffman, Morris B. "Peremptory Challenges: Lawyers Are from Mars, Judges Are from Venus." 3 *Green Bag* 2d 135 (winter 2000). Available at www.lexis-nexis.com/universe.

Holmes, Malcolm D., Harmon M. Hosch, Howard C. Daudistel, Dolores A. Perez, and Joseph B. Graves. "Judges' Ethnicity and Minority Sentencing: Evidence Concerning Hispanics." *Social Science Quarterly* 74 (1993): 496–506.

———. "Ethnicity, Legal Resources, and Felony Dispositions in Two Southwestern Jurisdictions." *Justice Quarterly* 13 (1996): 11–30.

Huff, C. Ronald, ed. *Gangs in America.* Newbury Park, CA: Sage, 1990.

Huizinga, David, and Delbert S. Elliot. "Juvenile Offenders: Prevalence, Offender Incidence, and Arrest Rates by Race." *Crime and Delinquency* 33 (1987): 206–223.

Human Rights Watch. *Shielded from Justice: Police Brutality and Accountability in the United States.* New York: Human Rights Watch, 1998.

———. *Punishment and Prejudice: Racial Disparities in the War on Drugs.* Vol. 12, no. 2 (G) (May 2000). Available at www.hrw.org/reports/2000/usa/.

Humphries, Drew, John Dawson, Valerie Cronin, Phyllis Keating, Chris Wisniewski, and Jennine Eichfeld. "Mothers and Children, Drugs and Crack: Reactions to Maternal Drug Dependency." In *The Criminal Justice System and Women,* 2d ed., edited by Barbara Raffel Price and Natalie J. Sokoloff. New York: McGraw-Hill, 1995.

Jacobs, James. *New Perspectives on Prison and Imprisonment.* Ithaca, NY: Cornell University Press, 1983.

Jaynes, Gerald David, and Robin M. Williams Jr., eds. *A Common Destiny: Blacks and American Society.* Washington, DC: National Academy Press, 1992.

Jenkins, Phillip. "'The Ice Age': The Social Construction of a Drug Panic." *Justice Quarterly* 11 (1994): 7–31.

Johnson, Elmer H. "Selective Factors in Capital Punishment." *Social Forces* 36 (1957): 165.

Johnson, Guy. "The Negro and Crime." *Annals of the American Academy* 217 (1941): 93–104.

Johnson, Sheri Lynn. "Black Innocence and the White Jury." *University of Michigan Law Review* 83 (1985): 1611–1708.

Johnstone, J. W. C. "Youth Gangs and Black Suburbs." *Pacific Sociological Review* 24 (1981): 355–375.

Kalven, Harry, Jr., and Hans Zeisel. *The American Jury.* Boston: Little, Brown, 1966.

Kautt, Paula, and Cassia Spohn. "Cracking Down on Black Drug Offenders? Testing for Interactions among Offenders' Race, Drug Type, and Sentencing Strategy in Federal Drug Sentences." *Justice Quarterly* 19 (2002): 2–35.

Keil, Thomas, and Gennaro Vito. "Race and the Death Penalty in Kentucky Murder Trials: An Analysis of Post-*Gregg* Outcomes." *Justice Quarterly* (1990): 189–207.

Kempf, Kimberly Leonard, and Henry Sontheimer. "The Role of Race in Juvenile Justice in Pennsylvania." In *Minorities and Juvenile Justice,* edited by Kimberly Kempf Leonard, Carl E. Pope, and William H. Feyerherm. Thousand Oaks, CA: Sage, 1995.

Kennedy, Randall. "Changing Images of the State: Criminal Law and Racial Discrimination: A Comment." *Harvard Law Review* 107 (1994): 1255–1278.

———. *Race, Crime, and the Law.* New York: Vintage Books, 1997.

Kerner Commission. *Report of the National Advisory Commission on Civil Disorders.* New York: Bantam Books, 1968.

Kleck, Gary. "Racial Discrimination in Criminal Sentencing: A Critical Evaluation of the Evidence with Additional Evidence on the Death Penalty." *American Sociological Review* 46 (1981): 783–805.

Klein, Kitty, and Blanche Creech. "Race, Rape, and Bias: Distortion of Prior Odds and Meaning Changes." *Basic and Applied Social Psychology* 3 (1982): 21.

Klein, Malcolm W., Cheryl Maxson, and Lea C. Cunningham, et al. "'Crack,' Street Gangs and Violence." *Criminology* 29 (1991): 623–650.

Klein, Stephen, Joan Petersilia, and Susan Turner. "Race and Imprisonment Decisions in California." *Science* 247 (1990): 812–816.

Klinger, David. "Demeanor or Crime? Why 'Hostile' Citizens Are More Likely to Be Arrested." *Criminology* 32 (1994): 475–493.

Knepper, Paul. "Race, Racism and Crime Statistics." *Southern Law Review* 24 (1996): 71–112.

Kramer, John H., and Jeffery T. Ulmer. "Sentencing Disparity and Departures from Guidelines." *Justice Quarterly* 13 (1996): 81–105.

LaFree, Gary D. "The Effect of Sexual Stratification by Race on Official Reactions to Rape." *American Sociological Review* 45 (1980): 842–854.

———. *Rape and Criminal Justice: The Social Construction of Sexual Assault.* Belmont, CA: Wadsworth, 1989.

Leadership Conference on Civil Rights. *Justice on Trial: Racial Disparities in the American Criminal Justice System.* Washington, DC: Leadership Conference on Civil Rights, 2000.

Leiber, Michael J. "A Comparison of Juvenile Court Outcomes for Native Americans, African Americans, and Whites." *Justice Quarterly* 11 (1994): 255–279.

Levin, Martin Howard. "The Jury in a Criminal Case: Obstacles to Impartiality." *Criminal Law Bulletin* 24 (1988): 492–520.

Levine, James P. *Juries and Politics.* Pacific Grove, CA: Brooks/Cole, 1992.

Lujan, Carol Chiago. "Stereotyping by Politicians: Or 'The Only Real Indian Is the Stereotypical Indian.'" In *Images of Color, Images of Crime,* edited by Coramae Richey Mann and Marjorie Zatz. Los Angeles: Roxbury, 1998.

Lynch, Michael J., and E. Britt Patterson, eds. *Race and Criminal Justice.* New York: Harrow & Heston, 1991.

Mann, Coramae Richey. *Unequal Justice: A Question of Color.* Bloomington: University of Indiana Press, 1993.

Mason, Alpheus Thomas, and William M. Beaney. *American Constitutional Law.* Englewood Cliffs, NJ: Prentice-Hall, 1972.

Mather, Lynn. *Plea Bargaining or Trial?* Lexington, MA: Heath, 1979.

Mauer, Marc. *Young Black Men and the Criminal Justice System: A Growing National Problem.* Washington, DC: The Sentencing Project, 1990.

———. *Americans behind Bars: A Comparison of International Rates of Incarceration.* Washington, DC: The Sentencing Project, 1991.

———. *Race to Incarcerate.* New York: New Press, 1999.

Mauer, Marc, and Tracy Huling. *Young Black Americans and the Criminal Justice System: Five Years Later.* Washington, DC: The Sentencing Project, 1995.

Maxfield, Linda Drazga, and John H. Kramer. *Substantial Assistance: An Empirical Yardstick Gauging Equity in Current Federal Policy and Practices.* Washington, DC: United States Sentencing Commission, 1998.

McDonald, Douglas C., and Kenneth E. Carlson. *Sentencing in the Federal Courts: Does Race Matter?* Washington, DC: U.S. Department of Justice, 1993.

Melossi, Dario. "An Introduction: Fifty Years Later, Punishment and Social Structure in Comparative Analysis." *Contemporary Crises* 13 (1989): 311–326.

Melton, Ada Pecos. "Crime and Punishment: Traditional and Contemporary Tribal Justice." In *Images of Color, Images of Crime,* edited by Coramae Richey Mann and Marjorie S. Zatz. Los Angles: Roxbury, 1998.

Michalowski, Raymond J., and Susan J. Carlson. "Unemployment, Imprisonment and Social Structures of Accumulation: Historical Contingency in the Rushe-Kirchheimer Hypothesis." *Criminology* 37 (1999): 217–250.

Michalowski, Raymond J., and Michael A. Pearson. "Punishment and Social Structure at the State Level: A Cross-Sectional Comparison of 1970 and 1980." *Journal of Research in Crime and Delinquency* 27 (1990): 52–78.

Miethe, Terance D., and Charles A. Moore. "Socioeconomic Disparities under Determinate Sentencing Systems: A Comparison of Preguideline and Postguideline Practices in Minnesota." *Criminology* 23 (1985): 337–363.

Miller, Jerome. *Search and Destroy: African-American Males in the Criminal Justice System.* Cambridge: Cambridge University Press, 1996.

Moore, J. D., and Vigil R. Garcia. "Residence and Territoriality in Chicano Gangs." *Social Problems* 31 (1983): 182–194.

Morrison, Toni. *Beloved: A Novel.* New York: Plume, 1988.

Murphy, Clyde E. "Racial Discrimination in the Criminal Justice System." *North Carolina Central Law Journal* 17 (1988): 171–190.

Myers, Martha. "Symbolic Policy and the Sentencing of Drug Offenders." *Law & Society Review* 23 (1989): 295–315.

———. *Race, Labor and Punishment in the South.* Columbus: Ohio State University Press, 1999.

Myrdal, Gunnar. *An American Dilemma: The Negro Problem and Modern Democracy.* New York: Harper & Brothers, 1944.

NAACP Legal Defense and Educational Fund. *Death Row USA, Winter 2002.* Available at www.deathpenaltyinfo .org/DEATHROWUSArecent.pdf.

Nardulli, Peter F., James Eisenstein, and Roy B. Flemming. *The Tenor of Justice: Criminal Courts and the Guilty Plea Process.* Chicago: University of Chicago Press, 1988.

Nobiling, Tracy, Cassia Spohn, and Miriam DeLone. "A Tale of Two Counties: Unemployment and Sentence Severity." *Justice Quarterly* 15 (1998): 459–485.

Note. "*Batson v. Kentucky:* Challenging the Use of the Peremptory Challenge." *American Journal of Criminal Law* 15 (1988): 298.

O'Brien, Robert M. "The Interracial Nature of Violent Crimes: A Reexamination." *American Journal of Sociology* 92 (1987): 817–835.

Olsen, Jack. *Last Man Standing: The Tragedy and Triumph of Geronimo Pratt.* New York: Doubleday, 2000.

Panel on Juvenile Crime. *Juvenile Crime Juvenile Justice.* Washington, DC: National Academy Press, 2001.

Pate, Anthony M., and Lorie Fridell. *Police Use of Force.* 2 vols. Washington, DC: The Police Foundation, 1993.

Paternoster, Raymond. "Discrimination Revisited: An Exploration of Front-stage and Backstage Criminal Justice Decision Making." *Sociology and Social Research* 69 (1984a): 90–108.

———. "Prosecutorial Discretion in Requesting the Death Penalty: A Case of Victim-Based Racial Discrimination." *Law & Society Review* 18 (1984b): 437–478.

———. *Capital Punishment in America.* New York: Lexington Books, 1991.

Peak, K., and J. Spencer. "Crime in Indian Country: Another Trail of Tears." *Journal of Criminal Justice* 15 (1987): 485–494.

Petersilia, Joan. *Racial Disparities in the Criminal Justice System.* Santa Monica, CA: Rand Corporation, 1983.

Peterson, Ruth D., and John Hagan. "Changing Conceptions of Race: Towards an Account of Anomalous Findings of Sentencing Research." *American Sociological Review* 49 (1984): 56–70.

Platt, Anthony M. *The Child Saver: The Invention of Delinquency.* 2d ed. Chicago: University of Chicago Press, 1977.

Police Executive Research Forum. *Racially Biased Policing: A Principled Response.* Washington, DC: PERF, 2001.

PolicyLink. *Community-Centered Policing: A Force for Change.* Oakland, CA: PolicyLink, 2001.

Pommersheim, Frank, and Steve Wise. "Going to the Penitentiary: A Study of Disparate Sentencing in South Dakota." *Criminal Justice and Behavior* 16 (1989): 155–165.

Pope, Carl E., and William H. Feyerherm. "Minority Status and Juvenile Justice Processing: An Assessment of the Research Literature (Part I)." *Criminal Justice Abstracts* 22 (1990): 327–335.

Quinney, Richard. *The Social Reality of Crime.* Boston: Little, Brown, 1970.

Radelet, Michael L. "Racial Characteristics and the Imposition of the Death Penalty." *American Sociological Review* 46 (1981): 918–927.

———. "Executions of Whites for Crimes against Blacks: Exceptions to the Rule?" *The Sociological Quarterly* 30 (1989): 529–544.

Radelet, Michael L., and Glenn L. Pierce. "Race and Prosecutorial Discretion in Homicide Cases." *Law & Society Review* 19 (1985): 587–621.

Ralph, Paige H., Jonathan R. Sorensen, and James W. Marquart. "A Comparison of Death-Sentenced and Incarcerated Murderers in Pre-*Furman* Texas." *Justice Quarterly* 9 (1992): 185–209.

Ramirez, Deborah A. "Affirmative Jury Selection: A Proposal to Advance Both the Deliberative Ideal and Jury Diversity." *University of Chicago Legal Forum* (1998): 161.

Ramirez, Deborah A., Jack McDevitt, and Amy Farrell. *A Resource Guide on Racial Profiling Data Collection Systems: Promising Practices and Lessons Learned.* Washington, DC: U.S. Department of Justice, 2000.

Reddy, Marlita A., ed. *Statistical Record of African Americans.* Detroit, MI: Gale Research.

———. *Statistical Record of Hispanic Americans.* Detroit, MI: Gale Research, 1993.

Reiman, Jeffrey. *The Rich Get Richer and Poor Get Prison.* Boston: Allyn & Bacon, 1995.

Reiss, Albert J. *The Police and the Public.* New Haven, CT: Yale University Press, 1971.

Rennison, Callie Marie. *Violent Victimization and Race, 1993–1998.* Available at www.ojp.usdoj/bjs.

Rise, Eric W. *The Martinsville Seven: Race, Rape, and Capital Punishment.* Charlottesville: University Press of Virginia, 1995.

Roberts, Dorothy. "Punishing Drug Addicts Who Have Babies: Women of Color, Equality, and the Right of Privacy." *Harvard Law Review* 104 (1991): 1419–1454.

Ruback, R. Barry, and Paula J. Vardaman. "Decision Making in Delinquency Cases: The Role of Race and Juveniles' Admission/Denial of the Crime." *Law and Human Behavior* 21 (1997): 47–69.

Sarat, Austin. "Recapturing the Spirit of *Furman:* The American Bar Association and the New Abolitionist Politics." *Law and Contemporary Problems* 61 (1998): 5–28.

———. *When the State Kills: Capital Punishment and the American Condition.* Princeton, NJ: Princeton University Press, 1998.

Secret, Philip E., and James B. Johnson. "The Effect of Race on Juvenile Justice Decision Making in Nebraska: Detention, Adjudication, and Disposition, 1988–1993." *Justice Quarterly* 14 (1997): 445–478.

Sentencing Project, The. *Facts about Prison and Prisoners.* Available at www.sentencingproject.org (April 2002).

———. *Felony Disenfranchisement Laws in the United States.* Available at www.sentencingproject.org (November 2002).

Serr, Brian J., and Mark Maney. "Racism, Peremptory Challenges, and the Democratic Jury: The Jurisprudence of a Delicate Balance." *Journal of Criminal Law and Criminology* 79 (1988): 1–65.

Silberman, Charles E. *Criminal Violence, Criminal Justice.* New York: Random House, 1978.

Skogan, Wesley G., and Susan M. Hartnett. *Community Policing: Chicago Style.* New York: Oxford University Press, 1997.

Smith, Brent L., and Kelly R. Damphouse. "Punishing Political Offenders: The Effect of Political Motive on Federal Sentencing Decisions." *Criminology* 34 (1996): 289–321.

Smith, Douglas A., Christy Visher, and Laura A. Davidson. "Equity and Discretionary Justice: The Influence of Race on Police Arrest Decisions." *Journal of Criminal Law and Criminology* 75 (1984): 234–249.

Smith, Michael David. *Race versus Robe: The Dilemma of Black Judges.* Port Washington, NY: Associated Faculty Press, 1983.

Snell, Tracy. *Correctional Populations in the United States 1992.* Washington, DC: Department of Justice, 1995.

Song, John Huey-Long. "Attitudes of Chinese Immigrants and Vietnamese Refugees toward Law Enforcement in the United States." *Justice Quarterly* 9 (1992): 703–719.

Spears, Jeffrey W. *Diversity in the Courtroom: A Comparison of the Sentencing Decisions of Black and White Judges and Male and Female Judges in Cook County Circuit Court.* Ph.D. diss., University of Nebraska at Omaha, 1999.

Spitzer, Steven. "Toward a Marxian Theory of Deviance." *Social Problems* 22 (1975): 638–651.

Spohn, Cassia. "Decision Making in Sexual Assault Cases: Do Black and Female Judges Make a Difference?" *Women & Criminal Justice* 2 (1990a): 83–105.

———. "The Sentencing Decisions of Black and White Judges: Expected and Unexpected Similarities." *Law & Society Review* 24 (1990b): 1197–1216.

———. "Crime and the Social Control of Blacks: Offender/Victim Race and the Sentencing of Violent Offenders." In *Inequality, Crime & Social Control,* edited by George S. Bridges and Martha A. Myers. Boulder, CO: Westview Press, 1994.

———. "Thirty Years of Sentencing Reform: A Quest for a Racially Neutral Sentencing Process." In *Policies, Processes, and Decisions of the Criminal Justice System.* Vol. 3, *Criminal Justice 2000.* Washington, DC: U.S. Department of Justice, 2000.

Spohn, Cassia, and Jerry Cederblom. "Race and Disparities in Sentencing: A Test of the Liberation Hypothesis." *Justice Quarterly* 8 (1991): 305–327.

Spohn, Cassia, and Miriam DeLone. "When Does Race Matter? An Analysis of the Conditions under Which Race Affects Sentence Severity." *Sociology of Crime, Law, and Deviance* 2 (2000): 3–37.

Spohn, Cassia, John Gruhl, and Susan Welch. "The Effect of Race on Sentencing: A Re-Examination on an Unsettled Question." *Law & Society Review* 16 (1981–1982): 71–88.

———. "The Impact of the Ethnicity and Gender of Defendants on the Decision to Reject or Dismiss Felony Charges." *Criminology* 25 (1987): 175–191.

Spohn, Cassia, and David Holleran. "The Imprisonment Penalty Paid by Young Unemployed Black and Hispanic Male Offenders." *Criminology* 38 (2000): 281–306.

Spohn, Cassia, and Jeffrey Spears. "The Effect of Offender and Victim Characteristics on Sexual Assault Case Processing Decisions." *Justice Quarterly* 13 (1996): 649–679.

———. "Sentencing of Drug Offenders in Three Cities: Does Race/Ethnicity Make a Difference?" In *Crime Control and Criminal Justice: The Delicate Balance,* edited by Darnell F. Hawkins, Samuel L. Meyers Jr., and Randolph N. Stone. Westport, CT: Greenwood, 2002.

Steffensmeier, Darrell, and Stephen Demuth. "Ethnicity and Sentencing Outcomes in U.S. Federal Courts: Who Is Punished More Harshly?"

American Sociological Review 65 (2000): 705–729.

Steffensmeier, Darrell, John Kramer, and Cathy Streifel. "Gender and Imprisonment Decisions." *Criminology* 31 (1993): 411–443.

Steffensmeier, Darrell, John Kramer, and Jeffery Ulmer. "Age Differences in Criminal Sentencing." *Justice Quarterly* 12 (1995): 701–719.

Steffensmeier, Darrell, Jeffery Ulmer, and John Kramer. "The Interaction of Race, Gender, and Age in Criminal Sentencing: The Punishment Cost of Being Young, Black, and Male." *Criminology* 36 (1998): 363–397.

Sudnow, David. "Normal Crimes: Sociological Features of the Penal Code in the Public Defender's Office." *Social Problems* 12 (1965): 255–277.

Swift, B., and G. Bickel. *Comparative Parole Treatment of American Indians and Non-Indians at United States Federal Prisons.* Washington, DC: Bureau of Social Science Research, 1974.

Texas Civil Rights Project. *The Death Penalty in Texas: Due Process and Equal Justice . . . or Rush to Execution?* Austin: Texas Civil Rights Project, 2000.

Thernstrom, Stephan, and Abigail Thernstrom. *America in Black and White: One Nation, Indivisible.* New York: Simon & Schuster, 1997.

Thomas, Jim. "Racial Codes in Prison Culture: Snapshots in Black and White." In *Race and Criminal Justice,* edited by Michael Lynch and Britt Patterson. New York: Harrow & Heston, 1991.

Tonry, Michael. *Malign Neglect: Race, Crime and Punishment in America.* New York: Oxford University Press, 1995.

———. *Sentencing Matters.* New York: Oxford University Press, 1996.

Toy, Calvin. "A Short History of Asian Gangs in San Francisco." *Justice Quarterly* 9 (1992): 645–665.

Tuch, Steven A., and Ronald Weitzer, "Racial Differences in Attitudes toward the Police." *Public Opinion Quarterly* 61 (1997): 643–663.

Turner, Billy M., Rickie D. Lovell, John C. Young, and William F. Denny. "Race and Peremptory Challenges during Voir Dire: Do Prosecution and Defense Agree?" *Journal of Criminal Justice* 14 (1986): 61–69.

Uhlman, Thomas M. "Black Elite Decision Making: The Case of Trial Judges." *American Journal of Political Science* 22 (1978): 884–895.

———. *Racial Justice: Black Judges and Defendants in an Urban Trial Court.* Lexington, MA: Lexington Books, 1979.

Ulmer, Jeffery T., and John H. Kramer. "Court Communities under Sentencing Guidelines: Dilemmas of Formal Rationality and Sentencing Disparity." *Criminology* 34 (1996): 383–407.

U.S. Department of Justice. *The Police and Public Opinion.* Washington, DC: U.S. Government Printing Office, 1977.

———. *The Federal Death Penalty System: A Statistical Survey (1988–2000).* Washington, DC: U.S. Department of Justice, 2000.

———. *The Federal Death Penalty System: Supplementary Data Analysis and Revised Protocols for Capital Case Review.* Washington, DC: U.S. Department of Justice, 2001.

U.S. Department of Justice, Bureau of Justice Statistics. *Comparing Federal and State Inmates, 1991.* Washington, DC: U.S. Government Printing Office, 1993.

———. *Sourcebook of Criminal Justice Statistics, 1999.* Washington, DC: U.S. Government Printing Office, 2000.

———. *Capital Punishment 2000.* Washington, DC: U.S. Government Printing Office, 2001.

U.S. General Accounting Office. *Death Penalty Sentencing: Research Indicates Pattern of Racial Disparities.* Washington, DC: General Accounting Office, 1990.

United States Sentencing Commission. *Special Report to the Congress: Mandatory Minimum Penalties in the Federal Criminal Justice System.* Washington, DC: U.S. Sentencing Commission, 1991.

————. *Substantial Assistance Departures in the United States Courts.* Washington, DC: U.S. Sentencing Commission, 1995.

————. *Report to the Congress: Cocaine and Federal Sentencing Policy.* Washington, DC: U.S. Sentencing Commission, 2002.

van den Haag, Ernest. *Punishing Criminals: Confronting a Very Old and Painful Question.* New York: Basic Books, 1975.

Vigil, James D. *Barrio Gangs.* Austin: University of Texas Press, 1988.

von Hirsch, Andrew. *Doing Justice: The Choice of Punishments.* New York: Hill & Wang, 1976.

Wakeling, Stewart, Miriam Jorgensen, Susan Michaelson, and Manley Begay. *Policing on American Indian Reservations: A Report to the National Institute of Justice.* Washington, DC: U.S. Government Printing Office, 2001.

Walker, Samuel. "Racial Minority and Female Employment in Policing: The Implications of 'Glacial' Change." *Crime and Delinquency* 31 (1985): 555–572.

————. *Taming the System: The Control of Discretion in Criminal Justice, 1950–1990.* New York: Oxford University Press, 1993.

————. "Complaints against the Police: A Focus Group Study of Citizen Perceptions, Goals, and Expectations." *Criminal Justice Review* 22 (1997): 207–225.

————. *Police Interactions with Racial and Ethnic Minorities: Assessing the Evidence and Allegations.* Washington, DC: Police Executive Research Forum, 2000.

————. *Police Accountability: The Role of Citizen Oversight.* Belmont, CA: Wadsworth, 2001.

————. "Searching for the Denominator: Problems with Police Traffic Stop Data and an Early Warning System Solution." *Justice Research and Policy* 3 (spring 2001): 63–95.

Walker, Samuel, and Molly Brown. "A Pale Reflection of Reality: The Neglect of Racial and Ethnic Minorities in Introductory Criminal Justice Textbooks." *Journal of Criminal Justice Education* 6, no. 1 (spring 1995): 61–83.

Walker, Samuel, and K. B. Turner. *A Decade of Modest Progress: Employment of Black and Hispanic Police Officers, 1982–1992.* Omaha: University of Nebraska Press, 1992.

Walker, Thomas G., and Deborah J. Barrow. "The Diversification of the Federal Bench: Policy and Process Ramifications." *Journal of Politics* 47 (1985): 596–617.

Walsh, Anthony. "The Sexual Stratification Hypothesis in Light of Changing Conceptions of Race." *Criminology* 25 (1987): 153–173.

Washington, Linn. *Black Judges on Justice: Perspectives from the Bench.* New York: New Press, 1994.

Way, H. Frank. *Criminal Justice and the American Constitution.* North Scituate, MA: Duxbury Press, 1980.

Weisburd, David, et al. *The Abuse of Police Authority: A National Study of Police Officers' Attitudes.* Washington, DC: The Police Foundation, 2001.

Weisenburger, Steven. *Modern Medea.* New York: Hill & Wang, 1998.

Weitzer, Ronald. "Racialized Policing: Residents' Perceptions in Three Neighborhoods." *Law & Society Review* 34, no. 1 (2000): 129–156.

Welch, Susan, Michael Combs, and John Gruhl. "Do Black Judges Make a Difference?" *American Journal of Political Science* 32 (1988): 126–136.

Werthman, Carl, and Irving Piliavin. "Gang Members and the Police." In *The Police: Six Sociological Essays,* edited by David J. Bordua. New York: Wiley, 1967.

Wheeler, Gerald R., and Carol L. Wheeler. "Reflections on Legal Representation of the Economically Disadvantaged: Beyond Assembly Line Justice." *Crime and Delinquency* 26 (1980): 319–332.

Wilbanks, William. "Is Violent Crime Intraracial?" *Crime and Delinquency* 31 (1985): 117–128.

————. *The Myth of a Racist Criminal Justice System.* Monterey, CA: Brooks/Cole, 1987.

Wilson, James Q. *Thinking about Crime.* New York: Basic Books, 1975.

Wilson, William Julius. *The Truly Disadvantaged.* Chicago: University of Chicago Press, 1987.

Wishman, Seymour. *Anatomy of a Jury: The System on Trial.* New York: Times Books, 1986.

Wolfgang, Marvin E., and Marc Reidel. "Race, Judicial Discretion, and the Death Penalty." *Annals of the American Academy of Political and Social Science* 407 (1973): 119–133.

————. "Rape, Race and the Death Penalty in Georgia." *American Journal of Orthopsychiatry* 45 (1975): 658–668.

Wriggins, Jennifer. "Rape, Racism, and the Law." *Harvard Women's Law Journal* 6 (1983): 103–141.

Wright, Bruce McM. "A Black Broods on Black Judges." *Judicature* 57 (1973): 22–23.

Young, Iris Marion. *Justice and the Politics of Difference.* Princeton, NJ: Princeton University Press, 1990.

Zatz, Marjorie S. "Pleas, Priors and Prison: Racial/Ethnic Differences in Sentencing." *Social Science Research* 14 (1985): 169–193.

————. "The Changing Form of Racial/Ethnic Biases in Sentencing." *Journal of Research in Crime and Delinquency* 25 (1987): 69–92.

————. "The Convergence of Race, Ethnicity, Gender, and Class on Court Decisionmaking: Looking Toward the 21st Century." In *Policies, Processes, and Decisions of the Criminal Justice System,* vol. 3: *Criminal Justice 2000.* Washington, DC: U.S. Department of Justice, 2000.

Zatz, Marjorie S., Carol Chiago Lujan, and Zoann K. Snyder-Joy. "American Indians and Criminal Justice: Some Conceptual and Methodological Considerations." In *Race and Criminal Justice,* edited by Michael J. Lynch and E. Britt Patterson. New York: Harrow & Heston, 1995.

Zorn, Eric. "Dark Truths Buried in Nicarico Case May Yet See Light." *Chicago Tribune* (October 19, 1995), sec. 2, p. 1.

Index